W9-BXN-399

C: The Complete Reference
Third Edition

Herbert Schildt

Osborne **McGraw-Hill**

Berkeley New York St. Louis San Francisco
Auckland Bogotá Hamburg London Madrid
Mexico City Milan Montreal New Delhi Panama City
Paris São Paulo Singapore Sydney
Tokyo Toronto

Osborne **McGraw-Hill**
2600 Tenth Street
Berkeley, California 94710
U.S.A.

C: The Complete Reference, Third Edition

Publisher
  Lawrence Levitsky

Acquisitions Editor
  Bob Myren

Copy Editor
  Carl Wikander

Proofreader
  Vicki Van Ausdall

Indexer
  Sheryl Schildt

Computer Designer
  Jani Beckwith

Illustrator
  Rhys Elliot

Quality Control Specialist
  Joe Scuderi

Cover Design
  Compass Marketing

34567890 DOC 998765

ISBN 0-07-882101-0

Contents

Part I

The C Language

Part II

The C Standard Library

Part IV

Software Development Using C

Part V

A C Interpreter

Preface

This is the third edition of *C: The Complete Reference*. In the years since the first edition was written, much has transpired in the programming world. Here are some examples. When the first edition was being written, C was not yet standardized. Many competing implementations were fighting for dominance, with each compiler being slighty different than the next. When the second edition was prepared, the ANSI C standard had just been adopted. Today, standard C code is simply a given. (And, with standardization the promise of truly portable C code was finally fulfilled.) When the first edition of this book was written, DOS was the only operating system that had a sizable user base and Windows was simply an odd backwater. Today, both Windows and DOS environments exist in numbers larger than many ever imagined possible. Finally, when the first edition was published, C++ was an experimental language attracting the attention of only a few programmers that sought to push at the limits of programming. By the time the second edition was created, C++ was settling down, but the object-oriented paradigm was still not widely accepted or used. At the time of this writing, C++ has entered the mainstream of computer languages and rivals C for the top position.

Today, C is both standard and stable. It is also the most popular professional programming language in the world. However, the environments in which C is being extensively used continue to expand. For example, it is the language of choice for applications created for DOS, Windows, OS/2, and UNIX (to name few).

I must admit that when I wrote the first edition of *C: The Complete Reference,* I did not envision all of the changes and advancements that were to follow. (Although some, like the success of C++, were obvious from the start.) However, the one thing that I knew then is the same thing that I know now: C is the finest programming language that I have ever encountered. It is graceful, elegant, consistent, and (most importantly) powerful. Its continued success is a source of constant enjoyment for me.

A Book for All Programmers

This C reference is designed for all C programmers, regardless of their experience level. It does assume, however, a reader able to create at least a simple C program. If you are just learning C, this book will make an excellent companion to any C tutorial and serve as a source of answers to your specific questions.

Because C++ (C's object-oriented enhancement) is built upon C, this book is also appropriate for C++ programmers wishing to have a detailed reference to the foundation upon which C++ is constructed.

Therefore, whether you are programming in C or C++, whether you are a newcomer to programming or a seasoned pro, you will find this book to be of value.

What's New in the Third Edition

For the most part, I have left the basic structure of this book unchanged from its two preceding editions. Since C is a stable, standardized language, there was no reason to perform any major alterations. Most of the changes found in this edition reflect two things: the changes in the environment in which C is used and the emergence of C++ as a mainstream language.

Of the original 29 chapters, 26 are structurally unchanged from the previous edition. Three have been replaced. The ones replaced dealt with low-level DOS-based interfacing, DOS-based graphics functions, and an overview of C++. The DOS-based chapters have been replaced with an overview of Windows 95 programming. Since the last revision to this book, Windows has moved from relative obscurity into virtual dominance. Further, C is the most commonly used language for Windows programming. Therefore, coverage of this important C programming arena seemed necessary.

Both the first and second editions of this book concluded with an overview of C++. At the time when the earlier editions were prepared, C++ was still largely an experimental language. However, in the five years that have elapsed since the last revision, use of C++ has exploded. C++ is now a mainstream programming language on par with C. For this reason, a short overview of this important topic no longer seemed valuable. (The subject had simply become too large, requiring a complete book of its own!) Instead, the interested reader is directed to my book *C++: The*

Complete Reference, which covers C++ in full detail. In place of the chapter on C++, I have subsitituted the description of a C interpreter. I think that you will find the creation of the C interpreter one of the most interesting sections of this book.

What's Inside

This books covers in detail all aspects of the C language and its libraries. Its main emphasis is on ANSI standard C. However, the older, de facto "K & R" standard is also discussed when appropriate.

The book is divided into five parts, covering

- The C language
- The C libraries
- Common algorithms and applications
- The C programming environment
- The creation of a C interpreter

Part One provides a thorough discussion of the keywords, preprocessor directives, and features that define the C language.

Part Two discusses the standard C library. This section describes all functions specified by the ANSI C standard as well as several common, but non-standard functions.

Part Three covers some of the more common and important algorithms and applications that all C programmers should have in their toolbox. It also includes a discussion of AI-based problem solving and Windows 95 programming.

Part Four examines the C programming environment, including such things as interfacing to assembly code, efficiency, porting, and debugging.

Part Five illustrates the C language by creating an interpreter for it. This is easily the most exciting, challenging, and, at the same time, fun chapter in the book. If you are like most C programmers, exploring, enhancing, and otherwise tinkering with the C interpreter in Part Five will be irresistible! There is also no better way to understand the purity and elegance of the C language than by building an interpreter for it.

HS
January 11, 1995
Mahomet, IL

Diskette Offer

There are many useful and interesting functions, algorithms, and programs contained in this book. If you're like me, you probably would like to try them, but hate typing them into the computer. When I key in routines from a book it always seems that I type something wrong and spend hours trying to get the program to work. For this reason, I am offering the source code on diskette for all the programs contained in this book for $24.95. Just fill in the order blank on the next page and mail it, along with your payment, to the address shown. Or, if you're in a hurry, just call (217) 586-4021 (the number of my consulting office) and place your order by telephone. You can FAX your order to (217) 586-4997. (Visa and Mastercard accepted.)

Please send me _____ copies, at $24.95 each, of the programs in C: *The Complete Reference, Third Edition* on an IBM compatible diskette.

Foreign orders only: Checks must be drawn on a U.S bank and please add $5 shipping and handling.

_____
Name

_____
Address

_____ _____ _____
City   State   Zip

_____
Telephone

Diskette size (check one): 5 1/4" _____ 3 1/2"_____
Method of payment: Check_____ Visa_____ MC_____
Credit card number: _____
Expiration date: _____
Signature: _____

Send to:

Herbert Schildt
398 County Rd 2500 N
Mahomet, IL 61853

or phone: (217) 586-4021
FAX: (217) 586-4997

For Further Study

C: The Complete Reference, Third Edition is just one of the many programming books written by Herbert Schildt. Here are some others that you will find of interest.

■ If you want to learn more about the C language, we recommend the following titles.

> *The Annotated ANSI C Standard*
> *Teach Yourself C, Second Edition*

■ To learn about C++, you will find these books especially helpful.

> *C++: The Complete Reference*
> *Teach Yourself C++, Second Edition*
> *C++ From the Ground Up*
> *Turbo C/C++: The Complete Reference*

■ If you are interested in programming Windows 95, Schildt has written the definitive guide to this latest version of Windows:

> *Schildt's Windows 95 Programming in C and C++*

■ To learn more about Windows programming, we recommend the *Osborne Windows Programming Series*, co-authored by Herbert Schildt. You will find it to be invaluable when trying to understand the complexities of Windows. The series titles are:

> *Volume 1: Programming Fundamentals*
> *Volume 2: General Purpose API Functions*
> *Volume 3: Special Purpose API Functions*

When you need solid answers, fast, turn to Herbert Schildt, the recognized authority on programming.

PART ONE

The C Language

The first part of this reference guide presents a thorough discussion of the C programming language. Chapter 1 provides a quick overview of the C language—the more knowledgeable programmer may wish to skip directly to Chapter 2. Chapter 2 examines C's built-in data types, variables, operators, and expressions. Next, Chapter 3 presents program control statements. Chapter 4 discusses arrays and strings. Chapter 5 looks at pointers. Chapter 6 deals with functions, and Chapter 7 discusses structures, unions, and user-defined types. Chapter 8 examines console I/O. Chapter 9 covers file I/O, and Chapter 10 discusses the C preprocessor and comments.

The material in this section (and most of the material in the book) reflects the ANSI standard for C. Therefore, it is applicable to virtually all modern C compilers.

Chapter One

An Overview of C

The purpose of this chapter is to present an overview of the C programming language, its origins, its uses, and its underlying philosophy. This chapter is mainly for newcomers to C.

The Origins of C

C was invented and first implemented by Dennis Ritchie on a DEC PDP-11 that used the UNIX operating system. C is the result of a development process that started with an older language called BCPL. BCPL was developed by Martin Richards, and it influenced a language called B, which was invented by Ken Thompson. B led to the development of C in the 1970s.

For many years, the de facto standard for C was the version supplied with the UNIX version 5 operating system. It was first described in *The C Programming Language* by Brian Kernighan and Dennis Ritchie (Englewood Cliffs, N.J.: Prentice-Hall, 1978). With the rise in popularity of personal computers, a large number of C implementations were created. In a near miracle, most of these implementations were highly compatible. (That is, a program written for one of them could usually be successfully compiled using another.) However, because no standard existed, there were discrepancies. To remedy this situation, a committee was established in the summer of 1983 to create an ANSI (American National Standards Institute) standard that would define the C language once and for all. The standardization process took 6 years (much longer than anyone reasonably expected). The ANSI C standard was finally adopted in December of 1989, with the first copies becoming available in early 1990. Today, all mainstream C compilers comply with the ANSI C standard. This book fully covers and emphasizes the ANSI C standard. At the same time, it still contains information on features associated with the old UNIX version of C. In other words, no matter what C compiler you are using or what environment you are using it in, you will find applicable material here.

C Is a Middle-Level Language

C is often called a *middle-level* computer language. This does not mean that C is less powerful, harder to use, or less developed than a high-level language such as BASIC or Pascal, nor does it imply that C has the cumbersome nature of assembly language (and its associated troubles). Rather, C is thought of as a middle-level language because it combines the best elements of high-level languages with the control and flexibility of assembly language. Table 1-1 shows how C fits into the spectrum of computer languages.

Highest level	Ada
	Modula-2
	Pascal
	COBOL
	FORTRAN
	BASIC
Middle level	C++
	C
	FORTH
	Macro-assembler
Lowest level	Assembler

Table 1-1. *C's Place in the World of Languages*

As a middle-level language, C allows the manipulation of bits, bytes, and addresses—the basic elements with which the computer functions. Despite this fact, C code is also very portable. *Portability* means that it is easy to adapt software written for one type of computer or operating system to another. For example, if you can easily convert a program written for DOS so that it runs under Windows, that program is portable.

All high-level programming languages support the concept of data types. A *data type* defines a set of values that a variable can store along with a set of operations that can be performed on that variable. Common data types are integer, character, and real. Although C has five basic built-in data types, it is not a strongly typed language, as are Pascal and Ada. C permits almost all type conversions. For example, you may freely intermix character and integer types in an expression.

Unlike a high-level language, C performs almost no run-time error checking. For example, no check is performed to ensure that array boundaries are not overrun. These types of checks are the responsibility of the programmer.

In the same vein, C does not demand strict type compatibility between a parameter and an argument. As you may know from your other programming experience, a high-level computer language will typically require that the type of an argument be (more or less) exactly the same type as the parameter that will receive the argument. However, such is not the case for C. Instead, C allows an argument to be of any type so long as it can be reasonably converted into the type of the parameter. Further, C provides all of the automatic conversions to accomplish this.

C is special in that it allows the direct manipulation of bits, bytes, words, and pointers. This makes it well suited for system-level programming, where these operations are common.

Another important aspect of C is that it has only 32 keywords (27 from the Kernighan and Ritchie de facto standard, and 5 added by the ANSI standardization committee), which are the commands that make up the C language. High-level languages typically have several times more keywords. As a comparison, consider that most versions of BASIC have well over 100 keywords!

C Is a Structured Language

In your previous programming experience, you may have heard the term *block-structured* applied to a computer language. Although the term block-structured language does not strictly apply to C, C is commonly referred to simply as a *structured* language. It has many similarities to other structured languages, such as ALGOL, Pascal, and Modula-2.

> **NOTE:** *The reason that C is not, technically, a block-structured language is that block-structured languages permit procedures or functions to be declared inside other procedures or functions. However, since C does not allow the creation of functions within functions, it cannot formally be called block-structured.*

The distinguishing feature of a structured language is *compartmentalization* of code and data. This is the ability of a language to section off and hide from the rest of the program all information and instructions necessary to perform a specific task. One way that you achieve compartmentalization is by using subroutines that employ local (temporary) variables. By using local variables, you can write subroutines so that the events that occur within them cause no side effects in other parts of the program. This capability makes it very easy for your C programs to share sections of code. If you develop compartmentalized functions, you only need to know what a function does, not how it does it. Remember, excessive use of global variables (variables known throughout the entire program) may allow bugs to creep into a program by allowing unwanted side effects. (Anyone who has programmed in standard BASIC is well aware of this problem.)

A structured language allows you a variety of programming possibilities. It directly supports several loop constructs, such as **while**, **do-while**, and **for**. In a structured language, the use of **goto** is either prohibited or discouraged and is not the common form of program control (as is the case in standard BASIC and traditional FORTRAN, for example). A structured language allows you to place statements anywhere on a line and does not require a strict field concept (as some older FORTRANs do).

Here are some examples of structured and nonstructured languages:

Nonstructured	Structured
FORTRAN	Pascal
BASIC	Ada
COBOL	C++
	C
	Modula-2

Structured languages tend to be modern. In fact, a mark of an old computer language is that it is nonstructured. Today, most programmers consider structured languages easier to program in and the programs written in those languages easier to maintain.

C's main structural component is the function—C's stand-alone subroutine. In C, functions are the building blocks in which all program activity occurs. They allow you to define and code separately the separate tasks in a program, thus allowing your programs to be modular. After you have created a function, you can rely on it to work properly in various situations without creating side effects in other parts of the program. Being able to create stand-alone functions is extremely critical in larger projects where one programmer's code must not accidentally affect another's.

Another way to structure and compartmentalize code in C is through the use of code blocks. A *code block* is a logically-connected group of program statements that is treated as a unit. In C, you create a code block by placing a sequence of statements between opening and closing curly braces. In this example,

```
if (x < 10)   {
    printf("too low, try again\n");
    scanf("%d", &x);
}
```

the two statements after the **if** and between the curly braces are both executed if **x** is less than 10. These two statements together with the braces represent a code block. They are a logical unit: One of the statements cannot execute without the other executing also. Note that every statement in C can be either a single statement or a block of statements. Code blocks allow many algorithms to be implemented with clarity, elegance, and efficiency. Moreover, they help the programmer better conceptualize the true nature of the algorithm being implemented.

C Is a Programmer's Language

Surprisingly, not all computer programming languages are for programmers. Consider the classic examples of nonprogrammer languages, COBOL and BASIC. COBOL was designed not to better the programmer's lot, not to improve the reliability of the code produced, and not even to improve the speed with which code can be written. Rather, COBOL was designed, in part, to enable nonprogrammers to read and presumably (however unlikely) to understand the program. BASIC was created essentially to allow nonprogrammers to program a computer to solve relatively simple problems.

In contrast, C was created, influenced, and field-tested by working programmers. The end result is that C gives the programmer what the programmer wants: few restrictions, few complaints, block structures, stand-alone functions, and a compact set of keywords. By using C, you can nearly achieve the efficiency of assembly code combined with the structure of ALGOL or Modula-2. It is no wonder that C is easily the most popular language among topflight professional programmers.

The fact that you can often use C in place of assembly language is a major factor in its popularity among programmers. Assembly language uses a symbolic representation of the actual binary code that the computer executes directly. Each assembly-language operation maps into a single task for the computer to perform. Although assembly language gives programmers the potential to accomplish tasks with maximum flexibility and efficiency, it is notoriously difficult to work with when developing and debugging a program. Furthermore, since assembly language is unstructured, the final program tends to be spaghetti code—a tangled mess of jumps, calls, and indexes. This lack of structure makes assembly-language programs difficult to read, enhance, and maintain. Perhaps more important, assembly-language routines are not portable between machines with different central processing units (CPUs).

Initially, C was used for systems programming. A *systems program* forms a portion of the operating system of the computer or its support utilities. For example, the following are usually called systems programs:

- Operating systems
- Interpreters
- Editors
- Compilers
- Databases
- Spreadsheets

As C grew in popularity, many programmers began to use it to program all tasks because of its portability and efficiency. Because there are C compilers for virtually all computers, you can take code written for one machine and compile and run it on another with relatively few changes. This portability saves both time and money. C compilers also tend to produce very tight, fast object code—tighter and faster than that of most COBOL compilers, for example.

In addition, programmers use C in all types of programming tasks because they like it! C offers the speed of assembly language and the extensibility of FORTH, but has few of the restrictions of Pascal or Modula-2. Each C programmer can create and maintain a unique library of functions that have been tailored to his or her own programming style and that can be used in many different programs. Because it allows—indeed, encourages—separate compilation, C enables programmers to manage large projects easily, with minimal duplication of effort.

Compilers Versus Interpreters

It is important to understand that a computer language defines the nature of a program and not the way that the program will be executed. There are two general methods by which a program can be executed. It can be *compiled* or it can be *interpreted*. While programs written in any computer language can be compiled or interpreted, some languages are designed more for one form of execution than the other. For example, BASIC was designed to be interpreted and C was designed to be compiled. However, in the case of C, it is important to understand that it was specifically optimized as a compiled language. Although C interpreters have been written and are available in some environments (especially as debugging aids or experimental platforms like the one developed in Part Five), C was developed with compilation in mind. Therefore, you will almost certainly be using a C compiler and not a C interpreter when developing your C programs. Since the difference between a compiler and interpreter may not be clear to all readers, the following brief description will clarify matters.

An interpreter reads the source code of your program one line at a time, performing the specific instructions contained in that line. A compiler reads the entire program and converts it into *object code*, which is a translation of the program source code into a form that the computer can execute directly. Object code is also referred to as binary code or machine code. Once the program is compiled, a line of source code is no longer meaningful in the execution of your program.

When you use an interpreter, it must be present each time you wish to run your program. For example, when using a BASIC interpreter, you have to execute the interpreter, load your program, and type **RUN** each time you want to use it. The BASIC interpreter examines your program one line at a time for correctness and then executes it. This slow process occurs every time the program runs. A compiler, by contrast, converts your program into object code that your computer can execute directly. Because the compiler translates your program one time, all you need to do is execute your program directly, usually just by typing its name. Therefore, compilation is a one-time cost, while interpreted code incurs this overhead each time a program runs.

The Form of a C Program

Table 1-2 lists the 32 keywords that, combined with the formal C syntax, form the C programming language. Of these, 27 were defined by the original version of C. These five were added by the ANSI C committee: **enum, const, signed, void,** and **volatile**.

In addition, many C compilers have added several keywords that better exploit their operating environment. For example, several compilers include keywords to manage the memory organization of the 8086 family of processors, to support inter-language programming, and to access interrupts. Here is a list of some commonly used extended keywords:

asm	_cs	_ds	_es
_ss	cdecl	far	huge
interrupt	near	pascal	

Your compiler may also support other extensions that help it take better advantage of its specific environment.

All C keywords are lowercase. In C, uppercase and lowercase are different: **else** is a keyword; **ELSE** is not. You may not use a keyword for any other purpose in a C program—that is, you may not use it as a variable or function name.

All C programs consist of one or more functions. The only function that must be present is called **main( )**, which is the first function called when program execution begins. In well-written C code, **main( )** contains what is, in essence, an outline of what the program does. The outline is composed of function calls. Although **main( )** is not a keyword, treat it as if it were. For example, don't try to use **main( )** as the name of a variable because you will probably confuse the compiler.

The general form of a C program is illustrated in Figure 1-1, where **f1( )** through **fN( )** represent user-defined functions.

auto	double	int	struct
break	else	long	switch
case	enum	register	typedef
char	extern	return	union
const	float	short	unsigned
continue	for	signed	void
default	goto	sizeof	volatile
do	if	static	while

Table 1-2.   *A List of ANSI C Keywords*

```
    Global declarations

    return-type main(parameter list)
    {
      statement sequence
    }

    return-type f1(parameter list)
    {
      statement sequence
    }

    return-type f2(parameter list)
    {
      statement sequence
    }
      .
      .
      .
    return-type fN(parameter list)
    {
      statement sequence
    }
```

Figure 1-1.   *The general form of a C program*

The Library and Linking

Technically speaking, you can create a useful, functional C program that consists solely of the statements that you actually created. However, this is quite rare because C does not, within the actual definition of the language, provide any method of performing input/output (I/O) operations. As a result, most programs include calls to various functions contained in C's *standard library*.

All C compilers come with a standard C library of functions that perform most commonly needed tasks. The ANSI C standard specifies a minimal set of functions that will be contained in the library. However, your compiler will probably contain many other functions. For example, the ANSI C standard does not define any graphics functions, but your compiler will probably include some.

In some implementations of C, the library actually exists in one large file; in others, it is contained in many smaller files, a configuration that increases efficiency and practicality. However, for the sake of simplicity, this book uses the singular form in reference to the library.

The implementors of your C compiler have already written most of the general-purpose functions that you will use. When you call a function that is not part of your program, the C compiler "remembers" its name. Later, the linker combines the code you wrote with the object code already found in the standard library. This process is called *linking*. Some C compilers have their own linker while others use the standard linker supplied by your operating system.

The functions in the library are in *relocatable* format. This means that the memory addresses for the various machine-code instructions have not been absolutely defined—only offset information has been kept. When your program links with the functions in the standard library, these memory offsets are used to create the actual addresses used. There are several technical manuals and books that explain this process in more detail. However, you do not need any further explanation of the actual relocation process to program in C.

Many of the functions that you will need as you write programs are in the standard library. They act as building blocks that you combine. If you write a function that you will use again and again, you can place it into a library too. Some compilers allow you to place your function in the standard library; others make you create an additional library. Either way, the code will be there for you to use repeatedly.

Remember that the ANSI C standard only specifies a minimum standard library. Most compilers supply libraries that contain far more functions than those defined by ANSI. Moreover, some functions found in the original UNIX version of C are not defined by ANSI because they are redundant. This book covers all functions defined by ANSI as well as the most important and widely used functions defined by the old UNIX C standard. It also examines several widely used functions not defined by ANSI or the old UNIX standard. (Non-ANSI functions are marked to avoid any confusion.)

Separate Compilation

Most short C programs are completely contained within one source file. However, as a program's length grows, so does its compile time (and long compile times make for short tempers). Hence, C allows a program to be contained in many files and lets you compile each file separately. Once you have compiled all files, they are linked, along with any library routines, to form the complete object code. The advantage of separate compilation is that if you change the code of one file, you do not need to recompile the entire program. On all but the most simple projects, this saves a substantial amount of time. (Strategies for separate compilation are discussed in Part Four.)

Compiling a C Program

Creating an executable form of your C program consists of these three steps:

1. Creating your program

2. Compiling your program

3. Linking your program with whatever functions are needed from the library

Today, most C compilers supply integrated programming environments that include an editor. Most also include stand-alone compilers. For stand-alone versions, you must have a separate editor to create your program. In either case, be careful: compilers only accept standard text files for input. For example, your compiler will not accept files created by certain word processors because they contain control codes and nonprinting characters.

The exact method you use to compile your program will depend upon what C compiler you are using. Also, how linking is accomplished will vary between compilers and environments. For example, it may be included as part of the compiler or as a stand-alone application. Consult your user's manual for details.

C's Memory Map

A compiled C program creates and uses four logically distinct regions of memory that serve distinct functions. The first region is the memory that actually holds your program code. The next region is memory where global variables are stored. The remaining two regions are the stack and the heap. The *stack* is used for a great many things while your program executes. It holds the return addresses of function calls, arguments to functions, and local variables. It will also save the current state of the CPU. The *heap* is a region of free memory that your program can use via C's dynamic allocation functions for things like linked lists and trees.

The exact layout of your program may vary from compiler to compiler and environment to environment. For example, most C compilers for the 8086 family of processors have several different ways to organize memory because of the segmented memory architecture of the 8086. (The memory models of the 8086 family of processors are discussed later in this book.)

Although the exact physical layout of each of the four regions of memory differs among CPU types and C implementations, the diagram in Figure 1-2 shows conceptually how your C programs appear in memory.

C Versus C++

Before concluding this chapter, a few words about C++ are in order. Newcomers are sometimes confused about what C++ is and how it differs from C. In short, C++ is an extended and enhanced version of C that is designed to support object-oriented programming (OOP). C++ contains and supports the entire C language in addition to a set of object-oriented extensions. (That is, C++ is a superset of C.) Because C++ is built upon the foundation of C, you cannot program in C++ unless you understand C. Therefore, virtually all of the material in this book also applies to C++.

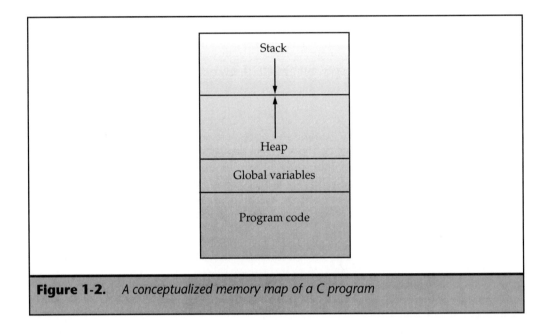

Figure 1-2.   *A conceptualized memory map of a C program*

NOTE: *For a complete description of the C++ language, see* C++: The Complete Reference, *by Herbert Schildt (Berkeley, CA: Osborne/McGraw-Hill).*

Today, and for many years to come, most programmers will still write, maintain, and utilize C, not C++, programs. As mentioned, C supports structured programming. Structured programming has been proven effective over the 25 years that it has been widely used. C++ is designed primarily to support OOP, which incorporates structured programming principles, but adds objects. While OOP is very effective for a certain class of programming tasks, many programs simply do not benefit from its application. Therefore, "straight C code" will be around for a very long time.

Will a C++ Compiler Work with C Programs?

Today it is rare to see a compiler advertised or described as simply a "C compiler." Instead, it is common to see a compiler advertised as a "C/C++ compiler," or sometimes just as a "C++ compiler." This situation naturally gives rise to the question, "Will a C++ compiler work with a C program?" The answer is "Yes!" Any and all compilers than can compile C++ programs can also compile C programs. Therefore, if your compiler calls itself a "C++ compiler," don't worry, it is also a full, ANSI-standard C compiler as well.

A Review of Terms

The terms that follow will be used frequently throughout the remainder of this reference. You should be completely familiar with them.

- *Source Code*   The text of a program that a user can read, commonly thought of as the program. The source code is input into the C compiler.

- *Object Code*   Translation of the source code of a program into machine code, which the computer can read and execute directly. Object code is the input to the linker.

- *Linker*   A program that links separately-compiled functions into one program. It combines the functions in the standard C library with the code that you wrote. The output of the linker is an executable program.

- *Library*   The file containing the standard functions that your program may use. These functions include all I/O operations as well as other useful routines.

- *Compile Time*   The events that occur while your program is being compiled.

- *Run Time*   The events that occur while your program is executing.

Chapter Two

C Expressions

This chapter examines the most fundamental element of the C language: the *expression*. As you will see, expressions in C are substantially more general and more powerful than in most other computer languages. Expressions are formed from the atomic elements of C: data and operators. Data may be represented either by variables or by constants. C, like most other computer languages, supports a number of different types of data. It also provides a wide variety of operators.

The Five Basic Data Types

There are five atomic data types in C: character, integer, floating-point, double floating-point, and valueless (**char**, **int**, **float**, **double**, and **void**, respectively). As you will see, all other data types in C are based upon one of these types. The size and range of these data types may vary with each processor type and between implementations of C. However, in all cases a character is 1 byte. Although an integer is often 2 bytes, you cannot make this assumption if you want your programs to be portable to the widest range of environments. It is important to understand that the ANSI C standard only stipulates the minimal *range* of each data type, not its size in bytes.

The exact format of floating-point values will depend upon how they are implemented. Integers will generally correspond to the natural size of a word on the host computer. Values of type **char** are generally used to hold values defined by the ASCII character set. Values outside that range may be handled differently between C implementations.

The range of **float** and **double** will depend upon the method used to represent the floating-point numbers. Whatever the method, the range is quite large. The ANSI standard specifies that the minimum range for a floating-point value is 1E–37 to 1E+37. The minimum number of digits of precision for each floating-point type is shown in Table 2-1.

The type **void** either explicitly declares a function as returning no value or creates generic pointers. Both of these uses are discussed in subsequent chapters.

Modifying the Basic Types

Except type **void**, the basic data types may have various modifiers preceding them. You use a *modifier* to alter the meaning of the base type to fit various situations more precisely. The list of modifiers is shown here:

signed
unsigned
long
short

You can apply the modifiers **signed**, **short**, **long**, and **unsigned** to character and integer base types. However, you may also apply **long** to **double**.

Type	Approximate Size in Bits	Minimal Range
char	8	−127 to 127
unsigned char	8	0 to 255
signed char	8	−127 to 127
int	16	−32,767 to 32,767
unsigned int	16	0 to 65,535
signed int	16	Same as **int**
short int	16	Same as **int**
unsigned short int	16	0 to 65,535
signed short int	16	Same as **short int**
long int	32	−2,147,483,647 to 2,147,483,647
signed long int	32	Same as **long int**
unsigned long int	32	0 to 4,294,967,295
float	32	Six digits of precision
double	64	Ten digits of precision
long double	80	Ten digits of precision

Table 2-1.   *All Data Types Defined by the ANSI C Standard*

Table 2-1 shows all data type combinations that adhere to the ANSI C standard, along with their minimal ranges and approximate bit widths.

The use of **signed** on integers is allowed, but redundant because the default integer declaration assumes a signed number. The most important use of **signed** is to modify **char** in implementations in which **char** is unsigned by default.

Some implementations may allow you to apply **unsigned** to the floating-point types (as in **unsigned double**). However, this reduces the portability of your code and is generally not recommended. Any additional or expanded types not defined by the ANSI standard will probably not be supported on every C implementation.

The difference between signed and unsigned integers is in the way that the high-order bit of the integer is interpreted. If you specify a signed integer, the C compiler generates code that assumes that the high-order bit of an integer is to be used as a *sign flag*. If the sign flag is 0, the number is positive; if it is 1, the number is negative.

In general, negative numbers are represented using the *two's complement* approach, which reverses all bits in the number (except the sign flag), adds 1 to this number, and sets the sign flag to 1.

Signed integers are important for a great many algorithms, but they only have half the absolute magnitude of their unsigned brothers. For example, here is 32,767:

0 1 1 1 1 1 1 1   1 1 1 1 1 1 1 1

If the high-order bit were set to 1, the number would be interpreted as –1. However, if you declare this to be an **unsigned int**, the number becomes 65,535 when the high-order bit is set to 1.

Identifier Names

In C, the names of variables, functions, labels, and various other user-defined objects are called *identifiers*. These identifiers can vary from one to several characters. The first character must be a letter or an underscore and subsequent characters must be either letters, digits, or underscores. Here are some correct and incorrect identifier names:

Correct	Incorrect
count	1count
test23	hi!there
high_balance	high...balance

The ANSI C standard states that identifiers may be of any length. However, not all characters will necessarily be significant. If the identifier will be involved in an external link process, then at least the first six characters will be significant. These identifiers, called *external names*, include function names and global variables that are shared between files. If the identifier is not used in an external link process, then at least the first 31 characters will be significant. This type of identifier is called an *internal name* and includes the names of local variables, for example. Consult the user manual to see exactly how many significant characters are allowed for the compiler that you are using.

An identifier name may be longer than the number of significant characters recognized by the compiler. However, characters past the limit will be ignored. For example, if your compiler recognizes 31 significant characters, the following identifiers will appear the same to it:

overly_long_identifiers_are_cumbersome
overly_long_identifiers_are_cumbersome_to_use

In C, upper- and lowercase are treated as distinct. Hence, **count**, **Count**, and **COUNT** are three separate identifiers. In some environments, the case of function names and global variables may be ignored if the linker is not case sensitive (but most contemporary environments support case-sensitive linking).

An identifier cannot be the same as a C keyword, and should not have the same name as functions that are in the C library.

Variables

As you probably know, a *variable* is a named location in memory that is used to hold a value that may be modified by the program. All C variables must be declared before they can be used. The general form of a declaration is

> *type variable_list;*

Here, *type* must be a valid C data type plus any modifiers and *variable_list* may consist of one or more identifier names separated by commas. Here are some declarations:

```
int i,j,l;
short int si;
unsigned int ui;
double balance, profit, loss;
```

Remember, in C the name of a variable has nothing to do with its type.

Where Variables Are Declared

Variables will be declared in three basic places: inside functions, in the definition of function parameters, and outside of all functions. These are local variables, formal parameters, and global variables.

Local Variables

Variables that are declared inside a function are called *local variables*. In some C literature, these variables are referred to as *automatic* variables. This book uses the more common term local variable. Local variables may be referenced only by statements that are inside the block in which the variables are declared. In other words, local variables are not known outside their own code block. Remember, a block of code begins with an opening curly brace and terminates with a closing curly brace.

Local variables exist only while the block of code in which they are declared is executing. That is, a local variable is created upon entry into its block and destroyed upon exit.

The most common code block in which local variables are declared is the function. For example, consider the following two functions:

```
void func1(void)
{
   int x;

   x = 10;
}
```

```
void func2(void)
{
  int x;

  x = -199;
}
```

The integer variable **x** is declared twice, once in **func1( )** and once in **func2( )**. The **x** in **func1( )** has no bearing on or relationship to the **x** in **func2( )**. This is because each **x** is only known to the code within the same block as the variable declaration.

The C language contains the keyword **auto**, which you can use to declare local variables. However, since all nonglobal variables are, by default, assumed to be **auto**, this keyword is virtually never used. Hence, the examples in this book will not use it. (It has been said that **auto** was included in C to provide for source-level compatibility with its predecessor B.)

Most programmers declare all the local variables used by a function immediately after the function's opening curly brace and before any other statements. However, you may declare local variables within any code block. The block defined by a function is simply a special case. For example,

```
void f(void)
{
  int t;

  scanf("%d",&t);

  if(t==1) {
    char s[80];  /* this is created only upon
                     entry into this block */
    printf("enter name:");
    gets(s);
    /* do something ... */
  }
}
```

Here, the local variable **s** is created upon entry into the **if** code block and destroyed upon exit. Furthermore, **s** is known only within the **if** block and may not be referenced elsewhere—even in other parts of the function that contains it.

One advantage of declaring a local variable within a conditional block is that memory for the variable will only be allocated if needed. This is because local variables do not come into existence until the block in which they are declared is entered. You might need to worry about this when producing code for dedicated controllers (like a garage door opener that responds to a digital security code) in which RAM is in short supply, for example.

Declaring variables within the block of code that uses them also helps prevent unwanted side effects. Since the variable does not exist outside the block in which it is declared, it cannot be accidentally altered. However, when each function performs one well-defined, logical task, you may not need to "protect" variables inside a function from the code that makes up the function. This is why all the variables used by a function are generally declared at the start of the function.

Remember that you must declare all local variables at the start of the block in which they are defined, prior to any program statements. For example, the following function is technically incorrect and will not compile on most compilers.

```
/* This function is in error. */
void f(void)
{
  int i;

  i = 10;

  int j;   /* this line will cause an error */

  j = 20;
}
```

However, if you had declared **j** within its own block of code or before the **i = 10** statement, the function would have been accepted. For example, either version shown here is syntactically correct:

```
/* Define j inside its own code block. */
void f(void)
{
  int i;

  i = 10;

  {  /* define j in its own block */
    int j;

    j = 20;
  }
```

```
}

/* Define j at start of function block. */
void f(void)
{
  int i;
  int j;

  i = 10;
  j = 20;
}
```

> **NOTE:** *As a point of interest, the restriction requiring that all variables be declared at the start of a block has been removed in C++. In C++, variables may be declared anywhere within a block.*

Because local variables are created and destroyed with each entry and exit from the block in which they are declared, their content is lost once the block is left. This is especially important to remember when calling a function. When a function is called, its local variables are created, and upon its return they are destroyed. This means that local variables cannot retain their values between calls. (However, you can direct the compiler to retain their values by using the **static** modifier.)

Unless otherwise specified, local variables are stored on the stack. The fact that the stack is a dynamic and changing region of memory explains why local variables cannot, in general, hold their values between function calls.

You can initialize a local variable to some known value. This value will be assigned to the variable each time the block of code in which it is declared is entered. For example, the following program prints the number 10 ten times:

```
#include <stdio.h>

void f(void);

void main(void)
{
  int i;

  for(i=0; i<10; i++)  f();
}

void f(void)
```

```
{
  int j = 10;

  printf("%d ", j);

  j++;  /* this line has no lasting effect */
}
```

Formal Parameters

If a function is to use arguments, it must declare variables that will accept the values of the arguments. These variables are called the *formal parameters* of the function. They behave like any other local variables inside the function. As shown in the following program fragment, their declarations occur after the function name and inside parentheses:

```
/* Return 1 if c is part of string s; 0 otherwise */
is_in(char *s, char c)
{
  while(*s)
    if(*s==c) return 1;
    else s++;

  return 0;
}
```

The function **is_in( )** has two parameters: **s** and **c**. This function returns 1 if the character specified in **c** is contained within the string **s**; 0 if it is not.

You must tell C what type of variables the formal parameters are by declaring them as just shown. Then you may use them inside the function as normal local variables. Keep in mind that, as local variables, they are also dynamic and are destroyed upon exit from the function.

Make sure that the formal parameters you declare are of the same type as the arguments you use to call the function. If there is a type mismatch, unexpected results can occur. Unlike many other languages, C will generally attempt to accommodate what you have requested even if it is highly unusual or suspect. This especially applies to type mismatches between arguments and parameters. As the programmer, you have to make sure that type mismatch errors do not occur.

Although C provides for *function prototypes*, which you can use to help verify that the arguments used to call a function are compatible with its parameters, problems can still occur. (That is, function prototypes do not fully eliminate argument-parameter type mismatches.) Also, you must explicitly include function prototypes in your program to receive their added benefit. They are not automatic. (Function prototyping is discussed in depth in Chapter 6.)

As with local variables, you may make assignments to a function's formal parameters or use them in any allowable C expression. Even though these variables receive the value of the arguments passed to the function, you can use them like any other local variable.

Global Variables

Unlike local variables, *global variables* are known throughout the program and may be used by any piece of code. Also, they will hold their value throughout the program's execution. You create global variables by declaring them outside of any function. Any expression may access them, regardless of what block of code that expression is in.

In the following program, the variable **count** has been declared outside of all functions. Although its declaration occurs before the **main( )** function, you could have placed it anywhere before its first use as long as it was not in a function. However, it is best to declare global variables at the top of the program.

```c
#include <stdio.h>
int count;   /* count is global   */

void func1(void);
void func2(void);

void main(void)
{
  count = 100;
  func1();
}

void func1(void)
{
  int temp;

  temp = count;
  func2();
  printf("count is %d", count); /* will print 100 */
}

void func2(void)
{
  int count;
```

```
    for(count=1; count<10; count++)
      putchar('.');
}
```

Look closely at this program. Notice that although neither **main( )** nor **func1( )** has declared the variable **count**, both may use it. **func2( )**, however, has declared a local variable called **count**. When **func2( )** references **count**, it references only its local variable, not the global one. If a global variable and a local variable have the same name, all references to that variable name inside the code block in which the local variable is declared will refer to that local variable and have no effect on the global variable. This can be convenient, but forgetting this can cause your program to act strangely, even though it looks correct.

Storage for global variables is in a fixed region of memory set aside for this purpose by the C compiler. Global variables are helpful when many functions in your program use the same data. You should avoid using unnecessary global variables, however. They take up memory the entire time your program is executing, not just when they are needed. In addition, using a global where a local variable would do makes a function less general because it relies on something that must be defined outside itself. Finally, using a large number of global variables can lead to program errors because of unknown and unwanted side effects. This is evidenced in standard BASIC, where all variables are global. A major problem in developing large programs in BASIC is the accidental changing of a variable's value because it was used elsewhere in the program. This can happen in C if you use too many global variables in your programs.

One of the principal reasons for a structured language is to compartmentalize code and data. In C, compartmentalization is achieved through the use of local variables and functions. For example, Figure 2-1 shows two ways to write **mul( )**—a simple function that computes the product of two integers.

Both functions return the product of the variables **x** and **y**. However, you can use the generalized, or *parameterized*, version to return the product of *any* two numbers, while you can use the specific version to find only the product of the global variables **x** and **y**.

Access Modifiers

C defines two modifiers (also referred to as *qualifiers*) that control how variables may be accessed or modified. These qualifiers are **const** and **volatile**. They must precede the type modifiers and the type names that they qualify.

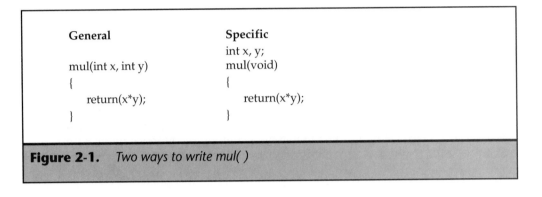

Figure 2-1. *Two ways to write mul( )*

const

Variables of type **const** may not be changed by your program. (A **const** variable can be given an initial value, however.) The compiler is free to place variables of this type into read-only memory (ROM). For example,

```
const int a=10;
```

creates an integer variable called **a** with an initial value of 10 that your program may not modify. However, you can use the variable **a** in other types of expressions. A **const** variable will receive its value either from an explicit initialization or by some hardware-dependent means.

The **const** qualifier can be used to protect the objects pointed to by the arguments to a function from being modified by that function. That is, when a pointer is passed to a function, that function can modify the actual variable pointed to by the pointer. However, if the pointer is specified as **const** in the parameter declaration, the function code won't be able to modify what it points to. For example, the **sp_to_dash( )** function in the following program prints a dash for each space in its string argument. That is, the string "this is a test" will be printed as "this-is-a-test". The use of **const** in the parameter declaration ensures that the code inside the function cannot modify the object pointed to by the parameter.

```
#include <stdio.h>

void sp_to_dash(const char *str);

void main(void)
{
   sp_to_dash("this is a test");
```

```
  }

  void sp_to_dash(const char *str)
  {
    while(*str) {
      if(*str== ' ') printf("%c", '-');
      else printf("%c", *str);
      str++;
    }
  }
```

If you had written **sp_to_dash( )** in such a way that the string would be modified, it would not compile. For example, if you had coded **sp_to_dash( )** as follows, you would receive a compile-time error:

```
  /* this is wrong */
  void sp_to_dash(const char *str)
  {
    while(*str) {
      if(*str==' ' ) *str = '-'; /* can't do this */
      printf("%c", *str);
      str++;
    }
  }
```

Many functions in the C standard library use **const** in their parameter declarations. For example, the **strlen( )** function has this prototype:

size_t strlen(const char *str);

Specifying *str* as **const** ensures that **strlen( )** will not modify the string pointed to by *str*. In general, when a standard library function has no need to modify an object pointed to by a calling argument, it is declared as **const.**

You can also use **const** to verify that your program does not modify a variable. Remember, a variable of type **const** can be modified by something outside your program. For example, a hardware device may set its value. However, by declaring a variable as **const**, you can prove that any changes to that variable occur because of external events.

volatile

The modifier **volatile** tells the compiler that a variable's value may be changed in ways not explicitly specified by the program. For example, a global variable's address may be passed to the operating system's clock routine and used to hold the real time of the system. In this situation, the contents of the variable are altered without any explicit assignment statements in the program. This is important because most C compilers automatically optimize certain expressions by assuming that a variable's content is unchanging if it does not occur on the left side of an assignment statement; thus, it might not be reexamined each time it is referenced. Also, some compilers change the order of evaluation of an expression during the compilation process. The **volatile** modifier prevents these changes.

You can use **const** and **volatile** together. For example, if 0x30 is assumed to be the value of a port that is changed by external conditions only, the following declaration would prevent any possibility of accidental side effects:

```
const volatile unsigned char *port=0x30;
```

Storage Class Specifiers

There are four storage class specifiers supported by C:

    extern
    static
    register
    auto

These specifiers tell the compiler how to store the subsequent variable. The storage specifier precedes the rest of the variable declaration. Its general form is

storage_specifier type var_name

extern

Because C allows separate modules of a large program to be separately compiled and linked together, there must be some way of telling all the files about the global variables required by the program. As a general rule, you can declare a global variable only once. If you declared two global variables with the same name inside the same file, your C compiler might print an error message, like "duplicate variable name," or it might simply choose one variable over the other. But a worse problem occurs if you try to declare all the global variables needed by your program in each file of a multi-file program. Although the compiler does not issue any error messages at compile time, you are actually trying to create two (or more) copies of each variable. The trouble starts when you attempt to link your modules. The linker displays an error message such as "duplicate label" because it does not know which variable to use. The solution is to declare all of your global variables in one file and use **extern** declarations in the other, as in Figure 2-2.

In File 2, the global variable list was copied from File 1 and the **extern** specifier was added to the declarations. The **extern** specifier tells the compiler that the variable types and names that follow it have been declared elsewhere. In other words, **extern** lets the compiler know what the types and names are for these global variables without actually creating storage for them again. When the linker links the two modules, all references to the external variables are resolved.

There is another, optional use of **extern** that you may occasionally see. When you use a global variable inside a function, you can declare it as **extern**, as shown here:

```
int first, last;   /* global definition of first
                      and last */

void main(void)
{
  extern int first;   /* optional use of the
                         extern declaration */

  .
  .
  .

}
```

Although **extern** variable declarations as shown in this example are allowed, they are not necessary. If the C compiler finds a variable that has not been declared, the compiler checks if it matches any of the global variables. If it does, the compiler assumes that the global variable is being referenced.

static Variables

static variables are permanent variables within their own function or file. Unlike global variables, they are not known outside their function or file, but they maintain their values between calls. This feature makes them useful when you write generalized functions and function libraries that other programmers may use. **static** has different effects upon local variables and global variables.

static Local Variables

When you apply the **static** modifier to a local variable, the compiler creates permanent storage for it, much as it creates storage for a global variable. The key difference between a **static** local variable and a global variable is that the **static** local variable

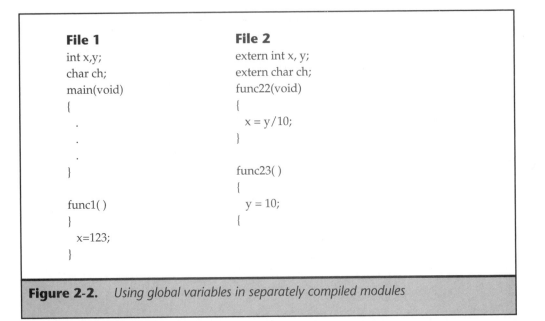

Figure 2-2. *Using global variables in separately compiled modules*

remains known only to the block in which it is declared. In simple terms, a **static** local variable is a local variable that retains its value between function calls.

static local variables are very important to the creation of stand-alone functions because several types of routines must preserve a value between calls. If **static** variables were not allowed, globals would have to be used, opening the door to possible side effects. An example of a function that benefits from a **static** local variable is a number-series generator that produces a new value based on the previous one. You could use a global variable to hold this value. However, each time the function is used in a program, you would have to declare that global variable and make sure that it did not conflict with any other global variables already in place. Also, using a global variable would make this function difficult to put into a function library. The better solution is to declare the variable that holds the generated number to be **static**, as in this program fragment:

```
series(void)
{
  static int series_num;

  series_num = series_num+23;
  return series_num;
}
```

In this example, the variable **series_num** stays in existence between function calls, instead of coming and going the way a normal local variable would. This means that each call to **series( )** can produce a new member of the series based on the preceding number without declaring that variable globally.

You can give a **static** local variable an initialization value. This value is assigned only once—not each time the block of code is entered, as with normal local variables. For example, this version of **series( )** initializes **series_num** to 100:

```
series(void)
{
  static int series_num = 100;

  series_num = series_num+23;
  return series_num;
}
```

As the function now stands, the series will always begin with the value 123. While this is acceptable for some applications, most series generators need to let the user specify the starting point. One way to give **series_num** a user-specified value is to make **series_num** a global variable and then set its value as specified. However, not defining **series_num** as global was the point of making it **static**. This leads to the second use of **static.**

static Global Variables

Applying the specifier **static** to a global variable instructs the compiler to create a global variable that is known only to the file in which you declared it. This means that even though the variable is global, routines in other files may have no knowledge of it or alter its contents directly, keeping it free from side effects. For the few situations where a local **static** cannot do the job, you can create a small file that contains only the functions that need the global **static** variable, separately compile that file, and use it without fear of side effects.

To illustrate a global **static**, the series generator example from the previous section is recoded so that a seed value initializes the series through a call to a second function called **series_start( )**. The entire file containing **series( )**, **series_start( )**, and **series_num** is shown here:

```
/* This must all be in one file - preferably by itself. */

static int series_num;
void series_start(int seed);
int series(void);
```

```
series(void)
{
  series_num = series_num+23;
  return series_num;
}

/* initialize series_num */
void series_start(int seed)
{
  series_num = seed;
}
```

Calling **series_start( )** with some known integer value initializes the series generator. After that, calls to **series( )** generate the next element in the series.

To review: The names of local **static** variables are known only to the block of code in which they are declared; the names of global **static** variables are known only to the file in which they reside. If you place the **series( )** and **series_start( )** functions in a library, you can use the functions but cannot reference the variable **series_num**, which is hidden from the rest of the code in your program. In fact, you can even declare and use another variable called **series_num** in your program (in another file, of course). In essence, the **static** modifier permits variables that are known only to the functions that need them, without confusing other functions.

static variables enable you to hide portions of your program from other portions. This can be a tremendous advantage when you are trying to manage a very large and complex program.

register Variables

The **register** storage specifier traditionally applied only to variables of type **int** and **char**. However, the ANSI C standard broadened its definition so that you can apply **register** to any type of variable.

Originally, the **register** specifier requested that the C compiler keep the value of a variable in a register of the CPU rather than in memory, where normal variables are stored. This meant that operations on a **register** variable could occur much faster than on a normal variable because the value of the **register** variable was actually held in the CPU and did not require a memory access to determine or modify its value.

Today, the definition of **register** has been greatly expanded and it now may be applied to any type of variable. The ANSI standard simply states "that access to the object be as fast as possible." In practice, characters and integers are still stored in registers in the CPU. Larger objects like arrays obviously cannot be stored in a register, but they may still receive preferential treatment by the compiler. Depending upon the implementation of the C compiler and its operating environment, **register** variables may be handled in any way deemed fit by the compiler's implementor. In fact, it is technically permissible for a compiler to ignore the **register** specifier altogether and treat variables modified by it as if they weren't, but this is seldom done in practice.

You can only apply the **register** specifier to local variables and to the formal parameters in a function. Hence, global **register** variables are not allowed. Here is an example that uses **register** variables. This function computes the result of M^e for integers:

```
int_pwr(register int m,  register int e)
{
  register int temp;

  temp = 1;

  for(; e; e--) temp = temp * m;
  return temp;
}
```

In this example, **e**, **m**, and **temp** are declared as **register** variables because they are all used within the loop. The fact that **register** variables are optimized for speed makes them ideal for control of or use in loops. Generally, **register** variables are used where they will do the most good, which are often places where many references will be made to the same variable. This is important because you can declare any number of variables as being of type **register**, but not all will receive the same access speed optimization.

The number of **register** variables optimized for speed allowed within any one code block is determined by both the environment and the specific implementation of C. You don't have to worry about declaring too many **register** variables because the C compiler automatically transforms **register** variables into nonregister variables when the limit is reached. (This ensures portability of C code across a broad line of processors.)

Usually at least two **register** variables of type **char** or **int** can actually be held in the registers of the CPU. Because environments vary widely, consult your compiler's user manual to determine if you can apply any other types of optimization options.

Because a **register** variable may be stored in a register of the CPU, **register** variables do not have addresses. That is, you may not find the address of a **register** variable using the **&** operator (discussed later in this chapter).

Although the ANSI C standard has broadened the description of **register** beyond its traditional meaning, in practice it still generally has a significant effect only with integer and character types. Thus, you should probably not count on substantial speed improvements for other variable types.

Variable Initializations

You can give most variables in C a value as you declare them by placing an equal sign and a constant after the variable name. The general form of initialization is

type variable_name = constant;

Some examples are

```
char ch = 'a';

int first = 0;

float balance = 123.23;
```

Global and **static** local variables are initialized only at the start of the program. Local variables (excluding **static** local variables) are initialized each time the block in which they are declared is entered. Local variables that are not initialized have unknown values before the first assignment is made to them. Uninitialized global and **static** local variables are automatically set to zero.

Constants

In C, *constants* refer to fixed values that the program may not alter. C constants can be of any of the basic data types. The way each constant is represented depends upon its type. Character constants are enclosed between single quotes. For example 'a' and '%' are both character constants. C also defines multi-byte characters (used mostly in non-English language environments).

Integer constants are specified as numbers without fractional components. For example, 10 and –100 are integer constants. Floating-point constants require the decimal point followed by the number's fractional component. For example, 11.123 is a floating-point constant. C also allows you to use scientific notation for floating-point numbers.

There are two floating-point types: **float** and **double**. There are also several variations of the basic types that you can generate using the type modifiers. By default, the C compiler fits a numeric constant into the smallest compatible data type that will hold it. Therefore, 10 is **int** by default, but 60,000 is **unsigned,** and 100,000 is **long**. Even though the value 10 could fit into a character type, the compiler will not cross type boundaries. The only exception to the smallest type rule are floating-point constants, which are assumed to be **doubles**.

For most programs you will write, the compiler defaults are adequate. However, you can specify precisely the type of numeric constant you want by using a suffix. For floating-point types, if you follow the number with an F, the number is treated as a **float**. If you follow it with an L, the number becomes a **long double**. For integer types, the U suffix stands for **unsigned** and the L for **long**. Here are some examples:

Data type	Constant examples
int	1 123 21000 –234
long int	35000L –34L
short int	10 –12 90
unsigned int	10000U 987U 40000
float	123.23F 4.34e–3F
double	123.23 12312333 –0.9876324
long double	1001.2L

Hexadecimal and Octal Constants

It is sometimes easier to use a number system based on 8 or 16 rather than 10 (our standard decimal system). The number system based on 8 is called *octal* and uses the digits 0 through 7. In octal, the number 10 is the same as 8 in decimal. The base 16 number system is called *hexadecimal* and uses the digits 0 through 9 plus the letters A through F, which stand for 10, 11, 12, 13, 14, and 15, respectively. For example, the hexadecimal number 10 is 16 in decimal. Because these two number systems are used frequently, C allows you to specify integer constants in hexadecimal or octal instead of decimal. A hexadecimal constant must consist of a 0x followed by the constant in hexadecimal form. An octal constant begins with a 0. Here are some examples:

```
int hex = 0x80;    /* 128 in decimal */
int oct = 012;     /* 10 in decimal */
```

String Constants

C supports one other type of constant: the string. A *string* is a set of characters enclosed in double quotes. For example, "this is a test" is a string. You have seen examples of strings in some of the **printf( )** statements in the sample programs. Although C allows you to define string constants, it does not formally have a string data type.

You must not confuse strings with characters. A single character constant is enclosed in single quotes, as in 'a'. However, "a" is a string containing only one letter.

Backslash Character Constants

Enclosing character constants in single quotes works for most printing characters. A few, however, such as the carriage return, are impossible to enter into a string from the keyboard. For this reason, C includes the special *backslash character constants*.

C supports several special backslash codes (listed in Table 2-2) so that you may easily enter these special characters as constants. You should use the backslash codes instead of their ASCII equivalents to help ensure portability.

For example, the following program outputs a new line and a tab and then prints the string **this is a test**.

```
#include <stdio.h>
void main(void)
{
   printf("\n\tThis is a test");
}
```

Operators

C is very rich in built-in operators. (In fact, C places more significance on operators than do most other computer languages.) C defines four classes of operators: *arithmetic*, *relational*, *logical*, and *bitwise*. In addition, C has some special operators for particular tasks.

Code	Meaning
\b	Backspace
\f	Form feed
\n	New line
\r	Carriage return
\t	Horizontal tab
\"	Double quote
\'	Single quote
\0	Null
\\	Backslash
\v	Vertical tab
\a	Alert
\N	Octal constant (where N is an octal constant)
\xN	Hexadecimal constant (where N is a hexadecimal constant)

Table 2-2. *Backslash Codes*

The Assignment Operator

In C, you can use the assignment operator within any valid C expression. This is not the case with most computer languages (including Pascal, BASIC, and FORTRAN), which treat the assignment operator as a special case statement. The general form of the assignment operator is

variable_name = expression;

where an expression may be as simple as a single constant or as complex as you require. Like BASIC and FORTRAN, C uses a single equal sign to indicate assignment (unlike Pascal or Modula-2, which use the := construct). The *target*, or left part, of the assignment must be a variable or a pointer, not a function or a constant.

Frequently in literature on C and in compiler error messages you will see these two terms: lvalue and rvalue. Simply put, an *lvalue* is any object that can occur on the left side of an assignment statement. For all practical purposes, "lvalue" means "variable." The term *rvalue* refers to expressions on the right side of an assignment and simply means the value of an expression.

Type Conversion in Assignments

When variables of one type are mixed with variables of another type, a *type conversion* will occur. In an assignment statement, the type conversion rule is easy: The value of the right side (expression side) of the assignment is converted to the type of the left side (target variable), as illustrated here:

```
int x;
char ch;
float  f;

void func(void)
{
  ch = x;    /* line 1 */
  x = f;     /* line 2 */
  f = ch;    /* line 3 */
  f = x;     /* line 4 */
}
```

In line 1, the left high-order bits of the integer variable **x** are lopped off, leaving **ch** with the lower 8 bits. If **x** were between 256 and 0, **ch** and **x** would have identical values. Otherwise, the value of **ch** would reflect only the lower-order bits of **x**. In line 2, **x** will receive the nonfractional part of **f**. In line 3, **f** will convert the 8-bit integer value stored in **ch** to the same value in the floating-point format. This also happens in line 4, except that **f** will convert an integer value into floating-point format.

When converting from integers to characters and long integers to integers, the appropriate amount of high-order bits will be removed. In many environments, this means that 8 bits will be lost when going from an integer to a character and 16 bits will be lost when going from a long integer to an integer.

Table 2-3 summarizes the assignment type conversions. Remember that the conversion of an **int** to a **float**, or a **float** to a **double**, and so on, does not add any precision or accuracy. These kinds of conversions only change the form in which the value is represented. In addition, some C compilers (and processors) always treat a **char** variable as positive, no matter what value it has, when converting it to an **int** or **float**. Other compilers treat **char** variable values greater than 127 as negative numbers when converting. Generally speaking, you should use **char** variables for characters, and use **int**s, **short int**s, or **signed char**s when needed to avoid possible portability problems.

To use Table 2-3 to make a conversion not shown, simply convert one type at a time until you finish. For example, to convert from **double** to **int**, first convert from **double** to **float** and then from **float** to **int**.

Since some computer languages, such as Pascal, prohibit automatic type conversions, the fact that C allows them is sometimes surprising. However, C was designed to simplify the life of the programmer by allowing work to be done in C rather than assembler. To replace assembler, C has to allow such type conversions.

Multiple Assignments

C allows you to assign many variables the same value by using multiple assignments in a single statement. For example, this program fragment assigns **x**, **y**, and **z** the value 0:

```
x = y = z = 0;
```

Target Type	Expression Type	Possible Info Loss
signed char	char	If value > 127, target is negative
char	short int	High-order 8 bits
char	int	High-order 8 bits
char	long int	High-order 24 bits
int	long int	High-order 16 bits
int	float	Fractional part and possibly more
float	double	Precision, result rounded
double	long double	Precision, result rounded

Table 2-3. *Common Type Conversions (Assuming a 16-Bit Word)*

In professional programs, variables are frequently assigned common values using this method.

Arithmetic Operators

Table 2-4 lists C's arithmetic operators. In C, the operators +, −, *, and / work as they do in most other computer languages. You can apply them to almost any built-in data type allowed by C. When you apply / to an integer or character, any remainder will be truncated. For example, 5/2 will equal 2 in integer division.

The modulus operator % also works in C as it does in other languages, yielding the remainder of an integer division. However, you cannot use it on floating-point types. The following code fragment illustrates %:

```
int x, y;

x = 5;
y = 2;

printf("%d", x/y);   /* will display 2 */
printf("%d", x%y);   /* will display 1, the remainder of
                        the integer division */

x = 1;
y = 2;

printf("%d %d", x/y, x%y); /*  will display 0 1 */
```

The last line prints a 0 and a 1 because 1/2 in integer division is 0 with a remainder of 1.

Operator	Action
−	Subtraction, also unary minus
+	Addition
*	Multiplication
/	Division
%	Modulus
− −	Decrement
++	Increment

Table 2-4. *Arithmetic Operators*

The unary minus multiplies its operand by –1. That is, any number preceded by a minus sign switches its sign.

Increment and Decrement

C includes two useful operators not generally found in other computer languages. These are the increment and decrement operators, **++** and **– –**. The operator **++** adds 1 to its operand, and **– –** subtracts one. In other words:

```
x = x+1;
```

is the same as

```
++x;
```

and

```
x = x-1;
```

is the same as

```
x--;
```

Both the increment and decrement operators may either precede (prefix) or follow (postfix) the operand. For example,

```
x = x+1;
```

can be written

```
++x;
```

or

```
x++;
```

There is, however, a difference between the prefix and postfix forms when you use these operators in an expression. When an increment or decrement operator precedes its operand, C performs the increment or decrement operation before obtaining the value of the operand for use in the expression. If the operator follows its operand, C obtains the value of the operand before incrementing or decrementing it. For instance,

```
x = 10;
y = ++x;
```

sets **y** to 11. However, if you write the code as

```
x = 10;
y = x++;
```

y is set to 10. Either way, **x** is set to 11; the difference is in when it happens.

Most C compilers produce very fast, efficient object code for increment and decrement operations—code that is better than that generated by using the equivalent assignment statement. For this reason, you should use the increment and decrement operators when you can.

Here is the precedence of the arithmetic operators:

highest	++ −−
	- (unary minus)
	* / %
lowest	+ −

Operators on the same level of precedence are evaluated by the compiler from left to right. Of course, you can use parentheses to alter the order of evaluation. C treats parentheses in the same way as virtually all other computer languages. Parentheses force an operation, or set of operations, to have a higher level of precedence.

Relational and Logical Operators

In the term *relational operator*, relational refers to the relationships that values can have with one another. In the term *logical operator*, logical refers to the ways these relationships can be connected. Because the relational and logical operators often work together, they are discussed together here.

The idea of true and false underlies the concepts of relational and logical operators. In C, true is any value other than zero. False is zero. Expressions that use relational or logical operators return zero for false and 1 for true.

Table 2-5 shows the relational and logical operators. The truth table for the logical operators is shown here using 1's and 0's.

p	q	p && q	p ¦¦ q	!p
0	0	0	0	1
0	1	0	1	1
1	1	1	1	0
1	0	0	1	0

Both the relational and logical operators are lower in precedence than the arithmetic operators. That is, an expression like 10 > 1+12 is evaluated as if it were written 10 > (1+12). Of course, the result is false.

You can combine several operations together into one expression, as shown here:

10>5 && !(10<9) ¦¦ 3<=4

In this case, the result is true.

Although C does not contain an exclusive OR (XOR) logical operator, you can easily create a function that performs this task using the other logical operators. The outcome of an XOR operation is true if and only if one operand (but not both) is true.

Relational Operators

Operator	Action
>	Greater than
>=	Greater than or equal
<	Less than
<=	Less than or equal
==	Equal
!=	Not equal

Logical Operators

Operator	Action
&&	AND
¦¦	OR
!	NOT

Table 2-5. *Relational and Logical Operators*

The following program contains the function **xor( )**, which returns the outcome of an exclusive OR operation performed on its two arguments:

```c
#include <stdio.h>

int xor(int a, int b);

void main(void)
{
  printf("%d", xor(1, 0));
  printf("%d", xor(1, 1));
  printf("%d", xor(0, 1));
  printf("%d", xor(0, 0));
}


/* Perform a logical XOR operation using the
   two arguments. */
xor(int a, int b)
{
  return (a || b) && !(a && b);
}
```

The following table shows the relative precedence of the relational and logical operators:

highest	!
	> >= < <=
	== !=
	&&
lowest	||

As with arithmetic expressions, you can use parentheses to alter the natural order of evaluation in a relational and/or logical expression. For example,

!0 && 0 || 0

is false. However, when you add parentheses to the same expression, as shown here, the result is true:

!(0 && 0) ¦¦ 0

Remember, all relational and logical expressions produce a result of either 0 or 1. Therefore, the following program fragment is not only correct, but will print the number 1.

```
int x;

x = 100;
printf("%d", x>10);
```

Bitwise Operators

Unlike many other languages, C supports a full complement of bitwise operators. Since C was designed to take the place of assembly language for most programming tasks, it needed to be able to support many operations that can be done in assembler, including operations on bits. *Bitwise operation* refers to testing, setting, or shifting the actual bits in a byte or word, which correspond to C's standard **char** and **int** data types and variants. You cannot use bitwise operations on **float**, **double**, **long double**, **void**, or other more complex types. Table 2-6 lists the operators that apply to bitwise operations. These operations are applied to the individual bits of the operands.

Operator	Action
&	AND
¦	OR
^	Exclusive OR (XOR)
~	One's complement
>>	Shift right
<<	Shift left

Table 2-6.   *Bitwise Operators*

The bitwise AND, OR, and NOT (one's complement) are governed by the same truth table as their logical equivalents, except that they work bit by bit. The exclusive OR (^) has the truth table shown here:

p	q	p ^q
0	0	0
1	0	1
1	1	0
0	1	1

As the table indicates, the outcome of an XOR is true only if exactly one of the operands is true; otherwise, it is false.

Bitwise operations most often find application in device drivers—such as modem programs, disk file routines, and printer routines—because the bitwise operations can be used to mask off certain bits, such as parity. (The parity bit confirms that the rest of the bits in the byte are unchanged. It is usually the high-order bit in each byte.)

Think of the bitwise AND as a way to clear a bit. That is, any bit that is 0 in either operand causes the corresponding bit in the outcome to be set to 0. For example, the following function reads a character from the modem port using the function **read_modem( )** and resets the parity bit to 0:

```
char get_char_from_modem(void)
{
  char ch;

  ch = read_modem(); /* get a character from the
                          modem port */
  return(ch & 127);
}
```

Parity is often indicated by the eighth bit, which is set to 0 by ANDing it with a byte that has bits 1 through 7 set to 1 and bit 8 set to 0. The expression **ch & 127** means to AND together the bits in ch with the bits that make up the number 127. The net result is that the eighth bit of **ch** is set to 0. In the following example, assume that **ch** had received the character "A" and had the parity bit set:

Parity bit

	1 1 0 0 0 0 0 1	**ch** containing an "A" with parity set
	0 1 1 1 1 1 1 1	127 in binary
&	————————	do bitwise AND
	0 1 0 0 0 0 0 1	"A" without parity

The bitwise OR, as the reverse of AND, can be used to set a bit. Any bit that is set to 1 in either operand causes the corresponding bit in the outcome to be set to 1. For example, the following is 128 | 3:

```
    1 0 0 0 0 0 0 0     128 in binary
    0 0 0 0 0 0 1 1     3 in binary
|   _____         bitwise OR
    1 0 0 0 0 0 1 1     result
```

An exclusive OR, usually abbreviated XOR, will set a bit on if and only if the bits being compared are different. For example, 127^120 is

```
    0 1 1 1 1 1 1 1     127 in binary
    0 1 1 1 1 0 0 0     120 in binary
^   _____         bitwise XOR
    0 0 0 0 0 1 1 1     result
```

Remember, relational and logical operators always produce a result that is either 0 or 1, whereas the similar bitwise operations may produce any arbitrary value in accordance with the specific operation. In other words, bitwise operations may produce values other than 0 or 1, while logical operators will always evaluate to 0 or 1.

The bit shift operators, >> and <<, move all bits in a variable to the right or left as specified. The general form of the shift-right statement is

variable >> number of bit positions

The general form of the shift-left statement is

variable << number of bit positions

As bits are shifted off one end, zeroes are brought in the other end. (In the case of a signed, negative integer, a right shift will cause a 1 to be brought in so that the sign bit is preserved.) Remember, a shift is not a rotate. That is, the bits shifted off one end do not come back around to the other. The bits shifted off are lost.

Bit-shift operations can be very useful when you are decoding input from an external device, like a D/A converter, and reading status information. The bitwise shift operators can also quickly multiply and divide integers. A shift right effectively divides a number by 2 and a shift left multiplies it by 2, as shown in Table 2-7. The following program illustrates the shift operators:

```
/* A bit shift example. */
#include <stdio.h>

void main(void)
{
  unsigned int i;
  int j;

  i = 1;

  /* left shifts */
  for(j=0; j<4; j++) {
    i = i << 1;   /* left shift i by 1,
                which is same as a multiply by 2 */
    printf("left shift %d: %d\n", j, i);
  }

  /* right shifts */
  for(j=0; j<4; j++) {
    i = i >> 1;   /* right shift i by 1,
                which is same as a division by 2 */
    printf("right shift %d: %d\n", j, i);
  }
}
```

unsigned char x;	x as each statement executes	value of x
x=7;	0 0 0 0 0 1 1 1	7
x=x<<1;	0 0 0 0 1 1 1 0	14
x=x<<3;	0 1 1 1 0 0 0 0	112
x=x<<2;	1 1 0 0 0 0 0 0	192
x=x>>1;	0 1 1 0 0 0 0 0	96
x=x>>2;	0 0 0 1 1 0 0 0	24

Each left shift multiplies by 2. Notice that information has been lost after x<<2 because a bit was shifted off the end.

Each right shift divides by 2. Notice that subsequent divisions do not bring back any lost bits.

Table 2-7.   *Multiplication and Division with Shift Operators*

The one's complement operator,~, reverses the state of each bit in its operand. That is, all 1's are set to 0, and all 0's are set to 1.

The bitwise operators are often used in cipher routines. If you want to make a disk file appear unreadable, perform some bitwise manipulations on it. One of the simplest methods is to complement each byte by using the one's complement to reverse each bit in the byte, as is shown here:

Original byte	00101100	
After 1st complement	11010011	Same
After 2nd complement	00101100	

Notice that a sequence of two complements in a row always produces the original number. Hence, the first complement represents the coded version of that byte. The second complement decodes the byte to its original value.

You could use the **encode( )** function shown here to encode a character.

```
/* A simple cipher function. */
char encode(char ch)
{
  return(~ch); /* complement it */
}
```

The ? Operator

C contains a very powerful and convenient operator that replaces certain statements of the if-then-else form. The ternary operator **?** takes the general form

Exp1 ? Exp2 : Exp3;

where *Exp1*, *Exp2*, and *Exp3* are expressions. Notice the use and placement of the colon. The **?** operator works like this: *Exp1* is evaluated. If it is true, *Exp2* is evaluated and becomes the value of the expression. If *Exp1* is false, *Exp3* is evaluated and its value becomes the value of the expression. For example, in

```
x = 10;

y = x>9 ? 100 : 200;
```

y is assigned the value 100. If **x** had been less than 9, **y** would have received the value 200. The same code written using the **if-else** statement is

```
x = 10;

if(x>9) y = 100;
else y = 200;
```

The **?** operator will be discussed more fully in Chapter 3 in relationship to C's other conditional statements.

The & and * Pointer Operators

A *pointer* is the memory address of a variable. A *pointer variable* is a variable that is specifically declared to hold a pointer to an object of its specified type. Knowing a variable's address can be of great help in certain types of routines. However, pointers have three main functions in C. They can provide a fast means of referencing array elements. They allow C functions to modify their calling parameters. Lastly, they support linked lists and other dynamic data structures. Chapter 5 is devoted exclusively to pointers. However, this chapter briefly covers the two operators that are used to manipulate pointers.

The first pointer operator is **&**, a unary operator that returns the memory address of its operand. (Remember, a unary operator only requires one operand.) For example,

```
m = &count;
```

places into **m** the memory address of the variable **count**. This address is the computer's internal location of the variable. It has nothing to do with the value of **count**. You can think of **&** as meaning "the address of." Therefore, the preceding assignment statement means "**m** receives the address of **count**."

To better understand this assignment, assume that the variable **count** is at memory location 2000. Also assume that **count** has a value of 100. Then, after the previous assignment, **m** will have the value 2000.

The second pointer operator is *, which is the complement of **&**. The * is a unary operator that returns the value of the variable located at the address that follows it. For example, if **m** contains the memory address of the variable **count**,

```
q = *m;
```

places the value of **count** into **q**. Now **q** has the value 100 because 100 is stored at location 2000, the memory address that was stored in **m**. Think of * as meaning "at address." In this case, you could read the statement as "**q** receives the value at address **m**."

Unfortunately, the multiplication symbol and the "at address" symbol are the same, and the symbol for the bitwise AND and the "address of" symbol are the same. These operators have no relationship to each other. Both **&** and ***** have a higher precedence than all other arithmetic operators except the unary minus, with which they share equal precedence.

Variables that will hold pointers must be declared as such. Variables that will hold memory addresses, or pointers as they are called in C, must be declared by putting ***** in front of the variable name. This indicates to the compiler that it will hold a pointer to that type of variable. For example, to declare **ch** as a pointer to a character, write

```
char *ch;
```

Here, **ch** is not a character but a pointer to a character—there is a big difference. The type of data that a pointer points to, in this case **char**, is called the *base type* of the pointer. However, the pointer variable itself is a variable that holds the address to an object of the base type. Hence, a character pointer (or any pointer) is of sufficient size to hold an address as defined by the architecture of the computer that it is running on. However, remember that a pointer should only point to data that is of that pointer's base type.

You can mix both pointer and nonpointer variables in the same declaration statement. For example,

```
int x, *y, count;
```

declares **x** and **count** as integer types and **y** as a pointer to an integer type.

The following program uses ***** and **&** operators to put the value 10 into a variable called **target**. As expected, this program displays the value 10 on the screen.

```
#include <stdio.h>

void main(void)
{
  int target, source;
  int *m;

  source = 10;
  m = &source;
  target = *m;

  printf("%d", target);
}
```

The Compile-Time Operator sizeof

sizeof is a unary compile-time operator that returns the length, in bytes, of the variable or parenthesized type-specifier that it precedes. For example, assuming that integers are 2 bytes and **float**s are 8 bytes,

```
float f;

printf("%f ", sizeof f);
printf("%d", sizeof(int));
```

will display **8 2**.

Remember, to compute the size of a type, you must enclose the type name in parentheses. This is not necessary for variable names, although there is no harm done if you do so.

C defines (using **typedef**) a special type called **size_t**, which corresponds loosely to an unsigned integer. Technically, the value returned by **sizeof** is of type **size_t**. For all practical purposes, however, you can think of it (and use it) as if it were an unsigned integer value.

sizeof primarily helps to generate portable code that depends upon the size of the C built-in data types. For example, imagine a database program that needs to store six integer values per record. If you want to port the database program to a variety of computers, you must not assume the size of an integer, but must determine its actual length using **sizeof**. This being the case, you could use the following routine to write a record to a disk file:

```
/* Write 6 integers to a disk file. */
void put_rec(int rec[6], FILE *fp)
{
  int len;

  len = fwrite(rec, sizeof rec, 1, fp);
  if(len != 1) printf("write error");
}
```

Coded as shown, **put_rec( )** compiles and runs correctly on any computer, no matter how many bytes are in an integer.

The Comma Operator

You use the comma operator to string together several expressions. The left side of the comma operator is always evaluated as **void**. This means that the expression on the right side becomes the value of the total comma-separated expression. For example,

```
x = (y=3, y+1);
```

first assigns **y** the value 3 and then assigns **x** the value 4. The parentheses are necessary because the comma operator has a lower precedence than the assignment operator.

Essentially, the comma causes a sequence of operations. When you use it on the right side of an assignment statement, the value assigned is the value of the last expression of the comma-separated list.

The comma operator has somewhat the same meaning as the word "and" in normal English as used in the phrase "do this and this and this."

The Dot (.) and Arrow (–>) Operators

The . (dot) and the ->(arrow) operators reference individual elements of structures and unions. *Structures* and *unions* are aggregate data types that may be referenced under a single name (see Chapter 7).

The dot operator is used when working with the actual structure or union. The arrow operator is used when a pointer to a structure or union is used. For example, given the fragment,

```
struct employee
{
  char name[80];
  int age;
  float wage;
} emp;

struct employee *p = &emp; /* address of emp into p */
```

you would write the following code to assign the value 123.23 to the **wage** member of structure variable **emp**:

```
emp.wage = 123.23;
```

However, the same assignment using a pointer to **emp** would be

```
p->wage = 123.23;
```

Parentheses and Square Brackets as Operators

In C, parentheses are operators that increase the precedence of the operations inside them.

Square brackets perform array indexing (arrays will be discussed fully in Chapter 4). Given an array, the expression within square brackets provides an index into that array. For example,

```
#include <stdio.h>
char s[80];

void main(void)
{
  s[3] = 'X';
  printf("%c", s[3]);
}
```

first assigns the value **'X'** to the fourth element (remember all arrays in C begin at 0) of array **s**, and then prints that element.

Precedence Summary

Table 2-8 lists the precedence of all C operators. Note that all operators, except the unary operators and **?**, associate from left to right. The unary operators (*, &, –) and **?** associate from right to left.

Highest	() [] -> .
	! ~ ++ -- – (type) * & sizeof
	* / %
	+ –
	<< >>
	< <= > >=
	== !=
	&
	^
	¦
	&&
	¦¦
	?:
	= += -= *= /= etc.
Lowest	,

Table 2-8.   *The Precedence of C Operators*

Expressions

Operators, constants, and variables are the constituents of expressions. An *expression* in C is any valid combination of these elements. Because most expressions tend to follow the general rules of algebra, they are often taken for granted. However, a few aspects of expressions relate specifically to C.

Order of Evaluation

The ANSI C standard does not specify the order in which the subexpressions of an expression are evaluated. This leaves the C compiler free to rearrange an expression to produce more optimal code. However, it also means that your code should never rely upon the order in which subexpressions are evaluated. For example, the expression

```
x = f1() + f2();
```

does not ensure that **f1( )** will be called before **f2( )**.

Type Conversion in Expressions

When constants and variables of different types are mixed in an expression, they are all converted to the same type. The C compiler converts all operands up to the type of the largest operand, which is called *type promotion*. First, all **char** and **short int** values are automatically elevated to **int**. (This process is called *integral promotion*.) Once this step has been completed, all other conversions are done operation by operation, as described in the following type conversion algorithm:

IF an operand is a **long double**
THEN the second is converted to **long double**
ELSE IF an operand is a **double**
THEN the second is converted to **double**
ELSE IF an operand is a **float**
THEN the second is converted to **float**
ELSE IF an operand is an **unsigned long**
THEN the second is converted to **unsigned long**
ELSE IF an operand is **long**
THEN the second is converted to **long**
ELSE IF an operand is **unsigned int**
THEN the second is converted to **unsigned int**

There is one additional special case: If one operand is **long** and the other is **unsigned int**, and if the value of the **unsigned int** cannot be represented by a **long**, both operands are converted to **unsigned long**.

Once these conversion rules have been applied, each pair of operands is of the same type and the result of each operation is the same as the type of both operands.

For example, consider the type conversions that occur in Figure 2-3. First, the character **ch** is converted to an integer and **float f** is converted to **double**. Then the outcome of **ch/i** is converted to a **double** because **f*d** is **double**. The final result is **double** because, by this time, both operands are **double**.

Casts

You can force an expression to be of a specific type by using a *cast*. The general form of a cast is

(type) expression

where *type* is a valid C data type. For example, to make sure that the expression **x/2** evaluates to type **float**, write

```
(float) x/2
```

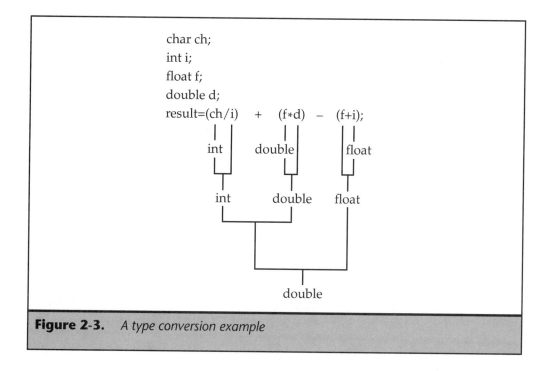

Figure 2-3. *A type conversion example*

Casts are technically operators. As an operator, a cast is unary and has the same precedence as any other unary operator.

Although casts are not usually used a great deal in programming, they can be very useful when needed. For example, suppose you wish to use an integer for loop control, yet to perform computation on it requires a fractional part, as in the following program:

```
#include <stdio.h>

void main(void) /* print i and i/2 with fractions */
{
  int i;

  for(i=1; i<=100; ++i)
    printf("%d / 2 is: %f\n", i, (float) i /2);
}
```

Without the cast **(float)**, only an integer division would have been performed. The cast ensures that the fractional part of the answer is displayed.

Spacing and Parentheses

You can add tabs and spaces to C expressions to make them easier to read. For example, the following two expressions are the same:

```
x=10/y ~ (127/x);

x = 10 / y ~ (127/x);
```

Redundant or additional parentheses do not cause errors or slow down the execution of an expression. You should use parentheses to clarify the exact order of evaluation, both for yourself and for others. For example, which of the following two expressions is easier to read?

```
x=y/2-34*temp&127;
x = (y/3) - ((34*temp) & 127);
```

C Shorthand

There is a variation on the assignment statement, sometimes refered to as *C shorthand*, that simplifies the coding of a certain type of assigment operation. For example,

```
x = x+10;
```

can be written as

```
x += 10;
```

The operator **+=** tells the compiler to assign to **x** the value of **x** plus 10.

This shorthand works for all the binary operators in C (those that require two operands). In general, statements like:

var = var operator expression

can be rewritten as

var operator = expression

For another example,

```
x = x-100;
```

is the same as

```
x -= 100;
```

Shorthand notation is widely used in professionally written C programs; you should become familiar with it.

Chapter Three

Program Control Statements

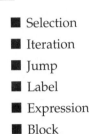his chapter discusses C's rich and varied program control statements. The ANSI standard categorizes C's statements into these groups:

- Selection
- Iteration
- Jump
- Label
- Expression
- Block

Included in the selection statements are **if** and **switch**. (The term "conditional statement" is often used in place of "selection statement." However, the ANSI standard uses "selection" as will this book.) The iteration statements are **while, for**, and **do-while**. These are also commonly called *loop statements*. The jump statements are **break, continue, goto**, and **return**. The label statements include the **case** and **default** statements (discussed along with the **switch** statement) and the label statement (discussed with **goto**). Expression statements are statements composed of a valid C expression. Block statements are simply blocks of code. (Remember, a block begins with a { and ends with a }.)

Since many C statements rely upon the outcome of some conditional test, let's begin by reviewing the concepts of true and false in C.

True and False in C

Many C statements rely upon a conditional expression that determines what course of action is to be taken. A conditional expression evaluates to either a true or false value. In C, unlike many other computer languages, a true value is any nonzero value, including negative numbers. A false value is 0. This approach to true and false allows a wide range of routines to be coded extremely efficiently, as you will see shortly.

Selection Statements

C supports two types of selection statements: **if** and **switch**. In addition, the **?** operator is an alternative to **if** in certain circumstances.

if

The general form of the **if** statement is

    if (*expression*) *statement*;
    else *statement*;

where a *statement* may consist of a single statement, a block of statements, or nothing (in the case of empty statements). The **else** clause is optional.

If *expression* evaluates to true (anything other than 0), the statement or block that forms the target of **if** is executed; otherwise, the statement or block that is the target of **else** will be executed, if it exists. Remember, only the code associated with **if** or the code associated with **else** executes, never both.

The conditional statement controlling **if** must produce a scalar result. A *scalar* is either an integer, character, pointer, or floating-point type. However, it is rare to use a floating-point number to control a conditional statement because this slows execution time considerably. (It takes several instructions to perform a floating-point operation. It takes relatively few instructions to perform an integer or character operation.)

The following program contains an example of **if**. The program plays a very simple version of the "guess the magic number" game. It prints the message **** Right **** when the player guesses the magic number. It generates the magic number using C's random number generator **rand( )**, which returns an arbitrary number between 0 and **RAND_MAX** (which defines an integer value that is 32,767 or larger). **rand( )** requires the header file **stdlib.h**.

```
/* Magic number program #1. */
#include <stdio.h>
#include <stdlib.h>

void main(void)
{
  int magic; /* magic number */
  int guess; /* user's guess */

  magic = rand(); /* generate the magic number */

  printf("Guess the magic number: ");
  scanf("%d", &guess);

  if(guess == magic) printf("** Right **");
}
```

Taking the magic-number program further, the next version illustrates the use of the **else** statement to print a message in response to the wrong number.

```
/* Magic number program #2. */
#include <stdio.h>
#include <stdlib.h>
```

```
void main(void)
{
  int magic; /* magic number */
  int guess; /* user's guess */

  magic = rand(); /* generate the magic number */

  printf("Guess the magic number: ");
  scanf("%d", &guess);

  if(guess == magic) printf("** Right **");
  else printf("Wrong");
}
```

Nested ifs

A nested **if** is an **if** that is the target of another **if** or **else**. Nested **if**s are very common in programming. In C, an **else** statement always refers to the nearest **if** statement that is within the same block as the **else** and that is not already associated with an **else**. For example,

```
if(i)
{
  if(j) statement 1;
  if(k) statement 2; /* this if */
  else  statement 3; /* is associated with this else */
}
else statement 4; /* associated with if(i) */
```

As noted, the final **else** is not associated with **if(j)** because it is not in the same block. Rather, the final **else** is associated with **if(i)**. Also, the inner **else** is associated with **if(k)**, which is the nearest **if**.

The ANSI C standard specifies that at least 15 levels of nesting must be supported. In practice, most compilers allow substantially more.

You can use a nested **if** to further improve the magic number program by providing the player with feedback about a wrong guess.

```
/* Magic number program #3. */
#include <stdio.h>
#include <stdlib.h>
```

```
void main(void)
{
  int magic; /* magic number */
  int guess; /* user's guess */

  magic = rand(); /* get a random number */

  printf("Guess the magic number: ");
  scanf("%d", &guess);

  if (guess == magic) {
    printf("** Right **");
    printf(" %d is the magic number\n", magic);
  }
  else {
    printf("Wrong, ");
    if(guess > magic) printf("too high\n");
    else printf("too low\n");
  }
}
```

The if-else-if Ladder

A common programming construct is the *if-else-if ladder*, sometimes called the *if-else-if staircase* because of its appearance. Its general form is

if *(expression) statement;*
else
  if *(expression) statement;*
  else
    if *(expression) statement;*
.
.
.
      else *statement;*

The conditions are evaluated from the top downward. As soon as a true condition is found, the statement associated with it is executed and the rest of the ladder is bypassed. If none of the conditions are true, the final **else** is executed. That is, if all other conditional tests fail, the last **else** statement is performed. If the final **else** is not present, no action takes place if all other conditions are false.

Although the indentation of the preceding if-else-if ladder is technically correct, it can lead to overly deep indentation. For this reason, the if-else-if ladder is generally indented like this:

if *(expression)*
    statement;
else if*(expression)*
    statement;
else if*(expression)*
    statement;
    .
    .
    .
else
    statement;

Using an if-else-if ladder, the magic number program becomes

```c
/* Magic number program #4. */
#include <stdio.h>
#include <stdlib.h>

void main(void)
{
  int magic; /* magic number */
  int guess; /* user's guess */

  magic = rand(); /* generate the magic number */

  printf("Guess the magic number: ");
  scanf("%d", &guess);

  if(guess == magic) {
    printf("** Right ** ");
    printf("%d is the magic number", magic);
  }
  else if(guess > magic)
    printf("Wrong, too high");
  else printf("Wrong, too low");
}
```

The ? Alternative

You can use the **?** operator to replace **if-else** statements of the general form:

> if(*condition*) *expression;*
> else *expression;*

However, the target of both **if** and **else** must be a single expression—not another C statement.

The **?** is called a *ternary operator* because it requires three operands. It takes the general form

> *Exp1 ? Exp2 : Exp3*

where *Exp1*, *Exp2*, and *Exp3* are expressions. Notice the use and placement of the colon. The value of a **?** expression is determined as follows: *Exp1* is evaluated. If it is true, *Exp2* is evaluated and becomes the value of the entire **?** expression. If *Exp1* is false, then *Exp3* is evaluated and its value becomes the value of the expression. For example, consider

```
x = 10;
y = x>9 ? 100 : 200;
```

In this example, **y** is assigned the value 100. If **x** had been less than 9, **y** would have received the value 200. The same code written with the **if-else** statement would be

```
x = 10;
if(x>9) y = 100;
else y = 200;
```

The following program uses the **?** operator to square an integer value entered by the user. However, this program preserves the sign (10 squared is 100 and –10 squared is –100).

```
#include <stdio.h>

void main(void)
{
  int isqrd, i;

  printf("Enter a number: ");
```

```
    scanf("%d", &i);

    isqrd = i>0 ? i*i : -(i*i);

    printf("%d squared is %d", i, isqrd);
}
```

The use of the **?** operator to replace **if-else** statements is not restricted to
assignments only. Remember, all functions (except those declared as **void**) may return
a value. Hence, you can use one or more function calls in a C expression. When the
function's name is encountered, the function is executed so that its return value may
be determined. Therefore, you can execute one or more function calls using the **?**
operator by placing the calls in the expressions that form the **?**'s operands, as in

```
#include <stdio.h>

int f1(int n);
int f2(void);

void main(void)
{
  int t;

  printf("Enter a number: ");
  scanf("%d", &t);

  /* print proper message */
  t ? f1(t) + f2() : printf("zero entered");
}

f1(int n)
{
  printf("%d ", n);
  return 0;
}

f2(void)
{
  printf("entered");
  return 0;
}
```

Entering a 0 in this example calls the **printf( )** function and displays the message **zero entered**. If you enter any other number, both **f1( )** and **f2( )** execute. Note that the value of the **?** expression is discarded in this example. You don't need to assign it to anything.

A word of warning: Some C compilers rearrange the order of evaluation of an expression in an attempt to optimize the object code. This could cause functions that form the operands of the **?** operator to execute in an unintended sequence.

Using the **?** operator, you can rewrite the magic number program yet again.

```c
/* Magic number program #5. */
#include <stdio.h>
#include <stdlib.h>

void main(void)
{
  int magic;
  int guess;

  magic = rand(); /* generate the magic number */

  printf("Guess the magic number: ");
  scanf("%d", &guess);

  if(Guess == magic) {
    printf("** Right ** ");
    printf("%d is the magic number", magic);
  }
  else
    guess > magic ? printf("High") : printf("Low");
}
```

Here, the **?** operator displays the proper message based on the outcome of the test **guess > magic**.

The Conditional Expression

Sometimes newcomers to C are confused by the fact that you can use any valid C expression to control the **if** or the **?** operator. That is, you are not restricted to expressions involving the relational and logical operators (as is the case in languages like BASIC or Pascal). The expression must simply evaluate to either a zero or nonzero value. For example, the following program reads two integers from the keyboard and displays the quotient. It uses an **if** statement, controlled by the second number, to avoid a divide-by-zero error.

```
/* Divide the first number by the second. */

#include <stdio.h>

void main(void)
{
   int a, b;

   printf("Enter two numbers: ");
   scanf("%d%d", &a, &b);

   if(b) printf("%d\n", a/b);
   else printf("Cannot divide by zero.\n");
}
```

This approach works because if **b** is 0, the condition controlling the **if** is false and the **else** executes. Otherwise, the condition is true (nonzero) and the division takes place. However, writing the **if** statement like this:

```
if(b != 0) printf("%d\n", a/b);
```

is redundant and potentially inefficient and is considered bad style.

switch

C has a built-in multiple-branch selection statement, called **switch**, which successively tests the value of an expression against a list of integer or character constants. When a match is found, the statements associated with that constant are executed. The general form of the **switch** statement is

```
switch (expression) {
   case constant1:
      statement sequence
      break;
   case constant2:
      statement sequence
      break;
   case constant3:
      statement sequence
      break;
      .
      .
      .
```

```
  default
    statement sequence
}
```

The value of *expression* is tested, in order, against the values of the constants specified in the **case** statements. When a match is found, the *statement sequence* associated with that **case** is executed until the **break** statement or the end of the **switch** statement is reached. The **default** statement is executed if no matches are found. The **default** is optional and, if it is not present, no action takes place if all matches fail.

The ANSI C standard specifies that a **switch** can have at least 257 **case** statements. (Most compilers allow substantially more.) In practice, you will want to limit the number of **case** statements to a smaller amount for efficiency. Although **case** is a label statement, it cannot exist by itself, outside of a **switch**.

The **break** statement is one of C's jump statements. You can use it in loops as well as in the **switch** statement (see the section "Iteration Statements"). When **break** is encountered in a **switch**, program execution "jumps" to the line of code following the **switch** statement.

There are three important things to know about the **switch** statement:

■ The **switch** differs from the **if** in that **switch** can only test for equality whereas **if** can evaluate any type of relational or logical expression.

■ No two **case** constants in the same **switch** can have identical values. Of course, a **switch** statement enclosed by an outer **switch** may have **case** constants that are the same.

■ If character constants are used in the **switch** statement, they are automatically converted to integers.

The **switch** statement is often used to process keyboard commands, such as menu selection. As shown here, the function **menu( )** displays a menu for a spelling-checker program and calls the proper procedures:

```
void menu(void)
{
  char ch;

  printf("1. Check Spelling\n");
  printf("2. Correct Spelling Errors\n");
  printf("3. Display Spelling Errors\n");
  printf("Strike Any Other Key to Skip\n");
  printf("        Enter your choice: ");

  ch = getchar(); /* read the selection from
```

```
                        the keyboard */

  switch(ch) {
    case '1':
      check_spelling();
      break;
    case '2':
      correct_errors();
      break;
    case '3':
      display_errors();
      break;
    default :
      printf("No option selected");
  }
}
```

Technically, the **break** statements inside the **switch** statement are optional. They terminate the statement sequence associated with each constant. If the **break** statement is omitted, execution will continue on into the next **case**'s statements until either a **break** or the end of the **switch** is reached. For example, the following function uses the "drop through" nature of the **case**s to simplify the code for a device-driver input handler:

```
/* Process a value */
void inp_handler(int i)
{
  int flag;

  flag = -1;

  switch(i) {
    case 1:  /* these cases have common statement */
    case 2:  /* sequences */
    case 3:
      flag = 0;
      break;
    case 4:
      flag = 1;
    case 5:
      error(flag);
```

```
      break;
    default:
      process(i);
  }
}
```

This example illustrates two aspects of **switch**. First, you can have **case** statements that have no statement sequence associated with them. When this occurs, execution simply drops through to the next **case**. In this example, the first three **case**s all execute the same statements, which are

```
flag = 0;
break;
```

Second, execution of one statement sequence continues into the next **case** if no **break** statement is present. If **i** matches 4, **flag** is set to 1 and, because there is no **break** statement at the end of that **case**, execution continues and the call to **error(flag)** is executed. If **i** had matched 5, **error(flag)** would have been called with a flag value of –1 (rather than 1).

The fact that **case**s can run together when no **break** is present prevents the unnecessary duplication of statements, resulting in more efficient code.

Note that the statements associated with each **case** are not code blocks but are *statement sequences*. (Of course, the entire **switch** statement does define a block). This technical distinction is only important in certain situations. Here is one example. The following code fragment is in error and will not compile because you cannot declare a local variable within a statement sequence. (You may only declare local variables at the start of a block.)

```
/* This is incorrect.*/
switch(c) {
  case 1:
    int t;
      .
      .
      .
```

Although a bit odd, you could add a local variable as shown next. In this case, the declaration occurs at the start of the **switch** block.

```
/* Although strange, this is correct. */
switch(c)
{
  int t;
  case 1:
      .
      .
      .
```

Of course, you can create a block of code as one of the statements in a sequence and declare a local variable within it, as shown here:

```
/* This is correct. */
switch(c) {
  case 1:
      { /* create block */
        int t;
          .
          .
          .

      }
      .
      .
      .
```

Nested switch Statements

You can have a **switch** as part of the statement sequence of an outer **switch**. Even if the **case** constants of the inner and outer **switch** contain common values, no conflicts arise. For example, the following code fragment is perfectly acceptable:

```
switch(x) {
  case 1:
    switch(y) {
      case 0: printf("divide by zero error");
              break;
      case 1: process(x,y);
    }
    break;
  case 2:
      .
      .
      .
```

Iteration Statements

In C, and all other modern programming languages, iteration statements (also called loops) allow a set of instructions to be repeatedly executed until a certain condition is reached. This condition may be predefined (as in the **for** loop), or open ended (as in the **while** and **do-while** loops).

The for Loop

The general design of C's **for** loop is reflected in some form or another in all procedural programming languages. However, in C, it provides unexpected flexibility and power.

The general form of the **for** statement is

for(*initialization; condition; increment*) *statement;*

The **for** loop allows many variations. However, the *initialization* is generally an assignment statement that is used to set the loop control variable. The *condition* is a relational expression that determines when the loop exits. The *increment* defines how the loop control variable changes each time the loop is repeated. You must separate these three major sections by semicolons. The **for** loop continues to execute as long as the condition is true. Once the condition becomes false, program execution resumes on the statement following the **for**.

In the following program, a **for** loop is used to print the numbers 1 through 100 on the screen:

```c
#include <stdio.h>

void main(void)
{
  int x;

  for(x=1; x <= 100; x++) printf("%d ", x);
}
```

In the loop, **x** is initially set to 1 and then compared with 100. Since **x** is less than 100, **printf( )** is called and the loop iterates. This causes **x** to be increased by 1 and again tested to see if it is still less than or equal to 100. If it is, **printf( )** is called. This process repeats until **x** is greater than 100, at which point the loop terminates. In this example, **x** is the loop control variable, which is changed and checked each time the loop repeats.

The following example is a **for** loop that iterates multiple statements:

```c
for(x=100; x != 65; x-=5 ) {
  z = x*x;
  printf("The square of %d, %f", x, z);
}
```

Both the squaring of **x** and the call to **printf( )** are executed until **x** equals 65. Note that the loop is *negative running*: **x** is initialized to 100 and 5 is subtracted from it each time the loop repeats.

In **for** loops, the conditional test is always performed at the top of the loop. This means that the code inside the loop may not be executed at all if the condition is false to begin with. For example, in

```
x = 10;
for(y=10; y!=x; ++y) printf("%d", y);
printf("%d", y);  /* this is the only printf()
                     statement that will execute */
```

the loop will never execute because **x** and **y** are equal when the loop is entered. Because this causes the conditional expression to evaluate to false, neither the body of the loop nor the increment portion of the loop executes. Hence, **y** still has the value 10, and the only output produced by the fragment is the number 10 printed once on the screen.

for Loop Variations

The previous discussion described the most common form of the **for** loop. However, C offers several variations that increase the flexibility and applicability of the **for** loop.

One of the most common variations uses the comma operator to allow two or more variables to control the loop. (Remember, you use the comma operator to string together a number of expressions in a "do this and this" fashion. See Chapter 2.) For example, the variables **x** and **y** control the following loop, and both are initialized inside the **for** statement:

```
for(x=0, y=0; x+y<10; ++x) {
  y = getchar();
  y = y-'0'; /* subtract the ASCII code for 0
              from y */
      .
      .
      .
}
```

Commas separate the two initialization statements. Each time the loop repeats, **x** is incremented and **y**'s value is set by keyboard input. Both **x** and **y** must be at the correct value for the loop to terminate. Even though **y**'s value is set by keyboard input, **y** must be initialized to 0 so that its value is defined before the first evaluation of the conditional expression. (If **y** were not defined, it could by chance contain the value 10, making the conditional test false and preventing the loop from executing.)

The **converge( )** function shown next demonstrates multiple loop control variables. The **converge( )** function displays a string by printing characters from both ends, converging in the middle at the specified line. This requires positioning the cursor at various disconnected points on the screen. Because C runs under a wide variety of environments, it does not define a cursor positioning function. However, virtually all C compilers supply one, although its name may vary. The following program uses Borland's cursor positioning function, which is called **gotoxy( )**. (It requires the header **conio.h**.)

```c
/* Borland version. */
#include <stdio.h>
#include <conio.h>
#include <string.h>

void converge(int line, char *message);

void main(void)
{
  converge(10, "This is a test of converge().");
}

/* This function displays a string starting at the left
   side of the specified line.  It writes characters
   from both the ends converging at the middle. */
void converge(int line, char *message)
{
  int i, j;

  for(i=1, j=strlen(message); i<j; i++, j--) {
    gotoxy(i, line); printf("%c", message[i-1]);
    gotoxy(j, line); printf("%c", message[j-1]);
  }
}
```

The Microsoft equivalent of **gotoxy( )** is **_settextposition( )**, which uses the header file **graph.h**. The previous program, recoded for Microsoft C, is shown here:

```c
/* Microsoft version. */
#include <stdio.h>
#include <graph.h>
```

```
#include <string.h>

void converge(int line, char *message);

void main(void)
{
  converge(10, "This is a test of converge().");
}

/* This function displays a string starting at the left
    side of the specified line.  It writes characters
    from both the ends converging at the middle. */
void converge(int line, char *message)
{
  int i, j;

  for(i=1, j=strlen(message); i<j; i++, j--) {
    _settextposition(line, i);
    printf("%c", message[i-1]);
    _settextposition(line, j);
    printf("%c", message[j-1]);
  }
}
```

If you use a different C compiler, you will need to check your user manuals for the name of your cursor positioning function.

In both versions of **converge( )**, the **for** loop uses two loop control variables, **i** and **j**, to index the string from opposite ends. As the loop iterates, **i** is increased and **j** is decreased. The loop stops when **i** is equal to or greater than **j**, thus ensuring that all characters are written.

The conditional expression does not have to involve testing the loop control variable against some target value. In fact, the condition may be any relational or logical statement. This means that you can test for several possible terminating conditions.

For example, you could use the following function to log a user onto a remote system. The user has three tries to enter the password. The loop terminates when the three tries are used up or the user enters the correct password.

```
void sign_on(void)
{
  char str[20];
```

```
    int x;

    for(x=0; x<3 && strcmp(str, "password"); ++x) {
      printf("Enter password please:");
      gets(str);
    }

    if(x==3) return;
    /* else log user in ... */
}
```

This function uses **strcmp( )**, the standard library function that compares two strings and returns 0 if they match.

Remember, each of the three sections of the **for** loop may consist of any valid C expression. The expressions need not actually have anything to do with what the sections are generally used for. With this in mind, consider the following example:

```
#include <stdio.h>

int sqrnum(int num);
int readnum(void);
int prompt(void);

void main(void)
{
  int t;

  for(prompt(); t=readnum(); prompt())
    sqrnum(t);
}

prompt(void)
{
  printf("Enter a number: ");
  return 0;
}

readnum(void)
{
  int t;
```

```
    scanf("%d", &t);
    return t;
}

sqrnum(int num)
{
    printf("%d\n", num*num);
    return num*num;
}
```

Look closely at the **for** loop in **main( )**. Notice that each part of the **for** loop is composed of function calls that prompt the user and read a number entered from the keyboard. If the number entered is 0, the loop terminates because the conditional expression will be false. Otherwise, the number is squared. Thus, this **for** loop uses the initialization and increment portions in a nontraditional but completely valid sense.

Another interesting trait of the **for** loop is that pieces of the loop definition need not be there. In fact, there need not be an expression present for any of the sections—the expressions are optional. For example, this loop will run until the user enters **123**:

```
for(x=0; x!=123; ) scanf("%d", &x);
```

Notice that the increment portion of the **for** definition is blank. This means that each time the loop repeats, **x** is tested to see if it equals 123, but no further action takes place. If you type **123** at the keyboard, however, the loop condition becomes false and the loop terminates.

The initialization often occurs outside the **for** statement. This most frequently happens when the initial condition of the loop control variable must be computed by some complex means as in this example:

```
gets(s);  /* read a string into s */
if(*s) x = strlen(s); /* get the string's length */
else x = 10;

for( ; x<10; ) {
    printf("%d", x);
    ++x;
}
```

The initialization section has been left blank and **x** is initialized before the loop is entered.

The Infinite Loop

Although you can use any loop statement to create an infinite loop, **for** is traditionally used for this purpose. Since none of the three expressions that form the **for** loop are required, you can make an endless loop by leaving the conditional expression empty, as here:

```
for( ; ; ) printf(" This loop will run forever.\n");
```

You may have an initialization and increment expression, but C programmers more commonly use the **for(;;)** construct to signify an infinite loop.

Actually, the **for(;;)** construct does not guarantee an infinite loop because C's **break** statement, encountered anywhere inside the body of a loop, causes immediate termination (**break** is discussed later in this chapter). Program control then resumes at the code following the loop, as shown here:

```
ch = '\0';

for( ; ; ) {
  ch = getchar(); /* get a character */
  if(ch=='A') break; /* exit the loop */
}

printf("you typed an A");
```

This loop will run until the user types an **A** at the keyboard.

for Loops with No Bodies

As defined by the C syntax, a statement may be empty. This means that the body of the **for** loop (or any other loop) may also be empty. You can use this fact to improve the efficiency of certain algorithms and to create time delay loops.

Removing spaces from an input stream is a common programming task. For example, a database program may allow a query such as "show all balances less than 400." The database needs to have each word fed to it separately, without spaces. That is, the database input processor recognizes "**show**" but not " **show**". The following loop removes leading spaces from the stream pointed to by **str**.

```
for( ; *str == ' '; str++) ;
```

As you can see, this loop has no body—and no need for one either.

Time delay loops are often used in programs. The following code shows how to create one by using **for**:

```
for(t=0; t<SOME_VALUE; t++) ;
```

The while Loop

The second loop available in C is the **while** loop. Its general form is

while(*condition*) *statement*;

where *statement* is either an empty statement, a single statement, or a block of statements. The *condition* may be any expression, and true is any nonzero value. The loop iterates while the condition is true. When the condition becomes false, program control passes to the line of code immediately following the loop.

The following example shows a keyboard input routine that simply loops until the user types **A**:

```
wait_for_char(void)
{
  char ch;

  ch = '\0';  /* initialize ch */
  while(ch != 'A') ch = getchar();
  return ch;
}
```

First, **ch** is initialized to null. As a local variable, its value is not known when **wait_for_char( )** is executed. The **while** loop then checks to see if **ch** is not equal to **A**. Because **ch** was initialized to null, the test is true and the loop begins. Each time you press a key, the condition is tested again. Once you enter an **A**, the condition becomes false because **ch** equals **A**, and the loop terminates.

Like **for** loops, **while** loops check the test condition at the top of the loop, which means that the body of the loop will not execute if the condition is false to begin with. This feature may eliminate the need to perform a separate conditional test before the loop. The **pad( )** function provides a good illustration of this. It adds spaces to the end of a string to fill the string to a predefined length. If the string is already at the desired length, no spaces are added.

```
#include <stdio.h>
#include <string.h>

void pad(char *s, int length);
```

```
void main(void)
{
  char str[80];

  strcpy(str, "this is a test");
  pad(str, 40);
  printf("%d", strlen(str));
}

/* Add spaces to the end of a string. */
void pad(char *s, int length)
{
  int l;

  l = strlen(s); /* find out how long it is */

  while(l<length) {
    s[l] = ' '; /* insert a space */
    l++;
  }
  s[l]= '\0'; /* strings need to be
                  terminated in a null */
}
```

The two arguments of **pad( )** are **s**, a pointer to the string to lengthen, and **length**, the number of characters that **s** should have. If the length of string **s** is already equal to or greater than **length**, the code inside the **while** loop does not execute. If **s** is shorter than **length**, **pad( )** adds the required number of spaces. The **strlen( )** function, part of the standard library, returns the length of the string.

If several separate conditions need to terminate a **while** loop, a single variable commonly forms the conditional expression. The value of this variable is set at various points throughout the loop. In this example

```
void func1(void)
{
  int working;

  working = 1; /* i.e., true */

  while(working) {
    working = process1();
```

```
   if(working)
      working = process2();
   if(working)
      working = process3();
 }
}
```

any of the three routines may return false and cause the loop to exit.

There need not be any statements in the body of the **while** loop. For example,

```
while((ch=getchar()) != 'A') ;
```

will simply loop until the user types **A**. If you feel uncomfortable putting the assignment inside the **while** conditional expression, remember that the equal sign is just an operator that evaluates to the value of the right-hand operand.

The do-while Loop

Unlike **for** and **while** loops, which test the loop condition at the top of the loop, the **do-while** loop checks its condition at the bottom of the loop. This means that a **do-while** loop always executes at least once. The general form of the **do-while** loop is

```
do{
    statement;
} while(condition);
```

Although the curly braces are not necessary when only one statement is present, they are usually used to avoid confusion (to you, not the compiler) with the **while**. The **do-while** loop iterates until *condition* becomes false.

The following **do-while** loop will read numbers from the keyboard until it finds a number less than or equal to 100.

```
do {
   scanf("%d", &num);
} while(num > 100);
```

Perhaps the most common use of the **do-while** loop is in a menu selection function. When the user enters a valid response, it is returned as the value of the function. Invalid responses cause a reprompt. The following code shows an improved version of the spelling-checker menu developed earlier in this chapter:

```c
void menu(void)
{
  char ch;

  printf("1. Check Spelling\n");
  printf("2. Correct Spelling Errors\n");
  printf("3. Display Spelling Errors\n");
  printf("       Enter your choice: ");

  do {
    ch = getchar(); /* read the selection from
                        the keyboard */
    switch(ch) {
      case '1':
        check_spelling();
        break;
      case '2':
        correct_errors();
        break;
      case '3':
        display_errors();
        break;
    }
  } while(ch!='1' && ch!='2' && ch!='3');
}
```

Here, the **do-while** loop is a good choice because you will always want a menu function to execute at least once. After the options have been displayed, the program will loop until a valid option is selected.

Jump Statements

C has four statements that perform an unconditional branch: **return, goto, break,** and **continue**. Of these, you may use **return** and **goto** anywhere in your program. You may use the **break** and **continue** statements in conjunction with any of the loop statements. As discussed earlier in this chapter, you can also use **break** with **switch**.

The return Statement

The **return** statement is used to return from a function. It is categorized as a jump statement because it causes execution to return (jump back) to the point at which the call to the function was made. If **return** has a value associated with it, that value becomes the return value of the function. If no return value is specified, assume that a garbage value is returned. (Some C compilers will automatically return 0 if no value is specified, but do not count on this.)

The general form of the **return** statement is

return *expression*;

Remember, the *expression* is optional. However, if present, it will become the return value of the function.

You can use as many **return** statements as you like within a function. However, the function will stop executing as soon as it encounters the first **return**. The } that ends a function also causes the function to return. It is the same as a **return** without any specified value.

A function declared as **void** may not contain a **return** statement that specifies a value. (Since a **void** function has no return value, it makes sense that no **return** statement within a **void** function can return a value.)

See Chapter 6 for more information on **return**.

The goto Statement

Since C has a rich set of control structures and allows additional control using **break** and **continue**, there is little need for **goto**. Most programmers' chief concern about the **goto** is its tendency to render programs unreadable. Nevertheless, although the **goto** statement fell out of favor some years ago, it has managed to polish its tarnished image somewhat. There are no programming situations that require **goto**. Rather, it is a convenience, which, if used wisely, can be a benefit in a narrow set of programming situations. As such, **goto** is not used outside of this section.

The **goto** statement requires a label for operation. (A *label* is a valid C identifier followed by a colon.) Furthermore, the label must be in the same function as the **goto** that uses it—you cannot jump between functions. The general form of the **goto** statement is

goto *label*;
.
.
.
label:

where *label* is any valid label either before or after **goto**. For example, you could create a loop from 1 to 100 using the **goto** and a label, as shown here:

```
x = 1;
loop1:
  x++;
  if(x<100) goto loop1;
```

The break Statement

The **break** statement has two uses. You can use it to terminate a **case** in the **switch** statement (covered in the section on **switch** earlier in this chapter). You can also use it to force immediate termination of a loop, bypassing the normal loop conditional test.

When the **break** statement is encountered inside a loop, the loop is immediately terminated and program control resumes at the next statement following the loop. For example,

```
#include <stdio.h>

void main(void)
{
  int t;

  for(t=0; t<100; t++) {
    printf("%d ", t);
    if(t==10) break;
  }
}
```

prints the numbers 0 through 10 on the screen. Then the loop terminates because **break** causes immediate exit from the loop, overriding the conditional test **t<100**.

Programmers often use the **break** statement in loops in which a special condition can cause immediate termination. For example, here a keypress can stop the execution of the **look_up( )** function:

```
look_up(char *name)
{
  do {
      /* look up names ... */
      if(kbhit()) break;
  } while(!found);
  /* process match */
}
```

The **kbhit( )** function returns 0 if you do not press a key. Otherwise, it returns a nonzero value. Because of the wide differences between computing environments, the ANSI C standard does not define **kbhit( )**, but you will almost certainly have it (or one with a slightly different name) supplied with your compiler.

A **break** causes an exit from only the innermost loop. For example,

```
for(t=0; t<100; ++t) {
  count = 1;
  for(;;) {
    printf("%d ", count);
    count++;
    if(count==10) break;
  }
}
```

prints the numbers 1 through 10 on the screen 100 times. Each time the compiler encounters **break**, control is passed back to the outer **for** loop.

A **break** used in a **switch** statement will affect only that **switch**. It does not affect any loop the **switch** happens to be in.

The exit( ) Function

Although **exit( )** is not a program control statement, a short digression that discusses it is in order at this time. Just as you can break out of a loop, you can break out of a program by using the standard library function **exit( )**. This function causes immediate termination of the entire program, forcing a return to the operating system. In effect, the **exit( )** function acts as if it were breaking out of the entire program.

The general form of the **exit( )** function is

void exit(int *return_code*);

The value of *return_code* is returned to the calling process, which is usually the operating system. Zero is generally used as a return code to indicate normal program termination. Other arguments are used to indicate some sort of error.

Programmers frequently use **exit( )** when a mandatory condition for program execution is not satisfied. For example, imagine a virtual reality computer game that requires a special graphics adapter. The **main( )** function of this game might look like this:

```
void main(void)
{
  if(!virtual_graphics()) exit(1);
  play();
}
```

where **virtual_graphics( )** is a user-defined function that returns true if the virtual-reality graphics adapter is present. If the adapter is not in the system, **virtual_graphics( )** returns false and the program terminates.

As another example, this version of **menu( )** uses **exit( )** to quit the program and return to the operating system:

```c
void menu(void)
{
  char ch;

  printf("1. Check Spelling\n");
  printf("2. Correct Spelling Errors\n");
  printf("3. Display Spelling Errors\n");
  printf("4. Quit\n");
  printf("      Enter your choice: ");

  do {
    ch=getchar(); /* read the selection from
                     the keyboard */
      switch(ch) {
        case '1':
          check_spelling();
          break;
        case '2':
          correct_errors();
          break;
        case '3':
          display_errors();
          break;
        case '4':
          exit(0); /* return to OS */
      }
    } while(ch!='1' && ch!='2' && ch!='3');
}
```

The continue Statement

The **continue** statement works somewhat like the **break** statement. Instead of forcing termination, however, **continue** forces the next iteration of the loop to take place, skipping any code in between. For the **for** loop, **continue** causes the conditional test and then the increment portions of the loop to execute. For the **while** and **do-while** loops, program control passes to the conditional tests. For example, the following program counts the number of spaces contained in the string entered by the user:

```
/* Count spaces */
#include <stdio.h>

void main(void)
{
  char s[80], *str;
  int space;

  printf("Enter a string: ");
  gets(s);
  str = s;

  for(space=0; *str; str++) {
    if(*str != ' ') continue;
    space++;
  }
  printf("%d spaces\n", space);
}
```

Each character is tested to see if it is a space. If it is not, the **continue** statement forces the **for** to iterate again. If the character *is* a space, **space** is incremented.

The following example shows how you can use **continue** to expedite the exit from a loop by forcing the conditional test to be performed sooner:

```
void code(void)
{
  char done, ch;

  done = 0;
  while(!done) {
    ch = getchar();
    if(ch=='$') {
      done = 1;
      continue;
    }
    putchar(ch+1); /* shift the alphabet one
                      position higher */

  }
}
```

This function codes a message by shifting all characters you type one letter higher. For example, an **A** becomes a **B** . The function will terminate when you type a **$**. After a **$** has been input, no further output will occur because the conditional test, brought into effect by **continue**, will find **done** to be true and will cause the loop to exit.

Expression Statements

Chapter 2 covers C expressions thoroughly. However, a few special points are mentioned here. Remember, an expression statement is simply a valid C expression followed by a semicolon, as in

```
func();  /* a function call */
a = b+c; /* an assignment statement */
b+f();   /* a valid, but strange statement */
;        /* an empty statement */
```

The first expression statement executes a function call. The second is an assignment. The third expression, though strange, is still evaluated by the C compiler because the function **f( )** may perform some necessary task. The final example shows that C allows a statement to be empty (sometimes called a *null statement*).

Block Statements

Block statements are simply groups of related statements that are treated as a unit. The statements that make up a block are logically bound together. A block is begun with a { and terminated by its matching }. Programmers use block statements most commonly to create a multi-statement target for some other statement, such as **if**. However, you may place a block statement anywhere you would put any other statement. For example, this is perfectly valid (although unusual) C code:

```
#include <stdio.h>

void main(void)
{
  int i;

  {  /* a block statement */
    i = 120;
    printf("%d", i);
  }
}
```

Chapter Four

Arrays and Strings

n *array* is a collection of variables of the same type that are referenced by a common name. A specific element in an array is accessed by an index. In C, all arrays consist of contiguous memory locations. The lowest address corresponds to the first element and the highest address to the last element. Arrays may have from one to several dimensions. The most common array in C is the *string*, which is simply an array of characters terminated by a null. This approach to strings gives C greater power and efficiency than other languages.

In C, arrays and pointers are closely related; a discussion of one usually refers to the other. This chapter focuses on arrays, while Chapter 5 looks closely at pointers. You should read both to understand fully these important C constructs.

Single-Dimension Arrays

The general form for declaring a single-dimensioned array is

type var_name[size];

Like other variables, arrays must be explicitly declared so that the compiler may allocate space for them in memory. Here, *type* declares the base type of the array, which is the type of each element in the array. *size* defines how many elements the array will hold. For example, to declare a 100-element array called **balance**, and of type **double**, use this statement:

```
double balance[100];
```

In C, all arrays have 0 as the index of their first element. Therefore, when you write

```
char p[10];
```

you are declaring a character array that has ten elements, **p[0]** through **p[9]**. For example, the following program loads an integer array with the numbers 0 through 99:

```
void main(void)
{
  int x[100]; /* this declares a 100-integer array */
  int t;

  for(t=0; t<100; ++t) x[t] = t;
}
```

The amount of storage required to hold an array is directly related to its type and size. For a single-dimension array, the total size in bytes is computed as shown here:

total bytes = sizeof(type) * size of array

C has no bounds checking on arrays. You could overwrite either end of an array and write into some other variable's data or even into the program's code. As the programmer, it is your job to provide bounds checking where needed. For example, this code will compile without error, but is incorrect because the **for** loop will cause the array **count** to be overrun.

```
int count[10], i;

/* this causes count to be overrun */
for(i=0; i<100; i++) count[i] = i;
```

Single-dimension arrays are essentially lists of information of the same type that are stored in contiguous memory locations in index order. For example, Figure 4-1 shows how array **a** appears in memory if it starts at memory location 1000 and is declared as shown here:

```
char a[7];
```

Generating a Pointer to an Array

You can generate a pointer to the first element of an array by simply specifying the array name, without any index. For example, given

```
int sample[10];
```

Element	a[0]	a[1]	a[2]	a[3]	a[4]	a[5]	a[6]
Address	1000	1001	1002	1003	1004	1005	1006

Figure 4-1. *A seven-element character array beginning at location 1000*

you can generate a pointer to the first element by using the name **sample**.
For example, the following program fragment assigns **p** the address of the first
element of **sample**:

```
int *p;
int sample[10];

p = sample;
```

You can also specify the address of the first element of an array using the **&**
operator. For example, **sample** and **&sample[0]** both produce the same results.
However, in professionally written C code, you will almost never see **&sample[0]**.

Passing Single-Dimension Arrays to Functions

In C, you cannot pass an entire array as an argument to a function. You can, however,
pass to the function a pointer to an array by specifying the array's name without an
index. For example, the following program fragment passes the address of **i** to **func1( )**:

```
void main(void)
{
  int i[10];

  func1(i);
  .
  .
  .
}
```

If a function receives a single-dimension array, you may declare its formal
parameter in one of three ways: as a pointer, as a sized array, or as an unsized array.
For example, to receive **i**, a function called **func1( )** can be declared as

```
void func1(int *x) /* pointer */
{
  .
  .
  .
}
```

or

```
void func1(int x[10]) /* sized array */
{
    .
    .
    .
}
```

or finally as

```
void func1(int x[]) /* unsized array */
{
    .
    .
    .
}
```

All three declaration methods produce similar results because each tells the compiler that an integer pointer is going to be received. The first declaration actually uses a pointer. The second employs the standard array declaration. In the final version, a modified version of an array declaration simply specifies that an array of type **int** of some length is to be received. As you can see, the length of the array doesn't matter as far as the function is concerned because C performs no bounds checking. In fact, as far as the compiler is concerned,

```
void func1(int x[32])
{
    .
    .
    .
}
```

also works because the C compiler generates code that instructs **func1( )** to receive a pointer—it does not actually create a 32-element array.

Strings

By far the most common use of one-dimensional arrays is as character strings. Remember, in C, a string is defined as a character array that is terminated by a null. A null is specified as '\0' and is zero. For this reason, you need to declare character arrays to be one character longer than the largest string that they are to hold. For example, to declare an array **str** that can hold a 10-character string, you would write

```
char str[11];
```

This makes room for the null at the end of the string.

Although C does not have a string data type, it allows string constants. A *string constant* is a list of characters enclosed in double quotes. For example,

"hello there"

You do not need to add the null to the end of string constants manually—the C compiler does this for you automatically.

C supports a wide range of string manipulation functions. The most common are

Name	Function
strcpy(s1, s2)	Copies s2 into s1.
strcat(s1, s2)	Concatenates s2 onto the end of s1.
strlen(s1)	Returns the length of s1.
strcmp(s1, s2)	Returns 0 if s1 and s2 are the same; less than 0 if s1<s2; greater than 0 if s1>s2.
strchr(s1, ch)	Returns a pointer to the first occurrence of ch in s1.
strstr(s1, s2)	Returns a pointer to the first occurrence of s2 in s1.

These functions use the standard header file **string.h**. (These and other string functions are discussed in detail in Part Two.) The following program illustrates the use of these string functions:

```
#include <stdio.h>
#include <string.h>

void main(void)
{
  char s1[80], s2[80];

  gets(s1);
  gets(s2);

  printf("lengths: %d %d\n", strlen(s1), strlen(s2));

  if(!strcmp(s1, s2)) printf("The strings are equal\n");
```

```
    strcat(s1, s2);
    printf("%s\n", s1);

    strcpy(s1, "This is a test.\n");
    printf(s1);
    if(strchr("hello", 'e')) printf("e is in hello\n");
    if(strstr("hi there", "hi")) printf("found hi");
}
```

If you run this program and enter the strings "**hello**" and "**hello**", the output is

lengths: 5 5
The strings are equal
hellohello
This is a test.
e is in hello
found hi

Remember, **strcmp( )** returns false if the strings are equal. Be sure to use the logical operator **!** to reverse the condition, as just shown, if you are testing for equality.

Two-Dimensional Arrays

C supports multidimensional arrays. The simplest form of the multidimensional array is the two-dimensional array. A two-dimensional array is, essentially, an array of one-dimensional arrays. To declare a two-dimensional integer array **d** of size 10,20, you would write

```
int d[10][20];
```

Pay careful attention to the declaration. Most other computer languages use commas to separate the array dimensions; C, in contrast, places each dimension in its own set of brackets.

Similarly, to access point 1,2 of array **d**, you would use

```
d[1][2]
```

The following example loads a two-dimensional array with the numbers 1 through 12 and prints them row by row.

```
#include <stdio.h>

void main(void)
{
   int t, i, num[3][4];

   for(t=0; t<3; ++t)
     for(i=0; i<4; ++i)
       num[t][i] = (t*4)+i+1;

   /* now print them out */
   for(t=0; t<3; ++t) {
     for(i=0; i<4; ++i)
       printf("%3d ", num[t][i]);
     printf("\n");
   }
}
```

In this example, **num[0][0]** has the value 1, **num[0][1]** the value 2, **num[0][2]** the value 3, and so on. The value of **num[2][3]** will be 12. You can visualize the **num** array as shown here:

num [t] [i]

	0	1	2	3
0	1	2	3	4
1	5	6	7	8
2	9	10	11	12

Two-dimensional arrays are stored in a row-column matrix, where the first index indicates the row and the second indicates the column. This means that the rightmost index changes faster than the leftmost when accessing the elements in the array in the order in which they are actually stored in memory. See Figure 4-2 for a graphic representation of a two-dimensional array in memory.

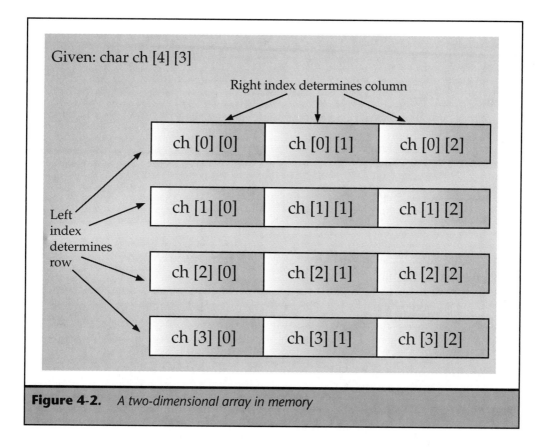

Figure 4-2. *A two-dimensional array in memory*

In the case of a two-dimensional array, the following formula yields the number of bytes of memory needed to hold it:

bytes = size of 1st index * size of 2nd index * sizeof(base type)

Therefore, assuming 2-byte integers, an integer array with dimensions 10,5 would have

10 * 5 * 2

or 100 bytes allocated.

When a two-dimensional array is used as an argument to a function, only a pointer to the first element is actually passed. However, the parameter receiving a two-dimensional array must define at least the size of the rightmost dimension. This is because the C compiler needs to know the length of each row if it is to index the array correctly. For example, a function that receives a two-dimensional integer array with dimensions 10,10 is declared like this:

```
void func1(int x[][10])
{
     .
     .
     .
}
```

You can specify the left dimension if you like, but it is not necessary. In either case, the C compiler needs to know the size of the right dimension in order to correctly execute expressions such as

```
x[2][4]
```

inside the function. If the length of the rows is not known, the compiler cannot determine where the third row begins.

The following short program uses a two-dimensional array to store the numeric grade for each student in a teacher's classes. The program assumes that the teacher has three classes and a maximum of 30 students per class. Notice the way the array **grade** is accessed by each of the functions.

```
#include <stdio.h>
#include <ctype.h>
#include <stdlib.h>

/* A simple student grades database. */

#define CLASSES  3
#define GRADES   30

int grade[CLASSES][GRADES];

void enter_grades(void);
int get_grade(int num);
void disp_grades(int g[][GRADES]);

void main(void)
{
  char ch, str[80];

  for(;;) {
    do {
```

```c
      printf("(E)nter grades\n");
      printf("(R)eport grades\n");
      printf("(Q)uit\n");
      gets(str);
      ch = toupper(*str);
    } while(ch!='E' && ch!='R' && ch!='Q');

    switch(ch) {
      case 'E':
        enter_grades();
        break;
      case 'R':
        disp_grades(grade);
        break;
      case 'Q':
        exit(0);
    }
  }
}

/* Enter the student's grades. */
void enter_grades(void)
{
  int t, i;

  for(t=0; t<CLASSES; t++) {
    printf("Class # %d:\n", t+1);
    for(i=0; i<GRADES; ++i)
      grade[t][i] = get_grade(i);
  }
}

/* Read a grade. */
get_grade(int num)
{
  char s[80];

  printf("Enter grade for student # %d:\n", num+1);
  gets(s);
  return(atoi(s));
}
```

```
/* Display grades. */
void disp_grades(int g[][GRADES])
{
  int t, i;

  for(t=0; t<CLASSES; ++t) {
    printf("Class # %d:\n", t+1);
    for(i=0; i<GRADES; ++i)
      printf("Student #%d is %d\n", i+1, g[t][i]);
  }
}
```

Arrays of Strings

It is not uncommon in programming to use an array of strings. For example, the input processor to a database may verify user commands against an array of valid commands. To create an array of strings, use a two-dimensional character array. The size of the left index determines the number of strings and the size of the right index specifies the maximum length of each string. The following code declares an array of 30 strings, each with a maximum length of 79 characters.

```
char str_array[30][80];
```

It is easy to access an individual string: You simply specify only the left index. For example, the following statement calls **gets( )** with the third string in **str_array**.

```
gets(str_array[2]);
```

The preceding statement is functionally equivalent to

```
gets(&str_array[2][0]);
```

but the first of the two forms is much more common in professionally written C code.

To understand better how string arrays work, study the following short program, which uses a string array as the basis for a very simple text editor:

```
#include <stdio.h>

#define MAX 100
#define LEN 80

char text[MAX][LEN];

/* A very simple text editor. */
void main(void)
{
  register int t, i, j;

  printf("Enter an empty line to quit.\n");

  for(t=0; t<MAX; t++) {
    printf("%d: ", t);
    gets(text[t]);
    if(!*text[t]) break; /* quit on blank line */
  }

  for(i=0; i<t; i++) {
    for(j=0; text[i][j]; j++) putchar(text[i][j]);
    putchar('\n');
  }
}
```

This program inputs lines of text until a blank line is entered. Then it redisplays each line one character at a time.

Multidimensional Arrays

C allows arrays of more than two dimensions. The exact limit, if any, is determined by your compiler. The general form of a multidimensional array declaration is

type name[Size1][Size2][Size3]. . .[SizeN];

Arrays of three or more dimensions are not often used because of the amount of memory they require. For example, a four-dimensional character array with dimensions 10,6,9,4 requires

> 10 * 6 * 9 * 4

or 2,160 bytes. If the array held 2-byte integers, 4,320 bytes would be needed. If the array held **doubles** (assuming 8 bytes per **double**), 17,280 bytes would be required. The storage required increases exponentially with the number of dimensions. Large multidimensional arrays are often dynamically allocated a piece at a time using C's dynamic allocation functions. This approach is called a *sparse array* and is discussed in Chapter 21.

In multidimensional arrays, it takes the computer time to compute each index. This means that accessing an element in a multidimensional array can be slower than accessing an element in a single-dimension array.

When passing multidimensional arrays into functions, you must declare all but the leftmost dimension. For example, if you declare array **m** as

```
int m[4][3][6][5];
```

a function, **func1( )**, that receives **m**, would look like this:

```
void func1(int d[][3][6][5])
{
    .
    .
    .
}
```

Of course, you can include the first dimension if you like.

Indexing Pointers

In C, pointers and arrays are closely related. As you know, an array name without an index is a pointer to the first element in the array. For example, consider the following array.

```
char p[10];
```

The following statements are identical:

```
p
&p[0]
```

Put another way,

```
p == &p[0]
```

evaluates to true because the address of the first element of an array is the same as the address of the array.

As stated, an array name without an index generates a pointer. Conversely, a pointer can be indexed as if it were declared to be an array. For example, consider this program fragment:

```
int *p, i[10];
p = i;
p[5] = 100;   /* assign using index */
*(p+5) = 100; /* assign using pointer arithmetic */
```

Both assignment statements place the value 100 in the sixth element of **i**. The first statement indexes **p**; the second uses pointer arithmetic. Either way, the result is the same. (Chapter 5 discusses pointers and pointer arithmetic.)

This same concept also applies to arrays of two or more dimensions. For example, assuming that **a** is a 10-by-10 integer array, these two statements are equivalent:

```
a
&a[0][0]
```

Furthermore, the 0,4 element of **a** may be referenced two ways: either by array indexing, **a[0][4]**, or by the pointer, ***(a+4)**. Similarly, element 1,2 is either **a[1][2]** or ***(a+12)**. In general, for any two-dimensional array

a[j][k] is equivalent to *(a+(j * row length)+k)

Pointers are sometimes used to access arrays because pointer arithmetic is often faster than array indexing.

A two-dimensional array can be reduced to a pointer to an array of one-dimensional arrays. Therefore, using a separate pointer variable is one easy way to use pointers to access elements within a row of a two-dimensional array. The following function illustrates this technique. It will print the contents of the specified row for the global integer array **num**:

```
int num[10][10];
.
```

```
        .
        .
void  pr_row(int j)
{
   int *p, t;

   p = &num[j][0]; /* get address of first
                      element in row j */

   for(t=0; t<10; ++t) printf("%d ", *(p+t));
}
```

You can generalize this routine by making the calling arguments be the row, the row length, and a pointer to the first array element, as shown here:

```
void pr_row(int j, int row_dimension, int *p)
{
   int t;

   p = p + (j * row_dimension);

   for(t=0; t<row_dimension; ++t)
     printf("%d ", *(p+t));
}
```

Arrays of greater than two dimensions may be reduced in a similar way. For example, a three-dimensional array can be reduced to a pointer to a two-dimensional array, which can be reduced to a pointer to a single-dimension array. Generally, an n-dimensional array can be reduced to a pointer and an (n-1)-dimensional array. This new array can be reduced again with the same method. The process ends when a single-dimension array is produced.

Array Initialization

C allows the initialization of arrays at the time of their declaration. The general form of array initialization is similar to that of other variables, as shown here:

type_specifier array_name[size1]. . .[sizeN] = { value_list };

The *value_list* is a comma-separated list of constants whose type is compatible with *type_specifier*. The first constant is placed in the first position of the array, the second constant in the second position, and so on. Note that a semicolon follows the }.

In the following example, a 10-element integer array is initialized with the numbers 1 through 10:

```
int i[10] = {1, 2, 3, 4, 5, 6, 7, 8, 9, 10};
```

This means that **i[0]** will have the value 1 and **i[9]** will have the value 10.

Character arrays that hold strings allow a shorthand initialization that takes the form:

char *array_name*[*size*] = "*string*";

For example, this code fragment initializes **str** to the phrase "I like C".

```
char str[9] = "I like C";
```

This is the same as writing

```
char str[9] = {'I', ' ', 'l', 'i', 'k', 'e',' ', 'C', '\0'};
```

Because all strings in C end with a null, you must make sure that the array you declare is long enough to include the null. This is why **str** is nine characters long even though "I like C" is only eight. When you use the string constant, the compiler automatically supplies the null terminator.

Multidimensional arrays are initialized the same as single-dimension ones. For example, the following initializes **sqrs** with the numbers 1 through 10 and their squares.

```
int sqrs[10][2] = {
  1,1,
  2,4,
  3,9,
  4,16,
  5,25,
  6,36,
  7,49,
  8,64,
  9,81,
  10,100
};
```

Unsized Array Initializations

Imagine that you are using array initialization to build a table of error messages, as shown here:

```
char e1[12] = "Read error\n";
char e2[13] = "Write error\n";
char e3[18] = "Cannot open file\n";
```

As you might guess, it is tedious to count the characters in each message manually to determine the correct array dimension. You can let C automatically calculate the dimensions of the arrays by using unsized arrays. If, in an array initialization statement, the size of the array is not specified, the C compiler automatically creates an array big enough to hold all the initializers present. This is called an *unsized array*. Using this approach, the message table becomes

```
char e1[] = "Read error\n";
char e2[] = "Write error\n";
char e3[] = "Cannot open file\n";
```

Given these initializations, this statement

```
printf("%s has length %d\n",  e2,  sizeof e2);
```

will print

Write error has length 13

Besides being less tedious, unsized array initialization allows you to change any of the messages without fear of using incorrect array dimensions.

Unsized array initializations are not restricted to one-dimensional arrays. For multidimensional arrays, you must specify all but the leftmost dimension. (The other dimensions are needed to allow the C compiler to index the array properly.) In this way, you may build tables of varying lengths and the compiler automatically allocates enough storage for them. For example, the declaration of **sqrs** as an unsized array is shown here:

```
int sqrs[][2] = {
  1,1,
  2,4,
  3,9,
  4,16,
  5,25,
  6,36,
  7,49,
  8,64,
  9,81,
  10,100
};
```

The advantage of this declaration over the sized version is that you may lengthen or shorten the table without changing the array dimensions.

A Tic-Tac-Toe Example

The longer example that follows illustrates many of the ways that you can manipulate arrays with C. Two-dimensional arrays are commonly used to simulate board game matrices. This section develops a simple tic-tac-toe program.

The computer plays a very simple game. When it is the computer's turn, it uses **get_computer_move( )** to scan the matrix, looking for an unoccupied cell. When it finds one, it puts an **O** there. If it cannot find an empty location, it reports a draw game and exits. The **get_player_move( )** function asks you where you want to place an **X**. The upper-left corner is location 1,1; the lower-right corner is 3,3.

The matrix array is initialized to contain spaces. This makes it easy to display the matrix on the screen.

Each time a move has been made, the program calls the **check( )** function. This function returns a space if there is no winner yet, an X if you have won, or an O if the computer has won. It scans the rows, the columns, and then the diagonals, looking for one that contains either all X's or all O's.

The **disp_matrix( )** function displays the current state of the game. Notice how initializing the matrix with spaces simplified this function.

The routines in this example all access the **matrix** array differently. Study them to make sure that you understand each array operation.

```
/* A simple Tic Tac Toe game. */
#include <stdio.h>
#include <stdlib.h>

char matrix[3][3];  /* the tic tac toe matrix */

char check(void);
void init_matrix(void);
void get_player_move(void);
void get_computer_move(void);
void disp_matrix(void);

void main(void)
{
  char done;

  printf("This is the game of Tic Tac Toe.\n");
  printf("You will be playing against the computer.\n");

  done = ' ';
  init_matrix();
  do{
    disp_matrix();
    get_player_move();
    done = check(); /* see if winner */
    if(done!= ' ') break; /* winner!*/
    get_computer_move();
    done = check(); /* see if winner */
  } while(done== ' ');
  if(done=='X') printf("You won!\n");
  else printf("I won!!!!\n");
  disp_matrix(); /* show final positions */
}

/* Initialize the matrix. */
void init_matrix(void)
{
  int i, j;

  for(i=0; i<3; i++)
    for(j=0; j<3; j++) matrix[i][j] = ' ';
}
```

```c
/* Get a player's move. */
void get_player_move(void)
{
  int x, y;

  printf("Enter coordinates for your X: ");
  scanf("%d%d", &x, &y);

  x--; y--;

  if(matrix[x][y]!= ' '){
    printf("Invalid move, try again.\n");
    get_player_move();
  }
  else matrix[x][y] = 'X';
}

/* Get a move from the computer. */
void get_computer_move(void)
{
  int i, j;
  for(i=0; i<3; i++){
    for(j=0; j<3; j++)
      if(matrix[i][j]==' ') break;
    if(matrix[i][j]==' ') break;
  }

  if(i*j==9)  {
    printf("draw\n");
    exit(0);
  }
  else
    matrix[i][j] = 'O';
}

/* Display the matrix on the screen. */
void disp_matrix(void)
{
  int t;

  for(t=0; t<3; t++) {
```

```
    printf(" %c | %c | %c ",matrix[t][0],
             matrix[t][1], matrix [t][2]);
    if(t!=2) printf("\n---|---|---\n");
  }
  printf("\n");
}

/* See if there is a winner. */
char check(void)
{
  int i;

  for(i=0; i<3; i++)  /* check rows */
    if(matrix[i][0]==matrix[i][1] &&
       matrix[i][0]==matrix[i][2]) return matrix[i][0];

  for(i=0; i<3; i++)  /* check columns */
    if(matrix[0][i]==matrix[1][i] &&
       matrix[0][i]==matrix[2][i]) return matrix[0][i];

  /* test diagonals */
  if(matrix[0][0]==matrix[1][1] &&
     matrix[1][1]==matrix[2][2])
       return matrix[0][0];

  if(matrix[0][2]==matrix[1][1] &&
     matrix[1][1]==matrix[2][0])
       return matrix[0][2];

  return ' ';
}
```

Chapter Five

Pointers

The correct understanding and use of pointers is critical to successful C programming. There are three reasons for this: First, pointers provide the means by which functions can modify their calling arguments. Second, pointers support C's dynamic allocation routines. Third, pointers can improve the efficiency of certain routines.

Pointers are one of C's strongest but also one of its most dangerous features. For example, uninitialized pointers (or pointers containing invalid values) can cause your system to crash. Perhaps worse, it is easy to use pointers incorrectly, causing bugs that are very difficult to find.

What Are Pointers?

A *pointer* is a variable that holds a memory address. This address is the location of another object (typically another variable) in memory. For example, if one variable contains the address of another variable, the first variable is said to *point to* the second. Figure 5-1 illustrates this situation.

Pointer Variables

If a variable is going to hold a pointer, it must be declared as such. A pointer declaration consists of a base type, an *, and the variable name. The general form for declaring a pointer variable is

type *name;

where *type* is the base type of the pointer and may be any valid C type. The name of the pointer variable is specified by *name*.

The base type of the pointer defines what type of variables the pointer can point to. Technically, any type of pointer can point anywhere in memory. However, all pointer arithmetic is done relative to its base type, so it is important to declare the pointer correctly. (Pointer arithmetic is discussed later in this chapter.)

The Pointer Operators

There are two special pointer operators: * and **&**. The **&** is a unary operator that returns the memory address of its operand. (Remember, a unary operator only requires one operand.) For example,

```
m = &count;
```

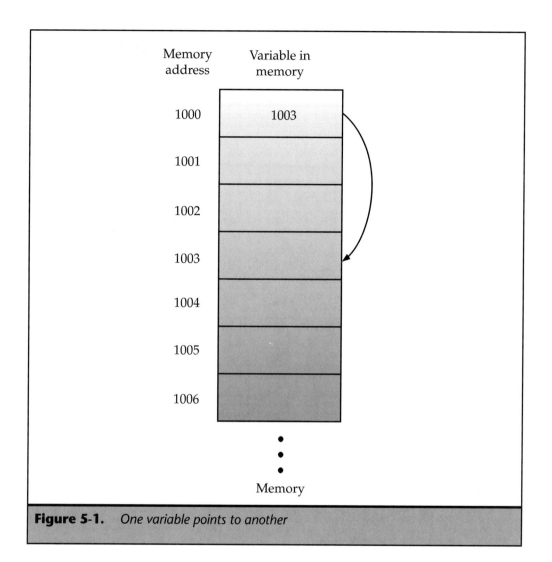

Memory address

Variable in memory

1000 — 1003

1001

1002

1003

1004

1005

1006

Memory

Figure 5-1. *One variable points to another*

places into **m** the memory address of the variable **count**. This address is the computer's internal location of the variable. It has nothing to do with the value of **count**. You can think of **&** as returning "the address of." Therefore, the preceding assignment statement means "**m** receives the address of **count**."

To understand the above assignment better, assume that the variable **count** uses memory location 2000 to store its value. Also assume that **count** has a value of 100. Then, after the preceding assignment, **m** will have the value 2000.

The second pointer operator, *****, is the complement of **&**. It is a unary operator that returns the value located at the address that follows.

For example, if **m** contains the memory address of the variable **count**,

```
q = *m;
```

places the value of **count** into **q**. Thus, **q** will have the value 100 because 100 is stored at location 2000, which is the memory address that was stored in **m**. You can think of * as "at address." In this case, the preceding statement means "**q** receives the value at address **m**."

It is sometimes confusing to beginners that the multiplication sign and the "at address" sign are the same, and the bitwise AND and the "address of" sign are the same. These operators have no relationship to each other. Both **&** and * have a higher precedence than all other arithmetic operators except the unary minus, with which they are equal.

You must make sure that your pointer variables always point to the correct type of data. For example, when you declare a pointer to be of type **int**, the compiler assumes that any address that it holds points to an integer variable—whether it actually does or not. Because C allows you to assign any address to a pointer variable, the following code fragment compiles with no error messages (or only warnings, depending upon your compiler) but does not produce the desired result:

```
void main(void)
{
  float x, y;
  int  *p;

  /* The next statement causes p (which is an
       integer pointer) to point to a float. */
  p = &x;

  /* The next statement does not operate as
       expected. */
  y = *p;
}
```

This will not assign the value of **x** to **y**. Because **p** is declared as an integer pointer, only 2 bytes of information will be transferred to **y**, not the 8 bytes that normally make up a floating-point number.

Pointer Expressions

In general, expressions involving pointers conform to the same rules as other C expressions. This section examines a few special aspects of pointer expressions.

Pointer Assignments

As with any variable, you may use a pointer on the right-hand side of an assignment statement to assign its value to another pointer. For example,

```
#include <stdio.h>

void main(void)
{
  int x;
  int *p1, *p2;

  p1 = &x;
  p2 = p1;

  printf(" %p", p2); /* print the address of x,
                        not x's value! */
}
```

Both **p1** and **p2** now point to **x**. The address of **x** is displayed by using the **%p printf( )** format specifier, which causes **printf( )** to display an address in the format used by the host computer.

Pointer Arithmetic

There are only two arithmetic operations that you may use on pointers: addition and subtraction. To understand what occurs in pointer arithmetic, let **p1** be an integer pointer with a current value of 2000. Also, assume integers are 2 bytes long. After the expression

```
p1++;
```

p1 contains 2002, not 2001. The reason for this is that each time **p1** is incremented, it will point to the next integer. The same is true of decrements. For example, assuming that **p1** has the value 2000, the expression

```
p1--;
```

causes **p1** to have the value 1998.

Generalizing from the preceding example, the following rules govern pointer arithmetic. Each time a pointer is incremented, it points to the memory location of the next element of its base type. Each time it is decremented, it points to the location of the previous element. When applied to character pointers, this will appear as "normal" arithmetic because characters are always 1 byte long. However, all other pointers will increase or decrease by the length of the data type they point to. For example, using 1-byte characters and 2-byte integers, when a character pointer is incremented, its value increases by one. However, when an integer pointer is incremented, its value increases by two. This is because pointers are incremented or decremented relative to the length of their base type. This approach ensures that a pointer is always pointing to an appropriate element of its base type. Figure 5-2 illustrates this concept.

You are not limited to the increment and decrement operators. For example, you may add or subtract integers to or from pointers. The expression

```
p1 = p1 + 12;
```

makes **p1** point to the twelfth element of **p1**'s type beyond the one it currently points to.

Besides addition and subtraction of a pointer and an integer, only one other arithmetic operation is allowed: you may subtract one pointer from another in order to find the number of objects of their base type that separate the two pointers. All other arithmetic operations are prohibited. Specifically, you may not multiply or divide pointers; you may not add two pointers; you may not apply the bitwise operators to them; and you may not add or subtract type **float** or **double** to or from pointers.

Pointer Comparisons

You can compare two pointers in a relational expression. For instance, given two pointers **p** and **q**, the following statement is perfectly valid:

```
if(p<q) printf("p points to lower memory than q\n");
```

Generally, pointer comparisons are used when two or more pointers point to a common object. As an example, a pair of stack routines are developed that store and

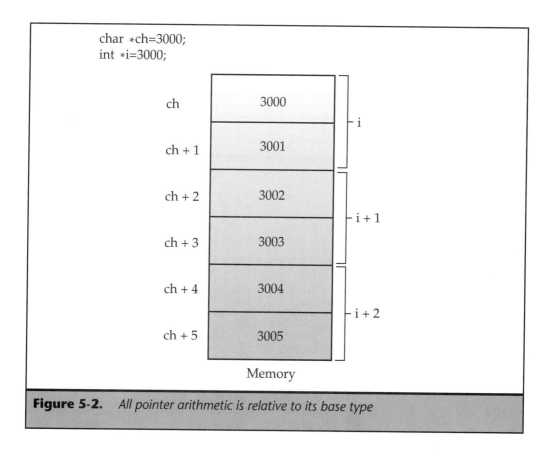

```
char *ch=3000;
int *i=3000;
```

ch   3000

   i

ch + 1   3001

ch + 2   3002

   i + 1

ch + 3   3003

ch + 4   3004

   i + 2

ch + 5   3005

Memory

Figure 5-2. *All pointer arithmetic is relative to its base type*

retrieve integer values. A stack is a list that uses first-in, last-out accessing. It is often compared to a stack of plates on a table—the first one set down is the last one to be used. Stacks are used frequently in compilers, interpreters, spreadsheets, and other system-related software. To create a stack, you need two functions: **push( )** and **pop( )**. The **push( )** function places values on the stack and **pop( )** takes them off. These routines are shown here with a simple **main( )** function to drive them. The program puts the values you enter into the stack. If you enter **0**, a value is popped from the stack. To stop the program, enter **–1**.

```
#include <stdio.h>
#include <stdlib.h>

#define SIZE 50

void push(int i);
```

```
int pop(void);

int  *tos, *p1, stack[SIZE];

void main(void)
{
  int value;

  tos = stack; /* tos points to the top of stack */
  p1 = stack; /* initialize p1 */

  do {
    printf("Enter value: ");
    scanf("%d", &value);
    if(value!=0) push(value);
    else printf("value on top is %d\n", pop());
  } while(value!=-1);
}

void push(int i)
{
  p1++;
  if(p1==(tos+SIZE)) {
    printf("Stack Overflow");
    exit(1);
  }
  *p1 = i;
}

pop(void)
{
  if(p1==tos) {
    printf("Stack Underflow");
    exit(1);
  }
  p1--;
  return *(p1+1);
}
```

You can see that memory for the stack is provided by the array **stack**. The pointer **p1** is set to point to the first byte in **stack**. The **p1** variable actually accesses the stack. The variable **tos** holds the memory address of the top of the stack. The value of **tos** prevents stack overflows and underflows. Once the stack has been initialized, **push( )** and **pop( )** may be used. Both the **push( )** and **pop( )** functions perform a relational test on the pointer **p1** to detect limit errors. In **push( )**, **p1** is tested against the end of stack by adding **SIZE** (the size of the stack) to **tos**. This prevents an overflow. In **pop( )**, **p1** is checked against **tos** to be sure that a stack underflow has not occurred.

In **pop( )**, the parentheses are necessary in the return statement. Without them, the statement would look like this:

```
return *p1 +1;
```

which would return the value at location **p1** plus one, not the value of the location **p1+1**.

Pointers and Arrays

There is a close relationship between pointers and arrays. Consider this program fragment:

```
char str[80], *p1;
p1 = str;
```

Here, **p1** has been set to the address of the first array element in **str**. To access the fifth element in **str**, you could write

```
str[4]
```

or

```
*(p1+4)
```

Both statements will return the fifth element. Remember, arrays start at 0. To access the fifth element, you must use 4 to index **str**. You also add 4 to the pointer **p1** to access the fifth element because **p1** currently points to the first element of **str**. (Recall that an array name without an index returns the starting address of the array, which is the address of the first element.)

C provides two methods of accessing array elements: pointer arithmetic and array indexing. Pointer arithmetic can be faster than array indexing. Since speed is often a consideration in programming, C programmers commonly use pointers to access array elements.

These two versions of **putstr( )**—one with array indexing and one with pointers—illustrate how you can use pointers in place of array indexing. The **putstr( )** function writes a string to the standard output device one character at a time.

```
/* Index s as an array. */
void putstr(char *s)
{
  register int t;
  for(t=0; s[t]; ++t) putchar(s[t]);
}

/* Access s as a pointer. */
void putstr(char *s)
{
  while(*s) putchar(*s++);
}
```

Most professional C programmers would find the second version easier to read and understand. In fact, the pointer version is the way routines of this sort are commonly written in C.

Arrays of Pointers

Pointers may be arrayed like any other data type. The declaration for an **int** pointer array of size 10 is

```
int *x[10];
```

To assign the address of an integer variable called **var** to the third element of the pointer array, write

```
x[2] = &var;
```

To find the value of **var**, write

```
*x[2]
```

If you want to pass an array of pointers into a function, you can use the same method that you use to pass other arrays—simply call the function with the array name without any indexes. For example, a function that receives array **x** looks like this:

```
void display_array(int *q[])
{
  int t;

  for(t=0; t<10; t++)
    printf("%d ", *q[t]);
}
```

Remember, **q** is not a pointer to integers, but rather a pointer to an array of pointers to integers. Therefore you need to declare the parameter **q** as an array of integer pointers, as just shown. You cannot declare **q** simply as an integer pointer because that is not what it is.

Pointer arrays are often used to hold pointers to strings. You can create a function that outputs an error message given its code number, as shown here:

```
void syntax_error(int num)
{
  static char *err[] = {
    "Cannot Open File\n",
    "Read Error\n",
    "Write Error\n",
    "Media Failure\n"
  };

  printf("%s", err[num]);
}
```

The array **err** holds pointers to each string. As you can see, **printf( )** inside **syntax_error( )** is called with a character pointer that points to one of the various error messages indexed by the error number passed to the function. For example, if **num** is passed a 2, the message **Write Error** is displayed.

As a point of interest, note that the command line argument **argv** is an array of character pointers. (See Chapter 6.)

Multiple Indirection

You can have a pointer point to another pointer that points to the target value. This situation is called *multiple indirection*, or *pointers to pointers*. Pointers to pointers can be confusing. Figure 5-3 helps clarify the concept of multiple indirection. As you can see, the value of a normal pointer is the address of the object that contains the value

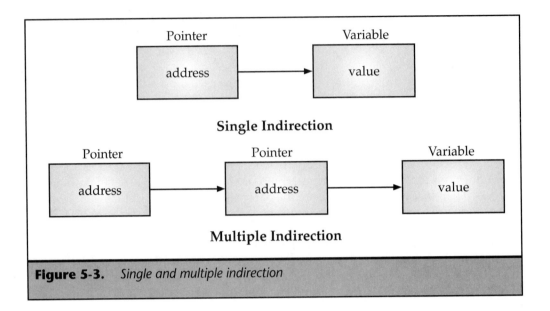

Figure 5-3. *Single and multiple indirection*

desired. In the case of a pointer to a pointer, the first pointer contains the address of the second pointer, which points to the object that contains the value desired.

Multiple indirection can be carried on to whatever extent desired, but more than a pointer to a pointer is rarely needed. In fact, excessive indirection is difficult to follow and prone to conceptual errors.

NOTE: Do not confuse multiple indirection with high-level data structures, such as linked lists, that use pointers. These are two fundamentally different concepts.

A variable that is a pointer to a pointer must be declared as such. You do this by placing an additional asterisk in front of the variable name. For example, the following declaration tells the compiler that **newbalance** is a pointer to a pointer of type **float**:

```
float **newbalance;
```

You should understand that **newbalance** is not a pointer to a floating-point number but rather a pointer to a **float** pointer.

To access the target value indirectly pointed to by a pointer to a pointer, you must apply the asterisk operator twice, as in this example:

```c
#include <stdio.h>

void main(void)
{
  int x, *p, **q;

  x = 10;
  p = &x;
  q = &p;

  printf("%d", **q); /* print the value of x */
}
```

Here, **p** is declared as a pointer to an integer and **q** as a pointer to a pointer to an integer. The call to **printf( )** prints the number **10** on the screen.

Initializing Pointers

After a pointer is declared but before it has been assigned a value, it may contain an unknown value. Should you try to use the pointer before giving it a valid value, you will probably crash your program—and possibly your computer's operating system as well—a very nasty type of error!

There is an important convention that most C programmers follow when working with pointers: A pointer that does not currently point to a valid memory location is given the value null (which is zero). By convention, any pointer that is null implies that it points to nothing and should not be used. However, just because a pointer has a null value does not make it "safe." The use of null is simply a convention that programmers follow. It is not part of the C language. For example, if you use a null pointer on the left side of an assignment statement, you still run the risk of crashing your program or operating system.

Because a null pointer is assumed to be unused, you can use the null pointer to make many of your pointer routines easier to code and more efficient. For example, you could use a null pointer to mark the end of a pointer array. A routine that accesses that array knows that it has reached the end when it encounters the null value. The **search( )** function shown here illustrates this type of approach.

```
/* look up a name */
search(char *p[], char *name)
{
  register int t;

  for(t=0; p[t]; ++t)
    if(!strcmp(p[t], name)) return t;

    return -1; /* not found */
}
```

The **for** loop inside **search( )** runs until either a match is found or a null pointer is encountered. Assuming the end of the array is marked with a null, the condition controlling the loop fails when it is reached.

C programmers commonly initialize strings. You saw an example of this in the **syntax_error( )** function in the section "Arrays of Pointers." Another variation on the initialization theme is the following type of string declaration:

```
char *p = "hello world";
```

As you can see, the pointer **p** is not an array. The reason this sort of initialization works is because of the way the compiler operates. All C compilers create what is called a *string table*, which is used internally by the compiler to store the string constants used by the program. Therefore, the preceding declaration statement places the address of **hello world**, as stored in the string table, into the pointer **p**. Throughout a program, **p** can be used like any other string. For example, the following program is perfectly valid:

```
#include <stdio.h>
#include <string.h>

char *p = "hello world";

void main(void)
{
  register int t;

  /* print the string forward and backwards */
  printf(p);
  for(t=strlen(p)-1; t>-1; t--) printf("%c", p[t]);
}
```

Pointers to Functions

A confusing yet powerful feature of C is the *function pointer*. Even though a function is not a variable, it has a physical location in memory that can be assigned to a pointer. A function's address is the entry point of the function. Because of this, a function pointer can be used to call a function.

To understand how function pointers work, you must know a little about how a function is compiled and called in C. First, as each function is compiled, source code is transformed into object code and an entry point is established. When a call is made to a function while your program is running, a machine-language call is made to this entry point. Therefore, if a pointer contains the address of a function's entry point, it can be used to call that function.

You obtain the address of a function by using the function's name without any parentheses or arguments. (This is similar to the way an array's address is obtained when only the array name, without indexes, is used.) To see how this is done, study the following program, paying close attention to the declarations:

```
#include <stdio.h>
#include <string.h>

void check(char *a, char *b,
           int (*cmp)(const char *, const char *));

void main(void)
{
  char s1[80], s2[80];
  int (*p)();

  p = strcmp;

  gets(s1);
  gets(s2);

  check(s1, s2, p);
}

void check(char *a, char *b,
           int (*cmp)(const char *, const char *))
{
  printf("testing for equality\n");
  if(!(*cmp)(a, b)) printf("equal");
  else printf("not equal");
}
```

When the **check( )** function is called, two character pointers and one function pointer are passed as parameters. Inside the function **check( )**, the arguments are declared as character pointers and a function pointer. Notice how the function pointer is declared. You must use a similar form when declaring other function pointers, although the return type of the function may differ. The parentheses around the ***cmp** are necessary for the compiler to interpret this statement correctly.

Inside **check( )**, the expression

```
(*cmp)(a, b)
```

calls **strcmp( )**, which is pointed to by **cmp**, with the arguments **a** and **b**. Again, the parentheses around *cmp are necessary. This example also illustrates the general method for using a function pointer to call the function it points to.

Note that you can call **check( )** by using **strcmp( )** directly, as shown here:

```
check(s1, s2, strcmp);
```

This eliminates the need for an additional pointer variable.

You may wonder why anyone would write a program in this way. Obviously, nothing is gained and significant confusion is introduced in the previous example. However, at times it is advantageous to pass functions as parameters or to create an array of functions. For example, when a compiler or interpreter is written, the parser (the part that evaluates expressions) often calls various support functions, such as those that compute mathematical operations (sine, cosine, tangent, etc.), perform I/O, or access system resources. Instead of having a large **switch** statement with all of these functions listed in it, an array of function pointers can be created. In this approach, the proper function is selected by its index. You can get the flavor of this type of usage by studying the expanded version of the previous example. In this program, **check( )** can be made to check for either alphabetical equality or numeric equality by simply calling it with a different comparison function.

```
#include <stdio.h>
#include <ctype.h>
#include <stdlib.h>
#include <string.h>

void check(char *a, char *b,
           int (*cmp)(const char *, const char *));
int numcmp(const char *a, const char *b);

void main(void)
```

```
{
  char s1[80], s2[80];

  gets(s1);
  gets(s2);

  if(isalpha(*s1))
        check(s1, s2, strcmp);
  else
        check(s1, s2, numcmp);
}

void check(char *a, char *b,
          int (*cmp)(const char *, const char *))
{
  printf("testing for equality\n");
  if(!(*cmp)(a, b)) printf("equal");
  else printf("not equal");
}

numcmp(const char *a, const char *b)
{
  if(atoi(a)==atoi(b)) return 0;
  else return 1;
}
```

C's Dynamic Allocation Functions

Pointers provide necessary support for C's powerful dynamic allocation system. *Dynamic allocation* is the means by which a program can obtain memory while it is running. As you know, global variables are allocated storage at compile time. Local variables use the stack. However, neither global nor local variables can be added during program execution. Yet there will be times when the storage needs of a program cannot be known ahead of time. For example, a word processor or a database should take advantage of all the RAM in a system. However, because the amount of available RAM varies between computers, such programs will not be able to do so using normal variables. Instead, these and other programs must allocate memory as they need it using C's dynamic allocation system.

Memory allocated by C's dynamic allocation functions is obtained from the *heap*—the region of free memory that lies between your program and its permanent storage area and the stack. Although the size of the heap is unknown, it generally contains a fairly large amount of free memory.

The core of C's allocation system consists of the functions **malloc( )** and **free( )**. (Most C compilers supply several other dynamic allocation functions, but these two are the most important.) These functions work together using the free memory region to establish and maintain a list of available storage. The **malloc( )** function allocates memory and the **free( )** function releases it. That is, each time a **malloc( )** memory request is made, a portion of the remaining free memory is allocated. Each time a **free( )** memory release call is made, memory is returned to the system. Any program that uses these functions should include the header file **stdlib.h**.

The **malloc( )** function has this prototype:

void *malloc(size_t *number_of_bytes*);

Here, *number_of_bytes* is the number of bytes of memory you wish to allocate. (The type **size_t** is defined in **stdlib.h** as (more or less) an **unsigned** integer.) The **malloc( )** function returns a pointer of type **void**, which means that you can assign it to any type of pointer. After a successful call, **malloc( )** returns a pointer to the first byte of the region of memory allocated from the heap. If there is not enough available memory to satisfy the **malloc( )** request, an allocation failure occurs and **malloc( )** returns a null.

The code fragment shown here allocates 1000 bytes of contiguous memory:

```
char *p;
p = malloc(1000); /* get 1000 bytes */
```

After the assignment, **p** points to the first of 1000 bytes of free memory.

The next example allocates space for 50 integers. Notice the use of **sizeof** to ensure portability.

```
int *p;
p = malloc(50*sizeof(int));
```

Since the heap is not infinite, whenever you allocate memory, you must check the value returned by **malloc( )** to make sure that it is not null before using the pointer. Using a null pointer will almost certainly crash your program. The proper way to allocate memory and test for a valid pointer is illustrated in this code fragment:

```
if(!(p=malloc(100)) {
    printf("Out of memory.\n");
    exit(1);
}
```

Of course, you can substitute some other sort of error handler in place of the call to **exit( )**. Just make sure that you do not use the pointer **p** if it is null.

The **free( )** function is the opposite of **malloc( )** in that it returns previously allocated memory to the system. Once the memory has been freed, it may be reused by a subsequent call to **malloc( )**. The function **free( )** has this prototype:

void free(void *p);

Here, *p* is a pointer to memory that was previously allocated using **malloc( )**. It is critical that you *never* call **free( )** with an invalid argument; this will destroy the free list.

C's dynamic allocation subsystem is used in conjunction with pointers to support a variety of important programming constructs, such as linked lists and binary trees. You will see several examples of these in Part Three. Another important use of dynamic allocation is the dynamic array, discussed next.

Dynamically Allocated Arrays

Sometimes you will want to allocate memory using **malloc( )**, but operate on that memory as if it were an array, using array indexing. In essence, you may want to create a *dynamically allocated array*. Since any pointer may be indexed as if it were a single-dimension array, this presents no trouble. For example, the following program shows how you can use a dynamically allocated array:

```c
/* Allocate space for a string dynamically, request user
   input, and then print the string backwards. */

#include <stdlib.h>
#include <stdio.h>
#include <string.h>

void main(void)
{
  char *s;
  register int t;

  s = malloc(80);

  if(!s) {
    printf("Memory request failed.\n");
    exit(1);
  }

  gets(s);
  for(t=strlen(s)-1; t>=0; t--) putchar(s[t]);
  free(s);
}
```

As the program shows, before its first use, **s** is tested to ensure that the allocation request succeeded and a valid pointer was returned by **malloc( )**. This is absolutely necessary to prevent accidental use of a null pointer, which, as stated earlier, will almost certainly cause a problem. Notice how the pointer **s** is used in the call to **gets( )** and then indexed as an array to print the string backwards.

Accessing allocated memory as if it were a single-dimension array is straightforward. However, multidimensional dynamic arrays pose some problems. Since the dimensions of the array have not been defined in your program, you cannot directly index a pointer as if it were a multidimensional array. To allow a dynamically allocated array, you must use this trick: Pass the pointer as a parameter to a function. This way, the function can define the dimensions of the parameter receiving the pointer, thus allowing normal array indexing. To see how this works, study the following example, which builds a table of the numbers 1 through 10 raised to their first, second, third, and fourth powers:

```
/* Display powers of the numbers 1 through 10.
   Note: even though this is a correct program,
   some compilers will issue a warning message
   concerning the argument to the functions
   table() and show(). If this happens, just
   ignore it. */

#include <stdio.h>
#include <stdlib.h>

int pwr(int a, int b);
void table(int p[4][10]);
void show(int p[4][10]);

void main(void)
{
  int *p;

  p = malloc(40*sizeof(int));

  if(!p) {
    printf("Memory request failed.\n");
    exit(1);
  }

  /* here, p is simply a pointer */
  table(p);
  show(p);
}
```

```
/* Build the table of powers. */
void table(int p[4][10]) /* Now the compiler has an array
                                to work with. */
{
  register int i, j;

  for(j=1; j<11; j++)
    for(i=1; i<5; i++) p[i-1][j-1] = pwr(j, i);
}


/* Display the table of integer powers. */
void show(int p[4][10]) /* Now the compiler has an array
                               to work with. */
{
  register int i, j;

  printf("%10s %10s %10s %10s\n",
         "N", "N^2", "N^3", "N^4");
  for(j=1; j<11; j++) {
    for(i=1; i<5; i++) printf("%10d ", p[i-1][j-1]);
    printf("\n");
  }
}

/* Raise an integer to the specified power. */
pwr(int a, int b)
{
  register int  t=1;

  for(; b; b--) t = t*a;
  return t;
}
```

The output produced by this program is shown in Table 5-1.

As this program illustrates, by defining a function parameter to the desired array dimensions, you can trick the C compiler into handling multidimensional dynamic arrays. Actually, as far as the C compiler is concerned, you do have a 4,10 integer array inside the functions **show( )** and **table( )**. The difference is that the storage for the array is allocated manually using the **malloc( )** statement, rather than automatically using the normal array declaration statement. Also, note the use of **sizeof** to compute the

N	N^2	N^3	N^4
1	1	1	1
2	4	8	16
3	9	27	81
4	16	64	256
5	25	125	625
6	36	216	1296
7	49	343	2401
8	64	512	4096
9	81	729	6561
10	100	1000	10000

Table 5-1.   *Output of the Powers Program*

number of bytes needed for a 4,10 integer array. This guarantees the portability of this program to computers with integers of a different size.

Problems with Pointers

Nothing will get you into more trouble than a wild pointer! Pointers are a mixed blessing. They give you tremendous power and are necessary for many programs. At the same time, when a pointer accidentally contains a wrong value, it can be the most difficult bug to find.

An erroneous pointer is difficult to find because the pointer, itself, is not the problem. The problem is that each time you perform an operation using the bad pointer, you are reading or writing to some unknown piece of memory. If you read from it, the worst that can happen is that you get garbage. However, if you write to it, you might be writing over other pieces of your code or data. This may not show up until later in the execution of your program, and may lead you to look for the bug in the wrong place. There may be little or no evidence to suggest that the pointer is the original cause of the problem. This type of bug causes programmers to lose sleep time and time again.

Because pointer errors are such nightmares, you should do your best never to generate one. To help you avoid them, a few of the more common errors are discussed here. The classic example of a pointer error is the *uninitialized pointer*. Consider this program.

```
/* This program is wrong. */
void main(void)
{
```

```
    int x, *p;

    x = 10;
    *p = x;
}
```

This program assigns the value 10 to some unknown memory location. Here is why. Since the pointer **p** has never been given a value, it contains an unknown value when the assignment ***p = x** takes place. This causes the value of **x** to be written to some unknown memory location. This type of problem often goes unnoticed when your program is small because the odds are in favor of **p** containing a "safe" address—one that is not in your code, data area, or operating system. However, as your program grows, the probability increases of **p** pointing to something vital. Eventually, your program stops working. The solution is to always make sure that a pointer is pointing at something valid before it is used.

A second common error is caused by a simple misunderstanding of how to use a pointer. Consider the following:

```
/* This program is wrong. */
#include <stdio.h>

void main(void)
{
   int x, *p;

   x = 10;
   p = x;

   printf("%d", *p);
}
```

The call to **printf( )** does not print the value of **x**, which is 10, on the screen. It prints some unknown value because the assignment

```
p = x;
```

is wrong. That statement assigns the value 10 to the pointer **p**. However, **p** is supposed to contain an address, not a value. To correct the program, write

```
p = &x;
```

Another error that sometimes occurs is caused by incorrect assumptions about the placement of variables in memory. You can never know where your data will be placed in memory, or if it will be placed there the same way again, or whether each compiler will treat it in the same way. For these reasons, making any comparisons between pointers that do not point to a common object may yield unexpected results. For example,

```
char s[80], y[80];
char *p1, *p2;

p1 = s;
p2 = y;
if(p1 < p2) . . .
```

is generally an invalid concept. (In very unusual situations, you might use something like this to determine the relative position of the variables. But this would be rare.)

A related error results when you assume that two adjacent arrays may be indexed as one by simply incrementing a pointer across the array boundaries. For example,

```
int first[10], second[10];
int *p, t;

p = first;
for(t=0; t<20; ++t)   *p++ = t;
```

This is not a good way to initialize the arrays **first** and **second** with the numbers 0 through 19. Even though it may work on some compilers under certain circumstances, it assumes that both arrays will be placed back to back in memory with **first** first. This may not always be the case.

The next program illustrates a very dangerous type of bug. See if you can find it.

```
/* This program has a bug. */
#include <string.h>
#include <stdio.h>

void main(void)
{
  char *p1;
  char s[80];

  p1 = s;
```

```
   do {
     gets(s);   /* read a string */

     /* print the decimal equivalent of each
        character */
     while(*p1) printf(" %d", *p1++);

   } while(strcmp(s, "done"));
 }
```

This program uses **p1** to print the ASCII values associated with the characters contained in **s**. The problem is that **p1** is assigned the address of **s** only once. The first time through the loop, **p1** points to the first character in **s**. However, the second time through, it continues where it left off because it is not reset to the start of **s**. This next character may be part of the second string, another variable, or a piece of the program! The proper way to write this program is

```
/* This program is now correct. */
#include <string.h>
#include <stdio.h>

void main(void)
{
  char *p1;
  char s[80];

  do {
    p1 = s;
    gets(s);   /* read a string */
    /* print the decimal equivalent of each
       character */
    while(*p1) printf(" %d", *p1++);

  } while(strcmp(s, "done"));
}
```

Here, each time the loop iterates, **p1** is set to the start of the string. In general, you should remember to reinitialize a pointer if it is to be reused.

The fact that handling pointers incorrectly can cause tricky bugs is no reason to avoid using them. Just be careful, and make sure that you know where each pointer is pointing before you use it.

Chapter Six

Functions

F unctions are the building blocks of C and the place where all program activity occurs. They are one of C's most important features.

The General Form of a Function

The general form of a function is

type_specifier function_name(parameter list)
{
    body of the function
}

The *type_specifier* specifies the type of data that the function returns. A function may return any type of data except an array. If no type is specified, the compiler assumes that the function returns an integer result. The *parameter list* is a comma-separated list of variable names and their associated types that receive the values of the arguments when the function is called. A function may be without parameters, in which case the parameter list is empty. However, even if there are no parameters, the parentheses are still required.

In variable declarations, you can declare many variables to be of a common type by using a comma-separated list of variable names. In contrast, all function parameters must be declared individually, each including both the type and name. That is, the parameter declaration list for a function takes this general form:

f(type varname1, type varname2, . . . , type varnameN)

Scope Rules of Functions

The *scope rules* of a language are the rules that govern whether a piece of code knows about or has access to another piece of code or data.

In C, each function is a discrete block of code. A function's code is private to that function and cannot be accessed by any statement in any other function except through a call to that function. (For instance, you cannot use **goto** to jump into the middle of another function.) The code that constitutes the body of a function is hidden from the rest of the program and, unless it uses global variables or data, it can neither affect nor be affected by other parts of the program. Stated another way, the code and data that are defined within one function cannot interact with the code or data defined in another function because the two functions have a different scope.

Variables that are defined within a function are called local variables. A local variable comes into existence when the function is entered and is destroyed upon exit.

That is, local variables cannot hold their value between function calls. The only exception to this rule is when the variable is declared with the **static** storage class specifier. This causes the compiler to treat the variable as if it were a global variable for storage purposes, but still to limit its scope to within the function. (Chapter 2 covers global and local variables in depth.)

In C, all functions are at the same scope level. That is, you cannot define a function within a function. This is why C is not technically a block-structured language.

Function Arguments

If a function is to use arguments, it must declare variables that accept the values of the arguments. These variables are called the *formal parameters* of the function. They behave like other local variables inside the function and are created upon entry into the function and destroyed upon exit. As shown in the following function, the parameter declarations occur after the function name:

```
/* Return 1 if c is part of string s; 0 otherwise. */
is_in(char *s,  char c)
{
  while(*s)
    if(*s==c) return 1;
    else s++;
  return 0;
}
```

The function **is_in( )** has two parameters: **s** and **c**. This function returns 1 if the character **c** is part of the string **s**; otherwise, it returns 0.

You must make sure that the arguments used to call a function are compatible with the type of its parameters. If the types are incompatible, the compiler will not necessarily issue an error message, but unexpected results are likely to occur. Unlike many other languages, C is robust and generally does something with any syntactically correct program, even if that program contains questionable type mismatches. For example, if a function expects a pointer but is called with a value, unanticipated results can occur. The use of function prototypes (discussed shortly) can help catch these types of errors, but they will not catch all type mismatches.

As with local variables, you may make assignments to a function's formal parameters or use them in any allowable C expression. Even though these variables perform the special task of receiving the value of the arguments passed to the function, you can use them as you do any other local variable.

Call by Value, Call by Reference

In general, subroutines can be passed arguments in one of two ways. The first is called *call by value*. This method copies the *value of* an argument into the formal parameter of the subroutine. In this case, changes made to the parameter have no effect on the argument.

Call by reference is the second way of passing arguments to a subroutine. In this method, the *address* of an argument is copied into the parameter. Inside the subroutine, the address is used to access the actual argument used in the call. This means that changes made to the parameter affect the argument.

With a few exceptions, C uses call by value to pass arguments. In general, this means that code within a function cannot alter the arguments used to call the function. Consider the following program:

```
#include <stdio.h>

int sqr(int x);

void main(void)
{
   int t=10;

   printf("%d %d", sqr(t), t);
}

sqr(int x)
{
   x = x*x;
   return(x);
}
```

In this example, the value of the argument to **sqr( )**, 10, is copied into the parameter **x**. When the assignment x = x*x takes place, only the local variable **x** is modified. The variable **t**, used to call **sqr( )**, still has the value 10. Hence, the output is **100 10**.

Remember that it is a copy of the value of the argument that is passed into the function. What occurs inside the function has no effect on the variable used in the call.

Creating a Call by Reference

Even though C's parameter-passing convention is call by value, you can create a call by reference by passing a pointer to an argument, instead of the argument itself. Since the address of the argument is passed to the function, code within the function can change the value of the argument outside the function.

Pointers are passed to functions just like any other value. Of course, you need to declare the parameters as pointer types. For example, the function **swap( )**, which exchanges the value of the two integer variables pointed to by its arguments, shows how.

```
void swap(int *x, int *y)
{
   int temp;

   temp = *x;   /* save the value at address x */
   *x = *y;     /* put y into x */
   *y = temp;   /* put x into y */
}
```

swap( ) is able to exchange the values of the two variables pointed to by **x** and **y** because their addresses (not their values) are passed. Thus, within the function, the contents of the variables can be accessed using standard pointer operations. Hence, the contents of the variables used to call the function are swapped.

Remember that **swap( )** (or any other function that uses pointer parameters) must be called with the addresses of the arguments. The following program shows the correct way to call **swap( )**:

```
void swap(int *x, int *y);

void main(void)
{
   int i, j;

   i = 10;
   j = 20;

   swap(&i, &j); /* pass the addresses of i and j */
}
```

In this example, the variable **i** is assigned the value 10 and **j** is assigned the value 20. Then **swap( )** is called with the addresses of **i** and **j**. (The unary operator **&** is used to produce the address of the variables.) Therefore, the addresses of **i** and **j**, not their values, are passed into the function **swap( )**.

Calling Functions with Arrays

Arrays are covered in detail in Chapter 4. However, this section discusses passing arrays as arguments to functions because it is an exception to the standard call-by-value parameter passing.

When an array is used as an argument to a function, only the address of the array is passed, not a copy of the entire array. When you call a function with an array name, a pointer to the first element in the array is passed into the function. (Don't forget, in C an array name without any index is a pointer to the first element in the array.) This means that the parameter declaration must be of a compatible pointer type. There are three ways to declare a parameter that is to receive an array pointer. First, it may be declared as an array, as shown here:

```
/* Print some numbers. */
#include <stdio.h>

void display(int num[10]);

void main(void)
{
  int t[10], i;

  for(i=0; i<10; ++i) t[i]=i;
  display(t);
}

void display(int num[10])
{
  int i;

  for(i=0; i<10; i++) printf("%d ", num[i]);
}
```

Even though the parameter **num** is declared as an integer array of ten elements, the C compiler automatically converts it to an integer pointer. This is necessary because no parameter can actually receive an entire array. Therefore, since only a pointer to an array is passed, a pointer parameter must be there to receive it.

The second way to declare an array parameter is to specify it as an unsized array, as shown here:

```
void display(int num[])
{
  int i;

  for(i=0; i<10; i++) printf("%d ", num[i]);
}
```

Here, **num** is declared as an integer array of unknown size. Since C provides no array-boundary checks, the actual size of the array is irrelevant to the parameter (but not to the program, of course). This method of declaration also actually defines **num** as an integer pointer.

The final way that **num** can be declared—the most common form in professionally written C programs—is as a pointer, as shown here:

```
void display(int *num)
{
  int i;

  for(i=0; i<10; i++) printf("%d ", num[i]);
}
```

This is allowed because any pointer may be indexed using [ ] as if it were an array.

Don't confuse passing arrays with passing array elements, however. An array element used as an argument is treated like any other simple variable. For example, the preceding program could have been written without passing the entire array, as shown here:

```
/* Print some numbers. */
#include <stdio.h>

void display(int num);

void main(void)
{
  int t[10], i;

  for(i=0; i<10; ++i) t[i] = i;
  for(i=0; i<10; i++) display(t[i]);
```

```
}

void display(int num)
{
  printf("%d ", num);
}
```

As you can see, the parameter to **display( )** is of type **int**. It is not relevant that
display( ) is called using an array element, because only that one value of the array
is used.

When an array is used as a function argument, its address is passed to a function.
This is an exception to C's call-by-value parameter passing convention. In this case,
the code inside the function is operating on, and potentially altering, the actual
contents of the array used to call the function. For example, consider the function
print_upper( ), which prints its string argument in uppercase:

```
#include <stdio.h>
#include <ctype.h>

void print_upper(char *string);

void main(void)
{
  char s[80];

  gets(s);
  print_upper(s);
}

/* Print a string in uppercase. */
void print_upper(char *string)
{
  register int t;

  for(t=0; string[t]; ++t)  {
    string[t] = toupper(string[t]);
    putchar(string[t]);
  }
}
```

After the call to **print_upper( )**, the contents of array **s** in **main( )** will change to uppercase. If this is not what you want, you could write the program like this:

```
#include <stdio.h>
#include <ctype.h>

void print_upper(char *string);

void main(void)
{
  char s[80];

  gets(s);
  print_upper(s);
}

void print_upper(char *string)
{
  register int t;

  for(t=0; string[t]; ++t)
    putchar(toupper(string[t]));
}
```

In this version, the contents of array **s** remain unchanged because its values are not altered.

The standard library function **gets( )** is a classic example of passing arrays into functions. Although the **gets( )** in your standard library is more sophisticated and complex, the following simpler version, called **xgets( )**, will give you an idea of how it works.

```
/* A very simple version of the standard
   gets() library function */
char *xgets(char *s)
{
  char ch, *p;
  int t;

  p = s;  /* gets() returns a pointer to s */
```

```
for(t=0; t<80; ++t){
  ch = getchar();

  switch(ch) {
    case '\n':
      s[t] = '\0'; /* terminate
                      the string */
      return p;
    case '\b':
      if(t>0) t--;
      break;
    default:
      s[t] = ch;
  }
}
s[80] = '\0';
return p;
}
```

The **xgets( )** function must be called with a character pointer, which can be either a variable declared as a character pointer, or the name of a character array, which by definition is a character pointer. Upon entry, **xgets( )** establishes a **for** loop from 0 to 80. This prevents larger strings from being entered at the keyboard. If more than 80 characters are entered, the function returns. (The real **gets( )** function does not have this restriction.) Because C has no built-in bounds checking, you should make sure that any array used to call **xgets( )** can accept at least 80 characters. As you type characters on the keyboard, they are placed in the string. If you type a backspace, the counter **t** is reduced by 1, effectively removing the previous character from the array. When you press ENTER, a null is placed at the end of the string, signaling its termination. Because the actual array used to call **xgets( )** is modified, upon return it contains the characters that you type.

argc and argv—Arguments to main( )

Sometimes it is useful to pass information into a program when you run it. Generally, you pass information into the **main( )** function via command line arguments. A *command line argument* is the information that follows the program's name on the command line of the operating system. For example, when you compile C programs, you might type something like the following:

cc *program_name*

where *program_name* is a command line argument that specifies the name of the program you wish to compile.

There are two special built-in arguments, **argv** and **argc**, that are used to receive command line arguments. The **argc** parameter holds the number of arguments on the command line and is an integer. It is always at least 1 because the name of the program qualifies as the first argument. The **argv** parameter is a pointer to an array of character pointers. Each element in this array points to a command line argument. All command line arguments are strings—any numbers will have to be converted by the program into the proper internal format. For example, this simple program prints **Hello** and your name on the screen if you type it directly after the program name.

```
#include <stdio.h>
#include <stdlib.h>

void main(int argc, char *argv[])
{
  if(argc!=2) {
    printf("You forgot to type your name.\n");
    exit(1);
  }
  printf("Hello %s", argv[1]);
}
```

If you called this program **name** and your name were Tom, you would type **name Tom** to run the program. The output from the program would be **Hello Tom**.

In many environments, each command line argument must be separated by a space or a tab. Commas, semicolons, and the like are not considered separators. For example,

```
run Spot, run
```

is made up of three strings, while

```
Herb,Rick,Fred
```

is a single string since commas are not generally legal separators.

Some environments allow you to enclose within double quotes a string containing spaces. This causes the entire string to be treated as a single argument. Check your operating system manual for details on the definition of command line parameters for your system.

You must declare **argv** properly. The most common method is

```
char *argv[];
```

The empty brackets indicate that the array is of undetermined length. You can now access the individual arguments by indexing **argv**. For example, **argv[0]** points to the first string, which is always the program's name; **argv[1]** points to the first argument, and so on.

Another short example using command line arguments is the program called **countdown**, shown here. It counts down from a starting value (which is specified on the command line) and beeps when it reaches 0. Notice that the first argument containing the number is converted into an integer by the standard function **atoi( )**. If the string "display" is the second command line argument, the countdown will also be displayed on the screen.

```
/* Countdown program. */
#include <stdio.h>
#include <stdlib.h>
#include <ctype.h>
#include <string.h>

void main(int argc, char *argv[])
{
  int disp, count;

  if(argc<2) {
    printf("You must enter the length of the count\n");
    printf("on the command line.  Try again.\n");
    exit(1);
  }

  if(argc==3 && !strcmp(argv[2], "display")) disp = 1;
  else disp = 0;

  for(count=atoi(argv[1]); count; --count)
    if(disp) printf("%d\n", count);

  putchar('\a');  /* this will ring the bell on most
                     computers */
```

```
    printf("Done");
}
```

Notice that if no command line arguments have been specified, an error message is printed. A program with command line arguments often issues instructions if the user attempts to run the program without entering the proper information.

To access an individual character in one of the command strings, add a second index to **argv**. For example, the next program displays all of the arguments with which it was called, one character at a time:

```
#include <stdio.h>

void main(int argc, char *argv[])
{
  int t, i;

  for(t=0; t<argc; ++t) {
    i = 0;

    while(argv[t][i]) {
      putchar(argv[t][i]);
      ++i;
    }
  }
}
```

Remember, the first index accesses the string and the second index accesses the individual characters of the string.

Usually, you use **argc** and **argv** to get initial commands into your program. In theory, you can have up to 32,767 arguments, but most operating systems do not allow more than a few. You normally use these arguments to indicate a filename or an option. Using command line arguments gives your program a professional appearance and facilitates its use in batch files.

When a program does not require command line parameters, it is common practice to explicitly declare **main( )** as having no parameters by using the **void** keyword in its parameter list. (This is the approach used by the programs in this book.) However, if you like, you may simply specify an empty parameter list.

The names **argc** and **argv** are traditional but arbitrary. You may name these two parameters to **main( )** anything you like. Also, some compilers may support additional arguments to **main( )**, so be sure to check your user's manual.

The return Statement

The **return** statement has two important uses. First, it causes an immediate exit from the function that it is in. That is, it causes program execution to return to the calling code. Second, it may be used to return a value.

Returning from a Function

There are two ways that a function terminates execution and returns to the caller. The first occurs when the last statement in the function has executed and, conceptually, the function's ending curly brace (}) is encountered. (Of course, the curly brace isn't actually present in the object code, but you can think of it in this way.) For example, the **pr_reverse( )** function in this program simply prints the string "I like C" backwards on the screen and then returns.

```
#include <string.h>
#include <stdio.h>

void pr_reverse(char *s);

void main(void)
{
  pr_reverse("I like C");
}

void pr_reverse(char *s)
{
  register int t;

  for(t=strlen(s)-1; t>=0; t--) putchar(s[t]);
}
```

Once the string has been displayed, there is nothing left for **pr_reverse( )** to do, so it returns to the place it was called from.

Actually, not many functions use this default method of terminating their execution. Most functions rely on the **return** statement to stop execution either because a value must be returned or to make a function's code simpler and more efficient.

Remember, a function may contain several **return** statements. For example, the **find_substr( )** function in the following program returns the starting position of a substring within a string, or returns –1 if no match is found.

```
#include <stdio.h>

int find_substr(char *s1, char *s2);

void main(void)
{
  if(find_substr("C is fun", "is") != -1)
    printf("substring is found");
}

/* Return index of first match of s2 in s1. */
find_substr(char *s1, char *s2)
{
  register int t;
  char *p, *p2;

  for(t=0; s1[t]; t++) {
    p = &s1[t];
    p2 = s2;

    while(*p2 && *p2==*p) {
      p++;
      p2++;
    }
    if(!*p2) return t; /* 1st return */
  }
   return -1; /* 2nd return */
}
```

Returning Values

All functions, except those of type **void**, return a value. This value is explicitly specified by the **return** statement. If no **return** statement is present, then the return value of the function is technically undefined. (Generally, C compiler implementers return 0 when no explicit return value is specified, but you should not count on this if portability is a concern.) In other words, as long as a function is not declared as **void**, you may use it as an operand in any valid C expression. Therefore, each of the following expressions is valid in C:

```
x = power(y);
if(max(x,y) > 100) printf("greater");
for(ch=getchar(); isdigit(ch); ) ... ;
```

However, a function cannot be the target of an assignment. A statement such as

```
swap(x,y) = 100; /* incorrect statement */
```

is wrong. The C compiler will flag it as an error and will not compile a program that contains it.

When you write programs, your functions generally will be of three types. The first type is simply computational. These functions are specifically designed to perform operations on their arguments and return a value based on that operation. A computational function is a "pure" function. Examples are the standard library functions **sqrt( )** and **sin( )**, which compute the square root and sine of their arguments.

The second type of function manipulates information and returns a value that simply indicates the success or failure of that manipulation. An example is the library function **fclose( )**, which is used to close a file. If the close operation is successful, the function returns 0; if the operation is unsuccessful, it returns an error code.

The last type of function has no explicit return value. In essence, the function is strictly procedural and produces no value. An example is **exit( )**, which terminates a program. All functions that do not return values should be declared as returning type **void**. By declaring a function as **void**, you keep it from being used in an expression, thus preventing accidental misuse.

Sometimes, functions that really don't produce an interesting result return something anyway. For example, **printf( )** returns the number of characters written. Yet, it would be unusual to find a program that actually checked this. In other words, although all functions, except those of type **void**, return values, you don't have to use the return value for anything. A common question concerning function return values is, "Don't I have to assign this value to some variable since a value is being returned?" The answer is no. If there is no assignment specified, the return value is simply discarded. Consider the following program, which uses the function **mul( )**:

```
#include <stdio.h>

int mul(int a, int b);

void main(void)
{
   int x, y, z;

   x = 10;    y = 20;
   z = mul(x, y);            /* 1 */
   printf("%d", mul(x,y));   /* 2 */
   mul(x, y);                /* 3 */
```

```
    }

mul(int a, int b)
{
    return a*b;
}
```

In line 1, the return value of **mul( )** is assigned to **z**. In line 2, the return value is not actually assigned, but it is used by the **printf( )** function. Finally, in line 3, the return value is lost because it is neither assigned to another variable nor used as part of an expression.

Functions That Return Noninteger Values

When the return type of a function is not explicitly declared, it automatically defaults to **int**. For many C functions, this default will work. However, when a different data type is required, the process involves two steps. First, the function must be given an explicit type specifier. Second, the return type of the function must be identified before the first call is made to it. Only in this way can the compiler generate correct code for functions returning noninteger values.

Functions may be declared to return any valid C data type (except arrays). Declaring functions is similar to declaring variables: the type specifier precedes the function name. The type specifier tells the compiler what type of data the function is to return. This information is critical if the program is going to run correctly because different data types have different sizes and internal representations.

Before you can use a function that returns a noninteger type, its type must be made known to the rest of the program. This is because, unless directed to the contrary, C assumes that a function will return an integer value. If your program calls a function that returns a different type prior to that function's declaration, the compiler mistakenly generates the wrong code for the function call. To prevent this, you must use a special form of declaration statement near the top of your program to tell the compiler what value that function is really returning.

There are two ways to declare a function before it is used: the traditional way and the modern prototype method. The traditional approach was the only method available when C was first invented, but is now obsolete. Prototypes were added by the ANSI C standard. The traditional approach is still allowed by the ANSI standard in order to provide compatibility with older code, but new uses of it are strongly discouraged.

In this section, the traditional approach is examined. Even though it is outdated, many existing programs still use it, so you should be familiar with it. Moreover, the prototype method is basically an extension of the traditional concept. (Function prototypes are discussed in the following section.)

Using the traditional approach, you specify the function's return type and name near the start of your program to inform the compiler that a function will return some type of value other than an integer, as illustrated here:

```
#include <stdio.h>

float sum();   /* declare the function */
float first, second;

void main(void)
{
  first = 123.23;
  second = 99.09;

  printf("%f", sum());
}

float sum()
{
  return first + second;
}
```

The first function type declaration tells the compiler that **sum( )** returns a floating-point data type. This allows the compiler to correctly generate code for calls to **sum( )**. Without the declaration, the compiler will flag a type mismatch error.

The traditional function type declaration statement has the general form

type_specifier function_name( );

Notice that the parameter list is empty. Even if the function takes arguments, none are listed in its type declaration.

Without the type declaration statement, a mismatch occurs between the type of data the function returns and the type of data the calling routine expects. The results will be bizarre and unpredictable. If both functions are in the same file, the compiler catches the type mismatch and does not compile the program. However, if the functions are in different files, the compiler does not detect the error. Type checking is not done at link time or run time, only at compile time. For this reason, you must make sure that both types are compatible.

NOTE: *When a character is returned from a function declared to be of type* ***int****, the character value is converted into an integer. Because C cleanly handles the conversion from character to integer and back again, a function that returns a character value is often not declared as returning a character value. The programmer instead relies upon the default type conversion of characters into integers and back again. This sort of thing is found frequently in older C code and is not technically considered an error.*

Function Prototypes

The traditional function declaration (described in the preceding section) only allowed the return type of a function to be declared. The ANSI C standard expanded the traditional function declaration by allowing the number and types of the function's arguments to be declared in addition to its return type. This expanded definition is called a *function prototype*. As mentioned, function prototypes were not part of the original C language. They are, however, one of the most important additions made to C when it was standardized. In this book, all examples include full function prototypes. Prototypes enable C to provide stronger type checking, somewhat like that provided by languages such as Pascal. When you use prototypes, the compiler can find and report any illegal type conversions between the type of arguments used to call a function and the type definition of its parameters. The compiler will also catch differences between the number of arguments used to call a function and the number of parameters in the function.

The general form of a function prototype definition is

type func_name(type parm_name1, type parm_name2,. . .,
        type parm_nameN);

The use of parameter names is optional. However, they enable the compiler to identify any type mismatches by name when an error occurs, so it is a good idea to include them.

The following program illustrates the value of function prototypes. It produces an error message because it contains an attempt to call **sqr_it( )** with an integer argument instead of the integer pointer required. (In C, the conversion of an integer into a pointer is not allowed.)

```
/* This program uses a function prototype to
   enforce strong type checking. */

void sqr_it(int *i); /* prototype */

void main(void)
```

```
{
  int x;

  x = 10;
  sqr_it(x);   /* type mismatch */
}

void sqr_it(int *i)
{
  *i = *i * *i;
}
```

Because of the need for compatibility with the original version of C, some special rules apply to function prototypes. First, when a function's return type is declared, but the parameter list is empty, the compiler simply assumes that *no parameter information* is given. As far as the compiler is concerned, the function could have several parameters or no parameters. Therefore, how does one prototype a function that does not have any parameters? The answer is this: When a function has no parameters, its prototype uses **void** inside the parameter list. For example, if a function called **f( )** returns a **float** and has no parameters, its prototype looks like this:

```
float f(void);
```

This tells the compiler that the function has no parameters, and any call to that function that has parameters is an error.

Prototyping affects C's automatic type promotions. When a nonprototyped function is called, all characters are converted to integers and all **float**s into **double**s. These somewhat odd type promotions have to do with the characteristics of the original environment in which C was developed. However, if you prototype a function, the types specified in the prototype are maintained and no type promotions will occur.

Function prototypes help you trap bugs before they occur. In addition, they help verify that your program is working correctly by not allowing functions to be called with mismatched arguments.

Keep one fact firmly in mind: Although the use of function prototypes is strongly recommended, it is not technically an error if there is no prototype for a function. This is necessary to support pre-prototype C code. Nevertheless, your code should, in general, include full prototyping information. (Also, it is possible that future revisions to the ANSI C standard will require prototypes, since the amount of pre-prototype code is diminishing.)

NOTE: *Although prototypes are optional in C, they are required by C's successor: C++.*

Returning Pointers

Although functions that return pointers are handled just like any other type of function, a few important concepts need to be discussed.

Pointers to variables are neither integers nor unsigned integers. They are the memory addresses of a certain type of data. The reason for this distinction is because pointer arithmetic is relative to the base type. For example, if an integer pointer is incremented, it will contain a value that is 2 greater than its previous value (assuming 2-byte integers). In general, each time a pointer is incremented (or decremented), it points to the next (or previous) data item of its type. Since each data type may be of different length, the compiler must know what type of data the pointer is pointing to. For this reason, a function that returns a pointer must declare explicitly what type of pointer it is returning.

To return a pointer, a function must be declared as having a pointer return type. For example, this function returns a pointer to the first occurrence of the character **c** in string **s**:

```
/* Return pointer of first occurrence of c in s. */
char *match(char c, char *s)
{
  while(c!=*s && *s) s++;
  return(s);
}
```

If no match is found, a pointer to the null terminator is returned. Here is a short program that uses **match( )**:

```
#include <stdio.h>

char *match(char c, char *s);  /* prototype */

void main(void)
{
  char s[80], *p, ch;
```

```
  gets(s);
  ch = getchar();
  p = match(ch, s);

  if(*p)   /* there is a match */
    printf("%s ", p);
  else
    printf("No match found.");
}
```

This program reads a string and then a character. If the character is in the string, the program prints the string from the point of match. Otherwise, it prints **No match found**.

Functions of Type void

One of **void**'s uses is to explicitly declare functions that do not return values. This prevents their use in any expression and helps avert accidental misuse. For example, the function **print_vertical( )** prints its string argument vertically down the side of the screen. Since it returns no value, it is declared as **void**.

```
void print_vertical(char *str)
{
  while(*str)
    printf("%c\n", *str++);
}
```

Before you can use any **void** function, you must declare its prototype. If you don't, C assumes that it is returning an integer and when the compiler actually reaches the function, it declares a type mismatch. The following program shows a proper example that prints a single command line argument vertically on the screen:

```
#include <stdio.h>

void print_vertical(char *str);   /* prototype */

void main(int argc, char *argv[])
{
  if(argc) print_vertical(argv[1]);
}
```

```
void print_vertical(char *str)
{
  while(*str)
    printf("%c\n", *str++);
}
```

Before the ANSI C standard defined **void**, functions that did not return values simply defaulted to type **int**. Therefore, don't be surprised to see many examples of this in older code.

What Does main( ) Return?

The **main( )** function returns an integer to the calling process, which is generally the operating system. Returning a value from **main( )** is the equivalent of calling **exit( )** with the same value. If **main( )** does not explicitly return a value, the value passed to the calling process is technically undefined. In practice, most C compilers automatically return 0, but do not rely on this if portability is a concern.

You may also declare **main( )** as **void** if it does not return a value. (Many of the programs in this book take this approach.) Some compilers issue a warning message if a function is not declared as **void** and also does not return a value. So, if you choose not to return a value from **main( )** you will want to declare its return type as **void.**

Recursion

In C, a function can call itself. A function is said to be *recursive* if a statement in the body of the function calls itself. Recursion is the process of defining something in terms of itself, and is sometimes called *circular definition*.

A simple example of a recursive function is **factr( )**, which computes the factorial of an integer. The factorial of a number **n** is the product of all the whole numbers between 1 and **n**. For example, 3 factorial is 1 x 2 x 3, or 6. Both **factr( )** and its iterative equivalent are shown here:

```
factr(int n)   /* recursive */
{
  int answer;

  if(n==1) return(1);
  answer = factr(n-1)*n; /* recursive call */
  return(answer);
}
```

```
fact(int n)     /* non-recursive */
{
  int t, answer;

  answer = 1;

  for(t=1; t<=n; t++)
    answer=answer*(t);

  return(answer);
}
```

The nonrecursive version of **fact( )** should be clear. It uses a loop that runs from 1 to **n** and progressively multiplies each number by the moving product.

The operation of the recursive **factr( )** is a little more complex. When **factr( )** is called with an argument of 1, the function returns 1. Otherwise, it returns the product of **factr(n-1)*n**. To evaluate this expression, **factr( )** is called with **n-1**. This happens until **n** equals 1 and the calls to the function begin returning.

Computing the factorial of 2, the first call to **factr( )** causes a second, recursive call with the argument of 1. This call returns 1, which is then multiplied by 2 (the original **n** value). The answer is then 2. Try working through the computation of 3 factorial on your own. (You might want to insert **printf( )** statements into **factr( )** to see the level of each call and what the intermediate answers are.)

When a function calls itself, a new set of local variables and parameters are allocated storage on the stack, and the function code is executed from the top with these new variables. A recursive call does not make a new copy of the function. Only the arguments are new. As each recursive call returns, the old local variables and parameters are removed from the stack and execution resumes at the point of the function call inside the function. Recursive functions could be said to "telescope" out and back.

Most recursive routines do not significantly reduce code size or improve memory utilization. Also, the recursive versions of most routines may execute a bit slower than their iterative equivalents because of the overhead of the repeated function calls. In fact, many recursive calls to a function could cause a stack overrun. Because storage for function parameters and local variables is on the stack and each new call creates a new copy of these variables, the stack could possibly overwrite some other data or program memory. However, you probably will not have to worry about this unless a recursive function runs wild.

The main advantage to recursive functions is that you can use them to create clearer and simpler versions of several algorithms. For example, the QuickSort in Part Three is quite difficult to implement in an iterative way. Also, some problems, especially ones related to artificial intelligence, lend themselves to recursive solutions. Finally, some people seem to think recursively more easily than iteratively.

When writing recursive functions, you must have an **if** statement somewhere to force the function to return without the recursive call being executed. If you don't, the function will never return once you call it. Omitting the **if** is a common error when writing recursive functions. Use **printf( )** and **getchar( )** liberally during program development so that you can watch what is going on and abort execution if you see a mistake.

Declaring Variable Length Parameter Lists

In C, you can specify a function that has a variable number of parameters. The most common example is **printf( )**. To tell the compiler that an unknown number of arguments may be passed to a function, you must end the declaration of its parameters using three periods. For example, this prototype specifies that **func( )** will have at least two integer parameters and an unknown number (including 0) of parameters after that.

```
func(int a, int b, ...);
```

This form of declaration is also used by a function's definition.

Any function that uses a variable number of parameters must have at least one actual parameter. For example, this is incorrect:

```
func(...);
```

For more on variable number of parameters, see Part Two, under the standard library function **va_arg( )**.

Classic Versus Modern Function Parameter Declarations

The original version of C used a different parameter declaration method, sometimes called the *classic* form. This book uses a declaration approach called the *modern* form. The ANSI standard for C supports both forms, but strongly recommends the modern form. However, you should know the classic form because many older programs still use it. (Also, some new programs use this form because it works with older compilers.)

The classic function parameter declaration consists of two parts: a parameter list, which goes inside the parentheses that follow the function name, and the actual parameter declarations, which go between the closing parentheses and the function's opening curly brace. The general form of the classic parameter definition is

```
type func_name(parm1, parm2, . . .parmN)
type parm1;
type parm2;
     .
     .
     .
type parmN;
{
  function code
}
```

For example, this modern declaration:

```
float f(int a, int b, char ch)
{
  /* ... */
}
```

will look like this in its classic form:

```
float f(a, b, ch)
int a, b;
char ch;
{
  /* ... */
}
```

Notice that the classic form allows the declaration of more than one parameter in a list after the type name.

Remember that the classic form of parameter declaration is obsolete. However, your compiler can still compile older programs that use the classic form with no trouble. This allows older code to be maintained.

Implementation Issues

There are a few important things to remember when you create C functions that affect their efficiency and usability. These issues are the subject of this section.

Parameters and General-Purpose Functions

A general-purpose function is one that will be used in a variety of situations, perhaps by many different programmers. Typically, you should not base general-purpose functions on global data. All of the information a function needs should be passed to it by its parameters. When this is not possible, you should use static variables.

Besides making your functions general-purpose, parameters keep your code readable and less susceptible to bugs resulting from side effects.

Efficiency

Functions are the building blocks of C and are crucial to all but the simplest programs. However, in certain specialized applications, you may need to eliminate a function and replace it with *in-line* code. In-line code performs the same actions as a function, but without the overhead associated with a function call. For this reason, in-line code is often used instead of function calls when execution time is critical.

In-line code is faster than a function call for two reasons. First, a CALL instruction takes time to execute. Second, if there are arguments to pass, these have to be placed on the stack, which also takes time. For most applications, this very slight increase in execution time is of no significance. But if it is, remember that each function call uses time that would be saved if the function's code were placed in line. For example, the following are two versions of a program that prints the square of the numbers from 1 to 10. The in-line version runs faster than the other because the function call takes time.

in line

```
#include <stdio.h>

void main(void)
{
  int x;

  for(x=1; x<11; ++x)
    printf("%d", x*x);
}
```

function call

```
#include <stdio.h>
int sqr(int a);
void main(void)
{
  int x;

  for(x=1; x<11; ++x)
    printf("%d", sqr(x));
}

sqr(int a)
{
  return a*a;
}
```

Libraries and Files

Once you have written a function, you can do three things with it: You can just leave it in the same file as the **main( )** function; you can put it in a separate file with other functions that you have written; or you can place it into a library. In this section, a few issues relating to these options are discussed.

Separate Files

While working on a large program, one of the most frustrating yet common tasks is searching each file to find where you put some function. A little preliminary organization will help you to avoid this problem.

First, group all functions that are conceptually related into one file. For example, if you are writing a text editor, you can put all functions for deleting text in one file, all for searching text in another, and so on.

Second, put all general-purpose functions together. For example, in database programs the input/output formatting functions are used by various other functions and belong in a separate file.

Third, group top-level functions in either a separate file or, if there is room, in the **main( )** file. Top-level functions initiate the general activity of the program, essentially defining its operation.

Libraries

Technically, a library of functions differs from a separately compiled file of functions. When routines in a library are linked with the rest of your program, only the functions that your program actually uses are loaded and linked with your program. In a separately compiled file, all of the functions are loaded and linked with your program whether used or not. For most files that you create, you will probably want all of the functions in the file anyway. In the case of the C standard library, you would never want *all* of the functions linked into your program because your object code would be huge!

At times, you may want to create a library. For example, suppose you had written a special set of statistical functions. You would not want to load all these functions if your program only needed to find the average of some set of values. In this case, a library would be useful.

Most C compilers include instructions for creating a library. Since this process varies from compiler to compiler, study your user's manual to determine what procedure you should follow.

How Big Should a Program File Be?

Because C allows separate compilation, the question of optimum file size naturally arises. This is important because compilation time is directly related to the size of the file that is being compiled. Generally, the linking process is much shorter than compiling and eliminates the need to constantly recompile working code. On the other hand, having to keep track of multiple files can be troublesome.

How large a file should be is different for every user, every compiler, and every operating environment. However, as a rule of thumb, no source file should be longer than 10,000 to 15,000 bytes. After that point, you should break it into two or more files.

Chapter Seven

Structures, Unions, Enumerations, and User-Defined Types

The C language allows you to create custom data types five different ways. The first is the *structure,* which is a grouping of variables under one name and is called an *aggregate* (or sometimes a *conglomerate*) data type. The second user-defined type is the *bit-field,* which is a variation on the structure and allows easy access to individual bits. The third is the *union,* which enables the same piece of memory to be defined as two or more different types of variables. A fourth custom data type is the *enumeration,* which is a list of named integer constants. The final user-defined type is created through the use of **typedef** and defines a new name for an existing type.

Structures

In C, a structure is a collection of variables referenced under one name, providing a convenient means of keeping related information together. A *structure declaration* forms a template that may be used to create structures. The variables that make up the structure are called *members* of the structure. (Structure members are also commonly referred to as *elements* or *fields.*)

Generally, all of the members of a structure are logically related. For example, the name and address information in a mailing list would normally be represented in a structure. The following code fragment shows how to declare a structure that defines the name and address fields. The keyword **struct** tells the compiler that a structure is being declared.

```
struct addr
{
  char name[30];
  char street[40];
  char city[20];
  char state[3];
  unsigned long int zip;
};
```

Notice that the declaration is terminated by a semicolon. This is because a structure declaration is a statement. Also, the structure tag **addr** identifies this particular data structure and is its type specifier.

At this point, *no variable has actually been created.* Only the form of the data has been defined. To declare a variable of type **addr**, write

```
struct addr addr_info;
```

This declares a variable of type **struct addr** called **addr_info**. When you define a structure, you are essentially defining a complex variable type, not a variable, itself. Not until you declare a variable of that type does one actually exist.

When a structure variable (such as **addr_info**) is declared, the C compiler automatically allocates sufficient memory to accommodate all of its members. Figure 7-1 shows how **addr_info** appears in memory assuming 1-byte characters and 4-byte long integers.

You may also declare one or more structure variables when you declare a structure. For example,

```
struct addr {
  char name[30];
  char street[40];
  char city[20];
  char state[3];
  unsigned long int zip;
} addr_info, binfo, cinfo;
```

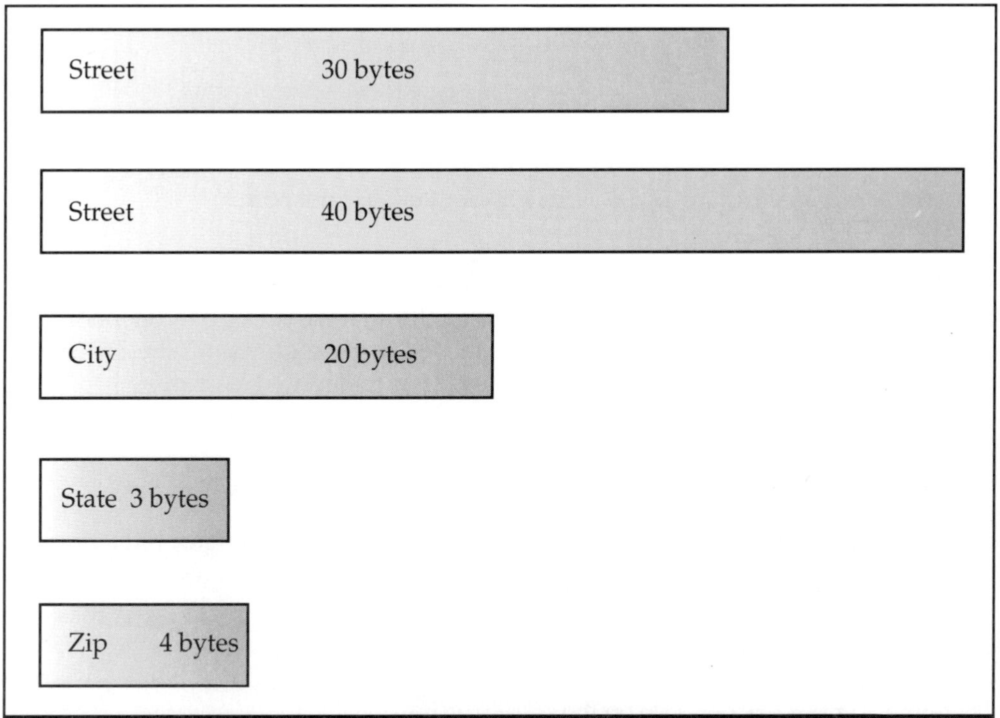

Street	30 bytes

Street	40 bytes

City	20 bytes

State 3 bytes

Zip	4 bytes

Figure 7-1.   *The **addr_info** structure in memory*

defines a structure type called **addr** and declares variables **addr_info**, **binfo**, and **cinfo** of that type.

If you only need one structure variable, the structure tag is not needed. That means that

```
struct {
  char name[30];
  char street[40];
  char city[20];
  char state[3];
  unsigned long int zip;
} addr_info;
```

declares one variable named **addr_info** as defined by the structure preceding it.

The general form of a structure declaration is

```
struct tag {
  type member_name;
  type member_name;
  type member_name;
    .
    .
    .
} structure_variables;
```

where either *tag* or *structure_variables* may be omitted, but not both.

Referencing Structure Members

Individual members of a structure are referenced through the use of the . operator (usually called the *dot operator*). For example, the following code assigns the ZIP code 12345 to the **zip** field of the structure variable **addr_info** declared earlier:

```
addr_info.zip = 12345;
```

The structure variable name followed by a period and the member name references that individual member. The general form for accessing a member of a structure is

   structure_name.member_name

Therefore, to print the ZIP code on the screen, write

```
printf("%d", addr_info.zip);
```

This prints the ZIP code contained in the **zip** member of the structure variable **addr_info**.

In the same fashion, the character array **addr_info.name** can be used to call **gets( )**, as shown here:

```
gets(addr_info.name);
```

This passes a character pointer to the start of **name**.

Since **name** is a character array, you can access the individual characters of **addr_info.name** by indexing **name**. For example, you can print the contents of **addr_info.name** one character at a time by using the following code:

```
register int t;

for(t=0; addr_info.name[t]; ++t)

  putchar(addr_info.name[t]);
```

Structure Assignments

The information contained in one structure may be assigned to another structure of the same type using a single assignment statement. That is, you do not need to assign the value of each member separately. The following program illustrates structure assignments:

```
#include <stdio.h>

void main(void)
{
  struct {
    int a;
    int b;
  } x, y;

  x.a = 10;
```

```
y = x;   /* assign one structure to another */

printf("%d", y.a);

}
```

After the assignment, **y.a** will contain the value 10.

Arrays of Structures

Perhaps the most common usage of structures is in arrays of structures. To declare an array of structures, you must first define a structure and then declare an array variable of that type. For example, to declare a 100-element array of structures of type **addr** that had been defined earlier, write

```
struct addr addr_info[100];
```

This creates 100 sets of variables that are organized as defined in the structure **addr**.

To access a specific structure, index the structure name. For example, to print the ZIP code of structure 3, write

```
printf("%d", addr_info[2].zip);
```

Like all array variables, arrays of structures begin indexing at 0.

A Mailing-List Example

To illustrate how structures and arrays of structures are used, this section develops a simple mailing-list program that uses an array of structures to hold the address information. In this example, the stored information includes name, street, city, state, and ZIP code.

To define the basic data structure, **addr**, that will hold this information, write

```
struct addr {
  char name[30];
  char street[40];
```

```
    char city[20];
    char state[3];
    unsigned long int zip;
} addr_info[MAX];
```

Notice that the ZIP code field is an unsigned long integer. This is because some ZIP codes are greater than 64,000—such as 94564—and cannot be represented by a 2-byte integer. Frankly, it is more common to store ZIP codes using a character string because it accommodates postal codes with letters as well as numbers (as used by Canada and other countries). However, this example stores the ZIP code in a integer as a means of illustrating a numeric structure element.

The first function needed for the program is **main( )**.

```
/* A simple mailing list example using an
   array of structures. */
#include <stdio.h>
#include <stdlib.h>

#define MAX 100

struct addr {
  char name[30];
  char street[40];
  char city[20];
  char state[3];
  unsigned long int zip;
} addr_info[MAX];

void init_list(void), enter(void);
void delete(void), list(void);
int menu_select(void), find_free(void);

void main(void)
{
  char choice;

  init_list(); /* initialize the structure array */

  for(;;) {
    choice = menu_select();
    switch(choice) {
      case 1: enter();
```

```
        break;
      case 2: delete();
        break;
      case 3: list();
        break;
      case 4: exit(0);
    }
  }
}
```

First, the function **init_list( )** prepares the structure array for use by putting a null character into the first byte of the **name** field for each structure in the array. The program assumes that an array element is not in use if **name** is empty. The **init_list( )** function is shown here:

```
/* Initialize the list. */
void init_list(void)
{
  register int t;

  for(t=0; t<MAX; ++t) addr_info[t].name[0] = '\0';
}
```

The **menu_select( )** function displays the options and returns the user's selection.

```
/* Get a menu selection. */
menu_select(void)
{
  char s[80];
  int c;

  printf("1. Enter a name\n");
  printf("2. Delete a name\n");
  printf("3. List the file\n");
  printf("4. Quit\n");

  do {
    printf("\nEnter your choice: ");
    gets(s);
    c = atoi(s);
  } while(c<0 || c>4);
```

```
    return c;
}
```

The **enter( )** function prompts the user for input and places the information entered
into the next free structure. If the array is full, the message **List Full** is printed on the
screen. **find_free( )** searches the structure array for an unused element.

```
/* Input addresses into the list. */
void enter(void)
{
  int slot;
  char s[80];

  slot = find_free();
  if(slot==-1) {
    printf("\nList Full");
    return;
  }

  printf("Enter name: ");
  gets(addr_info[slot].name);

  printf("Enter street: ");
  gets(addr_info[slot].street);

  printf("Enter city: ");
  gets(addr_info[slot].city);

  printf("Enter state: ");
  gets(addr_info[slot].state);

  printf("Enter zip: ");
  gets(s);
  addr_info[slot].zip = strtoul(s, '\0', 10);
}

/* Find an unused structure. */
find_free(void)
{
  register int t;
```

```
    for(t=0; addr_info[t].name[0] && t<MAX; ++t) ;

    if(t==MAX) return -1; /* no slots free */
    return t;
}
```

Notice that **find_free( )** returns a –1 if every structure array variable is in use. This is a safe number because there cannot be a –1 element in an array.

The **delete( )** function asks the user to specify the number of the address that needs to be deleted. The function then puts a null character in the first character position of the **name** field.

```
/* Delete an address. */
void delete(void)
{
  register int slot;
  char s[80];

  printf("Enter record #: ");
  gets(s);
  slot = atoi(s);
  if(slot>=0 && slot < MAX)
    addr_info[slot].name[0] = '\0';
}
```

The final function needed by the program is **list( )**, which prints the entire mailing list on the screen. C does not define a standard function that sends output to the printer because of the wide variation between computing environments. However, all C compilers provide some means to accomplish this. You might want to add printing capability to the mailing-list program on your own.

```
/* Display the list on the screen. */
void list(void)
{
  register int t;

  for(t=0; t<MAX; ++t) {
    if(addr_info[t].name[0]) {
      printf("%s\n", addr_info[t].name);
      printf("%s\n", addr_info[t].street);
```

```
        printf("%s\n", addr_info[t].city);
        printf("%s\n", addr_info[t].state);
        printf("%lu\n", addr_info[t].zip);
      }
    }
  printf("\n\n");
}
```

The complete mailing-list program is shown here. If you have any remaining doubts about structures, enter this program into your computer and study its execution, making changes and watching their effects.

```
/* A simple mailing list example using an
   array of structures. */
#include <stdio.h>
#include <stdlib.h>

#define MAX 100

struct addr {
  char name[30];
  char street[40];
  char city[20];
  char state[3];
  unsigned long int zip;
} addr_info[MAX];

void init_list(void), enter(void);
void delete(void), list(void);
int menu_select(void), find_free(void);

void main(void)
{
  char choice;

  init_list(); /* initialize the structure array */
  for(;;) {
    choice = menu_select();
    switch(choice) {
      case 1: enter();
        break;
```

```
      case 2: delete();
        break;
      case 3: list();
        break;
      case 4: exit(0);
    }
  }
}

/* Initialize the list. */
void init_list(void)
{
  register int t;

  for(t=0; t<MAX; ++t) addr_info[t].name[0] = '\0';
}

/* Get a menu selection. */
menu_select(void)
{
  char s[80];
  int c;

  printf("1. Enter a name\n");
  printf("2. Delete a name\n");
  printf("3. List the file\n");
  printf("4. Quit\n");
  do {
    printf("\nEnter your choice: ");
    gets(s);
    c = atoi(s);
  } while(c<0 || c>4);
  return c;
}

/* Input addresses into the list. */
void enter(void)
{
  int slot;
  char s[80];

  slot = find_free();
```

```
   if(slot==-1) {
     printf("\nList Full");
     return;
   }

   printf("Enter name: ");
   gets(addr_info[slot].name);

   printf("Enter street: ");
   gets(addr_info[slot].street);

   printf("Enter city: ");
   gets(addr_info[slot].city);

   printf("Enter state: ");
   gets(addr_info[slot].state);

   printf("Enter zip: ");
   gets(s);
   addr_info[slot].zip = strtoul(s, '\0', 10);
}

/* Find an unused structure. */
find_free(void)
{
  register int t;

  for(t=0; addr_info[t].name[0] && t<MAX; ++t) ;

  if(t==MAX) return -1; /* no slots free */
  return t;
}

/* Delete an address. */
void delete(void)
{
  register int slot;
  char s[80];

  printf("enter record #: ");
  gets(s);
  slot = atoi(s);
```

```
   if(slot>=0 && slot < MAX)
     addr_info[slot].name[0] = '\0';
}

/* Display the list on the screen. */
void list(void)
{
  register int t;

  for(t=0; t<MAX; ++t) {
    if(addr_info[t].name[0]) {
      printf("%s\n", addr_info[t].name);
      printf("%s\n", addr_info[t].street);
      printf("%s\n", addr_info[t].city);
      printf("%s\n", addr_info[t].state);
      printf("%lu\n", addr_info[t].zip);
    }
  }
  printf("\n\n");
}
```

Passing Structures to Functions

This section discusses passing structures and their members to functions.

Passing Structure Members to Functions

When you pass a member of a structure to a function, you are actually passing the value of that member to the function. Therefore, you are passing a simple variable (unless, of course, that element is complex, such as an array of characters). For example, consider this structure:

```
struct fred
{
  char x;
  int y;
  float z;
  char s[10];
} mike;
```

Here are examples of each member being passed to a function:

```
func(mike.x);   /* passes character value of x */
func2(mike.y); /* passes integer value of y */
func3(mike.z); /* passes float value of z */
func4(mike.s); /* passes address of string s */
func(mike.s[2]); /* passes character value of s[2] */
```

If you wish to pass the *address* of an individual structure member, put the **&** operator before the structure name. For example, to pass the address of the members of the structure **mike**, write

```
func(&mike.x);   /* passes address of character x */
func2(&mike.y); /* passes address of integer y */
func3(&mike.z); /* passes address of float z */
func4(mike.s); /* passes address of string s */
func(&mike.s[2]); /* passes address of character s[2] */
```

Remember that the **&** operator precedes the structure name, not the individual member name. Note also that **s** already signifies an address, so no **&** is required.

Passing Entire Structures to Functions

When a structure is used as an argument to a function, the entire structure is passed using the standard call-by-value method. Of course, this means that any changes made to the contents of the structure inside the function to which it is passed do not affect the structure used as an argument.

NOTE: *In some early versions of C, structures could not be passed to functions. Instead, they were treated like arrays, and only a pointer to the structure was passed. Keep this in mind if you ever use a very old C compiler.*

When using a structure as a parameter, remember that the type of the argument must match the type of the parameter. For example, in the following program both the argument **arg** and the parameter **parm** are declared as the same type of structure.

```
#include <stdio.h>

/* Define a structure type. */
struct struct_type {
  int a, b;
  char ch;
} ;
```

```
void f1(struct struct_type parm);

void main(void)
{
  struct struct_type arg;

  arg.a = 1000;

  f1(arg);
}

void f1(struct struct_type parm)
{
  printf("%d", parm.a);
}
```

As this program illustrates, if you will be declaring parameters that are structures, you must make the declaration of the structure type global so that all parts of your program can use it. For example, had **struct_type** been declared inside **main( )** (for example), then it would not have been visible to **f1( )**.

As just stated, when passing structures, the type of the argument must match the type of the parameter. It is not sufficient for them to simply be physically similar; their type names must match. For example, the following version of the preceding program is incorrect and will not compile because the type name of the argument used to call **f1( )** differs from the type name of its parameter.

```
/* This program is incorrect and will not compile. */
#include <stdio.h>

/* Define a structure type. */
struct struct_type {
  int a, b;
  char ch;
} ;

/* Define a structure similar to struct_type,
   but with a different name. */
struct struct_type2 {
  int a, b;
  char ch;
} ;
```

```
void f1(struct struct_type2 parm);

void main(void)
{
  struct struct_type arg;

  arg.a = 1000;

  f1(arg); /* type mismatch */
}

void f1(struct struct_type2 parm)
{
  printf("%d", parm.a);
}
```

Structure Pointers

C allows pointers to structures just as it allows pointers to any other type of variable. However, there are some special aspects to structure pointers that you should know.

Declaring a Structure Pointer

Like other pointers, structure pointers are declared by placing * in front of a structure variable's name. For example, assuming the previously defined structure **addr**, the following declares **addr_pointer** as a pointer to data of that type:

```
struct addr *addr_pointer;
```

Using Structure Pointers

There are two primary uses for structure pointers: to generate a call by reference parameter to a function, and to create linked lists and other dynamic data structures using C's allocation system. This chapter covers the first use. The second use is covered thoroughly in Part Three.

There is one major drawback to passing all but the simplest structures to functions: the overhead needed to push the structure onto the stack when the function call is executed. (Recall that arguments are passed to functions on the stack.) For simple structures with few members, this overhead is not too great. If the structure contains many members, however, or if some of its members are arrays, run-time performance may degrade to unacceptable levels. The solution to this problem is to pass only a pointer to the function.

When a pointer to a structure is passed to a function, only the address of the structure is pushed on the stack. This makes for very fast function calls. A second advantage, in some cases, is when a function needs to reference the actual structure used as the argument, instead of a copy. By passing a pointer, the function can modify the contents of the structure used in the call.

To find the address of a structure variable, place the & operator before the structure's name. For example, given the following fragment:

```
struct bal {
    float balance;
    char name[80];
} person;

struct bal *p;   /* declare a structure pointer */
```

then

```
p = &person;
```

places the address of the structure **person** into the pointer **p**.

To access the members of a structure using a pointer to that structure, you must use the –> operator. For example, this references the **balance** field:

```
p->balance
```

The –> is usually called the *arrow operator*, and consists of the minus sign followed by a greater than sign. The arrow is used in place of the dot operator when you are accessing a structure member through a pointer to the structure.

To see how a structure pointer can be used, examine this simple program, which prints the hours, minutes, and seconds on your screen using a software timer.

```
/* Display a software timer. */
#include <stdio.h>

#define DELAY 128000

struct my_time {
    int hours;
    int minutes;
    int seconds;
```

```
} ;

void display(struct my_time *t);
void update(struct my_time *t);
void delay(void);

void main(void)
{
  struct my_time systime;

  systime.hours = 0;
  systime.minutes = 0;
  systime.seconds = 0;

  for(;;) {
    update(&systime);
    display(&systime);
  }
}

void update(struct my_time *t)
{
  t->seconds++;
  if(t->seconds==60) {
    t->seconds = 0;
    t->minutes++;
  }

  if(t->minutes==60) {
    t->minutes = 0;
    t->hours++;
  }

  if(t->hours==24) t->hours = 0;
  delay();
}

void display(struct my_time *t)
{
  printf("%02d:", t->hours);
  printf("%02d:", t->minutes);
  printf("%02d\n", t->seconds);
```

```
   }

   void delay(void)
   {
     long int t;

     /* change this as needed */
     for(t=1; t<DELAY; ++t) ;
   }
```

The timing of this program is adjusted by changing the definition of **DELAY**.

As you can see, a global structure called **my_time** was defined but no variable was declared. Inside **main( )**, the structure **systime** is declared and initialized to 00:00:00. This means that **systime** is known directly only to the **main( )** function.

The functions **update( )** (which changes the time) and **display( )** (which prints the time) are passed the address of **systime**. In both functions, their arguments are declared as a pointer to a **my_time** structure.

Inside **update( )** and **display( )**, each member of **systime** is accessed via a pointer. Because **update( )** receives a pointer to the **systime** structure, it can update its value. For example, to set the hours back to 0 when 24:00:00 is reached, **update( )** contains this line of code:

```
   if(t->hours==24) t->hours = 0;
```

This tells the compiler to take the address of **t** (which points to **systime** in **main( )**) and to reset **hours** to zero.

Remember, use the dot operator to access structure elements when operating on the structure itself. When you have a pointer to a structure, use the arrow operator.

Arrays and Structures Within Structures

A member of a structure may be either a simple or complex type. A simple member is one that is of any of the built-in data types, such as integer or character. You have already seen one type of complex element: the character arrays used in **addr**. Other complex data types include one-dimensional and multidimensional arrays of the other data types and structures.

A member of a structure that is an array is treated as you might expect from the earlier examples. For example, consider this structure:

```
   struct x {
```

```
    int a[10][10]; /* 10 x 10 array of ints */
    float b;
} y;
```

To reference integer 3,7 in **a** of structure **y**, write

```
y.a[3][7]
```

When a structure is a member of another structure, it is called a *nested structure*. For example, the structure **address** is nested inside **emp** in this example:

```
struct emp {
    struct addr address; /* nested structure */
    float wage;
} worker;
```

Here, structure **emp** has been defined as having two members. The first is a structure of type **addr**, which contains an employee's address. The other is **wage**, which holds the employee's wage. The following code fragment assigns 93456 to the **zip** element of **address**.

```
worker.address.zip = 93456;
```

As you can see, the members of each structure are referenced from outermost to innermost. The ANSI C standard specifies that structures may be nested to at least 15 levels. Most compilers allow more.

Bit-Fields

Unlike most other computer languages, C has a built-in feature, called a *bit-field*, that allows you to access a single bit. Bit-fields can be useful for a number of reasons:

- If storage is limited you can store several *Boolean* (true/false) variables in one byte.
- Certain devices transmit information encoded into bits.
- Certain encryption routines need to access the bits within a byte.

Although these tasks can be performed using the bitwise operators, a bit-field can add more structure (and possibly efficiency) to your code.

To access bits, C uses a method based on the structure. In fact, a bit-field is really just a special type of structure member that defines how long, in bits, the field is to be. The general form of a bit-field definition is

```
struct tag {
   type name1 : length;
   type name2 : length;
     .
     .
     .
   type nameN : length;
} variable_list;
```

Here, *type* specifies the type of the bit-field, which must be either **int**, **unsigned**, or **signed**. Bit-fields of length 1 should be declared as **unsigned** because a single bit cannot have a sign. (Some compilers may only allow **unsigned** bit-fields.) The number of bits in the bit-field is specified by *length*.

Bit-fields are frequently used when analyzing input from a hardware device. For example, the status port of a serial communications adapter might return a status byte organized like this:

Bit	Meaning When Set
0	Change in clear-to-send line
1	Change in data-set-ready
2	Trailing edge detected
3	Change in receive line
4	Clear-to-send
5	Data-set-ready
6	Telephone ringing
7	Received signal

You can represent the information in a status byte using the following bit-field:

```
struct status_type {
   unsigned delta_cts: 1;
   unsigned delta_dsr: 1;
   unsigned tr_edge:   1;
   unsigned delta_rec: 1;
   unsigned cts:       1;
   unsigned dsr:       1;
   unsigned ring:      1;
```

```
    unsigned rec_line:  1;
} status;
```

You might use a routine similar to that shown here to enable a program to determine when it can send or receive data.

```
status = get_port_status();
if(status.cts) printf("clear to send");
if(status.dsr) printf("data ready");
```

To assign a value to a bit-field, simply use the form you would use for any other type of structure element. For example, this code fragment clears the **ring** field:

```
status.ring = 0;
```

As you can see from this example, each bit-field is accessed with the dot operator. However, if the structure is referenced through a pointer, you must use the –> operator.

You do not have to name each bit-field. This makes it easy to reach the bit you want, bypassing unused ones. For example, if you only care about the **cts** and **dsr** bits, you could declare the **status_type** structure like this:

```
struct status_type {
  unsigned :    4;
  unsigned cts: 1;
  unsigned dsr: 1;
} status;
```

Also, notice that the bits after **dsr** do not need to be specified if they are not used.

It is valid to mix normal structure members with bit-fields. For example,

```
struct emp {
  struct addr address;
  float pay;
  unsigned lay_off:    1; /* lay off or active */
  unsigned hourly:     1; /* hourly pay or wage */
  unsigned deductions: 3; /* IRS deductions */
};
```

defines an employee record that uses only 1 byte to hold three pieces of information: the employee's status, whether the employee is salaried, and the number of deductions. Without the bit-field, this information would have taken 3 bytes.

Bit-field variables have certain restrictions. You cannot take the address of a bit-field. Bit-field variables cannot be arrayed. You cannot know, from machine to machine, whether the fields will run from right to left or from left to right. In other words, any code that uses bit-fields may have some machine dependencies.

Unions

In C, a *union* is a memory location that is shared by two or more different variables, generally of different types, at different times. Declaring a **union** is similar to declaring a structure. Its general form is

union *tag* {
    type variable_name;
    type variable_name;
    type variable_name;
    .
    .
    .
} *union_variables;*

For example,

```
union u_type {
  int i;
  char ch;
};
```

This declaration does not create any variables. You may declare a variable either by placing its name at the end of the declaration or by using a separate declaration statement. To declare a **union** variable **cnvt** of type **u_type** using the definition just given, write

```
union u_type cnvt;
```

In **cnvt**, both integer **i** and character **ch** share the same memory location. (Of course, **i** occupies 2 bytes and **ch** uses only 1.) Figure 7-2 shows how **i** and **ch** share the same address. At any point in your program, you can refer to the data stored in **cnvt** as either an integer or a character.

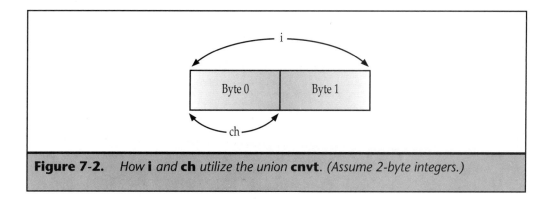

Figure 7-2. *How **i** and **ch** utilize the union **cnvt**. (Assume 2-byte integers.)*

When a **union** variable is declared, the compiler automatically allocates enough storage to hold the largest member of the **union**. For example, (assuming 2-byte integers) **cnvt** is two bytes long so that it can hold **i**, even though **ch** requires only one byte.

To access a member of a **union**, use the same syntax that you would use for structures: the dot and arrow operators. If you are operating on the **union** directly, use the dot operator. If the **union** is accessed through a pointer, use the arrow operator. For example, to assign the integer 10 to element **i** of **cnvt**, write

```
cnvt.i = 10;
```

In the next example, a pointer to **cnvt** is passed to a function:

```
void func1(union u_type *un)
{
  un->i = 10; /* assign 10 to cnvt using
                 function */
}
```

Using a **union** can aid in the production of machine-independent (portable) code. Because the compiler keeps track of the actual sizes of the **union** members, no machine dependencies are produced. That is, you need not worry about the size of an **int**, **long**, **float**, or whatever.

Unions are used frequently when specialized type conversions are needed because you can refer to the data held in the **union** in fundamentally different ways. For example, you may use a **union** to manipulate the bytes that comprise a **double** in order to alter its precision or to perform some unusual type of rounding.

To get an idea of the usefulness of a **union** when non-standard type conversions are needed, consider the problem of writing an integer to a disk file. The C standard library contains no function specifically designed to write an integer to a file. While you can write any type of data (including an integer) to a file using **fwrite( )**, using **fwrite( )** is overkill for such a simple operation. However, using a **union** you can easily create a function called **putw( )**, which writes the binary representation of an integer to a file one byte at a time. To see how, first create a **union** consisting of one integer and a 2-byte character array:

```
union pw {
  int i;
  char ch[2];
};
```

Now, **putw( )** can be written like this:

```
putw(union pw word, FILE *fp)
{
  putc(word->ch[0], fp); /* write first half */
  putc(word->ch[1], fp); /* write second half */
}
```

Although **putw( )** may be called with an integer, it can still use the standard function **putc( )** to write each byte in the integer to a disk file one byte at a time.

Enumerations

An *enumeration* is a set of named integer constants that specify all the legal values a variable of that type may have. Enumerations are common in everyday life. For example, an enumeration of the coins used in the United States is

penny, nickel, dime, quarter, half-dollar, dollar

Enumerations are defined much like structures; the keyword **enum** signals the start of an enumeration type. The general form for enumerations is

enum *tag* { *enumeration list* } *variable_list*;

Here, both the enumeration tag and the variable list are optional. As with structures, the enumeration tag name is used to declare variables of its type. The following code fragment defines an enumeration called **coin** and declares **money** to be of that type:

```
enum coin { penny, nickel, dime, quarter,
            half_dollar, dollar};
enum coin money;
```

Given these declarations, the following types of statements are perfectly valid:

```
money = dime;
if(money==quarter) printf("Money is a quarter.\n");
```

The key point to understand about an enumeration is that each of the symbols stands for an integer value. As such, they may be used anywhere that an integer may be used. Each symbol is given a value one greater than the symbol that precedes it. The value of the first enumeration symbol is 0. Therefore,

```
printf("%d %d", penny, dime);
```

displays **0 2** on the screen.

You can specify the value of one or more of the symbols by using an initializer. Do this by following the symbol with an equal sign and an integer value. Symbols that appear after initializers are assigned values greater than the previous initialization value. For example, the following code assigns the value of 100 to **quarter**:

```
enum coin { penny, nickel, dime, quarter=100,
            half_dollar, dollar};
```

Now, the values of these symbols are

penny	0
nickel	1
dime	2
quarter	100
half_dollar	101
dollar	102

One common but erroneous assumption about enumerations is that the symbols can be input and output directly. This is not the case. For example, the following code fragment will not perform as desired:

```
/* this will not work */
money = dollar;
printf("%s", money);
```

Remember, **dollar** is simply a name for an integer; it is not a string. For the same reason, you cannot use this code to achieve the desired results:

```
/* this code is wrong */
strcpy(money, "dime");
```

That is, a string that contains the name of a symbol is not automatically converted to that symbol.

Actually, creating code to input and output enumeration symbols is quite tedious (unless you are willing to settle for their integer values). For example, you need the following code to display, in words, the kind of coin that **money** contains:

```
switch(money) {
  case penny: printf("penny");
    break;
  case nickel: printf("nickel");
    break;
  case dime: printf("dime");
    break;
  case quarter: printf("quarter");
    break;
  case half_dollar: printf("half_dollar");
    break;
  case dollar: printf("dollar");
}
```

Sometimes, you can declare an array of strings and use the enumeration value as an index to translate that value into its corresponding string. For example, this code also outputs the proper string:

```
char name[][12]={
  "penny",
  "nickel",
  "dime",
  "quarter",
  "half_dollar",
```

```
    "dollar"
};
printf("%s", name[money]);
```

Of course, this only works if no symbol is initialized because the string array must be indexed starting at 0.

Since enumeration values must be converted manually to their human-readable string values for I/O operations, they are most useful in routines that do not make such conversions. An enumeration is often used to define a compiler's symbol table, for example. Enumerations are also used to help prove the validity of a program by providing a compile-time redundancy check confirming that a variable is assigned only valid values.

Using sizeof to Ensure Portability

You have seen that structures and unions can be used to create variables of different sizes, and that the actual size of these variables may change from machine to machine. The **sizeof** operator computes the size of any variable or type and can help eliminate machine-dependent code from your programs. This operator is especially useful where structures or unions are concerned.

For the following discussion, assume a C implementation, common to many C compilers, which has the sizes for data types shown here:

Type	Size in Bytes
char	1
int	2
float	4

Therefore, the following code will print the numbers 1, 2, and 4 on the screen:

```
char ch;
int i;
float f;

printf("%d", sizeof(ch));

printf("%d", sizeof(i));

printf("%d", sizeof(f));
```

The size of a structure is equal to *or greater than* the sum of the sizes of its members. For example,

```
struct s {
  char ch;
  int i;
  float f;
} s_var;
```

Here, **sizeof(s_var)** is at least 7 (4 + 2 + 1). However, the size of **s_var** might be greater because the compiler is allowed to pad a structure in order to achieve word or paragraph alignment. (A paragraph is 16 bytes.) Since the size of a structure may be greater than the sum of the sizes of its members, you should always use **sizeof** when you need to know the size of a structure.

Since **sizeof** is a compile-time operator, all the information necessary to compute the size of any variable is known at compile time. This is especially meaningful for **unions**, because the size of a **union** is always equal to the size of its largest member. For example, consider

```
union u {
  char ch;
  int i;
  float f;
} u_var;
```

Here, the **sizeof(u_var)** is 4. At run time, it does not matter what **u_var** is actually holding. All that matters is the size of its largest member, because any **union** must be as large as its largest element.

typedef

C allows you to explicitly define new data type names by using the keyword **typedef**. You are not actually *creating* a new data type, but rather defining a new name for an existing type. This process can help make machine-dependent programs more portable. If you define your own type name for each machine-dependent data type used by your program, then only the **typedef** statements have to be changed when compiling for a new environment. **typedef** also can aid in self-documenting your code by allowing descriptive names for the standard data types. The general form of the **typedef** statement is

typedef *type newname*;

where _type_ is any valid data type and _newname_ is the new name for this type. The new name you define is in addition to, not a replacement for, the existing type name.

For example, you could create a new name for **float** by using

```
typedef float balance;
```

This statement tells the compiler to recognize **balance** as another name for **float**. Next, you could create a **float** variable using **balance**:

```
balance over_due;
```

Here, **over_due** is a floating-point variable of type **balance**, which is another word for **float**.

Now that **balance** has been defined, it can be used in another **typedef**. For example,

```
typedef balance overdraft;
```

tells the compiler to recognize **overdraft** as another name for **balance**, which is another name for **float**.

There is one application of **typedef** that you may find especially useful: it can be used to simplify the declaration of structure, **union**, or enumeration variables. For example, consider the following declaration:

```
struct mystruct {
  unsigned x;
  float f;
};
```

To declare a variable of type **mystruct** you must use a declaration like this:

```
struct mystruct s;
```

While there is certainly nothing whatsoever wrong with this declaration, it does require the use of two identifiers: **struct** and **mystruct.** However, if you apply **typedef** to the declaration of **mystruct,** as shown here,

```
typedef struct _mystruct {
  unsigned x;
  float f;
} mystruct;
```

then you can declare variables of this structure using the following declaration:

```
mystruct s;
```

The point is that by **typedef**ing the declaration of **mystruct**, you have created a new, single-identifier type name. While this is technically only a convenience, it is certainly worth doing if you will be declaring several structure variables. This same technique can be applied to **union**s and enumerations, as well.

Using **typedef** can make your code easier to read and easier to port to a new machine. But remember, you are not creating any new data types.

Chapter Eight

Console I/O

C is practically unique in its approach to input/output operations. This is because the C language does not define any keywords that perform I/O. Instead, input and output are accomplished through library functions. C's I/O system is an elegant piece of engineering that offers a flexible yet cohesive mechanism for transferring data between devices. However, C's I/O system is quite large and involves several different functions.

In C, there are both console and file I/O. Technically, C makes little distinction between console I/O and file I/O. However, they are conceptually very different worlds. This chapter examines in detail the console I/O functions. The next chapter presents the file I/O system and describes how the two systems relate.

With one exception, this chapter covers only console I/O functions defined by the ANSI C standard. The ANSI C standard does not define any functions that perform various screen control operations (such as cursor positioning) or that display graphics, because these operations vary widely between machines. Instead, the standard C console I/O functions perform only TTY-based output. However, most compilers include in their libraries screen control and graphics functions that apply to the specific environment in which the compiler is designed to run. Part Two covers a representative sample of these functions.

This chapter refers to the console I/O functions as performing input from the keyboard and output to the screen. However, these functions actually have the standard input and standard output of the system as the target and/or source of their I/O operations. Furthermore, standard input and standard output may be redirected to other devices. These concepts are covered in Chapter 9.

Reading and Writing Characters

The simplest of the console I/O functions are **getchar( )**, which reads a character from the keyboard, and **putchar( )**, which prints a character to the screen. The **getchar( )** function waits until a key is pressed and then returns its value. The key pressed is also automatically echoed to the screen. The **putchar( )** function writes a character to the screen at the current cursor position. The prototypes for **getchar( )** and **putchar( )** are shown here:

```
int getchar(void);
int putchar(int c);
```

The header file for these functions is STDIO.H. As its prototype shows, the **getchar( )** function is declared as returning an integer. However, you can assign this value to a **char** variable, as is usually done, because the character is contained in the low-order byte. (The high-order byte is usually zero.) **getchar( )** returns **EOF** if an error occurs.

In the case of **putchar( )**, even though it is declared as taking an integer parameter, you will generally call it using a character argument. Only the low-order byte of its parameter is actually output to the screen. The **putchar( )** function returns the character written, or **EOF** if an error occurs. (The **EOF** macro is defined in STDIO.H and is generally equal to –1.)

The following program illustrates **getchar( )** and **putchar( ).** It inputs characters from the keyboard and displays them in reverse case. That is, it prints uppercase as lowercase and lowercase as uppercase. To stop the program, enter a period.

```
#include <stdio.h>
#include <ctype.h>

void main(void)
{
  char ch;

  printf("Enter some text (type a period to quit).\n");
  do {
    ch = getchar();

    if(islower(ch)) ch = toupper(ch);
    else ch = tolower(ch);

    putchar(ch);
  } while (ch != '.');
}
```

A Problem with getchar( )

There are some potential problems with **getchar( )**. The ANSI C standard defines **getchar( )** to be compatible with the original, UNIX-based version of C. Unfortunately, in its original form, **getchar( )** buffers input until ENTER is pressed. This is called _line-buffered_ input and it was the method used by the original UNIX systems—that is, you had to press ENTER before anything you typed was actually sent to your program. Also, since **getchar( )** inputs only one character each time it is called, line-buffering may leave one or more characters waiting in the input queue, which is annoying in interactive environments. Even though the ANSI standard specifies that **getchar( )** can be implemented as an interactive function, it seldom is. Therefore, if the preceding program did not behave as you expected, you now know why.

Alternatives to getchar( )

getchar( ) might not be implemented by your compiler in such a way that it is useful in an interactive environment. If this is the case, you will probably want to use a different function to read characters from the keyboard. The ANSI C standard does not define any function that is guaranteed to provide interactive input, but virtually all C compilers do. Although these functions are not defined by ANSI, they are commonly used since **getchar( )** does not fill the needs of most programmers.

Two of the most common alternative functions, **getch( )** and **getche( )**, have these prototypes:

```
int getch(void);
int getche(void);
```

For most compilers, the prototypes for these functions are found in CONIO.H. The **getch( )** function waits for a keypress after which it returns immediately. It does not echo the character to the screen. The **getche( )** function is the same as **getch( )**, but the key is echoed. This book often uses **getche( )** or **getch( )** instead of **getchar( )** when a character needs to be read from the keyboard in an interactive program. However, if your compiler does not support these alternative functions, or if **getchar( )** is implemented as an interactive function by your compiler, you should substitute **getchar( )** when necessary.

For example, the previous program is shown here using **getch( )** instead of **getchar( )**:

```c
#include <stdio.h>
#include <conio.h>
#include <ctype.h>

void main(void)
{
  char ch;

  printf("Enter some text (type a period to quit).\n");
  do {
    ch = getch();

    if(islower(ch)) ch = toupper(ch);
    else ch = tolower(ch);

    putchar(ch);
  } while (ch != '.');
}
```

Reading and Writing Strings

The next step up in console I/O, in terms of complexity and power, are the functions **gets( )** and **puts( )**. They enable you to read and write strings of characters at the console.

The **gets( )** function reads a string of characters entered at the keyboard and places them at the address pointed to by its argument. You may type characters at the keyboard until you strike a carriage return. The carriage return does not become part of the string; instead, a null terminator is placed at the end and **gets( )** returns. In fact, you cannot use **gets( )** to return a carriage return (although **getchar( )** can do so). You can correct typing mistakes by using the BACKSPACE key before pressing ENTER. The prototype for **gets( )** is

    char *gets(char *str);

where *str* is a character array that receives the characters input by the user. **gets( )** also returns *str*. The prototype for **gets( )** is in STDIO.H. The following program reads a string into the array **str** and prints its length:

```
#include <stdio.h>
#include <string.h>

void main(void)
{
  char str[80];

  gets(str);
  printf("Length is %d", strlen(str));
}
```

The **puts( )** function writes its string argument to the screen followed by a newline. Its prototype is:

    int puts(const char *str);

puts( ) recognizes the same backslash codes as **printf( )**, such as '\t' for tab. A call to **puts( )** requires far less overhead than the same call to **printf( )** because **puts( )** can only output a string of characters—it cannot output numbers or do format conversions. Therefore, **puts( )** takes up less space and runs faster than **printf( )**. For this reason, the **puts( )** function is often used when it is important to have highly optimized code. The **puts( )** function returns **EOF** if an error occurs. Otherwise, it returns a nonnegative value. However, when writing to the console, you can usually assume that no error will occur, so the return value of **puts( )** is seldom monitored. The following statement displays **hello**:

```
puts("hello");
```

Table 8-1 summarizes the basic console I/O functions.

The following program, a simple computerized dictionary, demonstrates several of the basic console I/O functions. It prompts the user to enter a word and then checks to see if the word matches one in its built-in database. If a match is found, the program prints the word's meaning. Pay special attention to the indirection used in this program. If you have any trouble understanding it, remember that the **dic** array is an array of pointers to strings. Notice that the list must be terminated by two nulls.

```c
/* A simple dictionary. */
#include <stdio.h>
#include <conio.h>
#include <string.h>
#include <ctype.h>

/* list of words and meanings */
char   *dic[][40] = {
  "atlas", "a volume of maps",
  "car", "a motorized vehicle",
  "telephone", "a communication device",
  "airplane", "a flying machine",
  "", ""   /* null terminate the list */
};

void main(void)
{
  char word[80], ch;
  char **p;
```

Function	Operation
getchar( )	Reads a character from the keyboard; waits for carriage return.
getche( )	Reads a character with echo; does not wait for carriage return; not defined by ANSI, but a common extension.
getch( )	Reads a character without echo; does not wait for carriage return; not defined by ANSI, but a common extension.
putchar( )	Writes a character to the screen.
gets( )	Reads a string from the keyboard.
puts( )	Writes a string to the screen.

Table 8-1. *The Basic I/O Functions*

```
do {
   puts("\nEnter word: ");
   gets(word);

   p = (char **)dic;

   /* find matching word and print its meaning */
   do {
     if(!strcmp(*p, word)) {
       puts("meaning:");
       puts(*(p+1));
       break;
     }
     if(!strcmp(*p, word)) break;
     p = p + 2;  /* advance through the list */
   } while(*p);
   if(!*p) puts("word not in dictionary");
   printf("another? (y/n): ");
   ch = getche();
 } while(toupper(ch) != 'N');
}
```

Formatted Console I/O

The functions **printf( )** and **scanf( )** perform formatted output and input—that is, they can read and write data in various formats that are under your control. The **printf( )** function writes data to the console. The **scanf( )** function, its complement, reads data from the keyboard. Both functions can operate on any of the built-in data types, including characters, strings, and numbers.

printf( )

The prototype for **printf( )** is

> int printf(const char *control_string, ...);

The prototype for **printf( )** is in STDIO.H. The **printf( )** function returns the number of characters written or a negative value if an error occurs.

The *control_string* consists of two types of items. The first type is composed of characters that will be printed on the screen. The second type contains format specifiers that define the way the subsequent arguments are displayed. A format specifier begins with a percent sign and is followed by the format code. There must be exactly the same number of arguments as there are format specifiers, and the format specifiers and the arguments are matched in order from left to right. For example, this **printf( )** call

```
printf("I like %c %s", 'C', "very much!");
```

displays

```
I like C very much!
```

The **printf( )** function accepts a wide variety of format specifiers, as shown in Table 8-2.

Code	Format
%c	Character
%d	Signed decimal integers
%i	Signed decimal integers
%e	Scientific notation (lowercase e)
%E	Scientific notation (uppercase E)
%f	Decimal floating point
%g	Uses %e or %f, whichever is shorter
%G	Uses %E or %F, whichever is shorter
%o	Unsigned octal
%s	String of characters
%u	Unsigned decimal integers
%x	Unsigned hexadecimal (lowercase letters)
%X	Unsigned hexadecimal (uppercase letters)
%p	Displays a pointer
%n	The associated argument is an integer pointer into which the number of characters written so far is placed
%%	Prints a % sign

Table 8-2. *printf( ) Format Specifiers*

Printing Characters

To print an individual character, use **%c**. This causes its matching argument to be output, unmodified, to the screen.

To print a string, use **%s**.

Printing Numbers

You may use either **%d** or **%i** to indicate a signed decimal number. These format specifiers are equivalent; both are supported for historical reasons.

To output an unsigned value, use **%u**.

The **%f** format specifier displays numbers in floating point.

The **%e** and **%E** specifiers tell **printf( )** to display a **double** argument in scientific notation. Numbers represented in scientific notation take this general form:

x.dddddE+/–yy

If you want to display the letter "E" in uppercase, use the **%E** format; otherwise use **%e**.

You can tell **printf( )** to use either **%f** or **%e** by using the **%g** or **%G** format specifiers. This causes **printf( )** to select the format specifier that produces the shortest output. Where applicable, use **%G** if you want "E" shown in uppercase; otherwise, use **%g**. The following program demonstrates the effect of the **%g** format specifier:

```c
#include <stdio.h>

void main(void)
{
  double f;

  for(f=1.0; f<1.0e+10; f=f*10)
    printf("%g ", f);
}
```

It produces the following output.

```
1 10 100 1000 10000 100000 1e+06 1e+07 1e+08 1e+09
```

You can display unsigned integers in octal or hexadecimal format using **%o** and **%x**, respectively. Since the hexadecimal number system uses the letters A through F to represent the numbers 10 through 15, you can display these letters in either upper- or lowercase. For uppercase, use the **%X** format specifier; for lowercase, use **%x**, as shown here:

```
#include <stdio.h>

void main(void)
{
  unsigned num;

  for(num=0; num<255; num++) {
    printf("%o ", num);
    printf("%x ", num);
    printf("%X\n", num);
  }
}
```

Displaying an Address

If you wish to display an address, use **%p**. This format specifier causes **printf( )** to display a machine address in a format compatible with the type of addressing used by the computer. The next program displays the address of **sample**:

```
#include <stdio.h>

int sample;

void main(void)
{
  printf("%p", &sample);
}
```

The %n Specifier

The **%n** format specifier is different from the others. Instead of telling **printf( )** to display something, it causes **printf( )** to load the variable pointed to by its corresponding argument with a value equal to the number of characters that have been output. In other words, the value that corresponds to the **%n** format specifier must be a pointer to a variable. After the call to **printf( )** has returned, this variable will hold the number of characters output, up to the point at which the **%n** was encountered. Examine this program to understand this somewhat unusual format code.

```
#include <stdio.h>

void main(void)
{
   int count;

   printf("this%n is a test\n", &count);
   printf("%d", count);
}
```

This program displays **this is a test** followed by the number 4. The **%n** format specifier is used primarily to enable your program to perform dynamic formatting.

Format Modifiers

Many format specifiers may take modifiers that alter their meaning slightly. For example, you can specify a minimum field width, the number of decimal places, and left justification. The format modifier goes between the percent sign and the format code. These modifiers are discussed next.

The Minimum Field Width Specifier

An integer placed between the % sign and the format code acts as a *minimum field width specifier*. This pads the output with spaces to ensure that it reaches a certain minimum length. If the string or number is longer than that minimum, it will still be printed in full. The default padding is done with spaces. If you wish to pad with 0's, place a 0 before the field width specifier. For example, **%05d** will pad a number of less than five digits with 0's so that its total length is five. The following program demonstrates the minimum field width specifier:

```
#include <stdio.h>

void main(void)
{
   double item;

   item = 10.12304;
```

```
    printf("%f\n", item);
    printf("%10f\n", item);
    printf("%012f\n", item);
}
```

This program produces the following output:

```
10.123040
 10.123040
00010.123040
```

The minimum field width modifier is most commonly used to produce tables in which the columns line up. For example, the next program produces a table of squares and cubes for the numbers between 1 and 19:

```
#include <stdio.h>

void main(void)
{
  int i;

  /* display a table of squares and cubes */
  for(i=1; i<20; i++)
    printf("%8d %8d %8d\n", i, i*i, i*i*i);
}
```

A sample of its output is shown here:

```
1         1         1
2         4         8
3         9        27
4        16        64
5        25       125
6        36       216
7        49       343
8        64       512
9        81       729
```

```
10      100     1000
11      121     1331
12      144     1728
13      169     2197
14      196     2744
15      225     3375
16      256     4096
17      289     4913
18      324     5832
19      361     6859
```

The Precision Specifier

The *precision specifier* follows the minimum field width specifier (if there is one). It consists of a period followed by an integer. Its exact meaning depends upon the type of data it is applied to.

When you apply the precision specifier to floating-point data using the **%f**, **%e**, or **%E** specifiers, it determines the number of decimal places displayed. For example, **%10.4f** displays a number at least ten characters wide with four decimal places. If you don't specify the precision, a default of six is used.

When the precision specifier is applied to **%g** or **%G,** it specifies the number of significant digits.

Applied to strings, the precision specifier specifies the maximum field length. For example, **%5.7s** displays a string at least five and not exceeding seven characters long. If the string is longer than the maximum field width, the end characters will be truncated.

When applied to integer types, the precision specifier determines the minimum number of digits that will appear for each number. Leading zeros are added to achieve the required number of digits.

The following program illustrates the precision specifier:

```c
#include <stdio.h>

void main(void)
{
  printf("%.4f\n", 123.1234567);
  printf("%3.8d\n", 1000);
  printf("%10.15s\n", "This is a simple test.");
}
```

It produces the following output:

```
123.1235
00001000
This is a simpl
```

Justifying Output

By default, all output is right-justified. That is, if the field width is larger than the data printed, the data will be placed on the right edge of the field. You can force output to be left-justified by placing a minus sign directly after the %. For example, **%–10.2f** left-justifies a floating-point number with two decimal places in a 10-character field.

The following program illustrates left justification:

```
#include <stdio.h>

void main(void)
{
  printf("right-justified:%8d\n", 100);
  printf("left-justified:%-8d\n", 100);
}
```

Handling Other Data Types

There are two format modifiers that allow **printf( )** to display **short** and **long** integers. These modifiers may be applied to the **d, i, o, u,** and **x** type specifiers. The **l** (*ell*) modifier tells **printf( )** that a **long** data type follows. For example, **%ld** means that a **long int** is to be displayed. The **h** modifier instructs **printf( )** to display a **short** integer. For instance, **%hu** indicates that the data is of type **short unsigned int**.

The **L** modifier may prefix the floating-point specifiers **e, f,** and **g** and indicates that a **long double** follows.

The * and # Modifiers

The **printf( )** function supports two additional modifiers to some of its format specifiers: * and #.

Preceding **g, G, f, E,** or **e** specifiers with a # ensures that there will be a decimal point even if there are not decimal digits. If you precede the **x** or **X** format specifier with a #, the hexadecimal number will be printed with a **0x** prefix. Preceding the **o** specifier with # causes the number to be printed with a leading zero. You cannot apply # to any other format specifiers.

Instead of constants, the minimum field width and precision specifiers may be provided by arguments to **printf( )**. To accomplish this, use an * as a placeholder. When the format string is scanned, **printf( )** will match the * to an argument in the order in which they occur. For example, in Figure 8-1, the minimum field width is 10, the precision is 4, and the value to be displayed is **123.3**.

The following program illustrates both # and *:

```
#include <stdio.h>

void main(void)
{
  printf("%x %#x\n", 10, 10);
  printf("%*.*f", 10, 4, 1234.34);
}
```

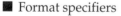

scanf( )

scanf( ) is the general-purpose console input routine. It can read all the built-in data types and automatically convert numbers into the proper internal format. It is much like the reverse of **printf( )**. The prototype for **scanf( )** is

    int scanf(const char *control_string, ...);

The prototype for **scanf( )** is in STDIO.H. The **scanf( )** function returns the number of data items successfully assigned a value. If an error occurs, **scanf( )** returns **EOF**. The *control_string* determines how values are read into the variables pointed to in the argument list.

The control string consists of three classifications of characters.

- Format specifiers
- White-space characters
- Non-white-space characters

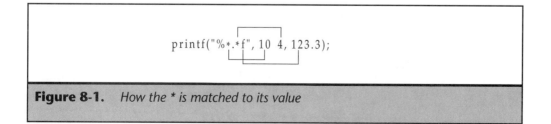

Figure 8-1.   *How the * is matched to its value*

Code	Meaning
%c	Read a single character
%d	Read a decimal integer
%i	Read a decimal integer
%e	Read a floating-point number
%f	Read a floating-point number
%g	Read a floating-point number
%o	Read an octal number
%s	Read a string
%x	Read a hexadecimal number
%p	Read a pointer
%n	Receives an integer value equal to the number of characters read so far
%u	Read an unsigned integer
%[]	Scan for a set of characters

Table 8-3. *scanf( ) Format Specifiers*

Let's take a look at each of these now.

Format Specifiers

The input format specifiers are preceded by a % sign and tell **scanf( )** what type of data is to be read next. These codes are listed in Table 8-3. The format specifiers are matched, in order from left to right, with the arguments in the argument list. Let's look at some examples.

Inputting Numbers

To read a decimal number, use the **%d** or **%i** specifiers. (These specifiers, which do the same thing, are both included for compatibility with older versions of C.)

To read a floating-point number represented in either standard or scientific notation, use **%e**, **%f**, or **%g**. (Again, these specifiers, which do precisely the same thing, are included for compatibility with older versions of C.)

You can use **scanf( )** to read integers in either octal or hexadecimal form by using the **%o** and **%x** format commands, respectively. The **%x** may be in either upper- or lowercase. Either way, you may enter the letters A through F in either case when entering hexadecimal numbers. The following program reads an octal and hexadecimal number:

```
#include <stdio.h>

void main(void)
{
  int i, j;

  scanf("%o%x", &i, &j);
  printf("%o %x", i, j);
}
```

The **scanf( )** function stops reading a number when the first non-numeric character is encountered.

Inputting Unsigned Integers

To input an unsigned integer, use the **%u** format specifier. For example,

```
unsigned num;
scanf("%u", &num);
```

reads an unsigned number and puts its value into **num**.

Reading Individual Characters Using scanf( )

As you learned earlier in this chapter, you can read individual characters using **getchar( )** or a derivative function. You can also use **scanf( )** for this purpose if you use the **%c** format specifier. However, like most implementations of **getchar( )**, **scanf( )** will generally line-buffer input when the %c specifier is used. This makes it somewhat troublesome in an interactive environment.

Although spaces, tabs, and newlines are used as field separators when reading other types of data, when reading a single character, white-space characters are read like any other character. For example, with an input stream of "**x y**," this code fragment

```
scanf("%c%c%c", &a, &b, &c);
```

returns with the character **x** in **a**, a space in **b**, and the character **y** in **c**.

Reading Strings

The **scanf( )** function can be used to read a string from the input stream using the **%s** format specifier. Using **%s** causes **scanf( )** to read characters until it encounters a white-space character. The characters that are read are put into the character array pointed to by the corresponding argument and the result is null terminated. As it applies to **scanf( )**, a white-space character is either a space, a newline, a tab, a vertical tab, or a form feed. Unlike **gets( )**, which reads a string until a carriage return is typed, **scanf( )** reads a string until the first white space is entered. This means that you cannot use **scanf( )** to read a string like "this is a test" because the first space terminates the reading process. To see the effect of the **%s** specifier, try this program using the string "hello there".

```
#include <stdio.h>

void main(void)
{
  char str[80];

  printf("Enter a string: ");
  scanf("%s", str);
  printf("Here's your string: %s", str);
}
```

The program responds with only the "hello" portion of the string.

Inputting an Address

To input a memory address, use the **%p** format specifier. This specifier causes **scanf( )** to read an address in the format defined by the architecture of the CPU. For example, this program inputs an address and then displays what is at that memory address:

```
#include <stdio.h>

void main(void)
{
  char *p;

  printf("Enter an address: ");
  scanf("%p", &p);
  printf("Value at location %p is %c\n", p, *p);
}
```

The %n Specifier

The **%n** specifier instructs **scanf( )** to assign the number of characters read from the input stream at the point at which the **%n** was encountered to the variable pointed to by the corresponding argument.

Using a Scanset

The **scanf( )** function supports a general purpose format specifier called a scanset. A *scanset* defines a set of characters. When **scanf( )** processes the scanset, it will input characters as long as those characters are part of the set defined by the scanset. The characters read will be assigned to the character array that is pointed to by the scanset's corresponding argument. You define a scanset by putting the characters to scan for inside square brackets. The beginning square bracket must be prefixed by a percent sign. For example, the following scanset tells **scanf( )** to read only the characters X, Y, and Z.

```
%[XYZ]
```

When you use a scanset, **scanf( )** continues to read characters and put them into the corresponding character array until it encounters a character that is not in the scanset. Upon return from **scanf( )**, this array will contain a null-terminated string that consists of the characters that have been read. To see how this works, try this program:

```
#include <stdio.h>

void main(void)
{
  int i;
  char str[80], str2[80];

  scanf("%d%[abcdefg]%s", &i, str, str2);
  printf("%d %s %s", i, str, str2);
}
```

Enter **123abcdtye** followed by ENTER The program will then display **123 abcd tye**. Because the "t" is not part of the scanset, **scanf( )** stops reading characters into **str** when it encounters the "t." The remaining characters are put into **str2**.

You can specify an inverted set if the first character in the set is a ^. The ^ instructs **scanf( )** to accept any character that is *not* defined by the scanset.

You can specify a range using a hyphen. For example, this tells **scanf( )** to accept the characters A through Z:

```
%[A-Z]
```

One important point to remember is that the scanset is case sensitive. If you want to scan for both upper- and lowercase letters, you must specify them individually.

Discarding Unwanted White Space

A white-space character in the control string causes **scanf( )** to skip over one or more white-space characters in the input stream. A white-space character is either a space, a tab, vertical tab, form feed, or a newline. In essence, one white-space character in the control string causes **scanf( )** to read, but not store, any number (including zero) of white-space characters up to the first non-white-space character.

Non-White-Space Characters in the Control String

A non-white-space character in the control string causes **scanf( )** to read and discard matching characters in the input stream. For example, **"%d,%d"** causes **scanf( )** to read an integer, read and discard a comma, and then read another integer. If the specified character is not found, **scanf( )** terminates. If you wish to read and discard a percent sign, use %% in the control string.

You Must Pass scanf( ) Addresses

All the variables used to receive values through **scanf( )** must be passed by their addresses. This means that all arguments must be pointers to the variables used as arguments. Recall that this is C's way of creating a call by reference, and it allows a function to alter the contents of an argument. For example, to read an integer into the variable **count**, you would use the following **scanf( )** call:

```
scanf("%d", &count);
```

Strings will be read into character arrays, and the array name, without any index, is the address of the first element of the array. So, to read a string into the character array **str**, you would use

```
scanf("%s", str);
```

In this case, **str** is already a pointer and need not be preceded by the **&** operator.

Format Modifiers

As with **printf( )**, **scanf( )** allows a number of its format specifiers to be modified.

The format specifiers can include a maximum field length modifier. This is an integer, placed between the % and the format specifier, that limits the number of characters read for that field. For example, to read no more than 20 characters into **str**, write

```
scanf("%20s", str);
```

If the input stream is greater than 20 characters, a subsequent call to input begins where this call leaves off. For example, if you enter

ABCDEFGHIJKLMNOPQRSTUVWXYZ

as the response to the **scanf( )** call in this example, only the first 20 characters, or up to the "T," are placed into **str** because of the maximum field width specifier. This means that the remaining characters, UVWXYZ, have not yet been used. If another **scanf( )** call is made, such as

```
scanf("%s", str);
```

the letters UVWXYZ are placed into **str**. Input for a field may terminate before the maximum field length is reached if a white space is encountered. In this case, **scanf( )** moves on to the next field.

To read a long integer, put an **l** (*ell*) in front of the format specifier. To read a short integer, put an **h** in front of the format specifier. These modifiers can be used with the **d, i, o, u**, and **x** format codes.

By default, the **f, e**, and **g** specifiers instruct **scanf( )** to assign data to a **float**. If you put an **l** (*ell*) in front of one of these specifiers, **scanf( )** assigns the data to a **double**. Using an **L** tells **scanf( )** that the variable receiving the data is a **long double**.

Suppressing Input

You can tell **scanf( )** to read a field but not assign it to any variable by preceding that field's format code with an *. For example, given

```
scanf("%d%*c%d", &x, &y);
```

you could enter the coordinate pair **10,10**. The comma would be correctly read, but not assigned to anything. Assignment suppression is especially useful when you need to process only a part of what is being entered.

Chapter Nine

File I/O

As you probably know, the C language does not contain any I/O statements. Instead, all I/O operations take place through calls to functions in the C standard library. This approach makes C's file system extremely powerful and flexible. C's I/O system is also unique because data may be transferred in either its internal binary representation or in a human-readable text format. This makes it easy to create files to fit any need.

ANSI C I/O Versus UNIX I/O

The ANSI C standard defines a complete set of I/O functions that can be used to read and write any type of data. In contrast, the old UNIX C standard contains two distinct file systems that handle I/O operations. The first method loosely parallels the one defined by the ANSI standard and is sometimes called the *buffered* file system (sometimes the terms *formatted* or *high-level* are used instead). The second is the *UNIX-like* file system (sometimes called either *unformatted* or *unbuffered*) and is defined under only the old UNIX standard. The ANSI C standard does not define the UNIX-like file system because, among other things, the two file systems are largely redundant and the UNIX-like file system may not be relevant to certain environments that could otherwise support C. This chapter emphasizes the ANSI C file system. The fact that the ANSI C standard does not define the UNIX-like I/O system suggests that its use will decline. In fact, it would be very hard to justify its use on any new project. However, because UNIX-like routines have been used in thousands of existing C programs, they are discussed briefly at the end of this chapter.

C Versus C++ I/O

Because C forms the foundation for C++ (C's object-oriented enhancement), there is sometimes a question of how C's I/O system relates to C++. The following short discussion answers this question.

C++ supports the entire ANSI C file system. Thus, if you will be porting code to C++ sometime in the future, you will not have to change all of your I/O routines. However, C++ also defines its own, object-oriented I/O system, which includes both I/O functions and I/O operators. The C++ I/O system completely duplicates the functionality of the ANSI C I/O system. In general, if you will be using C++ to write object-oriented programs, you will want to use the object-oriented I/O system. Otherwise, you are free to use either the object-oriented file system or the ANSI C file system. One advantage to using the latter is that it is currently standardized and will be recognized by all current C and C++ compilers.

NOTE: *For a complete discussion of C++, including its object-oriented I/O system, refer to the following books:* C++: The Complete Reference, *by Herbert Schildt (Berkeley, CA: Osborne/McGraw-Hill) and* C++ From the Ground Up, *by Herbert Schildt (Berkeley, CA: Osborne/McGraw-Hill).*

Streams and Files

Before beginning our discussion of the ANSI C file system it is important to understand the difference between the terms *streams* and *files*. The C I/O system supplies a consistent interface to the C programmer independent of the actual device being accessed. That is, the C I/O system provides a level of abstraction between the programmer and the device. This abstraction is called a *stream* and the actual device is called a *file*. It is important to understand how streams and files interact.

Streams

The C file system is designed to work with a wide variety of devices, including terminals, disk drives, and tape drives. Even though each device is very different, the buffered file system transforms each into a logical device called a stream. All streams behave similarly. Because streams are largely device independent, the same function that can write to a disk file can also be used to write to another type of device, such as the console. There are two types of streams: text and binary.

Text Streams

A *text stream* is a sequence of characters. The ANSI C standard allows (but does not require) a text stream to be organized into lines terminated by a newline character. However, the newline character is optional on the last line and is determined by the implementation (actually, most C compilers do not terminate text streams with newline characters). In a text stream, certain character translations may occur as required by the host environment. For example, a newline may be converted to a carriage return/linefeed pair. Therefore, there may not be a one-to-one relationship between the characters that are written (or read) and those on the external device. Also, because of possible translations, the number of characters written (or read) may not be the same as those on the external device.

Binary Streams

A *binary stream* is a sequence of bytes with a one-to-one correspondence to those on the external device—that is, no character translations occur. Also, the number of bytes written (or read) is the same as the number on the external device. However, an implementation-defined number of null bytes may be appended to a binary stream. These null bytes might be used to pad the information so that it fills a sector on a disk, for example.

Files

In C, a *file* may be anything from a disk file to a terminal or printer. You associate a stream with a specific file by performing an open operation. Once a file is open, information may be exchanged between it and your program.

Not all files have the same capabilities. For example, a disk file can support random access while a modem port cannot. This brings up an important point about the C I/O system: All streams are the same but all files are not.

If the file can support *position requests*, opening that file also initializes the *file position indicator* to the start of the file. As each character is read from or written to the file, the position indicator is incremented, ensuring progression through the file.

You disassociate a file from a specific stream with a close operation. If you close a file opened for output, the contents, if any, of its associated stream are written to the external device. This process is generally referred to as *flushing* the stream, and guarantees that no information is accidentally left in the disk buffer. All files are closed automatically when your program terminates normally, either by **main( )** returning to the operating system or by a call to **exit( )**. Files are not closed when a program terminates abnormally, such as when it crashes or when it calls **abort( )**.

Each stream that is associated with a file has a file control structure of type **FILE**. This structure is defined in the header STDIO.H. Never modify this file control block.

If you are new to programming, C's separation of streams and files may seem unnecessary or contrived. Just remember that its main purpose is to provide a consistent interface. In C, you need only think in terms of streams and use only one file system to accomplish all I/O operations. The C I/O system automatically converts the raw input or output from each device into an easily managed stream.

File System Basics

The ANSI C file system is composed of several interrelated functions. The most common of these are shown in Table 9-1. These functions require that the header file STDIO.H be included in any program in which they are used. Notice that most of the functions begin with the letter "f." This is a holdover from the UNIX C standard, which defined two file systems. The UNIX I/O functions did not begin with a prefix and most of the formatted I/O system functions were prefixed with the "f." The ANSI standardization committee elected to maintain this naming convention in the interest of continuity.

The header file STDIO.H provides the prototypes for the I/O functions and defines these three types: **size_t**, **fpos_t**, and **FILE**. The **size_t** type is some variety of unsigned integer, as is **fpos_t**. The **FILE** type is discussed in the next section.

STDIO.H also defines several macros. The ones relevant to this chapter are **NULL**, **EOF**, **FOPEN_MAX**, **SEEK_SET**, **SEEK_CUR**, and **SEEK_END**. The **NULL** macro defines a null pointer. The **EOF** macro is generally defined as –1 and is the value

Name	Function
fopen( )	Opens a file
fclose( )	Closes a file
putc( )	Writes a character to a file
fputc( )	Same as putc( )
getc( )	Reads a character from a file
fgetc( )	Same as getc( )
fseek( )	Seeks to a specified byte in a file
fprintf( )	Is to a file what printf( ) is to the console
fscanf( )	Is to a file what scanf( ) is to the console
feof( )	Returns true if end-of-file is reached
ferror( )	Returns true if an error has occurred
rewind( )	Resets the file position indictor to the beginning of the file
remove( )	Erases a file
fflush( )	Flushes a file

Table 9-1.   *The Most Common ANSI C File System Functions*

returned when an input function tries to read past the end of the file. **FOPEN_MAX** defines an integer value that determines the number of files that may be open at any one time. The other macros are used with **fseek( )**, which is the function that performs random access on a file.

The File Pointer

The file pointer is the common thread that unites the ANSI C I/O system. A *file pointer* is a pointer to information that defines various things about the file, including its name, status, and the current position of the file. In essence, the file pointer identifies a specific disk file and is used by the associated stream to direct the operation of the I/O functions. A file pointer is a pointer variable of type **FILE**. In order to read or write files, your program needs to use file pointers. To obtain a file pointer variable, use a statement like this:

```
FILE *fp;
```

Opening a File

The **fopen( )** function opens a stream for use and links a file with that stream. Then it returns the file pointer associated with that file. Most often (and for the rest of this discussion) the file is a disk file. The **fopen( )** function has this prototype:

FILE *fopen(const char *filename, const char *mode);

where *filename* is a pointer to a string of characters that make up a valid file name and may include a path specification. The string pointed to by *mode* determines how the file will be opened. Table 9-2 shows the legal values for *mode*. Strings like "r+b" may also be represented as "rb+."

As stated, the **fopen( )** function returns a file pointer. Your program should never alter the value of this pointer. If an error occurs when it is trying to open the file, **fopen( )** returns a null pointer.

As Table 9-2 shows, a file may be opened in either text or binary mode. In most implementations, in text mode, carriage return/linefeed sequences are translated to newline characters on input. On output, the reverse occurs: Newlines are translated to carriage return/linefeeds. No such translations occur on binary files.

The following code uses **fopen( )** to open a file named TEST for output.

```
FILE *fp;


fp = fopen("test", "w");
```

Mode	Meaning
r	Open a text file for reading
w	Create a text file for writing
a	Append to a text file
rb	Open a binary file for reading
wb	Create a binary file for writing
ab	Append to a binary file
r+	Open a text file for read/write
w+	Create a text file for read/write
a+	Append or create a text file for read/write
r+b	Open a binary file for read/write
w+b	Create a binary file for read/write
a+b	Append or create a binary file for read/write

Table 9-2.   *The Legal Values for Mode*

While technically correct, you will usually see the preceding code written like this:

```
FILE *fp;

if ((fp = fopen("test","w"))==NULL) {
  printf("Cannot open file.\n");
  exit(1);
}
```

This method will detect any error in opening a file, such as a write-protected or a full disk, before your program attempts to write to it. In general, you will always want to confirm that **fopen( )** succeeded before attempting any other operations on the file.

If you use **fopen( )** to open a file for writing, any preexisting file by that name will be erased and a new file started. If no file by that name exists, one will be created. If you want to add to the end of the file, you must use mode "a." You can only open existing files for read operations. If the file does not exist, an error is returned. Finally, if a file is opened for read/write operations, it will not be erased if it exists. However, if it does not exist it will be created.

The number of files that may be open at any one time is specified by **FOPEN_MAX.** This value will usually be at least 8, but you must check your compiler manual for its exact value.

Closing a File

The **fclose( )** function closes a stream that was opened by a call to **fopen( )**. It writes any data still remaining in the disk buffer to the file and does a formal operating-system-level close on the file. Failure to close a stream invites all kinds of trouble, including lost data, destroyed files, and possible intermittent errors in your program. An **fclose( )** also frees the file control block associated with the stream, making it available for reuse. In most cases, there is an operating system limit to the number of open files you may have at any one time, so you may have to close one file before opening another.

The **fclose( )** function has this prototype:

int fclose(FILE *fp);

where fp is the file pointer returned by the call to **fopen( )**. A return value of zero signifies a successful close operation. The function returns **EOF** if an error occurs. You can use the standard function **ferror( )** (discussed shortly) to determine and report any problems. Generally, **fclose( )** will only fail when a disk has been prematurely removed from the drive or there is no more space on the disk.

Writing a Character

The ANSI C I/O system defines two equivalent functions that output a character: **putc( )** and **fputc( )**. (Actually, **putc( )** is implemented as a macro.) There are two identical functions simply to preserve compatibility with older versions of C. This book uses **putc( )**, but you can use **fputc( )** if you like.

The **putc( )** function writes characters to a file that was previously opened for writing using the **fopen( )** function. The prototype of this function is

int putc(int *ch*, FILE **fp*);

where *fp* is the file pointer returned by **fopen( )** and *ch* is the character to be output. The file pointer tells **putc( )** which disk file to write to. For historical reasons, *ch* is defined as an **int** but only the low-order byte is used.

If a **putc( )** operation is successful, it returns the character written. Otherwise, it returns **EOF**.

Reading a Character

There are also two equivalent functions that input a character: **getc( )** and **fgetc( )**. Both are defined to preserve compatibility with older versions of C. This book uses **getc( )** (which is actually implemented as a macro), but you can use **fgetc( )** if you like.

The **getc( )** function reads characters from a file opened in read mode by **fopen( )**. The prototype of **getc( )** is

int getc(FILE **fp*);

where *fp* is a file pointer of type **FILE** returned by **fopen( )**. For historical reasons, **getc( )** returns an integer, but the high-order byte is zero.

The **getc( )** function returns **EOF** when the end of the file has been reached. Therefore, to read to the end of a text file, you could use the following code:

```
do {
  ch = getc(fp);
} while(ch!=EOF);
```

However, **getc( )** also returns **EOF** if an error occurs. You can use **ferror( )** to determine precisely what has occurred.

Using fopen( ), getc( ), putc( ), and fclose( )

The functions **fopen( )**, **getc( )**, **putc( )**, and **fclose( )** constitute the minimal set of file routines. The following program, KTOD, is a simple example of using **putc( )**, **fopen( )**, and **fclose( )**. It simply reads characters from the keyboard and writes them to a disk file until the user types a dollar sign. The file name is specified from the command line. For example, if you call this program KTOD, typing **KTOD TEST** allows you to enter lines of text into the file called TEST.

```c
/* KTOD: A key to disk program. */
#include <stdio.h>
#include <stdlib.h>

void main(int argc, char *argv[])
{
  FILE *fp;
  char ch;

  if(argc!=2) {
    printf("You forgot to enter the filename.\n");
    exit(1);
  }

  if((fp=fopen(argv[1], "w"))==NULL) {
    printf("Cannot open file.\n");
    exit(1);
  }

  do {
    ch = getchar();
    putc(ch, fp);
  } while (ch!='$');

  fclose(fp);
}
```

The complementary program DTOS reads any ASCII file and displays the contents on the screen.

```c
/* DTOS: A program that reads files and displays them
         on the screen. */
#include <stdio.h>
#include <stdlib.h>

void main(int argc, char *argv[])
{
```

```
FILE *fp;
char ch;

if(argc!=2) {
  printf("You forgot to enter the filename.\n");
  exit(1);
}

if((fp=fopen(argv[1], "r"))==NULL) {
  printf("Cannot open file.\n");
  exit(1);
}

ch = getc(fp);    /* read one character */

while (ch!=EOF) {
  putchar(ch);   /* print on screen */
  ch = getc(fp);
}

fclose(fp);
}
```

Try these two programs. First use KTOD to create a text file. Then read its contents using DTOS.

Using feof( )

As stated earlier, the ANSI C file system can also operate on binary data. When a file is opened for binary input, an integer value equal to the **EOF** mark may be read. This would cause the input routine to indicate an end-of-file condition even though the physical end of the file had not been reached. To solve this problem, C includes the function **feof( )**, which determines when the end of the file has been encountered. The **feof( )** function has this prototype:

   int feof(FILE *fp);

Like the other file functions, its prototype is in STDIO.H. **feof( )** returns true if the end of the file has been reached; otherwise, it returns 0. Therefore, the following routine reads a binary file until the end of the file is encountered:

```
while(!feof(fp)) ch = getc(fp);
```

Of course, you can apply this method to text files as well as binary files.

The following program, which copies text or binary files, contains an example of **feof( )**. The files are opened in binary mode and **feof( )** checks for the end of the file.

```
/* Copy a file. */
#include <stdio.h>
#include <stdlib.h>

void main(int argc, char *argv[])
{
  FILE *in, *out;
  char ch;

  if(argc!=3) {
    printf("You forgot to enter a filename.\n");
    exit(1);
  }

  if((in=fopen(argv[1], "rb"))==NULL) {
    printf("Cannot open source file.\n");
    exit(1);
  }
  if((out=fopen(argv[2], "wb")) == NULL) {
    printf("Cannot open destination file.\n");
    exit(1);
  }

  /* This code actually copies the file. */
  while(!feof(in)) {
    ch = getc(in);
    if(!feof(in)) putc(ch, out);
  }

  fclose(in);
  fclose(out);
}
```

Working with Strings: fputs( ) and fgets( )

In addition to **getc( )** and **putc( )**, C supports the related functions **fgets( )** and **fputs( )**, which read and write character strings from and to a disk file. These functions work just like **putc( )** and **getc( )**, but instead of reading or writing a single character, they read or write strings. They have the following prototypes:

    int fputs(const char *str, FILE *fp);
    char *fgets(char *str, int length, FILE *fp);

The prototypes for **fgets( )** and **fputs( )** are in STDIO.H.

The **fputs( )** function writes the string pointed to by *str* to the specified stream. It returns **EOF** if an error occurs.

The **fgets( )** function reads a string from the specified stream until either a newline character is read or *length*–1 characters have been read. If a newline is read, it will be part of the string (unlike the **gets( )** function). The resultant string will be null terminated. The function returns *str* if successful and a null pointer if an error occurs.

The following program demonstrates **fputs( ).** It reads strings from the keyboard and writes them to the file called TEST. To terminate the program, enter a blank line. Since **gets( )** does not store the newline character, one is added before each string is written to the file so that the file can be read more easily.

```c
#include <stdio.h>
#include <stdlib.h>
#include <string.h>

void main(void)
{
  char str[80];
  FILE *fp;

  if((fp = fopen("TEST", "w"))==NULL) {
    printf("Cannot open file.\n");
    exit(1);
  }

  do {
    printf("Enter a string (CR to quit):\n");
    gets(str);
    strcat(str, "\n");  /* add a newline */
    fputs(str, fp);
  } while(*str!='\n');
}
```

rewind( )

The **rewind( )** function resets the file position indicator to the beginning of the file specified as its argument. That is, it "rewinds" the file. Its prototype is

void rewind(FILE *fp);

where *fp* is a valid file pointer. The prototype for **rewind( )** is in STDIO.H.

To see an example of **rewind( )**, you can modify the program from the previous section so that it displays the contents of the file just created. To accomplish this, the program rewinds the file after input is complete and then uses **fgets( )** to read back the file. Notice that the file must now be opened in read/write mode using "w+" for the mode parameter.

```c
#include <stdio.h>
#include <stdlib.h>
#include <string.h>

void main(void)
{
  char str[80];
  FILE *fp;

  if((fp = fopen("TEST", "w+"))==NULL) {
    printf("Cannot open file.\n");
    exit(1);
  }

  do {
    printf("Enter a string (CR to quit):\n");
    gets(str);
    strcat(str, "\n");  /* add a newline */
    fputs(str, fp);
  } while(*str!='\n');

  /* now, read and display the file */
  rewind(fp);  /* reset file position indicator to
                  start of the file. */
  while(!feof(fp)) {
    fgets(str, 79, fp);
    printf(str);
  }
}
```

ferror( )

The **ferror( )** function determines whether a file operation has produced an error. The **ferror( )** function has this prototype:

int ferror(FILE *fp);

where *fp* is a valid file pointer. It returns true if an error has occurred during the last file operation; otherwise, it returns false. Because each file operation sets the error condition, **ferror( )** should be called immediately after each file operation; otherwise, an error may be lost. The prototype for **ferror( )** is in STDIO.H.

The following program illustrates **ferror( )** by removing tabs from a text file and substituting the appropriate number of spaces. The tab size is defined by **TAB_SIZE**. Notice how **ferror( )** is called after each disk operation. To use the program, specify the names of the input and output files on the command line.

```c
/* The program substitutes spaces for tabs
   in a text file and supplies error checking. */

#include <stdio.h>
#include <stdlib.h>

#define TAB_SIZE 8
#define IN 0
#define OUT 1

void err(int e);

void main(int argc, char *argv[])
{
  FILE *in, *out;
  int tab, i;
  char ch;

  if(argc!=3) {
    printf("usage: detab <in> <out>\n");
    exit(1);
  }

  if((in = fopen(argv[1], "rb"))==NULL) {
    printf("Cannot open %s.\n", argv[1]);
    exit(1);
  }
```

```
    if((out = fopen(argv[2], "wb"))==NULL) {
      printf("Cannot open %s.\n", argv[1]);
      exit(1);
    }

    tab = 0;
    do {
      ch = getc(in);
      if(ferror(in)) err(IN);

      /* if tab found, output appropriate number of spaces */
      if(ch=='\t') {
        for(i=tab; i<8; i++) {
          putc(' ', out);
          if(ferror(out)) err(OUT);
        }
        tab = 0;
      }
      else {
        putc(ch, out);
        if(ferror(out)) err(OUT);
        tab++;
        if(tab==TAB_SIZE) tab = 0;
        if(ch=='\n' || ch=='\r') tab = 0;
      }
    } while(!feof(in));
    fclose(in);
    fclose(out);
}

void err(int e)
{
  if(e==IN) printf("Error on input.\n");
  else printf("Error on output.\n");
  exit(1);
}
```

Erasing Files

The **remove( )** function erases the specified file. Its prototype is

    int remove(const char *filename);

It returns zero if successful. Otherwise, it returns a nonzero value.

The following program erases the file specified on the command line. However, it first gives you a chance to change your mind. A utility like this might be useful to new computer users.

```
/* Double check before erasing. */
#include <stdio.h>
#include <stdlib.h>
#include <ctype.h>

main(int argc, char *argv[])
{
  char str[80];
  if(argc!=2) {
    printf("usage: xerase <filename>\n");
    exit(1);
  }

  printf("Erase %s? (Y/N): ", argv[1]);
  gets(str);

  if(toupper(*str)=='Y')
    if(remove(argv[1])) {
      printf("Cannot erase file.\n");
      exit(1);
    }
  return 0;  /* return success to OS */
}
```

Flushing a Stream

If you wish to flush the contents of an output stream, use the **fflush( )** function, whose prototype is shown here:

int fflush(FILE *fp);

This function writes the contents of any buffered data to the file associated with *fp*. If you call **fflush( )** with *fp* being null, all files opened for output are flushed.

The **fflush( )** function returns 0 if successful; otherwise, it returns **EOF**.

fread( ) and fwrite( )

To read and write data types that are longer than one byte, the ANSI C file system provides two functions: **fread( )** and **fwrite( )**. These functions allow the reading and writing of blocks of any type of data. Their prototypes are

> size_t fread(void *buffer*, size_t *num_bytes*,
>   size_t *count*, FILE *fp*);
> size_t fwrite(const void *buffer*, size_t *num_bytes*,
>   size_t *count*, FILE *fp*);

For **fread( )**, *buffer* is a pointer to a region of memory that will receive the data from the file. For **fwrite( )**, *buffer* is a pointer to the information that will be written to the file. The value of *count* determines how many items are read or written, with each item being *num_bytes* bytes in length. (Remember, the type **size_t** is defined in STDIO.H and is more or less an unsigned integer.) Finally, *fp* is a file pointer to a previously opened stream. The prototypes of both of the functions are defined in STDIO.H.

The **fread( )** function returns the number of items read. This value may be less than *count* if the end of the file is reached or an error occurs. The **fwrite( )** function returns the number of items written. This value will equal *count* unless an error occurs.

Using fread( ) and fwrite( )

As long as the file has been opened for binary data, **fread( )** and **fwrite( )** can read and write any type of information. For example, the following program writes and then reads back a **double**, an **int**, and a **long** to and from a disk file. Notice how it uses **sizeof** to determine the length of each data type.

```
/* Write some non-character data to a disk file
   and read it back.  */
#include <stdio.h>
#include <stdlib.h>

void main(void)
{
  FILE *fp;
  double d = 12.23;
  int i = 101;
  long l = 123023L;

  if((fp=fopen("test", "wb+"))==NULL) {
    printf("Cannot open file.\n");
    exit(1);
```

```
    }

    fwrite(&d, sizeof(double), 1, fp);
    fwrite(&i, sizeof(int), 1, fp);
    fwrite(&l, sizeof(long), 1, fp);

    rewind(fp);

    fread(&d, sizeof(double), 1, fp);
    fread(&i, sizeof(int), 1, fp);
    fread(&l, sizeof(long), 1, fp);

    printf("%f %d %ld", d, i, l);

    fclose(fp);
}
```

As this program illustrates, the buffer can be (and often is) simply the memory used to hold a variable. In this simple program, the return values of **fread( )** and **fwrite( )** are ignored. In the real world, however, you should check their return values for errors.

One of the most useful applications of **fread( )** and **fwrite( )** involves reading and writing user-defined data types, especially structures. For example, given this structure:

```
struct struct_type {
  float balance;
  char name[80];
} cust;
```

the following statement writes the contents of **cust** to the file pointed to by **fp**.

```
fwrite(&cust, sizeof(struct struc_type), 1, fp);
```

To illustrate just how easy it is to write large amounts of data using **fread( )** and **fwrite( )**, a simple mailing list program is developed. The list will be stored in an array of structures of this type:

```
struct list_type {
  char name[40];
```

```
   char street[40];
   char city[30];
   char state[3];
   char zip[10];
} list[SIZE];
```

The value of **SIZE** determines how many addresses the list can hold.

When the program executes, the **name** field of each structure is initialized with a null. By convention, the program assumes that a structure is unused if the name is of 0 length.

The routines **save( )** and **load( )**, shown next, are used to save and load the mailing-list database. Note how little code is contained in each function because of the power of **fread( )** and **fwrite( )**. Notice also how these functions check the return values of **fread( )** and **fwrite( )** for errors.

```
/* Save the list. */
void save(void)
{
  FILE  *fp;
  register int i;

  if((fp=fopen("maillist", "wb"))==NULL) {
    printf("Cannot open file.\n");
    return;
  }


  for(i=0; i<SIZE; i++)
    if(*list[i].name)
      if(fwrite(&list[i],
          sizeof(struct list_type), 1, fp)!=1)
          printf("File write error.\n");

  fclose(fp);
}

/* Load the file. */
void load(void)
{
  FILE  *fp;
  register int i;
```

```
if((fp=fopen("maillist", "rb"))==NULL) {
  printf("Cannot open file.\n");
  return;
}

init_list();
for(i=0; i<SIZE; i++)
  if(fread(&list[i],
      sizeof(struct list_type), 1, fp)!=1) {
        if(feof(fp)) break;
        printf("File read error.\n");
    }

  fclose(fp);
}
```

Both functions confirm a successful file operation by checking the return value of **fread( )** or **fwrite( )**. Also, **load( )** must explicitly check for end-of-file via **feof( )** because **fread( )** returns the same value whether end-of-file has been reached or an error has occurred.

The entire mailing-list program is shown next. You may wish to use this as a core for further enhancements, including the ability to delete names and search for addresses.

```
/* A very simple mailing list database */

#include <stdio.h>
#include <ctype.h>
#include <stdlib.h>
#include <string.h>

#define SIZE 100

struct list_type {
  char name[40];
  char street[40];
  char city[30];
  char state[3];
  char zip[10];
} list[SIZE];
```

```c
int menu(void);
void init_list(void), enter(void);
void display(void), save(void);
void load(void);

void main(void)
{
  char choice;

  init_list();

  for(;;) {
    choice = menu();
    switch(choice) {
      case 'e': enter();
        break;
      case 'd': display();
        break;
      case 's': save();
        break;
      case 'l': load();
        break;
      case 'q': exit(0);
    }
  }
}

/* Initialize the list. */
void init_list(void)
{
  register int t;

  for(t=0; t<SIZE; t++) *list[t].name = '\0';
  /* a zero length name signifies empty */
}

/* Put names into list. */
void enter(void)
{
  register int i;

  for(i=0; i<SIZE; i++)
```

```c
    if(!*list[i].name) break;

  if(i==SIZE) {
    printf("List Full\n");
    return;
  }

  printf("Name: ");
  gets(list[i].name);

  printf("Street: ");
  gets(list[i].street);

  printf("City: ");
  gets(list[i].city);

  printf("State: ");
  gets(list[i].state);

  printf("ZIP: ");
  gets(list[i].zip);
}

/* Display the list. */
void display(void)
{
  register int t;

  for(t=0; t<SIZE; t++) {
    if(*list[t].name) {
      printf("%s\n", list[t].name);
      printf("%s\n", list[t].street);
      printf("%s\n", list[t].city);
      printf("%s\n", list[t].state);
      printf("%s\n\n", list[t].zip);
    }
  }
}

/* Save the list. */
void save(void)
{
```

```
    FILE  *fp;
    register int i;

    if((fp=fopen("maillist", "wb"))==NULL) {
      printf("Cannot open file.\n");
      return;
    }

    for(i=0; i<SIZE; i++)
      if(*list[i].name)

        if(fwrite(&list[i],
            sizeof(struct list_type), 1, fp)!=1)
              printf("File write error.\n");

    fclose(fp);
}

/* Load the file. */
void load(void)
{
  FILE  *fp;
  register int i;

  if((fp=fopen("maillist", "rb"))==NULL) {
    printf("Cannot open file.\n");
    return;
  }

  init_list();
  for(i=0; i<SIZE; i++)
    if(fread(&list[i],
        sizeof(struct list_type), 1, fp)!=1) {
          if(feof(fp)) break;
          printf("File read error.\n");
      }

  fclose(fp);
}

/* Get a menu selection. */
menu(void)
```

```
{
  char s[80];

  do {
    printf("(E)nter\n");
    printf("(D)isplay\n");
    printf("(L)oad\n");
    printf("(S)ave\n");
    printf("(Q)uit\n\n");
    printf("choose one: ");
    gets(s);
  } while(!strchr("edlsq", tolower(*s)));
  return tolower(*s);
}
```

fseek( ) and Random-Access I/O

You can perform random read and write operations using the buffered I/O system with the help of **fseek( )**, which sets the file position indicator. Its prototype type is shown here:

   int fseek(FILE *fp, long *numbytes*, int *origin*);

Here, *fp* is a file pointer returned by a call to **fopen( )**. *numbytes* is the number of bytes from *origin* which will become the new current position, and *origin* is one of the following macros defined in STDIO.H:

Origin	Macro Name
Beginning of file	SEEK_SET
Current position	SEEK_CUR
End of file	SEEK_END

Therefore, to seek *numbytes* from the start of the file, *origin* should be **SEEK_SET**. To seek from the current position use **SEEK_CUR**, and to seek from the end of the file use **SEEK_END**. The **fseek( )** function returns 0 when successful and a nonzero value if an error occurs.

   The following fragment illustrates **fseek( )**. It seeks to and displays the specified byte in the specified file. Specify the file name and then the byte to seek to on the command line.

```
#include <stdio.h>
#include <stdlib.h>

void main(int argc, char *argv[])
{
  FILE *fp;

  if(argc!=3) {
    printf("Usage: SEEK filename byte\n");
    exit(1);
  }

  if((fp = fopen(argv[1], "r"))==NULL) {
    printf("Cannot open file.\n");
    exit(1);
  }

  if(fseek(fp, atol(argv[2]), SEEK_SET)) {
    printf("Seek error.\n");
    exit(1);
  }

  printf("Byte at %ld is %c.\n", atol(argv[2]), getc(fp));
  fclose(fp);
}
```

You can use **fseek( )** to seek in multiples of any type of data by simply multiplying the size of the data by the number of the item you want to reach. For example, if you have a mailing-list file produced by the example in the previous section, the following code fragment seeks to the tenth address.

```
fseek(fp, 9*sizeof(struct list_type), SEEK_SET);
```

fprintf( ) and fscanf( )

In addition to the basic I/O functions already discussed, the buffered I/O system includes **fprintf( )** and **fscanf( )**. These functions behave exactly like **printf( )** and **scanf( )** except that they operate with files. The prototypes of **fprintf( )** and **fscanf( )** are

int fprintf(FILE *fp, const char *control_string,. . .);
int fscanf(FILE *fp, const char *control_string,. . .);

where *fp* is a file pointer returned by a call to **fopen( )**. **fprintf( )** and **fscanf( )** direct their I/O operations to the file pointed to by *fp*.

As an example, the following program reads a string and an integer from the keyboard and writes them to a disk file called TEST. The program then reads the file and displays the information on the screen. After running this program, examine the TEST file. As you will see, it contains human-readable text.

```c
/* fscanf() - fprintf() example */
#include <stdio.h>
#include <io.h>
#include <stdlib.h>

void main(void)
{
  FILE *fp;
  char s[80];
  int t;

  if((fp=fopen("test", "w")) == NULL) {
    printf("Cannot open file.\n");
    exit(1);
  }

  printf("Enter a string and a number: ");
  fscanf(stdin, "%s%d", s, &t); /* read from
                                   keyboard */

  fprintf(fp, "%s %d", s, t); /* write to file */
  fclose(fp);

  if((fp=fopen("test","r")) == NULL) {
    printf("Cannot open file.\n");
    exit(1);
  }

  fscanf(fp, "%s%d", s, &t); /* read from file */
  fprintf(stdout, "%s %d", s, t); /* print on
                                     screen */
}
```

A word of warning: Although **fprintf( )** and **fscanf( )** often are the easiest way to write and read assorted data to disk files, they are not always the most efficient. Because formatted ASCII data is being written as it would appear on the screen (instead of in binary), extra overhead is incurred with each call. So, if speed or file size is a concern, you should probably use **fread( )** and **fwrite( )**.

The Standard Streams

Whenever a C program starts execution, three streams are opened automatically. They are **stdin** (standard input), **stdout** (standard output), and **stderr** (standard error). Normally, these streams refer to the console, but they may be redirected by the operating system to some other device in environments that support redirectable I/O. (Redirectable I/O is supported by Windows, DOS, UNIX and OS/2, for example.)

Because the standard streams are file pointers, they may be used by the ANSI C I/O system to perform I/O operations on the console. For example, **putchar( )** could be defined like this:

```
putchar(char c)
{
   return putc(c, stdout);
}
```

In general, **stdin** is used to read from the console, and **stdout** and **stderr** are used to write to the console. You may use **stdin**, **stdout**, and **stderr** as file pointers in any function that uses a variable of type **FILE ***. For example, you can use **fputs( )** to output a string to the console using a call like this:

```
fputs("hello there", stdout);
```

Keep in mind that **stdin**, **stdout**, and **stderr** are not variables in the normal sense and may not be assigned a value using **fopen( )**. Also, just as these file pointers are created automatically at the start of your program, they are closed automatically at the end; you should not try to close them.

The Console I/O Connection

Recall from Chapter 8 that C makes little distinction between console I/O and file I/O. The console I/O functions described in Chapter 8 actually direct their I/O operations to either **stdin** or **stdout**. In essence, the console I/O functions are simply special versions of their parallel file functions. The reason they exist is as a convenience to you, the programmer.

As described in the previous section, you can perform console I/O using any of C's file system functions. However, what might surprise you is that you can perform disk file I/O using console I/O functions, such as **printf( )**! This is because all of the console I/O functions described in Chapter 8 operate on **stdin** and **stdout**. In environments that allow redirection of I/O, this means that **stdin** and **stdout** could refer to a device other than the keyboard and screen. For example, consider this program:

```
#include <stdio.h>

void main(void)
{
  char str[80];

  printf("Enter a string: ");
  gets(str);
  printf(str);
}
```

Assume that this program is called TEST. If you execute TEST normally, it displays its prompt on the screen, reads a string from the keyboard, and displays that string on the display. However, in an environment that supports I/O redirection, either **stdin**, **stdout**, or both could be redirected to a file. For example, in a DOS or Windows environment, executing TEST like this:

```
TEST > OUTPUT
```

causes the output of TEST to be written to a file called OUTPUT. Executing TEST like this:

TEST < INPUT > OUTPUT

directs **stdin** to the file called INPUT and sends output to the file called OUTPUT.
When a C program terminates, any redirected streams are reset to their default status.

Using freopen( ) to Redirect the Standard Streams

You can redirect the standard streams by using the **freopen( )** function. This function associates an existing stream with a new file. Hence, you can use it to associate a standard stream with a new file. Its prototype is

FILE *freopen(const char *filename,
            const char *mode, FILE *stream);

where *filename* is a pointer to the file name you wish associated with the stream pointed to by *stream*. The file is opened using the value of *mode*, which may have the same values as those used with **fopen( )**. **freopen( )** returns *stream* if successful or NULL on failure.

The following program uses **freopen( )** to redirect **stdout** to a file called OUTPUT:

```
#include <stdio.h>

void main(void)
{
  char str[80];

  freopen("OUTPUT", "w", stdout);

  printf("Enter a string: ");
  gets(str);
  printf(str);
}
```

In general, redirecting the standard streams by using **freopen( )** is useful in special situations, such as debugging. However, performing disk I/O using redirected **stdin** and **stdout** is not as efficient as using functions like **fread( )** or **fwrite( )**.

The UNIX-Like File System

Because C was originally developed under the UNIX operating system, many implementations include a second disk file I/O system that closely mirrors the UNIX low-level disk file routines. The UNIX-like file system uses functions that are separate from the ANSI C file system functions. The most common UNIX-like functions are shown in Table 9-3.

Remember, the UNIX-like file system is sometimes called the unbuffered file system. This is because you must provide and maintain all disk buffers—the system will not do it for you. Therefore, the UNIX-like file system does not contain functions such as **getc( )** and **putc( )** (which read and write characters from or to a stream of data). Instead, it contains the **read( )** and **write( )** functions, which read or write one complete buffer of information with each call.

Recall that the unbuffered file system is not defined by the ANSI C standard and its use will probably diminish over the next few years. For this reason, it is not recommended for new projects. However, a great many existing C programs use it and it is supported by virtually all existing C compilers.

Name	Function
rea d( )	Reads a buffer of data
write( )	Writes a buffer of data
open( )	Opens a disk file
creat( )	Creates a disk file
close( )	Closes a disk file
lseek( )	Seeks to the specified byte in a file
unlink( )	Removes a file from the directory

Table 9-3. *The UNIX-Like Unbuffered I/O Functions*

The header file used by the UNIX-like file system is called IO.H in many implementations. For some functions, you will also need to include the header file FNCTL.H.

NOTE: Many implementations of C do not allow you to use the ANSI file functions and the UNIX-like file functions in the same program. Just to be safe, use either one system or the other.

open( )

Unlike the high-level I/O system, the low-level system does not use file pointers of type **FILE**, but rather file descriptors of type **int**. The prototype for **open( )** is

    int open(const char *filename, int mode);

where *filename* is any valid file name and *mode* is one of the following macros, which are defined in the header file FCNTL.H.

Mode	Effect
O_RDONLY	Read
O_WRONLY	Write
O_RDWR	Read/Write

Many compilers have additional modes—such as text, binary, and the like—so check your user's manual. A successful call to **open( )** returns a positive integer. A return value of –1 means that the file cannot be opened.

A call to **open( )** is usually written similar to this:

```
int fd;
if((fd=open(filename, mode)) == -1) {
  printf("Cannot open file.\n");
  exit(1);
}
```

In most implementations, the operation fails if the file specified in the **open( )** statement does not exist on the disk. (That is, **open( )** won't create a new file.) To create a new file, you will normally call **creat( )**, which is described next. However, depending upon the exact implementation of your C compiler, you may be able to use **open( )** to create a file that is currently nonexistent. (Check your user's manual for details.)

creat( )

If your compiler does not allow you to create a new file using **open( )**, or if you want to ensure portability, you must use **creat( )** to create a new file for write operations. The prototype for **creat( )** is

int creat(const char *filename, int mode);

where filename is any valid file name. The mode argument specifies an access code for the file. Consult your compiler's user manual for specific details. **creat( )** returns a valid file descriptor if successful or –1 on failure.

close( )

The prototype for **close( )** is

int close(int fd);

Here, fd must be a valid file descriptor previously obtained through a call to **open( )** or **creat( )**. **close( )** returns a –1 if unable to close the file. It returns 0 if successful.

The **close( )** function releases the file descriptor so that it can be reused for another file. There is always some limit to the number of open files that may exist simultaneously, so you should close a file when it is no longer needed. More important, a close operation forces any information in the internal disk buffers of the operating system to be written to disk. Failure to close a file may lead to loss of data.

read( ) and write( )

Once a file has been opened for writing, it may be accessed by **write( )**. The prototype for the **write( )** function is int write(int *fd*, const void **buf*, unsigned *size*);

Each time a call to **write( )** is executed, *size* number of bytes are written to the disk file specified by *fd* from the buffer pointed to by *buf*.

The **write( )** function returns the number of bytes written after a successful write operation. Upon failure, most implementations return an **EOF**, but check your user's manual.

The **read( )** function is the complement of **write( )**. Its prototype is

int read(int *fd*, void **buf*, unsigned *size*);

where *fd*, *buf*, and *size* are the same as for **write( )**, except that **read( )** places the data read into the buffer pointed to by *buf*. If **read( )** is successful, it returns the number of characters actually read. It returns 0 upon the physical end-of-file, and –1 if errors occur.

The following program illustrates several aspects of the UNIX-like I/O system. It reads lines of text from the keyboard and writes them to a disk file. After they are written, the program reads them back.

```c
/* Read and write using unbuffered I/O */
#include <stdio.h>
#include <io.h>
#include <stdlib.h>
#include <string.h>
#include <fcntl.h>

#define BUF_SIZE  128

void input(char *buf, int fd1);
void display(char *buf, int fd2);

void main(void)
{
  char buf[BUF_SIZE];
  int fd1, fd2;

  if((fd1=open("test", O_WRONLY))==-1){ /* open for write */
    printf("Cannot open file.\n");
    exit(1);
  }

  input(buf, fd1);
```

```
    /* now close file and read back */
    close(fd1);

    if((fd2=open("test", O_RDONLY))==-1){ /* open for read */
      printf("Cannot open file.\n");
      exit(1);
    }

    display(buf, fd2);
    close(fd2);
}

/* Input text. */
void input(char *buf, int fd1)
{
  register int t;
  do {
    for(t=0; t<BUF_SIZE; t++) buf[t] = '\0';
    gets(buf); /* input chars from keyboard */
    if(write(fd1, buf, BUF_SIZE)!=BUF_SIZE) {
      printf("Error on write.\n");
      exit(1);
    }
  } while (strcmp(buf, "quit"));
}

/* Display file. */
void display(char *buf, int fd2)
{
  for(;;) {
    if(read(fd2, buf, BUF_SIZE)==0) return;
    printf("%s\n", buf);
  }
}
```

unlink( )

If you wish to erase a file, use **unlink( )**. Its prototype is

int unlink(const char *filename);

where *filename* is a character pointer to any valid file name. **unlink( )** returns zero if successful and –1 if it is unable to erase the file. This could happen if the file is not on the disk to begin with or if the disk is write-protected.

Random Access Using lseek( )

The UNIX-like file system supports random access via calls to **lseek( )**. The prototype for **lseek( )** is

long lseek(int *fd*, long *offset*, int *origin*);

where *fd* is a file descriptor returned by **creat( )** or **open( )**. The *offset* is generally of type **long**, but check your C compiler's user's manual. *origin* may be one of these macros (defined in IO.H): **SEEK_SET**, **SEEK_CUR**, or **SEEK_END**. These are the effects of each value for *origin*:

SEEK_SET: Seek *offset* bytes from the start of the file.
SEEK_CUR: Seek *offset* bytes from the current position.
SEEK_END: Seek *offset* bytes from the end of the file.

The **lseek( )** function returns the current file position as measured from the start of the file. Upon failure, a –1 is returned.

The program shown here uses **lseek( )**. To run it, specify a file from the command line. You are prompted for the buffer you wish to read. Enter a negative number to exit. You may want to change the buffer size to match the sector size of your system, although this is not necessary. Here, the buffer size is 128:

```
/* Demonstrate lseek(). */
#include <stdio.h>
#include <io.h>
#include <stdlib.h>
#include <fcntl.h>

#define BUF_SIZE   128

void main(int argc, char *argv[])
{
  char buf[BUF_SIZE+1], s[10];
  int fd, sector;

 if(argc!=2) {
    printf("usage: dump <sector>\n");
```

```
    exit(1);
  }

  buf[BUF_SIZE] = '\0'; /* null terminate buffer */

  if((fd=open(argv[1], O_RDONLY))==-1) {
    printf("Cannot open file.\n");
    exit(1);
  }

  do {
    printf("\nBuffer: ");
    gets(s);

    sector = atoi(s); /* get the sector to read */

    if(lseek(fd, (long)sector*BUF_SIZE, 0)==-1L)
      printf("Seek Error\n");

    if(read(fd, buf, BUF_SIZE)==0) {
      printf("Sector Out Of Range\n");
    }
    else
      printf(buf);
  } while(sector>=0);
  close(fd);
}
```

Chapter Ten

The C Preprocessor
and Comments

Y ou can include various instructions to the compiler in the source code for a C program. These are called *preprocessor directives*, and although not actually part of the C language, they expand the scope of the C programming environment. This chapter also examines comments.

The C Preprocessor

As defined by the ANSI C standard, the C preprocessor contains the following directives:

#if	#include
#ifdef	#define
#ifndef	#undef
#else	#line
#elif	#error
#endif	#pragma

As you can see, all preprocessor directives begin with a # sign. In addition, each preprocessing directive must be on its own line. For example,

```
#include <stdio.h>  #include <stdlib.h>
```

will not work.

#define

The **#define** directive defines an identifier and a character sequence (i.e., a set of characters) that will be substituted for the identifier each time the identifier is encountered in the source file. The ANSI C standard refers to the identifier as a *macro name* and to the replacement process as *macro replacement*. The general form of the directive is

#define *macro_name char-sequence*

Notice that there is no semicolon in this statement. There may be any number of spaces between the identifier and the character sequence but once the character sequence begins, it is terminated only by a newline.

For example, if you wish to use the word **TRUE** for the value 1 and the word **FALSE** for the value 0, you could declare these two macro **#defines**

```
#define TRUE 1
#define FALSE 0
```

This causes the compiler to substitute a 1 or a 0 each time **TRUE** or **FALSE** is encountered in your source file. For example, the following prints **0 1 2** on the screen:

```
printf("%d %d %d", FALSE, TRUE, TRUE+1);
```

Once a macro name has been defined, it may be used as part of the definition of other macro names. For example, this code defines the values of **ONE**, **TWO**, and **THREE**:

```
#define ONE     1
#define TWO     ONE+ONE
#define THREE   ONE+TWO
```

Macro substitution is simply the replacement of an identifier by the character sequence associated with it. Therefore, if you wish to define a standard error message, you might write something like this:

```
#define E_MS "standard error on input\n"

printf(E_MS);
```

The compiler will actually substitute the string "standard error on input\n" when the identifier **E_MS** is encountered. To the compiler, the **printf( )** statement will actually appear to be

```
printf("standard error on input\n");
```

No text substitutions occur if the identifier is within a quoted string. For example,

```
#define XYZ this is a test

printf("XYZ");
```

does not print **this is a test**, but rather **XYZ**.

If the string is longer than one line, you may continue it on the next by placing a backslash at the end of the line, as shown here:

```
#define LONG_STRING "this is a very long \
string that is used as an example"
```

C programmers commonly use uppercase letters for defined identifiers. This convention helps anyone reading the program know at a glance that a macro replacement will take place. Also, it is best to put all **#define**s at the start of the file or in a separate header file rather than sprinkling them throughout the program.

Macros are most frequently used to define names for "magic numbers" that occur in a program. For example, you may have a program that defines an array and has several routines that access that array. Instead of "hard-coding" the array's size with a constant, you should define the size using a **#define** statement and then use that macro name whenever the array size is needed. In this way, if you need to change the size of the array, you will only need to change the **#define** statement and then recompile your program. For example,

```
#define MAX_SIZE 100

/* ... */

float balance[MAX_SIZE];

/* ... */

for(i=0; i<MAX_SIZE; i++) printf("%f", balance[i]);
```

Since **MAX_SIZE** defines the size of the array **balance**, if the size of **balance** needs to be changed in the future, you need only change the definition of **MAX_SIZE**. All subsequent references to it will be automatically updated when you recompile your program.

Defining Function-like Macros

The **#define** directive has another powerful feature: The macro name can have arguments. Each time the macro name is encountered, the arguments used in its definition are replaced by the actual arguments found in the program. This form of a macro is called a *function-like macro*. For example,

```
#include <stdio.h>

#define ABS(a)   (a)<0 ? -(a) : (a)

void main(void)
{
  printf("abs of -1 and 1: %d %d", ABS(-1), ABS(1));
}
```

When this program is compiled, **a** in the macro definition will be substituted with the values –1 and 1. The parentheses that enclose **a** ensure proper substitution in all cases. For example, if the parentheses around **a** were removed, this expression

```
ABS(10-20)
```

would be converted to

```
10-20<0 ? -10-20 : 10-20
```

and would yield the wrong result.

The use of a function-like macro in place of real functions has one major benefit: It increases the execution speed of the code because there is no function call overhead. However, if the size of the function-like macro is very large, this increased speed may be paid for with an increase in the size of the program because of duplicated code.

#error

The **#error** directive forces the compiler to stop compilation. It is used primarily for debugging. The general form of the **#error** directive is

#error *error_message*

The *error_message* is not between double quotes. When the **#error** directive is encountered, the error message is displayed, possibly along with other information defined by the creator of the compiler.

#include

The **#include** directive instructs the compiler to read another source file in addition to the one that contains the **#include** directive. The name of the additional source file must be enclosed between double quotes or angle brackets. For example,

```
#include "stdio.h"
#include <stdio.h>
```

both instruct the C compiler to read and compile the header for the file system library functions.

Include files can have **#include** directives in them. This is referred to as *nested includes*. The number of levels of nesting allowed varies between compilers. However, the ANSI C standard stipulates that at least eight nested inclusions will be available.

Whether the file name is enclosed by quotes or by angle brackets determines how the search for the specified file is conducted. If the file name is enclosed in angle brackets, the file is searched for in a manner defined by the creator of the compiler. Often, this means searching some special directory set aside for include files. If the file name is enclosed in quotes, the file is looked for in another implementation-defined manner. For many compilers, this means searching the current working directory. If the file is not found, the search is repeated as if the file name had been enclosed in angle brackets.

Typically, most programmers use angle brackets to include the standard header files. The use of quotes is generally reserved for including files specifically related to the program at hand. However, there is no hard and fast rule that demands this usage.

Conditional Compilation Directives

There are several directives that allow you to selectively compile portions of your program's source code. This process is called *conditional compilation* and is used widely by commercial software houses that provide and maintain many customized versions of one program.

#if, #else, #elif, and #endif

Perhaps the most commonly used conditional compilation directives are the **#if**, **#else**, **#elif**, and **#endif**. These directives allow you to conditionally include portions of code based upon the outcome of a constant expression.

The general form of **#if** is

```
#if constant_expression
   statement sequence
#endif
```

If the constant expression following **#if** is true, the code that is between it and **#endif** is compiled. Otherwise, the intervening code is skipped. The **#endif** directive marks the end of an **#if** block. For example,

```
/* Simple #if example. */
#include <stdio.h>

#define MAX 100

void main(void)
{
#if MAX>99
  printf("compiled for array greater than 99\n");
#endif
}
```

This program displays the message on the screen because **MAX** is greater than 99. This example illustrates an important point. The expression that follows the **#if** is evaluated at compile time. Therefore, it must contain only previously defined identifiers and constants—no variables may be used.

The **#else** directive works much like the **else** that is part of the C language: It establishes an alternative if **#if** fails. The previous example can be expanded as shown here:

```
/* Simple #if/#else example. */
#include <stdio.h>

#define MAX 10

void main(void)
{
#if MAX>99
  printf("compiled for array greater than 99\n");
#else
  printf("compiled for small array\n");
#endif
}
```

In this case, **MAX** is defined to be less than 99 so the **#if** portion of the code is not compiled. The **#else** alternative is compiled, however, and the message **compiled for small array** is displayed.

Notice that **#else** is used to mark both the end of the **#if** block and the beginning of the **#else** block. This is necessary because there can only be one **#endif** associated with any **#if**.

The **#elif** directive means "else if" and establishes an if-else-if chain for multiple compilation options. **#elif** is followed by a constant expression. If the expression is true, that block of code is compiled and no other **#elif** expressions are tested. Otherwise, the next block in the series is checked. The general form for **#elif** is

```
#if expression
    statement sequence
#elif expression 1
    statement sequence
#elif expression 2
    statement sequence
#elif expression 3
    statement sequence
#elif expression 4
        .
        .
        .
#elif expression N
    statement sequence
#endif
```

For example, the following fragment uses the value of **ACTIVE_COUNTRY** to define the currency sign:

```
#define US 0
#define ENGLAND 1
#define FRANCE 2

#define ACTIVE_COUNTRY US

#if ACTIVE_COUNTRY == US
  char currency[] = "dollar";
#elif ACTIVE_COUNTRY == ENGLAND
  char currency[] = "pound";
#else
  char currency[] = "franc";
#endif
```

The ANSI C standard states that **#ifs** and **#elifs** may be nested at least eight levels. (Your compiler will probably allow more.) When nested, each **#endif**, **#else**, or **#elif** associates with the nearest **#if** or **#elif**. For example, the following is perfectly valid:

```
#if MAX>100
  #if SERIAL_VERSION
    int port=198;
  #elif
    int port=200;
  #endif
#else
  char out_buffer[100];
#endif
```

#ifdef and #ifndef

Another method of conditional compilation uses the directives **#ifdef** and **#ifndef**, which mean "if defined" and "if not defined," respectively. The general form of **#ifdef** is

```
#ifdef macro_name
   statement sequence
#endif
```

If *macro_name* has been previously defined in a **#define** statement, the block of code will be compiled.

The general form of **#ifndef** is

```
#ifndef macro_name
   statement sequence
#endif
```

If *macro_name* is currently undefined by a **#define** statement, the block of code is compiled.

Both **#ifdef** and **#ifndef** may use an **#else** statement, but not **#elif**.

For example,

```
#include <stdio.h>

#define TED 10
```

```
void main(void)
{
#ifdef TED
  printf("Hi Ted\n");
#else
  printf("Hi anyone\n");
#endif
#ifndef RALPH
  printf("RALPH not defined\n");
#endif
}
```

will print **Hi Ted** and **RALPH not defined**. However, if **TED** were not defined, **Hi anyone** would be displayed, followed by **RALPH not defined**.

You may nest **#ifdefs** and **#ifndefs**.

#undef

The **#undef** directive removes a previously defined definition of the macro name that follows it. That is, it "undefines" a macro. The general form for **#undef** is

#undef *macro_name*

For example,

```
#define LEN 100
#define WIDTH 100

char array[LEN][WIDTH];

#undef LEN
#undef WIDTH
/* at this point both LEN and WIDTH are undefined */
```

Both **LEN** and **WIDTH** are defined until the **#undef** statements are encountered.

#undef is used principally to allow macro names to be localized to only those sections of code that need them.

Using defined

In addition to **#ifdef**, there is a second way to determine if a macro name is defined. You can use the **#if** directive in conjunction with the **defined** compile-time operator. The **defined** operator has this general form:

defined *macro-name*

If *macro-name* is currently defined, then the expression is true. Otherwise, it is false. For example, to determine if the macro **MYFILE** is defined, you can use either of these two preprocessing commands:

```
#if defined MYFILE
```

or

```
#ifdef MYFILE
```

You may also precede **defined** with the ! to reverse the condition. For example, the following fragment is compiled only if **DEBUG** is not defined.

```
#if !defined DEBUG
  printf("Final version!\n");
#endif
```

One reason for using **defined** is that it allows the existence of a macro name to be determined by a **#elif** statement.

#line

The **#line** directive changes the contents of __**LINE**__ and __**FILE**__, which are predefined identifiers in the compiler. The __**LINE**__ identifier contains the line number of the currently compiled line of code. The __**FILE**__ identifier is a string that contains the name of the source file being compiled. The general form for **#line** is

#line *number "filename"*

where *number* is any positive integer and becomes the new value of __LINE__, and the optional *filename* is any valid file identifier, which becomes the new value of the __FILE__. **#line** is primarily used for debugging and special applications.

For example, the following code specifies that the line count will begin with 100 and the **printf( )** statement displays the number 102 because it is the third line in the program after the **#line 100** statement.

```
#include <stdio.h>

#line 100                        /* reset the line counter */
void main(void)                  /* line 100 */
{                                /* line 101 */
  printf("%d\n",__LINE__);       /* line 102 */
}
```

#pragma

The **#pragma** directive is an implementation-defined directive that allows various instructions to be given to the compiler. For example, a compiler may have an option that supports program execution tracing. A trace option would then be specified by a **#pragma** statement. You must check the compiler's user's manual for details and options.

The # and ## Preprocessor Operators

There are two preprocessor operators: **#** and **##**. These operators are used with the **#define** statement.

The **#** operator, which is generally called the *stringize* operator, turns the argument it precedes into a quoted string. For example, consider this program.

```
#include <stdio.h>

#define mkstr(s)    # s

void main(void)
{
  printf(mkstr(I like C));
}
```

The C preprocessor turns the line

```
printf(mkstr(I like C));
```

into

```
printf("I like C");
```

The ## operator, called the *pasting* operator, concatenates two tokens. For example,

```
#include <stdio.h>

#define concat(a, b)   a ## b

void main(void)
{
  int xy = 10;
  printf("%d", concat(x, y));
}
```

The preprocessor transforms

```
printf("%d", concat(x, y));
```

into

```
printf("%d", xy);
```

If these operators seem strange to you, keep in mind that they are not needed or used in most C programs. They exist primarily to allow the preprocessor to handle some special cases.

Predefined Macro Names

The ANSI C standard specifies five built-in predefined macro names. They are

```
__LINE__
__FILE__
__DATE__
__TIME__
__STDC__
```

If your compiler is nonstandard, some or all of these macros may be missing. Your compiler may also supply more predefined macros. The **__LINE__** and **__FILE__** macros were discussed in the section on **#line**.

The **__DATE__** macro contains a string of the form *month/day/year*. This string represents the date of the translation of the source file into object code.

The time of the translation of the source code into object code is contained as a string in **__TIME__**. The form of the string is *hour:minute:second*.

The macro **__STDC__** contains the decimal constant 1. This means that the implementation conforms to the ANSI C standard. If the macro contains any other number (or is not defined), the implementation varies from the standard.

Comments

In C, all comments begin with the character pair /* and end with */. There must be no spaces between the asterisk and the slash. The compiler ignores any text between the beginning and ending comment symbols. For example, this program prints only **hello** on the screen:

```c
#include <stdio.h>

void main(void)
{
  printf("hello");
  /* printf("there"); */
}
```

Comments may be placed anywhere in a program, as long as they do not appear in the middle of keyword or identifier. That is, this comment is valid:

```c
x = 10+ /* add the numbers */5;
```

while

```
swi/*this will not work*/tch(c) { ...
```

is incorrect because a C keyword cannot contain a comment. However, you should not generally place comments in the middle of expressions because it obscures their meaning.

Comments may not be nested. That is, one comment may not contain another comment. For example, this code fragment causes a compile-time error:

```
/* this is an outer comment
   x = y/a;
   /* this is an inner comment - and causes an error */
*/
```

You should include comments whenever they are needed to explain the operation of the code. All but the most obvious functions should have a comment at the top that states what the function does, how it is called, and what it returns.

NOTE: *In C++ (C's object-oriented enhancement), you may define a single-line comment. Single line comments begin with a // and end at the end of the line. Because the single-line comment is quite popular and easily implemented, most C compilers today allow you to embed single line comments into a C program. However, doing so renders your program non-standard. For this reason it is best to use only C-style comments in C programs.*

PART TWO

The C Standard Library

Part Two of this book examines the C standard library. Chapter 11 discusses linking, libraries, and header files. Chapters 12 through 18 describe the functions in the standard library—each chapter concentrates on a specific function subsystem.

Part Two discusses three types of functions. First, it includes all of the library functions as defined by the ANSI C standard. These functions are included in all standard C implementations and code using them is portable to all standard environments. The second category of functions are those defined by the original UNIX version of C. Several of the most commonly used UNIX-based functions are described here. Finally, although no standard exists for graphics, screen control, or operating system interfacing functions, they are included in virtually all C implementations. For this reason, a representative sample is examined.

When exploring the standard library remember this: Most compiler implementors take great pride in the completeness of their library. Your compiler's library will probably contain many additional functions beyond those described here. Therefore, it is always a good idea to browse through your user's manual.

Chapter Eleven

Linking, Libraries, and Header Files

When a C compiler is written, there are actually two parts to the job. First, the compiler itself must be created. Second, the standard library must be coded. Somewhat surprisingly, the compiler itself is relatively easy to develop. It is the library functions that generally take the most time and effort. One reason for this is that many functions (such as the I/O system) must interface with the operating system for which the compiler is being written. In addition, the C standard library defines a large and diverse set of functions. Indeed, it is the richness and flexibility of the standard library that sets C apart from many other languages. To fully understand the nature of the C standard library and how it is used to produce executable programs, you should know how the linker works, how libraries differ from object files, and the role of header files.

The Linker

The linker has two functions. The first, as the name implies, is to combine (link) various pieces of object code. The second is to resolve the addresses of jump and call instructions found in the relocatable format of an object file. To understand its operation, let's look more closely at the process of separate compilation.

Separate Compilation

In *separate compilation*, parts of a program are compiled separately and then linked to form the finished executable program. The output of the compiler is a relocatable object file, and the output of the linker is an executable file. The role the linker plays is twofold. First, it physically combines the files specified in the link list into one program file. Second, it also resolves external references. An external reference is created any time the code in one file refers to code in another file. This may be through either a function call or a reference to a global variable. For example, when the two files shown here are linked, file 2's reference to **count** (which is declared in file 1) must be resolved. The linker tells the code in file 2 where **count** will be found.

File 1:

```
int count;
void display(void);

void main(void)
{
  count = 10;
  display();
}
```

File 2:

```
#include <stdio.h>

extern int count;

void display(void)
{
  printf("%d", count);
}
```

In a similar fashion, the linker tells file 1 where the function **display( )** is located so that it may be called.

   When the compiler generates the object code for **display( )**, it substitutes a placeholder for the address of **count** because the compiler has no way of knowing where **count** is. The same sort of thing occurs when **main( )** is compiled. The address of **display( )** is unknown, so a placeholder is used. This process forms the basis for relocatable code.

Relocatable Code

Relocatable code is simply object code that may run in any available memory region that is large enough to hold it. In a relocatable object file, the address of each call, jump, or global variable is not fixed, but is relative. To understand how relocatable code is created, you need to understand *absolute code*. For this discussion it is necessary to work with the actual machine instructions that would be generated by the C compiler, using a pseudo-assembly code fragment that somewhat resembles 8086 assembly code. (Don't worry if you don't know assembly language; this example is very simple.)

   The pseudo-assembly code shown here corresponds to the C code shown after it:

```
        mov a,0
label1: out a,123   ; send it out port 123
        inc a        ; increment the a register
        cmp a,100    ; is it equal to 100?
        out 123      ; output to port 123
        jnz label1   ; jmp not zero


/* C code version */
for(x=0; x<100; x++) out(x, 123);
```

In this example, the **a** register is initialized to zero. Then the program loops 100 times, each time sending the value in register **a** out port 123. The **inc** instruction increments the **a** register, and **cmp** compares the **a** register with the value 100. If the **a** register is equal to 100, the zero flag is set. The **jnz** instruction is read "jump not zero" and means to jump to the specified address if the zero flag is not set. The function **out( )** in the C code version is assumed to translate into the corresponding **out** instruction in the pseudo-assembly code.

   If an absolute assembler is used, the code is assembled to run at some specified absolute location. For example, assume the **mov** instruction requires 3 bytes. If the code were assembled to run at address 100, the label associated with the **jnz** instruction would be replaced by the address 103. This also implies that the object code for this program only runs correctly if it is placed in memory starting at 100. It cannot be loaded anywhere else.

Absolute addressing is fairly common in simple microcomputer systems. However, it is inadequate for general use because it requires that the location in memory where the program will be run is known at the time of assembly. This not only prevents the code from being linked with other code later on, but keeps the operating system from making the most efficient use of its resources. For these reasons, relocatable object code is generally used instead.

Relocatable code is created by using a *relocating assembler*. It uses no fixed address, only offsets from the beginning of the file. (An *offset* represents the number of bytes a label is from the start of the file.) The offsets are stored by the assembler in a table along with the label name. This table is sometimes called an *offset table*. The offset table is then used during the linking process to determine actual addresses. Using the previous assembly code example, the table entry for **label1** looks like the following illustration.

label1	3

When the linker links the code fragment containing **label1** with the rest of the code that makes up the program, the offset 3 is added to the current value of the location counter to compute the correct value to use in the **jnz** instruction. For example, if the location counter is 230 when the label is resolved, value 233 becomes the target address of the jump instruction. This discussion of the relocation process is, of course, an abstraction. Although the general principles are correct, the actual implementation will vary widely between environments.

Address relocation is needed for all types of jump instructions as well as for call instructions because both use memory addresses. In addition, all global data requires relocation. Even though you will be working with C and not assembler, the relocation process is handled in essentially the same way.

Linking with Overlays

Although not as common as they once were, some C compilers supply an overlay linker in addition to a standard linker. An *overlay linker* works like a regular linker but can also create overlays. An *overlay* is a piece of object code that is stored in a disk file and loaded and executed only when needed. The place in memory into which an overlay is loaded is called the *overlay region*. Overlays allow you to create and run programs that would be larger than available memory, because only the parts of the program that are currently in use are in memory.

To understand how overlays work, imagine that you have a program consisting of seven object files called F1 through F7. Assume also that there is insufficient free memory to run the program if the object files were all linked together in the normal way—you can only link the first five files before running out of memory. To remedy this situation, instruct the linker to create overlays consisting of files F5, F6, and F7. Each time a function in one of these files is invoked, the *overlay manager* (provided by the linker) finds the proper file and places it into the overlay region, allowing execution to proceed. The code in files F1 through F4 remains resident at all times. Figure 11-1 illustrates this situation.

As you might guess, the principal advantage of overlays is that they enable you to write very large programs. The main disadvantage—and the reason that overlays are usually a last resort—is that the loading process takes time and has a significant impact on the overall speed of execution. For this reason, you should group related functions together if you have to use overlays, so that the number of overlay loads is minimized. For example, if the application is a mailing list, it makes sense to place all sorting routines in one overlay, printing routines in another, and so on.

Sometimes a better alternative to overlays is *chaining*. In a chaining approach, one program instructs the operating system to load and execute another program. When the second program terminates, the original program resumes execution. Chaining

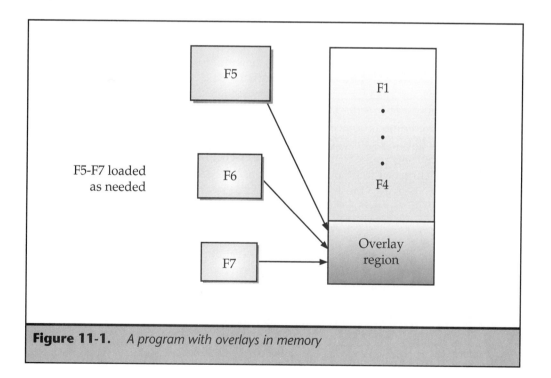

Figure 11-1. *A program with overlays in memory*

can be accomplished using the standard **system( )** function, which is described in Chapter 18.

Linking with DLLs

With the advent of operating systems such as Windows, another form of linking called *dynamic linking* has become a common part of the C landscape. Dynamic linking is the process by which the actual code for a function remains in a separate file on disk until a program that uses it is executed. When the program is executed, the dynamically linked functions required by the program are also loaded. Dynamically linked functions reside in a special type of library called a *Dynamic Link Library*, or DLL, for short.

The main advantage to using dynamically linked libraries is that the size of executable programs is dramatically reduced because each program does not have to store redundant copies of the library functions that is uses. Also, when DLL functions are updated, programs that use them will automatically obtain their benefits.

While the C standard library is not generally contained in a dynamic link library, many other types of functions are. For example, when you program for Windows, the entire set of API (Application Program Interface) functions are stored in DLLs. Fortunately, relative to your C program, it does not matter whether a library function is stored in a DLL or in a regular library file.

The C Standard Library

The ANSI C standard has defined both the content and form of the C standard library. That is, the ANSI C standard names and describes a set of functions which all ANSI-standard compilers must support. However, a compiler is free to supply additional functions not specified by the standard. (And, indeed, most compilers do.) For example, it is common for a compiler to have graphics functions, mouse-handler routines, and the like, even though none of these is defined by ANSI C. As long as you will not be porting your programs to a new environment, you can use these nonstandard functions without any negative consequences. However, if your code must be portable, the use of these functions must be restricted. From a practical point of view, virtually all non-trivial C programs will make use of non-standard functions, so you should not necessarily shy away from their use just because they are not part of the standard function library.

For most C compilers, the standard library is contained in one file. However, some implementations have grouped related functions in their own libraries for reasons of efficiency or because of size restrictions.

Library Files Versus Object Files

Although libraries are similar to object files, they have one crucial difference: Not all the code in the library is added to your program. When you link a program that consists of several object files, all of the code in each object file becomes part of the finished executable program. This happens whether the code is actually used or not. In other words, all object files specified at link time are combined to form the finished program. However, this is not the case with library files.

A library is a collection of functions. Unlike an object file, a library file stores each function, individually. When your program references a function contained in a library, the linker looks up that function and adds its code to your program. In this way, only functions that you actually use in your program are added to the executable file—not the entire library. Because functions are selectively added to your program when a library is used, the C standard functions are contained in libraries rather than object files. (If they were in object files, every program you wrote would be several hundred thousand bytes long!)

Header Files

Each function defined in the C standard library has a header file associated with it. The header files that relate to the functions that you use in your programs should (and in some cases, *must*) be included (using **#include**) in your program. There are two reasons for this. First, many functions in the standard library work with their own specific data types, to which your program must have access. These data types are defined in the header file related to each function. One of the most common examples is the file STDIO.H, which provides the type **FILE** that is necessary for disk file operations.

The second reason to include header files is to obtain the prototypes for the standard library functions. If the header files conform to the ANSI C standard (as virtually all modern compilers do), then they contain the prototypes for the standard library. Function prototypes allow stronger type checking to be performed by the compiler. By including the header files that correspond to the standard functions used by your program, you can catch potential type-mismatch errors. For example, since it includes STRING.H (the string function's header), the following code produces a warning message when compiled:

```
#include <string.h>

char s1[] = "hello ";
char s2[] = "there.";

void main(void)
{
  int p;

  p = strcat(s1, s2);
}
```

Because **strcat( )** is declared as returning a character pointer in its prototype, the compiler issues a warning that an error may have been made on the line that assigns it to the integer **p**.

Table 11-1 shows the standard header files defined by the ANSI C standard.

The ANSI C standard reserves identifier names beginning with an underscore and followed by either a second underscore or a capital letter for use in header files.

The remaining chapters in this section, which describe each function in the standard library, will indicate which of these header files are necessary for each function.

Macros in Header Files

Many of the C standard functions can be implemented either as actual functions or as function-like macros defined in a header file. For example, **abs( )**, which returns the absolute value of its integer argument, could be defined as a macro, as shown here:

```
#define abs(i) (i)<0 ? -(i) : (i)
```

Header File	Purpose
ASSERT.H	Defines the **assert( )** macro
CTYPE.H	Character handling
ERRNO.H	Error reporting
FLOAT.H	Defines implementation-dependent floating-point values
LIMITS.H	Defines various implementation-dependent limits
LOCALE.H	Supports localization
MATH.H	Various definitions used by the math library
SETJMP.H	Supports nonlocal jumps
SIGNAL.H	Supports signal handling
STDARG.H	Supports variable-length argument lists
STDDEF.H	Defines some commonly used constants
STDIO.H	Supports file I/O
STDLIB.H	Miscellaneous declarations
STRING.H	Supports string functions
TIME.H	Supports system time functions

Table 11-1. *The Standard Header Files*

Whether a standard function is defined as a macro or as a regular C function is usually of no consequence. However, in rare situations where a macro is unacceptable—for example, where code size is to be minimized or where an argument must not be evaluated more than once—you will have to create a real function and substitute it for the macro. Sometimes the C library itself also has a real function that you can use to replace a macro.

To force the compiler to use the real function (either from the library or written by you), you need to prevent the compiler from substituting the macro when the function name is encountered. Although there are several ways to do this, by far the best is simply to undefine the macro name using **#undef**. For example, to force the compiler to substitute the real **abs( )** function for the previously defined macro, you would insert this line of code near the beginning of your program:

```
#undef abs
```

Then, since **abs** is no longer defined as a macro, the function version is used.

Redefinition of Library Functions

Although linkers may vary slightly between implementations, they all operate in essentially the same way. For example, if your program consists of three files called F1, F2, and F3, the linker command line looks something like this:

LINK F1 F2 F3 LIBC

where LIBC is the name of the standard library.

NOTE: Some linkers automatically use the standard library and do not require that it be specified explicitly. Also, most integrated programming environments automatically include the appropriate library files.

As the link process begins, the linker generally first attempts to resolve all external references by using only the files F1, F2, and F3. Once this is done, the library is searched if unresolved external references still exist.

Because most linkers proceed in the order just described, you can redefine a function in the standard library. Your function is found first and used to resolve all references to it. Therefore, by the time the library is scanned, there are no unresolved references to the redefined function, and it is not loaded from the library.

You must be very careful when you redefine library functions because you could be creating unexpected side effects. This is because the library functions often use other library functions. For example, the **fwrite( )** function might use **putc( )**. Therefore, a redefinition of **putc( )** could cause **fwrite( )** to behave unexpectedly. A better idea is simply to use a different name for the functions that you want to redefine. This averts unexpected side effects.

Chapter Twelve

I/O Functions

M ost C compilers support at least two different I/O systems: the ANSI C file system and the UNIX-like file system. Many compilers—especially those that are DOS-based or DOS-compatible—support a third I/O system: direct console I/O. This chapter describes all functions that are part of the ANSI C file system, the most important functions that are part of the UNIX-like file system, and several of the DOS-based direct console I/O functions.

> **NOTE:** *Compilers designed for operating systems that support graphical user interfaces (GUI), such as Windows or OS/2, may provide I/O functions that relate specifically to those environments. However, such functions are not within the scope of this reference. If you are interested in programming for a GUI environment, you will need to consult guides that address those operating systems directly.*

The functions that make up the ANSI C I/O system can be grouped into two major categories: console I/O and file I/O. Strictly speaking, console I/O is made up of functions that are special-case versions of the more general functions found in the file system. However, console I/O and file I/O are different enough that they are often thought of as separate. For this reason, the first part of this book treated console I/O and file I/O as somewhat distinct systems to emphasize their differences. However this section makes no such distinction because both I/O types use a common logical interface: the stream.

The header file associated with the I/O functions defined by ANSI is called STDIO.H. It defines several macros and types used by the file system. The most important type is **FILE**, which is used to declare a file pointer. Two other types are **size_t** and **fpos_t**. The **size_t** type is essentially some variety of unsigned integer. The **fpos_t** type defines an object that can hold all the information needed to uniquely specify every position within a file. Other items defined within STDIO.H are discussed when the functions that use them are described.

Many of the functions defined by ANSI set the built-in global integer variable **errno** when an error occurs. Your program can check this variable to obtain more information about the error. The values that **errno** may take are implementation-dependent.

The UNIX-like I/O system is not defined by the ANSI C standard and is expected to decline in popularity. The most commonly used UNIX-like I/O system functions are included in this chapter because they are still widely used in existing programs. For many C compilers, the header file related to the UNIX-like file system is called IO.H. However, check your user's manual for details.

For DOS-compatible compilers, the direct console I/O functions generally use the CONIO.H header file. (Be sure to check your user's manual, however, because the header file might have a different name.)

For an overview of the C I/O system and a detailed discussion of the most important I/O functions, refer to Chapters 8 and 9 in Part One.

#include <conio.h>
char *cgets(char *str);

The **cgets( )** function is not defined by the ANSI C standard. It is commonly included in the library of DOS-compatible compilers.

The **cgets( )** function reads a string entered from the keyboard into the array pointed to by *str*. Prior to the call to **cgets( )**, the first byte of *str* must be set to the maximum length of the string you want to read. Upon return, the second byte of *str* will contain the number of characters actually read. Therefore, the array pointed to by *str* must be at least 2 bytes longer than the largest string you want to read. When you have finished entering a string, enter a carriage return, which is converted into a null to terminate the string. The string will begin at the third byte of the array.

The **cgets( )** function returns a pointer to **str[2]**.

In some implementations, **cgets( )** does not allow redirection to devices other than the keyboard. Also, **cgets( )** may operate relative to a window rather than the screen. Check your user's manual for details.

Example

This program reads from the keyboard a string of up to 20 characters in length:

```
#include <conio.h>

void main(void)
{
  char s[23];

  s[0] = 20;
  cputs("enter a string: ");
  cgets(s);
  cputs(&s[2]);
}
```

Related Functions

cputs( ), gets( ), fgets( ), puts( )

#include <stdio.h>
void clearerr(FILE *stream);

The **clearerr( )** function resets (turns off) the error flag associated with *stream*. The end-of-file indicator is also reset.

The error flags for each stream are initially set to zero by a successful call to **fopen( )**. Once an error has occurred, the flags stay set until an explicit call to either **clearerr( )** or **rewind( )** is made.

File errors can occur for a wide variety of reasons, many of which are system dependent. You can determine the exact nature of the error by calling **perror( )**, which displays what error has occurred (see **perror( )**).

Example

This program copies one file to another. If an error is encountered, a message is printed and the error is cleared.

```c
/* Copy one file to another. */
#include <stdio.h>
#include <stdlib.h>

void main(int argc, char *argv[])
{
  FILE *in, *out;
  char ch;

  if(argc!=3) {
    printf("You forgot to enter a filename.\n");
    exit(1);
  }

  if((in=fopen(argv[1], "rb")) == NULL) {
    printf("Cannot open file.\n");
    exit(1);
  }
  if((out=fopen(argv[2], "wb")) == NULL) {
    printf("Cannot open file.\n");
    exit(1);
  }

  while(!feof(in)) {
    ch = getc(in);
    if(ferror(in)) {
      printf("Read Error");
      clearerr(in);
      break;
    } else {
      if(!feof(in)) putc(ch, out);
```

```
        if(ferror(out)) {
          printf("Write Error");
          clearerr(out);
          break;
        }
      }
    }
  }
  fclose(in);
  fclose(out);
}
```

Related Functions

feof( ), ferror( ), and perror( )

#include <io.h>
int close(int fd);

The **close( )** function belongs to the UNIX-like file system and is not defined by the ANSI C standard.

When **close( )** is called with a valid file descriptor, it closes the file associated with it and flushes the write buffer if applicable. (File descriptors are created through a successful call to **open( )** or **creat( )** and do not relate to streams or file pointers.)

When successful, **close( )** returns zero; otherwise, it returns –1. There are several reasons that you may not be able to close a file. The most common is the premature removal of the medium. For example, if you remove a disk from the drive before the file is closed, an error results.

Example

This program opens and closes a file by using the UNIX-like file system:

```
#include <fcntl.h>
#include <io.h>
#include <stdio.h>
#include <stdlib.h>

void main(int argc, char *argv[])
{
  int fd;
```

```
  if((fd=open(argv[1], O_RDONLY))==-1) {
    printf("Cannot open file.");
    exit(1);
  }

  printf("File is existent.\n");
  if(close(fd)) printf("Error in closing file.\n");
}
```

Related Functions

open( ), creat( ), read( ), write( ), unlink( )

#include <conio.h>
int cprintf(const char *format, . . .);

The **cprintf( )** function is not defined by the ANSI C standard. It is commonly included in the library of DOS-compatible compilers.

The **cprintf( )** function operates exactly like **printf( )**, but in many implementations its output is not directable to devices other than the screen. Also, in some environments **cprintf( )** operates relative to a window instead of the screen. Check your user's manual for details.

Example

This program displays the string **I like C** on the screen:

```
#include <conio.h>

void main(void)
{
  cprintf("I like C");
}
```

Related Functions

cscanf( ), cputs( )

#include <conio.h>
int cputs(const char *str);

The **cputs( )** function is not defined by the ANSI C standard. It is commonly included in the library of DOS-compatible compilers.

The **cputs( )** function outputs to the screen the string pointed to by *str*. In some implementations, its output may not be redirected. Also, for some environments, **cputs( )** may output its string relative to a window rather than the screen. Refer to your user's manual for details.

cputs( ) returns the last character written if successful; it returns **EOF** if unsuccessful.

Example

This program writes **this is a test** on the screen:

```
#include <conio.h>

void main(void)
{
  cputs("this is a test");
}
```

Related Function

cprintf( )

#include <io.h>
int creat(const char *filename, int pmode);

The **creat( )** function is part of the UNIX-like file system and is not defined by the ANSI C standard.

The purpose of **creat( )** is to create a new file with the name pointed to by *filename* and to open it for writing. On success, **creat( )** returns a file descriptor that is greater than or equal to zero; on failure, it returns a –1. (File descriptors are integers and do not relate to streams or file pointers).

The value of *pmode* determines the file's access setting, sometimes called its *permission mode*. The value of *pmode* is highly dependent upon the operating system; check your user's manual for details. In general, the access mode may be read-only, write-only, or read/write. Also, in some environments, a security access descriptor may also be part of a file's access mode. For many compilers, the values of *pmode* are defined as macros in the header file called STAT.H (sometimes found in the SYS directory). The commonly used names and their meanings are shown here:

S_IWRITE	Allow output
S_IREAD	Allow input
S_IREAD ¦ S_IWRITE	Allow input/output

If the specified file already exists at the time of the call to **creat( )**, it is erased and all previous contents are lost.

Example

The following code fragment creates a file called TEST.

```
#include <io.h>
#include <sys\stat.h>
#include <stdio.h>
#include <stdlib.h>

void main(void)
{
  int fd;

  if((fd=creat("test", S_IWRITE))==-1) {
    printf("Cannot open file.\n");
    exit(1);
  }
}
```

Related Functions

open( ), **close( )**, **read( )**, **write( )**, **unlink( )**, **eof( )**

#include <conio.h>
int cscanf(const char *format, . . .);

The **cscanf( )** function is not defined by the ANSI C standard. It is commonly included in the library of DOS-compatible compilers.

The **cscanf( )** function operates exactly like **scanf( )**, but in many implementations its input cannot be directed to any device other than the keyboard. Also, in some environments **cscanf( )** operates relative to a window instead of the screen. Check your user's manual for details.

Example

This program reads a string entered from the keyboard:

```
#include <conio.h>

void main(void)
{
  char str[80];
```

```
   cprintf("enter a string: ");
   cscanf("%s", str);
   cprintf(str);
}
```

Related Functions

cprintf( ), cgets( )

#include <io.h>
int eof(int fd);

The **eof( )** function is part of the UNIX-like file system and is not defined by the ANSI C standard.

When called with a valid file descriptor, **eof( )** returns 1 if the end of the file has been reached; otherwise, it returns zero. If an error has occurred, **eof( )** returns –1.

Example

The following program displays a text file on the console using **eof( )** to determine when the end of the file has been reached:

```
#include <fcntl.h>
#include <io.h>
#include <stdio.h>
#include <stdlib.h>

void main(int argc, char *argv[])
{
  int fd;
  char ch;

  if((fd=open(argv[1], O_RDONLY))==-1) {
    printf("Cannot open file.\n");
    exit(1);
  }

  while(!eof(fd)) {
    read(fd, &ch, 1); /* read one char at a time */
    printf("%c", ch);
```

```
    }
    close(fd);
}
```

Related Functions

open( ), close( ), read( ), write( ), unlink( )

#include <stdio.h>
int fclose(FILE *stream);

The **fclose( )** function closes the file associated with *stream* and flushes its buffer. After an **fclose( )**, *stream* is no longer connected with a file and any automatically allocated buffers are deallocated.

If **fclose( )** is successful, it returns zero; otherwise, it returns **EOF**. Trying to close a file that has already been closed is an error. Removing the storage media before closing a file also generates an error, as does lack of sufficient free disk space.

Example

The following code opens and closes a file:

```
#include <stdio.h>
#include <stdlib.h>

void main(void)
{
  FILE *fp;

  if((fp=fopen("test", "rb"))==NULL) {
    printf("Cannot open file.\n");
    exit(1);
  }

  if(fclose(fp)) printf("File close error.\n");
}
```

Related Functions

fopen( ), freopen( ), fflush( )

#include <stdio.h>
int feof(FILE *stream);

The **feof( )** function checks the file position indicator to determine if the end of the file associated with *stream* has been reached. A nonzero value is returned if the file position indicator is at end-of-file; otherwise, the function returns zero.

Once the end of the file has been reached, subsequent read operations return **EOF** until either **rewind( )** is called or the file position indicator is moved using **fseek( )**. EOF is defined in STDIO.H.

The **feof( )** function is particularly useful when you are working with binary files because the end-of-file marker is also a valid binary integer. Thus, explicit calls must be made to **feof( )** to determine when the end of a binary file has been reached.

Example

This code fragment shows the proper way to read to the end of a binary file:

```
/*
    Assume that fp has been opened as a binary file
    for read operations.
*/
while(!feof(fp)) getc(fp);
```

Related Functions

clearerr( ), ferror( ), perror( ), putc( ), getc( )

#include <stdio.h>
int ferror(FILE *stream);

The **ferror( )** function checks for a file error on the given *stream*. A return value of zero indicates that no error has occurred, while a nonzero value means an error.

The error flags associated with *stream* stay set until either the file is closed or **rewind( )** or **clearerr( )** is called.

To determine the exact nature of the error, use the **perror( )** function.

Example

The following code fragment aborts program execution if a file error occurs:

```
/*
   Assume that fp points to a stream opened for write
   operations.
*/

while(!done) {
  putc(info, fp);
  if(ferror(fp)) {
    printf("File Error\n");
    exit(1);
  }
}
```

Related Functions

clearerr( ), feof( ), perror( )

#include <stdio.h>
int fflush(FILE *stream);

If *stream* is associated with a file opened for writing, a call to **fflush( )** physically writes to the file the contents of the output buffer. If *stream* points to an input file, the contents of the input buffer are cleared. In either case, the file remains open.

A return value of zero indicates success; **fflush( )** returns **EOF** if a write error has occurred.

All buffers are automatically flushed either upon normal program termination or when they are full. Closing a file also flushes its buffer.

Example

The following code fragment flushes the buffer after each write operation:

```
/*
   Assume that fp is associated with an output file.
*/
  .
  .
  .
fwrite(buf, sizeof(data_type), 1, fp);
fflush(fp);
  .
  .
  .
```

Related Functions

fclose( ), fopen( ), fread( ), fwrite( ), getc( ), putc( )

#include <stdio.h>
int fgetc(FILE *stream);

The **fgetc( )** function returns the next character from the input stream specified by *stream* and increments the file position indicator. The character is read as an **unsigned char** that is converted to an integer.

If the end of the file is reached, **fgetc( )** returns **EOF**. However, since **EOF** is a valid integer value, you must use **feof( )** to check for end-of-file when working with binary files. If **fgetc( )** encounters an error, **EOF** is also returned. Again, if working with binary files you must use **ferror( )** to check for file errors.

Example

The following program reads and displays the contents of a text file.

```
#include <stdio.h>
#include <stdlib.h>

void main(int argc, char *argv[])
{
  FILE *fp;
  char ch;

  if((fp=fopen(argv[1],"r"))==NULL) {
    printf("Cannot open file.\n");
    exit(1);
  }

  while((ch=fgetc(fp))!=EOF) {
    printf("%c", ch);
  }
  fclose(fp);
}
```

Related Functions

fputc( ), getc( ), putc( ), fopen( )

#include <stdio.h>
int fgetpos(FILE *stream, fpos_t *position);

The **fgetpos( )** function stores the current value of the file position indicator associated with *stream* in the object pointed to by *position*. The object pointed to by *position* must be of type **fpos_t**, a type defined in STDIO.H. The value stored there is useful only in a subsequent call to **fsetpos( )**.

If an error occurs, **fgetpos( )** returns nonzero; otherwise, it returns zero.

Example

The following fragment stores the current file location in **file_loc:**

```
FILE *fp;
fpos_t file_loc;
.
.
.
fgetpos(fp, &file_loc);
```

Related Functions

fsetpos( ), **fseek( )**, **ftell( )**

#include <stdio.h>
char *fgets(char *str, int num, FILE *stream);

The **fgets( )** function reads up to *num*–1 characters from *stream* and places them into the character array pointed to by *str*. Characters are read until either a newline or an **EOF** is received or until the specified limit is reached. If a newline character is entered, it is retained and becomes part of the string pointed to by *str*. After the characters have been read, a null is placed in the array immediately after the last character.

If successful, **fgets( )** returns *str*; a null pointer is returned upon failure. If a read error occurs, the contents of the array pointed to by *str* are indeterminate. Because a null pointer is returned either when an error has occurred or when the end of the file is reached, you should use **feof( )** or **ferror( )** to determine what has actually happened.

Example

This program uses **fgets( )** to display the contents of the text file specified in the first command line argument:

```
#include <stdio.h>
#include <stdlib.h>

void main(int argc, char *argv[])
{
  FILE *fp;
  char str[128];

  if((fp=fopen(argv[1], "r"))==NULL) {
    printf("Cannot open file.\n");
    exit(1);
  }

  while(!feof(fp)) {
    if(fgets(str, 126, fp)) printf("%s", str);
  }

  fclose(fp);
}
```

Related Functions

fputs( ), fgetc( ), gets( ), puts( )

#include <stdio.h>
FILE *fopen(const char *fname, const char *mode);

The **fopen( )** function opens a file whose name is pointed to by *fname* and returns the stream that is associated with it. The type of operations that are allowed on the file are defined by the value of *mode*. The legal values for *mode* as specified by the ANSI C standard are shown in Table 12-1. The file name must be a string of characters that constitutes a valid file name as defined by the operating system and may include a path specification if the environment supports it.

If **fopen( )** opens the specified file, a **FILE** pointer is returned. If the file cannot be opened, a null pointer is returned.

As Table 12-1 shows, a file may be opened in either text or binary mode. In text mode, some character translations may occur. For example, newlines may be converted into carriage return/linefeed sequences. No such translations occur on binary files.

This code fragment illustrates the correct way to open a file:

```
FILE *fp;

if ((fp = fopen("test", "w"))==NULL) {
  puts("Cannot open file.\n");
  exit(1);
}
```

This method detects any error in opening a file (such as trying to open a file on a write-protected or a full disk), before attempting to write to it. **NULL** is returned when an error occurs because no file pointer ever has that value. **NULL** is defined in STDIO.H.

If you use **fopen( )** to open a file for output, any preexisting file by that name is erased and a new file started. If no file by that name exists, one is created. If you want to add to the end of the file, you must use mode "a". Opening a file for read operations requires that the file exists. If it does not, an error is returned. Finally,

Mode	Meaning
"r"	Open text file for reading
"w"	Create text file for writing
"a"	Append to text file
"rb"	Open binary file for reading
"wb"	Create binary file for writing
"ab"	Append to binary file
"r+"	Open text file for read/write
"w+"	Create text file for read/write
"a+"	Open text file for read/write
"rb+"	Open binary file for read/write
"wb+"	Create binary file for read/write
"ab+"	Open binary file for read/write

Table 12-1. *The Legal Values for Mode*

if a file is opened for read/write operations it is not erased if it exists; however, if it does not exist it is created.

When accessing a file opened for read/write operations, you may not follow an output operation with an input operation without an intervening call to either **fflush( )**, **fseek( )**, **fsetpos( )**, or **rewind( )**. Also, you may not follow an input operation with an output operation without an intervening call to one of the previously mentioned functions.

Example

This fragment opens a file called TEST for binary read/write operations:

```
FILE *fp;

if((fp=fopen("test", "rb+"))==NULL) {
  printf("Cannot open file.\n");
  exit(1);
}
```

Related Functions

fclose( ), fread( ), fwrite( ), putc( ), getc( )

#include <stdio.h>
int fprintf(FILE *stream, const char *format, . . .);

The **fprintf( )** function outputs to the stream pointed to by *stream* the values of the arguments in its argument list as specified in the *format* string. The return value is the number of characters actually printed. If an error occurs, a negative number is returned.

There may be from zero to several arguments—the maximum number is system dependent.

The operations of the format control string and commands are identical to those in **printf( )**; see the **printf( )** function for a complete description.

Example

This program creates a file called TEST and writes **this is a test 10 20.01** into the file using **fprintf( )** to format the data.

```
#include <stdio.h>
#include <stdlib.h>

void main(void)
{
  FILE *fp;
```

```
if((fp=fopen("test", "wb"))==NULL) {
  printf("Cannot open file.\n");
  exit(1);
}

fprintf(fp, "this is a test %d %f", 10, 20.01);
fclose(fp);
}
```

Related Functions

printf( ), fscanf( )

#include <stdio.h>
int fputc(int ch, FILE *stream);

The **fputc( )** function writes the character *ch* to the specified stream at the current file position and then advances the file position indicator.

Even though *ch* is declared as an **int** for historical purposes, it is converted by **fputc( )** into an **unsigned char**. Because all character arguments are automatically elevated to integers at the time of the call, character variables are generally used as arguments. If an integer were used, the high-order byte would simply be discarded.

The value returned by **fputc( )** is the value of the character written. If an error occurs, **EOF** is returned. For files opened for binary operations, an **EOF** may be a valid character and you must use the **ferror( )** function to determine whether an error has actually occurred.

Example

This function writes the contents of a string to the specified stream:

```
void write_string(char *str, FILE *fp)
{
  while(*str) if(!ferror(fp)) fputc(*str++, fp);
}
```

Related Functions

fgetc( ), fopen( ), fprintf( ), fread( ), fwrite( )

#include <stdio.h>
int fputchar(int ch);

The **fputchar( )** function writes the character *ch* to **stdout**. This function is not defined by the ANSI C standard, but is a common addition. Even though *ch* is declared to be an **int** for historical purposes, it is converted by **fputchar( )** into an **unsigned char**. Because all character arguments are automatically elevated to integers at the time of the call, character variables are usually used as arguments. If an integer were used, the high-order byte would simply be discarded. A call to **fputchar( )** is the functional equivalent of a call to **fputc(ch, stdout)**.

The value returned by **fputchar( )** is the value of the character written. If an error occurs, **EOF** is returned. For files opened for binary operations, **EOF** may be a valid character and you need to use the **ferror( )** function to determine whether an error has actually occurred.

Example

This function writes the contents of a string to **stdout**:

```
void write_string(char *str)
{
  while(*str) if(!ferror(fp)) fputchar(*str++);
}
```

Related Functions

fgetc( ), fopen( ), fprintf( ), fread( ), fwrite( )

#include <stdio.h>
int fputs(const char *str, FILE *stream);

The **fputs( )** function writes to the specified stream the contents of the string pointed to by *str*. The null terminator is not written.

The **fputs( )** function returns nonnegative on success and **EOF** on failure.

If the stream is opened in text mode, certain character translations may take place. This means that there may not be a one-to-one mapping of the string onto the file. However, if the stream is opened in binary mode, no character translations occur and there will be a one-to-one mapping between the string and the file.

Example

This code fragment writes the string **this is a test** to the stream pointed to by **fp**.

```
fputs("this is a test", fp);
```

Related Functions

fgets( ), gets( ), puts( ), fprintf( ), fscanf( )

#include <stdio.h>
size_t fread(void *buf, size_t size, size_t count, FILE *stream);

The **fread( )** function reads *count* number of objects, each *size* bytes in length, from the stream pointed to by *stream* and places them in the array pointed to by *buf*. The file position indicator is advanced by the number of characters read.

The **fread( )** function returns the number of items actually read. If fewer items are read than are requested in the call, either an error has occurred or the end of the file has been reached. You must use **feof( )** or **ferror( )** to determine what has taken place.

If the stream is opened for text operations, certain character translations may occur (such as carriage return and linefeed sequences being transformed into newlines).

Example

The following program reads ten floating-point numbers from a disk file called TEST into the array **bal**.

```c
#include <stdio.h>
#include <stdlib.h>

void main(void)
{
  FILE *fp;
  float bal[10];

  if((fp=fopen("test", "rb"))==NULL) {
    printf("Cannot open file.\n");
    exit(1);
  }

  if(fread(bal, sizeof(float), 10, fp)!=10) {
    if(feof(fp)) printf("Premature end of file.");
    else printf("File read error.");
  }

  fclose(fp);
}
```

Related Functions

fwrite( ), fopen( ), fscanf( ), fgetc( ), getc( )

#include <stdio.h>
FILE *freopen(const char *fname, const char *mode, FILE *stream);

The **freopen( )** function associates an existing stream with a different file. The new file's name is pointed to by *fname*, the access mode is pointed to by *mode*, and the stream to be reassigned is pointed to by *stream*. The string *mode* uses the same format as **fopen( )**. For a complete discussion, see the description of **fopen( )**.

When called, **freopen( )** first tries to close a file that may currently be associated with *stream*. However, if the attempt to close the file fails, the **freopen( )** function still continues to open the other file.

The **freopen( )** function returns a pointer to *stream* on success; otherwise, the function returns a null pointer.

The main use of **freopen( )** is to redirect the system-defined streams **stdin**, **stdout**, and **stderr** to some other file.

Example

The program shown here uses **freopen( )** to redirect the stream **stdout** to the file called OUT. Because **printf( )** writes to **stdout**, the first message is displayed on the screen and the second is written to the disk file.

```
#include <stdio.h>
#include <stdlib.h>

void main(void)
{
  FILE *fp;

  printf("This will display on the screen.\n");

  if((fp=freopen("OUT", "w" ,stdout))==NULL) {
    printf("Cannot open file.\n");
    exit(1);
  }

  printf("This will be written to the file OUT.");

  fclose(fp);
}
```

Related Functions

fopen( ), fclose( )

#include <stdio.h>
int fscanf(FILE *stream, const char *format, . . .);

The **fscanf( )** function works exactly like the **scanf( )** function, but it reads the information from the stream specified by *stream* instead of **stdin**. See the **scanf( )** function for details.

The **fscanf( )** function returns the number of arguments actually assigned values. This number does not include skipped fields. A return value of **EOF** means that a failure occurred before the first assignment was made.

Example

This code fragment reads a string and a **float** from the stream **fp**.

```
char str[80];
float f;

fscanf(fp, "%s%f", str, &f);
```

Related Functions

scanf( ), fprintf( )

#include <stdio.h>
int fseek(FILE *stream, long offset, int origin);

The **fseek( )** function sets the file position indicator associated with *stream* according to the values of *offset* and *origin*. That is, it supports random I/O operations. The *offset* is the number of bytes from *origin* to seek to. The values for *origin* must be one of these macros (defined in STDIO.H):

Name	Meaning
SEEK_SET	Seek from start of file
SEEK_CUR	Seek from current location
SEEK_END	Seek from end of file

A return value of zero means that **fseek( )** succeeded. A nonzero value indicates failure.

In most implementations, and as specified by the ANSI C standard, *offset* must be a long integer in order to support files larger than 64K.

You may use **fseek( )** to move the position indicator anywhere in the file (possibly even beyond the end). However, it is an error to attempt to set the position indicator before the beginning of the file.

The **fseek( )** function clears the end-of-file flag associated with the specified stream. Furthermore, it nullifies any prior **ungetc( )** on the same stream. (See **ungetc( )**.)

Example

The following function seeks to the specified structure of type **addr**. Notice the use of **sizeof** to obtain the size of the structure.

```
struct addr {
  char name[40];
  char street[40];
  char city[40];
  char state[3];
  char zip[10];
} info;

void find(long client_num)
{
  FILE *fp;

  if((fp=fopen("mail", "rb")) == NULL) {
    printf("Cannot open file.\n");
    exit(1);
  }

  /* find the proper structure */
  fseek(fp, client_num*sizeof(struct addr), SEEK_SET);

  /* read the data into memory */
  fread(&info, sizeof(struct addr), 1, fp);

  fclose(fp);
}
```

Related Functions

ftell( ), rewind( ), fopen( ), fgetpos( ), fsetpos( )

#include <stdio.h>
int fsetpos(FILE *stream, const fpos_t *position);

The **fsetpos( )** function moves the file position indicator associated with *stream* to the point specified by the object pointed to by *position*. This value must have been previously obtained through a call to **fgetpos( )**. The type **fpos_t** is defined in STDIO.H. After **fsetpos( )** is executed, the end-of-file indicator is reset. Also, any previous call to **ungetc( )** is nullified.

If **fsetpos( )** fails, it returns nonzero. On success, it returns zero.

Example

This code fragment resets the current file position indicator to the value stored in **file_loc**.

```
fsetpos(fp, &file_loc);
```

Related Functions

fgetpos( ), **fseek( )**, **ftell( )**

#include <stdio.h>
long ftell(FILE *stream);

The **ftell( )** function returns the current value of the file position indicator for the specified stream. For binary streams, the value is the number of bytes the indicator is from the beginning of the file. For text streams, the return value may not be meaningful except as an argument to **fseek( )**. The reason for this is that text files are subject to character translations. For instance, carriage return/linefeeds may be translated into newlines, which affects the apparent size of a text file.

The **ftell( )** function returns –1 when an error occurs. If the stream is incapable of random seeks—if it is a terminal, for instance—the return value is undefined.

Example

This code fragment returns the current value of the file position indicator for the stream pointed to by **fp**:

```
long i;

if((i=ftell(fp))==-1L)
    printf("A file error has occurred.\n");
```

Related Functions

fseek( ), fgetpos( )

#include <stdio.h>
size_t fwrite(const void *buf, size_t size, size_t count, FILE *stream);

The **fwrite( )** function writes *count* number of objects (each *size* bytes in length) to the stream pointed to by *stream* from the buffer pointed to by *buf*. The file position indicator is advanced by the number of characters written.

The **fwrite( )** function returns the number of items actually written, which will equal the number requested if the function is successful. If fewer items are written than are requested, an error has occurred. For text streams, various character translations may take place but will not affect the return value.

Example

This program writes a **float** to the file TEST. Notice that **sizeof** is used both to determine the number of bytes in a **float** variable and to ensure portability.

```
#include <stdio.h>
#include <stdlib.h>

void main(void)
{
  FILE *fp;
  float f=12.23;

  if((fp=fopen("test", "wb"))==NULL) {
    printf("Cannot open file.\n");
    exit(1);
  }

  fwrite(&f, sizeof(float), 1, fp);

  fclose(fp);
}
```

Related Functions

fread( ), fscanf( ), getc( ), fgetc( )

#include <stdio.h>
int getc(FILE *stream);

The **getc( )** function returns the next character from the input *stream* and increments the file position indicator. The character is read as an **unsigned char** that is converted to an integer.

If the end of the file is reached, **getc( )** returns **EOF**. However, since **EOF** is a valid integer value, you must use **feof( )** to check for end-of-file when working with binary files. If **getc( )** encounters an error, **EOF** is also returned. When working with binary files, you must use **ferror( )** to check for file errors.

The **getc( )** and **fgetc( )** functions are identical; in most implementations, **getc( )** is simply defined as the macro shown here:

```
#define getc(fp) fgetc(fp)
```

This causes the **fgetc( )** function to be substituted for the **getc( )** macro.

Example

The following program reads and displays the contents of a text file.

```
#include <stdio.h>
#include <stdlib.h>

void main(int argc, char *argv[])
{
  FILE *fp;
  char ch;

  if((fp=fopen(argv[1], "r"))==NULL) {
    printf("Cannot open file.\n");
    exit(1);
  }

  while((ch=getc(fp))!=EOF) {
    printf("%c", ch);
  }

  fclose(fp);
}
```

Related Functions

fputc( ), fgetc( ), putc( ), fopen( )

#include <conio.h>
int getch(void);
int getche(void);

The **getch( )** and **getche( )** functions are not defined by the ANSI C standard. However, they are commonly included with DOS-compatible compilers. (These functions may be called **_getch( )** and **_getche( )** by your compiler.)

The **getch( )** function returns the next character read from the console but does not echo that character to the screen.

The **getche( )** function returns the next character read from the console and echoes that character to the screen.

Both of these functions bypass C's standard I/O functions and work directly with the operating system. Essentially, **getch( )** and **getche( )** perform direct keyboard input.

Example

This code fragment uses **getch( )** to read the user's menu selection for a spelling checker program:

```
do {
  printf("1: Check spelling\n");
  printf("2: Correct spelling\n");
  printf("3: Lookup a word in the dictionary\n");
  printf("4: Quit\n");

  printf("\nEnter your selection: ");
  choice = getch();
} while (!strchr("1234", choice));
```

Related Functions

getc( ), getchar( ), fgetc( )

#include <stdio.h>
int getchar(void);

The **getchar( )** function returns the next character from **stdin**. The character is read as an **unsigned char** that is converted to an integer.

If the end of the file is reached, **getchar( )** returns **EOF**. However, since **EOF** is a valid integer value, you must use **feof( )** to check for end-of-file when working with binary files. If **getchar( )** encounters an error, **EOF** is also returned. If you are working with binary files, you must use **ferror( )** to check for file errors.

The **getchar( )** function is functionally equivalent to **getc(stdin)**.

Example

This program reads characters from **stdin** into the array **s** until the user presses ENTER. Finally, the string is displayed.

```
#include <stdio.h>

void main(void)
{
  char s[256], *p;

  p = s;

  while((*p++ = getchar())!= '\n') ;
  *p = '\0'; /* add null terminator */
  printf(s);
}
```

Related Functions

fputc( ), **fgetc( )**, **putc( )**, **fopen( )**

#include <stdio.h>
char *gets(char *str);

The **gets( )** function reads characters from **stdin** and places them into the character array pointed to by *str*. Characters are read until a newline or an **EOF** is received. The newline character is not made part of the string; instead, it is translated into a null to terminate the string.

If successful, **gets( )** returns *str*; a null pointer is returned upon failure. If a read error occurs, the contents of the array pointed to by *str* are indeterminate. Because a null pointer is returned when either an error has occurred or when the end of the file is reached, use **feof( )** or **ferror( )** to determine what has actually happened.

There is no limit to the number of characters that **gets( )** will read. For this reason, it is your job to make sure that the array pointed to by *str* is not overrun.

Example

This program uses **gets( )** to read a file name:

```
#include <stdio.h>
#include <stdlib.h>

void main(void)
{
  FILE *fp;
  char fname[128];

  printf("Enter filename: ");
  gets(fname);

  if((fp=fopen(fname, "r"))==NULL) {
    printf("Cannot open file.\n");
    exit(1);
  }

  fclose(fp);
}
```

Related Functions

fputs( ), fgetc( ), fgets( ), puts( )

#include <stdio.h>
int getw(FILE *stream);

The **getw( )** function is not defined by the ANSI C standard, but is included with many C compilers. (It may be called **_getw( )** by your compiler.)

The **getw( )** function returns the next integer from *stream* and advances the file position indicator appropriately.

Because the integer read may have a value equal to **EOF**, you must use **feof( )** or **ferror( )** to determine when end-of-file is reached or whether an error has occurred.

Example

This program reads integers from the file INTTEST and reports their sum:

```
#include <stdio.h>
#include <stdlib.h>

void main(void)
{
  FILE *fp;
```

```
int sum=0;

if((fp=fopen("inttest", "rb"))==NULL) {
  printf("Cannot open file.\n");
  exit(1);
}

while(!feof(fp))
  sum = getw(fp)+sum;

printf("the sum is %d", sum);

fclose(fp);
}
```

Related Functions

putw( ), fread( )

#include <conio.h>
int kbhit(void);

The **kbhit( )** function is not defined by the ANSI C standard. However, it is found, under various names, in virtually all C implementations. It returns a nonzero value if a key has been pressed at the console. Otherwise, it returns zero. (Under no circumstances does it wait for a key to be pressed.)

Example

This **for** loop exits if a key is pressed:

```
for(;;) {
  if(kbhit()) break;
  .
  .
  .
}
```

Related Functions

fgetc( ), getc( )

#include <io.h>
long lseek(int fd, long offset, int origin);

The **lseek( )** function is part of the UNIX-like I/O system and is not defined by the ANSI C standard.

The **lseek( )** function sets the file position indicator of the file described by *fd* to the location specified by *offset* and *origin*. The *offset* is the number of bytes from *origin* to seek to. The values for *origin* must be one of these macros (defined in IO.H):

Name	Meaning
SEEK_SET	Seek from start of file
SEEK_CUR	Seek from current location
SEEK_END	Seek from end of file

The **lseek( )** function returns the new location of the file position indicator (in bytes from the start of the file) if successful. Upon failure, it returns –1.

Example

The example shown here allows you to examine a file one sector at a time by using the UNIX-like I/O system. You will want to change the buffer size to match the sector size of your system.

```c
#include <io.h>
#include <fcntl.h>
#include <stdlib.h>
#include <stdio.h>

#define BUF_SIZE 128

void main(int argc, char *argv[])
{
  char buf[BUF_SIZE+1], s[10];
  int fd, sector;

  buf[BUF_SIZE] = '\0'; /* null terminate buffer for printf */

  if((fd=open(argv[1], O_RDONLY))==-1) { /* open for read */
    printf("Cannot open file.\n");
    exit(1);
  }

  do {
```

```
    printf("Buffer: ");
    gets(s);

    sector = atoi(s); /* get the sector to read */

    if(lseek(fd, (long)sector*BUF_SIZE, SEEK_SET)==-1L)
      printf("Seek Error\n");

    if(read(fd, buf, BUF_SIZE)==0) {
      printf("Sector out of range.\n");
    }
    else
      printf("%s\n", buf);
  } while(sector>0);
  close(fd);
}
```

Related Functions

read( ), write( ), open( ), close( )

#include <fcntl.h>
#include <io.h>
int open(const char *fname, int mode);

The **open( )** function is part of the UNIX-like I/O system and is not defined by the ANSI C standard.

Unlike the buffered I/O system, the UNIX-like system does not use file pointers of type **FILE**; instead it uses file descriptors of type **int**. The **open( )** function opens a file whose name is pointed to by *fname* and sets its access mode as specified by *mode*. The values *mode* may have are shown here (these macros are defined in FCNTL.H):

Mode	Effect
O_RDONLY	Open for reading
O_WRONLY	Open for writing
O_RDWR	Open for reading and writing

NOTE: Many compilers have additional modes—such as text, binary, and the like—so check your user's manual.

A successful call to **open( )** returns a positive integer that is the file descriptor associated with the file. A return value of –1 means that the file cannot be opened.

In most implementations, the operation fails if the file specified in the **open( )** statement does not appear on the disk. However, depending upon the implementation, you may be able to use **open( )** to create a file that is currently nonexistent. Check your user's manual.

Example

You will usually see the call to **open( )** written like this:

```
int fd;

if((fd=open(filename, mode)) == -1) {
  printf("Cannot open file.\n");
  exit(1);
}
```

Related Functions

close( ), **read( )**, **write( )**

#include <stdio.h>
void perror(const char *str);

The **perror( )** function maps the value of the built-in global variable **errno** onto a string and writes that string to **stderr**. If the value of *str* is not null, this string is written first, followed by a colon and the implementation-defined error message.

Example

In this fragment, an error is reported if it occurs.

```
#include <stdio.h>
  .
  .
  .
if(ferror(fp)) perror("File error ");
```

#include <stdio.h>
int printf(const char *format, . . .);

The **printf( )** function writes to **stdout** the arguments that make up the argument list under the control of the string pointed to by *format*.

The string pointed to by *format* contains two types of items. The first type consists of characters that will be printed on the screen. The second type contains format commands that define the way the arguments are displayed. A format command consists of a percent sign followed by the format code. The format commands are shown in Table 12-2. There must be exactly the same number of arguments as there are format commands, and the format commands and arguments are matched in order. For example, this **printf( )** call:

```
printf("Hi %c %d %s", 'c', 10, "there!");
```

displays **Hi c 10 there!**.

If there are insufficient arguments to match the format commands, the output is undefined. If there are more arguments than format commands, the remaining arguments are discarded.

The **printf( )** function returns the number of characters actually printed. A negative return value indicates an error.

Code	Format
%c	Character
%d	Signed decimal integers
%i	Signed decimal integers
%e	Scientific notation (lowercase e)
%E	Scientific notation (uppercase E)
%f	Decimal floating point
%g	Uses %e or %f, whichever is shorter (if %e, uses lowercase e)
%G	Uses %E or %f, whichever is shorter (if %E, uses uppercase E)
%o	Unsigned octal
%s	String of characters
%u	Unsigned decimal integers
%x	Unsigned hexadecimal (lowercase letters)
%X	Unsigned hexadecimal (uppercase letters)
%p	Displays a pointer
%n	Associated argument is a pointer to an integer into which is placed the number of characters written so far
%%	Prints a % sign

Table 12-2. *printf( ) Format Commands*

The format commands may have modifiers that specify the field width, the precision, and a left-justification flag. An integer placed between the percent sign and the form at command acts as a *minimum field-width specifier*, padding the output with blanks or zeros to ensure that it is a minimum length. If the string or number is greater than that minimum, it will be printed in full. The default padding is done with spaces. For numeric values, if you wish to pad with zeros, place a zero before the field width specifier. For example, **%05d** pads a number of less than five digits with zeros so that its total length is five digits.

The effect of the *precision modifier* depends upon the type of format command being modified. To add a precision modifier, place a decimal point followed by the precision after the field-width specifier. For **e**, **E**, and **f** formats, the precision modifier determines the number of decimal places printed. For example, **%10.4f** displays a number at least ten characters wide with four decimal places. However, when used with the **g** or **G** specifier, the precision determines the maximum number of significant digits displayed.

When the precision modifier is applied to integers, it specifies the minimum number of digits that will be displayed. (Leading zeros are added, if necessary.)

When the precision modifier is applied to strings, the number following the period specifies the maximum field length. For example, **%5.7s** displays a string that is at least five characters long and does not exceed seven. If the string is longer than the maximum field width, the end characters are truncated.

By default, all output is right justified. That is, if the field width is larger than the data printed, the data will be placed on the right edge of the field. You can force the information to be left justified by placing a minus sign directly after the percent sign. For example, **%–10.2f** left justifies a floating-point number with two decimal places in a ten-character field.

There are two format specifiers that allow **printf( )** to display **short** and **long** integers. These specifiers may be applied to the **d, i, o, u, x,** and **X** type specifiers. The **l** specifier tells **printf( )** that a **long** data type follows. For example, **%ld** means that a **long int** is to be displayed. The **h** specifier instructs **printf( )** to display a **short int**. Therefore, **%hu** indicates that the data is of type **short unsigned int**.

Although not technically required, in most implementations the **l** modifier may also prefix the floating-point specifiers **e, E, f, g,** and **G** and indicates that a **double** follows. **L** is used to indicate a **long double**.

The **n** format causes the number of characters written so far to be put into the integer variable pointed to by the argument corresponding to the **n** specifier. For example, this code fragment displays the number **15** after the line **this is a test**.

```
int i;

printf("this is a test %n", &i);
printf("%d", i);
```

The # has a special meaning when used with some **printf( )** format specifiers. Preceding a **g, G, f, e** or **E** specifier with a # ensures that the decimal point will be present even if there are no decimal digits. If you precede the **x** format specifier with a #, the hexadecimal number will be printed with a **0x** prefix. When used with the **o** specifier, it causes a leading 0 to be printed. The # cannot be applied to any other format specifiers.

The minimum field width and precision specifiers may be provided by arguments to **printf( )** instead of by constants. To accomplish this, use an * as a placeholder. When the format string is scanned, **printf( )** will match *'s to arguments in the order in which they occur.

See the discussion of **printf( )** in Chapter 8 for further details.

Example

This program displays the output shown in its comments:

```c
#include <stdio.h>

void main(void)
{
  /* This prints "this is a test" left justified
     in 20 character field.
  */
  printf("%-20s", "this is a test");

  /* This prints a float with 3 decimal places in a 10
     character field. The output will be "    12.235".
  */
  printf("%10.3f", 12.234657);
}
```

Related Functions

scanf( ), fprintf( )

#include <stdio.h>
int putc(int ch, FILE *stream);

The **putc( )** function writes the character contained in the least significant byte of *ch* to the output stream pointed to by *stream*. Because character arguments are elevated to integer at the time of the call, you may use character variables as arguments to **putc( )**.

The **putc( )** function returns the character written; it returns **EOF** if an error occurs. If the output stream has been opened in binary mode, **EOF** is a valid value for *ch*. This means that you must use **ferror( )** to determine if an error has occurred.

The **putc( )** function is functionally equivalent to **fputc( )**. In fact, **putc( )** is often implemented as a macro, with **fputc( )** being substituted.

Example

The following loop writes the characters in string **str** to the stream specified by **fp**. The null terminator is not written.

```
for(; *str; str++) putc(*str, fp);
```

Related Functions

fgetc( ), fputc( ), getchar( ), putchar( )

#include <conio.h>
int putch(int ch);

The **putch( )** function is not defined by the ANSI C standard. However, it is commonly included in the standard library of DOS-compatible compilers.

The **putch( )** function outputs to the screen the character specified in the low-order byte of *ch*. In many implementations, its output may not be redirected. Also, in some environments it may operate relative to a window rather than the screen.

Example

This outputs the character **A** to the screen.

```
putch('A');
```

Related Functions

putc( ), putchar( )

#include <stdio.h>
int putchar(int ch);

The **putchar( )** function writes to **stdout** the character contained in the least significant byte of *ch*. The **putchar( )** function is functionally equivalent to **putc(ch,stdout)**. Because character arguments are elevated to integer at the time of the call, you may use characters as arguments to **putchar( )**.

On success, the **putchar( )** function returns the character written. It returns **EOF** if an error occurs. If the output stream has been opened in binary mode, **EOF** is a valid value for *ch*. This means that you must use **ferror( )** to determine if an error has occurred.

Example

The following loop writes to **stdout** the characters in string **str**. The null terminator is not written.

```
for(; *str; str++) putchar(*str);
```

Related Function

putc( )

#include <stdio.h>
int puts(const char *str);

The **puts( )** function writes the string pointed to by *str* to the standard output device. The null terminator is translated to a newline.

The **puts( )** function returns a nonnegative value if successful and **EOF** upon failure.

Example

The following code writes the string **this is an example** to **stdout**.

```
#include <stdio.h>
#include <string.h>

void main(void)
{
    char str[80];

    strcpy(str, "this is an example");

    puts(str);
}
```

Related Functions

putc( ), gets( ), printf( )

#include <stdio.h>
int putw(int i, FILE *stream);

The **putw( )** function is not defined by the ANSI C standard, but is commonly included in the standard library.

The **putw( )** function writes the integer *i* to *stream* at the current file position and increments the file position pointer appropriately.

The **putw( )** function returns the value written. A return value of **EOF** means an error has occurred in the stream if it is in text mode. Because **EOF** is also a valid integer value, you must use **ferror( )** to detect an error in a binary stream.

Example

This code fragment writes the value **100** to the stream pointed to by **fp**:

```
putw(100, fp);
```

Related Functions

getw( ), printf( ), fwrite( )

#include <io.h>
int read(int fd, void *buf, unsigned count);

The **read( )** function is part of the UNIX-like I/O system and is not defined by the ANSI C standard.

The **read( )** function reads *count* number of bytes from the file described by *fd* into the buffer pointed to by *buf*. The file position indicator is increased by the number of bytes read. If the file is opened in text mode, character translations may take place.

The return value will be equal to the number of bytes actually read. This number may be smaller than *count* if either an end-of-file or an error is encountered. A value of –1 means an error; a value of zero is returned if an attempt is made to read at end-of-file.

The **read( )** function tends to be implementation-dependent and may behave somewhat differently than stated here. Please check your user's manual for details.

Example

This program reads the first 100 bytes from the file TEST into the array **buffer**.

```
#include <fcntl.h>
#include <io.h>
#include <stdlib.h>
#include <stdio.h>

void main(void)
{
  int fd;
  char buffer[100];
```

```
    if((fd=open("test", O_RDONLY))==-1) {
      printf("Cannot open file.\n");
      exit(1);
    }

    if(read(fd, buffer, 100)!=100) printf("Read Error");
}
```

Related Functions
open( ), close( ), write( ), lseek( )

#include <stdio.h>
int remove(const char *fname);

The **remove( )** function erases the file specified by *fname*. It returns zero if the file is successfully deleted and nonzero if an error occurs.

Example

This program removes the file whose name is specified on the command line:

```
#include <stdio.h>

void main(int argc, char *argv[])
{
   if(remove(argv[1])) printf("Remove Error");
}
```

Related Function
rename( )

#include <stdio.h>
int rename(const char *oldfname, const char *newfname);

The **rename( )** function changes the name of the file specified by *oldfname* to *newfname*. The *newfname* must not match any existing directory entry.

The **rename( )** function returns zero if successful and nonzero if an error has occurred.

Example

This program renames the file specified as the first command line argument to that specified by the second command line argument. Assuming the program is called CHANGE, a command line consisting of CHANGE THIS THAT will change the name of a file called THIS to THAT.

```
#include <stdio.h>

void main(int argc, char *argv[])
{
  if(rename(argv[1], argv[2])!=0) printf("Rename Error");
}
```

Related Function

remove( )

#include <stdio.h>
void rewind(FILE *stream);

The **rewind( )** function moves the file position indicator to the start of the specified stream. It also clears the end-of-file and error flags associated with *stream*. It has no return value.

Example

This function twice reads the stream pointed to by **fp**, displaying the file each time.

```
void re_read(FILE *fp)
{
  /* read once */
  while(!feof(fp)) putchar(getc(fp));
  rewind(fp);

  /* read twice */
  while(!feof(fp)) putchar(getc(fp));
}
```

Related Function

fseek( )

#include <stdio.h>
int scanf(const char *format, . . .);

The **scanf( )** function is a general-purpose input routine that reads the stream **stdin**. It can read all the built-in data types and automatically convert them into the proper internal format. It is the complement of **printf( ).**

The control string pointed to by *format* consists of three types of characters:

- Format specifiers
- White-space characters
- Non-white-space characters

The format specifiers are preceded by a percent sign and tell **scanf( )** what type of data is to be read next. These codes are listed in Table 12-3. For example, **%s** reads a string while **%d** reads an integer.

The format string is read left to right and the format codes are matched, in order, with the arguments that make up the argument list.

A white-space character in the control string causes **scanf( )** to skip over one or more white-space characters in the input stream. A white-space character is either a space, a tab, or a newline. In essence, one white-space character in the control string

Code	Meaning
%c	Read a single character
%d	Read a decimal integer
%i	Read a decimal integer
%e	Read a floating-point number
%f	Read a floating-point number
%g	Read a floating-point number
%o	Read an octal number
%s	Read a string
%x	Read a hexadecimal number
%p	Read a pointer
%n	Receives an integer value equal to the number of characters read so far
%u	Read an unsigned integer
%[ ]	Scan for a set of characters
%%	Read a % sign

Table 12-3. *scanf( ) Format Codes*

causes **scanf( )** to read, but not store, any number (including zero) of white-space characters up to the first non-white-space character.

A non-white-space character causes **scanf( )** to read and discard a matching character. For example, **"%d,%d"** causes **scanf( )** to read an integer, read and discard a comma, and then read another integer. If the specified character is not found, **scanf( )** terminates.

All the variables used to receive values through **scanf( )** must be passed by their addresses. This means that all arguments must be pointers to the variables used as arguments. This is C's way of creating a call by reference, and it allows a function to alter the contents of an argument. For example, to read an integer into the variable **count**, you would use the following **scanf( )** call:

```
scanf("%d", &count);
```

Strings are read into character arrays, and the array name, without any index, is the address of the first element of the array. So, to read a string into the character array **address**, use

```
scanf("%s", address);
```

In this case, **address** is already a pointer and need not be preceded by the **&** operator.

The input data items must be separated by spaces, tabs, or newlines. Punctuation such as commas, semicolons, and the like do not count as separators. This means that

```
scanf("%d%d", &r, &c);
```

accepts an input of **10 20**, but fails with **10,20**.

An * placed after the % and before the format specifier reads data of the specified type but suppresses its assignment. Thus,

```
scanf("%d%*c%d", &x, &y);
```

given the input **10/20** places the value 10 into **x**, discards the division sign, and gives **y** the value 20.

The format commands can specify a maximum field-length modifier. This is an integer placed between the % and the format specifier that limits the number of characters read for any field. For example, if you wish to read no more than 20 characters into **address**, you would write

```
scanf("%20s", address);
```

If the input stream were greater than 20 characters, a subsequent call to input would begin where this call left off. Input for a field may terminate before the maximum field length is reached if a white space is encountered. In this case, **scanf( )** moves on to the next field.

Although spaces, tabs, and newlines are used as field separators, they are read like any other character when reading a single character. For example, with an input stream of **"x y"**,

```
scanf("%c%c%c", &a, &b, &c);
```

returns with the character **x** in **a**, a space in **b**, and the character **y** in **c**.

Be careful: Any other characters in the control string—including spaces, tabs, and newlines—are used to match and discard characters from the input stream. For example, given the input stream **"10t20"**,

```
scanf("%st%s", &x, &y);
```

places 10 into **x** and 20 into **y**. The **t** is discarded because of the **t** in the control string.

The ANSI C standard added to **scanf( )** a feature called a *scanset* that was not part of the original UNIX version. A scanset defines a set of characters that will be read by **scanf( )** and assigned to the scanset's corresponding character array. You define a scanset by putting inside square brackets the characters for which you want to scan. The beginning square bracket must be prefixed by a percent sign. For example, this scanset tells **scanf( )** to read only the characters **A, B,** and **C:**

```
%[ABC]
```

The argument corresponding to the scanset must be a pointer to a character array. When you use a scanset, **scanf( )** continues to read characters and put them into the array until a character that is not part of the scanset is encountered. (That is, a scanset reads only matching characters.) Upon return from **scanf( )**, the array will contain a null-terminated string.

You can specify an inverted set if the first character in the set is a ^ . When the ^ is present, it instructs **scanf( )** to accept any character that *is not* defined by the scanset.

You can specify a range using a hyphen. For example, this tells **scanf( )** to accept the letters A through Z:

```
%[A-Z]
```

Remember that the scanset is case sensitive. Therefore, if you want to scan for both upper- and lowercase letters, you must specify them individually.

The **scanf( )** function returns a number equal to the number of fields that were successfully assigned values. This number does not include fields that were read but not assigned because the * modifier was used to suppress the assignment. **EOF** is returned if an error occurs before the first field is assigned.

Example

The operation of these **scanf( )** statements is explained in their comments:

```
char str[80], str2[80];
int i;

/* read a string and an integer */
scanf("%s%d", str, &i);

/* read up to 79 chars into str */
scanf("%79s", str);

/* skip the integer between the two strings */
scanf("%s%*d%s", str, str2);
```

Related Functions

printf( ), fscanf( )

#include <stdio.h>
void setbuf(FILE *stream, char *buf);

The **setbuf( )** function either specifies the buffer the specified stream will use, or, if called with *buf* set to null, turns off buffering. If a programmer-defined buffer is to be specified, it must be **BUFSIZ** characters long. **BUFSIZ** is defined in STDIO.H.

The **setbuf( )** function returns no value.

Example

The following fragment associates a programmer-defined buffer with the stream pointed to by **fp**.

```
char buffer[BUFSIZ];
.
.
.
setbuf(fp, buffer);
```

Related Functions

fopen( ), fclose( ), setvbuf( )

#include <stdio.h>
int setvbuf (FILE *stream, char *buf, int mode, size_t size);

The **setvbuf( )** function allows the programmer to specify the buffer, its size, and its mode for the specified stream. The character array pointed to by *buf* is used as *stream*'s buffer for I/O operations. The size of the buffer is set by *size*, and *mode* determines how buffering will be handled. If *buf* is null, **setvbuf( )** will allocate its own buffer.

The legal values of *mode* are **_IOFBF**, **_IONBF**, and **_IOLBF**. These are defined in STDIO.H. When the mode is set to **_IOFBF**, full buffering takes place. If the mode is **_IOLBF**, the stream is line buffered, which for output streams means that the buffer is flushed each time a newline character is written; for input streams, an input request reads all characters up to a newline. In either case, the buffer is also flushed when full. When the mode is set to **_IONBF**, no buffering takes place.

The value of *size* must be greater than zero.

The **setvbuf( )** function returns zero on success; nonzero on failure.

Example

This code fragment sets the stream **fp** to line-buffered mode with a buffer size of 128:

```
#include <stdio.h>
char buffer[128];
.
.
.
setvbuf(fp, buffer, _IOLBF, 128);
```

Related Function

setbuf( )

#include <stdio.h>
int sprintf(char *buf, const char *format, . . .);

The **sprintf( )** function is identical to **printf( )**, but the output is put into the array pointed to by *buf*. See **printf( )** for details.

The return value is equal to the number of characters actually placed into the array.

Example

After this code fragment executes, **str** holds **one 2 3**:

```
char str[80];

sprintf(str,"%s %d %c", "one", 2, 3);
```

Related Functions

printf( ), **fsprintf( )**

#include <stdio.h>
int sscanf(const char *buf, const char *format, . . .);

The **sscanf( )** function is identical to **scanf( )**, but data is read from the array pointed to by *buf* rather than **stdin**. See **scanf( )** for details.

The return value is equal to the number of variables that were actually assigned values. This number does not include input that is skipped through the use of the * format modifier. A value of zero means that no fields were assigned; **EOF** indicates that an error occurred before the first assignment.

Example

This program prints the message **hello 1** on the screen:

```
#include <stdio.h>

void main(void)
{
  char str[80];
  int i;

  sscanf("hello 1 2 3 4 5", "%s%d", str, &i);
  printf("%s %d", str, i);
}
```

Related Functions

scanf( ), fscanf( )

#include <io.h>
long tell(int fd);

The **tell( )** function is part of the UNIX-like I/O system and is not defined by the ANSI C standard.

The **tell( )** function returns the current value of the file position indicator associated with the file descriptor *fd*. This value is the number of bytes the position indicator is from the start of the file. A return value of –1 indicates an error.

Example

This code fragment prints the current value of the position indicator for the file described by **fd**:

```
long pos;
.
.
.
pos = tell(fd);
printf("Position is %ld bytes from the start.", pos);
```

Related Functions

ftell( ), lseek( ), open( ), close( ), read( ), write( )

#include <stdio.h>
FILE *tmpfile(void);

The **tmpfile( )** function opens a temporary file for update and returns a pointer to its associated stream. The function automatically uses a unique file name to avoid conflicts with existing files. The file is automatically opened with binary, read-write access.

The **tmpfile( )** function returns a null pointer on failure; otherwise it returns a pointer to the stream.

The temporary file created by **tmpfile( )** is automatically removed when the file is closed or the program terminates.

Example

The following fragment creates a temporary working file.

```
FILE *temp;

if((temp=tmpfile())==NULL) {
  printf("Cannot open temporary work file.\n");
  exit(1);
}
```

Related Function

tmpnam( )

#include <stdio.h>
char *tmpnam(char *name);

The **tmpnam( )** function generates a unique file name and stores it in the array pointed to by *name*. The main purpose of **tmpnam( )** is to generate a temporary file name that is different from any other file in the directory.

The function may be called up to **TMP_MAX** times. **TMP_MAX** is defined in STDIO.H. Each time **tmpnam( )** is called, it generates a new temporary file name.

A pointer to *name* is returned on success; otherwise, a null pointer is returned. If *name* is NULL, then a pointer to a region of statically allocated memory that contains the file name is returned.

Example

This program displays three unique temporary file names:

```
#include <stdio.h>

void main(void)
{
  char name[40];
  int i;

  for(i=0; i<3; i++) {
    tmpnam(name);
    printf("%s ", name);
  }
}
```

Related Function

tmpfile( )

#include <stdio.h>
int ungetc(int ch, FILE *stream);

The **ungetc( )** function returns the character specified by the low-order byte of *ch* to the input stream *stream*. This character is then returned by the next read operation on *stream*. A call to **fflush( )**, **fseek( )**, **rewind( )**, or **fsetpos( )** undoes an **ungetc( )** operation and discards the character.

A one-character pushback is guaranteed; however, some implementations will accept more.

You may not "unget" an **EOF** character.

A call to **ungetc( )** clears the end-of-file flag associated with the specified stream. The value of the file position indicator for a text stream is undefined until all pushed-back characters are read, in which case it is the same as it was before the first **ungetc( )** call. For binary streams, each **ungetc( )** call decrements the file position indicator.

The return value is equal to *ch* on success and **EOF** on failure.

Example

This function reads words from the input stream pointed to by **fp**. The terminating character is returned to the stream for later use. For example, given the input **count/10**, the first call to **read_word( )** returns **count** and puts the "/" back into the input stream.

```
void read_word(FILE *fp, char *token)
{

  while(isalpha(*token=getc(fp))) token++;
  ungetc(fp, *token);
}
```

Related Function

getc( )

#include <io.h>
int unlink(const char *fname);

The **unlink( )** function is part of the UNIX-like I/O system and is not defined by the ANSI C standard.

The **unlink( )** function removes the specified file from the directory. It returns zero on success and –1 on failure.

Example

This program deletes the file specified as the first command line argument.

```
#include <io.h>
#include <stdio.h>

void main(int argc, char *argv[])
{
   if(unlink(argv[1])==-1) printf("Cannot remove file.");
}
```

Related Functions

open( ), close( )

#include <stdarg.h>
#include <stdio.h>
int vprintf(const char *format, va_list arg_ptr);
int vfprintf (FILE *stream, const char *format, va_list arg_ptr);
int vsprintf(char *buf, const char *format, va_list arg_ptr);

The functions **vprintf( )**, **vfprintf( )**, and **vsprintf( )** are functionally equivalent to **printf( )**, **fprintf( )**, and **sprintf( )**, respectively. However, the argument list has been replaced by a pointer to a list of arguments. This pointer must be of type **va_list** and is defined in STDARG.H. See **va_arg( )**, **va_start( )**, and **va_end( )** in Chapter 18 for further information on passing variable length arguments to functions.

Example

This code fragment shows how to set up a call to **vprintf( )**. The call to **va_start( )** creates a variable-length argument pointer to the start of the argument list. This pointer must be used in the call to **vprintf( )**. The call to **va_end( )** clears the variable-length argument pointer.

```
#include <stdio.h>
#include <stdarg.h>

void print_message(char *format, ...);

void main(void)
{
   print_message("Cannot open file %s.", "test");
}

void print_message(char *format, ...)
{
```

```
    va_list ptr; /* get an arg ptr */

    /* initialize ptr to point to the first argument after the
       format string
    */
    va_start(ptr, format);

    /* print out message */
    vprintf(format, ptr);

    va_end(ptr);
}
```

Related Functions

va_list( ), va_start( ), va_end( )

#include <io.h>
int write(int fd, char *buf, unsigned count);

The **write( )** function is part of the UNIX-like I/O system and is not defined by the ANSI C standard.

The **write( )** function writes *count* number of bytes to the file described by *fd* from the buffer pointed to by *buf*. The file position indicator is increased by the number of bytes written. If the file is opened in text mode, character translations may take place.

The return value will be equal to the number of bytes actually written. This number may be smaller than *count* if an error is encountered. A value of –1 means a fundamental error has occurred.

The **write( )** function tends to be implementation-dependent and may behave somewhat differently than stated here. Check your user's manual for details.

Example

This program writes 100 bytes from **buffer** to the file TEST.

```
#include <io.h>
#include <stdlib.h>
#include <stdio.h>
#include <fcntl.h>

void main(void)
{
```

```
int fd;
char buffer[100];

if((fd=open("test", O_WRONLY))==-1) {
  printf("Cannot open file.\n");
  exit(1);
}

gets(buffer);

if(write(fd, buffer, 100)!=100) printf("Write Error");
close(fd);
}
```

Related Functions

read( ), close( ), fwrite( ), lseek( )

Chapter Thirteen

String and Character Functions

The C standard library has a rich and varied set of string- and character-handling functions. In C, a string is a null-terminated array of characters. In a standard implementation, the string functions require the header file STRING.H to provide their prototypes. The character functions use CTYPE.H as their header file. All of the functions described in this chapter are defined by the ANSI C standard.

Because C has no bounds checking on array operations, it is the programmer's responsibility to prevent an array overflow. According to the ANSI C standard, if an array has overflowed, its "behavior is undefined"—a nice way of saying that your program is about to crash!

In C, a *printable character* is one that can be displayed on a terminal. These are usually the characters between a space (0x20) and tilde (0x7E). *Control characters* have values between 0 and 0x1F as well as DEL (0x7F).

The parameters to the character functions are declared as integers. However, only the low-order byte is used; a character function automatically converts its argument to **unsigned char**. Nevertheless, you can call these functions with character arguments because characters are automatically elevated to integers at the time of the call.

The header file STRING.H defines the **size_t** type, which is some variety of unsigned integer.

#include <ctype.h>
int isalnum(int ch);

The **isalnum( )** function returns nonzero if its argument is a letter or a digit. If the character is not an alphanumeric, **isalnum( )** returns zero.

Example

This program checks each character read from **stdin** and reports all alphanumeric characters:

```
#include <ctype.h>
#include <stdio.h>

void main(void)
{
  char ch;

  for(;;) {
    ch = getc(stdin);
    if(ch == ' ') break;
    if(isalnum(ch)) printf("%c is alphanumeric\n", ch);
  }
}
```

Related Functions

isalpha( ), iscntrl( ), isdigit( ), isgraph( ), isprint( ), ispunct( ), isspace( )

#include <ctype.h>
int isalpha(int ch);

The **isalpha( )** function returns nonzero if *ch* is a letter of the alphabet; otherwise, it returns zero. What constitutes a letter may vary from language to language—in English, it is upper- and lowercase letters from "A" to "Z."

Example

This program checks each character read from **stdin** and reports all letters:

```
#include <ctype.h>
#include <stdio.h>

void main(void)
{
  char ch;

  for(;;) {
    ch = getchar();
    if(ch == ' ') break;
    if(isalpha(ch)) printf("%c is a letter\n", ch);
  }
}
```

Related Functions

isalnum( ), iscntrl( ), isdigit( ), isgraph( ), isprint( ), ispunct( ), isspace( )

#include <ctype.h>
int iscntrl(int ch);

The **iscntrl( )** function returns nonzero if *ch* is between 0 and 0x1F or is equal to 0x7F (DEL); otherwise, it returns zero.

Example

This program checks each character read from **stdin** and reports all control characters:

```
#include <ctype.h>
#include <stdio.h>

void main(void)
{
  char ch;
  for(;;) {
    ch = getchar( );
    if(ch == ' ') break;
    if(iscntrl(ch)) printf("%c is a control char\n", ch);
  }
}
```

Related Functions

isalnum( ), isalpha( ), isdigit( ), isgraph( ), isprint( ), ispunct( ), isspace( )

#include <ctype.h>
int isdigit(int ch);

The **isdigit( )** function returns nonzero if *ch* is a digit (that is, 0 through 9). Otherwise, it returns zero.

Example

This program checks each character read from **stdin** and reports all digits:

```
#include <ctype.h>
#include <stdio.h>

void main(void)
{
  char ch;

  for(;;) {
    ch = getchar();
    if(ch == ' ') break;
    if(isdigit(ch)) printf("%c is a digit\n", ch);
  }
}
```

Related Functions

isalnum( ), isalpha( ), iscntrl( ), isgraph( ), isprint( ), ispunct( ), isspace( )

#include <ctype.h>
int isgraph(int ch);

The **isgraph( )** function returns nonzero if *ch* is any printable character other than a space; otherwise, it returns zero. Although implementation-dependent, printable characters are generally in the range 0x21 through 0x7E.

Example

This program checks each character read from **stdin** and reports all printable characters:

```
#include <ctype.h>
#include <stdio.h>

void main(void)
{
  char ch;

  for(;;) {
    ch = getchar();
    if(isgraph(ch)) printf("%c is printable\n", ch);
    if(ch == ' ') break;
  }
}
```

Related Functions

isalnum( ), isalpha( ), iscntrl( ), isdigit( ), isprint( ), ispunct( ), isspace( )

#include <ctype.h>
int islower(int ch);

The **islower( )** function returns nonzero if *ch* is a lowercase letter; otherwise, it returns zero.

Example

This program checks each character read from **stdin** and reports all lowercase letters.

```
#include <ctype.h>
#include <stdio.h>

void main(void)
{
```

```
  char ch;

  for(;;) {
    ch = getchar();
    if(ch == ' ') break;
    if(islower(ch)) printf("%c is lowercase\n", ch);
  }
}
```

Related Function

isupper( )

#include <ctype.h>
int isprint(int ch);

The **isprint( )** function returns nonzero if *ch* is a printable character, including a space; otherwise, it returns zero. Although implementation-dependent, printable characters are often in the range 0x20 through 0x7E.

Example

This program checks each character read from **stdin** and reports all printable characters:

```
#include <ctype.h>
#include <stdio.h>

void main(void)
{
  char ch;

  for(;;) {
    ch = getchar();
    if(isprint(ch)) printf("%c is printable\n",ch);
    if(ch == ' ') break;
  }
}
```

Related Functions

isalnum( ), isalpha( ), iscntrl( ), isdigit( ), isgraph( ), ispunct( ), isspace( )

#include <ctype.h>
int ispunct(int ch);

The **ispunct( )** function returns nonzero if *ch* is a punctuation character; otherwise, it returns zero. The term *punctuation*, as defined by this function, includes all printing characters that are neither alphanumeric nor a space.

Example

This program checks each character read from **stdin** and reports all punctuation:

```
#include <ctype.h>
#include <stdio.h>

void main(void)
{
  char ch;

  for(;;) {
    ch = getchar();
    if(ch == ' ') break;
    if(ispunct(ch)) printf("%c is punctuation\n", ch);
  }
}
```

Related Functions

isalnum( ), isalpha( ), iscntrl( ), isdigit( ), isgraph( ), isspace( )

#include <ctype.h>
int isspace(int ch);

The **isspace( )** function returns nonzero if *ch* is either a space, horizontal tab, vertical tab, formfeed, carriage return, or newline character; otherwise, it returns zero.

Example

This program checks each character read from **stdin** and reports all white-space characters:

```
#include <ctype.h>
#include <stdio.h>

void main(void)
{
```

```
  char ch;

  for(;;) {
    ch = getchar();
    if(isspace(ch)) printf("%c is white space\n", ch);
    if(ch == ' ') break;
  }
}
```

Related Functions

isalnum( ), isalpha( ), iscntrl( ), isdigit( ), isgraph( ), ispunct( )

#include <ctype.h>
int isupper(int ch);

The **isupper( )** function returns nonzero if *ch* is uppercase; otherwise, it returns zero.

Example

This program checks each character read from **stdin** and reports all uppercase letters:

```
#include <ctype.h>
#include <stdio.h>

void main(void)
{
  char ch;

  for(;;) {
    ch = getchar();
    if(ch == ' ') break;
    if(isupper(ch)) printf("%c is uppercase\n", ch);
  }
}
```

Related Function

islower( )

#include <ctype.h>
int isxdigit(int ch);

The **isxdigit( )** function returns nonzero if *ch* is a hexadecimal digit; otherwise, it returns zero. A hexadecimal digit will be in the range "A" through "F," "a" through "f," or 0 through 9.

Example

This program checks each character read from **stdin** and reports all hexadecimal digits:

```
#include <ctype.h>
#include <stdio.h>

void main(void)
{
  char ch;

  for(;;) {
    ch = getchar();
    if(ch == ' ') break;
    if(isxdigit(ch)) printf("%c is hexadecimal digit\n", ch);
  }
}
```

Related Functions

isalnum( ), isalpha( ), iscntrl( ), isdigit( ), isgraph( ), ispunct( ), isspace( )

#include <string.h>
void *memchr(const void *buffer, int ch, size_t count);

The **memchr( )** function searches the array pointed to by *buffer* for the first occurrence of *ch* in the first *count* characters.

The **memchr( )** function returns a pointer to the first occurrence of *ch* in *buffer*, or a null pointer if *ch* is not found.

Example

This program prints **is a test** on the screen:

```
#include <stdio.h>
#include <string.h>

void main(void)
```

```
{
  char *p;

  p = memchr("this is a test", ' ', 14);
  printf(p);
}
```

Related Functions

memcpy( ), memmove( )

#include <string.h>
int memcmp(const void *buf1, const void *buf2, size_t count);

The **memcmp( )** function compares the first *count* characters of the arrays pointed to by *buf1* and *buf2*. The comparison is done alphabetically.

The **memcmp( )** function returns an integer that is interpreted as follows:

Value	Meaning
Less than zero	*buf1* is less than *buf2*
Zero	*buf1* is equal to *buf2*
Greater than zero	*buf1* is greater than *buf2*

Example

This program shows the outcome of a comparison of its two command line arguments:

```
#include <stdio.h>
#include <string.h>
#include <stdlib.h>

void main(int argc, char *argv[])
{
  int outcome, len, l1, l2;

  if(argc!=3) {
    printf("Incorrect number of arguments.");
    exit(1);
  }

  /* find the length of shortest string */
  l1 = strlen(argv[1]);
  l2 = strlen(argv[2]);
```

```
    len = 11 < 12 ? 11:12;

    outcome = memcmp(argv[1], argv[2], len);
    if(!outcome) printf("Equal");
    else if(outcome<0) printf("First less than second.");
    else printf("First greater than second.");
}
```

Related Functions

memchr( ), memcpy( ), strcmp( )

#include <string.h>
void *memcpy(void *to, const void *from, size_t count);

The **memcpy( )** function copies *count* characters from the array pointed to by *from* into the array pointed to by *to*. If the arrays overlap, the behavior of **memcpy( )** is undefined.

The **memcpy( )** function returns *to*.

Example

This program copies the contents of **buf1** into **buf2** and displays the result:

```
#include <stdio.h>
#include <string.h>

#define SIZE 80

void main(void)
{
  char buf1[SIZE], buf2[SIZE];

  strcpy(buf1, "When, in the course of...");
  memcpy(buf2, buf1, SIZE);
  printf(buf2);
}
```

Related Function

memmove( )

#include <string.h>
void *memmove(void *to, const void *from, size_t count);

The **memmove( )** function copies *count* characters from the array pointed to by *from* into the array pointed to by *to*. If the arrays overlap, the copy will take place correctly, placing the correct contents into *to* but leaving *from* modified.

The **memmove( )** function returns *to*.

Example

This program copies the contents of **str1** into **str2** and displays the result:

```
#include <stdio.h>
#include <string.h>

#define SIZE 80

void main(void)
{
  char str1[SIZE], str2[SIZE];

  strcpy(str1, "When, in the course of...");
  memmove(str2, str1, SIZE);
  printf(str2);
}
```

Related Function

memcpy( )

#include <string.h>
void *memset(void *buf, int ch, size_t count);

The **memset( )** function copies the low-order byte of *ch* into the first *count* characters of the array pointed to by *buf*. It returns *buf*.

memset( ) is most commonly used to initialize a region of memory to some known value.

Example

This fragment initializes to null the first 100 bytes of the array pointed to by **buf**. Then it sets the first 10 bytes to **X** and displays the string **XXXXXXXXXX**.

```
memset(buf, '\0', 100);
memset(buf, 'X', 10);
printf(buf);
```

Related Functions

memcmp( ), memcpy( ), memmove( )

#include <string.h>
char *strcat(char *str1, const char *str2);

The **strcat( )** function concatenates a copy of *str2* to *str1* and terminates *str1* with a null. The null terminator that originally ended *str1* is overwritten by the first character of *str2*. The string *str2* is untouched by the operation. If the arrays overlap, the behavior of **strcat( )** is undefined.

The **strcat( )** function returns *str1*.

Remember, no bounds checking takes place. It is your responsibility to ensure that *str1* is large enough to hold both its original contents and those of *str2*.

Example

This program appends the first string read from **stdin** to the second. For example, assuming the user enters **hello** and **there**, the program prints **therehello**.

```
#include <stdio.h>
#include <string.h>

void main(void)
{
  char s1[80], s2[80];

  gets(s1);
  gets(s2);

  strcat(s2, s1);
  printf(s2);
}
```

Related Functions

strchr( ), strcmp( ), strcpy( )

#include <string.h>
char *strchr(const char *str, int ch);

The **strchr( )** function returns a pointer to the first occurrence of the low-order byte of *ch* in the string pointed to by *str*. If no match is found, a null pointer is returned.

Example

This program prints the string **is a test**:

```
#include <stdio.h>
#include <string.h>

void main(void)
{
  char *p;

  p = strchr("this is a test", ' ');
  printf(p);
}
```

Related Functions

strpbrk( ), **strspn( )**, **strstr( )**, **strtok( )**

#include <string.h>
int strcoll(const char *str1, const char *str2);

The **strcoll( )** function compares the string pointed to by *str1* with the one pointed to by *str2*. The comparison is performed relative to the current locale. (The locale may be specified by using the **setlocale( )** function. See **setlocale( )** for details.)

The **strcoll( )** function returns an integer that is interpreted as follows:

Value	Meaning
Less than zero	*str1* is less than *str2*
Zero	*str1* is equal to *str2*
Greater than zero	*str1* is greater than *str2*

Example

This code fragment prints **equal** on the screen:

```
if(!strcoll("hi", "hi")) printf("Equal");
```

Related Functions

memcmp( ), strcmp( )

#include <string.h>
int strcmp(const char *str1, const char *str2);

The **strcmp( )** function alphabetically compares two strings and returns an integer based on the outcome, as shown here:

Value	Meaning
Less than zero	str1 is less than str2
Zero	str1 is equal to str2
Greater than zero	str1 is greater than str2

Example

You can use the following function as a password-verification routine. It returns zero on failure and 1 on success.

```
password(void)
{
  char s[80];

  printf("Enter password: ");
  gets(s);

  if(strcmp(s, "pass")) {
    printf("Invalid Password\n");
    return 0;
  }
  return 1;
}
```

Related Functions

strchr( ), strcpy( ), strncmp( )

#include <string.h>
char *strcpy(char *str1, const char *str2);

The **strcpy( )** function copies the contents of the array pointed to by str2 into the array pointed to by str1. str2 must point to a null-terminated string. The **strcpy( )** function returns str1.

If *str1* and *str2* overlap, the behavior of **strcpy( )** is undefined. Also, the array pointed to by *str1* must be large enough to hold the contents of the string pointed to by *str2*.

Example

The following code fragment copies **hello** into string **str**:

```
char str[80];
strcpy(str, "hello");
```

Related Functions

memcpy( ), **strchr( )**, **strcmp( )**, **strncmp( )**

#include <string.h>
size_t strcspn(const char *str1, const char *str2);

The **strcspn( )** function returns the length of the initial substring of the string pointed to by *str1* that is made up of only those characters not contained in the string pointed to by *str2*. Stated differently, **strcspn( )** returns the index of the first character in the string pointed to by *str1* that matches any of the characters in the string pointed to by *str2*.

Example

The following program prints the number 8:

```
#include <string.h>
#include <stdio.h>

void main(void)
{
  int len;

  len = strcspn("this is a test", "ab");
  printf("%d", len);
}
```

Related Functions

strpbrk( ), **strrchr( )**, **strstr( )**, **strtok( )**

#include <string.h>
char *strerror(int errnum);

The **strerror( )** function returns a pointer to an implementation-defined error message that is associated with the value of *errnum*. Under no circumstances should you modify this string.

Example

This code fragment prints an implementation-defined error message on the screen:

```
printf(strerror(10));
```

#include <string.h>
size_t strlen(const char *str);

The **strlen( )** function returns the length of the null-terminated string pointed to by *str*. The null terminator is not counted.

Example

The following code fragment prints **5** on the screen:

```
printf("%d", strlen("hello"));
```

Related Functions

memcpy( ), strchr( ), strcmp( ), strncmp( )

#include <string.h>
char *strncat(char *str1, const char *str2, size_t count);

The **strncat( )** function concatenates not more than *count* characters of the string pointed to by *str2* to the string pointed to by *str1* and terminates *str1* with a null. The null terminator that originally ended *str1* is overwritten by the first character of *str2*. The string *str2* is untouched by the operation. If the strings overlap, the behavior of **strncat( )** is undefined.

The **strncat( )** function returns *str1*.

Remember, no bounds checking takes place, so it is your responsibility to ensure that *str1* is large enough to hold its original contents as well as those of *str2*.

Example

This program appends the first string read from **stdin** to the second and prevents an array overflow from occurring to **s1**. For example, assuming the user enters **hello** and **there**, the program prints **therehello**.

```
#include <stdio.h>
#include <string.h>

void main(void)
{
  char s1[80], s2[80];
  unsigned int len;

  gets(s1);
  gets(s2);

  /* compute how many chars will actually fit */
  len = 79-strlen(s2);

  strncat(s2, s1, len);
  printf(s2);
}
```

Related Functions

strcat( ), strnchr( ), strncmp( ), strncpy( )

#include <string.h>
int strncmp(const char *str1, const char *str2, size_t count);

The **strncmp( )** function alphabetically compares not more than *count* characters from the two null-terminated strings and returns an integer based on the outcome, as shown here:

Value	Meaning
Less than zero	*str1* is less than *str2*
Zero	*str1* is equal to *str2*
Greater than zero	*str1* is greater than *str2*

If there are fewer than *count* characters in either string, the comparison ends when the first null is encountered.

Example

The following function compares the first eight characters of two command line arguments and reports if they are equal:

```
#include <stdio.h>
#include <string.h>
```

```
#include <stdlib.h>

void main(int argc, char *argv[])
{
  if(argc!=3) {
    printf("Incorrect number of arguments.");
    exit(1);
  }

  if(!strncmp(argv[1], argv[2], 8))
    printf("The strings are the same.\n");
}
```

Related Functions

strcmp( ), strnchr( ), strncpy( )

#include <string.h>
char *strncpy(char *str1, const char *str2, size_t count);

The **strncpy( )** function copies up to *count* characters from the string pointed to by *str2* into the array pointed to by *str1*. *str2* must be a pointer to a null-terminated string.

If *str1* and *str2* overlap, the behavior of **strncpy( )** is undefined.

If the string pointed to by *str2* has fewer than *count* characters, nulls will be appended to *str1* until *count* characters have been copied.

Alternately, if the string pointed to by *str2* is longer than *count* characters, the resultant string pointed to by *str1* is not null terminated.

The **strncpy( )** function returns *str1*.

Example

The following code fragment copies at most 79 characters of **str1** into **str2**, thus ensuring that no array boundary overflow occurs:

```
char str1[128], str2[80];

gets(str1);
strncpy(str2, str1, 79);
```

Related Functions

memcpy( ), strchr( ), strncat( ), strncmp( )

#include <string.h>
char *strpbrk(const char *str1, const char *str2);

The **strpbrk( )** function returns a pointer to the first character in the string pointed to by *str1* that matches any character in the string pointed to by *str2*. Null terminators are not included. If there are no matches, a null pointer is returned.

Example

This program prints the message **s is a test** on the screen:

```
#include <stdio.h>
#include <string.h>

void main(void)
{
  char *p;

  p = strpbrk("this is a test", " absj");
  printf(p);
}
```

Related Functions

strrchr( ), strspn( ), strstr( ), strtok( )

#include <string.h>
char *strrchr(const char *str, int ch);

The **strrchr( )** function returns a pointer to the last occurrence of the low-order byte of *ch* in the string pointed to by *str*. If no match is found, a null pointer is returned.

Example

This program prints the string **is a test**:

```
#include <string.h>
#include <stdio.h>

void main(void)
{
  char *p;

  p = strrchr("this is a test", 'i');
  printf(p);
}
```

Related Functions

strpbrk( ), strspn( ), strstr( ), strtok( )

#include <string.h>
size_t strspn(const char *str1, const char *str2);

The **strspn( )** function returns the length of the initial substring of the string pointed to by *str1* that consists only of those characters contained in the string pointed to by *str2*. Stated differently, **strspn( )** returns the index of the first character in the string pointed to by *str1* that does not match any of the characters in the string pointed to by *str2*.

Example

This program prints **8**:

```
#include <string.h>
#include <stdio.h>

void main(void)
{
  int len;

  len = strspn("this is a test", "siht ");
  printf("%d", len);
}
```

Related Functions

strpbrk( ), strrchr( ), strstr( ), strtok( )

#include <string.h>
char *strstr(const char *str1, const char *str2);

The **strstr( )** function returns a pointer to the first occurrence of the string pointed to by *str2* in the string pointed to by *str1*. It returns a null pointer if no match is found.

Example

This program displays the message **is is a test**:

```
#include <string.h>
#include <stdio.h>

void main(void)
```

```
{
  char *p;

  p = strstr("this is a test", "is");
  printf(p);
}
```

Related Functions

strchr( ), strcspn( ), strpbrk( ), strrchr( ), strspn( ), strtok( )

#include <string.h>
char *strtok(char *str1, const char *str2);

The **strtok( )** function returns a pointer to the next token in the string pointed to by *str1*. The characters that make up the string pointed to by *str2* define the delimiters that separate each token from the next. For example, given this string:

One, two, and three.

The tokens are **One**, **two**, **and**, and **three**. The delimiters are the spaces, the commas, and the period.

strtok( ) returns a null pointer when there are no more tokens remaining in *str1*.

The first time **strtok( )** is called, *str1* is actually used in the call. Subsequent calls must use a null pointer for the first argument.

It is important to understand that the **strtok( )** function modifies the string pointed to by *str1*. Each time a token is found, the delimiter that terminates the token is replaced by a null. In this way, **strtok( )** can continue to advance through the string.

You can use a different set of delimiters for each call to **strtok( )**.

Example

This program tokenizes the string, "The summer soldier, the sunshine patriot", with spaces and commas being the delimiters. The output is

The ¦ summer ¦ soldier ¦ the ¦ sunshine ¦ patriot

```
#include <stdio.h>
#include <string.h>

void main(void)
{
```

```
    char *p;

    p = strtok("The summer soldier, the sunshine patriot", " ");
    printf(p);
    do {
      p = strtok('\0', ", ");
      if(p) printf("|%s", p);
    } while(p);
}
```

Related Functions

strchr( ), strcspn( ), strpbrk( ), strrchr( ), strspn( )

#include <string.h>
size_t strxfrm(char *str1, const char *str2, size_t count);

The **strxfrm( )** function transforms the string pointed to by *str2* so that it can be used by the **strcmp( )** function. **strxfrm( )** then puts up to *count* characters of the result into the string pointed to by *str1*. After the transformation, the outcome of a **strcmp( )** using *str1* and a **strcoll( )** using the original string pointed to by *str2* will be the same. The main use for the **strxfrm( )** function is in foreign language environments that do not use the ASCII collating sequence.

The **strxfrm( )** function returns the length of the transformed string.

Example

The following line transforms the first ten characters of the string pointed to by **s2** and puts the result in the string pointed to by **s1**:

```
    strxfrm(s1, s2, 10);
```

Related Function

strcoll( )

#include <ctype.h>
int tolower(int ch);

The **tolower( )** function returns the lowercase equivalent of *ch* if *ch* is a letter; otherwise, *ch* is returned unchanged.

Example

This code fragment displays **q**:

```
putchar(tolower('Q'));
```

Related Function

toupper( )

#include <ctype.h>
int toupper(int ch);

The **toupper( )** function returns the uppercase equivalent of *ch* if *ch* is a letter; otherwise, *ch* is returned unchanged.

Example

This code displays **A**:

```
putchar(toupper('a'));
```

Related Function

tolower( )

Chapter Fourteen

Mathematical Functions

The ANSI C standard defines 22 mathematical functions that fall into the following categories:

■ Trigonometric functions

■ Hyperbolic functions

■ Exponential and logarithmic functions

■ Miscellaneous

These functions are described in this chapter. Even if your compiler is not completely standard, the math functions described here are probably applicable.

All the math functions require the header MATH.H. In addition to declaring the prototypes for the math functions, this header defines the macro **HUGE_VAL**. The math functions also make frequent use of the macros **EDOM** and **ERANGE**, which are defined in the header file ERRNO.H. If an argument to a math function is not in the domain for which it is defined, an implementation-defined value is returned and the built-in global integer variable **errno** is set to **EDOM**. If a function produces a result too large to be represented by a **double**, an overflow occurs. This causes the function to return **HUGE_VAL** and sets **errno** to **ERANGE**, indicating a range error. If an underflow occurs, the function returns zero and (generally) sets **errno** to **ERANGE**. If your compiler does not comform to the ANSI C standard, the exact operation of the routines in error situations may be different.

As relating to the mathematical functions, all angles are in terms of radians.

*NOTE: To have access to **errno** and the macros **EDOM** and **ERANGE** you must include ERRNO.H in your program.*

#include <math.h>
double acos(double arg);

The **acos( )** function returns the arc cosine of *arg*. The argument to **acos( )** must be in the range –1 to 1; otherwise, a domain error occurs.

Example

This program prints the arc cosines of the values –1 through 1, in increments of one tenth:

```
#include <math.h>
#include <stdio.h>
```

```
void main(void)
{
  double val = -1.0;

  do {
    printf("Arc cosine of %f is %f.\n", val, acos(val));
    val += 0.1;
  } while(val<=1.0);
}
```

Related Functions

asin( ), atan( ), atan2( ), cos( ), cosh( ), sin( ), sinh( ), tan( ), tanh( )

#include <math.h>
double asin(double arg);

The **asin( )** function returns the arc sine of *arg*. The argument to **asin( )** must be in the range –1 to 1; otherwise, a domain error occurs.

Example

This program prints the arc sines of the values –1 through 1, in increments of one tenth:

```
#include <math.h>
#include <stdio.h>

void main(void)
{
  double val = -1.0;

  do {
    printf("Arc sine of %f is %f.\n", val, asin(val));
    val += 0.1;
  } while(val<=1.0);
}
```

Related Functions

acos( ), atan( ), atan2( ), cos( ), cosh( ), sin( ), sinh( ), tan( ), tanh( )

#include <math.h>
double atan(double arg);

The **atan( )** function returns the arc tangent of *arg*.

Example

This program prints the arc tangents of the values –1 through 1, in increments of one tenth:

```
#include <math.h>
#include <stdio.h>

void main(void)
{
  double val = -1.0;

  do {
    printf("Arc tangent of %f is %f.\n", val, atan(val));
    val += 0.1;
  } while(val<=1.0);
}
```

Related Functions

acos( ), asin( ), atan2( ), cos( ), cosh( ), sin( ), sinh( ), tan( ), tanh( )

#include <math.h>
double atan2(double y, double x);

The **atan2( )** function returns the arc tangent of *y/x*. It uses the signs of its arguments to compute the quadrant of the return value.

Example

This program prints the arc tangents of *y*, from –1 through 1, in increments of one tenth:

```
#include <math.h>
#include <stdio.h>

void main(void)
{
  double val = -1.0;

  do {
```

```
      printf("Atan2 of %f is %f.\n", val, atan2(val,1.0));
      val += 0.1;
   } while(val<=1.0);
}
```

Related Functions

acos( ), asin( ), atan( ), cos( ), cosh( ), sin( ), sinh( ), tan( ), tanh( )

#include <math.h>
double ceil(double num);

The **ceil( )** function returns the smallest integer (represented as a **double**) that is not less than *num*. For example, given 1.02, **ceil( )** returns **2.0**. Given –1.02, **ceil( )** returns **–1**.

Example

This code fragment prints **10** on the screen:

```
printf("%f", ceil(9.9));
```

Related Functions

floor( ), fmod( )

#include <math.h>
double cos(double arg);

The **cos( )** function returns the cosine of *arg*. The value of *arg* must be in radians.

Example

This program prints the cosines of the values –1 through 1, in increments of one tenth:

```
#include <math.h>
#include <stdio.h>

void main(void)
{
  double val = -1.0;

  do {
```

```
      printf("Cosine of %f is %f.\n", val, cos(val));
      val += 0.1;
   } while(val<=1.0);
}
```

Related Functions

acos( ), asin( ), atan( ), atan2( ), cosh( ), sin( ), sinh( ), tan( ), tanh( )

#include <math.h>
double cosh(double arg);

The **cosh( )** function returns the hyperbolic cosine of *arg*.

Example

The following program prints the hyperbolic cosines of the values –1 through 1, in increments of one tenth:

```
#include <math.h>
#include <stdio.h>

void main(void)
{
  double val = -1.0;

  do {
    printf("Hyperbolic cosine of %f is %f.\n", val, cosh(val));
    val += 0.1;
  } while(val<=1.0);
}
```

Related Functions

acos( ), asin( ), atan( ), atan2( ), cos( ), sin( ), tan( ), tanh( )

#include <math.h>
double exp(double arg);

The **exp( )** function returns the natural logarithm **e** raised to the *arg* power.

Example

This fragment displays the value of **e** (rounded to 2.718282):

```
printf("Value of e to the first: %f.", exp(1.0));
```

Related Function

log( )

#include <math.h>
double fabs(double num);

The **fabs( )** function returns the absolute value of *num*.

Example

This program prints **1.0 1.0** on the screen:

```
#include <math.h>
#include <stdio.h>

void main(void)
{
   printf("%1.1f %1.1f", fabs(1.0), fabs(-1.0));
}
```

Related Function

abs( )

#include <math.h>
double floor(double num);

The **floor( )** function returns the largest integer (represented as a **double**) that is not greater than *num*. For example, given 1.02, **floor( )** returns **1.0**. Given −1.02, **floor( )** returns **−2.0**.

Example

This code fragment prints **10** on the screen:

```
printf("%f", floor(10.9));
```

Related Functions

fceil( ), fmod( )

#include <math.h>
double fmod(double x, double y);

The **fmod( )** function returns the remainder of *x/y*.

Example

The following program prints **1.0** on the screen—the remainder of 10/3:

```
#include <math.h>
#include <stdio.h>

void main(void)
{
   printf("%1.1f", fmod(10.0, 3.0));
}
```

Related Functions

ceil( ), fabs( ), floor( )

#include <math.h>
double frexp(double num, int *exp);

The **frexp( )** function decomposes *num* into a mantissa in the range 0.5 to less than 1, and an integer exponent such that $num=mantissa*2^{exp}$. The mantissa is returned by the function and the exponent is stored at the variable pointed to by *exp*.

Example

This code fragment prints **0.625** for the mantissa and **4** for the exponent:

```
int e;
double f;

f = frexp(10.0, &e);
printf("%f %d", f, e);
```

Related Function

ldexp( )

#include <math.h>
double ldexp(double num, int exp);

The **ldexp( )** function returns the value of $num*2^{exp}$. If overflow occurs, **HUGE_VAL** is returned.

Example

This program displays the number **4**:

```
#include <math.h>
#include <stdio.h>

void main(void)
{
  printf("%f", ldexp(1,2));
}
```

Related Functions

frexp( ), modf( )

#include <math.h>
double log(double num);

The **log( )** function returns the natural logarithm for *num*. A domain error occurs if *num* is negative and a range error occurs if the argument is zero.

Example

The following program prints the natural logarithms for the numbers 1 through 10:

```
#include <math.h>
#include <stdio.h>

void main(void)
{
  double val = 1.0;

  do {
    printf("%f %f\n", val, log(val));
    val++;
  } while (val<11.0);
}
```

Related Function

log10( )

#include <math.h>
double log10(double num);

The **log10( )** function returns the base 10 logarithm for *num*. A domain error occurs if *num* is negative and a range error occurs if the argument is zero.

Example

This program prints the base 10 logarithms for the numbers 1 through 10:

```
#include <math.h>
#include <stdio.h>

void main(void)
{
  double val = 1.0;

  do {
    printf("%f %f\n", val, log10(val));
    val++;
  } while (val<11.0);
}
```

Related Function

log( )

#include <math.h>
double modf(double num, double *i);

The **modf( )** function decomposes *num* into its integer and fractional parts. It returns the fractional portion and places the integer part in the variable pointed to by *i*.

Example

This code fragment prints **10** and **0.123** on the screen:

```
double i;
double f;
```

```
f = modf(10.123, &i);
printf("%f %f",i , f);
```

Related Functions

frexp( ), ldexp( )

#include <math.h>
double pow(double base, double exp);

The **pow( )** function returns *base* raised to the *exp* power (*base^{exp}*). A domain error occurs if *base* is zero and *exp* is less than or equal to zero. This also happens if *base* is negative and *exp* is not an integer. An overflow produces a range error.

Example

The following program prints the first ten powers of 10:

```
#include <math.h>
#include <stdio.h>

void main(void)
{
  double x = 10.0, y = 0.0;

  do {
    printf("%f\n", pow(x, y));
    y++;
  } while(y<11.0);
}
```

Related Functions

exp( ), log( ), sqrt( )

#include <math.h>
double sin(double arg);

The **sin( )** function returns the sine of *arg*. The value of *arg* must be in radians.

Example

This program prints the sines of the values –1 through 1, in increments of one tenth:

```
#include <math.h>
#include <stdio.h>

void main(void)
{
  double val = -1.0;

  do {
    printf("Sine of %f is %f.\n", val, sin(val));
    val += 0.1;
  } while(val<=1.0);
}
```

Related Functions

acos( ), asin( ), atan( ), atan2( ), cos( ), cosh( ), sinh( ), tan( ), tanh( )

#include <math.h>
double sinh(double arg);

The **sinh( )** function returns the hyperbolic sine of *arg*.

Example

This program prints the hyperbolic sines of the values –1 through 1, in increments of one tenth:

```
#include <math.h>
#include <stdio.h>

void main(void)
{
  double val = -1.0;

  do {
    printf("Hyperbolic sine of %f is %f.\n", val, sinh(val));
    val += 0.1;
  } while(val<=1.0);
}
```

Related Functions

acos( ), asin( ), atan( ), atan2( ), cos( ), cosh( ), sin( ), tan( ), tanh( )

#include <math.h>
double sqrt(double num);

The **sqrt( )** function returns the square root of *num*. If it is called with a negative argument, a domain error occurs.

Example

This code fragment prints **4** on the screen:

```
printf("%f", sqrt(16.0));
```

Related Functions

exp( ), log( ), pow( )

#include <math.h>
double tan(double arg);

The **tan( )** function returns the tangent of *arg*. The value of *arg* must be in radians.

Example

This program prints the tangent of the values –1 through 1, in increments of one tenth:

```
#include <math.h>
#include <stdio.h>

void main(void)
{
  double val = -1.0;

  do {
    printf("Tangent of %f is %f.\n", val, tan(val));
    val += 0.1;
  } while(val<=1.0);
}
```

Related Functions

acos( ), asin( ), atan( ), atan2( ), cos( ), cosh( ), sin( ), sinh( ), tanh( )

#include <math.h>
double tanh(double arg);

The **tanh( )** function returns the hyperbolic tangent of *arg*.

Example

This program prints the hyperbolic tangent of the values −1 through 1, in increments of one tenth:

```
#include <math.h>
#include <stdio.h>

void main(void)
{
  double val = -1.0;

  do {
    printf("Hyperbolic tangent of %f is %f.\n", val, tanh(val));
    val += 0.1;
  } while(val<=1.0);
}
```

Related Functions

acos( ), asin( ), atan( ), atan2( ), cos( ), cosh( ), sin( ), sinh( ), tan( )

Chapter Fifteen

Time, Date, and Other System-Related Functions

This chapter covers functions that are, in one way or another, more closely tied to the operating system than are others in the C standard library. Of these, the functions defined by the ANSI C standard include the time and date functions as well as the localization functions **setlocale( )** and **localeconv( )**. These functions use the operating system's time and date information or, in the case of localization, its geo-political information.

This chapter also discusses a representative sampling of functions that allow direct operating system interfacing. None of these functions are defined by the ANSI C standard because each operating environment is different. The functions described in this chapter interface to DOS. DOS was chosen because it is widely used and commonly available. Also, C programs written for DOS frequently access its low-level functions. Of course, functions that interface to other operating systems will be different than those described here (but they will be similar in nature). Further, even among C compilers that operate under DOS, there may be slight differences in their approaches to the system-level interfacing functions. This chapter includes the most generalizable functions defined by Microsoft's DOS-compatible C/C++ compilers. But you should be able to generalize to the functions provided by your own compiler.

This chapter also discusses functions defined by Microsoft that interface with the ROM-BIOS of the PC. The BIOS provides the lowest level support for the computer's various hardware devices. In a sense, the BIOS is the lowest level of any operating system found on a PC. The BIOS functions are not defined by the ANSI C standard but the ones included here are a representative sample of the type of functions provided with most DOS and PC-based C compilers.

The ANSI C standard defines several functions that handle the date and time of the system as well as elapsed time. These functions require the header file TIME.H. This header defines four types: **size_t**, **clock_t**, **time_t**, and **tm**. **size_t** is some variety of unsigned integer. The types **clock_t** and **time_t** can represent the system time and date as a long integer. The ANSI C standard refers to this as *calendar time*. The structure type **tm** holds the date and time broken down into their elements. The **tm** structure is defined as shown here:

```
struct tm {
   int tm_sec;   /* seconds, 0-59 */
   int tm_min;   /* minutes, 0-59 */
   int tm_hour;  /* hours, 0-23 */
   int tm_mday;  /* day of the month, 1-31 */
   int tm_mon;   /* months since Jan, 0-11 */
   int tm_year;  /* years from 1900 */
   int tm_wday;  /* days since Sunday, 0-6 */
   int tm_yday;  /* days since Jan 1, 0-365 */
   int tm_isdst; /* Daylight Saving Time indicator */
};
```

The value of **tm_isdst** is positive if daylight saving time is in effect, zero if it is not in effect, and negative if no information is available. The ANSI C standard refers to this form of the time and date as *broken-down time.*

In addition, TIME.H defines the macro **CLOCKS_PER_SEC**, which is the number of system clock ticks per second.

The localization functions require the header file LOCALE.H.

The DOS interfacing functions defined by Microsoft C/C++ require the header DOS.H. This defines a union that corresponds to the registers of the 8086 family of CPUs and is used by some of the system-interfacing functions. This union is defined as the union of two structures to allow each register to be accessed either by word or byte. The structures and union are shown here, as defined by Microsoft:

```
/*   Copyright (c) 1985-1992, Microsoft Corporation.
     All rights reserved.
*/

/* word registers */
struct _WORDREGS {
  unsigned int ax;
  unsigned int bx;
  unsigned int cx;
  unsigned int dx;
  unsigned int si;
  unsigned int di;
  unsigned int cflag;
};

/* byte registers */
struct _BYTEREGS {
  unsigned char al, ah;
  unsigned char bl, bh;
  unsigned char cl, ch;
  unsigned char dl, dh;
};

/* general purpose registers union -
     overlays the corresponding word and byte registers.
*/

union _REGS {
  struct _WORDREGS x;
  struct _BYTEREGS h;
};
```

DOS.H also defines the structure type **_SREGS**, which some functions use to set the segment registers. This structure is defined by Microsoft as:

```
/*    Copyright (c) 1985-1992, Microsoft Corporation.
      All rights reserved.
*/

/* segment registers */

struct _SREGS {
  unsigned int es;
  unsigned int cs;
  unsigned int ss;
  unsigned int ds;
};
```

The BIOS interface functions require the header file BIOS.H.

Several functions described in this chapter assign the built-in global integer variable **errno** an error-code value when an error occurs. (You must include ERRNO.H to access **errno**.) Consult your user's manual for details.

#include <time.h>
char *asctime(const struct tm *ptr);

The **asctime( )** function converts the information stored in the structure pointed to by *ptr* into a string of the following form:

day month date hours:minutes:seconds year\n\0

Here is an example of such a string:

Wed Jun 19 12:05:34 1999

asctime( ) returns a pointer to the conversion string.

The structure pointer passed to **asctime( )** is generally obtained from either **localtime( )** or **gmtime( )**.

The buffer used by **asctime( )** to hold the string is a statically allocated character array and is overwritten each time the function is called. To save the contents of the string, you need to copy it elsewhere.

Example

This program displays the local time defined by the system:

```
#include <time.h>
#include <stdio.h>

void main(void)
{
  struct tm *ptr;
  time_t lt;

  lt = time(NULL);
  ptr = localtime(&lt);
  printf(asctime(ptr));
}
```

Related Functions

ctime( ), gmtime( ), localtime( ), time( )

#include <dos.h>
int _bdos(int fnum, unsigned dx, unsigned al);

The **_bdos( )** function is not defined by the ANSI C standard and only applies to DOS-based C compilers. It may also have a slightly different name, so check your user's manual.

The **_bdos( )** function accesses the DOS system function specified by *fnum*. It first places *dx* into the **DX** register and *al* into the **AL** register and then executes an INT 21H instruction.

The **_bdos( )** function returns the value of the **AX** register, which is used by DOS to return information.

The **_bdos( )** function can only be used to access system functions that either take no argument or require only **DX** and/or **AL** as their arguments.

Example

This program reads characters directly from the keyboard, bypassing all of C's I/O functions, until the user presses ENTER:

```
/* Do raw keyboard reads. */
#include <dos.h>
```

```
void main(void)
{
  while((255 & _bdos(1, 0, 0)) != '\r') ;
}
```

Related Functions

intdos( ), intdosx( )

#include <bios.h>
unsigned _bios_disk(unsigned cmd, struct _diskinfo_t *info);

The _bios_disk( ) function is not defined by the ANSI C standard and only applies to DOS-based C compilers. It may also have a slightly different name, so check your user's manual.

The _bios_disk( ) function performs BIOS-level disk operations using interrupt 0x13. These operations ignore the logical structure of the disk, including files. All operations take place on sectors.

Microsoft defines the _diskinfo_t structure as follows.

```
struct _diskinfo_t {
  unsigned drive;
  unsigned head;
  unsigned track;
  unsigned sector;
  unsigned nsectors;
  void __far *buffer;
};
```

The drive affected is specified in **drive**, with 0 corresponding to A, 1 to B, and so on for floppy drives. The first fixed disk is drive 0x80, the second 0x81, and so forth. The part of the disk operated upon is specified in **head**, **track**, and **sector**. The **nsectors** field specifies the number of sectors to read or write and **buffer** points to a buffer that holds information written to or read from the disk. Refer to a PC technical manual for details on the operation and options of the BIOS-level disk routines. Remember, direct control of the disk requires thorough and intimate knowledge of the hardware and DOS. It is best avoided except in unusual situations.

Related Functions

fread( ), fwrite( )

#include <bios.h>
unsigned _bios_equiplist(void);

The **_bios_equiplist( )** function is not defined by the ANSI C standard and only applies to DOS-based C compilers. It may also have a slightly different name, so check your user's manual.

The **_bios_equiplist( )** function returns a value that specifies what equipment is in the computer. This value is encoded as shown here:

Bit	Equipment
0	System has disk drives
1	80x87 math coprocessor installed
2, 3	Motherboard RAM size
	0 0: 16k
	0 1: 32k
	1 0: 48k
	1 1: 64k
4, 5	Initial video mode
	0 0: unused
	0 1: 40x25 BW, color adapter
	1 0: 80x25 BW, color adapter
	1 1: 80x25, monochrome adapter
6, 7	Number of floppy drives
	0 0: one
	0 1: two
	1 0: three
	1 1: four
8	Cleared if DMA chip installed
9, 10, 11	Number of serial ports
	0 0 0: zero
	0 0 1: one
	0 1 0: two
	0 1 1: three
	1 0 0: four
	1 0 1: five
	1 1 0: six
	1 1 1: seven
12	Set if game adapter is installed
13	Set if modem is installed
14, 15	Number of printers
	0 0: zero
	0 1: one
	1 0: two
	1 1: three

Example

This program displays the number of floppy drives installed in the computer:

```
#include <bios.h>
#include <stdio.h>

void main(void)
{
  unsigned eq;

  eq = _bios_equiplist();

  eq >>= 6; /* shift bits 6 and 7 into lowest position */

  printf("Floppy disk drives: %d", (eq & 3) + 1);
}
```

Related Function

_bios_serialcom( )

#include <bios.h>
unsigned _bios_keybrd(unsigned cmd);

The **_bios_keybrd( )** function is not defined by the ANSI C standard and only applies to DOS-based C compilers. It may have a slightly different name, so check your user's manual.

The **_bios_keybrd( )** function performs direct keyboard operations. The value of *cmd* determines what operation is executed.

If *cmd* is zero, **_bios_keybrd( )** returns the next key pressed. (It waits until a key is pressed.) It returns a 16-bit quantity that consists of two different values. The low-order byte contains the ASCII character code if a normal key is pressed and contains zero if a special key is pressed. Special keys include the arrow keys and the function keys. The high-order byte contains the scan code of the key, which corresponds loosely to the key's position on the keyboard.

If *cmd* is 1, **_bios_keybrd( )** checks to see if a key has been pressed. It returns nonzero if a key has been pressed; otherwise, it returns zero.

When *cmd* is 2, the shift status is returned and is encoded as shown here:

Bit	Meaning
0	Right SHIFT pressed
1	Left SHIFT pressed
2	Any CTRL key pressed

Bit	Meaning
3	Any ALT key pressed
4	SCROLL LOCK ON
5	NUM LOCK ON
6	CAPS LOCK ON
7	INSERT ON
8	Left CTRL pressed
9	Left ALT pressed
10	Right CTRL pressed
11	Right ALT pressed
12	SCROLL LOCK pressed
13	NUM LOCK pressed
14	CAPS LOCK pressed
15	SYSRQ pressed

Example

This code fragment generates random numbers until a key is pressed. It allows you to start **rand( )**, the random number generator, from a random point.

```
while(!_bios_keybrd(1)) rand();
```

Related Functions

getche( ), kbhit( )

#include <bios.h>
unsigned _bios_memsize(void);

The **_bios_memsize( )** function is not defined by the ANSI C standard and only applies to DOS-based C compilers. It may also have a slightly different name, so check your user's manual.

The **_bios_memsize( )** function returns the amount of memory (in units of 1K) installed in the system that is available to DOS. (This will be no larger than 640K.)

Example

This program reports the amount of memory in the system:

```
#include <bios.h>
#include <stdio.h>
void main(void)
{
  printf("%uK bytes of ram", _bios_memsize());
}
```

Related Function

_bios_equiplist( )

#include <bios.h>
unsigned _bios_printer(unsigned cmd, unsigned port,
unsigned data);

The **_bios_printer( )** function is not defined by the ANSI C standard and only applies to DOS-based C compilers. It may also have a slightly different name, so check your user's manual.

The **_bios_printer( )** function controls the printer port specified in *port*. If *port* is zero, LPT1 is used; if *port* is 1, LPT2 is accessed, etc. The exact function performed is contingent upon the value of *cmd*. The legal values for *cmd* are shown here:

Value	Meaning
0	Print the character passed in *data*
1	Initialize the printer port
2	Return the status of the port

The printer port status is encoded into the high-order byte of the return value, as shown here:

Bit	Meaning
0	Time-out error
1	Unused
2	Unused
3	I/O error
4	Printer selected
5	Out-of-paper error
6	Acknowledge
7	Print NOT busy

Example

This fragment prints the string **hello** on the printer connected to LPT1:

```
char p[] = "hello";
while(*p) _bios_printer(0, 0, *p++);
```

Related Function

_bios_serialcom( )

#include <bios.h>
unsigned _bios_serialcom(unsigned cmd, unsigned port, unsigned data);

The **_bios_serialcom( )** function is not defined by the ANSI C standard and only applies to DOS-based C compilers. It may also have a slightly different name, so check your user's manual.

The **_bios_serialcom( )** function manipulates the RS232 asynchronous communication port specified in *port*. Its operation is determined by the value of *cmd*, whose values are shown here:

cmd	Meaning
0	Initialize the port
1	Send a character
2	Receive a character
3	Return the port status

For access to COM1, *port* must be zero. For access to COM2, *port* must be 1, etc.

Before using the serial port, you will probably want to initialize it to something other than its default setting. To do this, call **_bios_serialcom( )** with *cmd* set equal to zero. The way the port is set up is determined by the value of the low-order byte of *data*, which is encoded with initialization parameters, as shown here:

The baud is encoded as shown here:

Baud	Bit Pattern
9600	111
4800	110
2400	101
1200	100
600	011
300	010
150	001
110	000

The parity bits are encoded as shown here:

Parity	Bit Pattern
No parity	0 0 or 1 0
Odd	0 1
Even	1 1

The number of stop bits is determined by bit 2 of the serial port initialization byte. If it is 1, two stop bits are used; otherwise, one stop bit is used. Finally, the number of data bits is set in bits 1 and 0 of the initialization byte. Of the four possible bit patterns, only two are valid. If bits 1 and 0 contain the pattern 1 0, seven data-bits are used. If they contain 1 1, eight data-bits are used.

For example, if you want to set the port to 9600 baud, even parity, one stop-bit, and eight data-bits, you would use this bit pattern:

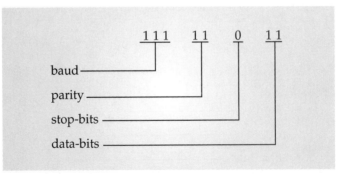

In decimal, this works out to 251.

The return value of **_bios_serialcom( )** is always a 16-bit quantity. The high-order byte contains the status bits, which have these values:

Meaning When Set	Bit
Data ready	0
Overrun error	1
Parity error	2
Framing error	3
Break-detect error	4
Transfer holding register empty	5
Transfer shift register empty	6
Time-out error	7

If *cmd* is set to 0, 1, or 3, the low-order byte is encoded as shown here:

Meaning When Set	Bit
Change in clear-to-send	0
Change in data-set-ready	1
Trailing-edge ring detector	2
Change in line signal	3
Clear to send	4
Data set ready	5
Ring indicator	6
Line signal detected	7

When *cmd* has a value of 2, the lower-order byte contains the value received by the port.

Example

This initializes port 0 to 9600 baud, even parity, one stop-bit, and eight data-bits:

```
_bios_serialcom(0, 0, 251);
```

Related Function

bioskey( )

#include <bios.h>
unsigned _bios_timeofday(unsigned cmd, long *newtime);

The **_bios_timeofday( )** function is not defined by the ANSI C standard and only applies to DOS-based C compilers. It may also have a slightly different name, so check your user's manual.

The **_bios_timeofday( )** function reads or sets the system clock. The system clock ticks at a rate of about 18.2 ticks per second. Its value is zero at midnight and increases until reset at midnight again or manually set to some value. If *cmd* is zero, **_bios_timeofday( )** returns the current value of the timer in the variable pointed to by *newtime*. If *cmd* is 1, the timer is set to the value pointed to by *newtime*.

The function returns the value of the AX register as set by the BIOS routine.

Example

This program prints the current value of the timer:

```
#include <bios.h>
#include <stdio.h>

void main(void)
{
  long t;

  _bios_timeofday(0, &t);
  printf("Timer value is %ld", t);
}
```

Related Functions

ctime( ), time( )

#include <time.h>
clock_t clock(void);

The **clock( )** function returns a value that approximates the amount of time the calling program has been running. To transform this value into seconds, divide it by **CLOCKS_PER_SEC**. A value of –1 is returned if the time is not available.

Example

The following function displays the current execution time, in seconds, for the program calling it:

```
void elapsed_time(void)
{
  printf("Elapsed time: %u secs.\n", clock()/CLOCKS_PER_SEC);
}
```

Related Functions

asctime( ), ctime( ), time( )

#include <time.h>
char *ctime(const time_t *time);

Given a pointer to the calendar time, the **ctime( )** function returns a pointer to a string in the form

day month date hours:minutes:seconds year\n\0

Here is an example of such a string:

Mon Dec 5 12:03:03 1994

The calendar time is generally obtained through a call to **time( )**.

The buffer used by **ctime( )** to hold the formatted output string is a statically allocated character array and is overwritten each time the function is called. To save the contents of the string, you need to copy it elsewhere.

Example

This program displays the local time defined by the system:

```c
#include <time.h>
#include <stdio.h>

void main(void)
{
  time_t lt;

  lt = time(NULL);
  printf(ctime(&lt));
}
```

Related Functions

asctime( ), gmtime( ), localtime( ), time( )

#include <time.h>
double difftime(time_t time2, time_t time1);

The **difftime( )** function returns the difference, in seconds, between *time1* and *time2*. That is, it returns *time2 – time1*.

Example

This program determines the number of seconds that it takes for the empty **for** loop to go from 0 to 500,000:

```
#include <time.h>
#include <stdio.h>

void main(void)
{
  time_t start,end;
  long unsigned t;

  start = time(NULL);
  for(t=0; t<500000; t++) ;
  end = time(NULL);
  printf("Loop used %f seconds.\n", difftime(end, start));
}
```

Related Functions

asctime( ), gmtime( ), localtime( ), time( )

#include <dos.h>
void _disable(void);

The **_disable( )** function is not defined by the ANSI C standard and only applies to DOS-based C compilers. It may also have a slightly different name, so check your user's manual.

The **_disable( )** function disables interrupts. The only interrupt that it allows is the NMI (nonmaskable interrupt). Use this function with care because many devices in the system use interrupts.

Related Function

_enable( )

#include <dos.h>
unsigned _dos_allocmem(unsigned size, unsigned *seg);

The **_dos_allocmem( )** function is not defined by the ANSI C standard and only applies to DOS-based C compilers. It may also have a slightly different name, so check your user's manual.

The **_dos_allocmem( )** function allocates a paragraph aligned block of memory. It puts the segment address of the block into the unsigned integer pointed to by *seg*. The *size* argument specifies the number of paragraphs to be allocated (a paragraph is 16 bytes).

If the requested memory can be allocated, a zero is returned. If insufficient free memory exists, the size of the maximum amount of available memory is put into the unsigned integer pointed to by *seg* and **errno** is set to **ENOMEM** (insufficient memory).

Example

This code fragment allocates 100 paragraphs of memory:

```
unsigned i;

i = 0;

if((_dos_allocmem(100, &i)==0)
   printf("Allocation Successful\n");
else
   printf("Allocation Failed\n");
```

Related Functions

_dos_freemem( ), _dos_setblock( )

#include <dos.h>
unsigned _dos_close(int fd);

The **_dos_close( )** function is not defined by the ANSI C standard and only applies to DOS-based C compilers. It may also have a slightly different name, so check your user's manual.

The **_dos_close( )** function closes the file specified by the file descriptor *fd*. It is functionally equivalent to the UNIX-like **close( )** function. Remember, file descriptors are used by the UNIX-like file system and do not relate to the ANSI C file system. The function returns zero if successful. Otherwise, it returns nonzero and sets **errno** to **EBADF** (bad file descriptor).

Example

This fragment closes the file associated with the file descriptor **fd**:

```
_dos_close(fd);
```

Related Functions

_dos_creat( ), **_dos_open( )**

#include <dos.h>
unsigned _dos_creat(char *fname, unsigned attr, int *fd);
unsigned _dos_creatnew(char *fname, unsigned attr, int *fd);

The **_dos_creat( )** and **_dos_creatnew( )** functions are not defined by the ANSI C standard and only apply to DOS-based C compilers. They may have slightly different names, so check your user's manual.

The **_dos_creat( )** function creates a file that will have the name pointed to by *fname* with the attributes specified by *attr*. It returns a file descriptor to the file in the integer pointed to by *fd*. (File descriptors are used by the UNIX-like file system, not the ANSI C file system.) If the file already exists, it is erased. The **_dos_creatnew( )** function is the same as **_dos_creat( )**, but if the file already exists, it is not erased and **_dos_creatnew( )** returns an error.

The valid values for *attr* are shown here (the macros are defined in DOS.H):

Macro	Meaning
_A_NORMAL	Normal file
_A_RDONLY	Read-only file
_A_HIDDEN	Hidden file
_A_SYSTEM	System file
_A_VOLID	Volume label
_A_SUBDIR	Subdirectory
_A_ARCH	Archive bit set

Both functions return zero if successful and nonzero on failure. On failure, **errno** contains one of these values: **ENOENT** (file not found), **EMFILE** (too many open files), **EACCES** (access denied), or **EEXIST** (file already exists).

The **_dos_creat( )** and **_dos_creatnew( )** functions are similar to the UNIX-like **creat( )** function.

Example

This fragment opens a file called TEST.TST for output:

```
int fd;

if(_dos_creat("test.tst", _A_NORMAL, &fd))
  printf("Cannot open file.");
```

Related Function

_dos_open( )

#include <dos.h>
int _dosexterr(struct _DOSERROR *err);

The **_dosexterr( )** function is not defined by the ANSI C standard and only applies to DOS-based C compilers. It may also have a slightly different name, so check your user's manual.

The **_dosexterr( )** function fills the structure pointed to by *err* with extended error information when a DOS call fails. The **_DOSERROR** structure is defined like this:

```
struct _DOSERROR {
  int exterror; /* error code */
  char class; /* class of error */
  char action; /* suggested action */
  char locus; /* location of error */
};
```

For the proper interpretation of the information returned by DOS, refer to a DOS technical reference.

Related Function

ferror( )

#include <dos.h>
unsigned _dos_findfirst(char *fname, unsigned attr,
struct _find_t *ptr);
unsigned _dos_findnext(struct _find_t *ptr);

The **_dos_findfirst( )** and **_dos_findnext( )** functions are not defined by the ANSI C standard and only apply to DOS-based C compilers. They may also have slightly different names, so check your user's manual.

The **_dos_findfirst( )** function searches for the first file name that matches the one pointed to by *fname*. The file name may include both a drive specifier and a path name. Also, the file name may include the wildcard characters * and ?. If a match is found, the structure pointed to by *ptr* is filled with information about the file.

Microsoft defines the **_find_t** structure as follows:

```
struct _find_t {
  char reserved[21];/* used by DOS */
  char attrib;      /* attribute of file */
  unsigned wr_time; /* last time file was written to */
  unsigned wr_date; /* last date file was written to */
  long size;        /* size in bytes */
  char name[13];    /* filename */
};
```

The *attrib* parameter determines what type of files are found by **_dos_findfirst**. *attrib* can be one or more of the following macros (defined in DOS.H):

Macro	Meaning
_A_NORMAL	Normal file
_A_RDONLY	Read-only file
_A_HIDDEN	Hidden file
_A_SYSTEM	System file
_A_VOLID	Volume label
_A_SUBDIR	Subdirectory
_A_ARCH	Archive bit set

The **_dos_findnext( )** function continues a search started by **_dos_findfirst( )**. The buffer pointed to by *ptr* must be the one used in the call to **_dos_findfirst( )**.

Both the **_dos_findfirst( )** and **_dos_findnext( )** functions return zero on success and nonzero on failure or when no more matches are found. On failure, **errno** is set to **ENOENT** (file name not found).

Example

This program displays all files that have .C extension in the current working directory:

```
#include <dos.h>
#include <stdio.h>

void main(void)
{
  struct _find_t f;
  register int done;

  done = _dos_findfirst("*.c", _A_NORMAL, &f);
  while(!done) {
    printf("%s %ld\n", f.name, f.size);
    done = _dos_findnext(&f);
  }
}
```

#include <dos.h>
unsigned _dos_freemem(unsigned seg);

The **_dos_freemem( )** function is not defined by the ANSI C standard and only applies to DOS-based C compilers. It may also have a slightly different name, so check your user's manual.

The **_dos_freemem( )** function frees the block of memory whose segment is in *seg*. This memory must have been previously allocated using **_dos_allocmem( )**. The function returns zero on success; upon failure, it returns nonzero and sets **errno** to **ENOMEM** (insufficient memory).

Example

This code fragment illustrates how to allocate and free memory using **_dos_allocmem( )** and **_dos_freemem( )**:

```
unsigned i;

if(_dos_allocmem(some, &i)!=0)
  printf("Allocation Error");
else
    _dos_freemem(i);
```

Related Functions

_dos_allocmem( ), _dos_setblock( )

#include <dos.h>
void _dos_getdate(struct _dosdate_t *d);
void _dos_gettime(struct _dostime_t *t);

The _dos_getdate( ) and _dos_gettime( ) functions are not defined by the ANSI C standard and only apply to DOS-based C compilers. They may also have slightly different names, so check your user's manual.

The _dos_getdate( ) function fills the structure pointed to by *d* with the DOS form of the current system date. The _dos_gettime( ) function fills the structure pointed to by *t* with the DOS form of the current system time.

Microsoft defines the **_dosdate_t** structure as follows:

```
struct _dosdate_t {
  unsigned char day;
  unsigned char month;
  unsigned int year;
  unsigned char dayofweek;  /* Sunday is 0 */
};
```

Microsoft defines the **_dostime_t** structure as shown here:

```
struct _dostime_t {
  unsigned char hour;
  unsigned char minute;
  unsigned char second;
  unsigned char hsecond; /* hundredths of second */
};
```

Example

This program displays the date and time using DOS system calls:

```
#include <dos.h>
#include <stdio.h>

void main(void)
{
  struct _dostime_t t;
```

```
    struct _dosdate_t d;

    _dos_getdate(&d);
    _dos_gettime(&t);

    printf("Date: %d/%d/%d\n", d.day, d.month, d.year);
    printf("Time: %d:%d:%d\n", t.hour, t.minute,
            t.second);
}
```

Related Functions

_dos_setdate( ), _dos_settime( )

#include <dos.h>
unsigned _dos_getdiskfree(unsigned drive,
struct _diskfree_t *dfptr);

The **_dos_getdiskfree( )** function is not defined by the ANSI C standard and only applies to DOS-based C compilers. It may also have a slightly different name, so check your user's manual.

The **_dos_getdiskfree( )** function returns the amount of free disk space in the structure pointed to by *dfptr* for the drive specified by *drive*. The drives are numbered from 1 beginning with A. You can specify the default drive by calling **_dos_getdiskfree( )** with a value of zero. The **_diskfree_t** structure is defined by Microsoft as follows:

```
struct _diskfree_t {
  unsigned total_clusters;
  unsigned avail_clusters;
  unsigned sectors_per_cluster;
  unsigned bytes_per_sector;
};
```

The function returns zero if successful and nonzero if an error occurs. On failure, **errno** is assigned the value **EINVAL** (invalid drive).

Example

The following program prints the number of free clusters available for use on drive C:

```
#include <dos.h>
#include <stdio.h>

void main(void)
{
  struct _diskfree_t p;

  _dos_getdiskfree(3, &p); /* drive C */

  printf("Number of free clusters is %u.",
         p.avail_clusters);
}
```

Related Function

_dos_getftime( )

#include <dos.h>
void _dos_getdrive(unsigned *drive);

The **_dos_getdrive( )** function is not defined by the ANSI C standard and only applies to DOS-based C compilers. It may also have a slightly different name, so check your user's manual.

The **_dos_getdrive( )** function returns the number of the current disk drive in the integer pointed to by *drive*. Drive A is encoded as 1, drive B as 2, and so on.

Example

This code fragment displays the current disk drive:

```
unsigned d;

_dos_getdrive(&d);
printf("Drive is %c", d+'A'-1);
```

Related Function

_dos_setdrive( )

#include <dos.h>
unsigned _dos_getfileattr(const char *fname, unsigned *attrib);

The **_dos_getfileattr( )** function is not defined by the ANSI C standard and only applies to DOS-based C compilers. It may also have a slightly different name, so check your user's manual.

The **_dos_getfileattr( )** function returns the attribute of the file specified by *fname* in the unsigned integer pointed to by *attrib*. The attribute will be one or more of the following values (the macros are defined in DOS.H):

Macro	Meaning
_A_NORMAL	Normal file
_A_RDONLY	Read-only file
_A_HIDDEN	Hidden file
_A_SYSTEM	System file
_A_VOLID	Volume label
_A_SUBDIR	Subdirectory
_A_ARCH	Archive bit set

The **_dos_getfileattr( )** function returns zero if successful and nonzero otherwise. If failure occurs, **errno** is set to **ENOENT** (invalid file).

Example

This code fragment determines if the file TEST.TST is a normal file:

```
unsigned attr;
if(_dos_getfileattr("test.tst", &attr))
  printf("File Error");

if(attr & _A_NORMAL) printf("File is normal.");
```

Related Function

_dos_setfileattr( )

#include <dos.h>
unsigned _dos_getftime(int fd, unsigned *fdate, unsigned *ftime);

The **_dos_getftime( )** function is not defined by the ANSI C standard and only applies to DOS-based C compilers. It may also have a slightly different name, so check your user's manual.

The function **_dos_getftime( )** returns the time and date of creation (or last modification) for the file associated with file descriptor *fd* in the integers pointed to by *ftime* and *fdate*.

The bits in the object pointed to by *ftime* are encoded as shown here:

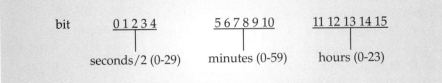

The bits in the object pointed to by *fdate* are encoded like this:

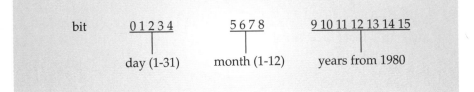

As indicated, the year is represented as the number of years from 1980. Therefore, if the year is 2000, the value of bits 9 through 15 will be 20.

The **_dos_getftime( )** function returns zero if successful. If an error occurs, it returns nonzero and sets **errno** to **EBADF** (bad file number).

Remember that files associated with file descriptors use the UNIX-like I/O system, which is not defined by or related to the ANSI C file system.

Example

This program prints the year that the file TEST.TST was created:

```c
#include <io.h>
#include <dos.h>
#include <fcntl.h>
#include <stdio.h>
#include <stdlib.h>

void main(void)
{
  struct {
    unsigned day: 5;
    unsigned month: 4;
    unsigned year: 7;
```

```
   } d;

   unsigned t;
   int fd;

   if((fd=open("TEST.TST", O_RDONLY))==-1) {
     printf("Cannot open file.");
     exit(1);
   }

   _dos_getftime(fd, (unsigned *) &d, &t);

   printf("Year of creation: %u", d.year+1980);
 }
```

Related Function

_dos_setftime( )

#include <dos.h>
void (__interrupt __far *_dos_getvect(unsigned intr))(void);

The **_dos_getvect( )** function is not defined by the ANSI C standard and only applies to DOS-based C compilers. It may also have a slightly different name, so check your user's manual.

The **_dos_getvect( )** function returns the address of the interrupt service routine associated with the interrupt specified in *intr*. This value is returned as a far pointer.

Example

The following code fragment returns the address of the print screen function (which is associated with interrupt 5).

```
   void (__interrupt __far *p)(void);

   p = _dos_getvect(5);
```

Related Function

_dos_setvect( )

#include <dos.h>
void _dos_keep(unsigned status, unsigned size);

The _dos_keep( ) function is not defined by the ANSI C standard and only applies to DOS-based C compilers. It may also have a slightly different name, so check your user's manual.

The _dos_keep( ) function executes an interrupt 0x31, which causes the current program to terminate but stay resident. The value of *status* is returned to DOS as a return code. The size of the program that is to stay resident is specified in *size*. The size is specified in paragraphs (16 bytes). The rest of the memory is freed for use by DOS.

Because terminate and stay resident programs are quite complex, there is no example here. However, my book, *The Craft of C* (Berkeley, CA: Osborne/McGraw-Hill, 1992), covers this topic in depth.

#include <dos.h>
unsigned _dos_open(const char *fname, unsigned mode, int *fd);

The _dos_open( ) function is not defined by the ANSI C standard and only applies to DOS-based C compilers. It may also have a slightly different name, so check your user's manual.

The _dos_open( ) function opens the file whose name is pointed to by *fname* in the mode specified by *mode* and returns a file descriptor to the file in the integer pointed to by *fd*. Remember, file descriptors are used by the UNIX-like file system and do not relate to the ANSI C file system.

The most common values for *mode* are

Value	Meaning
O_RDONLY	Read-only
O_WRONLY	Write-only
O_RDWR	Read/write

These macros are defined in FCNTL.H.

The _dos_open( ) function returns zero if successful and nonzero on failure. If an error occurs, **errno** is set to **EINVAL** (access mode invalid), **EACCES** (access denied), **EMFILE** (too many open files), or **ENOENT** (file not found).

Example

The following code fragment opens a file called TEST.TST for read/write operations:

```
int fd;

if(_dos_open("test.tst", O_RDWR, &fd))
    printf("Error opening file.");
```

Related Functions

_dos_close( ), _dos_creat( ), _dos_creatnew( )

#include <dos.h>
unsigned _dos_read(int fd, void __far *buf, unsigned count, unsigned *numread);

The **_dos_read( )** function is not defined by the ANSI C standard and only applies to DOS-based C compilers. It may also have a slightly different name, so check your user's manual.

The **_dos_read( )** function reads up to *count* bytes from the file specified by the file descriptor *fd* into the buffer pointed to by *buf*. The number of bytes actually read is returned in the variable pointed to by *numread*.

Upon success, **_dos_read( )** returns zero; it returns nonzero on failure. The return value is determined by DOS. (You will need DOS technical documentation to determine the nature of any errors that occur.) Also, on failure, **errno** will be set to either **EACCES** (access denied) or **EBADF** (file does not exist).

Example

This fragment reads up to 128 characters from the file described by **fd**:

```
unsigned count
char *buf[128];

if(_dos_read(fd, buf, 128, &count))
  printf("Error reading file.");
```

Related Function

_dos_write( )

#include <dos.h>
unsigned _dos_setblock(unsigned size, unsigned seg, unsigned *max);

The **_dos_setblock( )** function is not defined by the ANSI C standard and only applies to DOS-based C compilers. It may also have a slightly different name, so check your user's manual.

The **_dos_setblock( )** function changes the size of the block of memory whose segment address is *seg*. The new *size* is specified in paragraphs (16 bytes). The block of memory must have been previously allocated with **_dos_allocmem( )**.

If the size adjustment cannot be made, **_dos_setblock( )** returns the largest block (in paragraphs) that can be allocated in the variable pointed to by *max*.

On success, **_dos_setblock( )** returns zero; on failure, it returns nonzero and sets **errno** to **ENOMEM** (insufficient memory).

Example

This code fragment attempts to resize to 100 paragraphs the block of memory whose segment address is in **seg**:

```
unsigned max;

if(_dos_setblock(seg, 100, &max)!=0)
    printf("Resize error, largest block is %u.", max);
```

Related Functions

_dos_allocmem( ), **_dos_freemem( )**

#include <dos.h>
unsigned _dos_setdate(struct _dosdate_t *d);
unsigned _dos_settime(struct _dostime_t *t);

The **_dos_setdate( )** and **_dos_settime( )** functions are not defined by the ANSI C standard and only apply to DOS-based C compilers. They may also have slightly different names, so check your user's manual.

The **_dos_setdate( )** function sets the DOS system date as specified in the structure pointed to by *d*. The **_dos_settime( )** function sets the DOS system time as specified in the structure pointed to by *t*.

Microsoft defines the **_dosdate_t** structure as follows:

```
struct _dosdate_t {
    unsigned char day;
    unsigned char month;
    unsigned int year;
    unsigned char dayofweek;  /* Sunday is 0 */
};
```

Microsoft defines the **_dostime_t** structure as shown here:

```
struct _dostime_t {
  unsigned char hour;
  unsigned char minute;
  unsigned char second;
  unsigned char hsecond; /* hundredths of second */
};
```

The functions return zero if successful and nonzero if an error occurs.

Example

This code sets the system time to 10:10:10.0:

```
struct dostime_t t;

t.hour = 10;
t.minute  = 10;
t.second  = 10;
t.hsecond = 0;

_dos_settime(&t);
```

Related Functions

_dos_getdate( ), _dos_gettime( )

#include <dos.h>
void _dos_setdrive(unsigned drive, unsigned *num);

The **_dos_setdrive( )** function is not defined by the ANSI C standard and only applies to DOS-based C compilers. It may also have a slightly different name, so check your user's manual.

The **_dos_setdrive( )** function changes the current disk drive to the one specified by *drive*. Drive A corresponds to 1, drive B to 2, and so on. The number of drives in the system is returned in the integer pointed to by *num*.

Example

This fragment makes drive B the current drive:

```
unsigned num;

_dos_setdrive(2, &num);
```

Related Function

_dos_getdrive( )

#include <dos.h>
unsigned _dos_setfileattr(char *fname, unsigned *attrib);

The **_dos_setfileattr( )** function is not defined by the ANSI C standard and only applies to DOS-based C compilers. It may also have a slightly different name, so check your user's manual.

The **_dos_setfileattr( )** function sets the attribute of the file specified by *fname* to the attribute specified by *attrib*, which must be one or more of the following values (the macros are defined by Microsoft in DOS.H):

Macro	Meaning
_A_NORMAL	Normal file
_A_RDONLY	Read-only file
_A_HIDDEN	Hidden file
_A_SYSTEM	System file
_A_VOLID	Volume label
_A_SUBDIR	Subdirectory
_A_ARCH	Archive bit set

The **_dos_setfileattr( )** function returns zero if successful and nonzero otherwise. If failure occurs, **errno** is set to **ENOENT** (file not found) or **EACCES** (access denied).

Example

The following fragment sets the file TEST.TST to read-only:

```
unsigned attr;

attr = _A_RDONLY;

if(_dos_setfileattr("test.tst", &attr))
  printf("File Error");
```

Related Function

_dos_getfileattr( )

#include <dos.h>
unsigned _dos_setftime(int fd, unsigned fdate, unsigned ftime);

The **_dos_setftime( )** function is not defined by the ANSI C standard and only applies to DOS-based C compilers. It may also have a slightly different name, so check your user's manual.

The **_dos_setftime( )** function sets the date and time of the file specified by *fd*, which must be a valid file descriptor.

The bits in the object pointed to by *ftime* are encoded as shown here:

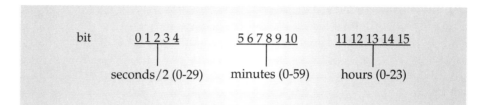

The bits in the object pointed to by *fdate* are encoded like this:

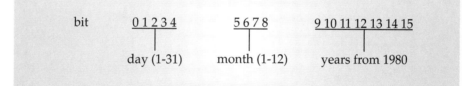

As indicated, the year is represented as the number of years from 1980. Therefore, to set the year to 2000, the value of bits 9 through 15 must be 20.

The **_dos_setftime( )** function returns zero if successful. If an error occurs, it returns nonzero and sets **errno** to **EBADF** (bad file number).

Remember that files associated with file descriptors use the UNIX-like I/O system, which is not defined by or related to the ANSI C file system.

Example

This code changes the year of the file's creation date to 2000:

```
#include <io.h>
#include <dos.h>
#include <fcntl.h>
#include <stdlib.h>
#include <stdio.h>

void main(void)
{
  union {
    struct {
      unsigned day: 5;
      unsigned month: 4;
      unsigned year: 7;
    } d;
    unsigned u;
  } date;

  unsigned t;
  int fd;

  if((fd=open("TEST.TST", O_RDONLY))==-1) {
    printf("Cannot open file.");
    exit(1);
  }

  _dos_getftime(fd, &date.u, &t);
  date.d.year = 20;

  _dos_setftime(fd, date.u, t);

  close(fd);
}
```

Related Function

_dos_getftime( )

#include <dos.h>
void _dos_setvect(unsigned intr, void (__interrupt __far *isr)( ));

The **_dos_setvect( )** function is not defined by the ANSI C standard and only applies to DOS-based C compilers. It may also have a slightly different name, so check your user's manual.

The **_dos_setvect( )** function puts the address of the interrupt service routine specified by *isr* into the vectored interrupt table at the location specified by *intr*.

Related Function

_dos_getvect( )

#include <dos.h>
unsigned _dos_write(int fd, void __far *buf, unsigned count, unsigned *numwritten);

The **_dos_write( )** function is not defined by the ANSI C standard and only applies to DOS-based C compilers. It may also have a slightly different name, so check your user's manual.

The **_dos_write( )** function writes up to *count* bytes to the file specified by the file descriptor *fd* from the buffer pointed to by *buf*. The number of bytes actually written is returned in the variable pointed to by *numwritten*.

Upon success, **_dos_write( )** returns zero; it returns nonzero on failure. The return value is determined by DOS; you will need DOS technical documentation to determine the nature of any errors that occur. Also, on failure, **errno** will be set to either **EACCES** (access denied) or **EBADF** (file does not exist).

Example

This fragment writes 128 characters to the file described by **fd**:

```
unsigned count
char *buf[128];
  .
  .
  .
if(_dos_write(fd, buf, 128, &count))
  printf("Error writing file.");
```

Related Function

_dos_read( )

#include <dos.h>
void _enable(void);

The **_enable( )** function is not defined by the ANSI C standard and only applies to DOS-based C compilers. It may also have a slightly different name, so check your user's manual.

The **_enable( )** function enables interrupts.

Related Function

_disable( )

#include <dos.h>
unsigned FP_OFF(void __far *ptr)
unsigned FP_SEG (void __far *ptr);

The **FP_OFF( )** and **FP_SEG( )** macros are not defined by the ANSI C standard and only apply to DOS-based C compilers. They may also have slightly different names, so check your user's manual.

The **FP_OFF( )** macro returns the offset portion of the far pointer *ptr*. The **FP_SEG( )** macro returns the segment of the far pointer *ptr*.

Example

This program prints the segment and offset of the far pointer **ptr**:

```
#include <dos.h>
#include <stdlib.h>
#include <stdio.h>


void main(void)
{
  char __far *ptr;

  ptr = (char __far *) malloc(100);

  printf("Segment:offset of ptr: %u %u", FP_SEG(ptr),
        FP_OFF(ptr));
}
```

#include <time.h>
struct tm *gmtime(const time_t *time);

The **gmtime( )** function returns a pointer to a **tm** structure that contains the broken-down form of *time*. The time is represented in Coordinated Universal Time (UTC). The *time* value is generally obtained through a call to **time( )**. If UTC is not supported by the system, a null pointer is returned.

The structure used by **gmtime( )** to hold the broken-down time is statically allocated and is overwritten each time the function is called. To save the contents of the structure, you need to copy it elsewhere.

Example

This program prints both the local time and the UTC of the system:

```
#include <time.h>
#include <stdio.h>

/* Print local and UTC time. */
void main(void)
{
  struct tm *local, *gm;
  time_t t;

  t = time(NULL);
  local = localtime(&t);
  printf("Local time and date: %s\n", asctime(local));
  gm = gmtime(&t);
  printf("Coordinated Universal Time and date: %s", asctime(gm));
}
```

Related Functions

asctime( ), localtime( ), time( )

#include <dos.h>
void _harderr(void (__far *int_handler)( ));
void _hardresume(int code);
void _hardretn(int code);

The **_harderr( )**, **_hardresume( )**, and **_hardretn( )** functions are not defined by the ANSI C standard and only apply to DOS-based C compilers. They may have slightly different names, so check your user's manual.

The **_harderr( )** function allows you to replace DOS's default critical error handler with one of your own. The function is called with the address of the function that is to become the new error handling routine. The error handler is executed each time an interrupt 0x24 occurs.

The error interrupt handler can exit in one of three ways: First, the **_hardresume( )** function causes the handler to exit to DOS, returning the value of *code*. Second, the handler can execute a **return**, which causes an exit to DOS. Third, the handler can return to the program via a call to **_hardretn( )**, with a return value of *code*.

Interrupt service functions are complex, so no example is shown. Also, the implementation of these functions varies greatly from compiler to compiler. Refer to your user's manual for details.

#include <dos.h>
int _int86(int int_num, union _REGS *in_regs, union _REGS *out_regs);
int _int86x(int int_num, union _REGS *in_regs,
union _REGS *out_regs, struct _SREGS *sregs);

The _int86( ) and _int86x( ) functions are not defined by the ANSI C standard and only apply to DOS-based C compilers. They may also have slightly different names, so check your user's manual.

The _int86( ) function executes the software interrupt specified by *int_num*. The contents of the union *in_regs* are first copied into the registers of the processor; then the proper interrupt is executed.

Upon return, the union *out_regs* contains the values of the registers that the CPU has upon return from the interrupt. The value returned by _int86( ) is the value of the AX register at the time of the return.

The union _REGS is defined in the header DOS.H.

The _int86x( ) function is identical to _int86( ), but you can set the values of the ES and DS segment registers by using the *sregs* parameter. Upon return from the call, the contents of the object pointed to by *sregs* contains the values of the current segment registers.

Example

The _int86( ) function is often used to call ROM routines in the BIOS. For example, this function executes an INT 10H function code 0, which sets the video mode to the mode specified by the argument **mode**.

```
#include <dos.h>

set_mode(char mode)
{
  union _REGS in, out;

  in.h.al = mode;
  in.h.ah = 0; /* set mode function number */

  _int86(0x10, &in, &out);
}
```

Related Functions

_bdos( ), _intdos( )

#include <dos.h>
int _intdos(union _REGS *in_regs, union _REGS *out_regs);
int _intdosx(union _REGS *in_regs, union _REGS *out_regs,
struct _SREGS *segregs);

The **_intdos( )** and **_intdosx( )** functions are not defined by the ANSI C standard and only apply to DOS-based C compilers. They may also have slightly different names, so check your user's manual.

The **_intdos( )** function accesses the DOS system function specified by the contents of the union pointed to by *in_regs*. It executes an INT 21H instruction and the outcome of the operation is placed in the union pointed to by *out_regs*. The **_intdos( )** function returns the value of the **AX** register, which is used by DOS to return information. Upon return, an error has occurred if the carry flag is set.

The **_intdos( )** function accesses system calls that either require arguments in registers other than **DX** or **AL**, or that return information in a register other than **AX**.

The union **_REGS** defines the registers of the 8086 family of processors and is found in the DOS.H header file.

For **_intdosx( )**, the value of *segregs* specifies the **DS** and **ES** registers. This function is principally for use in programs compiled with the large data models.

Example

The following program reads the time directly from the system clock, bypassing all of C's time functions:

```
#include <dos.h>
#include <stdio.h>

void main(void)
{
  union _REGS in, out;

  in.h.ah = 0x2c;  /* get time function number */
  intdos(&in, &out);
  printf("Time is %.2d:%.2d:%.2d", out.h.ch, out.h.cl, out.h.dh);
}
```

Related Functions

_bdos( ), **_int86( )**

#include <locale.h>
struct lconv *localeconv(void);

The **localeconv( )** function obtains the current locale settings that relate to numeric values, putting them into a statically allocated structure of type **lconv**. It returns a pointer to that structure. This structure must not be changed by your program.

The **lconv** structure is defined like this:

```
struct lconv {
  char *decimal_point;      /* decimal point character
                             for non-monetary values */
  char *thousands_sep;      /* thousands separator
                             for non-monetary values */
  char *grouping;           /* specifies grouping for
                             non-monetary values */
  char *int_curr_symbol;    /* international currency symbol */
  char *currency_symbol;    /* local currency symbol */
  char *mon_decimal_point;  /* decimal point character
                             for monetary values */
  char *mon_thousands_sep;  /* thousands separator
                             for monetary values */
  char*mon_grouping;        /* specifies grouping for
                             monetary values */
  char *positive_sign;      /* positive value indicator
                             for monetary values */
  char *negative_sign;      /* negative value indicator
                             for monetary values */
  char int_frac_digits;     /* number of digits displayed
                             to the right of the decimal
                             point for monetary values
                             displayed using international
                             format */
  char frac_digits;         /* number of digits displayed
                             to the right of the decimal
                             point for monetary values
                             displayed using local format */
  char p_cs_precedes;       /* 1 if currency symbol precedes
                             positive value,
                             0 if currency symbol
                             follows value */
  char p_sep_by_space;      /* 1 if currency symbol is
                             separated from value by a
                             space, 0 otherwise */
```

```
    char n_cs_precedes;        /* 1 if currency symbol precedes
                                  a negative value, 0 if
                                  currency symbol follows value */
    char n_sep_by_space;       /* 1 if currency symbol is
                                  separated from a negative
                                  value by a space, 0 if
                                  currency symbol follows value */
    char p_sign_posn;          /* indicates position of positive
                                  value symbol */
    char n_sign_posn;          /* indicates position of negative
                                  value symbol */
};
```

Example

The following program displays the decimal point character used by the current locale:

```
#include <stdio.h>
#include <locale.h>

void main(void)
{
  struct lconv lc;

  lc = *localeconv();

  printf("Decimal symbol is: %s\n", lc.decimal_point);
}
```

Related Function

setlocale( )

#include <time.h>
struct tm *localtime(const time_t *time);

The **localtime( )** function returns a pointer to the broken-down form of *time* in the form of a **tm** structure. The time is represented in local time. The *time* value is generally obtained through a call to **time( )**.

The structure used by **localtime( )** to hold the broken-down time is statically allocated and is overwritten each time the function is called. To save the contents of the structure, you need to copy it elsewhere.

Example

This program prints both the local time and the Coordinated Universal Time (UTC) of the system:

```
#include <time.h>
#include <stdio.h>

/* Print local and UTC time. */
void main(void)
{
  struct tm *local;
  time_t t;

  t = time(NULL);
  local = localtime(&t);
  printf("Local time and date: %s\n", asctime(local));
  local = gmtime(&t);
  printf("UTC time and date: %s\n", asctime(local));
}
```

Related Functions

asctime( ), **gmtime( )**, **time( )**

#include <time.h>
time_t mktime(struct tm *time);

The **mktime( )** function returns the calendar time equivalent of the broken-down time specified in the structure pointed to by *time*. This function is primarily used to initialize the system time. The elements **tm_wday** and **tm_yday** are set by the function, so they need not be defined prior to the call.

If **mktime( )** cannot represent the information as a valid calendar time, it returns a –1.

Example

This program tells you what day of the week January 3, 1999 is:

```
#include <time.h>
#include <stdio.h>
```

```
void main(void)
{
  struct tm t;
  time_t t_of_day;

  t.tm_year = 1999-1900;
  t.tm_mon = 0;
  t.tm_mday = 3;
  t.tm_hour = 0;   /* hour, min, sec don't matter */
  t.tm_min = 0;    /* as long as they don't cause a */
  t.tm_sec = 1;    /* new day to occur */
  t.tm_isdst = 0;

  t_of_day = mktime(&t);
  printf(ctime(&t_of_day));
}
```

Related Functions

asctime( ), ctime( ), gmtime( ), time( )

#include <dos.h>
void _segread(struct _SREGS *sregs);

The **_segread( )** function is not defined by the ANSI C standard and only applies to DOS-based C compilers. It may also have a slightly different name, so check your user's manual.

The **_segread( )** function copies the current values of the 8086 (family) segment registers into the structure pointed to by *sregs*.

#include <locale.h>
char *setlocale(int type, const char *locale);

The **setlocale( )** function allows you to query or set certain parameters that are sensitive to the geo-political location where a program is used. For example, in Europe, the comma is sometimes used in place of the decimal point.

If *locale* is null, **setlocale( )** returns a pointer to the current localization string associated with the information specified by *type*. Otherwise, **setlocale( )** attempts to use the specified localization string to set the locale parameters as specified by *type*.

At the time of the call, *type* must be one of the following macros:

LC_ALL
LC_COLLATE
LC_CTYPE
LC_MONETARY
LC_NUMERIC
LC_TIME

LC_ALL refers to all localization categories. **LC_COLLATE** affects the operation of the **strcoll( )** function. **LC_CTYPE** alters the way the character functions work. **LC_MONETARY** determines the monetary format. **LC_NUMERIC** changes the decimal-point character for formatted input/output functions. Finally, **LC_TIME** determines the behavior of the **strftime( )** function.

The ANSI C standard defines two possible strings for *locale*. The first is "C", which specifies a minimal environment for C compilation. The second is " ", the null string, which specifies the implementation-defined default environment. All other values for *locale* are implementation defined and affect portability.

The **setlocale( )** function returns a pointer to a string associated with the *type* parameter. If the request cannot be met, **setlocale( )** returns null.

Example

This program displays the current locale setting:

```
#include <locale.h>
#include <stdio.h>

void main(void)
{
  printf(setlocale(LC_ALL, ""));
}
```

Related Functions

localeconv( ), strcoll( ), strftime( ), time( )

#include <time.h>
size_t strftime(char *str, size_t maxsize, const char *fmt, const struct tm *time);

The **strftime( )** function places formatted time and date information, along with other information, into the string pointed to by *str*. **strftime( )** uses the format commands found in the string pointed to by *fmt* and the broken-down time pointed to by *time*. A maximum of *maxsize* characters is placed into *str*.

The **strftime( )** function works a little like **sprintf( )**. It recognizes a set of format commands that begin with the percent sign (%) and places its formatted output into a string. The format commands specify the exact way various time and date information is represented in *str*. Any other characters found in the format string are placed into *str* unchanged. The time and date displayed are in local time. The format commands are shown in Table 15-1. Notice that many of them are case sensitive.

The **strftime( )** function returns the number of characters placed in the string pointed to by *str*. If an error occurs, the function returns zero.

Command	Replaced by
%a	Abbreviated weekday name
%A	Full weekday name
%b	Abbreviated month name
%B	Full month name
%c	Standard date and time string
%d	Day-of-month as decimal (1-31)
%H	Hour, range (0-23)
%I	Hour, range (1-12)
%j	Day-of-year as decimal (1-366)
%m	Month as decimal (1-12)
%M	Minute as decimal (0-59)
%p	Locale's equivalent of AM or PM
%S	Second as decimal (0-61)
%U	Week-of-year, Sunday being first day (0-52)
%w	Weekday as decimal (0-6, Sunday being 0)
%W	Week-of-year, Monday being first day (0-53)
%x	Standard date string
%X	Standard time string
%y	Year in decimal without century (00-99)
%Y	Year including century as decimal
%Z	Timezone name
%%	The percent sign

Table 15-1. The **strftime( )** Format Commands

Example

Assuming that **ltime** points to a structure that contains 10:00:00 AM, the following fragment prints **It is now 10 AM**:

```
strftime(str, 100, "It is now %H %p.", ltime)
printf(str);
```

Related Functions

gmtime( ), **localtime( )**, **time( )**

#include <time.h>
time_t time(time_t *time);

The **time( )** function returns the current calendar time of the system. If the system has no time, **time( )** returns −1.

The **time( )** function can be called either with a null pointer or with a pointer to a variable of type **time_t**. If the latter is used, the variable pointed to by *time* is also assigned the calendar time.

Example

This program displays the local time defined by the system:

```
#include <time.h>
#include <stdio.h>

void main(void)
{
  struct tm *ptr;
  time_t lt;

  lt = time(NULL);
  ptr = localtime(&lt);
  printf(asctime(ptr));
}
```

Related Functions

ctime( ), **gmtime( )**, **localtime( )**, **strftime( )**

Chapter Sixteen

Dynamic Allocation

There are two primary ways in which a C program can store information in the main memory of the computer. The first method involves global and local variables—including arrays and structures. Storage for global (and static local) variables is fixed at compile time and remains constant throughout your program's run time. Storage for a local variable is allocated from the stack each time the variable comes into existence. Although global and local variables are efficiently implemented in C, they require that the programmer know, in advance, the amount of storage needed for every situation that the program may encounter—something that is not always possible. In fact, some programs need to be able to adjust their storage requirements in response to events that can only be known at run time.

To provide a means by which a program can obtain storage at run time, C includes a *dynamic allocation* subsystem. Dynamic allocation is the second way that a program can acquire storage for data. In this method, storage is allocated from free memory as needed during the execution of the program. The region of free memory that is used for dynamic allocation is called the *heap*. Traditionally, the heap lies between your program and its permanent storage area, and the stack. Figure 16-1 shows conceptually how a C program would appear in memory. (For the 8086 family of processors, the location of the heap changes depending upon what memory model is used. 8086 memory models are discussed shortly.) The stack grows downward as it is used. The amount of memory it needs is determined by how your program is

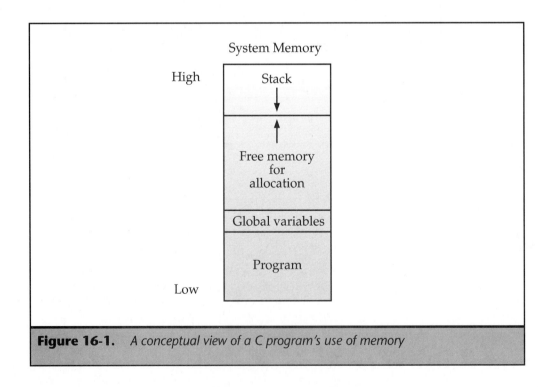

Figure 16-1. *A conceptual view of a C program's use of memory*

designed. For example, a program with many recursive functions makes much greater demands on the stack than one that does not have recursive functions, because local variables are stored on the stack. The memory required for the program's code and global data is fixed during program execution. Memory to satisfy a dynamic allocation request is taken from the heap, starting just above the global variables and growing towards the stack. As you might guess, under fairly extreme cases the stack may run into the heap. The fact that the heap may become exhausted implies that a memory allocation request may fail. (And, indeed, it can.)

At the core of C's dynamic allocation system are the functions **malloc( )** and **free( )** which are part of the standard C library. Each time a **malloc( )** memory request is made, a portion of the remaining free memory is allocated. Each time **free( )** is called, memory is returned to the system. The most common way to implement **malloc( )** and **free( )** is to organize the free memory into a linked list. However, the memory management method is implementation-dependent.

The ANSI C standard specifies that the prototypes for those dynamic allocation functions defined by the standard are in STDLIB.H.

The ANSI C standard defines only four functions for the dynamic allocation system: **calloc( )**, **malloc( )**, **free( )**, and **realloc( )**. However, this book examines several others that are in wide use—especially in the 8086 family of CPU environments. The basis for the nonstandard functions are those defined by Microsoft C/C++, but most compilers will have similar functions. (But the names may differ.) The nonstandard functions use the header file MALLOC.H.

Some of these additional allocation functions are necessary to support the segmented architecture of the 8086 family of processors efficiently. (These functions do not apply to other types of processors or to the newer members of the 8086 family when not running in DOS-compatibility mode.) Because of the segmented memory of the 8086 family of processors, three nonstandard type modifiers are generally supported by compilers built for these processors. For many compilers, these new types are called **near**, **far,** and **huge**. However, Microsoft has called these __**near**, __**far**, and __**huge**. Since the Microsoft version of the 8086-based allocation functions are discussed in this chapter, the Microsoft version of these keywords is used. (The leading underscores ensure ANSI compatibility.) These types are used to create pointers of a type other than that normally used by the memory model used to compile the program. The following discussion explains the 8086 segmented memory models.

8086 Segmented Memory Models

When operating in segmented mode, the 8086 family of processors views memory as a collection of 64K chunks, each called a *segment*. Each byte of memory is defined by its segment address (held in a segment register of the CPU) and its offset (held in another register) within that segment. Both the segment and offset use 16-bit values. When a memory address being accessed lies within the current segment, only the 16-bit offset need be loaded to access a specific byte of memory. However, if the memory address lies outside the current segment, both the 16-bit segment and the 16-bit offset need to be loaded. Thus, when accessing memory within the current segment, the C compiler can treat a pointer or a call or jump instruction as a 16-bit object. When accessing memory outside the current segment, the compiler must treat a pointer or call or jump instruction as a 32-bit entity.

Given the segmented nature of the 8086 family, you can organize memory into one of these six models (shown in order of increasing execution time):

Tiny	All segment registers are set to the same value and all addressing is done using 16 bits. This means that the code, data, and stack must all fit within the same 64K segment. Fastest program execution.
Small	All code must fit in one 64K segment and all data must fit in a second 64K segment. All pointers are 16 bits. As fast as tiny model.
Medium	All data must fit in one 64K segment, but the code may use multiple segments. All pointers to data are 16 bits, but all jumps and calls require 32-bit addresses. Quick access to data, slower code execution.
Compact	All code must fit in one 64K segment, but the data may use multiple segments. However, no data item can exceed 64K. All pointers to data are 32 bits, but jumps and calls may use 16-bit addresses. Slow access to data, faster code execution.
Large	Both code and data may use multiple segments. All pointers are 32 bits. However, no single data item can exceed 64K. Slower program execution.
Huge	Both code and data may use multiple segments. All pointers are 32 bits. Single data items can exceed 64K. Slowest program execution.

As you might guess, it is much faster to access memory via 16-bit pointers than 32-bit pointers because half as many bits need to be loaded into the CPU for each memory reference.

Occasionally, you will need to reference a pointer that is different from the default provided by your memory model. Many 8086-based C compilers allow pointers of either 16 or 32 bits to be explicitly created by the program, thus overriding the default memory model. Typically, this occurs when a program requires a lot of data for one specific operation. In such cases, a **far** pointer is created and the memory is allocated with a nonstandard version of **malloc( )** that allocates memory from outside the default data segment. In this way, all other memory accesses remain fast and execution time does not suffer as much as if a larger model were used. The reverse can also happen: A program that uses a larger model may establish a **near** pointer to a piece of frequently accessed memory to enhance performance. Because the actual methods of overriding the default memory model differ from compiler to compiler, check your user's manual for details.

Many 8086-based C compilers restrict the size of a single data item to 64K—the size of one segment. However, you can use the __**huge** modifier to create a pointer that can point to an object larger than 64K.

#include <malloc.h>
void *_alloca(size_t size);

The **_alloca( )** function is not defined by the ANSI C standard. It may also have a slightly different name, so check your user's manual.

The **_alloca( )** function allocates *size* bytes of memory from the system stack (not the heap) and returns a character pointer to it. A null pointer is returned if the allocation request cannot be honored.

Memory allocated with **_alloca( )** is automatically released when the function that called **_alloca( )** returns. This means that you should never use a pointer generated by **_alloca( )** as an argument to **free( )**.

Example

The following code allocates 80 bytes from the stack by using **_alloca( )**:

```
#include <malloc.h>
#include <stdio.h>

void main(void)
{
  char *str;

  if(!(str = _alloca(80))) {
    printf("Allocation error - aborting.");
    exit(1);
  }
  .
  .
  .
}
```

Related Functions

malloc( ), stackavail( )

#include <stdlib.h>
void *calloc(size_t num, size_t size);

The **calloc( )** function allocates an amount of memory equal to *num* * *size*. That is, **calloc( )** allocates sufficient memory for an array of *num* objects, each object being *size* bytes long.

The **calloc( )** function returns a pointer to the first byte of the allocated region. If there is not enough memory to satisfy the request, a null pointer is returned. You should always verify that the return value is not a null pointer before using it. Memory allocated using **calloc( )** is freed using **free( )**.

Example

This function returns a pointer to a dynamically allocated array of 100 **floats**:

```
#include <stdlib.h>
#include <stdio.h>

float *get_mem(void)
{
  float *p;

  p = calloc(100, sizeof(float));
  if(!p) {
    printf("Allocation error - aborting.");
    exit(1);
  }
  return p;
}
```

Related Functions

free( ), **malloc( )**, **realloc( )**

#include <malloc.h>
void __far * _fcalloc(size_t num, size_t size);

The **_fcalloc( )** function is not defined by the ANSI C standard and applies mostly to 8086-based C compilers. It may also have a slightly different name, so check your user's manual.

The **_fcalloc( )** function allocates an amount of memory equal to *num * size*. That is, **_fcalloc( )** allocates sufficient memory for an array of *num* objects, each object being *size* bytes long. The memory is allocated from outside the default data segment. (It is otherwise similar to **calloc( )**. See **calloc( )** for an example.)

The **_fcalloc( )** function returns a pointer to the first byte of the allocated region. If there is not enough memory to satisfy the request, a null pointer is returned. You should always verify that the return value is not a null pointer before using it.

Related Functions

_ffree( ), **_fmalloc( )**, **_frealloc( )**

#include <malloc.h>
void _ffree(void __far *ptr);

The **_ffree( )** function is not defined by the ANSI C standard and applies mostly to 8086-based compilers. It may also have a slightly different name, so check your user's manual.

The **_ffree( )** function returns to the system the memory pointed to by the **far** pointer *ptr*. This makes the memory available for future allocation. The pointer must have previously been allocated by using **_fmalloc( )**, **_frealloc( )**, or **_fcalloc( )**. It cannot free pointers allocated by other allocation functions. Using an invalid pointer in the call usually destroys the memory management mechanism and causes a system crash.

Example

This program allocates memory from outside the default data segment and then frees it. Note the use of __**far** to establish a **far** pointer. Remember that __**far** is not part of standard C and relates mostly to compilers that run on the 8086 family of processors.

```
#include <malloc.h>
#include <stdio.h>
#include <stdlib.h>

void main(void)
{
  char __far *str;

  if((str = _fmalloc(128))==NULL) {
    printf("Allocation error - aborting.");
    exit(1);
  }

  /* now free the memory */
  _ffree(str);
}
```

Related Functions

_fcalloc( ), _fmalloc( ), _frealloc( )

#include <malloc.h>
void __far *_fmalloc(size_t size);

The _fmalloc( ) function is not defined by the ANSI C standard and applies mostly to 8086-based C compilers. It may also have a slightly different name, so check your user's manual.

The _fmalloc( ) function returns a **far** pointer to the first byte of a region of memory of size *size* that has been allocated from outside the default data segment. If there is insufficient memory outside the default data segment, **_fmalloc( )** returns a null pointer. You must always verify that the return value is not a null pointer before using it.

Example

This function allocates sufficient memory from outside the default data segment to hold structures of type **addr**. Note the use of __far to establish a **far** pointer. Remember that __far is not part of standard C and relates mostly to compilers that run on the 8086 family of processors.

```
#include <malloc.h>
#include <stdlib.h>
#include <stdio.h>

struct addr {
  char name[40];
  char street[40];
  char city[40];
  char state[3];
  char zip[10];
};

struct addr __far *get_struct(void)
{
  struct addr __far *p;

  if((p = _fmalloc(sizeof(struct addr)))==NULL) {
    printf("Allocation error - aborting.");
    exit(1);
  }
  return p;
}
```

Related Functions

_fcalloc( ), _ffree( ), _frealloc( )

#include <malloc.h>
size_t _fmsize(void __far *ptr);

The **_fmsize( )** function is not defined by the ANSI C standard and applies mostly to 8086-based compilers. It may also have a slightly different name, so check your user's manual.

The **_fmsize( )** function returns the number of bytes in the allocated block of memory pointed to by the **far** pointer *ptr*. This memory must have been allocated with **_fmalloc( )**, **_frealloc( )**, or **_fcalloc( )**.

Example

This program displays the size of the block of memory required to hold the structure **addr**:

```
#include <malloc.h>
#include <stdio.h>

struct addr {
  char name[40];
  char street[40];
  char city[40];
  char state[3];
  char zip[10];
};

void main(void)
{
  struct addr __far *p;

  p = _fmalloc(sizeof(struct addr));

  printf("Size of block is %u.", _fmsize(p));
}
```

Related Function

_fmalloc( )

#include <malloc.h>
void __far*_frealloc(void __far *ptr, size_t size);

The _frealloc( ) function is not defined by the ANSI C standard and applies mostly to 8086-based compilers. It may also have a slightly different name, so check your user's manual.

The _frealloc( ) function changes the size of the previously allocated memory pointed to by *ptr* to that specified by *size*. The value of *size* may be greater or less than the original. The memory pointed to by *ptr* must have been previously allocated using _fmalloc( ) or _fcalloc( ).

_frealloc( ) may need to move the original block of memory in order to increase its size. If this occurs, the contents of the old block are copied into the new block—no information is lost. If *ptr* is null, _frealloc( ) simply allocates *size* bytes of memory, and returns a pointer to it. If *size* is zero, the memory pointed to by *ptr* is freed.

_frealloc( ) returns a pointer to the resized block of memory, which will be allocated from the **far** heap. If there is not enough free memory in the heap to allocate *size* bytes, a null pointer is returned and the original block is left unchanged.

_frealloc( ) is the **far** version of **realloc( )**. See **realloc( )** for an example.

Related Functions

_fcalloc( ), _ffree( ), _fmalloc( )

#include <stdlib.h>
void free(void *ptr);

The **free( )** function returns to the heap the memory pointed to by *ptr*, making the memory available for future allocation.

free( ) must only be called with a pointer that was previously allocated with one of the dynamic allocation system's functions (either **malloc( )**, **realloc( )**, or **calloc( )**). Using an invalid pointer in the call will probably destroy the memory management mechanism and cause a system crash.

Example

This program allocates room for the strings entered by the user and then frees the memory:

```c
#include <stdlib.h>
#include <stdio.h>

void main(void)
```

```
{
  char *str[100];
  int i;

  for(i=0; i<100; i++) {
    if((str[i] = malloc(128))==NULL) {
      printf("Allocation error - aborting.");
      exit(1);
    }
    gets(str[i]);
  }

  /* now free the memory */
  for(i=0; i<100; i++) free(str[i]);
}
```

Related Functions

calloc( ), malloc( ), realloc( )

#include <malloc.h>
unsigned _freect(size_t size);

The **_freect( )** function is not defined by the ANSI C standard. It may also have a slightly different name, so check your user's manual.

The **_freect( )** function returns the approximate number of items of size *size* that can be allocated from the free memory left in the heap.

Example

This program displays the number of floating-point values that may be stored in the heap:

```
#include <malloc.h>
#include <stdio.h>

void main(void)
{
  printf("Number of floats that will fit in the heap: ");
  printf("%u.\n", _freect(sizeof(float)));
}
```

Related Functions

malloc( ), _memavl( )

#include <malloc.h>
void __huge *_halloc(long num, size_t size);

The **_halloc( )** function is not defined by the ANSI C standard and applies mostly to 8086-based C compilers. It may also have a slightly different name, so check your user's manual.

The **_halloc( )** function returns a **__huge** pointer to the first byte of a region of memory of size *size * num* that has been allocated from outside the default data segment. That is, *num* objects of size *size* bytes are allocated. If the allocation request fails due to insufficient free memory, **_halloc( )** returns a null pointer. You should always verify that the return value is not a null pointer before using it.

The **_halloc( )** function may be used to allocate a block of memory larger than 64K on 8086-based computers. The value of *size* may need to be an even number.

Example

This function allocates sufficient memory from outside the default data segment to hold 128,000 bytes. Note the use of **__huge** to establish a **huge** pointer. Remember that **__huge** is not part of standard C and relates mostly to compilers that run on the 8086 family of processors.

```
#include <malloc.h>
#include <stdio.h>
#include <stdlib.h>

char __huge *get_ram(void)
{
  char __huge *p;

  if((p = _halloc(1, 128000))==NULL) {
    printf("Allocation error - aborting.");
    exit(1);
  }
  return p;
}
```

Related Functions

calloc( ), _hfree( ), malloc(), realloc( )

#include <malloc.h>
void _hfree(void __huge *ptr);

The **_hfree( )** function is not defined by the ANSI C standard and applies mostly to 8086-based C compilers. It may also have a slightly different name, so check your user's manual.

The **_hfree( )** function returns to the system the memory pointed to by the **huge** pointer *ptr*. This makes the memory available for future allocation. The pointer must have previously been allocated with **_halloc( )**. Using an invalid pointer in the call will probably destroy the memory management mechanism and cause a system crash.

Example

This program first allocates memory from outside the default data segment and then frees it:

```
#include <malloc.h>
#include <stdlib.h>
#include <stdio.h>

void main(void)
{
  char __huge *large;

  if((large = _halloc(1, 128000))==NULL) {
    printf("Allocation error - aborting.");
    exit(1);
  }

  /* now free the memory */
  _hfree(large);
}
```

Related Functions

calloc( ), _halloc( ), malloc( ), realloc( )

#include <stdlib.h>
void *malloc(size_t size);

The **malloc( )** function returns a pointer to the first byte of a region of memory of size *size* that has been allocated from the heap. If there is insufficient memory in the heap to satisfy the request, **malloc( )** returns a null pointer. You must always verify that the return value is not a null pointer before using it. Attempting to use a null pointer will usually result in a system crash.

Example

This function allocates sufficient memory to hold structures of type **addr**:

```
struct addr {
  char name[40];
  char street[40];
  char city[40];
  char state[3];
  char zip[10];
};

struct addr *get_struct(void)
{
  struct addr *p;

  if((p = malloc(sizeof(struct addr)))==NULL) {
    printf("Allocation error - aborting.");
    exit(1);
  }
  return p;
}
```

Related Functions

calloc( ), free( ), realloc( )

#include <malloc.h>
size_t _memavl(void);

The **_memavl( )** function is not defined by the ANSI C standard. It may also have a slightly different name, so check your user's manual.

The **_memavl( )** function returns the approximate number of bytes of free memory left in the heap.

Example

This program prints the number of bytes available for allocation:

```
#include <malloc.h>
#include <stdio.h>

void main(void)
{
  printf("Number of bytes available for allocation: ");
  printf("%u.", _memavl());
}
```

Related Functions

free( ), _freect( ), malloc( )

#include <malloc.h>
size_t _msize(void *ptr);

The **_msize( )** function is not defined by the ANSI C standard. It may also have a slightly different name, so check your user's manual.

The **_msize( )** function returns the number of bytes in the allocated block of memory pointed to by *ptr*. This memory must have been allocated with **malloc( )**, **realloc( )**, or **calloc( )**.

Example

This program displays the size of the block of memory that is required to hold the structure **addr**:

```
#include <malloc.h>
#include <stdio.h>

struct addr {
  char name[40];
  char street[40];
  char city[40];
  char state[3];
  char zip[10];
};

void main(void)
{
```

```
    struct addr *p;

    p = malloc(sizeof(struct addr));

    printf("Size of block is %u.", _msize(p));
}
```

Related Functions

malloc( ), realloc( )

#include <malloc.h>
void __near *_ncalloc(size_t num, size_t size);

The _ncalloc( ) function is not defined by the ANSI C standard and applies mostly to 8086-based C compilers. It may also have a slightly different name, so check your user's manual.

The _ncalloc( ) function allocates an amount of memory equal to *num* * *size*. That is, _ncalloc( ) allocates sufficient memory for an array of *num* objects, each object being *size* bytes long. The memory is allocated from inside the default data segment. (It is otherwise similar to **calloc( )**. See **calloc( )** for an example.)

The _ncalloc( ) function returns a pointer to the first byte of the allocated region. If there is not enough memory to satisfy the request, a null pointer is returned. You should always verify that the return value is not a null pointer before using it.

Related Functions

_nfree( ), _nmalloc( ), _nrealloc( )

#include <malloc.h>
void _nfree(char __near *ptr);

The _nfree( ) function is not defined by the ANSI C standard and applies mostly to 8086-based C compilers. It may also have a slightly different name, so check your user's manual.

The _nfree( ) function returns to the system the memory pointed to by the **near** pointer *ptr*. This makes the memory available for future allocation. The pointer must have previously been allocated with **_nmalloc( )**, **_ncalloc( )**, or **_nrealloc( )**. Using an invalid pointer in the call will probably destroy the memory management mechanism and cause a system crash.

Example

This program first allocates memory from inside the default data segment and then frees it. Note the use of __near to establish a near pointer. Remember that __near is not part of standard C and relates mostly to compilers that run on the 8086 family of processors.

```
#include <malloc.h>
#include <stdio.h>
#include <stdlib.h>

void main(void)
{
  char __near *str;

  if((str = _nmalloc(128))==NULL) {
    printf("Allocation error - aborting.");
    exit(1);
  }

  /* now free the memory */
  _nfree(str);
}
```

Related Functions

_ncalloc( ), _nmalloc( ), _nrealloc( )

#include <malloc.h>
char __near *_nmalloc(size_t size);

The _nmalloc( ) function is not defined by the ANSI C standard and applies mostly to 8086-based C compilers. It may also have a slightly different name, so check your user's manual.

The _nmalloc( ) function returns a near pointer to the first byte of a region of memory of size *size* that has been allocated from inside the default data segment. This is only meaningful for programs compiled for one of the 8086 large data model addressing modes. Using a near pointer allows data to be accessed using a 16-bit (rather than a 32-bit) pointer. If the allocation request fails due to insufficient free memory, _nmalloc( ) returns a null pointer. You must always verify that the return value is not a null pointer before using it.

Example

This function allocates sufficient memory from inside the default data segment to hold 128 bytes. Note the use of __**near** to establish a **near** pointer. Remember that __**near** is not part of standard C and relates mostly to compilers that run on the 8086 family of processors.

```
char __near *get_near_ram(void)
{
  char __near *p;

  if((p = _nmalloc(128))==NULL) {
    printf("Allocation error - aborting.");
    exit(1);
  }
  return p;
}
```

Related Functions

_ncalloc( ), _nfree( ), _nrealloc( )

#include <malloc.h>
size_t _nmsize(void __near *ptr);

The _nmsize( ) function is not defined by the ANSI C standard and applies mostly to 8086-based compilers. It may also have a slightly different name, so check your user's manual.

The _nmsize( ) function returns the number of bytes in the allocated block of memory pointed to by the **near** pointer *ptr*. This memory must have been allocated with _nmalloc( ), _nrealloc( ), or _ncalloc( ).

Example

This program displays the size of the block of memory that is required to hold the structure **addr**:

```
#include <malloc.h>
#include <stdio.h>

struct addr {
  char name[40];
  char street[40];
  char city[40];
```

```
   char state[3];
   char zip[10];
};

void main(void)
{
   struct addr __near *p;

   p = _nmalloc(sizeof(struct addr));

   printf("Size of block is %u.", _nmsize(p));
}
```

Related Function

_nmalloc( )

#include <malloc.h>
void __near*_nrealloc(void __near *ptr, size_t size);

The **_nrealloc( )** function is not defined by the ANSI C standard and applies mostly to 8086-based compilers. It may also have a slightly different name, so check your user's manual.

The **_nrealloc( )** function changes the size of the previously allocated memory pointed to by *ptr* to that specified by *size*. The value of *size* may be greater or less than the original. The memory pointed to by *ptr* must have been previously allocated using **_nmalloc( )** or **_ncalloc( )**.

_nrealloc( ) may need to move the original block of memory in order to increase its size. If this occurs, the contents of the old block are copied into the new block—no information is lost. If *ptr* is null, **_nrealloc( )** simply allocates *size* bytes of memory, and returns a pointer to it. If *size* is zero, the memory pointed to by *ptr* is freed.

_nrealloc( ) returns a pointer to the resized block of memory, which will be allocated from the **near** heap. If there is not enough free memory in the heap to allocate *size* bytes, a null pointer is returned and the original block is left unchanged.

_nrealloc( ) is the **near** version of **realloc( )**. See **realloc( )** for an example.

Related Functions

_ncalloc( ), _nfree( ), _nmalloc( )

#include <stdlib.h>
void *realloc(void *ptr, size_t size);

The **realloc( )** function changes the size of the previously allocated memory pointed to by *ptr* to that specified by *size*. The value of *size* may be greater or less than the original.

realloc( ) may need to move the original block of memory in order to increase its size. If this occurs, the contents of the old block are copied into the new block—no information is lost. If *ptr* is null, **realloc( )** simply allocates *size* bytes of memory, and returns a pointer to it. If *size* is zero, the memory pointed to by *ptr* is freed.

realloc( ) returns a pointer to the resized block of memory. If there is not enough free memory in the heap to allocate *size* bytes, a null pointer is returned and the original block is left unchanged.

Example

This program first allocates 17 characters, copies the string "This is 16 chars" into them, and then uses **realloc( )** to increase the size to 18 in order to place a period at the end.

```
#include <stdlib.h>
#include <stdio.h>
#include <string.h>

void main(void)
{
  char *p;

  p = malloc(17);
  if(!p) {
    printf("Allocation error - aborting.");
    exit(1);
  }

  strcpy(p, "This is 16 chars");

  p = realloc(p, 18);
  if(!p) {
    printf("Allocation error - aborting.");
    exit(1);
  }

  strcat(p, ".");

  printf(p);

  free(p);
}
```

Related Functions

calloc( ), free( ), malloc( )

#include <malloc.h>
size_t _stackavail(void)

The _stackavail( ) function is not defined by the ANSI C standard. It may also have a slightly different name, so check your user's manual.

The _stackavail( ) function returns the approximate number of bytes available on the stack that may be allocated using _alloca( ).

You can also use _stackavail( ) to predict possible heap-stack collisions that could be generated by recursive routines, as illustrated by the example that follows.

Example

The function **recurse( )** calls itself indefinitely, using up stack space with each call, until the stack size has reached a dangerously low level.

```
#include <malloc.h>
#include <stdio.h>

void recurse(void);

void main(void)
{
  recurse();
}

/* This routine will call itself until a heap-stack
   collision becomes a "real threat".
*/
void recurse(void)
{
  printf("%u\n", stackavail());
  if(stackavail() < 1000) return;
  recurse();
}
```

Related Functions

_alloca( ), _freect( ), _memavl( )

Chapter Seventeen

Screen and Graphics Functions

A lthough the ANSI standard for C does not define screen control or graphics functions, they are important to most contemporary programming tasks. The ANSI C standard does not define these types of functions because of wide differences between the capabilities and interfaces of different types of hardware. Even compilers designed for the same environment usually implement screen and graphics functions very differently. However, because of their importance and widespread use, coverage of a representative set of these functions is required. Towards this end, this chapter describes the most generalizable screen and graphics functions as defined by Microsoft C/C++. These functions are designed for DOS, but are similar in nature to those engineered for other operating systems. Remember, the graphics functions supplied with your compiler may differ, but the principles will be similar.

NOTE: The functions described in this chapter do not apply to Windows. Windows provides its own set of graphics functions, which are part of Windows' API (Application Program Interface). If you will be creating graphics programs in a Windows environment, you will need to use the API graphics functions.

The prototypes for Microsoft's screen and graphics functions are contained in GRAPH.H, along with several structure types, which are discussed as required.

This chapter first discusses various video modes available for the PC. This information relates to a number of the graphics functions.

PC Video Modes

As you probably know, there are several different types of PC video adapters in common use, including the monochrome, the CGA (Color Graphics Adapter), the EGA (Enhanced Graphics Adapter), the VGA (Video Graphics Array), and the Super VGA. Together, these adapters support several different modes of video operation. Table 17-1 summarizes these video modes. As you can see, some modes are for text and some are for graphics. In a text mode, only text may be displayed. In a graphics mode, both text and graphics can be displayed.

NOTE: If your system has a Super VGA, then it can support high-resolution graphics modes beyond those described in Table 17-1. These extended modes are non-standard and may differ among Super VGA adapters. You will need to consult your compiler manual for details concerning support for these extended modes.

The smallest user-addressable part of the screen in a text mode is one character. The smallest user-addressable part of the screen in a graphics mode is one pixel.

Mode	Type	Graphics Dimensions	Text Dimensions
0	Text, b/w	n/a	40x25
1	Text, 16 colors	n/a	40x25
2	Text, b/w	n/a	80x25
3	Text, 16 colors	n/a	80x25
4	Graphics, 4 colors	320x200	40x25
5	Graphics, 4 gray tones	320x200	40x25
6	Graphics, 2 colors	640x200	80x25
7	Text, b/w	n/a	80x25
8	PC*jr* graphics 16 colors (Obsolete)	160x200	20x25
8	Hercules Graphics, 2 colors	720x348	80x25
9	PC*jr* graphics 16 colors (Obsolete)	320x200	40x25
10	Reserved		
11	Reserved		
12	Reserved		
13	Graphics, 16 colors	320x200	40x25
14	Graphics, 16 colors	640x200	80x25
15	Graphics, 2 colors	640x350	80x25
16	Graphics, 16 colors	640x350	80x25
17	Graphics, 2 colors	640x480	80x30
18	Graphics, 16 colors	640x480	80x30
19	Graphics, 256 colors	320x200	40x25

Table 17-1. *Screen Modes for Various Video Adapters*

Actually, the term *pixel* originally referred to the smallest individual phosphor element on the video monitor that could be individually energized by the scan beam. However, the term has been generalized to refer to the smallest addressable point on a graphics display, given the current graphics mode.

In a text mode, individual character locations on the screen are referenced by their row and column numbers. For many implementations, the coordinate of the upper-left corner is location 1,1 when operating in a text mode. In a graphics mode, individual pixels are referenced by their X,Y coordinates, with X being the horizontal axis. In graphics modes, the upper-left corner of the screen is usually location 0,0. (The Microsoft screen and graphics functions described here reflect the common usage: the text origin is 1,1 and the graphics origin is 0,0.)

The text screen examples in this chapter use video mode 3, the 80-column color mode. The graphics routines use video mode 18. If your hardware does not support one or both of these modes, you will have to make the appropriate changes to the examples.

When in a color text mode, you may specify what color the text is displayed in. The colors and their integer equivalents are shown here:

Text Color	Value
Black	0
Blue	1
Green	2
Cyan	3
Red	4
Magenta	5
Brown	6
Lightgray	7
Darkgray	8
Lightblue	9
Lightgreen	10
Lightcyan	11
Lightred	12
Lightmagenta	13
Yellow	14
White	15

Setting the high-order bit by adding 128 to the color makes the text blink.

The text background colors are shown here:

Background Color	Value
Black	0
Blue	1
Green	2
Cyan	3
Red	4
Magenta	5
Brown	6

For the color graphics modes, the background colors are shown here:

Background Color	Value
Black	0
Blue	1
Green	2
Cyan	3
Red	4
Magenta	5
Brown	6
Lightgray	7
Darkgray	8
Lightblue	9
Lightgreen	10
Lightcyan	11
Lightred	12
Lightmagenta	13
Yellow	14
White	15

In a color graphics mode, the foreground color is determined by both the value of the color and the currently selected palette. In CGA four-color graphics video mode 4, you have four colors per palette and four palettes from which to choose. The colors are numbered 0 through 3, with 0 always being the background color. The palettes are also numbered 0 through 3. The palettes and their associated colors are shown in Table 17-2. The **_selectpalette( )** function allows you to change palettes.

In EGA/VGA 16-color mode, a palette consists of 16 colors, selected out of a possible 64 colors. The default values are shown here:

Color	Value
Black	0
Blue	1
Green	2
Cyan	3
Red	4
Magenta	5
Brown	6
Lightgray	7
Darkgray	8
Lightblue	9
Lightgreen	10
Lightcyan	11
Lightred	12
Lightmagenta	13
Yellow	14
White	15

Palette	Color Number		
	1	2	3
0	Green	Red	Brown
1	Cyan	Magenta	White
2	Lightgreen	Lightred	Yellow
3	Lightcyan	Lightmagenta	White

Table 17-2.   *The Palettes and Colors in Video Mode 4*

To change an EGA/VGA palette, use **_remapallpalette( )**, which maps the colors that you select onto the palette.

#include <graph.h>
short __far _arc(short x1, short y1, short x2, short y2,
short x3, short y3, short x4, short y4);

The **_arc( )** function draws an arc. The arc is a portion of an ellipse defined by a bounding rectangle whose upper-left corner is at *x1, y1* and whose lower-right corner is at *x2, y2*. (The rectangle is not displayed.) The arc begins at the point at which a line drawn from the center of the ellipse to *x3,y3* intersects the ellipse and ends at the point at which a line drawn from the center of the ellipse to *x4,y4* intersects the ellipse. (This process is depicted in Figure 17-1.) The arc is displayed in the current drawing color.

The **_arc( )** function returns true if successful; it returns zero if an error occurs.

Example

This program displays an arc:

```
#include <graph.h>
#include <conio.h>

void main(void)
{
  _setvideomode(_VRES16COLOR);

  _arc(100, 100, 200, 200, 100, 100, 200, 200);
  getche();

  _setvideomode(_DEFAULTMODE);
}
```

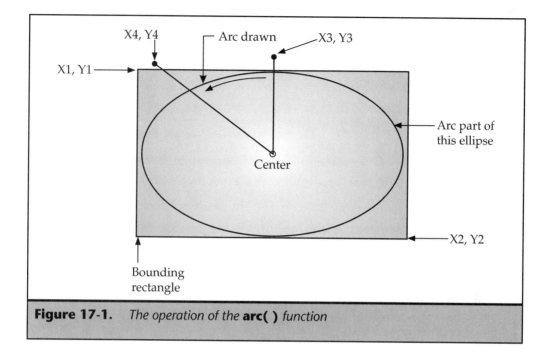

Figure 17-1. *The operation of the* **arc( )** *function*

Related Functions
_ellipse( ), _lineto( ), _rectangle( )

#include <graph.h>
void __far _clearscreen(short region);

The **_clearscreen( )** function clears the specified region of the screen using the current background color. This function works for both text and graphics video modes. The values of *region* are **_GCLEARSCREEN**, which clears the entire screen; **_GVIEWPORT**, which clears a graphics viewport; and **_GWINDOW**, which clears a text window. These macros are defined by Microsoft in GRAPH.H.

Example
This program clears the screen:

```
#include <graph.h>

void main(void)
{
  _clearscreen(_GCLEARSCREEN);
}
```

Related Functions

_settextwindow( ), _setviewport( )

#include <graph.h>
short __far _ellipse(short fill, short x1, short y1,
short x2, short y2);

The **_ellipse( )** function draws an ellipse using the current drawing color bounded by the rectangle defined by *x1,y1* and *x2,y2*. (The rectangle is not displayed.) If *fill* has the value **_GFILLINTERIOR**, the ellipse is filled using the current fill color and style. If *fill* has the value **_GBORDER**, the ellipse is not filled. These macros are defined by Microsoft in GRAPH.H.

If the ellipse can be drawn, **_ellipse( )** returns true. Otherwise, it returns zero.

Example

The following program draws an ellipse.

```
#include <graph.h>
#include <conio.h>

void main(void)
{
  _setvideomode(_VRES16COLOR);
  _setcolor(3);
  _ellipse(_GBORDER, 100, 100, 300, 200);
  getche();

  _setvideomode(_DEFAULTMODE);
}
```

Related Functions

_arc( ), _lineto( ), _rectangle( )

#include <graph.h>
short _ _far _floodfill(short x, short y, short color);

The **_floodfill( )** function fills an enclosed region with the current fill color and style. The region filled must be completely enclosed by the color specified by *color*. (That is, *color* specifies the color of the region's boundary.) The point specified by *x,y* must be inside the region to be filled.

The **_floodfill( )** function returns true if successful, and zero if an error occurs.

Example

This program draws an ellipse and then uses **_floodfill( )** to fill it:

```
#include <graph.h>
#include <conio.h>

void main(void)
{
  short color;

  _setvideomode(_VRES16COLOR);
  color = _getcolor();
  _ellipse(_GBORDER, 100, 100, 300, 200);
  _setcolor(2);
  _floodfill(150, 150, color);
  getche();

  _setvideomode(_DEFAULTMODE);
}
```

Related Function

_setfillmask( )

#include <graph.h>
long __far _getbkcolor(void);

The **_getbkcolor( )** function returns the value of the current background color.

Example

This program displays the default background color:

```
#include <graph.h>
#include <conio.h>
#include <stdio.h>

void main(void)
{
  _setvideomode(_VRES16COLOR);

  printf("Background color is %ld.", _getbkcolor());
  getche();

  _setvideomode(_DEFAULTMODE);
}
```

Related Function

_setbkcolor( )

#include <graph.h>
short __far _getcolor(void);

The _getcolor( ) function returns the value of the current drawing color. By default, the current drawing color has the highest value allowed by the video mode currently in use. You can use this fact to determine the valid range of colors (starting at zero) for a given mode.

Example

This program displays the value of the maximum drawing color:

```
#include <graph.h>
#include <conio.h>
#include <stdio.h>

void main(void)
{
  short color;

  _setvideomode(_VRES16COLOR);

  color = _getcolor();
  printf("Color is %hd.", color);
  getche();

  _setvideomode(_DEFAULTMODE);
}
```

Related Function

_setcolor( )

#include <graph.h>
struct _xycoord __far _getcurrentposition(void);

The _getcurrentposition( ) function returns the x,y location of the current graphics position. The current position is the point at which the next graphics output event will begin. The current graphics position is not related to the current text position in any way.

Microsoft defines the **_xycoord** structure like this:

```
struct _xycoord {
  short xcoord;
  short ycoord;
};
```

Example

This fragment displays the current graphics location:

```
struct _xycoord xy;
.
.
.
xy = _getcurrentposition();
printf("Current X,Y is %d %d.", xy.xcoord, xy.ycoord);
```

Related Functions

_gettextposition( ), **_moveto( )**

#include <graph.h>
unsigned char __far *__far _getfillmask(unsigned char __far *buf);

The **_getfillmask( )** function copies the current fill pattern into the buffer pointed to by *buf*. The buffer must be 8 bytes long.

The fill pattern defines the way an object is filled by **_floodfill( )** or one of the other functions that can fill an object. The mask is treated as an 8-byte by 8-bit array. This array is then repeatedly mapped onto the region being filled. When a bit is set, the corresponding pixel is set to the current fill color. If the bit is off, the pixel is left unchanged.

The **_getfillmask( )** function returns **NULL** if no mask is available.

Example

The following program saves the original fill mask, generates a new one randomly, fills an ellipse using the new mask, and, finally, resets the fill mask to its previous value.

```
#include <graph.h>
#include <conio.h>
#include <stdlib.h>

void main(void)
{
  short color, i;
  unsigned char oldmask[8];
  unsigned char newmask[8];

  /* obtain some random values for newmask */
  for(i=0; i<8; i++) newmask[i] = rand()%255;

  _setvideomode(_VRES16COLOR);

  color = _getcolor();
  _ellipse(_GBORDER, 100, 100, 300, 200);
  _setcolor(2);
  _getfillmask(oldmask);
  _setfillmask(newmask);
  _floodfill(150, 150, color);
  _setfillmask(oldmask);
  getche();

  _setvideomode(_DEFAULTMODE);
}
```

Related Function

_setfillmask( )

#include <graph.h>
void __far _getimage(short x1, short y1, short x2, short y2, char __huge *buf);

The **_getimage( )** function copies the contents of the rectangle defined by *x1,y1* and *x2,y2* into the buffer pointed to by *buf*. To determine how big, in bytes, the buffer must be, use the **_imagesize( )** function.

Example

This program copies the image of an ellipse from one part of the screen to another:

```
#include <stdio.h>
#include <graph.h>
#include <conio.h>
#include <stdlib.h>

void main(void)
{
  long size;
  char *buf;

  _setvideomode(_VRES16COLOR);

  size = _imagesize(100, 100, 300, 200);
  buf = malloc((size_t) size);
  if(!buf) {
    printf("Allocation error.\n");
    exit(1);
  }

  _ellipse(_GBORDER, 100, 100, 300, 200);
  _getimage(100, 100, 300, 200, buf);
  _putimage(0, 0, buf, _GPSET);
  getche();

  _setvideomode(_DEFAULTMODE);
}
```

Related Functions

_imagesize( ), _putimage( )

#include <graph.h>
unsigned short __far _getlinestyle(void);

The **_getlinestyle( )** function returns the current line style. This mask determines how lines will appear. The line style mask is 16 bits long. If a bit is set, the pixel corresponding to that bit is set to the current drawing color. If the bit is off, the pixel is left unchanged.

Example

The following program saves the current line style, uses a new style to draw a rectangle, restores the old line style, and draws another rectangle.

```
#include <graph.h>
#include <conio.h>

void main(void)
{
  short oldstyle;

  _setvideomode(_VRES16COLOR);

  oldstyle = _getlinestyle();
  _moveto(0, 0);

  /* default line style */
  _lineto(100, 100);

  /* new line style */
  _setlinestyle(12345);
  _rectangle(_GBORDER, 100, 100, 200, 200);

  /* old style restored */
  _setlinestyle(oldstyle);
  _rectangle(_GBORDER, 200, 200, 300, 300);
  getche();

  _setvideomode(_DEFAULTMODE);
}
```

Related Function

_setlinestyle( )

#include <graph.h>
short __far _getpixel(short x, short y);

The **_getpixel( )** function returns the color of the pixel specified by *x,y*. If the value of either *x* or *y* is invalid, **_getpixel( )** returns –1.

Example

This code fragment prints the current color of the pixel at 0,0:

```
printf("%d", _getpixel(0, 0));
```

Related Function

_setpixel( )

#include <graph.h>
short __far _gettextcolor(void);

The **_gettextcolor( )** function returns the current text color. This is the color in which textual output will be written.

Example

The following program displays text in the default color and a new color.

```
#include <graph.h>
#include <conio.h>
#include <stdio.h>

void main(void)
{
  int color;

  _setvideomode(_VRES16COLOR);

  color = _gettextcolor();
  printf("Default text color is %d.", color);
  _settextcolor(3);
  _settextposition(10, 1);
  _outtext("This is in a different color.\n");
  getche();

  _setvideomode(_DEFAULTMODE);
}
```

Related Function

_settextcolor( )

#include <graph.h>
struct _rccoord __far _gettextposition(void);

The **_gettextposition( )** function returns the current text position. The current text position is the location at which the next textual output will begin. The current text position does not relate to the current graphics position.

The **_gettextposition( )** function returns the row and column coordinates in a structure of type **_rccoord**, defined by Microsoft like this:

```
struct _rccoord {
  short row;
  short col;
};
```

Example

This fragment displays the current text position.

```
struct _rccoord loc;

loc = _gettextposition();

printf("%d,%d", loc.row, loc.col);
```

Related Function

_settextposition( )

#include <graph.h>
struct _videoconfig __far *__far _getvideoconfig(struct _videoconfig __far *buf);

The **_getvideoconfig( )** function copies the system's current video configuration into the structure pointed to by *buf*. The configuration information includes the dimension of the screen in pixels, the number of text columns and rows, the number of different colors, the bits per pixel, the number of video pages, and so on.

Microsoft defines the **_videoconfig** structure as follows:

```
struct _videoconfig {
  short numxpixels;    /* number of pixels horizontally */
  short numypixels;    /* number of pixels vertically */
  short numtextcols;   /* number of text columns */
  short numtextrows;   /* number of text rows */
  short numcolors;     /* number of colors */
  short bitsperpixel;  /* number bits in a pixel */
  short numvideopages; /* number of video pages */
  short mode;          /* video mode */
```

```
    short adapter;        /* video adapter */
    short monitor;        /* video monitor */
    short memory;         /* kilobytes of video memory */
};
```

Example

This fragment displays the number of text columns available in the current video mode:

```
struct _videoconfig c;

_getvideoconfig(&c);

printf("Text columns: %d.", c.numtextcols);
```

Related Function

_setvideomode( )

#include <graph.h>
long __far _imagesize(short x1, short y1, short x2, short y2);

The **_imagesize( )** function returns the size, in bytes, of memory needed to hold the rectangular region of the screen defined by *x1,y1* and *x2,y2* relative to the current video mode. It is principally used in conjunction with **_getimage( )**.

Example

The following code fragment returns the number of bytes of memory needed to store an image.

```
size = _imagesize(0, 0, 10, 10);
```

Related Functions

_getimage( ), _putimage( )

#include <graph.h>
short __far _lineto(short x, short y);

The **_lineto( )** function draws a line in the current drawing color from the current graphics position to that specified by *x,y*. The current graphics position is then set to *x,y*.

The **_lineto( )** function returns true if successful. If the coordinates specified by *x,y* are invalid for the current video mode, **_lineto( )** returns zero.

Example

This program draws a diagonal line starting in the upper-left corner of the screen:

```
#include <graph.h>
#include <conio.h>

void main(void)
{
  _setvideomode(_VRES16COLOR);

  _moveto(0, 0);
  _setcolor(3);
  _lineto(600, 400);
  getche();

  _setvideomode(_DEFAULTMODE);
}
```

Related Functions

_ellipse( ), _moveto( ), _rectangle( )

#include <graph.h>
struct _xycoord __far _moveto(short x, short y);

The **_moveto( )** function changes the current graphics position to that specified by *x,y*. It does not affect the current text position. The **_moveto( )** function returns a structure of type **_xycoord** that holds the coordinates of the previous graphics position.

The **_xycoord** structure is defined by Microsoft as:

```
struct _xycoord {
  short xcoord;
  short ycoord;
};
```

Example

This fragment makes the upper-left corner of the screen the current graphics location:

```
_moveto(0, 0);
```

Related Functions

_lineto( ), _settextposition( )

#include <graph.h>
void __far _outtext(const char __far *str);

The _outtext( ) function outputs the string pointed to by *str* to the screen at the current text position using the current text foreground and background colors. It also recognizes viewport and window boundaries.

Example

The following fragment outputs **Hello** to the screen.

```
_outtext("Hello");
```

Related Functions

_gettextposition( ), _settextposition( )

#include <graph.h>
short __far _pie(short fill, short x1, short y1, short x2, short y2, short x3, short y3, short x4, short y4);

The _pie( ) function draws a slice of a pie graph. The pie slice is a portion of an ellipse defined by a bounding rectangle whose upper-left corner is at *x1, y1* and whose lower-right corner is at *x2, y2*. The center of the pie is at the center of the bounding rectangle. The rectangle is not displayed. The pie slice begins at the point at which a line drawn from the center of the ellipse to *x3,y3* intersects the ellipse and ends at the point at which a line drawn from the center of the ellipse to *x4,y4* intersects the ellipse. (This process is depicted in Figure 17-2.) The pie slice is displayed in the current drawing color. If *fill* has the value **_GBORDER**, the pie slice is not filled. If *fill* has the value **_GFILLINTERIOR**, the slice is filled using the current fill color and style. (These macros are defined by Microsoft in GRAPH.H.)

Example

This program draws a pie slice:

```
#include <graph.h>
#include <conio.h>

void main(void)
{
  _setvideomode(_VRES16COLOR);

  _pie(_GBORDER, 100, 100, 300, 300, 300, 10, 100, 300);
  getche();

  _setvideomode(_DEFAULTMODE);
}
```

Related Functions

_ellipse( ), _rectangle( )

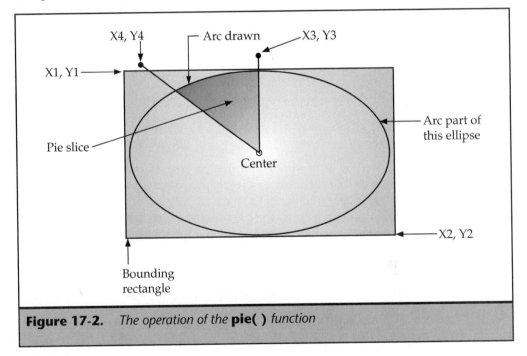

Figure 17-2. *The operation of the* **pie( )** *function*

#include <graph.h>
void __far _putimage(short x, short y, const char __huge *buf, short how);

The **_putimage( )** function copies an image to the screen. Frequently, this image was previously saved by **_getimage( )**. The memory that holds the image is pointed to by *buf*. The image is copied to the screen with its upper-left corner positioned at location *x,y*.

How the image will be copied to the screen is determined by *how*. Microsoft defines in GRAPH.H the five values it may have. If it is **_GPSET**, the image is copied to the screen, overwriting any previous contents. If *how* is **_GPRESET**, the image is copied to the screen in reverse video. If *how* is **_GXOR**, each pixel in the image is XORed with the current contents of the screen. If *how* is **_GOR**, each pixel is ORed with the current contents of the screen. Finally, if *how* is **_GAND**, each pixel in the image is ANDed with the current contents of the screen.

Example

This program copies the image of an ellipse from one part of the screen to another:

```
#include <stdio.h>
#include <graph.h>
#include <conio.h>
#include <stdlib.h>

void main(void)
{
  long size;
  char *buf;

  _setvideomode(_VRES16COLOR);

  size = _imagesize(100, 100, 300, 200);
  buf = malloc((size_t) size);
  if(!buf) {
    printf("allocation error\n");
    exit(1);
  }
  _ellipse(_GBORDER, 100, 100, 300, 200);
  _getimage(100, 100, 300, 200, buf);
  _putimage(0, 0, buf, _GPSET);
  getche();

  _setvideomode(_DEFAULTMODE);
}
```

Related Function

_getimage( )

#include <graph.h>
short __far _rectangle(short fill, short x1, short y1, short x2, short y2);

The **_rectangle( )** function draws a rectangle in the current drawing color. The upper-left corner of the rectangle is specified by *x1,y1* and the lower-right corner by *x2,y2*.

If *fill* has the value **_GFILLINTERIOR**, the rectangle is filled using the current fill color. If *fill* has the value **_GBORDER**, the rectangle is not filled. (These macros are defined by Microsoft in GRAPH.H.)

The **_rectangle( )** function returns true if the coordinates are within range, and zero otherwise.

Example

This code fragment draws a rectangle on the screen:

```
#include <graph.h>
#include <conio.h>

void main(void)
{
  _setvideomode(_VRES16COLOR);
  _rectangle(_GBORDER, 0, 0, 100, 100);
  getche();
  _setvideomode(_DEFAULTMODE);
}
```

Related Functions

_ellipse( ), _lineto( )

#include <graph.h>
short __far _remapallpalette(long __far *colors);
long __far _remappalette(short index, short newcolor);

The **_remapallpalette( )** function changes the values of the colors supported by the current video mode to the values specified in the array pointed to by *colors*, which must contain as many colors as there are in the current palette. The **_remappalette( )** function changes the value of one color, specified by *index*, to that specified by *newcolor*.

Both of these functions require either an EGA or better video adapter.

When successful, **_remappalette( )** returns the previously selected color. On failure, it returns –1. When successful, **_remapallpalette( )** returns nonzero. Upon failure, it returns 0.

Example

The following fragment maps color 3 onto color index 4:

```
_remappalette(4, 3);
```

Related Function

_selectpalette( )

#include <graph.h>
short __far _selectpalette(short palette);

The **_selectpalette( )** function selects one of four palettes when the video system is in mode 4 (four-color, medium resolution). The number of the palette is passed in *palette*. The current palette determines exactly what colors are available for display. The function returns the previously selected palette.

This function works only when the video system is in mode 4.

Example

This fragment selects palette 0:

```
_selectpalette(0);
```

Related Functions

_remapallpalette( ), _remappalette( )

#include <graph.h>
long __far _setbkcolor(long color);

The **_setbkcolor( )** function sets the background color to that specified by *color*. It returns the previous background color.

Example

This program displays **This is on cyan** on a cyan background:

```
#include <graph.h>
#include <conio.h>

void main(void)
{
  _setbkcolor(3L);
  _outtext("This is on cyan");
  getche();
}
```

Related Function

_getbkcolor( )

#include <graph.h>
short __far _setcolor(short color);

The **_setcolor( )** function changes the current drawing color to that specified by *color*. It returns the previous drawing color or –1 on failure.

Example

This program prints a line in each available foreground color:

```
#include <graph.h>
#include <conio.h>

void main(void)
{
  int i;

  _setvideomode(_VRES16COLOR);

  i = _getcolor();
  for( ; i; i--) {
    _setcolor(i);
    _moveto(i*10, 0);
    _lineto(i*10, 100);
  }
  getche();

  _setvideomode(_DEFAULTMODE);
}
```

Related Functions

_getbkcolor( ), _getcolor( ), _setbkcolor( )

#include <graph.h>
void __far _setfillmask(unsigned char __far *buf);

The _setfillmask( ) function sets the fill mask used by those routines that fill areas to that pointed to by *buf*, which must be an 8-byte by 8-bit array. This array is then repeatedly mapped onto the region being filled. When a bit is set, the corresponding pixel is set to the current fill color. If the bit is off, the pixel is left unchanged.

Example

This program creates a new randomly generated fill mask and uses it to fill an ellipse:

```
#include <graph.h>
#include <conio.h>
#include <stdlib.h>

void main(void)
{
  short i;
  unsigned char newmask[8];

  /* obtain some random values for newmask */
  for(i=0; i<8; i++) newmask[i] = rand()%255;

  _setvideomode(_VRES16COLOR);

  _setfillmask(newmask);
  _ellipse(_GFILLINTERIOR, 100, 100, 300, 200);
  getche();

  _setvideomode(_DEFAULTMODE);
}
```

Related Function

_getfillmask( )

#include <graph.h>
void __far _setlinestyle(unsigned short mask);

The _setlinestyle( ) function sets the current line style to that specified by *mask*. A line style mask is 16 bits long. If a bit is set, the pixel corresponding to that bit is set to the current drawing color. If the bit is off, the pixel is left unchanged.

Example

This program saves the current line style, uses a new one to draw a rectangle, restores the old line style, and draws another rectangle:

```
#include <graph.h>
#include <conio.h>

void main(void)
{
  short oldstyle;

  _setvideomode(_VRES16COLOR);

  oldstyle = _getlinestyle();
  _moveto(0, 0);

  /* default line style */
  _lineto(100, 100);

  /* new line style */
  _setlinestyle(12345);
  _rectangle(_GBORDER, 100, 100, 200, 200);

  /* old style restored */
  _setlinestyle(oldstyle);
  _rectangle(_GBORDER, 200, 200, 300, 300);
  getche();

  _setvideomode(_DEFAULTMODE);
}
```

Related Functions

_getlinestyle( ), _setfillmask( )

#include <graph.h>
short __far _setpixel(short x, short y);

The _setpixel( ) function changes the pixel specified by *x,y* to the current drawing color. It returns the pixel's previous color. If a coordinate specified is out of bounds, _setpixel( ) returns –1.

Example

This fragment sets the pixel at location 10,20 to the current drawing color:

```
_setpixel(10, 20);
```

Related Function

_getpixel( )

#include <graph.h>
short __far _settextcolor(short color);

The _settextcolor( ) function changes the current text color to that specified by *color*. It returns the previous text color.

Example

This program displays **This is in red** in red:

```
#include <graph.h>
#include <conio.h>
#include <stdio.h>

void main(void)
{
  _setvideomode(_VRES16COLOR);

  _settextcolor(4);
  _outtext("This is in red\n");
  getche();

  _setvideomode(_DEFAULTMODE);
}
```

Related Functions

_gettextcolor( ), _setcolor( )

#include <graph.h>
struct _rccoord __far _settextposition(short row, short col);

The **_settextposition( )** function sets the current text position to that specified by *row* and *col*. The current text position is the location at which the next textual output will begin. The current text position is not related to the current graphics position.

The **_settextposition( )** function returns the previous text position in the row and column coordinates in a structure of type **_rccoord**, defined by Microsoft like this:

```
struct _rccoord {
  short row;
  short col;
};
```

Example

This fragment sets the current text position to row 10, column 40:

```
_settextposition(10, 40);
```

Related Function

_gettextposition( )

#include <graph.h>
void __far _settextwindow(short row1, short col1, short row2, short col2);

The **_settextwindow( )** function defines a text window specified by *row1, col1* and *row2, col2*—the upper-left and lower-right corners of the window. Text written to the window with **_outtext( )** will appear relative to the window and not the screen. This means that text will scroll when the bottom of the window is written to. Also, text will be wrapped around to the next line when it attempts to go past the right edge of the window. The rest of the screen outside the window is untouched.

The standard console output functions ignore text windows.

Example

This function creates a small text window and writes output to it. Text will wrap and scroll within the window, but the rest of the screen will remain untouched.

```
#include <graph.h>
#include <conio.h>

void main(void)
{
  int i;

  _settextwindow(1, 1, 5, 40);

  for(i=0; i<100; i++)
    _outtext("This is a test. ");
}
```

Related Functions

_outtext( ), _setviewport( )

#include <graph.h>
short __far _setvideomode(short mode);

The **_setvideomode( )** function activates the video mode specified by *mode*. The valid modes are shown here. (The macros are defined by Microsoft in GRAPH.H.)

_TEXTBW40	_HERCMONO	_VRES16COLOR
_TEXTC40	_TEXTMONO	_MRES256COLOR
_TEXTBW80	_MRES16COLOR	_DEFAULTMODE
_TEXTC80	_HRES16COLOR	_MAXRESMODE
_MRES4COLOR	_ERESNOCOLOR	_MAXCOLORMODE
_MRESNOCOLOR	_ERESCOLOR	
_HRESBW	_VRES2COLOR	

You can restore the default video mode by calling **_setvideomode( )** with **_DEFAULTMODE**.

The **_setvideomode( )** function returns true if the mode change was successful. If the specified mode is not supported by the system's hardware, **_setvideomode( )** returns zero.

Example

The following fragment sets the video mode to 80-column color text:

```
_setvideomode(_TEXTC80);
```

Related Function

_getvideoconfig( )

#include <graph.h>
void __far _setviewport(short x1, short y1, short x2, short y2);

The **_setviewport( )** function creates a graphics window called a *viewport* whose upper-left corner is specified by *x1,y1* and whose lower-right corner is specified by *x2,y2*. Once a viewport has been defined, the graphics functions operate relative to it rather than the screen. Output is automatically clipped at the edges of the viewport.

Example

This program creates a viewport and draws a line within it.

```
#include <graph.h>
#include <conio.h>

void main(void)
{
  _setvideomode(_VRES16COLOR);

  _setviewport(200, 200, 300, 300);
  _moveto(0, 0); _setcolor(3);
  _lineto(600, 400); /* this line will be clipped */
  getche();

  _setvideomode(_DEFAULTMODE);
}
```

Related Function

_settextwindow( )

Chapter Eighteen

Miscellaneous Functions

This chapter discusses all of the ANSI standard functions that don't fit easily in any other category. They include functions that perform various conversions, support variable-length arguments, sorting, searching, and the like.

Many of these functions require the use of the header STDLIB.H. This header defines two types, **div_t** and **ldiv_t**, which are the types of the values returned by **div( )** and **ldiv( )**, respectively. STDLIB.H also defines the types **size_t**, which is the unsigned value returned by **sizeof**, and **wchar_t**, which is the data type of wide (16-bit) characters used by an extended character set. The header also defines these macros:

NULL	A null pointer
RAND_MAX	The maximum value that can be returned by the **rand( )** function
EXIT_FAILURE	The value returned to calling process if program termination is unsuccessful
EXIT_SUCCESS	The value returned to calling process if program termination is successful
MB_CUR_MAX	Maximum number of bytes in a multibyte character

If a function requires a different header file, that function description will discuss it.

#include <stdlib.h>
void abort(void);

The **abort( )** function causes immediate abnormal termination of a program. Generally, no files are flushed. In environments that support it, **abort( )** returns an implementation-defined value to the calling process (usually the operating system) indicating failure.

Example

This program terminates if the user enters an **A:**

```
#include <stdlib.h>
#include <stdio.h>

void main(void)
{
  for(;;)
    if(getchar()=='A') abort();
}
```

Related Functions

atexit( ), exit( )

#include <stdlib.h>
int abs(int num);

The **abs( )** function returns the absolute value of the integer *num*.

Example

This function converts the user-entered numbers into their absolute values:

```
#include <stdlib.h>
#include <stdio.h>

get_abs(void)
{
  char num[80];

  gets(num);
  return abs(atoi(num));
}
```

Related Function

labs( )

#include <assert.h>
void assert(int exp);

The **assert( )** macro, defined in its header ASSERT.H, writes error information to **stderr** and then aborts program execution if the expression *exp* evaluates to zero. Otherwise, **assert( )** does nothing. Although the exact output is implementation-defined, many compilers use a message similar to this:

Assertion failed: *<expression>*, file *<file>*, line *<linenum>*

The **assert( )** macro is generally used to help verify that a program is operating correctly. Therefore, the expression must be devised so that it evaluates to true only when no errors have taken place.

You need not remove the **assert( )** statements from the source code once a program is debugged because, if the macro **NDEBUG** is defined (as anything) prior to including ASSERT.H, the **assert( )** macros are ignored.

Example

This code fragment tests if the data read from a serial port is ASCII (that is, that it does not use the eighth bit):

```
    .
    .
    .
ch = read_port();
assert(!(ch & 128)); /* check bit 7 */
    .
    .
    .
```

Related Function

abort( )

#include <stdlib.h>
int atexit(void (*func)(void));

The **atexit( )** function registers the function pointed to by *func* as a function to be called upon normal program termination. That is, at the end of a program run, the specified function is called.

The **atexit( )** function returns zero if the function is successfully registered as a termination function; otherwise, it returns nonzero.

The ANSI C standard specifies that at least 32 termination functions may be established and that they be called in the reverse order of their establishment. In other words, the registration process is stack-like.

Example

This program prints **Hello There** on the screen when it terminates.

```
#include <stdlib.h>
#include <stdio.h>

void done(void);

void main(void)
{

   if(atexit(done)) printf("Error in atexit().");
}
```

```
void done(void)
{
   printf("Hello There");
}
```

Related Functions

abort( ), exit( )

#include <stdlib.h>
double atof(const char *str);

The **atof( )** function converts the string pointed to by *str* into a **double** value and returns the result. The string must contain a valid floating-point number. If not, the returned value is undefined.

The number may be terminated by any character that cannot be part of a valid floating-point number. This includes white space, punctuation other than periods, and characters other than "E" or "e." This means that if **atof( )** is called with "100.00HELLO", the value 100.00 is returned and the rest of the string is ignored.

Example

This program reads two floating-point numbers and displays their sum:

```
#include <stdlib.h>
#include <stdio.h>

void main(void)
{
   char num1[80], num2[80];

   printf("Enter first: ");
   gets(num1);
   printf("Enter second: ");
   gets(num2);
   printf("The sum is: %lf.", atof(num1) + atof(num2));
}
```

Related Functions

atoi( ), atol( )

#include <stdlib.h>
int atoi(const char *str);

The **atoi( )** function converts the string pointed to by *str* into an integer value and returns the result. The string must contain a valid integer. If not, the returned value is undefined; however, most implementations return zero.

The number may be terminated by any character that cannot be part of an integer. This includes white space, punctuation, and other non-digits. For example, if **atoi( )** is called with "123.23", the integer value 123 is returned and 0.23 is ignored.

Example

The following program reads two integers and displays their sum.

```
#include <stdlib.h>
#include <stdio.h>

void main(void)
{
  char num1[80], num2[80];

  printf("Enter first: ");
  gets(num1);
  printf("Enter second: ");
  gets(num2);
  printf("The sum is: %d.", atoi(num1)+atoi(num2));
}
```

Related Functions

atof( ), atol( )

#include <stdlib.h>
long atol(const char *str);

The **atol( )** function converts the string pointed to by *str* into a **long int** value and returns the result. The string must contain a valid **long** integer. If not, the returned value is undefined; however, most implementations return zero.

The number may be terminated by any character that cannot be part of an integer. This includes white space, punctuation, and other non-digits. For example, if **atol( )** is called with "123.23", the integer value 123 is returned and 0.23 is ignored.

Example

This program reads two long integers and displays their sum:

```
#include <stdlib.h>
#include <stdio.h>

void main(void)
{
  char num1[80], num2[80];

  printf("Enter first: ");
  gets(num1);
  printf("Enter second: ");
  gets(num2);
  printf("The sum is: %ld.", atol(num1)+atol(num2));
}
```

Related Functions

atof( ), atoi( )

#include <stdlib.h>
void *bsearch(const void *key, const void *buf, size_t num,
size_t size, int (*compare)(const void *, const void *));

The **bsearch( )** function performs a binary search on the sorted array pointed to by *buf*, returning a pointer to the first member that matches the key pointed to by *key*. The number of elements in the array is specified by *num*, and the size (in bytes) of each element is described by *size*.

The function pointed to by *compare* compares an element of the array with the key. The form of the *compare* function must be

int *compare*(const void *arg1, const void *arg2);

The function may be named anything you like. However, it must return the following values:

If *arg1* is less than *arg2*, return less than zero.
If *arg1* is equal to *arg2*, return zero.
If *arg1* is greater than *arg2*, return greater than zero.

The array must be sorted in ascending order with the lowest address containing the lowest element. If the array does not contain the key, a null pointer is returned.

Example

The following program reads characters entered at the keyboard and determines whether they belong to the alphabet.

```c
#include <stdlib.h>
#include <ctype.h>
#include <stdio.h>
#include <conio.h>

char *alpha = "abcdefghijklmnopqrstuvwxyz";

int comp(const void *ch, const void *s);

void main(void)
{
  char ch;
  char *p;

  do {
    printf("Enter a character: ");
    ch = getche();
    ch = tolower(ch);
    p = (char *) bsearch(&ch, alpha, 26, 1, comp);
    if(p) printf("is in alphabet\n");
    else printf("is not in alphabet\n");
  } while(p);
}

/* Compare two characters. */
comp(const void *ch, const void *s)
{
  return *(char *)ch - *(char *)s;
}
```

Related Function

qsort( )

#include <stdlib.h>
div_t div(int numerator, int denominator);

The **div( )** function returns the quotient and the remainder of the operation *numerator/denominator* in a structure of type **div_t**.

The structure type **div_t** is defined in STDLIB.H and has at least these two fields:

int quot; /* the quotient */
int rem; /* the remainder */

Example

This program displays the quotient and remainder of 10/3:

```
#include <stdlib.h>
#include <stdio.h>

void main(void)
{
  div_t n;

  n = div(10, 3);

  printf("Quotient and remainder: %d %d.\n", n.quot, n.rem);
}
```

Related Function

ldiv( )

#include <stdlib.h>
void exit(int exit_code);

The **exit( )** function causes immediate, normal termination of a program.

The value of *exit_code* is passed to the calling process, usually the operating system, if the environment supports it. By convention, if the value of *exit_code* is zero, normal program termination is assumed. A nonzero value may indicate an implementation-defined error. C also defines two values which may be used as parameters to **exit( )**: **EXIT_SUCCESS** and **EXIT_FAILURE.** These values will indicate successful and unsuccessful program termination in all environments.

Example

This function performs menu selection for a mailing list program. If **Q** is selected, the program is terminated.

```
menu(void)
{
  char choice;

  do {
    printf("Enter names (E)\n");
    printf("Delete name (D)\n");
    printf("Print (P)\n");
    printf("Quit (Q)\n");
    choice = getche();
  } while(!strchr("EDPQ", toupper(choice)));

  if(choice=='Q') exit(0);

  return choice;
}
```

Related Functions

abort( ), atexit( )

#include <stdlib.h>
char *getenv(const char *name);

The **getenv( )** function returns a pointer to environmental information associated with the string pointed to by *name* in the implementation-defined environmental information table. This string must never be changed by the program.

The environment of a program may include such things as path names and online devices. The exact nature of this data is implementation-defined. Refer to your compiler's user's manual for details.

If a call is made to **getenv( )** with an argument that does not match any of the environment data, a null pointer is returned.

Example

Assuming that a specific compiler maintains environmental information about the devices connected to the system, the following fragment returns a pointer to the list of devices:

```
char *p
  .
  .
  .
```

```
p = getenv("DEVICES");
   .
   .
   .
```

Related Function

system( )

#include <stdlib.h>
char *itoa(int num, const char *str, int radix);

The **itoa( )** function is not currently defined by the ANSI C standard, but is found with many compilers.

The **itoa( )** function converts the integer *num* into its string equivalent and places the result in the string pointed to by *str*. The base of the output string is determined by *radix*, which is generally in the range 2 through 16.

The **itoa( )** function returns *str*. Usually, there is no error return value. Be sure to call **itoa( )** with a string of sufficient length to hold the converted result.

Example

This program displays the value of 1423 in hexadecimal (58F):

```
#include <stdlib.h>
#include <stdio.h>

void main(void)
{
  char p[20];

  itoa(1423, p, 16);

  printf(p);
}
```

Related Functions

atoi( ), sscanf( )

#include <stdlib.h>
long labs(long num);

The **labs( )** function returns the absolute value of *num*.

Example

This function converts the number entered at the keyboard into its absolute value:

```
#include <stdlib.h>

long int get_labs()
{
  char num[80];

  gets(num);

  return labs(atol(num));
}
```

Related Function

abs( )

#include <stdlib.h>
ldiv_t ldiv(long numerator, long denominator);

The **ldiv( )** function returns the quotient and remainder of the operation *numerator/denominator* in an **ldiv_t** structure.

The structure type **ldiv_t** is defined in STDLIB.H and has at least these two fields:

long quot; /* the quotient */
long rem;   /* the remainder */

Example

This program displays the quotient and remainder of 100000L/3L:

```
#include <stdlib.h>
#include <stdio.h>

void main(void)
{
  ldiv_t n;
```

```
n = ldiv(100000L, 3L);

printf("Quotient & remainder: %ld %ld.\n", n.quot, n.rem);

}
```

Related Function

div( )

#include <setjmp.h>
void longjmp(jmp_buf envbuf, int status);

The **longjmp( )** function causes program execution to resume at the point of the last call to **setjmp( )**. These two functions are C's way of providing for a jump between functions. Notice that the header SETJMP.H is required.

The **longjmp( )** function resets the stack as described in *envbuf*, which must have been set by a prior call to **setjmp( )**. This causes program execution to resume at the statement following the **setjmp( )** invocation. That is, the computer is "tricked" into thinking that it never left the function that called **setjmp( )**. In effect, **longjmp( )** "warps" across time and (memory) space to a previous point in your program without having to perform the normal function-return process.

The buffer *evnbuf* is of type **jmp_buf**, which is defined in the header SETJMP.H. The buffer must have been set through a call to **setjmp( )** prior to calling **longjmp( )**.

The value of *status* becomes the return value of **setjump( )** and may be interrogated to determine where the long jump came from. The only value not allowed is zero.

The **longjmp( )** function must be called before the function that called **setjmp( )** returns. If not, the result is technically undefined. (Actually, a system crash will almost certainly occur.)

By far the most common use of **longjmp( )** is to return from a deeply nested set of routines when an error occurs.

Example

This program prints **1 2 3**:

```
#include <setjmp.h>
#include <stdio.h>

jmp_buf ebuf;
```

```
void f2(void);

void main(void)
{
  char first=1;
  int i;

  printf("1 ");
  i = setjmp(ebuf);
  if(first) {
    first =! first;
    f2();
    printf("This will not be printed.");
  }
  printf("%d", i);
}

void f2(void)
{
  printf("2 ");
  longjmp(ebuf, 3);
}
```

Related Function

setjmp( )

#include <stdlib.h>
char *ltoa(long num, const char *str, int radix);

The **ltoa( )** function is not currently defined by the ANSI C standard but is found in many C compilers.

The **ltoa( )** function converts the **long** integer *num* into its string equivalent, placing the result in the string pointed to by *str*. The base of the output string is determined by *radix*, which is usually in the range 2 through 16.

The **ltoa( )** function returns *str*. Generally, there is no error return value. Be sure to call **ltoa( )** with a string long enough to hold the converted result.

Example

This program displays the value of 1423 in hexadecimal (58F):

```
#include <stdlib.h>
#include <stdio.h>

void main(void)
{
  char p[20];

  ltoa(1423L, p, 16);

  printf(p);
}
```

Related Function

itoa( )

#include <stdlib.h>
int mblen(const char *str, size_t size)

The **mblen( )** function returns the length (in bytes) of a multibyte character pointed to by *str*. Only the first *size* number of characters are examined. It returns –1 on error.

If *str* is null, then **mblen( )** returns nonzero if multibyte characters have shift-state dependencies. If they do not, zero is returned.

Example

This statement displays the length of the multibyte character pointed to by **mb**.

```
printf("%d", mblen(mb, 2));
```

Related Functions

mbtowc( ), wctomb( )

#include <stdlib.h>
size_t mbstowcs(wchar_t *out, const char *in, size_t size)

The **mbstowcs( )** function converts the multibyte string pointed to by *in* into a wide character string and puts that result in the array pointed to by *out*. The type **wchar_t** is defined in STDLIB.H. Only *size* number of bytes will be stored in *out*.

The **mbstowcs( )** function returns the number of multibyte characters that are converted. If an error occurs, the function returns –1.

Example

This statement converts the first 4 characters in the multibyte string pointed to by **mb** and puts the result in **str**.

```
mbstowcs(str, mb, 4);
```

Related Functions

wcstombs( ), mbtowc( )

#include <stdlib.h>
int mbtowc(wchar_t *out, const char *in, size_t size)

The **mbtowc( )** function converts the multibyte character in the array pointed to by *in* into its wide character equivalent and puts that result in the object pointed to by *out*. The type **wchar_t** is defined in STDLIB.H. Only *size* number of characters will be examined.

This function returns the number of bytes that are put into *out*. –1 is returned if an error occurs. If *in* is null, then **mbtowc( )** returns nonzero if multibyte characters have shift-state dependencies. If they do not, zero is returned.

Example

This statement converts the multibyte character in **mbstr** into its equivalent wide character and puts the result in the array pointed to by **widenorm**. (Only the first 2 bytes of **mbstr** are examined.)

```
mbtowc(widenorm, mbstr, 2);
```

Related Functions

mblen( ), wctomb( )

#include <stdlib.h>
void qsort(void *buf, size_t num, size_t size,
int (*compare)(const void *, const void *));

The **qsort( )** function sorts the array pointed to by *buf* using a quicksort. The quicksort is generally considered the best general-purpose sorting algorithm. (See Chapter 19 for full coverage of sorting and searching in C.) Upon termination, the array is sorted. The number of elements in the array is specified by *num*, and the size (in bytes) of each element is described by *size*.

The function pointed to by *compare* is used to compare two elements of the array. The form of *compare* must be

int *compare*(const void **arg1*, const void **arg2*);

The function may be named anything you like. It must return the following values:

If *arg1* is less than *arg2*, return less than zero.
If *arg1* is equal to *arg2*, return zero.
If *arg1* is greater than *arg2*, return greater than zero.

The array is sorted into ascending order with the lowest address containing the lowest element.

Example

This program sorts a list of integers and displays the result:

```
#include <stdlib.h>
#include <stdio.h>

int num[10] = {
  1, 3, 6, 5, 8, 7, 9, 6, 2, 0
};

int comp(const void *, const void *);

void main(void)
{
  int i;

  printf("Original array: ");
  for(i=0; i<10; i++) printf("%d ", num[i]);

  qsort(num, 10, sizeof(int), comp);

  printf("Sorted array: ");
  for(i=0; i<10; i++) printf("%d ", num[i]);
}

/* compare the integers */
comp(const void *i, const void *j)
{
  return *(int *)i - *(int *)j;
}
```

Related Function

bsearch( )

#include <signal.h>
int raise(int signal);

The **raise( )** function sends the signal specified by *signal* to the executing program. It returns zero if successful; otherwise, it returns nonzero. Its uses the header file SIGNAL.H. The following standard signals are defined by the ANSI C standard. (However, a C implementation is free to support additional signals.)

Signal	Meaning
SIGABRT	Abnormal program termination
SIGFPE	Math error
SIGILL	Illegal instruction
SIGINT	Interactive attention required
SIGSEGV	Invalid memory access
SIGTERM	Program termination request

Example

The **raise( )** function is implementation-specific. Refer to your compiler's user's manual for details and examples.

Related Function

signal( )

#include <stdlib.h>
int rand(void);

The **rand( )** function generates a sequence of pseudorandom numbers. Each time it is called, an integer between zero and **RAND_MAX** is returned.

Example

The following program displays ten pseudorandom numbers.

```
#include <stdlib.h>
#include <stdio.h>

void main(void)
{
  int i;

  for(i=0; i<10; i++)
  printf("%d ", rand());
}
```

Related Function

srand( )

#include <setjmp.h>
int setjmp(jmp_buf envbuf);

The **setjmp( )** function saves the contents of the system stack in the buffer *envbuf* for later use by **longjmp( )**. It uses the header file SETJMP.H, which defines the type **jmp_buf**.

The **setjmp( )** function returns zero upon invocation. However, a **longjmp( )** passes an argument to **setjmp( )** when it executes; this value (always nonzero) appears to be **setjmp( )**'s value after a call to **longjmp( )**. See **longjmp( )** for additional information.

Example

This program prints **1 2 3**:

```
#include <setjmp.h>
#include <stdio.h>

jmp_buf ebuf;
void f2(void);

void main(void)
{
  char first=1;
  int i;

  printf("1 ");
  i = setjmp(ebuf);
  if(first) {
    first = !first;
    f2();
    printf("This will not be printed.");
  }
  printf("%d",i);
}

void f2(void)
{
  printf("2 ");
  longjmp(ebuf,3);
}
```

Related Function

longjmp( )

#include <signal.h>
void (*signal(int sig, void (*func)(int))) (int);

The **signal( )** function defines the function *func* to be executed if the specified signal *sig* is received. This function is somewhat implementation-specific. However, the value for *func* must be one of the following macros, defined in SIGNAL.H, or the address of a programmer-defined signal-handling function:

Macro	Meaning
SIG_DFL	Use default signal handling
SIG_IGN	Ignore the signal

If a function address is used, the specified function is executed. If a signal-handling function cannot process a signal, it must return **SIG_ERR** (which is a macro defined in SIGNAL.H.).

signal( ) is often used in setting up critical error handlers and control-C handlers.

Example

See your compiler's user's manual for details and examples relative to your system.

Related Function

raise( )

#include <stdlib.h>
void srand(unsigned seed);

The **srand( )** function sets a starting point for the sequence generated by **rand( )**, which returns pseudorandom numbers.

srand( ) is generally used to allow multiple program runs to use different sequences of pseudorandom numbers by specifying different starting points. However, you can generate the same pseudorandom sequence over and over by calling **srand( )** with the same seed before starting the sequence each time.

Example

This program uses the system time to randomly initialize the **rand( )** function by using **srand( )**:

```
#include <stdio.h>
#include <stdlib.h>
```

```
#include <time.h>

/* Seed rand with the system time
   and display the first 10 numbers.
*/
void main(void)
{
  int i, stime;
  long ltime;

  /* get the current calendar time */
  ltime = time(NULL);
  stime = (unsigned) ltime/2;
  srand(stime);

  for(i=0; i<10; i++) printf("%d ", rand());
}
```

Related Function

rand( )

#include <stdlib.h>
double strtod(const char *start, char **end);

The **strtod( )** function converts the string representation of a number stored in the string pointed to by *start* into a **double** and returns the result.

The **strtod( )** function works as follows. First, any leading white space in the string pointed to by *start* is stripped. Next, each character that constitutes the number is read. Any character that cannot be part of a floating-point number causes this process to stop. This includes white space, punctuation (other than periods), and characters other than "E" or "e." Finally, *end* is set to point to the remainder, if any, of the original string. This means that if **strtod( )** is called with "100.00 Pliers", the value 100.00 is returned and *end* points to the space that precedes the word "Pliers."

If a conversion error occurs, **strtod( )** returns either **HUGE_VAL** for overflow or **–HUGE_VAL** for underflow. If no conversion could take place, zero is returned. In either case, the global variable *errno* is set to **ERANGE**, indicating a range error.

Example

This program reads floating-point numbers from a character array:

```
#include <stdlib.h>
#include <ctype.h>
#include <stdio.h>

void main(void)
{
  char *end, *start = "100.00 pliers 200.00 hammers";

  end = start;
  while(*start) {
    printf("%f, ", strtod(start, &end));
    printf("Remainder: %s\n" ,end);
    start = end;
    /* move past the non-digits */
    while(!isdigit(*start) && *start) start++;
  }
}
```

The output is

    100.000000, Remainder: pliers 200.00 hammers
    200.000000, Remainder: hammers

Related Function

atof( )

#include <stdlib.h>
long strtol(const char *start, char **end, int radix);

The **strtol( )** function converts the string representation of a number stored in the string pointed to by *start* into a **long** and returns the result. The base of the number is determined by *radix*. If *radix* is zero, the base is determined by rules that govern constant specification. If the radix is other than zero, it must be in the range 2 through 36.

The **strtol( )** function works as follows. First, any leading white space in the string pointed to by *start* is stripped. Next, each character that constitutes the number is read. Any character that cannot be part of a **long** integer number causes this process to stop. This includes white space, punctuation, and characters. Finally, *end* is set to point to the remainder, if any, of the original string. This means that if **strtol( )** is called with "100 Pliers", the value **100L** will be returned and *end* will point to the space that precedes the word "Pliers."

If a conversion error occurs, **strtol( )** returns either **LONG_MAX** for overflow or **LONG_MIN** for underflow. The global **errno** is also set to **ERANGE**, indicating a range error. If no conversion could take place, zero is returned.

Example

This function reads base 10 numbers from standard input and returns their **long** equivalent.

```
#include <stdlib.h>
#include <stdio.h>

long read_long(void)
{
  char start[80], *end;

  printf("Enter a number: ");
  gets(start);
  return strtol(start, &end,10);
}
```

Related Function

atol( )

#include <stdlib.h>
unsigned long strtoul(const char *start, char **end, int radix);

The **strtoul( )** function converts the string representation of a number stored in the string pointed to by *start* into an **unsigned long** and returns the result. The base of the number is determined by *radix*. If *radix* is zero, the base is determined by rules that govern constant specification. If *radix* is specified, it must be in the range 2 through 36.

The **strtoul( )** function works as follows. First, any leading white space in the string pointed to by *start* is stripped. Next, each character that comprises the number is read. Any character that cannot be part of an **unsigned long** integer causes this process to stop. This includes white space, punctuation, and characters. Finally, *end* is set to point to the remainder, if any, of the original string. This means that if **strtoul( )** is called with "100 Pliers", the value **100L** will be returned and *end* will point to the space that precedes the word "Pliers."

If a conversion error occurs, then **strtoul( )** will return **ULONG_MAX** and the global variable **errno** is set to **ERANGE**, indicating a range error. If no conversion could take place, zero is returned.

Example

This function reads unsigned base 16 (hexadecimal) numbers from standard input and returns their **unsigned long** equivalent:

```
#include <stdlib.h>

unsigned long read_unsigned_long(void)
{
  char start[80], *end;

  printf("Enter a hex number: ");
  gets(start);
  return strtoul(start, &end, 16);
}
```

Related Function

strtol( )

#include <stdlib.h>
int system(const char *str);

The **system( )** function passes the string pointed to by *str* as a command to the command processor of the operating system.

If **system( )** is called with a null pointer, it returns nonzero if a command processor is present, zero otherwise. (Remember, some C code will be executed in dedicated systems that do not have operating systems and command processors.) The return value of **system( )** is implementation-defined when called with a pointer to a command string. However, generally it returns zero if the command was successfully executed, nonzero otherwise.

Example

Using the DOS operating system, this program displays the contents of the current working directory:

```
#include <stdlib.h>

void main(void)
{
  system("dir");
}
```

Related Function

exit( )

#include <stdarg.h>
void va_arg(va_list argptr, type);
type va_start(va_list argptr, last_parm);
void va_end(va_list argptr);

The **va_arg( )**, **va_start( )**, and **va_end( )** macros work together to allow a variable number of arguments to be passed to a function. The most common example of a function that takes a variable number of arguments is **printf( )**. The type **va_list** is defined by STDARG.H.

The general procedure for creating a function that can take a variable number of arguments is as follows. The function must have at least one known parameter prior to the variable parameter list, but may have more. The rightmost known parameter is *last_parm*. Before any of the variable length parameters may be accessed, the argument pointer *argptr* must be initialized through a call to **va_start( )**. After that, parameters are returned via calls to **va_arg( )**, with *type* being the type of the next parameter. Finally, after all of the parameters have been read and before returning from the function, a call to **va_end( )** must be made to ensure that the stack is properly restored. If **va_end( )** is not called, a program crash is very likely.

Example

This program uses **sum_series( )** to return the sum of a series of numbers. The first argument contains a count of the number of arguments to follow. In this example, the program sums the first five elements of the series:

$$\frac{1}{2} + \frac{1}{4} + \frac{1}{8} + \frac{1}{16} + \dots \frac{1}{2^N}$$

The output displayed is **0.968750**.

```
#include <stdio.h>
#include <stdarg.h>

double sum_series(int num, ...);

/* Variable length argument example - sum a series. */
void main(void)
```

```
{
  double d;

  d = sum_series(5, 0.5, 0.25, 0.125, 0.0625, 0.03125);

  printf("Sum of series is %f.\n", d);
}

double sum_series(int num, ...)
{
  double sum=0.0, t;
  va_list argptr;

  /* initialize argptr */
  va_start(argptr, num);

  /* sum the series */
  for( ; num; num--) {
    t = va_arg(argptr, double); /* get next argument */
    sum += t;
  }

  /* do orderly shutdown */
  va_end(argptr);
  return sum;
}
```

Related Function

vprintf( )

#include <stdlib.h>
size_t wcstombs(char *out, const wchar_t *in, size_t size)

The **wcstombs( )** function converts the array pointed to by *in* into its multibyte equivalent and puts the result in the array pointed to by *out*. Only the first *size* bytes of *in* are converted. Conversion stops before that if the null terminator is encountered.

If successful, **wcstombs( )** returns the number of bytes converted. On failure, –1 is returned.

Related Functions

wctomb( ), mbstowcs( )

#include <stdlib.h>
int wctomb(char *out, wchar_t in)

The **wctomb( )** function converts the wide character in *in* into its multibyte equivalent and puts the result in the object pointed to by *out*. The array pointed to by *out* must be **MB_CUR_MAX** characters long.

If successful, **wctomb( )** returns the number of bytes contained in the multibyte character. On failure, –1 is returned.

If *out* is NULL, then **wctomb( )** returns nonzero if the multibyte character is dependent on the shift-state and zero if it is not.

Related Functions

wcstombs( ), mbtowc( )

PART THREE

Algorithms and Applications

The purpose of Part Three is to show the various ways that C can be applied to a variety of programming tasks. In the process, it presents many common and useful algorithms and applications that illustrate several aspects of the C language. Many of the examples contained in Part Three can be useful starting points for your own C projects.

Chapter Nineteen

Sorting and Searching

In the world of computers, sorting and searching are perhaps the most fundamental and extensively analyzed tasks. These routines are used in almost all database programs as well as in compilers, interpreters, and operating systems. This chapter introduces the basics of sorting and searching. As you will see, sorting and searching illustrate several important C programming techniques.

Since the point of sorting data is generally to make searching that data easier and faster, sorting is discussed first.

Sorting

Sorting is the process of arranging a set of similar information into an increasing or decreasing order. Specifically, given a sorted list i of n elements, then

$$i_1 <= i_2 <= \ldots <= i_n$$

Even though most C compilers supply the function **qsort( )** as part of the standard library, you should understand sorting for three reasons. First, you cannot apply a generalized function like **qsort( )** to all situations. Second, because **qsort( )** is parameterized so that it may operate on a wide variety of data, it runs more slowly than a similar sort that operates on only one type of data. (Generalization inherently increases run time because of the extra processing time needed to handle various data types.) Finally, as you will see, although the quicksort algorithm (used by **qsort( )**) is very effective in the general case, it may not be the best sort for specialized situations.

There are two general categories of sorting algorithms: algorithms that sort arrays (both in memory and in random-access disk files), and algorithms that sort sequential disk or tape files. This chapter is concerned only with the first category, because it is most relevant to the average programmer.

Most often when information is sorted, only a portion of the information is used as the sort *key*. The key is that part of the data that determines which item comes before another. Thus, the key is used in comparisons, but when an exchange is made, the entire data structure is swapped. For example, in a mailing list the ZIP code field might be used as the key, but the entire address is sorted. For the sake of simplicity, the next few examples will sort character arrays as you learn about the various sorting methods. Later, you will learn how to adapt these methods to any type of data structure.

Classes of Sorting Algorithms

There are three general methods for sorting arrays:

- Exchange
- Selection
- Insertion

To understand these three methods, imagine a deck of cards. To sort the cards by using *exchange*, spread them on a table, face up, and then exchange out-of-order cards until the deck is ordered. Using *selection*, spread the cards on the table, select the card of lowest value, take it out of the deck, and hold it in your hand. Then, from the remaining cards on the table, select the lowest card and place it behind the one already in your hand. This process continues until all the cards are in your hand. The cards in your hand will be sorted when you finish the process. To sort the cards by using *insertion*, hold all the cards in your hand. Place one card at a time on the table, always inserting it in the correct position. The deck will be sorted when you have no cards in your hand.

Judging Sorting Algorithms

There are many different algorithms for each sorting method. They all have some merit, but the general criteria for judging a sorting algorithm are:

- How fast can it sort information in an average case?

- How fast are its best and worst cases?

- Does it exhibit natural or unnatural behavior?

- Does it rearrange elements with equal keys?

Look closely at these criteria now. Clearly, how fast a particular algorithm sorts is of great concern. The speed with which an array can be sorted is directly related to the number of comparisons and the number of exchanges that take place, with exchanges taking more time. A *comparison* occurs when one array element is compared to another; an *exchange* happens when two elements are swapped. As you will soon see, the run times of some sort routines increase exponentially, while some increase logarithmically relative to the number of items being sorted.

The best- and worst-case run times are important if you expect to encounter one of these situations frequently. Often a sort has a good average case but a terrible worst case.

A sort is said to exhibit *natural* behavior if it works least when the list is already in order, works harder as the list becomes less ordered, and works hardest when a list is in inverse order. How hard a sort works is based on the number of comparisons and exchanges that it executes.

To understand why rearranging elements with equal keys may be important, imagine a database such as a mailing list, which is sorted on a main key and a subkey. The main sort key is the ZIP code, and within ZIP codes the last name is the subkey. When a new address is added to the list and the list is re-sorted, you do not want the subkeys (that is, the last names within ZIP codes) to be rearranged. To guarantee that this doesn't happen, a sort must not exchange main keys of equal value.

The discussion that follows first examines the representative sorts from each category and then analyzes the efficiency of each. Later, you'll learn improved sorting methods.

Bubble Sort—The Demon of Exchange

The most well known (and infamous) sort is the *bubble sort*. Its popularity is derived from its catchy name and its simplicity. However, it is one of the worst sorts ever conceived.

The bubble sort is an exchange sort. It involves the repeated comparison and, if necessary, the exchange of adjacent elements. The elements are like bubbles in a tank of water—each seeks its own level. The simplest form of the bubble sort is shown here:

```c
/* The Bubble Sort. */
void bubble(char *item, int count)
{
  register int a, b;
  register char t;

  for(a=1; a<count; ++a)
    for(b=count-1; b>=a; --b) {
      if(item[b-1] > item[b]) {
        /* exchange elements */
        t = item[b-1];
        item[b-1] = item[b];
        item[b] = t;
      }
    }
}
```

In the preceding code, **item** is a pointer to the character array to be sorted and **count** is the number of elements in the array. The bubble sort is driven by two loops. Given that there are **count** elements in the array, the outer loop causes the array to be scanned **count**–1 times. This ensures that, in the worst case, every element is in its proper position when the function terminates. The inner loop actually performs the comparisons and exchanges. (A slightly improved version of the bubble sort terminates if no exchanges occur, but this adds another comparison in each pass through the inner loop.)

You can use this version of the bubble sort to sort a character array into ascending order. For example, the following short program sorts a string entered by the user:

```
/* Sort Driver */

#include <string.h>
#include <stdio.h>
#include <stdlib.h>

void bubble(char *item, int count);

void main(void)
{
  char s[80];

  printf("Enter a string:");
  gets(s);
  bubble(s, strlen(s));
  printf("The sorted string is: %s.\n", s);
}
```

To see how the bubble sort works, assume that the array to be sorted is **dcab**. Each pass is shown here:

initial   d c a b
pass 1   a d c b
pass 2   a b d c
pass 3   a b c d

In analyzing any sort, you should determine how many comparisons and exchanges will be performed for the best, average, and worst case. With the bubble sort, the number of comparisons is always the same because the two **for** loops repeat the specified number of times whether the list is initially ordered or not. This means that the bubble sort always performs

$1/2(n^2-n)$

comparisons, where n is the number of elements to be sorted. This formula is derived from the fact that the outer loop executes $n-1$ times and the inner loop executes an average of $n/2$ times. Multiplied together, these numbers result in the preceding formula.

The number of exchanges is zero for the best case, an already sorted list. The number of exchanges for the average- and worst-case exchanges are

average $3/4(n^2-n)$
worst $3/2(n^2-n)$

It is beyond the scope of this book to explain the derivation of the preceding formulas, but you can guess that as the list becomes less ordered, the number of elements out of order approaches the number of comparisons. (Remember that in a bubble sort there are three exchanges for every element out of order.)

The bubble sort is said to be an *n-squared algorithm* because its execution time is a multiple of the square of the number of elements. Frankly, this type of algorithm is very ineffective when applied to a large number of elements because execution time is directly related to the number of comparisons and exchanges. For example, ignoring the time that it takes to exchange any out-of-position element, assume that each comparison takes 0.001 seconds. Sorting ten elements takes about 0.05 seconds, sorting 100 elements takes about 5 seconds, and sorting 1000 elements takes about 500 seconds. A sort of 100,000 elements, the number in a small phone book, takes about 5,000,000 seconds, or about 1,400 hours—that is two months of continuous sorting! Figure 19-1 shows how execution time increases relative to the size of the array.

You can make slight improvements to the bubble sort in an attempt to speed it up. For example, the bubble sort has one peculiarity: An out-of-order element at the large

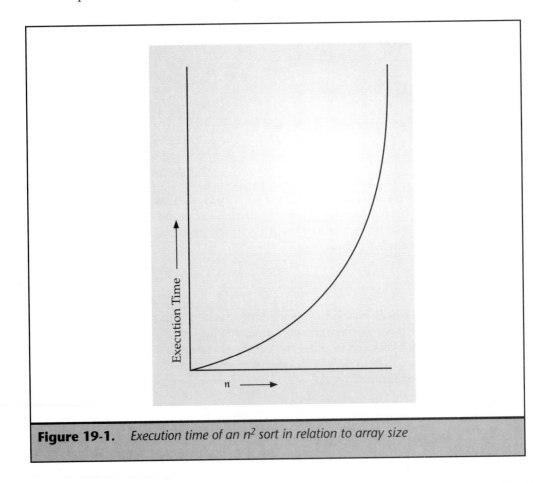

Figure 19-1. *Execution time of an n^2 sort in relation to array size*

end (such as "a" in the **dcab** example) goes to its proper position in one pass, but a misplaced element in the small end (such as "d") rises very slowly to its proper place. This suggests an improvement to the bubble sort. Instead of always reading the array in the same direction, subsequent passes could reverse direction. In this way greatly out-of-place elements travel quickly to their correct position. This version of the bubble sort is called the *shaker sort,* because it imparts the effect of a shaking motion to the array. The code that follows shows how a shaker sort works.

```
/* The Shaker Sort. */
void shaker(char *item, int count)
{
  register int a;
  int exchange;
  char t;

  do {
    exchange = 0;
    for(a=count-1; a>0; --a) {
      if(item[a-1]>item[a]) {
        t = item[a-1];
        item[a-1] = item[a];
        item[a] = t;
        exchange = 1;
      }
    }

    for(a=1; a<count; ++a) {
      if(item[a-1]>item[a]) {
        t = item[a-1];
        item[a-1] = item[a];
        item[a] = t;
        exchange = 1;
      }
    }
  } while(exchange); /* sort until no exchanges
                        take place */
}
```

Although the shaker sort improves the bubble sort, it still executes on the order of an *n*-squared algorithm. This is because the number of comparisons has not been changed and the number of exchanges has been reduced by only a relatively small constant. The shaker sort is better than the bubble sort, but better sorts exist.

Sorting by Selection

A selection sort selects the element with the lowest value and exchanges it with the first element. Then, from the remaining $n-1$ elements, the element with the smallest key is found and exchanged with the second element, and so forth. The exchanges continue to the last two elements. For example, if the selection method were used on the array **bdac**, each pass would look like this:

initial	b d a c
pass 1	a d b c
pass 2	a b d c
pass 3	a b c d

The code that follows shows the basic selection sort.

```c
/* The Selection Sort. */
void select(char *item, int count)
{
  register int a, b, c;
  int exchange;
  char t;

  for(a=0; a<count-1; ++a) {
    exchange = 0;
    c = a;
    t = item[a];
    for(b=a+1; b<count; ++b) {
      if(item[b]<t) {
        c = b;
        t = item[b];
        exchange = 1;
      }
    }
    if(exchange) {
      item[c] = item[a];
      item[a] = t;
    }
  }
}
```

Unfortunately, as with the bubble sort, the outer loop executes $n-1$ times and the inner loop averages $1/2n$ times. As a result, the selection sort requires

$1/2(n^2-n)$

comparisons, making it too slow for a large number of items. The number of exchanges for the best and worst cases are

best	$3(n-1)$
worst	$n^2/4+3\ (n-1)$

For the best case, only *n*-1 elements need to be moved if the list is ordered, and each move requires three exchanges. The worst case approximates the number of comparisons. The average case is difficult to determine and its derivation is beyond the scope of this book. However, it is

$n(\log n+y)$

where *y* is Euler's constant, about 0.577216.

Although the number of comparisons for both the bubble sort and the selection sort are the same, the number of exchanges in the average case is far less for the selection sort. However, better sorts exist.

Sorting by Insertion

The *insertion* sort is the third and last of the simple sorting algorithms. It initially sorts the first two members of the array. Next, the algorithm inserts the third member into its sorted position in relation to the first two members. Then it inserts the fourth element into the list of three elements. The process continues until all elements have been sorted. For example, given the array **dcab**, each pass of the insertion sort is shown here:

initial	d c a b
pass 1	c d a b
pass 2	a c d b
pass 3	a b c d

The code for a version of the insertion sort is

```c
/* The Insertion Sort. */
void insert(char *item, int count)
{

  register int a, b;
  char t;
```

```
for(a=1; a<count; ++a) {
  t = item[a];
  for(b=a-1; b>=0 && t<item[b]; b--)
    item[b+1] = item[b];
  item[b+1] = t;
  }
}
```

Unlike the bubble and selection sorts, the number of comparisons that occur during an insertion sort depends upon how the list is initially ordered. If the list is in order, the number of comparisons is $n–1$. If it is out of order, it is

$$1/2(n^2–n)$$

The average case is

$$1/4(n^2–n)$$

The number of exchanges are

best	$2(n–1)$
average	$1/4(n^2–n)$
worst	$1/2(n^2–n)$

Therefore, for worst cases the insertion sort is as bad as the bubble sort and selection sort, and for average cases it is only slightly better. However, the insertion sort does have two advantages. First, it behaves naturally. That is, it works the least when the array is already sorted and the hardest when the array is sorted in inverse order. This makes the insertion sort excellent for lists that are almost in order. The second advantage is that it leaves the order of equal keys the same. This means that if a list is sorted by two keys, it remains sorted for both keys after an insertion sort.

Even though the number of comparisons may be fairly low for certain sets of data, the array must always be shifted over each time an element is placed in its proper location. As a result, the number of moves can be significant. However, still better sorts exist.

Improved Sorts

All of the algorithms in the preceding section had the fatal flaw of executing in n-squared time. For large amounts of data, this makes the sorts very slow. In fact, at some point, the sorts would be too slow to use. Unfortunately, horror stories of "the sort that took three days" are often real. When a sort takes too long, it is usually the fault of the underlying algorithm. However, the first response is often "let's write it in assembly code." Using assembly language does sometimes speed up a routine by a constant factor. If the underlying algorithm is inefficient, however, the sort will be slow no matter how optimal the coding. *Remember*: When a routine is running relative to n^2, increasing the speed of the code or the computer only causes a small improvement because the rate at which the run time is increasing is exponential. (In essence, the n^2 curve in Figure 19-1 is shifted to the right slightly, but is otherwise unchanged.) The rule of thumb is that if the routine is not fast enough when written in C, it will not be fast enough in assembly language. The solution is to use a better sorting algorithm.

This section describes two excellent sorts. The first is the *Shell* sort. The second, the *quicksort*, is usually considered the best sorting routine. These sorts run so fast that if you blink, you miss them!

The Shell Sort

The Shell sort is named after its inventor, D. L. Shell. However, the name probably stuck because its method of operation is often described in terms of seashells piled upon one another.

The general sorting method is derived from the insertion sort and is based on diminishing increments. Consider the diagram in Figure 19-2. First, all elements that are three positions apart are sorted. Then, all elements that are two positions apart are sorted. Finally, all elements adjacent to each other are sorted.

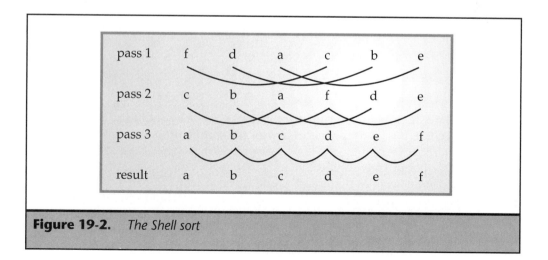

Figure 19-2.   *The Shell sort*

It is not easy to see that this method yields good results, or in fact that it even sorts the array. But it does. Each sorting pass involves relatively few elements, or elements that are already in reasonable order, so the Shell sort is efficient and each pass increases order.

The exact sequence for the increments can be changed. The only rule is that the last increment must be 1. For example, the sequence

9, 5, 3, 2, 1

works well and is used in the Shell sort shown here. Avoid sequences that are powers of 2—for mathematically complex reasons, they reduce the efficiency of the sorting algorithm (but the sort still works).

```c
/* The Shell Sort. */
void shell(char *item, int count)
{

  register int i, j, gap, k;
  char x, a[5];

  a[0]=9; a[1]=5; a[2]=3; a[3]=2; a[4]=1;

  for(k=0; k<5; k++) {
    gap = a[k];
    for(i=gap; i<count; ++i) {
      x = item[i];
      for(j=i-gap; x<item[j] && j>=0; j=j-gap)
        item[j+gap] = item[j];
      item[j+gap] = x;
    }
  }
}
```

You may have noticed that the inner **for** loop has two test conditions. The comparison **x<item[j]** is obviously necessary for the sorting process. The test **j>=0** keeps the sort from overrunning the boundary of the array **item**. These extra checks will degrade the performance of the Shell sort to some extent.

Slightly different versions of the sort employ special array elements called *sentinels*, which are not actually part of the array to be sorted. Sentinels hold special termination values that indicate the least and greatest possible element. In this way, the bounds checks are unnecessary. However, using sentinels requires a specific knowledge of the data, which limits the generality of the sort function.

The Shell sort presents some very difficult mathematical problems that are far beyond the scope of this discussion. Take it on faith that execution time is proportional to

$$n^{1.2}$$

for sorting n elements. This is a significant improvement over the n-squared sorts. To understand how great the improvement is, see Figure 19-3, which graphs both an n^2 and an $n^{1.2}$ sort. However, before getting too excited about the Shell sort, you should know that the quicksort is even better.

The Quicksort

The quicksort, invented and named by C.A.R. Hoare, is superior to all others in this book, and it is generally considered the best general-purpose sorting algorithm currently available. It is based on the exchange sort—surprising in light of the terrible performance of the bubble sort!

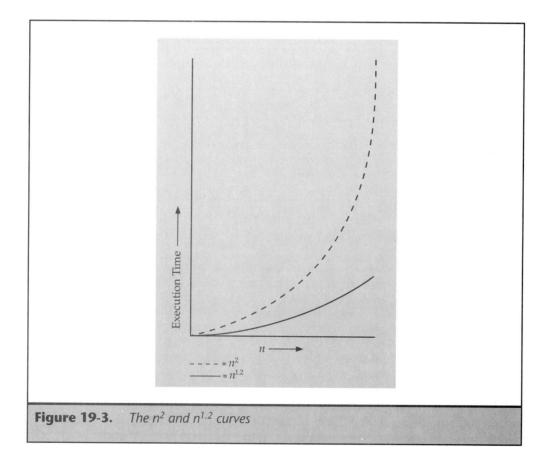

Figure 19-3.   *The n^2 and $n^{1.2}$ curves*

The quicksort is built on the idea of partitions. The general procedure is to select a value, called the *comparand*, and then to partition the array into two sections. All elements greater than or equal to the partition value are on one side and those less than the value are on the other. This process is then repeated for each remaining section until the array is sorted. For example, given the array **fedacb** and using the value **d** as the comparand, the first pass of the quicksort would rearrange the array as follows:

initial	f e d a c b
pass1	b c a d e f

This process is then repeated for each section—that is, **bca** and **def**. As you can see, the process is essentially recursive in nature and, indeed, the cleanest implementations of quicksort are recursive algorithms.

You can select the middle comparand value in two ways. You can either choose it at random or you can select it by averaging a small set of values taken from the array. For optimal sorting, you should select a value that is precisely in the middle of the range of values. However, this is not easy to do for most sets of data. In the worst case, the value chosen is at one extremity. Even in this case, however, quicksort still performs well. The following version of quicksort selects the middle element of the array as the comparand.

```c
/* Quicksort setup function. */
void quick(char *item, int count)
{
  qs(item, 0, count-1);
}

/* The Quicksort. */
void qs(char *item, int left, int right)
{
  register int i, j;
  char x, y;

  i = left; j = right;
  x = item[(left+right)/2];

  do {
    while(item[i]<x && i<right) i++;
    while(x<item[j] && j>left) j--;

    if(i<=j) {
      y = item[i];
```

```
        item[i] = item[j];
        item[j] = y;
        i++; j--;
      }
  } while(i<=j);

  if(left<j) qs(item, left, j);
  if(i<right) qs(item, i, right);
}
```

In this version, the function **quick( )** sets up a call to the main sorting function **qs( )**. This enables the same common interface of **item** and **count** to be maintained, but it is not essential because **qs( )** could have been called directly by using three arguments.

Deriving the number of comparisons and exchanges that quicksort performs requires mathematics beyond the scope of this book. However, the average number of comparisons is

$$n \log n$$

and the average number of exchanges is approximately

$$n/6 \log n$$

These numbers are significantly lower than those provided by any of the previous sorts.

You should be aware of one particularly problematic aspect to quicksort. If the comparand value for each partition is the largest value, quicksort degenerates into "slowsort" with an n-squared run time. Generally, however, this does not happen.

You must choose a method of defining the value of the comparand carefully. The method is frequently determined by the data that you are sorting. In very large mailing lists, where the sorting is often by ZIP code, the selection is simple because the ZIP codes are fairly evenly distributed—and a simple algebraic function can determine a suitable comparand. However, in certain databases, the keys may be the same or so close in value that a random selection is often the best one. A common and fairly effective method is to sample three elements from a partition and take the middle value.

Choosing a Sort

Generally, quicksort is the optimum sort because it is so fast. However, when only very small lists of data are to be sorted (less than 100), the overhead created by quicksort's recursive calls may offset the benefits of a superior algorithm. In rare cases like this, one of the simpler sorts—perhaps even the bubble sort—may be quicker.

Sorting Other Data Structures

Until now, you have been sorting only arrays of characters. Obviously, arrays of any of the built-in data types may be sorted by simply changing the data types of the parameters and variables to the sort function. Generally, however, complex data types like strings or groupings of information like structures need to be sorted. Most sorting involves a key and information linked to that key. To change the algorithms to accommodate a key, you need to alter the comparison section, the exchange section, or both. The algorithm itself remains unchanged.

Because quicksort is one of the best general-purpose routines available at this time, it is used in the following examples. However, the same techniques apply to any of the sorts described earlier.

Sorting Strings

Sorting strings is a common programming task. By far, strings are easiest to sort when they are contained in a string table. A *string table* is simply an array of strings. And, an array of strings is a two-dimensional character array in which the number of strings in the table is determined by the size of the left dimension and the maximum length of each string is determined by the size of the right dimension. (Refer to Chapter 4 for information about arrays of strings.) The string version of quicksort that follows accepts an array of strings in which each string is up to ten characters long. (You can change this length if you want.) This version sorts the strings in dictionary order.

```
/* A Quicksort for strings. */
void quick_string(char item[][10], int count)
{
  qs_string(item, 0, count-1);
}

void qs_string(char item[][10], int left, int right)
{
  register int i, j;
  char *x;
  char temp[10];

  i = left; j = right;
  x = item[(left+right)/2];
```

```
do {
  while(strcmp(item[i],x)<0 && i<right) i++;
  while(strcmp(item[j],x)>0 && j>left) j--;
  if(i<=j) {
    strcpy(temp, item[i]);
    strcpy(item[i], item[j]);
    strcpy(item[j], temp);
    i++; j--;
  }
} while(i<=j);

if(left<j) qs_string(item, left, j);
if(i<right) qs_string(item, i, right);
}
```

Notice that the comparison step has been changed to use the function **strcmp( )**. The function returns a negative number if the first string is lexicographically less than the second, zero if the strings are equal, and a positive number if the first string is lexicographically greater than the second. Also notice that when two strings must be swapped, three calls to **strcpy( )** are required.

Be aware that **strcmp( )** slows down the sort for two reasons. First, it involves a function call, which always takes time. Second, **strcmp( )** itself performs several comparisons to determine the relationship of the two strings. In the first case, if speed is absolutely critical, place the code for **strcmp( )** in line inside the routine by duplicating the **strcmp( )** code. In the second case, there is no way to avoid comparing the strings since, by definition, this is what the task involves. The same line of reasoning also applies to the **strcpy( )** function. The use of **strcpy( )** to exchange two strings involves a function call and a character-by-character exchange of the two strings—both of which add time. The overhead of the function call could be eliminated through the use of inline code. However, the fact that exchanging two strings means exchanging their individual characters (one-by-one) cannot be altered.

Sorting Structures

Most application programs that require a sort probably need to have a collection of data sorted. For example, mailing lists, databases, and employee records all contain collections of data. As you know, in C programs collections of data are typically stored in structures. Although a structure will generally contain several members, it will usually be sorted on the basis of only one member, which is used as the sort key. Aside from the selection of the key, the techniques used to sort other types of data also apply to sorting structures.

To see an example of sorting structures, let's use a structure, called **address**, that is capable of holding a mailing address. Such a structure could be used by a mailing list program. The **address** structure is shown here.

```
struct address {
   char name[40];
   char street[40];
   char city[20];
   char state[3];
   char zip[11];
};
```

Since it is reasonable to arrange a mailing list as an array of structures, assume for this example that the sort routine will sort an array of structures of type **address**. Such a routine is shown here. It sorts the addresses by ZIP code.

```
/* A Quicksort for structures of type address. */
void quick_struct(struct address item[], int count)
{
   qs_struct(item,0,count-1);
}

void qs_struct(struct address item[], int left, int right)
{

   register int i, j;
   char *x;
   struct address temp;

   i = left; j = right;
   x = item[(left+right)/2].zip;

   do {
     while(strcmp(item[i].zip,x)<0 && i<right) i++;
     while(strcmp(item[j].zip,x)>0 && j>left) j--;
     if(i<=j) {
       temp = item[i];
       item[i] = item[j];
       item[j] = temp;
       i++; j--;
     }
   } while(i<=j);
```

```
   if(left<j) qs_struct(item, left, j);
   if(i<right) qs_struct(item, i, right);
}
```

Sorting Random-Access Disk Files

There are two types of disk files: *sequential* and *random access*. If either type of disk file is small enough, it may be read into memory and the array sorting routines presented earlier will be able to sort it. However, many disk files are too large to be sorted easily in memory and require special techniques. Most database applications use random-access disk files. This section shows one way random-access disk files may be sorted.

Random-access disk files have two major advantages over sequential disk files. First, they are easy to maintain. You can update information without having to copy the entire list. Second, they can be treated as a very large array on disk, which greatly simplifies sorting.

Treating a random-access file as an array means that you can use the basic quicksort with just a few modifications. Instead of indexing an array, the disk version of the quicksort must use **fseek( )** to seek the appropriate records on the disk.

In reality, each sorting situation differs in relation to the exact data structure that is sorted and the key that is used. However, you can learn the general idea of sorting random-access disk files by using a short program to sort structures of type **address**, the mailing-list structure defined earlier. The sample program that follows first creates a disk file that contains unsorted addresses. It then sorts the file. The number of addresses to sort is specified by **NUM_ELEMENTS** (which is 4 for this program). However, for a real-world application, a record count would have to be maintained dynamically. You should experiment with this program on your own, trying different types of structures, containing different types of data.

```c
/* Disk sort for structures of type address. */
#include <stdio.h>
#include <stdlib.h>
#include <string.h>

#define NUM_ELEMENTS 4   /* This is an arbitrary number
                            that should be determined
                            dynamically for each list. */

struct address {
  char name[30];
  char street[40];
  char city[20];
```

```
    char state[3];
    char zip[11];
}ainfo;

struct address addrs[NUM_ELEMENTS] = {
  "A. Alexander", "101 1st St", "Olney", "Ga", "55555",
  "B. Bertrand", "22 2nd Ave", "Oakland", "Pa", "34232",
  "C. Carlisle", "33 3rd Blvd", "Ava", "Or", "92000",
  "D. Dodger", "4 Fourth Dr", "Fresno", "Mi", "45678"
};

void quick_disk(FILE *fp, int count);
void qs_disk(FILE *fp, int left, int right);
void swap_all_fields(FILE *fp, long i, long j);
char *get_zip(FILE *fp, long rec);

void main(void)
{
  FILE *fp;

  /* first, create a file to sort */
  if((fp=fopen("mlist", "wb"))==NULL) {
    printf("Cannot open file for write.\n");
    exit(1);
  }
  printf("Writing unsorted data to disk.\n");
  fwrite(addrs, sizeof(addrs), 1, fp);
  fclose(fp);

  /* now, sort the file */
  if((fp=fopen("mlist", "rb+"))==NULL) {
    printf("Cannot open file for read/write.\n");
    exit(1);
  }

  printf("Sorting disk file.\n");
  quick_disk(fp, NUM_ELEMENTS);
  fclose(fp);
  printf("List sorted.\n");
}

/* A Quicksort for files. */
```

```
void quick_disk(FILE *fp, int count)
{
  qs_disk(fp, 0, count-1);
}

void qs_disk(FILE *fp, int left, int right)
{
  long int i, j;
  char x[100];

  i = left; j = right;

  strcpy(x, get_zip(fp,(long)(i+j)/2)); /* get the middle zip */

  do {
    while(strcmp(get_zip(fp,i),x)<0 && i<right) i++;
    while(strcmp(get_zip(fp,j),x)>0 && j>left) j--;

    if(i<=j) {
      swap_all_fields(fp, i, j);
      i++; j--;
    }
  } while(i<=j);

  if(left<j) qs_disk(fp, left, (int) j);
  if(i<right) qs_disk(fp, (int) i, right);
}

void swap_all_fields(FILE *fp, long i, long j)
{
  char a[sizeof(ainfo)], b[sizeof(ainfo)];

  /* first read in record i and j */
  fseek(fp, sizeof(ainfo)*i, SEEK_SET);
  fread(a, sizeof(ainfo), 1, fp);

  fseek(fp, sizeof(ainfo)*j, SEEK_SET);
  fread(b, sizeof(ainfo), 1, fp);

  /* then write them back in opposite slots */
  fseek(fp, sizeof(ainfo)*j, SEEK_SET);
  fwrite(a, sizeof(ainfo), 1, fp);
```

```
    fseek(fp, sizeof(ainfo)*i, SEEK_SET);
    fwrite(b, sizeof(ainfo), 1, fp);
}

/* Return a pointer to the zip code */
char *get_zip(FILE *fp, long rec)
{
  struct address *p;

  p = &ainfo;

  fseek(fp, rec*sizeof(ainfo), SEEK_SET);
  fread(p, sizeof(ainfo), 1, fp);

  return ainfo.zip;
}
```

As you can see, several support functions had to be written to sort the address records. In the comparison section of the sort, the function **get_zip( )** was used to return a pointer to the ZIP code of the comparand and the record being checked. The function **swap_all_fields( )** performs the actual data exchange. Note that under most operating systems, the order of the reads and writes has a great impact on the speed of this sort. When an exchange occurs, the code, as it is shown, forces a seek to record **i**, then to **j**. While the head of the disk drive is still positioned at **j**, **i**'s data is written. This means that the head does not need to move a great distance. Had the code been written with **i**'s data written first, an extra seek would have been necessary.

Searching

Databases of information exist so that, from time to time, a user can locate a record by entering its key. There is only one method of finding information in an unsorted array and another for a sorted array. Most compilers supply search functions as part of the standard library. However, as with sorting, general-purpose routines sometimes are simply too inefficient for use in demanding situations because of the extra overhead created by their generalization.

Searching Methods

Finding information in an unsorted array requires a sequential search starting at the first element and stopping either when a match is found or at the end of the array. This method must be used on unsorted data but can be applied to sorted data as well.

However, if the data has been sorted, you can use a binary search, which helps you locate the data more quickly.

The Sequential Search

The sequential search is simple to code. The following function searches a character array of known length until a match of the specified key is found:

```
sequential_search(char *item, int count, char key)
{
  register int t;

  for(t=0; t<count; ++t)
    if(key==item[t]) return t;
  return -1; /* no match */
}
```

This function returns the index number of the matching entry if there is one; otherwise, it returns –1.

It is easy to see that a straight sequential search will, on the average, test $1/2n$ elements. In the best case, it tests only one element and in the worst case it tests n elements. If the information is stored on disk, the search time can be lengthy. But if the data is unsorted, you can only search sequentially.

The Binary Search

If the data to be searched is sorted, you can use a vastly superior method to find a match. It is the *binary search*, which uses the divide-and-conquer approach. To employ this method, test the middle element. If it is larger than the key, then test the middle element of the first half; otherwise, test the middle element of the second half. Repeat this procedure until a match is found or there are no more elements to test.

For example, to find the number 4 given the array

1 2 3 4 5 6 7 8 9

a binary search first tests the middle, which is 5. Since this is greater than 4, the search continues with the first half, or

1 2 3 4 5

The middle element is now 3. This is less than 4, so the first half is discarded. The search continues with

4 5

This time the match is found.

In a binary search, the number of comparisons in the worst case is

$$\log_2 n$$

In the average case, the number is somewhat lower and in the best case the number of comparisons is one.

A binary search function for character arrays follows. You can make this search for any arbitrary data structure by changing the comparison portion of the routine.

```c
/* The Binary search. */
binary(char *item, int count, char key)
{
  int low,high, mid;

  low = 0; high = count-1;
  while(low<=high) {
    mid = (low+high)/2;
    if(key<item[mid]) high = mid-1;
    else if(key>item[mid]) low = mid+1;
    else return mid; /* found */
  }
  return -1;
}
```

Chapter Twenty

Queues, Stacks, Linked Lists, and Trees

Programs consist of two things: algorithms and data structures. A good program is an effective blend of both. The choice and implementation of a data structure is as important as the routines that manipulate it. How information is organized and accessed is usually determined by the nature of the programming problem. For this reason, it is important for you to have the right storage and retrieval method for a variety of situations in your bag of tricks.

How closely a data type is bound to its machine representation has an inverse correlation to its abstraction. That is, as data types become more abstract, the way the programmer thinks of them bears an ever-decreasing resemblance to the way they are actually represented in memory. Simple types, such as **char** and **int**, are tightly bound to their machine representation. For example, the machine representation of an integer value closely approximates the programmer's concept of that value. Simple arrays, which are organized collections of basic data types, are not quite as tightly bound as the elemental types, but they exist in memory in much the same way as you visualize them.

As data types become more complex, they are conceptually less similar to their machine equivalents. For example, floating-point values are more abstract than are integers. The actual representation of a **float** inside the machine is little like the average programmer's conception of a floating-point number. Even more abstract is the structure, which is a conglomerate data type. The final level of abstraction transcends the mere physical aspects of the data by adding the mechanism by which that data may be accessed—that is, stored and retrieved. In essence, the physical data is linked with a *data engine*, which controls the way information can be accessed by your program. It is these data engines that are the subject of this chapter.

There are four basic types of data engines:

- A queue
- A stack
- A linked list
- A binary tree

Each of these methods provides a solution to a class of problems. These methods are essentially devices that perform a specific storage-and-retrieval operation on the information that they are given and the requests that they receive. They all store an item and retrieve an item, where an item is one informational unit. The rest of this chapter shows you how to build these data engines using the C language. In the process, several common C programming techniques are illustrated, including dynamic allocation and pointer manipulation.

Queues

A *queue* is simply a linear list of information that is accessed in *first-in, first-out* order, which is sometimes called FIFO. That is, the first item placed on the queue is the first item retrieved, the second item put in is the second item retrieved, and so on. This is

Action	Contents of the Queue
qstore(A)	A
qstore(B)	A B
qstore(C)	A B C
qretrieve( ) returns **A**	B C
qstore(D)	B C D
qretrieve( ) returns **B**	C D
qretrieve( ) returns **C**	D

Table 20-1.   *A Queue in Action*

the only means of storage and retrieval in a queue; random access of any specific item is not allowed.

Queues are very common in real life. For example, lines at a bank or a fast-food restaurant are queues (except when rude patrons push their way to the front!). To visualize how a queue works, consider two functions: **qstore( )** and **qretrieve( )**. The **qstore( )** function places an item onto the end of the queue, and **qretrieve( )** removes the first item from the queue and returns its value. Table 20-1 shows the effect of a series of these operations.

Keep in mind that a retrieval operation removes an item from the queue and destroys it if it is not stored elsewhere. Therefore, a queue may be empty because all items have been removed.

Queues are used in many programming situations. One of the most common is in simulations. Queues are also used by the task scheduler of an operating system and for I/O buffering.

To see an example of a queue in action, we will use a simple appointment-scheduler program. This program allows you to enter a number of appointments; then, as each appointment is met, it is taken off the list. For the sake of simplicity, each appointment description will be limited to 255 characters and the number of appointments is arbitrarily limited to 100.

First, the functions **qstore( )** and **qretrieve( )** shown here are needed for the simple scheduling program. They will store pointers to the strings that describe the appointments.

```
#define MAX 100

char *p[MAX];
int spos = 0;
```

```
int rpos = 0;

/* Store an appointment. */
void qstore(char *q)
{
  if(spos==MAX) {
    printf("List Full\n");
    return;
  }
  p[spos] = q;
  spos++;
}

/* Retrieve an appointment. */
char *qretrieve()
{
  if(rpos==spos) {
    printf("No more appointments.\n");
    return NULL;
  }
  rpos++;
  return p[rpos-1];
}
```

Notice that these functions require two global variables: **spos** (which holds the index of the next free storage location) and **rpos** (which holds the index of the next item to retrieve). You can use these functions to maintain a queue of other data types by simply changing the base type of the array that they operate on.

The function **qstore( )** places pointers to new appointments on the end of the list and checks to see if the list is full. The function **qretrieve( )** takes appointments off the queue while there are events to perform. With each new appointment scheduled, **spos** is incremented and, with each appointment completed, **rpos** is incremented. In essence, **rpos** chases **spos** through the queue. Figure 20-1 shows how this may appear in memory as the program executes. If **rpos** and **spos** are equal, there are no events left in the schedule. Even though the information stored in the queue is not actually destroyed by **qretrieve( )**, it is effectively destroyed because it can never be accessed again.

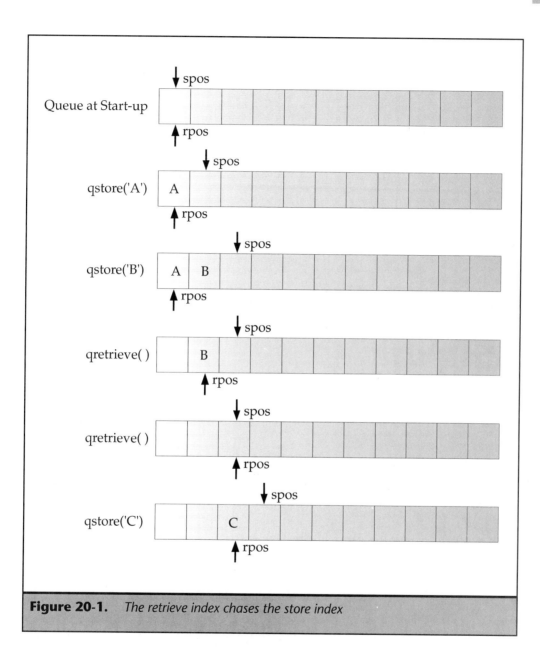

Figure 20-1. *The retrieve index chases the store index*

The entire program for this simple appointment scheduler is listed here. You may want to enhance this program for your own use.

```c
/* Mini Appointment-Scheduler */

#include <string.h>
#include <stdlib.h>
#include <stdio.h>
#include <ctype.h>

#define MAX 100

char *p[MAX], *qretrieve(void);
int spos = 0;
int rpos = 0;
void enter(void), qstore(char *q), review(void), delete(void);

void main(void)
{
  char s[80];
  register int t;

  for(t=0; t<MAX; ++t) p[t] = NULL; /* init array to nulls */

  for(;;) {
    printf("Enter, List, Remove, Quit: ");
    gets(s);
    *s = toupper(*s);

    switch(*s) {
      case 'E':
        enter();
        break;
      case 'L':
        review();
        break;
      case 'R':
        delete();
        break;
      case 'Q':
        exit(0);
    }
  }
}
```

```
}

/* Enter appointments in queue. */
void enter(void)
{
  char s[256], *p;

  do {
    printf("Enter appointment %d: ", spos+1);
    gets(s);
    if(*s==0) break; /* no entry */
    p = malloc(strlen(s)+1);
    if(!p) {
      printf("Out of memory.\n");
      return;
    }
    strcpy(p, s);
    if(*s) qstore(p);
  }while(*s);
}

/* See what's in the queue. */
void review(void)
{
  register int t;

  for(t=rpos; t<spos; ++t)
    printf("%d. %s\n", t+1, p[t]);
}

/* Delete an appointment from the queue. */
void delete(void)
{
  char *p;

  if((p=qretrieve())==NULL) return;
  printf("%s\n", p);
}

/* Store an appointment. */
void qstore(char *q)
{
```

```
   if(spos==MAX) {
     printf("List Full\n");
     return;
   }
   p[spos] = q;
   spos++;
 }

 /* Retrieve an appointment. */
 char *qretrieve(void)
 {
   if(rpos==spos) {
     printf("No more appointments.\n");
     return NULL;
   }
   rpos++;
   return p[rpos-1];
 }
```

The Circular Queue

In studying the preceding appointment scheduler program, an improvement may
have occurred to you. Instead of having the program stop when the limit of the array
used to store the queue is reached, you could have both the store index (**spos**) and the
retrieve index (**rpos**) loop back to the start of the array. In this way, any number of
items could be placed on the queue, so long as items were also being taken off. This
implementation of a queue is called a *circular queue* because it uses its storage array as
if it were a circle instead of a linear list.

To create a circular queue for use in the scheduler program, you need to change the
functions **qstore( )** and **qretrieve( )** as shown here:

```
 void qstore(char *q)
 {
   /* The queue is full if either spos is one less than rpos
      or if spos is at the end of the queue array and rpos
      is at the beginning.
   */
   if(spos+1==rpos || (spos+1==MAX && !rpos)) {
     printf("List Full\n");
     return;
   }
```

```
    p[spos] = q;
    spos++;
    if(spos==MAX) spos = 0; /* loop back */
  }

char *qretrieve(void)
{
  if(rpos==MAX) rpos = 0; /* loop back */
  if(rpos==spos) {
    printf("No events to retrieve.\n");
    return NULL;
  }
  rpos++;
  return p[rpos-1];
}
```

In essence, the queue is full when the store index is one less than the retrieve index; otherwise, there is room in the queue for another event. Conceptually, the array used for the circular version of the scheduler program looks like Figure 20-2.

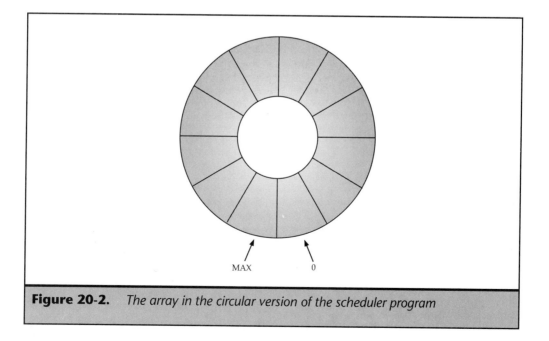

Figure 20-2.   *The array in the circular version of the scheduler program*

Perhaps the most common use of a circular queue is in operating systems, where a circular queue holds the information read from and written to disk files or the console. Circular queues are also used in real-time application programs, which must continue to process information while buffering I/O requests. Many word processors do this when they reformat a paragraph or justify a line. What is being typed is not displayed until the other process is complete. To accomplish this, the application program needs to check for keyboard entry during the other process's execution. If a key has been typed, it is quickly placed in the queue and the other process continues. Once the process is complete, the characters are retrieved from the queue.

To get a feel for this use of a circular queue, consider a simple program that contains two processes. The first process in the program prints the numbers **1** to **32,000** on the screen. The second process places characters into a circular queue as they are typed, without echoing them to the screen, until you press ENTER. The characters you type are not displayed because the first process is given priority over the screen. Once you have pressed ENTER, the characters in the queue are retrieved and printed.

For the program to function as described, it must use two functions not defined by the ANSI C standard: **kbhit( )** and **getch( )**. The **kbhit( )** function returns true if a key has been pressed; otherwise, it returns false. The **getch( )** function reads a keystroke but does not echo the character to the screen. The ANSI C standard does not define functions that check keyboard status or read keyboard characters without echoing them to the display because these functions are highly operating-system dependent. Nonetheless, most compilers supply routines to do these things. The short program shown here works with most compilers; however, the two nonstandard functions might have different names.

```c
/* A circular queue example using a keyboard buffer. */
#include <stdio.h>
#include <conio.h>
#include <stdlib.h>

#define MAX 80

char buf[MAX+1];
int spos=0;
int rpos=0;

void qstore(char q);
char qretrieve(void);

void main(void)
{
  register char ch;
```

```
   int t;

   buf[80] = NULL;

   /* Input characters until a carriage return is typed. */
   for(ch=' ',t=0; t<32000 && ch!='\r'; ++t) {
     if(kbhit()) {
       ch = getch();
       qstore(ch);
     }
     printf("%d ", t);
     if(ch=='\r') {
       /* Display and empty the key buffer. */
       printf("\n");
       while((ch=qretrieve())!=NULL) printf("%c", ch);
       printf("\n");
     }
   }
}

/* Store characters in the queue. */
void qstore(char q)
{
  if(spos+1==rpos || (spos+1==MAX && !rpos)) {
    printf("List Full\n");
    return;
  }
  buf[spos] = q;
  spos++;
  if(spos==MAX) spos = 0; /* loop back */
}

/* Retrieve a character. */
char qretrieve(void)
{
  if(rpos==MAX) rpos = 0; /* loop back */
  if(rpos==spos) return NULL;

  rpos++;
  return buf[rpos-1];
}
```

Stacks

A *stack* is the opposite of a queue because it uses last-in, first-out accessing, which is sometimes called LIFO. To visualize a stack, just imagine a stack of plates. The first plate on the table is the last to be used and the last plate placed on the stack is the first to be used. Stacks are used a great deal in system software, including compilers and interpreters. In fact, C compilers use the stack for passing arguments to functions.

When working with stacks, the two basic operations—store and retrieve—are traditionally called *push* and *pop*, respectively. Therefore, to implement a stack you need two functions: **push( )**, which places a value on the stack, and **pop( )**, which retrieves a value from the stack. You also need a region of memory to use as the stack. You can use an array for this purpose or allocate a region of memory using C's dynamic allocation functions. As with the queue, the retrieval function takes a value off the list and destroys it if it is not stored elsewhere. The general forms of **push( )** and **pop( )** that use an integer array follow. You may maintain stacks of other data types by changing the base type of the array on which **push( )** and **pop( )** operate.

```c
int stack[MAX];
int tos=0;    /* top of stack */

/* Put an element on the stack. */
void push(int i)
{

  if(tos>=MAX) {
    printf("Stack Full\n");
    return;
  }
  stack[tos] = i;
  tos++;
}

/* Retrieve the top element from the stack. */
pop(void)
{
  tos--;
  if(tos<0) {
    printf("Stack Underflow\n");
    return 0;
  }
  return stack[tos];
}
```

Action	Contents of Stack
push(A)	A
push(B)	B A
push(C)	C B A
pop( ) retrieves **C**	B A
push(F)	F B A
pop( ) retrieves **F**	B A
pop( ) retrieves **B**	A
pop( ) retrieves **A**	*empty*

Table 20-2. *A Stack in Action*

The variable **tos** is the index of the top of the stack. When implementing these functions, you must remember to prevent overflow and underflow. In these routines, an empty stack is signaled by **tos** being zero and a full stack by **tos** being greater than the last storage location. To see how a stack works, see Table 20-2.

An excellent example of stack usage is a four-function calculator. Most calculators today accept a standard form of an expression called *infix notation*, which takes the general form *operand-operator-operand*. For example, to add 200 to 100, enter **100**, then press the PLUS (+) key, then **200**, and press the EQUAL (=) key. In contrast, many early calculators (and some still made today) use *postfix notation*, in which both operands are entered first and then the operator is entered. For example, to add 200 to 100 by using postfix notation, you enter 100, then 200, and then press the PLUS key. As operands are entered, they are placed on a stack. Each time an operator is entered, two operands are removed from the stack and the result is pushed back on the stack. One advantage of the postfix form is that long, complex expressions can be easily entered by the user.

The following example demonstrates a stack by implementing a postfix calculator for integer expressions.To begin, the **push( )** and **pop( )** functions must be modified, as shown here. They also will use dynamically allocated memory (instead of a fixed-size array) for the stack. Although the use of dynamically allocated memory is not necessary for this simple example, it illustrates how dynamically allocated memory may be used to support a stack.

```
int *p;   /* will point to a region of free memory */
int *tos; /* points to top of stack */
int *bos; /* points to bottom of stack */
```

```
/* Store an element on the stack. */
void push(int i)
{
  if(p>bos) {
    printf("Stack Full\n");
    return;
  }
  *p = i;
  p++;
}

/* Retrieve the top element from the stack. */
pop(void)
{
  p--;
  if(p<tos) {
    printf("Stack Underflow\n");
    return 0;
  }
  return *p;
}
```

Before these functions can be used, a region of free memory must be allocated with **malloc( )**, the address of the beginning of that region assigned to **tos**, and the address of the end assigned to **bos**.

The entire postfix-based calculator program is shown here:

```
/* A simple four-function calculator. */

#include <stdio.h>
#include <stdlib.h>

#define MAX 100

int *p;    /* will point to a region of free memory */
int *tos; /* points to top of stack */
int *bos; /* points to bottom of stack */

void push(int i);
int pop(void);
```

```
void main(void)
{
  int a, b;
  char s[80];

  p = (int *) malloc(MAX*sizeof(int)); /* get stack memory */
  if(!p) {
    printf("Allocation Failure\n");
    exit(1);
  }
  tos = p;
  bos = p+MAX-1;

  printf("Four Function Calculator\n");
  printf("Enter 'q' to quit\n");

  do {
    printf(": ");
    gets(s);
    switch(*s) {
      case '+':
        a = pop();
        b = pop();
        printf("%d\n", a+b);
        push(a+b);
        break;
      case '-':
        a = pop();
        b = pop();
        printf("%d\n", b-a);
        push(b-a);
        break;
      case '*':
        a = pop();
        b = pop();
        printf("%d\n", b*a);
        push(b*a);
        break;
      case '/':
        a = pop();
        b = pop();
        if(a==0) {
```

```
            printf("divide by 0\n");
            break;
          }
          printf("%d\n", b/a);
          push(b/a);
          break;
      case '.': /* show contents of top of stack */
        a = pop();
        push(a);
        printf("Current value on top of stack: %d\n", a);
        break;
      default:
        push(atoi(s));
    }
  } while(*s!='q');
}

/* Put an element on the stack. */
void push(int i)
{
  if(p>bos) {
    printf("Stack Full\n");
    return;
  }
  *p = i;
  p++;
}

/* Retrieve the top element from the stack. */
pop(void)
{
  p--;
  if(p<tos) {
    printf("Stack Underflow\n");
    return 0;
  }
  return *p;
}
```

Linked Lists

Queues and stacks share two common traits: They both have very strict rules for referencing the data stored in them, and the retrieval operations are, by nature, consumptive. In other words, accessing an item in a stack or queue requires its removal, and unless the item is stored elsewhere it is destroyed. Also, stacks and queues both use a contiguous region of memory. Unlike a stack or a queue, a *linked list* may be accessed in a random fashion because each piece of information carries with it a link to the next data item in the chain. For this reason, a linked list requires a complex data structure—as opposed to a stack or queue, which can operate on both simple and complex data items. In addition, a linked-list retrieval operation does not remove and destroy an item from the list. In fact, you need to add a specific deletion operation to do this.

Linked lists can be either singly linked or doubly linked. A singly linked list contains a link to the next data item. A doubly linked list contains links to both the next and the previous element in the list. You will use one or the other of these linked list types, depending upon your application.

Singly Linked Lists

A singly linked list requires that each item of information contain a link to the next element in the list. Each data item usually consists of a structure that includes information fields and a link pointer. Conceptually, a singly linked list looks like that shown in Figure 20-3.

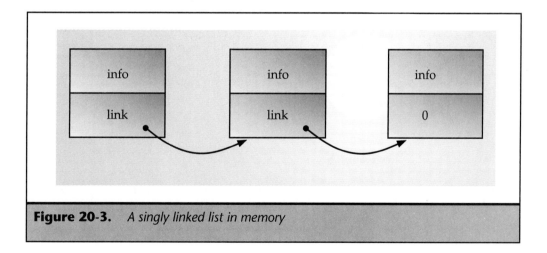

Figure 20-3.   *A singly linked list in memory*

Basically, there are two ways to build a singly linked list. The first is to simply put each new item on the end of the list. The other is to add items into specific places in the list—in ascending sorted order, for example. How you build the list determines the way the storage function is coded. Let's start with the simpler case of creating a linked list by adding items on the end.

The items stored in a linked list generally consist of structures because each item must carry with it a link to the next item in the list as well as the data itself. Therefore, we will need to define a structure that will be used in the examples that follow. Since mailing lists are commonly stored in a linked list, an address structure makes a good choice. The data structure for each element in the mailing list is defined here:

```
struct address {
   char name[40];
   char street[40];
   char city[20];
   char state[3];
   char zip[11];
   struct address *next;
} info;
```

The **slstore( )** function, shown next, builds a singly linked list by placing each new element on the end. It must be passed a pointer to a structure of type **address** as well as a pointer to the last element in the list. If the list is empty, then the pointer to the last element in the list must be null.

```
void slstore(struct address *i,
             struct address **last)
{
   if(!*last) *last = i; /* first item in list */
   else (*last)->next = i;
   i->next = NULL;
   *last = i;
}
```

Although you can sort the list created with the function **slstore( )** as a separate operation, it is easier to sort the list while building it by inserting each new item in the proper sequence of the chain. Also, if the list is already sorted, it would be advantageous to keep it sorted by inserting new items in their proper location. You do this by sequentially scanning the list until the proper location is found, inserting the new address at that point, and rearranging the links as necessary.

Three possible situations can occur when you insert an item in a singly linked list. First, it may become the new first item; second, it can go between two other items; or third, it can become the last element. Figure 20-4 diagrams how the links are changed for each case.

Keep in mind that if you change the first item in the list, you must update the entry point to the list elsewhere in your program. To avoid this overhead, you can use a *sentinel* as a first item. In this case, choose a special value that will always be first in the list to keep the entry point to the list from changing. This method has the disadvantage of using one extra storage location to hold the sentinel, but this is usually not an important factor.

The function shown next, **sls_store( )**, will insert **address** structures into the mailing list in ascending order based on the **name** field. It must be passed a pointer to the pointer to the first element and the last element in the list along with a pointer to the information

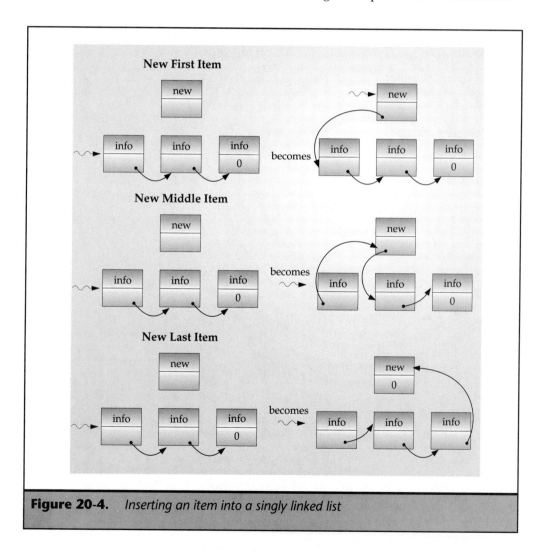

Figure 20-4.   *Inserting an item into a singly linked list*

to be stored. Since the first or last element in the list could change, **sls_store( )** automatically updates the pointers to the beginning and end of the list if they change. The first time your program calls **sls_store( )**, **first** and **last** must point to null.

```
/* Store in sorted order. */
void sls_store(struct address *i, /* new element to store */
               struct address **start, /* start of list */
               struct address **last) /* end of list */
{
  struct address *old, *p;

  p = *start;

  if(!*last) { /* first element in list */
    i->next = NULL;
    *last = i;
    *start = i;
    return;
  }

  old = NULL;
  while(p) {
    if(strcmp(p->name, i->name)<0) {
      old = p;
      p = p->next;
    }
    else {
      if(old) { /* goes in middle */
        old->next = i;
        i->next = p;
        return;
      }
      i->next = p; /* new first element */
      *start = i;
      return;
    }
  }
  (*last)->next = i; /* put on end */
  i->next = NULL;
  *last = i;
}
```

A linked list will rarely have a specific function dedicated to the retrieval process—that is, to returning item after item in list order. Usually this code is so short that it is simply placed inside another routine such as a search, delete, or display function. For example, the routine shown here displays all of the names in a mailing list:

```
void display(struct address *start)
{
  while(start) {
    printf("%s\n", start->name);
    start = start->next;
  }
}
```

When **display( )** is called, **start** must be a pointer to the first structure in the list.

Retrieving items from the list is as simple as following a chain. A search routine based on the **name** field could be written like this:

```
struct address *search(struct address *start, char *n)
{
  while(start) {
    if(!strcmp(n, start->name)) return start;
    start = start->next;
  }
  return NULL;   /* no match */
}
```

Because **search( )** returns a pointer to the list item that matches the search name, it must be declared as returning a structure pointer of type **address**. If there is no match, a null is returned.

Deleting an item from a singly linked list is straightforward. As with insertion, there are three cases: deleting the first item, deleting an item in the middle, and deleting the last item. Figure 20-5 shows each of these operations.

The function that follows deletes a given item from a list of structures of type **address**:

```
void sldelete(
    struct address *p, /* previous item */
    struct address *i, /* item to delete */
    struct address **start, /* start of list */
    struct address **last) /* end of list */
{
```

```
    if(p) p->next = i->next;
    else *start = i->next;

    if(i==*last && p) *last = p;

}
```

sldelete( ) must be sent pointers to the deleted item, the item before it in the chain, and the first and last items in the list. If the first item is to be removed, the previous pointer must be null. The function automatically updates **start** and **last** in the case where the item one of them points to is deleted.

Singly linked lists have one major drawback that prevents their extensive use: The list cannot be read in reverse order. For this reason, doubly linked lists are usually used.

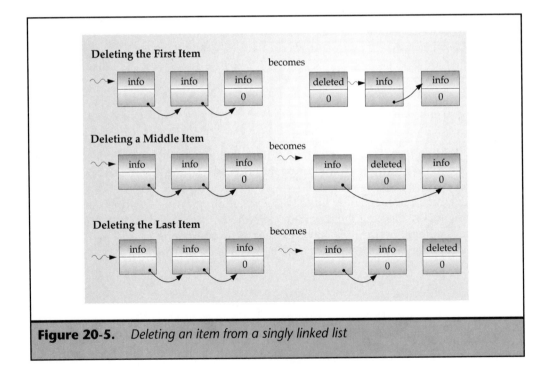

Figure 20-5.   *Deleting an item from a singly linked list*

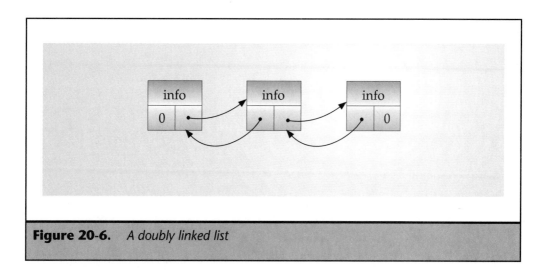

Figure 20-6.   *A doubly linked list*

Doubly Linked Lists

Doubly linked lists consist of data plus links to the next item as well as the preceding item. Figure 20-6 shows how these links are arranged.

Having two links instead of just one has several advantages. Perhaps the most important is that the list can be read in either direction. This simplifies list management, making insertions and deletions easier. It also allows a user to scan the list in either direction. Another advantage is meaningful only in the case of some type of failure. Since the entire list can be read using either forward links or backward links, should one of the links become invalid, the list could be reconstructed by using the other.

There are three ways a new element can be inserted into a doubly linked list: insert a new first element, insert in the middle, and insert a new last element. These operations are illustrated in Figure 20-7.

Building a doubly linked list is similar to building a singly linked list except that two links are maintained. Therefore, the structure must have room for both links. Using the mailing-list example again, you can modify structure **address** as shown here to accommodate both links:

```
struct address {
  char name[40];
  char street[40];
  char city[20];
  char state[3];
  char zip[11];
  struct address *next;
  struct address *prior;
} info;
```

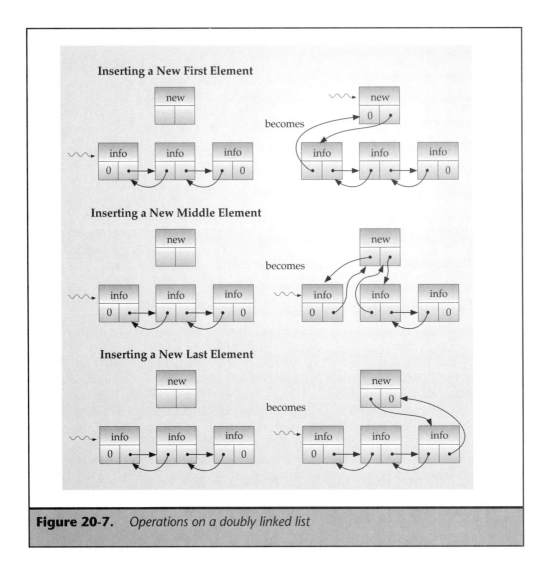

Figure 20-7.   *Operations on a doubly linked list*

Using **address** as the basic data item, the following function, **dlstore( )**, builds a doubly linked list:

```
void dlstore(struct address *i, struct address **last)
{

  if(!*last) *last = i; /* is first item in list */
  else (*last)->next = i;
  i->next = NULL;
```

```
    i->prior = *last;
    *last = i;
}
```

The function **dlstore( )** places each new entry on the end of the list. You must call it with a pointer to the data to be stored as well as a pointer to the end of the list, which must be null on the first call.

Like singly linked lists, a doubly linked list can be built by a function that stores each element in a specific location in the list instead of always placing each new item on the end. The function shown here, **dls_store( )**, creates a list that is sorted in ascending order:

```
/* Create a doubly linked list in sorted order. */
void dls_store(
  struct address *i,    /* new element */
  struct address **start, /* first element in list */
  struct address **last /* last element in list */
)
{
  struct address *old, *p;

  if(*last==NULL) { /* first element in list */
    i->next = NULL;
    i->prior = NULL;
    *last = i;
    *start = i;
    return;
  }

  p = *start; /* start at top of list */

  old = NULL;
  while(p) {
    if(strcmp(p->name, i->name)<0){
      old = p;
      p = p->next;
    }
    else {
      if(p->prior) {
        p->prior->next = i;
        i->next = p;
        i->prior = p->prior;
```

```
       p->prior = i;
       return;
    }
    i->next = p; /* new first element */
    i->prior = NULL;
    p->prior = i;
    *start = i;
    return;
  }
}
old->next = i; /* put on end */
i->next = NULL;
i->prior = old;
*last = i;
}
```

Because the first or last element in the list can change, the **dls_store( )** function automatically updates pointers to the beginning and ending elements of the list through the **start** and **last** parameters. You must call the function with a pointer to the data to be stored, and a pointer to the pointers to the first and last items in the list. When called the first time, the objects pointed to by **first** and **last** must be null.

As in singly linked lists, retrieving a specific data item in a doubly linked list is simply the process of following the links until the proper element is found.

There are three cases to consider when deleting an element from a doubly linked list: deleting the first item, deleting an item from the middle, and deleting the last item. Figure 20-8 shows how the links are rearranged. The function **dldelete( )**, shown here, deletes an item from a doubly linked list.

```
void dldelete(
  struct address *i, /* item to delete */
  struct address **start,  /* first item */
  struct address **last) /* last item */
{
  if(i->prior) i->prior->next = i->next;
  else { /* new first item */
    *start = i->next;
    if(start) start->prior = NULL;
  }

  if(i->next) i->next->prior = i->prior;
  else    /* deleting last element */
    *last = i->prior;
}
```

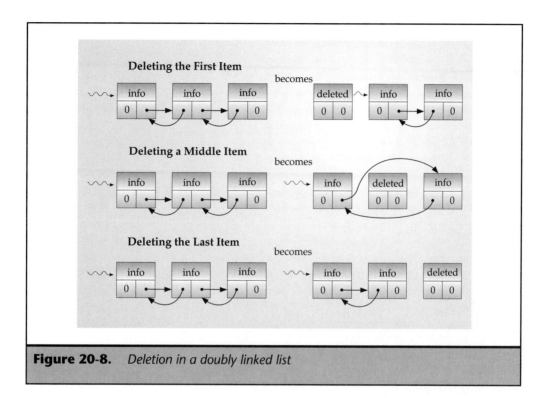

Figure 20-8. *Deletion in a doubly linked list*

Because the first or last element in the list could be deleted, the **dldelete( )** function automatically updates pointers to the beginning and ending elements of the list through the **start** and **last** parameters. You must call the function with a pointer to the data to be deleted, and a pointer to the pointers to the first and last items in the list.

A Mailing-List Example

To finish the discussion of doubly linked lists, this section presents a simple but complete mailing-list program. The entire list is kept in memory while in use. However, it can be stored in a disk file and loaded for later use.

```
/* A simple mailing list program that illustrates the
   use and maintenance of doubly linked lists.
*/
#include <stdio.h>
#include <stdlib.h>
#include <string.h>

struct address {
```

```
   char name[30];
   char street[40];
   char city[20];
   char state[3];
   char zip[11];
   struct address *next;  /* pointer to next entry */
   struct address *prior;  /* pointer to previous record */
} list_entry;

struct address *start;  /* pointer to first entry in list */
struct address *last;  /* pointer to last entry */
struct address *find(char *);

void enter(void), search(void), save(void);
void load(void), list(void);
void delete(struct address **, struct address **);
void dls_store(struct address *i, struct address **start,
               struct address **last);
void inputs(char *, char *, int), display(struct address *);
int menu_select(void);

void main(void)
{
  start = last = NULL;  /* initialize top and bottom pointers */

  for(;;) {
    switch(menu_select()) {
      case 1: enter();
        break;
      case 2: delete(&start, &last);
        break;
      case 3: list();
        break;
      case 4: search(); /* find a street */
        break;
      case 5: save();  /* save list to disk */
        break;
      case 6: load();  /* read from disk */
        break;
      case 7: exit(0);
```

```
      }
    }
}

/* Select an operation. */
menu_select(void)
{
  char s[80];
  int c;

  printf("1. Enter a name\n");
  printf("2. Delete a name\n");
  printf("3. List the file\n");
  printf("4. Search\n");
  printf("5. Save the file\n");
  printf("6. Load the file\n");
  printf("7. Quit\n");
  do {
    printf("\nEnter your choice: ");
    gets(s);
    c = atoi(s);
  } while(c<0 || c>7);
  return c;
}

/* Enter names and addresses. */
void enter(void)
{
  struct address *info;

  for(;;) {
    info = (struct address *)malloc(sizeof(list_entry));
    if(!info) {
      printf("\nout of memory");
      return;
    }

    inputs("Enter name: ", info->name, 30);
    if(!info->name[0]) break;  /* stop entering */
    inputs("Enter street: ", info->street, 40);
```

```
      inputs("Enter city: ", info->city, 20);
      inputs("Enter state: ", info->state, 3);
      inputs("Enter zip: ", info->zip, 10);

      dls_store(info, &start, &last);
  } /* entry loop */
}

/* This function will input a string up to
   the length in count and will prevent
   the string from being overrun.  It will also
   display a prompting message. */
void inputs(char *prompt, char *s, int count)
{
  char p[255];

  do {
    printf(prompt);
    gets(p);
    if(strlen(p)>count) printf("\nToo Long\n");
  } while(strlen(p)>count);
  strcpy(s, p);
}

/* Create a doubly linked list in sorted order. */
void dls_store(
  struct address *i,    /* new element */
  struct address **start, /* first element in list */
  struct address **last /* last element in list */
)
{
  struct address *old, *p;

  if(*last==NULL) {  /* first element in list */
    i->next = NULL;
    i->prior = NULL;
    *last = i;
    *start = i;
    return;
  }
```

```
     p = *start; /* start at top of list */

   old = NULL;
   while(p) {
     if(strcmp(p->name, i->name)<0){
       old = p;
       p = p->next;
     }
     else {
       if(p->prior) {
         p->prior->next = i;
         i->next = p;
         i->prior = p->prior;
         p->prior = i;
         return;
       }
       i->next = p; /* new first element */
       i->prior = NULL;
       p->prior = i;
       *start = i;
       return;
     }
   }
   old->next = i; /* put on end */
   i->next = NULL;
   i->prior = old;
   *last = i;
}

/* Remove an element from the list. */
void delete(struct address **start, struct address **last)
{
   struct address *info, *find();
   char s[80];

   inputs("enter name: ", s, 30);
   info = find(s);
   if(info) {
     if(*start==info) {
       *start=info->next;
       if(*start) (*start)->prior = NULL;
       else *last = NULL;
```

```
  }
  else {
    info->prior->next = info->next;
    if(info!=*last)
        info->next->prior = info->prior;
    else
      *last = info->prior;
  }
  free(info);  /* return memory to system */
 }
}

/* Find an address. */
struct address *find( char *name)
{
  struct address *info;

  info = start;
  while(info) {
    if(!strcmp(name, info->name)) return info;
    info = info->next;  /* get next address */
  }
  printf("Name not found.\n");
  return NULL;  /* not found */
}

/* Display the entire list. */
void list(void)
{
  struct address *info;

  info = start;
  while(info) {
    display(info);
    info = info->next;  /* get next address */
  }
  printf("\n\n");
}

/* This function actually prints the fields in each address. */
void display(struct address *info)
{
```

```
      printf("%s\n", info->name);
      printf("%s\n", info->street);
      printf("%s\n", info->city);
      printf("%s\n", info->state);
      printf("%s\n", info->zip);
      printf("\n\n");
}

/* Look for a name in the list. */
void search(void)
{
  char name[40];
  struct address *info, *find();

  printf("Enter name to find: ");
  gets(name);
  info = find(name);
  if(!info) printf("Not Found\n");
  else display(info);
}

/* Save the file to disk. */
void save(void)
{
  struct address *info;

  FILE *fp;

  fp = fopen("mlist", "wb");
  if(!fp) {
    printf("Cannot open file.\n");
    exit(1);
  }
  printf("\nSaving File\n");

  info = start;
  while(info) {
    fwrite(info, sizeof(struct address), 1, fp);
    info = info->next;  /* get next address */
  }
  fclose(fp);
}
```

```
/* Load the address file. */
void load()
{
  struct address *info;
  FILE *fp;

  fp = fopen("mlist", "rb");
  if(!fp) {
    printf("Cannot open file.\n");
    exit(1);
  }

  /* free any previously allocated memory */
  while(start) {
    info = start->next;
    free(info);
    start = info;
  }

  /* reset top and bottom pointers */
  start = last = NULL;

  printf("\nLoading File\n");
  while(!feof(fp)) {
    info = (struct address *) malloc(sizeof(struct address));
    if(!info) {
      printf("Out of Memory");
      return;
    }
    if(1!=fread(info, sizeof(struct address), 1, fp)) break;
    dls_store(info, &start, &last);
  }
  fclose(fp);
}
```

Binary Trees

The final data structure to be examined is the *binary tree*. Although there can be many different types of trees, binary trees are special because, when sorted, they lend themselves to rapid searches, insertions, and deletions. Each item in a tree consists of information along with a link to the left member and a link to the right member. Figure 20-9 shows a small tree.

Special terminology is needed when discussing trees. Computer scientists are not known for their grammar, and terminology for trees is a classic case of a confused metaphor. The *root* is the first item in the tree. Each data item is called a *node* of the tree, and any piece of the tree is called a *subtree*. A node that has no subtrees attached to it is called a *terminal node* or *leaf*. The *height* of the tree is equal to the number of layers that its roots grow. When working with trees, you can think of them existing in memory looking the way they do on paper. But remember: a tree is only a way to logically organize data in memory, and memory is linear.

In a sense, the binary tree is a special form of linked list. Items can be inserted, deleted, and accessed in any order. Also, the retrieval operation is nondestructive. Although trees are easy to visualize, they present some very difficult programming problems. This discussion only scratches the surface.

Most functions that use trees are recursive because the tree itself is a recursive data structure. That is, each subtree is itself a tree. Therefore, the routines that this discussion develops will be recursive. Remember, nonrecursive versions of these functions exist, but their code is much harder to understand.

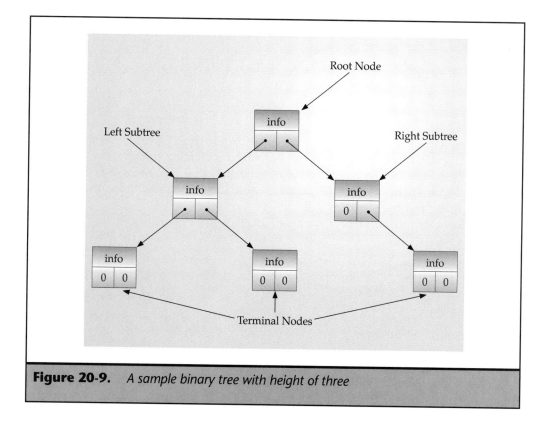

Figure 20-9.   *A sample binary tree with height of three*

How a tree is ordered depends on how it is going to be referenced. The process of accessing each node in a tree is called a *tree traversal*. Consider the following tree:

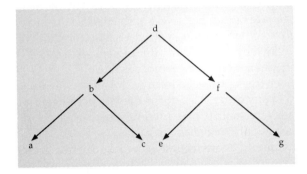

There are three ways to traverse a tree: *inorder, preorder,* and *postorder*. Using inorder, you visit the left subtree, the root, and then the right subtree. In preorder, you visit the root, the left subtree, and then the right subtree. With postorder, you visit the left subtree, the right subtree, and then the root. The order of access for the tree shown using each method is

inorder	a b c d e f g
preorder	d b a c f e g
postorder	a c b e g f d

Although a tree need not be sorted, most uses require this. Of course, what constitutes a sorted tree depends on how you will be traversing the tree. The rest of this chapter assumes inorder. Therefore, a sorted binary tree is one where the subtree on the left contains nodes that are less than or equal to the root, and those on the right are greater than the root.

The following function, **stree( )**, builds a sorted binary tree:

```
struct tree {
  char info;
  struct tree *left;
  struct tree *right;
};

struct tree *stree(
  struct tree *root,
  struct tree *r,
  char info)
```

```
{
  if(!r) {
    r = (struct tree *) malloc(sizeof(struct tree));
    if(!r) {
      printf("Out of Memory\n");
      exit(0);
    }
    r->left = NULL;
    r->right = NULL;
    r->info = info;
    if(!root) return r; /* first entry */
    if(info<root->info) root->left = r;
    else root->right = r;
    return r;
  }
  if(info<r->info) stree(r,r->left,info);
  else
    stree(r,r->right,info);
}
```

The preceding algorithm simply follows the links through the tree going left or right based on the **info** field. To use this function, you need a global variable that points to the root of the tree. This global must initially be set to **NULL**. The return value of the first call to **stree( )** must be assigned to this pointer. Subsequent calls do not need to reassign the root. Assuming the name of this global is **rt**, to call the function **stree( )** you use:

```
/* call stree()  */
if(!rt) rt = stree(rt, rt, info);
else stree(rt, rt, info);
```

In this way, both the first and subsequent elements can be inserted correctly.

The function **stree( )** is a recursive algorithm, as are most tree routines. The same routine would be several times longer if you employ iterative methods. The function must be called with the following arguments (proceeding left to right): a pointer to the root of the entire tree, a pointer to the root of the next subtree to search, and the information to be stored. The first time the function is called, the first two parameters are both pointers to the root of the entire tree. For the sake of clarity, only a character is used as the information stored in the tree. However, you could substitute any other data type.

To traverse in order the tree built by using **stree( )**, and to print the **info** field of each node, you could use the **inorder( )** function shown here:

```
void inorder(struct tree *root)
{
  if(!root) return;

  inorder(root->left);
  if(root->info) printf("%c ", root->info);
  inorder(root->right);
}
```

This recursive function returns when a terminal node (a null pointer) is encountered.

The functions for transversing the tree in preorder and postorder are shown in the following listing.

```
void preorder(struct tree *root)
{
  if(!root) return;

  if(root->info) printf("%c ", root->info);
  preorder(root->left);
  preorder(root->right);
}

void postorder(struct tree *root)
{
  if(!root) return;

  postorder(root->left);
  postorder(root->right);
  if(root->info) printf("%c ", root->info);
}
```

Now consider a short but interesting program that builds a sorted binary tree and then prints that tree inorder, sideways on your screen. The program requires only a small modification to the function **inorder( )** to print the tree. Because the tree is printed sideways on the screen, the right subtree must be printed before the left subtree for the tree to look correct. (This is technically the opposite of an inorder traversal.) This new function is called **print_tree( )** and is shown here.

```
void print_tree(struct tree *r, int l)
{
  int i;
```

```
  if(r==NULL) return;

  print_tree(r->right, l+1);
  for(i=0; i<l; ++i) printf(" ");
  printf("%c\n", r->info);
  print_tree(r->left, l+1);
}
```

The entire tree-printing program follows. Try entering various trees to see how each one is built.

```
/* This program displays a binary tree. */

#include <stdlib.h>
#include <stdio.h>

struct tree {
  char info;
  struct tree *left;
  struct tree *right;
};

struct tree *root; /* first node in tree */
struct tree *stree(struct tree *root,
                   struct tree *r, char info);
void print_tree(struct tree *root, int l);

void main(void)
{
  char s[80];

  root = NULL;  /* initialize the root */

  do {
    printf("Enter a letter: ");
    gets(s);
    if(!root) root = stree(root, root, *s);
    else stree(root, root, *s);
  } while(*s);
```

```
   print_tree(root, NULL);
}

struct tree *stree(
  struct tree *root,
  struct tree *r,
  char info)
{

  if(!r) {
    r = (struct tree *) malloc(sizeof(struct tree));
    if(!r) {
      printf("Out of Memory\n");
      exit(0);
    }
    r->left = NULL;
    r->right = NULL;
    r->info = info;
    if(!root) return r; /* first entry */
    if(info<root->info) root->left = r;
    else root->right = r;
    return r;
  }

  if(info<r->info) stree(r, r->left, info);
  else
    stree(r, r->right, info);
}

void print_tree(struct tree *r, int l)
{
  int i;

  if(!r) return;

  print_tree(r->right, l+1);
  for(i=0; i<l; ++i) printf(" ");
  printf("%c\n", r->info);
  print_tree(r->left, l+1);
}
```

This program is actually sorting the information that you give it. It is essentially a variation of the insertion sort that you saw in the previous chapter. In the average case, its performance can be quite good, but the quicksort is still a better general-purpose sorting method because it uses less memory and has lower processing overhead. However, if you have to build a tree from scratch or maintain an already sorted tree, you should always insert new entries in sorted order by using the **stree( )** function.

If you have run the tree-printing program, you have probably noticed that some trees are *balanced*—that is, each subtree is the same or nearly the same height as any other—and that others are very far out of balance. In fact, if you entered the tree **abcd**, it would have looked like this:

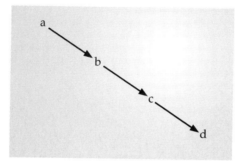

There would have been no left subtrees. This is called a *degenerate tree* because it has degenerated into a linear list. In general, if the data you are using as input to build a binary tree is fairly random, the tree produced approximates a balanced tree. However, if the information is already sorted, a degenerate tree results. (It is possible to readjust the tree with each insertion to keep the tree in balance, but this process is fairly complex and beyond the scope of this chapter.)

Search functions are easy to implement for binary trees. The following function returns a pointer to the node in the tree that matches the key; otherwise, it returns a null.

```
struct tree *search_tree(struct tree *root, char key)
{
  if(!root) return root;   /* empty tree */
  while(root->info!=key) {
    if(key<root->info) root = root->left;
    else root = root->right;
    if(root==NULL) break;
  }
  return root;
}
```

Unfortunately, deleting a node from a tree is not as simple as searching a tree. The deleted node may be either the root, a left node, or a right node. Also, the node may have from zero to two subtrees attached to it. The process of rearranging the pointers lends itself to a recursive algorithm, which is shown here:

```c
struct tree *dtree(struct tree *root, char key)
{
  struct tree *p,*p2;

  if(!root) return root; /* not found */

  if(root->info==key) { /* delete root */
    /* this means an empty tree */
    if(root->left==root->right){
      free(root);
      return NULL;
    }
    /* or if one subtree is null */
    else if(root->left==NULL) {
      p = root->right;
      free(root);
      return p;
    }
    else if(root->right==NULL) {
      p = root->left;
      free(root);
      return p;
    }
    /* or both subtrees present */
    else {
      p2 = root->right;
      p = root->right;
      while(p->left) p = p->left;
      p->left = root->left;
      free(root);
      return p2;
    }
  }
  if(root->info<key) root->right = dtree(root->right, key);
  else root->left = dtree(root->left, key);
  return root;
}
```

Remember to update the pointer to the root in the rest of your program code because the node deleted could be the root of the tree. The best way to accomplish this is to assign the return value from **dtree( )** to the variable in your program that points to the root, using a call similar to the following.

```
root = dtree(root,  key);
```

Binary trees offer tremendous power, flexibility, and efficiency when used with database management programs. This is because the information for these databases must reside on disk, and access times are important. Because a balanced binary tree has, as a worst case, $\log_2 n$ comparisons in searching, it is far better than a linked list, which must rely on a sequential search.

Chapter Twenty-One

Sparse Arrays

One of the more intriguing programming problems is the implementation of a sparse array. A *sparse array* is one in which not all the elements of the array are actually in use, present, or necessary. Sparse arrays are valuable when both of the following conditions are met: the array dimensions required by an application are quite large (possibly exceeding available memory), and when not all array locations will be used. Recall that arrays—especially multidimensional arrays—can consume vast quantities of memory because their storage needs are exponentially related to their dimensions. For example, a character array of 10 by 10 needs only 100 bytes of memory, a 100-by-100 array needs 10,000, but a 1000-by-1000 array needs 1,000,000 bytes of memory. Clearly, at some point a large array can exceed the capabilities of a given computer.

There are numerous examples of applications that require sparse-array processing. Many apply to matrix operations or to scientific and engineering problems that are easily understood only by experts in those fields. However, there is one very familiar application that uses sparse arrays: a spreadsheet program. Even though the matrix of the average spreadsheet is very large, say 999 by 999, only a portion of the matrix is actually in use at any one time. Spreadsheets use the matrix to hold formulas, values, and strings associated with each location. Using a sparse array, storage for each element is allocated from the pool of free memory as it is needed. Because only a small portion of the array elements are actually in use, the array (i.e., the spreadsheet) may appear very large—larger than would usually fit in the memory of the computer.

The rest of this discussion uses the terms *logical array* and *physical array*. The logical array is the array that you think of as existing in the system. For example, if a spreadsheet matrix has dimensions of 1000 by 1000, then the logical array that supports that matrix also has dimensions of 1000 by 1000—even though this array does not physically exist within the computer. The physical array is the array that actually exists inside the computer. Thus, if only 100 elements of a spreadsheet matrix are in use, the physical array is using space for only these 100 elements. The sparse-array techniques developed in this chapter provide the link between the logical and physical arrays.

This chapter examines four distinct techniques for creating a sparse array: the linked list, the binary tree, a pointer array, and hashing. Although no spreadsheet program is actually developed, all examples relate to a spreadsheet matrix that is organized as shown in Figure 21-1. In the figure, the X is located in cell B2.

The Linked-List Sparse Array

When you implement a sparse array by using a linked list, the first thing you must do is create a structure that holds the following items:

- The data that is being stored
- Its logical position in the array
- Links to the previous and next element

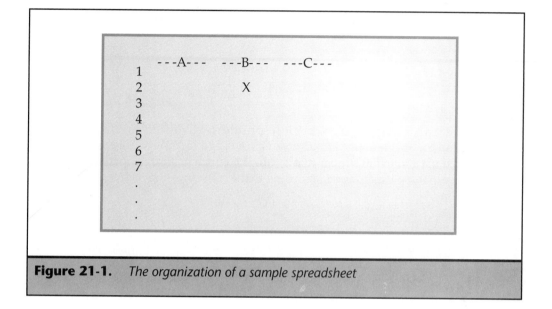

Figure 21-1. *The organization of a sample spreadsheet*

Each new structure is placed in the list with the elements inserted in sorted order based on the array index. The array is accessed by following the links.

For example, you can use the following structure as the basis of a sparse array in a spreadsheet program:

```
struct cell {
  char cell_name[9];  /* cell name e.g., A1, B34 */
  char  formula[128]; /* info e.g., 10/B2 */
  struct cell *next;  /* pointer to next entry */
  struct cell *prior; /* pointer to previous record */
} list_entry;
```

The field **cell_name** holds a string that contains a cell name such as A1, B34, Z19, or the like. The string **formula** holds the formula (i.e., data) that is assigned to each spreadsheet location.

An entire spreadsheet program would be far too large to use as an example. Instead this chapter examines the key functions that support the linked-list sparse array. Remember, there are many ways to implement a spreadsheet program. The data structure and routines here are just examples of sparse-array techniques.

The following global variables point to the beginning and end of the linked-list array.

```
struct cell *start; /* first element in list */
struct cell *last;  /* last element in list */
```

When you enter a formula into a cell in most spreadsheets, you are, in effect, creating a new element in the sparse array. If the spreadsheet uses a linked list, that new cell is inserted into it via a function similar to **dls_store( )**, which was developed in Chapter 20. Remember that the list is sorted according to the cell name; that is, A12 precedes A13, and so on.

```
/* Store cells in sorted order. */
void dls_store(struct cell *i,
               struct cell **start,
               struct cell **last)
{
  struct cell *old, *p;

  if(!*last) { /* first element in list */
    i->next = NULL;
    i->prior = NULL;
    *last = i;
    *start = i;
    return;
  }

  p = *start; /* start at top of list */

  old = NULL;
  while(p) {
    if(strcmp(p->cell_name, i->cell_name)<0){
      old = p;
      p = p->next;
    }
    else {
      if(p->prior) { /* is a middle element */
        p->prior->next = i;
        i->next = p;
        i->prior = p->prior;
        p->prior = i;
```

```
      return;
    }
    i->next = p; /* new first element */
    i->prior = NULL;
    p->prior = i;
    *start = i;
    return;
  }
}
old->next = i; /* put on end */
i->next = NULL;
i->prior = old;
*last = i;
return;
}
```

The **delete( )** function, which follows, removes from the list the cell whose name is an argument to the function:

```
void delete(char *cell_name,
            struct cell **start,
            struct cell **last)
{
  struct cell *info;

  info = find(cell_name, *start);
  if(info) {
    if(*start==info) {
      *start = info->next;
      if(*start) (*start)->prior = NULL;
      else *last = NULL;
    }
    else {
      if(info->prior) info->prior->next = info->next;
      if(info!=*last)
          info->next->prior = info->prior;
      else
        *last = info->prior;
    }
```

```
      free(info); /* return memory to system */
  }
}
```

The final function that you need to support a linked-list sparse array is **find( )**, which locates any specific cell. The function requires a linear search to locate each item, and, as you saw in Chapter 19, the average number of comparisons in a linear search is $n/2$, where n is the number of elements in the list. Here is **find( )**:

```
struct cell *find(char *cell_name, struct cell *start)
{
  struct cell *info;

  info = start;
  while(info) {
    if(!strcmp(cell_name, info->cell_name)) return info;
    info = info->next; /* get next cell */
  }
  printf("Cell not found.\n");
  return NULL; /* not found */
}
```

Analysis of the Linked-List Approach

The principal advantage of the linked-list approach to sparse arrays is that it makes efficient use of memory—memory is used only for those elements in the array that actually contain information. It is also simple to implement. However, it has one major drawback: It must use a linear search to access cells in the list. Also, the store routine uses a linear search to find the proper place to insert a new cell into the list. You can solve these problems by using a binary tree to support the sparse array, as shown next.

The Binary-Tree Approach to Sparse Arrays

In essence, the binary tree is simply a modified doubly linked list. Its major advantage over a list is that it can be searched quickly, which means that insertions and lookups can be very fast. In applications where you want a linked-list structure but need fast search times, the binary tree is perfect.

To use a binary tree to support the spreadsheet example, you must change the structure **cell** as shown in the code that follows:

```
struct cell {
  char cell_name[9];   /* cell name e.g., A1, B34 */
  char  formula[128]; /* info e.g., 10/B2 */
  struct cell *left;   /* pointer to left subtree */
  struct cell *right; /* pointer to right subtree */
} list_entry;
```

You can modify the **stree( )** function from Chapter 20 so that it builds a tree based on the cell name. Notice that the following assumes that the parameter **new** is a pointer to a new entry in the tree.

```
struct cell *stree(
        struct cell *root,
        struct cell *r,
        struct cell *new)
{
  if(!r) {     /* first node in subtree */
    new->left = NULL;
    new->right = NULL;
    if(!root) return new;  /* first entry in tree */
    if(strcmp(new->cell_name, root->cell_name)<0)
      root->left = new;
    else
      root->right = new;
    return new;
  }

  if(strcmp(r->cell_name, new->cell_name)<=0)
    stree(r, r->right, new);
  else
    stree(r, r->left, new);

  return root;
}
```

The **stree( )** function must be called with a pointer to the root node for the first two parameters and a pointer to the new cell for the third. It returns a pointer to the root.

To delete a cell from the spreadsheet, modify the **dtree( )** function as shown here to accept the name of the cell as a key:

```
struct cell *dtree(
        struct cell *root,
        char *key)
{
  struct cell *p, *p2;

  if(!root) return root; /* item not found */

  if(!strcmp(root->cell_name, key)) { /* delete root */
    /* this means an empty tree */
    if(root->left==root->right){
      free(root);
      return NULL;
    }
    /* or if one subtree is null */
    else if(root->left==NULL) {
      p = root->right;
      free(root);
      return p;
    }
    else if(root->right==NULL) {
      p = root->left;
      free(root);
      return p;
    }
    /* or both subtrees present */
    else {
      p2 = root->right;
      p = root->right;
      while(p->left) p = p->left;
      p->left = root->left;
      free(root);
      return p2;
    }
  }
  if(strcmp(root->cell_name, key)<=0)
    root->right = dtree(root->right, key);
  else root->left = dtree(root->left, key);
  return root;
}
```

Finally, you can use a modified version of the **search( )** function to locate quickly any cell in the spreadsheet if you specify the cell name.

```
struct cell *search_tree(
        struct cell *root,
        char *key)
{
  if(!root) return root;  /* empty tree */
  while(strcmp(root->cell_name, key)) {
    if(strcmp(root->cell_name, key)<=0)
      root = root->right;
    else root = root->left;
    if(root==NULL) break;
  }
  return root;
}
```

Analysis of the Binary-Tree Approach

A binary tree results in much faster insert and search times than a linked list. Remember, a sequential search requires, on average, $n/2$ comparisons, where n is the number of elements in the list. A binary search, in contrast, requires only $\log_2 n$ comparisons. Also, the binary tree is as memory efficient as a doubly linked list. However, in some situations, there is a better alternative than the binary tree.

The Pointer-Array Approach to Sparse Arrays

Suppose that your spreadsheet has the dimensions 26 by 100 (A1 through Z100), or a total of 2600 elements. In theory, you could use the following array of structures to hold the spreadsheet entries:

```
struct cell {
  char cell_name[9];
  char  formula[128];
} list_entry[2600];   /* 2,600 cells */
```

However, 2600 multiplied by 137 (the raw size of the structure) amounts to 356,200 bytes of memory. This is far too much memory to waste—especially if the array is not fully populated. Also, on processors that use segmented architectures, such as the 8086 family, memory access to such a large array is very slow because 32-bit pointers are required. So, this approach is often impractical. However, you could create an array of pointers to structures of type **cell**. This array of pointers would require significantly less permanent storage than the actual array. Each time an array location is assigned data, memory would be allocated for that data and the appropriate pointer in the pointer array would be set to point to that data. This scheme offers superior performance over the linked-list and binary-tree methods. The declaration that creates such an array of pointers is

```
struct cell {
  char cell_name[9];
  char formula[128];
} list_entry;

struct cell *sheet[2600]; /* array of 2,600 pointers */
```

You can use this smaller array to hold pointers to the information that is actually entered by the spreadsheet user. As each entry is made, a pointer to the information about the cell is stored in the proper location in the array. Figure 21-2 shows how this might appear in memory, with the pointer array providing support for the sparse array.

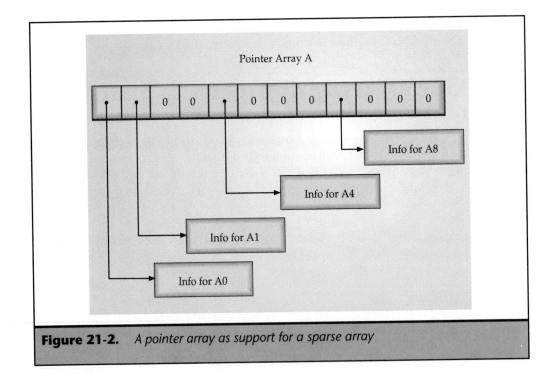

Figure 21-2. *A pointer array as support for a sparse array*

Before the pointer array can be used, each element must be initialized to null, which indicates that there is no entry in that location. The function that does this is

```
void init_sheet(void)
{
  register int t;

  for(t=0; t<2600; ++t) sheet[t] = NULL;
}
```

When the user enters a formula for a cell, the cell location (which is defined by its name) is used to produce an index for the pointer array **sheet**. The index is derived from the cell name by converting the name into a number, as shown in the following listing.

```
void store(struct cell *i)
{
  int loc;
  char *p;

  /* compute index given cell name */
  loc = *(i->cell_name) - 'A';
  p = &(i->cell_name[1]);
  loc += (atoi(p)-1) * 26;    /* WIDTH * rows */

  if(loc>=2600) {
    printf("Cell out of bounds.\n");
    return;
  }
  sheet[loc] = i; /* place pointer in the array */
}
```

When computing the index, **store( )** assumes that all cell names start with a capital letter and are followed by an integer—for example, B34, C19, and so on. Therefore, using the formula shown in **store( )**, the cell name A1 produces an index of zero, B1 produces an index of 1, A2 produces an index of 26, and so on. Because each cell name is unique, each index is also unique and the pointer to each entry is stored in the proper array element. If you compare this procedure to the linked-list or binary-tree version, you will see how much shorter and simpler it is.

The **delete( )** function also becomes very short. Called with the name of the cell to remove, it simply zeros the pointer to the element and returns the memory to the system.

```c
void delete(struct cell *i)
{
  int loc;
  char *p;

  /* compute index given cell name */
  loc = *(i->cell_name) - 'A';
  p = &(i->cell_name[1]);
  loc += (atoi(p)-1) * 26; /* WIDTH * rows */

  if(loc>=2600) {
    printf("Cell out of bounds.\n");
    return;
  }
  if(!sheet[loc]) return; /* don't free a null pointer */

  free(sheet[loc]);  /* return memory to system */
  sheet[loc] = NULL;
}
```

Once again, this code is much faster and simpler than the linked-list version.

The process of locating a cell given its name is simple because the name itself directly produces the array index. Therefore, the function **find( )** becomes

```c
struct cell *find(char *cell_name)
{
  int loc;
  char *p;

  /* compute index given name */
  loc = *(cell_name) - 'A';
  p = &(cell_name[1]);
  loc += (atoi(p)-1) * 26;    /* WIDTH * rows */

  if(loc>=2600 || !sheet[loc]) { /* no entry in that cell */
    printf("Cell not found.\n");
```

```
      return NULL;  /* not found */
  }
  else return sheet[loc];
}
```

Analysis of the Pointer-Array Approach

The pointer-array method of sparse-array handling provides much faster accessing to array elements than either the linked-list or binary-tree method. Unless the array is very large, the memory used by the pointer array is not usually a significant drain on the free memory of the system. However, the pointer array itself uses some memory for every location—whether the pointers are pointing to actual information or not. This may be a serious limitation for certain applications, although in general it is not a problem.

Hashing

Hashing is the process of extracting the index of an array element directly from the information that is stored there. The index generated is called the *hash*. Traditionally, hashing has been applied to disk files as a means of decreasing access time. However, you can use the same general methods to implement sparse arrays. The preceding pointer-array example used a special form of hashing called *direct indexing*, where each key maps onto one and only one array location. That is, each hashed index is unique. (The pointer-array method does not require a direct indexing hash—this was just an obvious approach given the spreadsheet problem.) In actual practice, such direct hashing schemes are few, and a more flexible method is required. This section shows how hashing can be generalized to allow greater power and flexibility.

The spreadsheet example makes clear that even in the most rigorous environments, not every cell in the sheet will be used. Suppose that for virtually all cases, no more than 10% of the potential locations are occupied by actual entries. That is, if the spreadsheet has dimensions 26x100 (2600 locations), only about 260 are actually used at any one time. This implies that the largest array necessary to hold all the entries will normally consist of only 260 elements. But how do the logical array locations get mapped onto and accessed from this smaller physical array? And what happens when this array is full? The following discussion describes one possible solution.

When data for a cell is entered by the user of the spreadsheet (which is the logical array), the cell location, defined by its name, is used to produce an index (a hash) into the smaller physical array. As it relates to hashing, the physical array is also called the *primary array*. The index is derived from the cell name, which is converted into a number, as in the pointer-array example. However, this number is then divided by 10 to produce an initial entry point into the primary array. (Remember, in this example the size of the physical array is only 10% that of the logical array.) If the location referenced by this index is free, the logical index and the value are stored there. However, since ten logical locations actually map onto one physical location, hash collisions can occur. When this happens, a linked list, sometimes called the *collision list*, is used to hold the entry. A separate collision list is associated with each entry in the primary array. Of course, these lists are zero length until a collision occurs, as depicted in Figure 21-3.

Suppose you want to find an element in the physical array, given its logical array index. First, transform the logical index into its hash value and check the physical

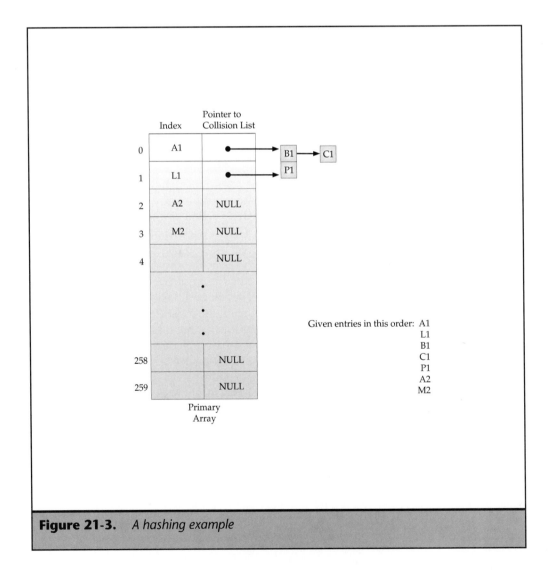

Figure 21-3. *A hashing example*

array at the index generated by the hash to see if the logical index stored there matches the one that you are searching for. If it does, return the information. Otherwise, follow the collision list until either the proper index is found or the end of the chain is reached.

Before you can understand how this procedure applies to the spreadsheet program, you need to define an array of structures, called **primary**, as shown here.

```
#define MAX 260

struct htype {

  int index;    /* logical index */
  int val;      /* actual value of the array element */
  struct htype *next; /* pointer to next value with same hash */
} primary[MAX];
```

Before this array can be used, it must be initialized. The following function initializes the **index** field to –1 (a value that, by definition, cannot be generated) to indicate an empty element. A **NULL** in the **next** field indicates an empty hash chain.

```
/* Initialize the hash array. */
void init(void)
{
  register int i;

  for (i=0; i<MAX; i++) {
    primary[i].index = -1;
    primary[i].next = NULL;   /* null chain */
    primary[i].val = 0;
  }
}
```

The **store( )** procedure converts a cell name into a hashed index into the **primary** array. If the location directly pointed to by the hashed value is occupied, the procedure automatically adds the entry to the collision list using a modified version of **slstore( )** developed in the preceding chapter. The logical index must be stored because it will be needed when that element is accessed again. These functions are shown here:

```
/* Compute hash and store value. */
void store(char *cell_name, int v)
{
```

```
   int h, loc;
   struct htype *p;

   /* produce the hash value */
   loc = *cell_name - 'A';
   loc += (atoi(&cell_name[1])-1) * 26;    /* WIDTH * rows */
   h = loc/10;

   /* Store in the location unless full or
      store there if logical indexes agree - i.e., update.
   */
   if(primary[h].index==-1 || primary[h].index==loc) {
     primary[h].index = loc;
     primary[h].val = v;
     return;
   }

   /* otherwise, create or add to collision list */
   p = malloc(sizeof(struct htype));
   if(!p) {
     printf("Out of Memory\n");
     return;
   }
   p->index = loc;
   p->val = v;
   slstore(p, &primary[h]);
}

/* Add elements to the collision list. */
void slstore(struct htype *i,
             struct htype *start)
{
  struct htype *old, *p;

  old = start;
  /* find end of list */
  while(start) {
    old = start;
    start = start->next;
  }
  /* link in new entry */
  old->next = i;
  i->next = NULL;
}
```

Before finding the value of an element, your program must first compute the hash and then check to see if the logical index stored in the physical array matches the index of the logical array that is requested. If it does, that value is returned; otherwise, the collision chain is searched. The **find( )** function, which performs these tasks, is shown here:

```
/* Compute hash and return value. */
int find(char *cell_name)
{
  int h, loc;
  struct htype *p;

  /* produce the hash value */
  loc = *cell_name - 'A';
  loc += (atoi(&cell_name[1])-1) * 26;    /* WIDTH * rows */
  h = loc/10;

  /* return the value if found */
  if(primary[h].index==loc)  return(primary[h].val);
  else { /* look in collision list */
    p = primary[h].next;
    while(p) {
      if(p->index == loc) return p->val;
      p = p->next;
    }
    printf("Not in Array\n");
    return -1;
  }
}
```

Creating a deletion function is left to you as an exercise. (*Hint*: Just reverse the insertion process.)

Keep in mind that the preceding hashing algorithm is very simple. Generally, you would use a more complex method to provide a more even distribution of indexes in the primary array, thus avoiding very long hash chains. However, the basic principle is the same.

Analysis of Hashing

In its best case (quite rare), each physical index created by the hash is unique and access times approximate that of direct indexing. This means that no collision lists are created and all lookups are essentially direct accesses. However, this will seldom be the case because it requires that the logical indexes be evenly distributed throughout the logical index space. In a worst case (also rare), a hashed scheme degenerates into a linked list. This can happen when the hashed values of the logical indexes are all the same. In the average (and the most likely) case, the hash method can access any specific element in the amount of time it takes to use a direct index plus some constant that is proportional to the average length of the hash chains. The most critical factor in using hashing to support a sparse array is to make sure that the hashing algorithm spreads the physical index evenly so that long collision lists are avoided.

Choosing an Approach

You must consider speed and memory efficiency when deciding whether to use a linked list, a binary tree, a pointer array, or a hashing approach to implement a sparse array.

When the array is very sparse, the most memory-efficient approaches are the linked lists and binary trees, because only array elements that are actually in use have memory allocated to them. The links themselves require very little additional memory and generally have a negligible effect. The pointer-array design requires that the entire pointer array exists, even if some of its elements are not used. Not only must the entire pointer array fit in memory, but enough memory must be left over for the application to use. This could be a serious problem for certain applications, whereas it may not be a problem at all for others. Usually you can calculate the approximate amount of free memory and determine whether it is sufficient for your program. The hashing method lies somewhere between the pointer-array and the linked-list/binary-tree approaches. Although it requires that all of the physical array exist even if it is not all used, it may still be smaller than a pointer array, which needs at least one pointer for each logical array location.

However, when the array is fairly full, the pointer array makes better use of memory. This is because the binary-tree and linked-list implementations need two pointers for each element, whereas the pointer array only has one pointer. For example, suppose that a 1000-element array were full and pointers were two bytes long. Both the binary tree and linked list would use 4000 bytes for pointers, but the pointer array would only need 2000—a savings of 2000 bytes. In the hashing method, even more memory is wasted to support the array.

By far the fastest approach, in terms of execution speed, is the pointer array. As in the spreadsheet example, there is often an easy method for indexing the pointer array and linking it with the sparse array elements. This makes accessing the elements of the sparse array nearly as fast as accessing a normal array. The linked-list version is very slow by comparison because it must use a linear search to locate each element. Even if extra information were added to the linked list to allow faster accessing of elements, it would still be slower than the pointer array's direct accessing capability. The binary tree certainly speeds up the search time, but it is sluggish compared with the pointer array's direct indexing capability. If you choose the hashing algorithm properly, the hashing method can often beat the binary tree in access times, but it will never be faster than the pointer-array approach.

The rule of thumb is to use a pointer-array implementation when possible because this method has the fastest access times. However, if memory usage is critical, you must use the linked-list or binary-tree approach.

Chapter Twenty-Two

Expression Parsing and Evaluation

How do you write a program that will take as input a string containing a numeric expression, such as (10 – 5) * 3, and compute the proper answer? If there is still a "high priesthood" among programmers, it must be those few who know how to do this. Many otherwise accomplished programmers are mystified by the way a high-level language converts complex expressions, such as 10 * 3 – (4 + count)/12, into instructions that a computer can execute. This procedure is called *expression parsing*, and it is the backbone of all language compilers and interpreters, spreadsheets, and anything else that needs to convert numeric expressions into a form that the computer can use. Expression parsing is generally thought of as off limits except to the enlightened few, but this need not be the case.

Although mysterious, expression parsing is actually very straightforward and is, in many ways, easier than other programming tasks. The reason for this is that the task is well defined and works according to the strict rules of algebra. This chapter will develop what is commonly referred to as a *recursive-descent parser* and all the necessary support routines that enable you to evaluate complex numeric expressions. Once you have mastered the operation of the parser, you can easily enhance and modify it to suit your needs. What's more, other programmers will think that you have entered the high priesthood!

NOTE: *The C interpreter presented in Part 5 of this book uses an enhanced form of the parser developed here. If you will be exploring the C interpreter, you will find the material in this chapter especially useful.*

Expressions

Although expressions can be made up of all types of information, this chapter deals only with numeric expressions. For our purposes, *numeric expressions* are composed of the following items:

- Numbers
- The operators +, –, /, *, ^, %, =
- Parentheses
- Variables

The operator ^ indicates exponentiation, as in BASIC, and = is the assignment operator. These items can be combined in expressions according to the rules of algebra. Here are some examples:

```
10 – 8
(100 – 5) * 14/6
a + b – c
```

10^5

a = 10 − b

Assume this precedence for each operator:

highest	unary +, −
	^
	*, /, %
	+, −
lowest	=

Operators of equal precedence evaluate from left to right.

In the examples in this chapter, all variables are single letters (in other words, 26 variables, **A** through **Z**, are available). The variables are not case sensitive (**a** and **A** are treated as the same variable). Each numeric value is a **double**, although you could easily write the routines to handle other types of values. Finally, to keep the logic clear and easy to understand, only a minimal amount of error checking is included in the routines.

In case you have not thought much about the process of expression parsing, try to evaluate this sample expression:

10 − 2 * 3

You know that this expression is equal to the value 4. Although you could easily create a program that would compute that *specific* expression, the question is how to create a program that gives the correct answer for any *arbitrary* expression. At first you might think of a routine something like this:

```
a = get first operand
while(operands present) {
        op = get operator
        b = get second operand
        a = a op b
}
```

This routine gets the first operand, the operator, and the second operand to perform the first operation and then gets the next operator and operand—if any—to perform the next operation, and so on. However, if you use this basic approach, the expression 10 − 2 * 3 evaluates to 24 (that is, 8 * 3) instead of 4 because this procedure neglects the precedence of the operators. You cannot just take the operands and operators in order from left to right because the rules of algebra dictate that multiplication must be done before subtraction. Some beginners think that this problem can be easily overcome, and sometimes—in very restricted cases—it can. But the problem only gets worse when you add parentheses, exponentiation, variables, function calls, and the like.

Although there are a few ways to write a routine that evaluates expressions, the one developed here is most easily written by a person. It is also the most common. (Some of the other methods used to write parsers employ complex tables that must be generated by another computer program. These are sometimes called *table-driven parsers*.) The method used here is called a *recursive-descent parser*, and in the course of this chapter you will see how it got its name.

Dissecting an Expression

Before you can develop a parser to evaluate expressions, you need to be able to break an expression into its components. For example, the expression

A * B – (W + 10)

contains the components A, *, B, –, (, W, +, 10, and). Each component represents an indivisible unit of the expression. In general, you need a routine that returns each item in the expression individually. The routine must also be able to skip over spaces and tabs and detect the end of the expression.

Each component of an expression is called a *token*. Therefore, the function that returns the next token in the expression is often called **get_token( )**. **get_token( )** requires a global character pointer to the string that holds the expression. In the version of **get_token( )** shown here, the global character pointer is **prog. prog** is global because it must maintain its value between calls to **get_token( )** and allow other functions to use it. Besides returning a token, you need to know what type of token is being returned. For the parser developed in this chapter, you need only three types: **VARIABLE**, **NUMBER**, and **DELIMITER**. (**DELIMITER** is used for both operators and parentheses.) Here is **get_token( )** along with its necessary globals, **#define**s, and support function:

```
#define DELIMITER   1
#define VARIABLE    2
#define NUMBER      3

extern char *prog;   /* points to the expression to be analyzed */
char token[80];
char tok_type;

/* Return the next token. */
void get_token(void)
{
  register char *temp;

  tok_type = 0;
```

```
    temp = token;
    *temp = '\0';

    if(!*prog) return; /* at end of expression */
    while(isspace(*prog)) ++prog;  /* skip over white space */

    if(strchr("+-*/%^=()", *prog)){
      tok_type = DELIMITER;
      /* advance to next char */
      *temp++ = *prog++;
    }
    else if(isalpha(*prog)) {
      while(!isdelim(*prog)) *temp++ = *prog++;
      tok_type = VARIABLE;
    }
    else if(isdigit(*prog)) {
      while(!isdelim(*prog)) *temp++ = *prog++;
      tok_type = NUMBER;
    }

    *temp = '\0';
}

/* Return true if c is a delimiter. */
isdelim(char c)
{
  if(strchr(" +-/*%^=()", c) || c==9 || c=='\r' || c==0)
    return 1;
  return 0;
}
```

Look closely at the preceding functions. After the first few initializations,
get_token( ) checks to see if the null terminating the expression has been found.
If it has, the end of the expression has been reached. If there are still more tokens to
retrieve from the expression, **get_token( )** first skips over any leading spaces. Once the
spaces have been skipped, **prog** is pointing to either a number, a variable, an operator,
or—if trailing spaces end the expression—a null. If the next character is an operator, it
is returned as a string in the global variable **token**, and **DELIMITER** is placed in
tok_type. If the next character is a letter instead, it is assumed to be one of the
variables. It is returned as a string in **token**, and **tok_type** is assigned the value
VARIABLE. If the next character is a digit, the entire number is read and placed
in the string **token** and its type is **NUMBER**. Finally, if the next character is none

of the preceding, it is assumed that the end of the expression has been reached. In this case, **token** is null, which signals the end of the expression.

As stated earlier, to keep the code in this function clean, a certain amount of error checking has been omitted and some assumptions have been made. For example, any unrecognized character may end an expression. Also, in this version, variables may be of any length, but only the first letter is significant. You can add more error checking and other details as your specific application dictates. You can easily modify or enhance **get_token( )** to enable character strings, other types of numbers, or whatever to be returned one token at a time from an input string.

To understand better how **get_token( )** works, study what it returns for each token and type in the following expression:

A + 100 – (B * C) /2

Token	Token Type
A	VARIABLE
+	DELIMITER
100	NUMBER
–	DELIMITER
(	DELIMITER
B	VARIABLE
*	DELIMITER
C	VARIABLE
)	DELIMITER
/	DELIMITER
2	NUMBER
null	Null

Remember that **token** always holds a null-terminated string, even if it contains just a single character.

Expression Parsing

There are a number of ways to parse and evaluate an expression. When working with a recursive-descent parser, think of expressions as *recursive data structures*—that is, expressions that are defined in terms of themselves. If, for the moment, expressions can only use +, –, *, /, and parentheses, all expressions can be defined with the following rules:

expression → term [+ term] [– term]
term→ factor [* factor] [/ factor]
factor→ variable, number, or (expression)

The square brackets designate an optional element, and → means produces. In fact, the rules are usually called the *production rules* of an expression. Therefore, you could say: "Term produces factor times factor or factor divided by factor" for the definition of *term*. Notice that the precedence of the operators is implicit in the way an expression is defined.

The expression

10 + 5 * B

has two terms: 10, and 5 * B. The second term contains of two factors: 5 and B. These factors consist of one number and one variable.

On the other hand, the expression

14 * (7 – C)

has two factors: 14 and (7 – C). The factors consist of one number and one parenthesized expression. The parenthesized expression contains two terms: one number and one variable.

This process forms the basis for a *recursive-descent parser*, which is basically a set of mutually recursive functions that work in a chainlike fashion. At each appropriate step, the parser performs the specified operations in the algebraically correct sequence. To see how this process works, parse the input expression that follows, using the preceding production rules, and perform the arithmetic operations at the appropriate time:

9/3 – (100 + 56)

If you parsed the expression correctly, you followed these steps:

1. Get the first term, 9/3.

2. Get each factor and divide the integers. The resulting value is 3.

3. Get the second term, (100 + 56). At this point, start recursively analyzing the second subexpression.

4. Get each term and add. The resulting value is 156.

5. Return from the recursive call and subtract 156 from 3. The answer is –153.

If you are a little confused at this point, don't feel bad. This is a fairly complex concept that takes some getting used to. There are two basic things to remember about this recursive view of expressions. First, the precedence of the operators is implicit in the way the production rules are defined. Second, this method of parsing and evaluating expressions is very similar to the way humans evaluate mathematical expressions.

A Simple Expression Parser

The remainder of this chapter develops two parsers. The first will parse and evaluate only constant expressions—that is, expressions with no variables. This example shows the parser in its simplest form. The second parser will include the 26 variables **A** through **Z**.

Here is the entire version of the simple recursive-descent parser for floating-point expressions:

```c
/* This module contains a simple expression parser
   that does not recognize variables.
*/

#include <stdlib.h>
#include <ctype.h>
#include <stdio.h>
#include <string.h>

#define DELIMITER  1
#define VARIABLE   2
#define NUMBER     3

extern char *prog;   /* holds expression to be analyzed */
char token[80];
char tok_type;

void eval_exp(double *answer), eval_exp2(double *answer);
void eval_exp3(double *answer), eval_exp4(double *answer);
void eval_exp5(double *answer);
void eval_exp6(double *answer), atom(double *answer);
void get_token(void), putback(void);
void serror(int error);
int isdelim(char c);

/* Parser entry point. */
void eval_exp(double *answer)
{
  get_token();
  if(!*token) {
    serror(2);
    return;
  }
  eval_exp2(answer);
```

```
    if(*token) serror(0); /* last token must be null */
}

/* Add or subtract two terms. */
void eval_exp2(double *answer)
{
  register char  op;
  double temp;

  eval_exp3(answer);
  while((op = *token) == '+' || op == '-') {
    get_token();
    eval_exp3(&temp);
    switch(op) {
      case '-':
        *answer = *answer - temp;
        break;
      case '+':
        *answer = *answer + temp;
        break;
    }
  }
}

/* Multiply or divide two factors. */
void eval_exp3(double *answer)
{
  register char op;
  double temp;

  eval_exp4(answer);
  while((op = *token) == '*' || op == '/' || op == '%') {
    get_token();
    eval_exp4(&temp);
    switch(op) {
      case '*':
        *answer = *answer * temp;
        break;
      case '/':
        *answer = *answer / temp;
        break;
      case '%':
```

```
        *answer = (int) *answer % (int) temp;
        break;
    }
  }
}

/* Process an exponent */
void eval_exp4(double *answer)
{
  double temp, ex;
  register int t;

  eval_exp5(answer);
  if(*token== '^') {
    get_token();
    eval_exp4(&temp);
    ex = *answer;
    if(temp==0.0) {
      *answer = 1.0;
      return;
    }
    for(t=temp-1; t>0; --t) *answer = (*answer) * (double)ex;
  }
}

/* Evaluate a unary + or -. */
void eval_exp5(double *answer)
{
  register char  op;

  op = 0;
  if((tok_type == DELIMITER) && *token=='+' || *token == '-') {
    op = *token;
    get_token();
  }
  eval_exp6(answer);
  if(op=='-') *answer = -(*answer);
}

/* Process a parenthesized expression. */
void eval_exp6(double *answer)
{
```

```
  if((*token == '(')) {
    get_token();
    eval_exp2(answer);
    if(*token != ')')
      serror(1);
    get_token();
  }
  else
    atom(answer);
}

/* Get the value of a number. */
void atom(double *answer)
{
  if(tok_type==NUMBER) {
    *answer = atof(token);
    get_token();
    return;
  }
  serror(0);  /* otherwise syntax error in expression */
}

/* Return a token to the input stream. */
void putback(void)
{
  char *t;

  t = token;
  for(; *t; t++) prog--;
}

/* Display a syntax error. */
void serror(int error)
{
  static char *e[]= {
      "Syntax Error",
      "Unbalanced Parentheses",
      "No Expression Present"
  };
  printf("%s\n", e[error]);
}
```

```
/* Return the next token. */
void get_token(void)
{
  register char *temp;

  tok_type = 0;
  temp = token;
  *temp = '\0';

  if(!*prog) return; /* at end of expression */
  while(isspace(*prog)) ++prog; /* skip over white space */

  if(strchr("+-*/%^=()", *prog)){
    tok_type = DELIMITER;
    /* advance to next char */
    *temp++ = *prog++;
  }
  else if(isalpha(*prog)) {
    while(!isdelim(*prog)) *temp++ = *prog++;
    tok_type = VARIABLE;
  }
  else if(isdigit(*prog)) {
    while(!isdelim(*prog)) *temp++ = *prog++;
    tok_type = NUMBER;
  }

  *temp = '\0';
}

/* Return true if c is a delimiter. */
isdelim(char c)
{

  if(strchr(" +-/*%^=()", c) || c==9 || c=='\r' || c==0)
    return 1;
  return 0;
}
```

The parser as it is shown can handle the following operators: +, −, *, /, %. In addition, it can handle integer exponentiation (^) and the unary minus. The parser can also deal with parentheses correctly. Notice that it has six levels as well as the

atom( ) function, which returns the value of a number. As discussed, the two globals **token** and **tok_type** return, respectively, the next token and its type from the expression string. The pointer **prog** points to the string that holds the expression.

The simple **main( )** function that follows demonstrates the use of the parser:

```
/* Parser demo program. */
#include <stdlib.h>
#include <ctype.h>
#include <stdio.h>
#include <string.h>

char *prog;
void eval_exp(double *answer);

void main(void)
{
  double answer;
  char *p;

  p = malloc(100);
  if(!p) {
    printf("Allocation failure.\n");
    exit(1);
  }

  /* Process expressions until a blank line
     is entered.
  */
  do {
    prog = p;
    printf("Enter expression: ");
    gets(prog);
    if(!*prog) break;
    eval_exp(&answer);
    printf("Answer is: %.2f\n", answer);
  } while(*p);
}
```

To understand exactly how the parser evaluates an expression, work through the following expression. (Assume that **prog** points to the start of the expression.)

$$10 - 3 * 2$$

When **eval_exp( )**, the entry point into the parser, is called, it gets the first token. If the token is null, the function prints the message **No Expression Present** and returns. However, in this case, the token contains the number **10**. Since the token is not null, **eval_exp2( )** is called. (**eval_exp1( )** is used when the assignment operator is added; it is not needed here.) As a result, **eval_exp2( )** calls **eval_exp3( )** and **eval_exp3( )** calls **eval_exp4( )**, which in turn calls **eval_exp5( )**. Then **eval_exp5( )** checks whether the token is a unary plus or minus, which in this case, it is not, so **eval_exp6( )** is called. At this point **eval_exp6( )** recursively calls either **eval_exp2( )** (in the case of a parenthesized expression) or **atom( )** to find the value of a number. Since the token is not a left parentheses, **atom( )** is executed and ***answer** is assigned the value 10. Next, another token is retrieved, and the functions begin to return up the chain. The token is now the operator –, and the functions return up to **eval_exp2( )**.

What happens next is very important. Because the token is –, it is saved in **op**. The parser then gets the next token, which is 3, and the descent down the chain begins again. As before, **atom( )** is entered. The value 3 is returned in ***answer** and the token ***** is read. This causes a return back up the chain to **eval_exp3( )**, where the final token 2 is read. At this point, the first arithmetic operation occurs—the multiplication of 2 and 3. The result is returned to **eval_exp2( )** and the subtraction is performed. The subtraction yields the answer 4. Although the process may at first seem complicated, work through some other examples to verify that this method functions correctly every time.

This parser would be suitable for use by a desktop calculator, as is illustrated by the previous program. It also could be used in a limited database. Before it could be used in a computer language or in a sophisticated calculator, however, it would need the ability to handle variables. This is the subject of the next section.

Adding Variables to the Parser

All programming languages, many calculators, and spreadsheets use variables to store values for later use. The simple parser in the preceding section needs to be expanded to include variables before it can store values. To include variables, you need to add several things to the parser. First, of course, are the variables themselves. As stated earlier, the parser recognizes only the variables **A** through **Z** (although you could expand that capability if you wanted to). Each variable uses one array location in a 26-element array of **double**s. Therefore, add the following to the parser:

```
double vars[26]= {    /* 26 user variables,  A-Z */
  0.0, 0.0, 0.0, 0.0, 0.0, 0.0, 0.0, 0.0, 0.0, 0.0,
  0.0, 0.0, 0.0, 0.0, 0.0, 0.0, 0.0, 0.0, 0.0, 0.0,
  0.0, 0.0, 0.0, 0.0, 0.0, 0.0
};
```

As you can see, the variables are initialized to 0 as a courtesy to the user.

You also need a routine to look up the value of a given variable. Because the variables are named **A** through **Z**, they can easily be used to index the array **vars** by subtracting the ASCII value for **A** from the variable name. The function **find_var( )** is shown here:

```
/* Return the value of a variable. */
double find_var(char *s)
{
  if(!isalpha(*s)){
    serror(1);
    return 0;
  }
  return vars[toupper(*token)-'A'];
}
```

As this function is written, it will actually accept long variable names, but only the first letter is significant. You may modify this to fit your needs.

You must also modify the **atom( )** function to handle both numbers and variables. The new version is shown here:

```
/* Get the value of a number or a variable. */
void atom(double *answer)
{
  switch(tok_type) {
    case VARIABLE:
      *answer = find_var(token);
      get_token();
      return;
    case NUMBER:
      *answer = atof(token);
      get_token();
      return;
    default:
      serror(0);
  }
}
```

Technically, these additions are all that is needed for the parser to use variables correctly; however, there is no way for these variables to be assigned a value. Often this is done outside the parser, but you can treat the equal sign as an assignment operator and make it part of the parser. There are various ways to do this. One method is to add **eval_exp1( )** to the parser, as shown here:

```
/* Process an assignment. */
void eval_exp1(double *result)
{
  int slot, ttok_type;
  char temp_token[80];

  if(tok_type==VARIABLE) {
    /* save old token */
    strcpy(temp_token, token);
    ttok_type = tok_type;

    /* compute the index of the variable */
    slot = toupper(*token) - 'A';

    get_token();
    if(*token != '=') {
      putback(); /* return current token */
      /* restore old token - not assignment */
      strcpy(token, temp_token);
      tok_type = ttok_type;
    }
    else {
      get_token(); /* get next part of exp */
      eval_exp2(result);
      vars[slot] = *result;
      return;
    }
  }

  eval_exp2(result);
}
```

As you can see, the function needs to look ahead to determine whether an assignment is actually being made. This is because a variable name always precedes an assignment, but a variable name alone does not guarantee that an assignment expression follows. That is, the parser will accept A = 100 as an assignment, but is also smart enough to know that A/10 is an expression. To accomplish this, **eval_exp1( )** reads the next token from the input stream. If it is not an equal sign, the token is returned to the input stream for later use by calling **putback( )**, shown here:

```
/* Return a token to the input stream. */
void putback(void)
{
  char *t;

  t = token;
  for(; *t; t++) prog--;
}
```

Here is the entire enhanced parser:

```
/* This module contains the recursive descent
   parser that recognizes variables.
*/

#include <stdlib.h>
#include <ctype.h>
#include <stdio.h>
#include <string.h>

#define DELIMITER  1
#define VARIABLE   2
#define NUMBER     3

extern char *prog;  /* points to the expression to be analyzed */
char token[80];
char tok_type;

double vars[26]= {     /* 26 user variables,  A-Z */
  0.0, 0.0, 0.0, 0.0, 0.0, 0.0, 0.0, 0.0, 0.0, 0.0,
  0.0, 0.0, 0.0, 0.0, 0.0, 0.0, 0.0, 0.0, 0.0, 0.0,
  0.0, 0.0, 0.0, 0.0, 0.0, 0.0
};

void eval_exp(double *answer), eval_exp2(double *answer);
void eval_exp1(double *result);
void eval_exp3(double *answer), eval_exp4(double *answer);
void eval_exp5(double *answer);
void eval_exp6(double *answer), atom(double *answer);
void get_token(void), putback(void);
void serror(int error);
double find_var(char *s);
```

```c
int isdelim(char c);

/* Parser entry point. */
void eval_exp(double *answer)
{
  get_token();
  if(!*token) {
    serror(2);
    return;
  }
  eval_exp1(answer);
  if(*token) serror(0); /* last token must be null */
}

/* Process an assignment. */
void eval_exp1(double *answer)
{
  int slot;
  char ttok_type;
  char temp_token[80];

  if(tok_type==VARIABLE) {
    /* save old token */
    strcpy(temp_token, token);
    ttok_type = tok_type;
    /* compute the index of the variable */
    slot = toupper(*token) - 'A';

    get_token();
    if(*token != '=') {
      putback(); /* return current token */
      /* restore old token - not assignment */
      strcpy(token, temp_token);
      tok_type = ttok_type;
    }
    else {
      get_token(); /* get next part of exp */
      eval_exp2(answer);
      vars[slot] = *answer;
      return;
    }
  }
```

```
    eval_exp2(answer);
}

/* Add or subtract two terms. */
void eval_exp2(double *answer)
{
  register char op;
  double temp;

  eval_exp3(answer);
  while((op = *token) == '+' || op == '-') {
    get_token();
    eval_exp3(&temp);
    switch(op) {
      case '-':
        *answer = *answer - temp;
        break;
      case '+':
        *answer = *answer + temp;
        break;
    }
  }
}

/* Multiply or divide two factors. */
void eval_exp3(double *answer)
{
  register char op;
  double temp;

  eval_exp4(answer);
  while((op = *token) == '*' || op == '/' || op == '%') {
    get_token();
    eval_exp4(&temp);
    switch(op) {
      case '*':
        *answer = *answer * temp;
        break;
      case '/':
        *answer = *answer / temp;
        break;
```

```
      case '%':
        *answer = (int) *answer % (int) temp;
        break;
    }
  }
}

/* Process an exponent */
void eval_exp4(double *answer)
{
  double temp, ex;
  register int t;

  eval_exp5(answer);
  if(*token== '^') {
    get_token();
    eval_exp4(&temp);
    ex = *answer;
    if(temp==0.0) {
      *answer = 1.0;
      return;
    }
    for(t=temp-1; t>0; --t) *answer = (*answer) * (double)ex;
  }
}

/* Evaluate a unary + or -. */
void eval_exp5(double *answer)
{
  register char  op;

  op = 0;
  if((tok_type == DELIMITER) && *token=='+' || *token == '-') {
    op = *token;
    get_token();
  }
  eval_exp6(answer);
  if(op=='-') *answer = -(*answer);
}

/* Process a parenthesized expression. */
void eval_exp6(double *answer)
```

```
{
  if((*token == '(')) {
    get_token();
    eval_exp2(answer);
    if(*token != ')')
      serror(1);
    get_token();
  }
  else atom(answer);
}

/* Get the value of a number or a variable. */
void atom(double *answer)
{
  switch(tok_type) {
    case VARIABLE:
      *answer = find_var(token);
      get_token();
      return;
    case NUMBER:
      *answer = atof(token);
      get_token();
      return;
    default:
      serror(0);
  }
}

/* Return a token to the input stream. */
void putback(void)
{
  char *t;

  t = token;
  for(; *t; t++) prog--;
}

/* Display a syntax error. */
void serror(int error)
{
  static char *e[]= {
      "Syntax Error",
```

```
      "Unbalanced Parentheses",
      "No Expression Present"
  };
  printf("%s\n", e[error]);
}

/* Return the next token. */
void get_token(void)
{
  register char *temp;

  tok_type = 0;
  temp = token;
  *temp = '\0';

  if(!*prog) return; /* at end of expression */

  while(isspace(*prog)) ++prog; /* skip over white space */

  if(strchr("+-*/%^=()", *prog)){
    tok_type = DELIMITER;
    /* advance to next char */
    *temp++ = *prog++;
  }
  else if(isalpha(*prog)) {
    while(!isdelim(*prog)) *temp++ = *prog++;
    tok_type = VARIABLE;
  }
  else if(isdigit(*prog)) {
    while(!isdelim(*prog)) *temp++ = *prog++;
    tok_type = NUMBER;
  }

  *temp = '\0';
}

/* Return true if c is a delimiter. */
isdelim(char c)
{
  if(strchr(" +-/*%^=()", c) || c==9 || c=='\r' || c==0)
    return 1;
  return 0;
```

```
    }

/* Return the value of a variable. */
double find_var(char *s)
{
  if(!isalpha(*s)){
    serror(1);
    return 0.0;
  }
  return vars[toupper(*token)-'A'];
}
```

You may still use the same **main( )** function that you used for the simple parser. With the enhanced parser, you can now enter expressions like

A = 10/4
A – B
C = A * (F – 21)

Syntax Checking in a Recursive-Descent Parser

In expression parsing, a syntax error is simply a situation in which the input expression does not conform to the strict rules required by the parser. Most of the time, this is caused by human error—usually typing mistakes. For example, the following expressions are not valid for the parsers in this chapter:

10 ** 8
(10 – 5) * 9)
/8

The first contains two operators in a row, the second has unbalanced parentheses, and the last has a division sign at the start of an expression. None of these conditions is allowed by the parsers in this chapter. Because syntax errors can cause the parser to give erroneous results, you need to guard against them.

As you studied the code of the parsers, you probably noticed the **serror( )** function, which is called under certain situations. Unlike many other parsers, the recursive-descent method makes syntax checking easy because, for the most part, it occurs in **atom( )**, **find_var( )**, or **eval_exp6( )**, where parentheses are checked. The only problem with the syntax checking as it now stands is that the entire parser is not aborted on syntax error. This can lead to multiple error messages.

The best way to implement the **serror( )** function is to have it execute some sort of reset. For example, all modern compilers come with a pair of companion functions called **setjmp( )** and **longjmp( )**. These two functions allow a program to branch to a *different* function. Therefore, **serror( )** could execute a **longjmp( )** to some safe point in your program outside the parser.

If you leave the code the way it is, multiple syntax-error messages may be issued. This can be an annoyance in some situations, but it can be a blessing in others because multiple errors may be caught. Generally, however, you will want to enhance the syntax checking before using it in commercial programs.

Chapter Twenty-Three

AI-Based Problem Solving

The field of artificial intelligence (AI) is composed of several different and exciting aspects. However, fundamental to most AI applications is problem solving.

Basically, there are two types of problems. The first type can be solved through the use of some sort of deterministic procedure that is guaranteed success—in other words, a *computation*. The methods used to solve these types of problems are often easily translated into an algorithm that a computer can execute. However, few real-world problems lend themselves to computational solutions. In fact, most problems are noncomputational. These problems are solved by *searching for a solution*—the method of problem solving with which AI is concerned.

One of the dreams of AI research is a general problem solver. A general problem solver is a program that can produce solutions to all sorts of different problems about which it has no specific designed-in knowledge. This chapter shows why the dream is as tantalizing as it is difficult to realize.

In early AI research, developing good search methods was a primary goal. There are two reasons for this: necessity and desire. One of the most difficult obstacles when applying AI techniques to real-world problems is the sheer magnitude and complexity of most situations. Solving these problems requires good search techniques. In addition, researchers believed then as they do now that searching is central to problem solving, which is a crucial ingredient of intelligence.

Representation and Terminology

Imagine that you have lost your car keys. You know that they are somewhere in your house, which looks like this:

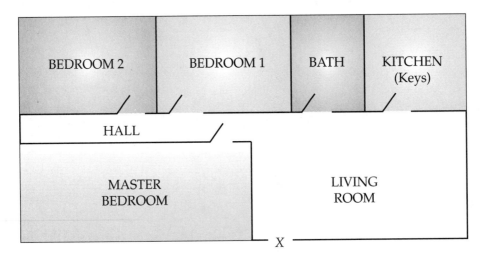

You are standing at the front door (where the X is). As you begin your search, you check the living room. Then you go down the hall to the first bedroom, through the hall to the second bedroom, back to the hall, and to the master bedroom. Not having found your keys, you backtrack further by going back through the living room. You find your keys in the kitchen. This situation is easily represented by a graph, as shown in Figure 23-1.

The fact that problems can be represented by a graph is important because a graph provides a means to visualize the way the different search techniques work. (Also, being able to represent problems by graphs allows AI researchers to apply various theorems from graph theory. However, these theorems are beyond the scope of this book.) With this in mind, study the following definitions:

Node	A Discrete Point
Terminal node	A node that ends a path
Search space	The set of all nodes
Goal	The node that is the object of the search
Heuristics	Information about whether any specific node is a better next choice than another
Solution path	A directed graph of the nodes visited en route to a solution

In the example of the lost keys, each room in the house is a node; the entire house is the search space; the goal, as it turns out, is the kitchen; and the solution path is shown in Figure 23-1. The bedrooms, kitchen, and the bath are terminal nodes because

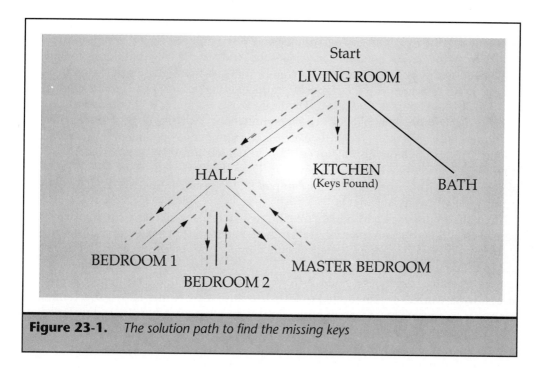

Figure 23-1. *The solution path to find the missing keys*

they lead nowhere. This example doesn't use heuristics, but you will see some later on in this chapter.

Combinatorial Explosions

At this point, you may think that searching for a solution is easy—you start at the beginning and work your way to the conclusion. In the extremely simple case of the lost keys, this is not a bad method. But in most problems that you would use a computer to solve, the situation is much different. In general, you use a computer to solve problems where the number of nodes in the search space is very large, and as the search space grows, so does the number of different possible paths to the goal. The trouble is that each node added to the search space adds more than one path. That is, the number of pathways to the goal increases faster as each node is added.

For instance, consider the number of ways three objects—A, B, and C—can be arranged on a table. The six possible permutations are

A	B	C
A	C	B
B	C	A
B	A	C
C	B	A
C	A	B

You can quickly prove to yourself that these six are the only ways that A, B, and C can be arranged. However, you can derive the same number by using a theorem from the branch of mathematics called *combinatorics*—the study of the way that things can be combined. According to the theorem, the number of ways that N objects can be arranged is equal to N! (N factorial). The factorial of a number is the product of all whole numbers equal to or less than itself down to 1. Therefore, 3! is 3 x 2 x 1, or 6. If you had four objects to arrange, there would be 4!, or 24, permutations. With five objects, the number is 120, and with six it is 720. With 1000 objects the number of possible permutations is huge! The graph in Figure 23-2 gives you a visual feel for what AI researchers commonly refer to as a *combinatoric explosion*. Once there are more than a handful of possibilities, it very quickly becomes impossible to examine (indeed, even to enumerate) all the arrangements.

In other words, each additional node in the search space increases the number of possible solutions by a number far greater than one. Hence, at some point there are too many possibilities to work with. Because the number of possibilities grows so quickly, only the simplest of problems lend themselves to exhaustive searches. An *exhaustive search* is one that examines all nodes—think of it as a "brute-force" technique. Brute force always works, but is not often practical because it consumes far too much time, too many computing resources, or both. For this reason, researchers have developed other search techniques.

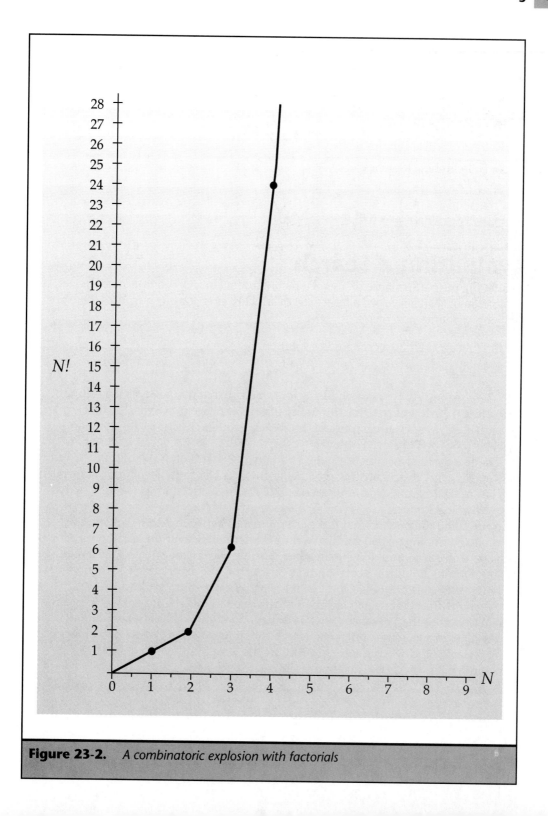

Figure 23-2. *A combinatoric explosion with factorials*

Search Techniques

There are several ways to search for a possible solution. The most important and common are

- Depth-first searches
- Breadth-first searches
- Hill-climbing searches
- Least-cost searches

This chapter examines each of these searches.

Evaluating a Search

Evaluating the performance of a search technique can be very complicated. In fact, the evaluation of searches forms a large part of AI. However, for our purposes there are two important measurements:

- How quickly the search finds a solution.
- How good the solution is.

There are several types of problems for which all that matters is that a solution, any solution, be found with the minimum effort. For these problems, the first measurement is especially important. However, in other situations, the solution must be good, perhaps even optimal.

The speed of a search is determined both by the length of the solution path and by the number of nodes actually traversed in the process of finding the solution. Remember that backtracking from dead ends is essentially wasted effort, so you want a search that seldom backtracks.

You should understand that there is a difference between finding an optimal solution and finding a good solution. Finding an optimal solution can imply an exhaustive search because sometimes this is the only way to know that the best solution has been found. Finding a good solution, in contrast, means finding a solution that is within a set of constraints—it does not matter if a better solution exists.

As you will see, the search techniques described in this chapter all work better in certain situations than in others. So, it is difficult to say whether one search method is *always* superior to another. But some search techniques have a greater probability of being better for the average case. In addition, the way a problem is defined can sometimes help you choose an appropriate search method.

First, consider a problem that we will use various searches to solve. Imagine that you are a travel agent and a rather quarrelsome customer wants you to book a flight from New York to Los Angeles with XYZ Airlines. You try to tell the customer that XYZ does not have a direct flight from New York to Los Angeles, but the customer insists that XYZ is the only airline that he will fly. XYZ's scheduled flights are as follows:

Flight	Distance
New York to Chicago	1000 miles
Chicago to Denver	1000 miles
New York to Toronto	800 miles
New York to Denver	1900 miles
Toronto to Calgary	1500 miles
Toronto to Los Angeles	1800 miles
Toronto to Chicago	500 miles
Denver to Urbana	1000 miles
Denver to Houston	1500 miles
Houston to Los Angeles	1500 miles
Denver to Los Angeles	1000 miles

You quickly see that there is a way to fly from New York to Los Angeles by using XYZ if you book connecting flights. You book the fellow his flights.

Your task is to write C programs that do the same thing even better.

A Graphic Representation

The flight information in XYZ's schedule book can be translated into the directed graph shown in Figure 23-3. A *directed graph* is simply a graph in which the lines connecting each node include an arrow to indicate the direction of motion. In a directed graph, you cannot travel in the direction against the arrow.

To make things easier to understand, this graph is redrawn as the tree in Figure 23-4. Refer to this version for the rest of this chapter. The goal, Los Angeles, is circled. Also notice that various cities appear more than once to simplify the construction of the graph.

Now you are ready to develop the various search programs that will find paths from New York to Los Angeles.

The Depth-First Search

The *depth-first search* explores each possible path to its conclusion before another path is tried. To understand exactly how this works, consider the tree that follows. F is the goal.

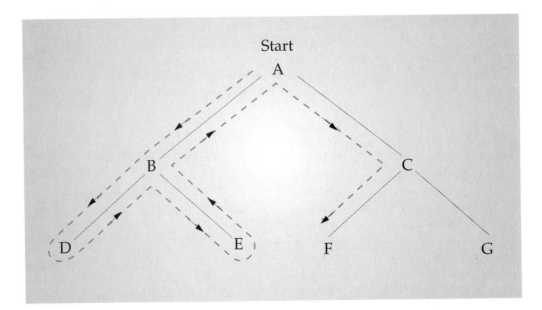

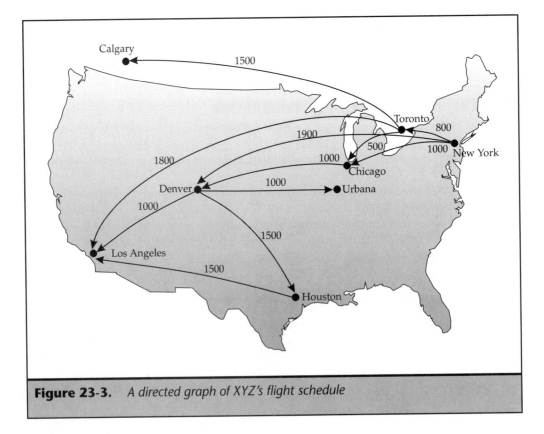

Figure 23-3. *A directed graph of XYZ's flight schedule*

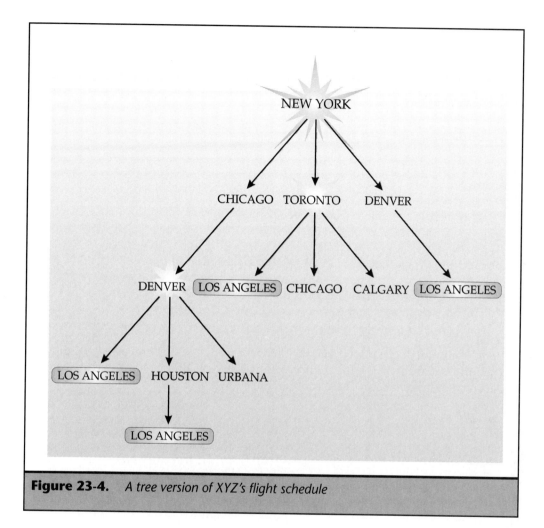

Figure 23-4. *A tree version of XYZ's flight schedule*

A depth-first search traverses the graph in the following order: ABDBEBACF. If you are familiar with trees, you recognize this type of search as an inorder tree traversal. That is, the path goes left until a terminal node is reached or the goal is found. If a terminal node is reached, the path backs up one level, goes right, and then left until either the goal or a terminal node is encountered. This procedure is repeated until the goal is found or the last node in the search space has been examined.

As you can see, a depth-first search is certain to find the goal because in the worst case it degenerates into an exhaustive search. In this example, an exhaustive search would result if G were the goal.

Writing a C program to find a route from New York to Los Angeles requires a database that contains the information about XYZ's flights. Each entry in the database must contain the departure and destination cities, the distance between them, and a flag that aids in backtracking (as you will see shortly). The following structure holds such information:

```c
#define MAX 100

/* structure of the flight database */
struct FL {
  char from[20];
  char to[20];
  int distance;
  char skip;  /* used in backtracking */
};

struct FL flight[MAX];  /* array of db structures */

int f_pos=0; /* number of entries in flight db */
int find_pos=0; /* index for searching flight db */
```

Individual entries are placed into the database using the function **assert_flight( )**, and **setup( )** initializes all the flight information. The global **f_pos** holds the index of the last item in the database. These routines are shown here:

```c
void setup(void)
{
  assert_flight("New York", "Chicago", 1000);
  assert_flight("Chicago", "Denver", 1000);
  assert_flight("New York", "Toronto", 800);
  assert_flight("New York", "Denver", 1900);
  assert_flight("Toronto", "Calgary", 1500);
  assert_flight("Toronto", "Los Angeles", 1800);
  assert_flight("Toronto", "Chicago", 500);
  assert_flight("Denver", "Urbana", 1000);
  assert_flight("Denver", "Houston", 1500);
  assert_flight("Houston", "Los Angeles", 1500);
  assert_flight("Denver", "Los Angeles", 1000);
}

/* Put facts into the database. */
void assert_flight(char *from, char *to, int dist)
{
```

```
   if(f_pos<MAX) {
     strcpy(flight[f_pos].from, from);
     strcpy(flight[f_pos].to, to);
     flight[f_pos].distance = dist;
     flight[f_pos].skip = 0;
     f_pos++;
   }
   else printf("Flight database full.\n");
}
```

In keeping with the spirit of AI, think of the database as containing facts. The program to be developed will use these facts to arrive at a solution. For this reason, many AI researchers refer to the database as a knowledge base. This chapter uses the two terms interchangeably.

Before you can write the actual code to find a route between New York and Los Angeles, you need several support functions. First, you need a routine that determines if there is a flight between the two cities. This function is called **match( )**, and it returns zero if no such flight exists or returns the distance between the two cities if there is a flight. This function is shown here:

```
/* If flight between from and to, then return
   the distance of flight; otherwise, return 0. */
match(char *from, char *to)
{
  register int t;

  for(t=f_pos-1; t>-1; t--)
    if(!strcmp(flight[t].from, from) &&
       !strcmp(flight[t].to, to)) return flight[t].distance;

  return 0;  /* not found */
}
```

Another necessary routine is **find( )**. Given a city, **find( )** searches the database for any connection. If a connection is found, the name of the destination city and its distance are returned; otherwise, zero is returned. The **find( )** routine follows:

```
/* Given from, find anywhere. */
find(char *from, char *anywhere)
{
  find_pos = 0;
  while(find_pos<f_pos) {
    if(!strcmp(flight[find_pos].from, from) &&
      !flight[find_pos].skip) {
        strcpy(anywhere, flight[find_pos].to);
        flight[find_pos].skip = 1; /* make active */
        return flight[find_pos].distance;
    }
    find_pos++;
  }
  return 0;
}
```

As you can see, cities that have the **skip** field set to 1 are not valid connections. Also, if a connection is found, its **skip** field is marked as active—this controls backtracking from dead ends.

Backtracking is a crucial ingredient in many AI techniques. Backtracking is accomplished through the use of recursive routines and a backtrack stack. Almost all backtracking situations are stacklike in operation—that is, they are first-in, last-out. As a path is explored, nodes are pushed onto the stack as they are encountered. At each dead end, the last node is popped off the stack and a new path, from that point, is tried. This process continues until either the goal is reached or all paths have been exhausted. The functions **push( )** and **pop( )**, which manage the backtrack stack, follow. They use the globals **tos** and **bt_stack** to hold the top-of-stack pointer and the stack array, respectively.

```
/* Stack Routines */
void push(char *from, char *to, int dist)
{
  if(tos<MAX) {
    strcpy(bt_stack[tos].from, from);
    strcpy(bt_stack[tos].to, to);
    bt_stack[tos].dist = dist;
    tos++;
  }
  else printf("Stack full.\n");
}
```

```
void pop(char *from, char *to, int *dist)
{
  if(tos>0) {
    tos--;
    strcpy(from, bt_stack[tos].from);
    strcpy(to, bt_stack[tos].to);
    *dist = bt_stack[tos].dist;
  }
  else printf("Stack underflow.\n");
}
```

Now that the required support routines have been developed, consider the code that follows. It defines the **isflight( )** function, the key routine in finding a route between New York and Los Angeles.

```
/* Determine if there is a route between from and to. */
void isflight(char *from, char *to)
{
  int d, dist;
  char anywhere[20];

  /* see if at destination */
  if(d=match(from, to)) {
    push(from, to, d);
    return;
  }

  /* try another connection */
  if(dist=find(from, anywhere)) {
    push(from, to, dist);
    isflight(anywhere, to);
  }
  else if(tos>0) {
    /* backtrack */
    pop(from, to, &dist);
    isflight(from, to);
  }
}
```

The routine works as follows: First, the database is checked by **match( )** to see if there is a flight between **from** and **to**. If there is, the goal has been reached—the connection is pushed onto the stack and the function returns. Otherwise, **find( )** checks if there is a connection between **from** and any place else. If there is, this connection is pushed onto the stack and **isflight( )** is called recursively. Otherwise, backtracking takes place. The previous node is removed from the stack and **isflight( )** is called recursively. This process continues until the goal is found. The **skip** field is necessary to backtracking to prevent the same connections from being tried over and over again.

Hence, if called with Denver and Houston, the first part of the routine would succeed and **isflight( )** would terminate. Say, however, that **isflight( )** is called with Chicago and Houston. In this case, the first part would fail because there is no direct flight connecting these two cities. The second part is tried by attempting to find a connection between the origin city and any other city. In this case, Chicago connects with Denver; therefore, **isflight( )** is called recursively with Denver and Houston. Once again, the first condition is tested. A connection is found this time. Finally, the recursive calls unravel and **isflight( )** terminates. Verify in your mind that, as **isflight( )** is presented here, it performs a depth-first search of the knowledge base.

It is important to understand that **isflight( )** does not actually *return* the solution—it *generates* it. Upon exit from **isflight( )**, the backtrack stack contains the route between Chicago and Houston—that is, the solution. In fact, the success or failure of **isflight( )** is determined by the state of the stack. An empty stack indicates failure; otherwise, the stack holds a solution. Hence, you need one more function to complete the entire program. The function is called **route( )**, and it prints both the path to follow as well as the total distance. The **route( )** function is shown here:

```c
/* Show the route and total distance. */
void route(char *to)
{
  int dist, t;

  dist = 0;
  t = 0;
  while(t<tos) {
    printf("%s to ", bt_stack[t].from);
    dist += bt_stack[t].dist;
    t++;
  }
  printf("%s\n", to);
  printf("Distance is %d.\n", dist);
}
```

The entire depth-first search program follows. Enter this program into your computer at this time.

```
/* Depth-first search. */
#include <stdio.h>
#include <string.h>

 #define MAX 100

/* structure of the flight database */
struct FL {
  char from[20];
  char to[20];
  int distance;
  char skip; /* used in backtracking */
};

struct FL flight[MAX]; /* array of db structures */

int f_pos=0; /* number of entries in flight db */
int find_pos=0; /* index for searching flight db */
int tos=0;      /* top of stack */
struct stack {
  char from[20];
  char to[20];
  int dist;
} ;
struct stack bt_stack[MAX]; /* backtrack stack */

void setup(void), route(char *to);
void assert_flight(char *from, char *to, int dist);
void push(char *from, char *to, int dist);
void pop(char *from, char *to, int *dist);
void isflight(char *from, char *to);
int find(char *from, char *anywhere);
int match(char *from, char *to);

void main(void)
{
  char from[20], to[20];

  setup();

  printf("From? ");
  gets(from);
  printf("To? ");
```

```
  gets(to);

  isflight(from,to);
  route(to);
}

/* Initialize the flight database. */
void setup(void)
{
  assert_flight("New York","Chicago",1000);
  assert_flight("Chicago","Denver",1000);
  assert_flight("New York","Toronto",800);
  assert_flight("New York","Denver",1900);
  assert_flight("Toronto","Calgary",1500);
  assert_flight("Toronto","Los Angeles",1800);
  assert_flight("Toronto","Chicago",500);
  assert_flight("Denver","Urbana",1000);
  assert_flight("Denver","Houston",1500);
  assert_flight("Houston","Los Angeles",1500);
  assert_flight("Denver","Los Angeles",1000);
}

/* Put facts into the database. */
void assert_flight(char *from, char *to, int dist)
{

  if(f_pos<MAX) {
    strcpy(flight[f_pos].from, from);
    strcpy(flight[f_pos].to, to);
    flight[f_pos].distance = dist;
    flight[f_pos].skip = 0;
    f_pos++;
  }
  else printf("Flight database full.\n");
}

/* Show the route and total distance. */
void route(char *to)

{
  int dist, t;
```

```
  dist = 0;
  t = 0;
  while(t<tos) {
    printf("%s to ", bt_stack[t].from);
    dist += bt_stack[t].dist;
    t++;
  }
  printf("%s\n", to);
  printf("Distance is %d.\n", dist);
}

/* If flight between from and to, then return
   the distance of flight; otherwise, return 0. */
match(char *from, char *to)
{
  register int t;

  for(t=f_pos-1; t>-1; t--)
    if(!strcmp(flight[t].from, from) &&
       !strcmp(flight[t].to, to)) return flight[t].distance;

  return 0; /* not found */
}

/* Given from, find anywhere. */
find(char *from, char *anywhere)
{
  find_pos=0;
  while(find_pos<f_pos) {
    if(!strcmp(flight[find_pos].from,from) &&
       !flight[find_pos].skip) {
        strcpy(anywhere,flight[find_pos].to);
        flight[find_pos].skip=1; /* make active */
        return flight[find_pos].distance;
      }
    find_pos++;
  }
  return 0;
}

/* Determine if there is a route between from and to. */
void isflight(char *from, char *to)
```

```
{
  int d, dist;
  char anywhere[20];

  /* see if at destination */
  if(d=match(from, to)) {
    push(from, to, d);
    return;
  }
  /* try another connection */
  if(dist=find(from, anywhere)) {
    push(from, to, dist);
    isflight(anywhere, to);
  }
  else if(tos>0) {
    /* backtrack */
    pop(from, to, &dist);
    isflight(from, to);
  }
}

/* Stack Routines */
void push(char *from, char *to, int dist)
{
  if(tos<MAX) {
    strcpy(bt_stack[tos].from,from);
    strcpy(bt_stack[tos].to,to);
    bt_stack[tos].dist=dist;
    tos++;
  }
  else printf("Stack full.\n");
}

void pop(char *from, char *to, int *dist)
{
  if(tos>0) {
    tos--;
    strcpy(from,bt_stack[tos].from);
    strcpy(to,bt_stack[tos].to);
    *dist=bt_stack[tos].dist;
  }
  else printf("Stack underflow.\n");
}
```

Notice that **main( )** prompts you for both the city of origin and the city of destination. This means that you can use the program to find routes between any two cities. However, the rest of this chapter assumes that New York is the origin and Los Angeles is the destination.

Compile the program now. For certain compilers, you will need to increase the amount of memory allocated for the stack because, for certain solutions, the routines are highly recursive.

When run with New York as the origin and Los Angeles as the destination, the solution is

New York to Chicago to Denver to Los Angeles
Distance is 3000.

Figure 23-5 shows the path of the search.

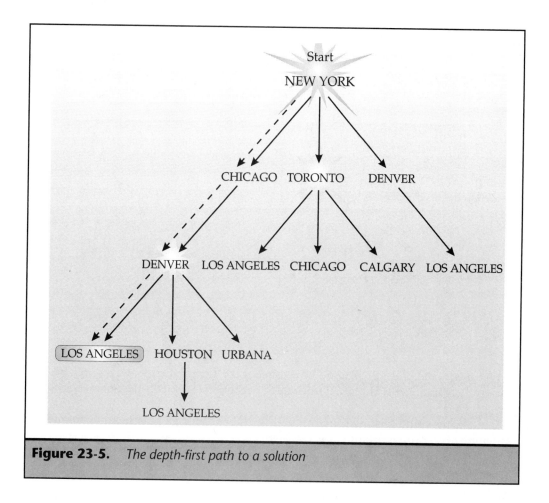

Figure 23-5.   *The depth-first path to a solution*

If you refer to Figure 23-5 you see that this is indeed the first solution that would be found by a depth-first search. It is not the optimal solution—which is New York to Toronto to Los Angeles with a distance of 2600 miles—but it is not bad.

An Analysis of the Depth-First Search

As you can see, the depth-first approach found a fairly good solution. Also, relative to this specific problem, depth-first searching found a solution on its first try with no backtracking—this is very good. But it would have had to traverse nearly all the nodes to arrive at the optimal solution—this is not so good.

Note that the performance of depth-first searches can be quite poor when a particularly long branch with no solution at the end is explored. In this case, a depth-first search wastes considerable time not only exploring this chain, but also backtracking to the goal.

The Breadth-First Search

The opposite of the depth-first search is the *breadth-first search*. In this method, each node on the same level is checked before the search proceeds to the next deeper level. This traversal method is shown here with C as the goal:

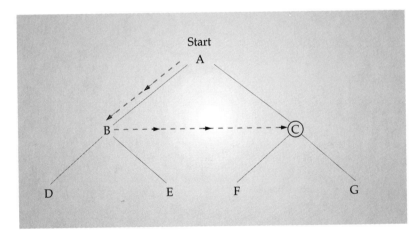

As you can see, the nodes A, B, and C are visited. Like a depth-first search, a breadth-first search guarantees a solution, if one exists, because it eventually degenerates into an exhaustive search.

To make the route-seeking program perform a breadth-first search, you only need to alter the procedure **isflight( )** as shown here:

```
void isflight(char *from, char *to)
{
  int d, dist;
  char anywhere[20];

  while(dist=find(from, anywhere)) {
    /* breadth-first modification */
    if(d=match(anywhere, to)) {
      push(from, to, dist);
      push(anywhere, to, d);
      return;
    }
  }
  /* try any connection */
  if(dist=find(from, anywhere)) {
    push(from, to, dist);
    isflight(anywhere, to);
  }
  else if(tos>0) {
    pop(from, to, &dist);
    isflight(from, to);
  }
}
```

As you can see, only the first condition has been altered. Now all connecting cities to the departure city are checked to see if they connect with the destination city.

Substitute this version of **isflight( )** in the program and run it. The solution is

New York to Toronto to Los Angeles
Distance is 2600.

The solution is optimal. Figure 23-6 shows the breadth-first path to the solution.

An Analysis of the Breadth-First Search

In this example, the breadth-first search performed very well by finding the first solution without backtracking. As it turned out, this was also the optimal solution. In fact, the first three solutions that would be found are the best three routes there are. However, remember that this result does not generalize to other situations because the path depends upon the physical organization of the information as it is stored in the computer. The example does illustrate, however, how radically different depth-first and breadth-first searches are.

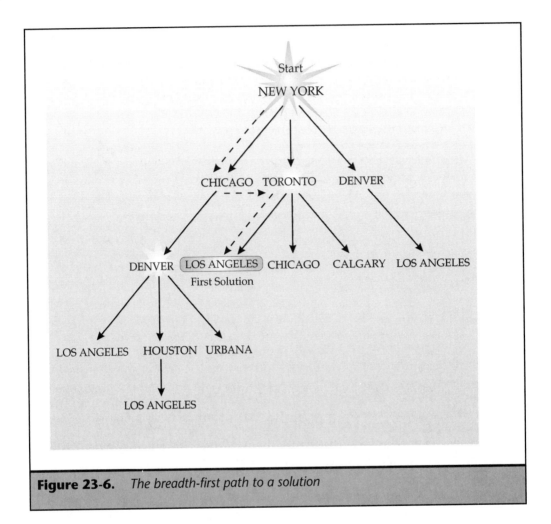

Figure 23-6.   *The breadth-first path to a solution*

A disadvantage to breadth-first searching becomes apparent when the goal is several layers deep. In this case a breadth-first search expends substantial effort to find the goal. In general, you choose between depth-first and breadth-first searching by making an educated guess about the most likely position of the goal.

Adding Heuristics

You have probably guessed by now that both the depth-first and breadth-first search routines are blind. They are methods of looking for a solution that rely solely upon moving from one goal to the other without any educated guesswork on the part of the computer. This may be fine for certain controlled situations where you know that one method is better than the other. However, a generalized AI program needs a search procedure that is on the average superior to either of these two techniques. The only way to achieve such a search is to add heuristic capabilities.

Recall that heuristics are simply rules that qualify the possibility that a search is proceeding in the correct direction. For example, imagine that you are lost in the woods and need a drink of water. The woods are so thick that you cannot see far ahead, and the trees are too big to climb and get a look around. However, you know that rivers, streams, and ponds are most likely in valleys; that animals frequently make paths to their watering places; that when you are near water it is possible to "smell" it; and that you can hear running water. So, you begin by moving downhill because water is unlikely to be uphill. Next you come across a deer trail that also runs downhill. Knowing that this may lead to water, you follow it. You begin to hear a slight rushing off to your left. Knowing that this may be water, you cautiously move in that direction. As you move, you begin to detect the increased humidity in the air; you can smell the water. Finally, you find a stream and have your drink. As you can see, heuristic information, although neither precise nor guaranteed, increases the chances that a search method will find a goal quickly, optimally, or both. In short, it ups the odds in favor of a quick success.

You may think that heuristic information could easily be included in programs designed for specific applications, but that it would be impossible to create generalized heuristic searches. This is not the case, as you will see.

Most often, heuristic search methods are based on maximizing or minimizing some aspect of the problem. In fact, the two heuristic approaches that we will look at use opposite heuristics and yield different results. Both of these searches will be built upon the depth-first search routines.

The Hill-Climbing Search

In the problem of scheduling a flight from New York to Los Angeles, there are two possible constraints that a passenger may want to minimize. The first is the number of connections that have to be made. The second is the length of the route. Remember, the shortest route does not necessarily imply the fewest connections. A search algorithm that attempts to find as a first solution a route that minimizes the number of connections uses the heuristic that the longer the distance of the flight, the greater the likelihood that it takes the traveler closer to the destination; therefore, the number of connections is minimized.

In the language of AI, this is called *hill climbing*. The hill-climbing algorithm chooses as its next step the node that appears to place it closest to the goal (that is, farthest away from the current position). It derives its name from the analogy of a hiker being lost in the dark halfway up a mountain. Assuming that the hiker's camp is at the top of the mountain, even in the dark the hiker knows that each step that goes up is a step in the right direction.

Working only with the information contained in the flight-scheduling knowledge base, here is how to incorporate the hill-climbing heuristic into the routing program: Choose the connecting flight that is as far away as possible from the current position in the hope that it will be closer to the destination. To do this, modify the **find( )** routine as shown here:

```
/* Given from, find the farthest away "anywhere". */
find(char *from, char *anywhere)
{
  int pos, dist;

  pos=dist = 0;
  find_pos = 0;

  while(find_pos<f_pos) {
    if(!strcmp(flight[find_pos].from, from) &&
      !flight[find_pos].skip) {
        if(flight[find_pos].distance>dist) {
        pos = find_pos;
        dist = flight[find_pos].distance;
      }
    }
    find_pos++;
  }
  if(pos) {
    strcpy(anywhere, flight[pos].to);
    flight[pos].skip = 1;
    return flight[pos].distance;
  }
  return 0;
}
```

The **find( )** routine now searches the entire database, looking for the connection that is farthest away from the departure city.

The entire hill-climbing program follows. Enter this program into your computer at this time:

```
/* Hill-climbing */
#include <stdio.h>
#include <string.h>

#define MAX 100
```

```
/* structure of the flight database */
struct FL {
  char from[20];
  char to[20];
  int distance;
  char skip; /* used for backtracking */
};

struct FL flight[MAX];  /* array of db structures */

int f_pos=0; /* number of entries in flight db */
int find_pos=0; /* index for searching flight db */

int tos=0;      /* top of stack */
struct stack {
  char from[20];
  char to[20];
  int dist;
} ;

struct stack bt_stack[MAX]; /* backtrack stack */

void setup(void), route(char *to);
void assert_flight(char *from, char *to, int dist);
void push(char *from, char *to, int dist);
void pop(char *from, char *to, int *dist);
void isflight(char *from, char *to);
int find(char *from, char *anywhere);
int match(char *from, char *to);

void main(void)
{
  char from[20], to[20];

  setup();

  printf("From? ");
  gets(from);
  printf("To? ");
  gets(to);

  isflight(from,to);
```

```
  route(to);
}

/* Initialize the flight database. */
void setup(void)
{
  assert_flight("New York", "Chicago", 1000);
  assert_flight("Chicago", "Denver", 1000);
  assert_flight("New York", "Toronto", 800);
  assert_flight("New York", "Denver", 1900);
  assert_flight("Toronto", "Calgary", 1500);
  assert_flight("Toronto", "Los Angeles", 1800);
  assert_flight("Toronto", "Chicago", 500);
  assert_flight("Denver", "Urbana", 1000);
  assert_flight("Denver", "Houston", 1500);
  assert_flight("Houston", "Los Angeles", 1500);
  assert_flight("Denver", "Los Angeles", 1000);
}

/* Put facts into the database. */
void assert_flight(char *from, char *to, int dist)
{

  if(f_pos<MAX) {
    strcpy(flight[f_pos].from, from);
    strcpy(flight[f_pos].to, to);
    flight[f_pos].distance = dist;
    flight[f_pos].skip = 0;
    f_pos++;
  }
  else printf("Flight database full.\n");
}

/* Show the route and the total distance. */
void route(char *to)
{
  int dist, t;

  dist = 0;
  t = 0;
  while(t<tos) {
    printf("%s to ", bt_stack[t].from);
```

```
      dist += bt_stack[t].dist;
      t++;
  }
  printf("%s\n", to);
  printf("Distance is %d.\n", dist);
}


/* If flight between from and to, then return
   the distance of flight; otherwise, return 0. */
match(char *from, char *to)
{
  register int t;

  for(t=f_pos-1; t>-1; t--)
    if(!strcmp(flight[t].from, from) &&
      !strcmp(flight[t].to, to)) return flight[t].distance;

  return 0;  /* not found */
}


/* Given from, find the farthest away "anywhere". */
find(char *from, char *anywhere)
{
  int pos, dist;

  pos=dist = 0;
  find_pos = 0;

  while(find_pos<f_pos) {
    if(!strcmp(flight[find_pos].from, from) &&
      !flight[find_pos].skip) {
        if(flight[find_pos].distance>dist) {
          pos = find_pos;
          dist = flight[find_pos].distance;
        }
    }
    find_pos++;
  }
  if(pos) {
    strcpy(anywhere, flight[pos].to);
    flight[pos].skip = 1;
    return flight[pos].distance;
```

```
  }
  return 0;
}

/* Determine if there is a route between from and to. */
void isflight(char *from, char *to)
{
  int d, dist;
  char anywhere[20];

  if(d=match(from, to)) {
    /* is goal */
    push(from, to, d);
    return;
  }

  /* find any connection */
  if(dist=find(from, anywhere)) {
    push(from, to, dist);
    isflight(anywhere, to);
  }
  else if(tos>0) {
    pop(from, to, &dist);
    isflight(from, to);
  }
}

/* Stack Routines */
void push(char *from, char *to, int dist)
{
  if(tos<MAX) {
    strcpy(bt_stack[tos].from, from);
    strcpy(bt_stack[tos].to, to);
    bt_stack[tos].dist = dist;
    tos++;
  }
  else printf("Stack full.\n");
}

void pop(char *from, char *to, int *dist)
{
  if(tos>0) {
```

```
      tos--;
      strcpy(from, bt_stack[tos].from);
      strcpy(to, bt_stack[tos].to);
      *dist = bt_stack[tos].dist;
    }
    else printf("Stack underflow.\n");
}
```

When the program is run, the solution is

New York to Denver to Los Angeles
Distance is 2900.

This is quite good! The route contains the minimal number of stops on the way (only one), and it is really quite close to the shortest route. Furthermore, the program arrives at the solution with no time or effort wasted through extensive backtracking.

However, if the Denver to Los Angeles connection did not exist, the solution would not be quite so good. It would be New York to Denver to Houston to Los Angeles—a distance of 4900 miles! This solution climbs a "false peak." As you can easily see, the route to Houston does not take us closer to the goal of Los Angeles. Figure 23-7 shows the first solution as well as the path to the false peak.

An Analysis of Hill Climbing

Actually, hill climbing provides fairly good solutions in many circumstances because it tends to reduce the number of nodes that need to be visited before a solution is reached. However, it can suffer from three maladies. First, there is the problem of false peaks, as you saw in the second solution in the example. In this case, extensive backtracking must be used to find the solution. The second problem relates to plateaus, a situation in which all next steps look equally good (or bad). In this case hill climbing is no better than depth-first searching. The final problem is that of a ridge. In this case, hill climbing really performs poorly because the algorithm causes the ridge to be crossed several times as backtracking occurs.

In spite of these potential troubles, hill climbing generally leads to a closer-to-optimal solution more quickly than any of the nonheuristic methods.

The Least-Cost Search

The opposite of a hill-climbing search is a *least-cost search*. This strategy is similar to standing in the middle of a street on a big hill while wearing roller skates. You have

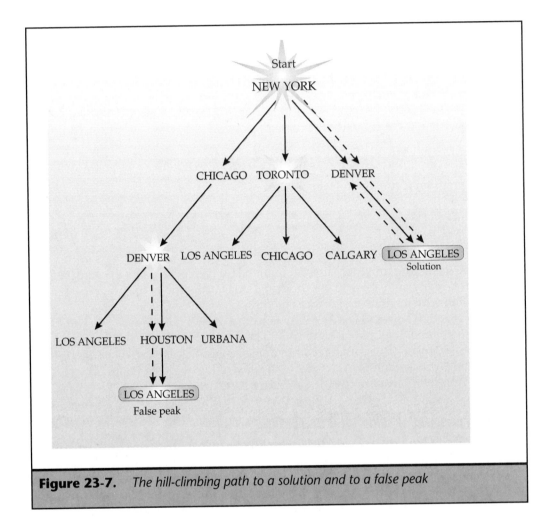

Figure 23-7.　*The hill-climbing path to a solution and to a false peak*

the definite feeling that it's a lot easier to go down rather than up! In other words, a least-cost search takes the path of least resistance.

Applying a least-cost search to the flight-scheduling problem implies that the shortest connecting flight is taken in all cases so that the route found has a good chance of covering the shortest distance. Unlike hill climbing, which minimized the number of connections, a least-cost search minimizes the number of miles.

To use a least-cost search, you must again alter **find( )** as shown:

```
/* Find closest "anywhere". */
find(char *from, char *anywhere)
{
  int pos, dist;

  pos = 0;
  dist = 32000;   /* larger than the longest route */
  find_pos = 0;

  while(find_pos<f_pos) {
    if(!strcmp(flight[find_pos].from, from) &&
       !flight[find_pos].skip) {
         if(flight[find_pos].distance<dist) {
         pos = find_pos;
         dist = flight[find_pos].distance;
       }
     }
     find_pos++;
  }
  if(pos) {
    strcpy(anywhere, flight[pos].to);
    flight[pos].skip = 1;
    return flight[pos].distance;
  }
  return 0;
}
```

Using this version of **find( )**, the solution is

New York to Toronto to Los Angeles
Distance is 2600.

As you can see, the search actually found the shortest route. Figure 23-8 shows the least-cost path to the goal.

An Analysis of the Least-Cost Search

The least-cost search and hill climbing have the same advantages and disadvantages, but in reverse. There can be false valleys, lowlands, and gorges, but a least-cost search usually works fairly well. However, don't assume that just because the least-cost

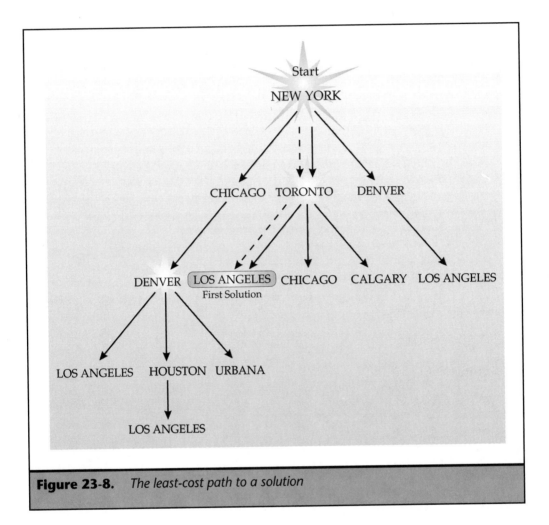

Figure 23-8. *The least-cost path to a solution*

search performed better than hill climbing in this problem that it is better. All that can be said is that on average it will outperform a blind search.

Choosing a Search Technique

As you have seen, the heuristic techniques tend, on the average, to work better than blind searching. However, it is not always possible to use a heuristic search because there may not be enough information to qualify the likelihood of the next node being on a path to the goal. Therefore, the rules for choosing a search method are separated into two categories: one for problems that can utilize a heuristic search and one for those that cannot.

If you cannot apply heuristics to a problem, depth-first searching is usually the best approach. The only exception to this is when you know something that indicates that a breadth-first search will be better.

The choice between hill climbing and a least-cost search is really one of deciding what constraint you are trying to minimize or maximize. In general, hill climbing produces a solution with the least nodes visited, but a least-cost search finds a path that requires the least effort.

If you are seeking a near-optimal solution but cannot apply an exhaustive search for the reasons already stated, an effective method is to apply each of the four searches and then use the best solution. Since the searches all work in substantially different ways, one should produce better results than the others.

Finding Multiple Solutions

Sometimes it is valuable to find several solutions to the same problem. This is not the same as finding all solutions (an exhaustive search), however. For instance, think about designing your dream house. You want to sketch several different floor plans to help you decide upon the best design, but you don't need sketches of all possible houses. In essence, multiple solutions can help you see many different ways to approach a solution before implementing one.

There are several ways to generate multiple solutions, but only two are examined here. The first is path removal and the second is node removal. As their names imply, generating multiple solutions without redundancy requires that already found solutions be removed from the system. Remember that neither of these methods attempts (or can even be used) to find all solutions. Finding all solutions is a different problem that is usually not attempted because it implies an exhaustive search.

Path Removal

The *path-removal method* of generating multiple solutions removes all nodes that form a current solution from the database and then attempts to find another. In essence, path removal prunes limbs from the tree.

To find multiple solutions by using path removal, you just need to alter **main( )** in the depth-first search, as shown here:

```
void main(void)
{
  char from[20], to[20];

  setup();
```

```
   printf("From? ");
   gets(from);
   printf("To? ");
   gets(to);
   do {
      isflight(from, to);
      route(to);
      tos = 0;  /* reset the backtrack stack */
   } while(getche()!='q');
}
```

Any connection that is part of a solution will have its **skip** field marked. Consequently, such a connection can no longer be found by **find( )** and all connections in a solution are effectively removed. You just need to reset **tos**, which effectively clears the backtrack stack.

The path-removal method finds the following solutions:

New York to Chicago to Denver to Los Angeles
Distance is 3000.

New York to Toronto to Los Angeles
Distance is 2600.

New York to Denver to Los Angeles
Distance is 2900.

The search found the three best solutions. However, this result cannot be generalized because it is based upon how the data is placed in the database and the actual situation under study.

Node Removal

The second way to force the generation of additional solutions, *node removal*, simply removes the last node in the current solution path and tries again. To do this, the function **main( )** must pop the last node off the backtrack stack and remove it from the database by using a new function called **retract( )**. Also, all the **skip** fields must be reset by using **clearmarkers( )** and the backtrack stack must be cleared. The functions **main( )**, **clearmarkers( )**, and **retract( )** are shown here:

```
void main(void)
{
  char from[20], to[20], c1[20], c2[20];
  int d;

  setup();

  printf("From? ");
  gets(from);
  printf("To? ");
  gets(to);
  do {
    isflight(from, to);
    route(to);
    clearmarkers();  /* reset the database */
    if(tos>0) pop(c1, c2, &d);
    retract(c1, c2);  /* remove last node from database */
    tos = 0;  /* reset the backtrack stack */
  } while(getche()!='q');
}

/* Reset the "skip" field - i.e., re-activate all nodes, */
void clearmarkers()
{
  int t;

  for(t=0; t<f_pos; ++t) flight[t].skip = 0;
}

/* Remove an entry from the database. */
void retract(char *from, char *to)

{
  int t;

  for(t=0; t<f_pos; t++)
    if(!strcmp(flight[t].from, from) &&
      !strcmp(flight[t].to, to)) {
        strcpy(flight[t].from, "");
        return;
    }
}
```

As you can see, retracting an entry is accomplished by simply using zero-length strings for the names of the cities. For your convenience, the entire node-removal program is shown here:

```c
/* Depth-first with multiple solutions
   using node removal */
#include <stdio.h>
#include <string.h>
#include <conio.h>

#define MAX 100

/* structure of the flight database */
struct FL {
  char from[20];
  char to[20];
  int distance;
  char skip;    /* used in backtracking */
};

struct FL flight[MAX];

int f_pos=0; /* number of entries in flight db */
int find_pos=0; /* index for searching flight db */

int tos=0;       /* top of stack */
struct stack {
  char from[20];
  char to[20];
  int dist;
} ;
struct stack bt_stack[MAX]; /* backtrack stack */

void retract(char *from, char *to);
void clearmarkers(void);
void setup(void), route(char *to);
void assert_flight(char *from, char *to, int dist);
void push(char *from, char *to, int dist);
void pop(char *from, char *to, int *dist);
void isflight(char *from, char *to);
int find(char *from, char *anywhere);
int match(char *from, char *to);
```

```
void main(void)
{
  char from[20],to[20], c1[20], c2[20];
  int d;

  setup();

  printf("From? ");
  gets(from);
  printf("To? ");
  gets(to);
  do {
    isflight(from,to);
    route(to);
    clearmarkers(); /* reset the database */
    if(tos>0) pop(c1,c2,&d);
    retract(c1,c2);  /* remove last node from database */
    tos=0;  /* reset the backtrack stack */
  } while(getche()!='q');
}

/* Initialize the flight database. */
void setup(void)
{
  assert_flight("New York","Chicago",1000);
  assert_flight("Chicago","Denver",1000);
  assert_flight("New York","Toronto", 800);
  assert_flight("New York","Denver", 1900);
  assert_flight("Toronto","Calgary",1500);
  assert_flight("Toronto","Los Angeles",1800);
  assert_flight("Toronto","Chicago",500);
  assert_flight("Denver","Urbana",1000);
  assert_flight("Denver","Houston",1500);
  assert_flight("Houston","Los Angeles",1500);
  assert_flight("Denver","Los Angeles",1000);
}

/* Put facts into the database. */
void assert_flight(char *from, char *to, int dist)
{
  if(f_pos<MAX) {
    strcpy(flight[f_pos].from, from);
```

```
      strcpy(flight[f_pos].to, to);
      flight[f_pos].distance = dist;
      flight[f_pos].skip = 0;
      f_pos++;
   }
   else printf("Flight database full.\n");
}
/* Reset the "skip" field - i.e., re-activate all nodes. */
void clearmarkers()
{
   int t;

   for(t=0; t<f_pos; ++t) flight[t].skip = 0;
}

/* Remove an entry from the database. */
void retract(char *from, char *to)
{
   int t;

   for(t=0; t<f_pos; t++)
     if(!strcmp(flight[t].from, from) &&
        !strcmp(flight[t].to, to)) {
          strcpy(flight[t].from,"");
          return;


     }
}

/* Show the route and the total distance. */
void route(char *to)
{
   int dist, t;

   dist=0;
   t=0;
   while(t<tos) {
     printf("%s to ", bt_stack[t].from);
     dist += bt_stack[t].dist;
     t++;
   }
   printf("%s\n",to);
```

```
      printf("Distance is %d.\n", dist);
    }

/* Given from, find anywhere. */
find(char *from, char *anywhere)
{
    find_pos = 0;
    while(find_pos<f_pos) {
      if(!strcmp(flight[find_pos].from, from) &&
         !flight[find_pos].skip) {
           strcpy(anywhere, flight[find_pos].to);
           flight[find_pos].skip = 1;
           return flight[find_pos].distance;
         }
      find_pos++;
    }
    return 0;
}

/* If flight between from and to, then return
   the distance of flight; otherwise, return 0. */
match(char *from, char *to)
{
    register int t;

    for(t=f_pos-1; t>-1; t--)
      if(!strcmp(flight[t].from, from) &&
         !strcmp(flight[t].to, to)) return flight[t].distance;

    return 0;  /* not found */
}

/* Determine if there is a route between from and to. */
void isflight(char *from, char *to)
{
    int d, dist;
    char anywhere[20];

    if(d=match(from, to)) {
      push(from, to, d); /* distance */
      return;
    }
```

```
   if(dist=find(from, anywhere)) {
     push(from, to, dist);
     isflight(anywhere, to);
   }
   else if(tos>0) {
     pop(from, to, &dist);
     isflight(from, to);
   }
}

/* Stack Routines */
void push(char *from, char *to, int dist)
{
  if(tos<MAX) {
    strcpy(bt_stack[tos].from, from);
    strcpy(bt_stack[tos].to, to);
    bt_stack[tos].dist = dist;
    tos++;
  }
  else printf("Stack full.\n");
}

void pop(char *from, char *to, int *dist)
{
  if(tos>0) {
  tos--;
    strcpy(from, bt_stack[tos].from);
    strcpy(to, bt_stack[tos].to);
    *dist = bt_stack[tos].dist;
  }
  else printf("Stack underflow.\n");
}
```

Using this method produces the following solutions:

New York to Chicago to Denver to Los Angeles
Distance is 3000.

New York to Chicago to Denver to Houston to Los Angeles
Distance is 5000.

New York to Toronto to Los Angeles
Distance is 2600.

In this case, the second solution is the worst possible route, but the optimal solution is still found. However, remember that you cannot generalize these results because they are based upon both the physical organization of data in the database and the specific situation under study.

Finding the "Optimal" Solution

All of the previous search techniques were concerned with finding a solution. As you saw with the heuristic searches, there were efforts to improve the likelihood of finding a good (and, hopefully, the optimal) solution. However, at times you may want *only* the optimal solution. Keep in mind, however, that *optimal*, as it is used here, simply means the best route that can be found by using one of the various multiple-solution generation techniques—it may not actually be the best solution. (Finding the true optimal solution would, of course, require the prohibitively time-consuming exhaustive search.)

Before leaving the well-worked scheduling example, consider a program that finds the optimal schedule with the condition that distance is to be minimized. Employ the path-removal method of generating multiple solutions, and use a least-cost search to minimize distance.

The key to finding the shortest schedule is to keep a solution that has a distance less than the previous one. Hence, when there are no more solutions to generate, the optimal solution remains.

To accomplish this, you must make a major change to the function **route( )** and create an additional stack. The new stack holds the current solution and, upon completion, the optimal solution. The new stack is called **solution**, and the modified **route( )** is shown here:

```
/* Find the shortest distance. */
route(void)
{
  int dist, t;
  static int old_dist=32000;

  if(!tos) return 0;   /* all done */
  t = 0;
  dist = 0;
  while(t<tos) {
    dist += bt_stack[t].dist;
    t++;
  }

  /* if shorter, then make new solution */
  if(dist<old_dist && dist) {
```

```
    t = 0;
    old_dist = dist;
    stos = 0; /* clear old route from location stack */
    while(t<tos) {
      spush(bt_stack[t].from, bt_stack[t].to, bt_stack[t].dist);
      t++;
    }
  }
  return dist;
}
```

The entire program follows. Notice the changes in **main( )** and the addition of **spush( )**, which places the new solution nodes onto the solution stack.

```
/* Optimal solution using least-cost with
   route removal.
*/
#include <stdio.h>
#include <string.h>

#define MAX 100

/* structure of the flight database */
struct FL {
  char from[20];
  char to[20];
  int distance;
  char skip;  /* used for backtracking */
};

struct FL flight[MAX];  /* array of db structures */

int f_pos=0; /* number of entries in flight db */
int find_pos=0; /* index for searching flight db */

int tos=0;     /* top of stack */
int stos=0;    /* top of solution stack */

struct stack {
  char from[20];
  char to[20];
```

```
    int dist;
} ;

struct stack bt_stack[MAX]; /* backtrack stack */
struct stack solution[MAX]; /* hold temporary solutions */

void setup(void);
int route(void);
void assert_flight(char *from, char *to, int dist);
void push(char *from, char *to, int dist);
void pop(char *from, char *to, int *dist);
void isflight(char *from, char *to);
void spush(char *from, char *to, int dist);
int find(char *from, char *anywhere);
int match(char *from, char *to);

void main(void)
{
  char from[20], to[20];
  int t, d;

  setup();

  printf("From? ");
  gets(from);
  printf("To? ");
  gets(to);
  do {
    isflight(from, to);
    d = route();
    tos = 0;  /* reset the backtrack stack */
  } while(d!=0);  /* while still finding solutions */

  t = 0;
  printf("Optimal solution is:\n");
  while(t<stos) {
    printf("%s to ", solution[t].from);
    d += solution[t].dist;
    t++;
  }
  printf("%s\n", to);
  printf("Distance is %d.\n", d);
```

```
}

/* Initialize the flight database. */
void setup(void)
{
  assert_flight("New York", "Chicago", 1000);
  assert_flight("Chicago", "Denver", 1000);
  assert_flight("New York", "Toronto", 800);
  assert_flight("New York", "Denver", 1900);
  assert_flight("Toronto", "Calgary", 1500);
  assert_flight("Toronto", "Los Angeles", 1800);
  assert_flight("Toronto", "Chicago", 500);
  assert_flight("Denver", "Urbana", 1000);
  assert_flight("Denver", "Houston", 1500);
  assert_flight("Houston", "Los Angeles", 1500);
  assert_flight("Denver", "Los Angeles", 1000);
}

/* Put facts into the database. */
void assert_flight(char *from, char *to, int dist)
{
  if(f_pos<MAX) {
    strcpy(flight[f_pos].from, from);
    strcpy(flight[f_pos].to, to);
    flight[f_pos].distance = dist;
    flight[f_pos].skip = 0;
    f_pos++;
  }
  else printf("Flight database full.\n");
}

/* Find the shortest distance. */
route(void)
{
  int dist, t;
  static int old_dist=32000;

  if(!tos) return 0;  /* all done */
  t = 0;
  dist = 0;
  while(t<tos) {
    dist += bt_stack[t].dist;
```

```
      t++;
    }

    /* if shorter then make new solution */
    if(dist<old_dist && dist) {
      t = 0;
      old_dist = dist;
      stos = 0; /* clear old route from location stack */
      while(t<tos)  {
        spush(bt_stack[t].from, bt_stack[t].to, bt_stack[t].dist);
        t++;
      }
    }
  }
  return dist;
}

/* If flight between from and to, then return
   the distance of flight; otherwise, return 0. */
match(char *from, char *to)
{
  register int t;

  for(t=f_pos-1; t>-1; t--)
    if(!strcmp(flight[t].from, from) &&
      !strcmp(flight[t].to, to)) return flight[t].distance;

  return 0;  /* not found */
}

/* Given from, find anywhere. */
find(char *from, char *anywhere)
{
  find_pos=0;
  while(find_pos<f_pos) {
    if(!strcmp(flight[find_pos].from, from) &&
      !flight[find_pos].skip) {
        strcpy(anywhere, flight[find_pos].to);
        flight[find_pos].skip = 1;
        return flight[find_pos].distance;
    }
    find_pos++;
  }
```

```
   return 0;
}

/* Determine if there is a route between from and to. */
void isflight(char *from, char *to)
{
  int d, dist;
  char anywhere[20];

  if(d=match(from, to)) {
    push(from, to, d); /* distance */
    return;
  }

  if(dist=find(from, anywhere)) {

    push(from, to, dist);
    isflight(anywhere, to);
  }
  else if(tos>0) {
    pop(from, to, &dist);
    isflight(from, to);
  }
}

/* Stack Routines */
void push(char *from, char *to, int dist)
{
  if(tos<MAX) {
    strcpy(bt_stack[tos].from, from);
    strcpy(bt_stack[tos].to, to);
    bt_stack[tos].dist = dist;
    tos++;
  }
  else printf("Stack full.\n");
}

void pop(char *from, char *to, int *dist)
{
  if(tos>0) {
    tos--;
    strcpy(from, bt_stack[tos].from);
```

```
    strcpy(to, bt_stack[tos].to);
    *dist = bt_stack[tos].dist;
  }
  else printf("Stack underflow.\n");
}


/* Solution Stack */
void spush(char *from, char *to, int dist)
{
  if(stos<MAX) {
    strcpy(solution[stos].from, from);
    strcpy(solution[stos].to, to);
    solution[stos].dist = dist;
    stos++;
  }
  else printf("Shortest distance stack full.\n");
}
```

The one inefficiency in the preceding method is that all paths are followed to their conclusion. An improved method would stop following a path as soon as the length equaled or exceeded the current minimum. You might want to modify this program to accommodate such an enhancement.

Back to the Lost Keys

To conclude this chapter on problem solving, it seems only fitting to provide a C program that finds the lost car keys described in the first example. The accompanying code employs the same techniques used in the problem of finding a route between two cities. By now, you should have a fairly good understanding of how to use C to solve problems, so the program is presented without further explanation.

```
/* Find the keys using a depth-first search. */
#include <stdio.h>
#include <string.h>

#define MAX 100

/* structure of the keys database */
struct FL {
  char from[20];
  char to[20];
```

```
   char skip;
};

struct FL keys[MAX];  /* array of db structures */

int f_pos=0; /* number of rooms in house */
int find_pos=0; /* index for searching keys db */

int tos=0;      /* top of stack */
struct stack {
  char from[20];
  char to[20];
} ;
struct stack bt_stack[MAX]; /* backtrack stack */

void setup(void), route(void);
void assert_keys(char *from, char *to);
void push(char *from, char *to);
void pop(char *from, char *to);
void iskeys(char *from, char *to);
int find(char *from, char *anywhere);
int match(char *from, char *to);

void main(void)
{
  setup();
  iskeys("front_door", "keys");
  route();
}

/* Initialize the database. */
void setup(void)
{
  assert_keys("front_door", "lr");
  assert_keys("lr", "bath");
  assert_keys("lr", "hall");
  assert_keys("hall", "bd1");
  assert_keys("hall", "bd2");
  assert_keys("hall", "mb");
  assert_keys("lr", "kitchen");
  assert_keys("kitchen", "keys");
}
```

```
/* Put facts into the database. */
void assert_keys(char *from, char *to)
{
  if(f_pos<MAX) {
    strcpy(keys[f_pos].from, from);
    strcpy(keys[f_pos].to, to);
    keys[f_pos].skip = 0;
    f_pos++;
  }
  else printf("Keys database full.\n");
}

/* Show the route to the keys. */
void route(void)
{
  int t;

  t = 0;
  while(t<tos) {
    printf("%s", bt_stack[t].from);
    t++;
    if(t<tos) printf(" to ");
  }
  printf("\n");
}

/* See if there is a match. */
match(char *from, char *to)
{
  register int t;

  for(t=f_pos-1; t>-1; t--)
    if(!strcmp(keys[t].from, from) &&
       !strcmp(keys[t].to, to)) return 1;

  return 0;  /* not found */
}

/* Given from, find anywhere. */
find(char *from, char *anywhere)
{
  find_pos = 0;
```

```
  while(find_pos<f_pos) {
    if(!strcmp(keys[find_pos].from, from) &&
      !keys[find_pos].skip) {
        strcpy(anywhere, keys[find_pos].to);
        keys[find_pos].skip = 1;
        return 1;
    }
    find_pos++;
  }
  return 0;
}

/* Determine if there is a route between from and to. */
void iskeys(char *from, char *to)
{
  char anywhere[20];

  if(match(from, to)) {
    push(from, to); /* distance */
    return;
  }

  if(find(from, anywhere)) {
    push(from, to);
    iskeys(anywhere, to);
  }
  else if(tos>0) {
    pop(from, to);
    iskeys(from, to);
  }
}

/* Stack Routines */
void push(char *from, char *to)
{
  if(tos<MAX) {
    strcpy(bt_stack[tos].from, from);
    strcpy(bt_stack[tos].to, to);
    tos++;
  }
  else printf("Stack full.\n");
```

```
}

void pop(char *from, char *to)
{
  if(tos>0) {
    tos--;
    strcpy(from, bt_stack[tos].from);
    strcpy(to, bt_stack[tos].to);
  }
  else printf("Stack underflow.\n");
}
```

Chapter Twenty-Four

Building a Windows 95 Skeleton

C is *the* language for Windows programming. As such, it seems only fitting to include an example of Windows programming in this book. However, Windows is a very large and complex environment to write programs for. In fact, just a description of Windows requires approximately 2000 pages of printed documentation! Although it is not possible to describe all details necessary to write a Windows application in one chapter, it is possible to introduce the basic elements common to all applications. Further, these basic elements can be combined into a minimal Windows application skeleton that can be used as the foundation for your own Windows applications.

Windows has gone through several incarnations since it was first introduced. At the time of this writing, the most current version of Windows is Windows 95. The material in this chapter is specifically tailored to this version of Windows. However, if you have a newer or older version of Windows, most of the discussion will still be applicable.

NOTE: *This chapter is adapted from my book* Schildt's Windows 95 Programming *in C and C++ (Berkeley, CA: Osborne/McGraw-Hill, 1995). If you are interested in learning more about Windows 95 programming, you will find this book especially useful. You will also find* The Osborne Windows Programming Series, volumes 1, 2, and 3, *by Schildt, Pappas, and Murray (Berkeley, CA: Osborne/McGraw-Hill, 1994) helpful.*

To begin, this chapter presents the Windows 95 programming perspective.

Windows 95 Programming Perspective

The goal of Windows 95 (and Windows in general) is to enable a person who has basic familiarity with the system to sit down and run virtually any application without prior training. To accomplish this end, Windows provides a consistent interface to the user. In theory, if you can run one Windows-based program, you can run them all. Of course, in actuality, most useful programs will still require some sort of training in order to be used effectively, but at least this instruction can be restricted to *what* the program *does*, not *how* the user must *interact* with it. In fact, much of the code in a Windows application is there just to support the user interface.

Before continuing, it must be stated that not every program that runs under Windows 95 will necessarily present the user with a Windows-style interface. It is possible to write Windows programs that do not take advantage of the Windows interface elements. To create a Windows-style program, you must purposely do so. Only those programs written to take advantage of Windows will look and feel like Windows programs. While you can override the basic Windows design philosophy, you had better have a good reason to do so, because the users of your programs will most likely be very disturbed. In general, any application programs you are writing for Windows 95 should utilize the normal Windows interface and conform to the standard Windows design practices.

Windows 95 is graphics-oriented, which means that it provides a Graphical User Interface (GUI). While graphics hardware and video modes are quite diverse, many of the differences are handled by Windows. This means that, for the most part, your program does not need to worry about what type of graphics hardware or video mode is being used. However, because of this graphical orientation, you as the programmer have added responsibility when creating Windows applications.

Let's look at a few of the more important features of Windows 95.

The Desktop Model

With few exceptions, the point of a window-based user interface is to provide the equivalent of a *desktop* on the screen. On a desk you might find several different pieces of paper, one on top of another, often with fragments of different pages visible beneath the top page. The equivalent of the desktop in Windows is the screen. The equivalents of pieces of paper are represented by *windows* on the screen. On a desk you may move pieces of paper about, maybe switching which piece of paper is on top or how much of another is exposed to view. Windows allows the same type of operations on its windows. By selecting a window, you can make it *current*, which means putting it on top of all the other open windows. You can enlarge or shrink a window, or move it about on the screen. In short, Windows lets you control the surface of the screen the way you control the items on your desk.

The Mouse

Like preceding versions of Windows, Windows 95 allows the use of the mouse for almost all control, selection, and drawing operations. Of course, to say that it *allows* the use of the mouse is an understatement. The fact is that the Windows 95 interface was *designed for the mouse*—it *allows* the use of the keyboard! Although it is certainly possible for an application program to ignore the mouse, it does so only in violation of a basic Windows design principle.

Icons and Bitmaps

Windows 95 encourages the use of icons and bitmaps (graphics images). The theory behind the use of icons and bitmaps is found in the old adage "a picture is worth a thousand words."

An icon is a small symbol that is used to represent some operation or program. Generally, the operation or program can be activated by selecting the icon. A bitmap is often used to convey information quickly and simply to the user. However, bitmaps can also be used as menu elements.

Menus, Toolbars, Status Bars, and Dialog Boxes

Aside from standard windows, Windows 95 also provides several special-purpose windows. The most common of these are the menu, the toolbar, the status bar, and the dialog box.

A *menu* is, as you would expect, a special window that contains only a menu from which the user makes a selection. However, instead of having to provide your own menu selection functions in your program, you simply create a standard menu using built-in menu-selection functions.

A *toolbar* is essentially a special type of menu that displays its options using small graphics images (icons). The user selects an object by clicking on the desired image. A *status bar* is a bar located on the bottom of a window that displays status information related to an application. Both toolbars and status bars are innovations added by Windows 95. They did not exist as standard elements in prior versions of Windows.

A *dialog box* is a special window that allows more complex interaction with the application than is allowed by a menu or toolbar. For example, your application might use a dialog box to request a filename. With few exceptions, non-menu input is accomplished via a dialog box.

How Windows 95 and Your Program Interact

When you write a program for many operating systems, it is your program that initiates interaction with the operating system. For example, in a DOS program, it is the program that requests such things as input and output. Put differently, programs written in the "traditional way" call the operating system. The operating system does not call your program. However, Windows 95 generally works in the opposite way. It is Windows 95 that calls your program. The process works like this: your program waits until it is sent a *message* by Windows. The message is passed to your program through a special function that is called by Windows. Once a message is received, your program is expected to take an appropriate action. While your program may call one or more Windows 95 API functions when responding to a message, it is still Windows 95 that initiates the activity. More than anything else, it is the message-based interaction with Windows 95 that dictates the general form of all Windows 95 programs.

There are many different types of messages that Windows 95 may send your program. For example, each time the mouse is clicked on a window belonging to your program, a mouse-clicked message will be sent to your program. Another type of message is sent each time a window belonging to your program must be redrawn. Still another message is sent each time the user presses a key when your program is the focus of input. Keep one fact firmly in mind: As far as your program is concerned, messages arrive randomly. This is why Windows 95 programs resemble interrupt-driven programs. You can't know what message will be next.

One final point: messages sent to your program are stored in a *message queue* associated with your program. Therefore, no message will be lost because your program is busy processing another message. The message will simply wait in the queue until your program is ready for it.

Windows 95 Uses Preemptive Multitasking

Since the start, Windows has been a multitasking operating system. This means that it can run two or more programs concurrently. Windows 95 uses *preemptive multitasking*. Using this approach, each active application receives a slice of CPU time. During its time slice, an application actually executes. When the application's time slice runs out, the next application begins executing. (The previously executing application enters a suspended state in which it awaits another time slice.) In this fashion, each application in the system receives a portion of CPU time. Although the application skeleton developed in this chapter is not concerned with the multitasking aspects of Windows 95, they will be an important part of any application that you create.

NOTE: Older versions of Windows used a form of multitasking called non-preemptive multitasking. With this approach, an application retained the CPU until it explicitly released it. This allowed applications to monopolize the CPU and effectively "lock out" other programs. Preemptive multitasking eliminates this problem.

The Win32 API: The Windows 95 API

In general, the Windows environment is accessed through a call-based interface called the *Application Program Interface* (API). The API consists of several hundred functions that your program calls as needed. The API functions provide all the system services performed by Windows 95. There is a subset to the API called the Graphics Device Interface (GDI), which is the part of Windows that provides device-independent graphics support. It is the GDI functions that make it possible for a Windows application to run on a variety of hardware.

Windows 95 programs use the Win32 API. For the most part, Win32 is a superset of the older Windows 3.1 API (Win16). Indeed, for the most part, the functions are called by the same name and are used in the same way. However, even though similar in spirit and purpose, the two APIs differ because Win32 supports 32-bit addressing while Win16 supports only the 16-bit, segmented-memory model. Because of this difference, several of the older API functions have been widened to accept 32-bit arguments and return 32-bit values. Also, a few API functions have had to be altered to accommodate the 32-bit architecture. API functions have also been added to support the new approach to multitasking, its new interface elements, and the other enhanced Windows 95 features. If you are new to Windows programming in general, these changes will not affect you significantly. However, if you will be porting code from Windows 3.1 to Windows 95, then you will need to carefully examine the arguments you pass to each API function.

Because Windows 95 supports 32-bit addressing, it makes sense that integers are also 32 bits long. This means that types **int** and **unsigned** are 32 bits long, not 16 bits, as is the case for Windows 3.1. If you want to use a 16-bit integer, it must be declared as **short**. (Windows 95 provides portable **typedef** names for these types, as you will see shortly.) Therefore, if you will be porting code from the 16-bit environment, you will need to check your use of integers because they will automatically be expanded from 16 to 32 bits, and side effects may result.

Another result of 32-bit addressing is that pointers no longer need to be declared as **near** or **far**. Any pointer can access any part of memory. In Windows 95, both **far** and **near** are defined as nothing. This means you can leave **far** and **near** in your programs when porting to Windows 95, but they will have no effect.

The Components of a Window

Before moving on to specific aspects of Windows 95 programming, a few important terms need to be defined. Figure 24-1 shows a standard window with each of its elements pointed out.

All windows have a border that defines the limits of the window; the borders are also used when resizing the window. At the top of the window are several items. On the far left is the system menu icon (also called the title bar icon). Clicking on this box displays the system menu. To the right of the system menu icon is the window's title. At the far right are the minimize, maximize, and close boxes. (Previous versions of Windows did not include a close box. This is a Windows 95 innovation.) The client area is the part of the window in which your program activity takes place. Most windows also have horizontal and vertical scroll bars that are used to move information through the window.

Some Windows 95 Application Basics

Before developing the Windows 95 application skeleton, some basic concepts common to all Windows 95 programs need to be discussed.

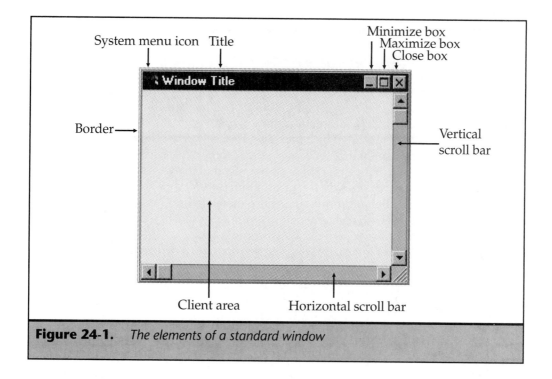

Figure 24-1.   *The elements of a standard window*

WinMain( )

All Windows 95 programs begin execution with a call to **WinMain( )**. (Windows programs do not have a **main( )** function.) **WinMain( )** has some special properties that differentiate it from other functions in your application. First, it must be compiled using the **WINAPI** calling convention. (You will see **APIENTRY** used as well. They both mean the same thing.) By default, functions in your C programs use the C calling convention. However, it is possible to compile a function so that it uses a different calling convention; Pascal is a common alternative. For various technical reasons, the calling convention Windows 95 uses to call **WinMain( )** is **WINAPI**. The return type of **WinMain( )** should be **int**.

The Window Function

All Windows 95 programs must contain a special function that is *not* called by your program, but is called by Windows 95. This function is generally called the *window function* or the *window procedure*. The window function is called by Windows 95 when it needs to pass a message to your program. It is through this function that Windows 95 communicates with your program. The window function receives the message in its parameters. All window functions must be declared as returning type **LRESULT CALLBACK**. The type **LRESULT** is a **typedef** that, at the time of this writing, is another name for a long integer. The **CALLBACK** calling convention is used with those functions that will be called by Windows 95. In Windows terminology, any function that is called by Windows is referred to as a *callback* function.

In addition to receiving the messages sent by Windows 95, the window function must initiate any actions indicated by a message. Typically, a window function's body consists of a **switch** statement that links a specific response to each message that the program will respond to. Your program need not respond to every message that Windows 95 sends. For messages that your program doesn't care about, you can let Windows 95 provide default processing. Since there are hundreds of different messages that Windows 95 can generate, it is common for most messages simply to be processed by Windows 95 and not by your program.

All messages are 32-bit integer values. Furthermore, all messages are linked with any additional information that the messages require.

Window Classes

When your Windows 95 program first begins execution, it will need to define and register a *window class*. When you register a window class, you are telling Windows 95 about the form and function of the window. However, registering the window class does not cause a window to come into existence. To actually create a window requires additional steps.

The Message Loop

As explained earlier, Windows 95 communicates with your program by sending it messages. All Windows 95 applications must establish a *message loop* inside the **WinMain( )** function. This loop reads any pending message from the application's message queue and dispatches that message back to Windows 95, which then calls your program's window function with that message as a parameter. This may seem to be an overly complex way of passing messages, but it is, nevertheless, the way that all Windows programs must function. (Part of the reason for this scheme is to return control to Windows 95 so that the scheduler can allocate CPU time as it sees fit rather than waiting for your application's time slice to end.)

Windows Data Types

As you will soon see, Windows 95 programs do not make extensive use of standard C data types, such as **int** or **char ***. Instead, all data types used by Windows 95 have been **typedef**ed within the WINDOWS.H file and/or its related files. The WINDOWS.H file is supplied by your Windows-compatible compiler and must be included in all Windows 95 programs. Some of the most common types are **HANDLE, HWND, BYTE, WORD, DWORD, UINT, LONG, BOOL, LPSTR,** and **LPCSTR. HANDLE** is a 32-bit integer that is used as a handle. As you will see, there are a number of handle types, but they are all the same size as **HANDLE**. A *handle* is simply a value that identifies some resource. Also, all handle types begin with an **H**. For example, **HWND** is a 32-bit integer used as a window handle. **BYTE** is an 8-bit unsigned character. **WORD** is a 16-bit unsigned short integer. **DWORD** is an unsigned long integer. **UINT** is a 32-bit unsigned integer. **LONG** is another name for **long**. **BOOL** is an integer. This type is used to indicate values that are either true or false. **LPSTR** is a pointer to a string, and **LPCSTR** is a **const** pointer to a string.

In addition to the basic types described above, Windows 95 defines several structures. The two that are needed by the skeleton program are **MSG** and **WNDCLASS**. The **MSG** structure holds a Windows 95 message, and **WNDCLASS** is a structure that defines a window class. These structures will be discussed later in this chapter.

A Windows 95 Skeleton

Now that the necessary background information has been covered, it's time to develop a minimal Windows 95 application. As stated, all Windows 95 programs have certain things in common. This section develops a Windows 95 skeleton that provides these necessary features. In the world of Windows programming, application skeletons are commonly used because there is a substantial "price of admission" when creating a Windows program. Unlike DOS programs that you may have written, in which a minimal program is about 5 lines long, a minimal Windows program is approximately 50 lines long.

A minimal Windows 95 program contains two functions: **WinMain( )** and the window function. The **WinMain( )** function must perform the following general steps:

1. Define a window class.

2. Register that class with Windows 95.

3. Create a window of that class.

4. Display the window.

5. Begin running the message loop.

The window function must respond to all relevant messages. Since the skeleton program does nothing but display its window, the only message that it must respond to is the one telling the application that the user has terminated the program.

Before considering the specifics, examine the following program, which is a minimal Windows 95 skeleton. It creates a standard window that includes a title. The window also contains the system menu and is, therefore, capable of being minimized, maximized, moved, resized, and closed. It also contains the standard minimize, maximize, and close boxes.

```c
/* A minimal Windows 95 skeleton. */

#include <windows.h>

LRESULT CALLBACK WindowFunc(HWND, UINT, WPARAM, LPARAM);

char szWinName[] = "MyWin"; /* name of window class */

int WINAPI WinMain(HINSTANCE hThisInst, HINSTANCE hPrevInst,
                   LPSTR lpszArgs, int nWinMode)
{
  HWND hwnd;
  MSG msg;
  WNDCLASS wcl;

  /* Define a window class. */
  wcl.hInstance = hThisInst; /* handle to this instance */
  wcl.lpszClassName = szWinName; /* window class name */
  wcl.lpfnWndProc = WindowFunc; /* window function */
  wcl.style = 0; /* default style */

  wcl.hIcon = LoadIcon(NULL, IDI_APPLICATION); /* icon style */
  wcl.hCursor = LoadCursor(NULL, IDC_ARROW); /* cursor style */
  wcl.lpszMenuName = NULL; /* no menu */

  wcl.cbClsExtra = 0; /* no extra */
  wcl.cbWndExtra = 0; /* information needed */

  /* Make the window background white. */
  wcl.hbrBackground = (HBRUSH) GetStockObject(WHITE_BRUSH);

  /* Register the window class. */
  if(!RegisterClass (&wcl)) return 0;

  /* Now that a window class has been registered, a window
     can be created. */
  hwnd = CreateWindow(
    szWinName, /* name of window class */
    "Windows 95 Skeleton", /* title */
    WS_OVERLAPPEDWINDOW, /* window style - normal */
    CW_USEDEFAULT, /* X coordinate - let Windows decide */
    CW_USEDEFAULT, /* Y coordinate - let Windows decide */
    CW_USEDEFAULT, /* width - let Windows decide */
```

```
      CW_USEDEFAULT, /* height - let Windows decide */
      HWND_DESKTOP, /* no parent window */
      NULL, /* no menu */
      hThisInst, /* handle of this instance of the program */
      NULL /* no additional arguments */
   );

   /* Display the window. */
   ShowWindow(hwnd, nWinMode);
   UpdateWindow(hwnd);

   /* Create the message loop. */
   while(GetMessage(&msg, NULL, 0, 0))
   {
     TranslateMessage(&msg); /* allow use of keyboard */
     DispatchMessage(&msg); /* return control to Windows */
   }
   return msg.wParam;
}


/* This function is called by Windows 95 and is passed
   messages from the message queue.
*/
LRESULT CALLBACK WindowFunc(HWND hwnd, UINT message,
                                WPARAM wParam, LPARAM lParam)
{
  switch(message) {
    case WM_DESTROY: /* terminate the program */
      PostQuitMessage(0);
      break;
    default:
      /* Let Windows 95 process any messages not specified in
         the preceding switch statement. */
      return DefWindowProc(hwnd, message, wParam, lParam);
  }
  return 0;
}
```

The window produced by this program is shown in Figure 24-2. Now let's go through this program step by step.

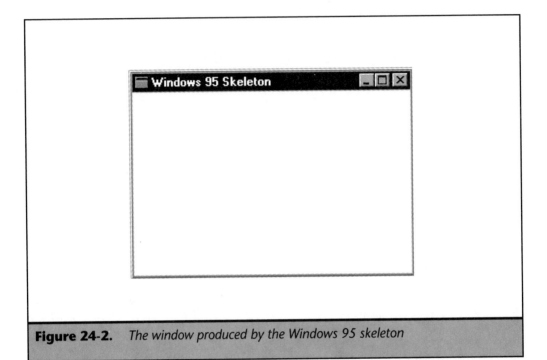

Figure 24-2. *The window produced by the Windows 95 skeleton*

First, all Windows 95 programs must include the header file WINDOWS.H. As was stated, this file (along with its support files) contains the API function prototypes and various types, macros, and definitions used by Windows 95. For example, the data types **HWND** and **WNDCLASS** are defined in WINDOWS.H.

The window function used by the program is called **WindowFunc( )**. It is declared as a callback function, because this is the function that Windows 95 calls to communicate with the program.

Program execution begins with **WinMain( )**, which is passed four parameters. **hThisInst** and **hPrevInst** are handles. **hThisInst** refers to the current instance of the program. Remember, Windows 95 is a multitasking system, so more than one instance of your program may be running at the same time. **hPrevInst** will always be **NULL**. (In Windows 3.1 programs, **hPrevInst** would be non-zero if there were other instances of the program currently executing, but this doesn't apply in Windows 95.) The **lpszArgs** parameter is a pointer to a string that holds any command line arguments specified when the application was begun. The **nWinMode** parameter contains a value that determines how the window will be displayed when your program begins execution.

Inside the function, three variables are created. The **hwnd** variable will hold the handle to the program's window. The **msg** structure variable will hold window messages, and the **wcl** structure variable will be used to define the window class.

Defining the Window Class

The first two actions that **WinMain( )** takes are to define a window class and then register it. A window class is defined by filling in the fields defined by the **WNDCLASS** structure. Its fields are shown here:

```
UINT style; /* type of window */
WNDPROC lpfnWndProc; /* address to window func */
int cbClsExtra; /* extra class info */
int cbWndExtra; /* extra window info */
HINSTANCE hInstance; /* handle of this instance */
HICON hIcon; /* handle of minimized icon */
HCURSOR hCursor; /* handle of mouse cursor */
HBRUSH hbrBackground; /* background color */
LPCSTR lpszMenuName; /* name of main menu */
LPCSTR lpszClassName; /* name of window class */
```

As you can see by looking at the program, the **hInstance** field is assigned the current instance handle as specified by **hThisInst**. The name of the window class is pointed to by **lpszClassName**, which points to the string "MyWin" in this case. The address of the window function is assigned to **lpfnWndProc**. No default style is specified, and no extra information is needed.

All Windows applications need to define a default shape for the mouse cursor and for the application's icon. An application can define its own custom version of these resources, or it may use one of the built-in styles, as the skeleton does. The style of the icon is loaded by the API function **LoadIcon( )**, whose prototype is shown here:

HICON LoadIcon(HINSTANCE *hInst*, LPCSTR *lpszName*);

This function returns a handle to an icon. Here, *hInst* specifies the handle of the module that contains the icon, and the icon name is specified in *lpszName*. However, to use one of the built-in icons, you must use **NULL** for the first parameter and specify one of the following macros for the second.

Icon Macro	Shape
IDI_APPLICATION	Default icon
IDI_ASTERISK	Information icon
IDI_EXCLAMATION	Exclamation point icon
IDI_HAND	Stop sign
IDI_QUESTION	Question mark icon

To load the mouse cursor, use the API **LoadCursor( )** function. This function has the following prototype:

HCURSOR LoadCursor(HINSTANCE *hInst*, LPCSTR *lpszName*);

This function returns a handle to a cursor resource. Here, *hInst* specifies the handle of the module that contains the mouse cursor, and the name of the mouse cursor is specified in *lpszName*. However, to use one of the built-in cursors, you must use **NULL** for the first parameter and specify one of the built-in cursors, using its macro, for the second parameter. Some of the most common built-in cursors are shown here.

Cursor Macro	Shape
IDC_ARROW	Default arrow pointer
IDC_CROSS	Cross hairs
IDC_IBEAM	Vertical I-beam
IDC_WAIT	Hourglass

The background color of the window created by the skeleton is specified as white, and a handle to this *brush* is obtained using the API function **GetStockObject( )**. A brush is a resource that paints the screen using a predetermined size, color, and pattern. The function **GetStockObject( )** is used to obtain a handle to a number of standard display objects, including brushes, pens (which draw lines), and character fonts. It has this prototype:

HGDIOBJ GetStockObject(int *object*);

The function returns a handle to the object specified by *object*. (The type **HGDIOBJ** is a GDI handle.) Here are some of the built-in brushes available to your program:

Brush Macro	Background Type
BLACK_BRUSH	Black
DKGRAY_BRUSH	Dark gray
HOLLOW_BRUSH	See-through window
LTGRAY_BRUSH	Light gray
WHITE_BRUSH	White

You can use these macros as parameters to **GetStockObject( )** to obtain a brush.

Once the window class has been fully specified, it is registered with Windows 95 using the API function **RegisterClass( )**, whose prototype is shown here:

ATOM RegisterClass(CONST WNDCLASS *lpWClass);

The function returns a value that identifies the window class. **ATOM** is a **typedef** that means **WORD**. Each window class is given a unique value. *lpWClass* must be the address of the **WNDCLASS** structure.

Creating a Window

Once a window class has been defined and registered, your application can actually create a window of that class using the API function **CreateWindow( )**, whose prototype is shown here.

```
HWND CreateWindow(
  LPCSTR lpClassName, /* name of window class */
  LPCSTR lpWinName, /* title of window */
  DWORD dwStyle, /* type of window */
  int X, int Y, /* upper-left coordinates */
  int Width, int Height, /* dimensions of window */
  HWND hParent, /* handle of parent window */
  HMENU hMenu, /* handle of main menu */
  HINSTANCE hThisInst, /* handle of creator */
  LPVOID lpszAdditional /* pointer to additional info */
);
```

As you can see by looking at the skeleton program, many of the parameters to **CreateWindow( )** may be defaulted or specified as **NULL**. In fact, most often the *X, Y, Width*, and *Height* parameters will simply use the macro **CW_USEDEFAULT**, which tells Windows 95 to select an appropriate size and location for the window. If the window has no parent, which is the case in the skeleton, then *hParent* must be specified as **HWND_DESKTOP**. (You may also use **NULL** for this parameter.) If the window does not contain a main menu, then *hMenu* must be **NULL**. Also, if no additional information is required, as is most often the case, then *lpszAdditional* is **NULL**. (The type **LPVOID** is **typedef**ed as **void ***. Historically, **LPVOID** stands for "long pointer to **void**.")

The remaining four parameters must be set explicitly by your program. First, *lpszClassName* must point to the name of the window class. (This is the name you gave it when it was registered.) The title of the window is a string pointed to by *lpszWinName*. This can be a null string, but usually a window will be given a title. The style (or type) of window actually created is determined by the value of *dwStyle*. The macro **WS_OVERLAPPEDWINDOW** specifies a standard window that has a system menu, a border, and minimize, maximize, and close boxes. While this style of window is the most common, you can construct one to your own specifications. To accomplish this, you simply OR together the various style macros that you want. Some other common styles are shown here:

Style Macros	Window Feature
WS_OVERLAPPED	Overlapped window with border
WS_MAXIMIZEBOX	Maximize box
WS_MINIMIZEBOX	Minimize box
WS_SYSMENU	System menu
WS_HSCROLL	Horizontal scroll bar
WS_VSCROLL	Vertical scroll bar

The *hThisInst* parameter must contain the current instance handle of the application.

The **CreateWindow( )** function returns the handle of the window it creates or **NULL** if the window cannot be created.

Once the window has been created, it still is not displayed on the screen. To cause the window to be displayed, call the **ShowWindow( )** API function. This function has the following prototype:

BOOL ShowWindow(HWND *hwnd*, int *nHow*);

The handle of the window to display is specified in *hwnd*. The display mode is specified in *nHow*. The first time the window is displayed, you will want to pass **WinMain( )**'s **nWinMode** as the *nHow* parameter. Remember, the value of **nWinMode** determines how the window will be displayed when the program begins execution. Subsequent calls can display (or remove) the window as necessary. Some common values for *nHow* are shown here:

Display Macros	Effect
SW_HIDE	Removes the window
SW_MINIMIZE	Minimizes the window into an icon
SW_MAXIMIZE	Maximizes the window
SW_RESTORE	Returns a window to normal size

The **ShowWindow( )** function returns the previous display status of the window. If the window was displayed, then non-zero is returned. If the window has not been displayed, zero is returned.

Although not technically necessary for the skeleton, a call to **UpdateWindow( )** is included because it is needed by virtually every Windows 95 application that you will create. It essentially tells Windows 95 to send a message to your application that the main window needs to be updated.

The Message Loop

The final part of the skeletal **WinMain( )** is the *message loop*. The message loop is a part of all Windows applications. Its purpose is to receive and process messages sent by Windows 95. When an application is running, it is continually being sent messages. These messages are stored in the application's message queue until they can be read and processed. Each time your application is ready to read another message, it must call the API function **GetMessage( )**, which has this prototype:

BOOL GetMessage(LPMSG *msg*, HWND *hwnd*, UINT *min*, UINT *max*);

The message will be received by the structure pointed to by *msg*. All Windows messages are of structure type **MSG**, shown here.

```
/* Message structure */
typedef struct tagMSG
{
  HWND hwnd; /* window that message is for */
  UINT message; /* message */
  WPARAM wParam; /* message-dependent info */
  LPARAM lParam; /* more message-dependent info */
  DWORD time; /* time message posted */
  POINT pt; /* X,Y location of mouse */
} MSG;
```

In **MSG**, the handle of the window for which the message is intended is contained in **hwnd**. All Win32 messages are 32-bit integers, and the message is contained in **message**. Additional information relating to each message is passed in **wParam** and **lParam**. The type **WPARAM** is a **typedef** for **UINT**, and **LPARAM** is a **typedef** for **LONG**.

The time the message was sent (posted) is specified in milliseconds in the **time** field.

The **pt** member will contain the coordinates of the mouse when the message was sent. The coordinates are held in a **POINT** structure, which is defined like this:

```
typedef struct tagPOINT {
  LONG x, y;
} POINT;
```

If there are no messages in the application's message queue, then a call to **GetMessage( )** will pass control back to Windows 95.

The *hwnd* parameter to **GetMessage( )** specifies the window for which messages will be obtained. It is possible, and even likely, that an application will contain several windows, but you only want to receive messages for a specific window. If you want to receive all messages directed at your application, this parameter must be **NULL**.

The remaining two parameters to **GetMessage( )** specify a range of messages that will be received. Generally, you want your application to receive all messages. To accomplish this, specify both *min* and *max* as 0, as the skeleton does.

GetMessage( ) returns zero when the user terminates the program, causing the message loop to terminate. Otherwise it returns non-zero.

Inside the message loop, two functions are called. The first is the API function **TranslateMessage( )**. This function translates virtual key codes generated by Windows 95 into character messages. (Virtual keys include function keys, arrow keys, etc.) Although it is not necessary for all applications, most applications call **TranslateMessage( )** because it is needed to allow full integration of the keyboard into your application program.

Once the message has been read and translated, it is dispatched back to Windows 95 using the **DispatchMessage( )** API function. Windows 95 then holds this message until it can be passed to the program's window function.

Once the message loop terminates, the **WinMain( )** function ends by returning the value of **msg.wParam** to Windows 95. This value contains the return code generated when your program terminates.

The Window Function

The second function in the application skeleton is its window function. In this case the function is called **WindowFunc( )**, but it could have any name you like. The window function is passed the first four members of the **MSG** structure as parameters. For the skeleton, the only parameter used is the message itself. However, actual applications will use the other parameters to this function.

The skeleton's window function responds to only one message explicitly: **WM_DESTROY**. This message is sent when the user terminates the program. When this message is received, your program must execute a call to the API function **PostQuitMessage( )**. The argument to this function is an exit code that is returned in

msg.wParam inside **WinMain( )**. Calling **PostQuitMessage( )** causes a **WM_QUIT** message to be sent to your application, which causes **GetMessage( )** to return false, thus stopping your program.

Any other messages received by **WindowFunc( )** are passed to Windows 95, via a call to **DefWindowProc( )**, for default processing. This step is necessary because all messages must be dealt with in one fashion or another.

Using a Definition File

If you are familiar with Windows 3.1 programming, then you have used *definition files*. In Windows 3.1, all programs need to have a definition file associated with them. A definition file is simply a text file that specifies certain information and settings needed by your Windows 3.1 program. However, because of the 32-bit architecture of Windows 95 (and other improvements), definition files are no longer needed. However, there is no harm in supplying a definition file, and if you want to include one for the sake of downward compatibility with Windows 3.1, then you are free to do so.

If you are new to Windows programming in general and you don't know what a definition file is, the following discussion gives a brief overview.

All definition files use the extension .DEF. For example, the definition file for the skeleton program could be called SKEL.DEF. Here is a definition file that you can use to provide downward compatibility with Windows 3.1:

```
DESCRIPTION 'Skeleton Program'
EXETYPE WINDOWS
CODE PRELOAD MOVEABLE DISCARDABLE
DATA PRELOAD MOVEABLE MULTIPLE
HEAPSIZE 8192
STACKSIZE 8192
EXPORTS WindowFunc
```

This file specifies the name of the program and its description, both of which are optional. It also states that the executable file will be compatible with Windows (rather than DOS, for example). The **CODE** statement tells Windows 95 to load all of the program at startup (**PRELOAD**), that the code may be moved in memory (**MOVEABLE**), and that the code may be removed from memory and reloaded if (and when) necessary (**DISCARDABLE**). The file states that your program's data must be loaded upon execution and may be moved about in memory. It also specifies that each instance of the program has its own data (**MULTIPLE**). Next, the size of the heap and stack allocated to the program are specified. Finally, the name of the window function is exported. Exporting allows Windows 3.1 to call the function.

> **NOTE:** *Definition files are not needed when programming for Windows 95. However, they cause no harm and may be included for downward compatibility to Windows 3.1. (The heap size and stack size may need to be increased for real applications.)*

Naming Conventions

Before concluding this chapter, a short comment on the naming of functions and variables needs to be made. If you are new to Windows programming, several of the variable and parameter names in the skeleton program and its description probably seemed rather unusual. This is because they follow a set of naming conventions that was invented for Windows programming by Microsoft. For functions, the name consists of a verb followed by a noun. The first character of the verb and noun are capitalized.

For variable names, Microsoft chose to use a rather complex system of imbedding the data type into the name. To accomplish this, a lowercase type prefix is added to the start of the variable's name. The name itself begins with a capital letter. The type prefixes are shown in Table 24-1. Frankly, the use of type prefixes is controversial and is not universally supported. Many Windows programmers use this method, but many do not. You are free to use any naming convention you like.

Prefix	Data Type
b	Boolean (one byte)
c	Character (one byte)
dw	Long unsigned integer
f	16-bit bitfield (flags)
fn	Function
h	Handle
l	Long integer
lp	Long pointer
n	Short integer
p	Pointer
pt	Long integer holding screen coordinates
w	Short unsigned integer
sz	Pointer to null-terminated string
lpsz	Long pointer to null-terminated string
rgb	Long integer holding RGB color values

Table 24-1.   *Variable Type Prefix Characters*

PART FOUR

Software
Development Using C

This part examines various aspects of the software-development process as they relate to the C programming environment. Chapter 25 covers the use of assembly-language subroutines and optimizations. Chapter 26 is an overview of the design process using C. Last, Chapter 27 provides a look at porting, efficiency, and debugging.

Chapter Twenty-Five

Interfacing to Assembly-Language Routines

A s powerful as C is, at times you must write a routine using assembler. The way you accomplish this will vary from compiler to compiler, but the general process described in this chapter applies to most compilers.

The interfacing of C and assembly language is fundamentally affected by two things: the type of CPU and the calling conventions of the compiler. Each CPU defines its own assembly language. Each C compiler is free to define its own calling convention, which determines how information is passed to and from a function. This chapter uses 8086-family assembly language. The assembly-language interfacing examples shown in this chapter use Microsoft C/C++ (plus one example using Borland C/C++), but you can generally apply the information to other C compilers. Even if you have a different CPU or compiler, the following discussion can serve as a guide. Remember, however, that interfacing to assembly language is an advanced technique.

Assembly-Language Interfacing

There are three reasons you might want to use a routine written in assembler:

- To gain speed and efficiency
- To perform some machine-specific function unavailable in C
- To use a third-party assembly-language routine

Let's take a closer look at these now.

Although C compilers tend to produce extremely fast, compact object code, no compiler consistently creates code as fast or compact as that written by an excellent programmer using assembler. Most of the time, the small difference does not matter, nor does it warrant the extra time needed to write in assembler. However, in special cases a specific function must be coded in assembler so that it runs very quickly. For example, you might code a floating-point math package in assembly language because it is used frequently and greatly affects a program's execution speed. Also, special hardware devices may need exact timing, which means that you must code in assembler to meet the strict timing requirement.

Many CPUs have certain instructions that most C compilers cannot execute. For example, when programming for an 8086-family processor, you cannot change data segments with any ANSI standard C instruction. Also, you cannot issue a software interrupt or control the contents of specific registers using a standard C statement.

It is very common in professional programming environments to purchase subroutine libraries for things like graphics, floating-point math, B-tree file routines, and the like. Sometimes it is necessary to take these in object format because the developer will not sell the source code. Occasionally, you can simply link these routines with code compiled by your compiler. At other times, you must write an interface module to correct any differences in the interface used by your compiler and the routines you purchased.

There are basically two ways to integrate assembly-code modules into your C programs. You can code the routine separately and link it with the rest of your program. Alternately, you can use the in-line assembly-code capabilities of many C compilers. This chapter explores both methods.

A word of warning: This chapter does *not* teach you how to code in assembler—it assumes that you already know how. If you do not, don't try the examples. It is extremely easy to do something slightly wrong and create a disaster. You could erase your hard disk, for example. Before trying to interface to an assembly language module that you create, you must consult your compiler's user's manual for details relating to your specific implementation.

The Calling Conventions of a C Compiler

A *calling convention* is the method that a particular C compiler uses to pass information into functions and return values. Virtually all C compilers use the stack to pass arguments to functions. If the argument is one of the built-in data types or a structure, union, or enumeration, the actual value is passed on the stack. If the argument is an array, its address is placed on the stack. When a C function begins execution, it retrieves its parameter's values from the stack. When a C function terminates, it passes a return value back to the calling routine. Typically, this value is returned in a register, although it could theoretically be passed on the stack.

The calling convention also determines exactly what registers must be preserved and which ones you can use freely. Often a compiler produces object code that needs only a portion of the available registers for a given CPU. You must preserve the contents of the registers used by your compiler, generally by pushing their contents on the stack before using them and then popping them when you are done. Any other registers are usually free for your use.

When you write an assembly-language module that must interface to code compiled by your C compiler, you need to follow the conventions defined and used by your compiler. Only in this way can you hope to have assembly-language routines interface correctly to your C code. The next section examines in detail the calling conventions of Microsoft C/C++.

The Calling Conventions of Microsoft C/C++

As is the case with most C compilers, Microsoft C/C++ passes arguments to functions on the stack. The arguments are pushed onto the stack from right to left. That is, given the call

    func(a, b, c);

c is pushed first, followed by **b**, and **a**. Table 25-1 shows the number of bytes occupied on the stack by each of the basis data types.

Upon entry into an assembly-code function, the contents of the **BP** register must be saved on the stack and the current value of the stack pointer (**SP**) is placed into **BP**. The only other registers that you must preserve are **SI, DI, SS**, and **DS** (if your routine uses them). Before returning, your assembly-language function must restore the value of **BP, SI, DI, SS**, and **DS** and reset the stack pointer.

If your assembly-language function returns an 8- or 16-bit value, it is placed into the **AX** register. Otherwise, it is returned according to Table 25-2.

One last point: A C program allocates space for local data on the stack. When you write your own assembly code functions, you must follow the same procedure for local variables.

Creating an Assembly-Code Function

Without a doubt, seeing how your compiler generates code is the easiest way to learn to create assembly-language functions that are compatible with your compiler's calling convention. Virtually all C compilers have a compile-time option that causes the compiler to output an assembly-language listing of the code that it generates. By

Type	Number of Bytes
char	2
short	2
signed char	2
signed short	2
unsigned char	2
unsigned short	2
int	2
signed int	2
unsigned int	2
long	4
unsigned long	4
float	4
double	8
long double	10
(near) pointer	2 (offset only)
(far) pointer	4 (segment and offset)

Table 25-1. *The Number of Bytes on the Stack Required for Each Data Type When Passed to a Function for Microsoft C/C++*

Type	Register(s) and Meaning
char	AL
unsigned char	AL
short	AX
unsigned short	AX
int	AX
unsigned int	AX
long	Low-order word in AX High-order word in DX
unsigned long	Low-order word in AX High-order word in DX
float & double	Address to value returned. AX contains offset, DX contains segment.
struct & union	Address to value returned. AX contains offset, DX contains segment.
(near) pointer	AX
(far) pointer	Offset in AX, segment in DX

Table 25-2. *Register Usage for Return Values Using Microsoft C/C++*

examining this file, you can learn a great deal about not only how to interface to the compiler, but also how the compiler actually works.

To produce an assembly language listing using the Microsoft C/C++ compiler, specify the **–Fa** option. The assembly code is contained in a file that has the same file name as the original C program but has the extension .ASM. This chapter uses the assembly code listings to show how Microsoft C/C++ generates code.

A Simple Assembly-Code Function

The program shown here illustrates how code is generated to call a function:

```
int sum;
int add(int a, int b);

void main(void)
{
  sum = add(10,12);
}
```

```
add(int a, int b)
{
  int t;

  t = a+b;
  return t;
}
```

The variable **sum** is intentionally declared as global so that you can see examples of both local and global data. If this program is called **test**, the following command line creates **test.asm**:

cl –Fa test.c

This causes the program to be compiled for the small memory model. (Memory Models are discussed in Chapter 16.) The contents of **test.asm** are shown here:

```
; File test.c
; Line 5
_main:
          push      bp
          mov       bp,sp
          mov       ax,OFFSET L00114
          call      __aNchkstk
          push      si
          push      di
; Line 6
          mov       ax,OFFSET 12
          push      ax
          mov       ax,OFFSET 10
          push      ax
          call      _add
          add       sp,OFFSET 4
          mov       WORD PTR _sum,ax
; Line 7
; Line 7
L00107:
          pop       di
          pop       si
          mov       sp,bp
          pop       bp
```

```
        ret     OFFSET 0
; Line 10
; a = 0004
; b = 0006
_add:
        push    bp
        mov     bp,sp
        mov     ax,OFFSET L00116
        call    __aNchkstk
        push    si
        push    di
; t = fffc
; Line 11
; Line 13
        mov     ax,WORD PTR 4[bp]
        add     ax,WORD PTR 6[bp]
        mov     WORD PTR -4[bp],ax
; Line 14
        mov     ax,WORD PTR -4[bp]
        jmp     L00112
; Line 15
; Line 15
L00112:
        pop     di
        pop     si
        mov     sp,bp
        pop     bp
        ret     OFFSET 0
```

The compiler adds the underscore in front of **sum**, **main**, and **add** to avoid confusion with any internal compiler names. In fact, the underscore is added to the front of all function and variable names. (This is common practice and is used by most compilers.)

The first thing that **_main** does is push **BP** and move **SP** into **BP**. Next, the compiler-supplied routine named **__aNchkstk** is called (this manages the stack). Next, **SI** and **DI** are saved. This step is technically unnecessary because they are not used in this program. Next, the two arguments to **_add** are pushed on the stack and **_add** is called. When **_add** returns, its return value is moved into **_sum**, and **_main** returns.

The function **_add** begins by saving **BP**, placing the value of **SP** into **BP**, setting the stack, and again saving **SI** and **DI**. (Again, the preservation of **SI** and **DI** is unnecessary in this case.) The next three lines of code add the numbers and place their sum in **t**'s location on the stack. (Remember, local data is stored on the stack in a C program.) Notice how the parameters to **_add** are accessed using **BP**. After the addition has been performed, the return value (in this case **t**) is loaded into **AX** and then the function returns.

In order to use this assembly language file, you will need to add to it the segment specifications, data declarations, and any other initializations required by your compiler. (Consult your compiler's user's manual.) However, after you have done this, you will be able to assemble this file, link it with the necessary library routines, and run it. Moreover, you can modify the file to make it run faster but leave the C source code untouched. For example, you could remove the instructions that load **AX** with the value of variable **t** prior to the **add( )**'s return—since **AX** already contains the result. This is called *hand optimization.* You could also remove the instructions that save and restore **SI** and **DI**, since they are not used in the program.

Keep in mind that different compilers generate somewhat different code. To see an example, examine the following assembly language program. This program was produced by compiling the preceding C program using Borland C/C++, using the **–S** option. Notice the similarities (and differences) with the code produced by the Microsoft compiler. (The file produced by the Borland compiler also includes the segment initialization code that was not included in the Microsoft version.) As a general rule, the calling conventions of Borland C/C++ are the same as those for Microsoft C/C++.

```
.286p
          ifndef   ??version
?debug    macro
          endm
publicdll macro name
          public   name
          endm
$comm     macro    name,dist,size,count
          comm     dist name:BYTE:count*size
          endm
          else
$comm     macro    name,dist,size,count
          comm     dist name[size]:BYTE:count
          endm
          endif
          ?debug   V 301h
          ?debug   S "test.c"
          ?debug   C E9225A981D056578312E63
_TEXT     segment byte public 'CODE'
_TEXT     ends
DGROUP    group    _DATA,_BSS
          assume   cs:_TEXT,ds:DGROUP
```

```
_DATA    segment word public 'DATA'
d@       label   byte
d@w      label   word
_DATA    ends
_BSS     segment word public 'BSS'
b@       label   byte
b@w      label   word
_BSS     ends
_TEXT    segment byte public 'CODE'
   ;
   ;     void main(void)
   ;
         assume  cs:_TEXT,ds:DGROUP
_main    proc    near
         push    bp
         mov     bp,sp
   ;
   ;     {
   ;        sum = add(10,12);
   ;
         push    12
         push    10
         call    near ptr _add
         add     sp,4
         mov     word ptr DGROUP:_sum,ax
   ;
   ;     }
   ;
         pop     bp
         ret
_main    endp
   ;
   ;     add(int a, int b)
   ;
         assume  cs:_TEXT,ds:DGROUP
_add     proc    near
         enter   2,0
   ;
   ;     {
   ;        int t;
   ;
```

```
;         t = a+b;
;
        mov      ax,word ptr [bp+4]
        add      ax,word ptr [bp+6]
        mov      word ptr [bp-2],ax
;
;        return t;
;
        mov      ax,word ptr [bp-2]
        leave
        ret
;
;        }
;
        leave
        ret
_add    endp
_TEXT   ends
_BSS    segment word public 'BSS'
_sum    label    word
        db       2 dup (?)
        ?debug   C E9
        ?debug   C FA00000000
_BSS    ends
_DATA   segment word public 'DATA'
s@      label    byte
_DATA   ends
_TEXT   segment byte public 'CODE'
_TEXT   ends
_s@     equ      s@
        public   _sum
        public   _add
        public   _main
        end
```

A Call-by-Reference Example

In the following program, the function **get_val( )** is called using the address of **a** to illustrate the code produced when pointers are used.

```c
#include <stdio.h>

void get_val(int *x);

void main(void)
{
  int a;

  get_val(&a);
  printf("%d", a);
}

void get_val(int *x)

{
  *x = 100;
}
```

The assembly-language file produced by Microsoft C/C++ is shown here:

```
; File test.c
; Line 6
_main:
        push    bp
        mov     bp,sp
        mov     ax,OFFSET L00184
        call    __aNchkstk
        push    si
        push    di
; a = fffc
; Line 7
; Line 9
        lea     ax,WORD PTR -4[bp]
        push    ax
        call    _get_val
        add     sp,OFFSET 2
; Line 10
        push    WORD PTR -4[bp]
        mov     ax,OFFSET L00180
        push    ax
        call    _printf
        add     sp,OFFSET 4
```

```
; Line 11
; Line 11
L00178:
        pop     di
        pop     si
        mov     sp,bp
        pop     bp
        ret     OFFSET 0
; Line 14
; x = 0004
_get_val:
        push    bp
        mov     bp,sp
        mov     ax,OFFSET L00186
        call    __aNchkstk
        push    si
        push    di
; Line 15
        mov     bx,WORD PTR 4[bp]
        mov     WORD PTR [bx],OFFSET 100
; Line 16
; Line 16
L00183:
        pop     di
        pop     si
        mov     sp,bp
        pop     bp
        ret     OFFSET 0
```

As you can see, **_get_val** is called by using the address of **a**. The address of **a** is found by using the LEA (load effective address) assembly-language instruction. Inside **_get_val**, this address loads the value **100** into **a** by using the indirect addressing mode of the 8086-family.

Using the Large Code and Data Memory Model

As a final example of the way a C compiler generates code, let's compile the same test program used by the previous section using the large memory model. This will cause references to library functions and global data to be **FAR**. To do this using the Microsoft compiler, specify the **–AH** compiler option. The following assembly-code module is produced:

```
; File test.c
; Line 6
_main:
        push    bp
        mov     bp,sp
        mov     ax,OFFSET L00184
        call    FAR PTR __aFchkstk
        push    si
        push    di
; a = fffc
; Line 7
; Line 9
        lea     ax,WORD PTR -4[bp]
        mov     dx,ss
        push    dx
        push    ax
        call    FAR PTR _get_val
        add     sp,OFFSET 4
; Line 10
        push    WORD PTR -4[bp]
        mov     ax,OFFSET L00180
        mov     dx,ds
        push    dx
        push    ax
        call    FAR PTR _printf
        add     sp,OFFSET 6
; Line 11
; Line 11
L00178:
        pop     di
        pop     si
        mov     sp,bp
        pop     bp
        ret     OFFSET 0
; Line 14
; x = 0006
_get_val:
        push    bp
        mov     bp,sp
        mov     ax,OFFSET L00186
        call    FAR PTR __aFchkstk
        push    si
        push    di
```

```
; Line 15
        les     bx,WORD PTR 6[bp]
        mov     WORD PTR es:[bx],OFFSET 100
; Line 16
; Line 16
L00183:
        pop     di
        pop     si
        mov     sp,bp
        pop     bp
        ret     OFFSET 0
```

Notice three important differences between this version and the previous one. First, the stack is now set with a call to __**aFchkstk** instead of __**aNchkstk**; __**aFchkstk** is used when a program is compiled for a large memory model. Second, the address of **a** now requires that 4 (not 2) bytes be pushed onto the stack prior to the call to **get_val( )**. This allows both the segment and the offset of **a** to be passed. Inside _**get_val**, **a** is accessed using its full 32-bit address. Third, the calls to _**get_val** and _**printf** are now **FAR**. If you want to link your own assembly-language functions with C code compiled for a large code and data model, you must generate compatible return code when returning from a **FAR** call. Confusing two different models will corrupt the stack and crash the program. Also, you must use **FAR** when referencing global data.

Creating An Assembly-Code Skeleton

Now that you have seen how C compilers call functions, it is just a short step to writing your own assembly-language functions. An easy method is to let the compiler generate an assembly-language skeleton for you. Once you have the skeleton, you just have to fill in the details. For example, suppose that you need to create an assembly-language routine that multiplies two integers. To have the compiler generate a skeleton for this function, first create a file that contains only this function.

```
mul(int a, int b)
{
}
```

Next, compile the file using the proper option to produce an assembly-language file. If you use the Microsoft compiler, this file is produced:

```
; File skel.c
; Line 2
; a = 0004
; b = 0006
_mul:
        push    bp
        mov     bp,sp
        mov     ax,OFFSET L00106
        call    __aNchkstk
        push    si
        push    di
; Line 3
; Line 3
L00105:
        pop     di
        pop     si
        mov     sp,bp
        pop     bp
        ret     OFFSET 0
```

Given this skeleton, all you have to do is fill in the details. The finished **mul( )** function is shown here:

```
; File skel.c with multiply added.
; Line 2
; a = 0004
; b = 0006
_mul:
        push    bp
        mov     bp,sp
        mov     ax,OFFSET L00106
        call    __aNchkstk
        push    si
        push    di
; Here is where the actual multiplication takes place.
        mov     ax,word ptr [bp+4]
        imul    word ptr [bp+6]
; AX now contains result, so return.
L00105:
        pop     di
        pop     si
        mov     sp,bp
```

```
pop     bp
ret     OFFSET 0
```

If your assembly-language function uses local variables, then you will need to allocate space for them on the stack. To do this, subtract the required number of bytes from **SP** after it has been saved in **BP**. Then, to access a local variable, index the stack appropriately using negative offsets to **BP**.

The best way to learn more about interfacing assembly-language code with your C programs is to write short functions in C that do approximately what you want the assembly-language version to do. Then, by using the assembly-language compiler option, create an assembly-language file. Most of the time, you will just need to hand-optimize this code instead of actually creating an assembly-language routine from the ground up.

Using asm

Although not part of standard C, many C compilers have added an extension to the C language that allows in-line assembly code to be part of a C program without using a completely separate assembly code module. The advantage to this is twofold. First, you don't need to write all of the interface code for each function. Second, all the code is in one place, which makes maintenance a little easier.

The common name for this extension is **asm**. (However, Microsoft C/C++ calls this extended keyword __asm.) To insert assembly code into a program, precede the assembly-code instruction with **asm**. That is, each line that contains assembly code must start with **asm**. The C compiler simply passes the assembly-code instruction through, untouched, to the assembler phase of the compiler.

> **NOTE:** While ANSI standard C does not define the **asm** keyword, C++ does.

For example, the following short function called **init_port1( )** moves the value 88 into **AX** and outputs it to ports 20 and 21:

```
void init_port1(void)
{
  printf("Initializing Port\n");
asm     mov AX, 88
asm     out 20, AX
asm     out 21, AX
}
```

Here, the compiler automatically provides the interface code to save registers and to return from the function. You just need to provide the code that runs inside the function.

You could use in-line assembly code to create a function that multiplies two numbers, called **mul( )**, without actually creating a separate assembly-language file. Using this approach, the code for **mul( )** is shown here:

```
mul(int a, int b)
{
asm      mov ax, word ptr [bp+4]
asm      imul word ptr [bp+6]
}
```

Remember, the C compiler provides all customary support for setting up and returning from a function call. You must simply provide the body of the function and follow the calling conventions to access the arguments.

Keep in mind that, whatever method you use, you are creating machine dependencies that will make your program difficult to port to another machine. However, for the demanding situations that require assembly code, it is usually worth the effort.

When to Code in Assembler

Because it is difficult to code in assembler, most programmers only do this when absolutely necessary. The general rule is: Don't do it; it creates too many problems! Nevertheless, there are two situations in which coding in assembler makes sense. The first is when there is absolutely no other way to achieve the desired result. For example, you may have to interface directly to a hardware device that cannot be handled with C. The second situation is when you must reduce a C program's execution time.

When you need to speed up a program, you should choose carefully which functions you code in assembler. If you code the wrong ones, you will see very little speed increase. If you choose the right ones, your program will fly! You can easily determine which functions to recode by reviewing how your program runs. The functions that are used inside loops are generally the ones to program in assembler. This is because they are executed repeatedly. Coding in assembler a function used only once or twice does not significantly speed up your program. But recoding a function used several times will. For example, consider the following **main( )** function:

```
#include <stdio.h>

void main(void)

{
  register int t;
  init();

  for(t=0; t<1000; ++t) {
    phase1();
    phase2();
    if(t==10) phase3();
  }
  byebye();
}
```

Clearly, recoding **init( )** and **byebye( )** will not measurably affect the speed of this program, because these functions execute only once. However, **phase1( )** and **phase2( )** execute 1000 times, and coding them in assembly language would definitely decrease this program's run time. **phase3( )** only executes once, even though it is inside the loop, so you should not recode this function into assembler.

With careful thought, you can make major improvements in the speed of your program by recoding only a few functions in assembler.

Chapter Twenty-Six

Software Engineering Using C

The entire discipline of computer science has emerged with astonishing speed. Before 1970, little distinction was made between engineers who designed computers and those who programmed them. If you understood computers, it was assumed that you could engineer the hardware as well as the software. This situation changed radically during the 1970s. Now, virtually all colleges offer separate curricula for computer engineers and software engineers.

The art and science of software engineering encompass a wide range of topics. Creating a large computer program is a little like designing a large building. There are so many bits and pieces that it almost seems impossible to make everything work together. Of course, what makes the creation of a large program possible is the application of the proper engineering methods. In this chapter, several techniques that relate specifically to the C programming environment and that make the creation and maintenance of a program much easier will be examined.

Top-Down Design

Without a doubt, the single most important thing that you can do to simplify the creation of a large program is to apply a solid approach. There are three general approaches to writing a program: top-down, bottom-up, and ad hoc. In the *top-down approach*, you start with the top-level routine and move downward to the low-level routines. The *bottom-up approach* works in the opposite direction: you begin with specific routines and build them progressively into more complex structures, ending at the top-level routine. The *ad hoc approach* has no predetermined method.

As a structured language, C lends itself to a top-down approach. The top-down method can produce clean, readable code that you can easily maintain. This approach also helps you clarify the overall structure of the program before you code low-level functions, reducing time wasted by false starts.

Outlining Your Program

Like an outline, the top-down method starts with a general description and works toward specifics. In fact, a good way to design a program is to first define exactly what the program will do at its top level and then fill in the details relating to each action. For example, assume that you have to write a mailing-list program. First you should make a list of the operations that the program will perform. Each entry in the list should contain only one functional unit. (You can think of a functional unit as a black box that performs a single task.) For example, your list might look like this:

- Enter a new address
- Delete an address
- Print the list
- Search for a name

- Save the list
- Load the list
- Quit the program

After you have defined the overall functionality of the program, you can sketch in the details of each functional unit, beginning with the main loop. One way to write the main loop of this program is like this:

```
main loop
{
  do {
    display menu
    get user selection
    process the selection
  } while selection does not equal quit
}
```

This type of algorithmic notation (sometimes called *pseudocode*) can help you clarify the general structure of your program before you sit down at the computer. C-like syntax has been used because it is familiar, but you can use any type of syntax that you like.

You should give a similar definition to each functional area. For example, you can define the function that writes the mailing list to a disk file like this:

```
save to disk {
  open disk file
  while data left to write {
    write data to disk
  }
  close disk file
}
```

At this point, the save-to-disk function has created new, more specific functional units. These units open a disk file, write data to disk, and close the disk file. You must define each of these. If, in the course of their definition, new functional units are created, they must also be defined, and so on. This process stops when no new functional units are created and all that is left to do is to actually write the C code that implements an action. For example, the unit that closes a disk file will probably consist of only a call to **fclose( )**.

Notice that the definition does not mention data structure or variables. This is intentional. So far, you only want to define what your program will do, not how it will actually do it. This definition process will help you decide on the actual structure of the data. (Of course, you need to determine the data structure before you can code all functional units.)

Choosing a Data Structure

After you have determined your program's general outline, you must decide how the data will be structured. The selection of a data structure and its implementation are critical because they help determine the design limits of your program.

A mailing list deals with collections of information: names, street addresses, cities, states, and ZIP codes. Using a top-down approach, this immediately suggests the use of a structure to hold the information. However, how will these structures be stored and manipulated? For a mailing-list program, you could use a fixed-size array of structures. But a fixed-size array has two serious drawbacks. First, the size of the array arbitrarily limits the length of the mailing list. Second, a fixed-size array will not take advantage of all the memory in your computer. Also, if you use a fixed size array and then memory is subtracted from the system (for example, if a memory card fails), the program may not work because the array may no longer fit in the remaining available memory. The solution to these problems is for the mailing-list program to allocate memory for each address dynamically, storing each address in some form of dynamic data structure (such as a linked list), which may grow as needed. In this way the list can be as large as free memory allows.

Although dynamic storage allocation has been chosen over a fixed-size array, the exact form of the data still has not been decided. There are several possibilities: You could use a singly linked list, a doubly linked list, a binary tree, or even a hashing method. Each method has its merits and its drawbacks. For the sake of discussion, assume that your particular mail list application requires especially fast search times, so you choose a binary tree. Only now can you define the structure that holds each name and address in the list, as shown here:

```
struct addr {
  char name[30];
  char street[40];
  char city[20];
  char state[3];
  char zip[11];
  struct addr *left;  /* pointer to left subtree */
  struct addr *right;  /* pointer to right subtree */
};
```

Once the data structure has been defined, you are ready to code your program. To do so, simply fill in the details described in the pseudocode outline you created earlier.

If you follow the top-down approach, your programs will not only be much easier to read, but will take less time to develop and less effort to maintain.

Bulletproof Functions

In large programs, especially those that control potentially life-threatening events, the potential for error has to be very slight. Although small programs can be verified as correct, this is not the case for large ones. (A verified program is proved to be free of errors and will never malfunction—in theory at least.) For example, consider a program that controls the wing flaps of a modern jet airplane. You cannot test all possible interactions of the numerous forces that will be exerted on the plane. This means that you cannot test the program exhaustively. At best, all that you can say is that it performed correctly in such and such situations. In a program of this type, the last thing that you (as a passenger or programmer) want is a crash (of the program or the plane).

After you have programmed for a few years, you learn that most program crashes can be attributed to one of a relatively few types of programmer errors. For example, many catastrophic program errors are caused by one of these relatively common mistakes:

- Some condition causes an unintended infinite loop to be entered.
- An array boundary has been violated, causing damage to adjacent code or data.
- A data type unexpectedly overflows.

In theory, these types of errors can be avoided by careful and thoughtful design and programming practices. (Indeed, professionally written programs should be reasonably free of these types of errors.)

However, there is another type of error that often appears after the initial development stage of a program, occurring either during final "fine tuning" or during the maintenance phase of the program. This error is caused by one function inadvertently interfering with another function's code or data. This type of error is especially hard to find because the code in both functions may appear to be correct. Instead, it is the interaction of the functions that causes the error. Therefore, to reduce the chance of a catastrophic failure, you will want your functions and their data to be as "bulletproof" as possible. The best way to achieve this is to keep the code and data related to each function hidden from the rest of the program. This is sometimes called *hiding code and data*.

Hiding code and data is similar to telling a secret only to those who need to know. Simply put, if a function does not need to know about another function or variable, don't let the function have access to it. You must follow four rules to accomplish this:

1. Each functional unit must have one entry point and one exit point.

2. Wherever possible, pass information to functions instead of using global variables.

3. Where global variables are required by a few related functions, you should place both the variables and the functions in a separate file. Also, the global variables must be declared as **static**.

4. Each function must be able to report the success or failure of its intended operation to the caller. That is, the code that calls a function must be able to know if that function succeeded or failed.

Rule 1 states that each functional area has one entry point and one exit point. This means that although a functional unit may contain several functions, the rest of the program communicates through only one of them. Think about the mailing-list program discussed earlier. There are seven functional areas. You could place all of the functions needed by each functional area in their own files and compile them separately. If done correctly, the only way in or out of each functional unit is through its top-level function. And, in the mailing-list program, these top-level functions are called only by **main( )**, thereby preventing one functional unit from accidentally damaging another. This situation is depicted in Figure 26-1.

Although it decreases performance in some cases, the best way to reduce the possibility of side effects is always to pass all information needed by a function to that

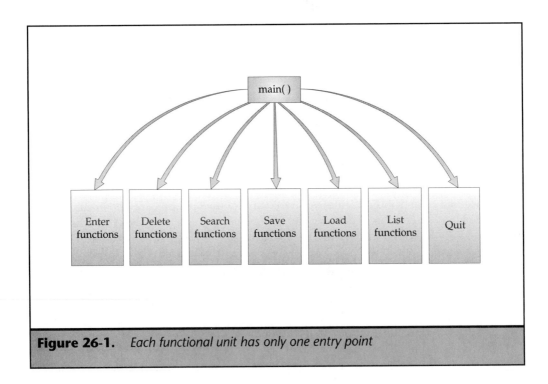

Figure 26-1. *Each functional unit has only one entry point*

function. Never use global data. This is rule 2, and if you have ever programmed a large program in standard BASIC—where every variable is global—you already understand its importance.

Rule 3 states that when global data must be used, the global data and the functions that need to access it should be placed in one file and compiled separately. The key is to declare the global data as **static**, thereby keeping knowledge of it from the other files. Also, the functions that access the **static** data can, themselves, be declared as **static**, preventing them from being called by other functions not declared within the same file.

Put simply, Rule 4 ensures that programs get a second chance by allowing the caller of a function to respond in a reasonable manner to an error condition. For example, if the function that controls the flaps on the airplane experiences an out-of-range condition, you do not want the entire program to fail (and the plane to crash). Rather, you want the program to know that an error occurred within the function. Since an out-of-range condition may be a temporary situation for a program that operates on real-time data, the program could respond to such an error by simply waiting a few clock ticks and trying again.

Keep in mind that strict adherence to these rules will not be applicable in every situation. However, you must follow the rules when the highest degree of fault tolerance is required. The goal of this approach is to create a program that has the highest likelihood of recovering unharmed from an error condition.

> *NOTE: If you are especially interested in the concepts supporting bulletproof functions, you will want to explore C++. C++ provides an even stronger protection mechanism called* encapsulation, *which further decreases the chance of one function damaging another.*

Using MAKE

Another type of error that tends to affect the creation of large programs occurs mostly during the development stage and can bring a project to a near standstill. This error occurs when one or more source files are out-of-date with their respective object files when the program is compiled. When this happens, the executable form of the program will not act in accordance with the current state of the source code. Anyone who has ever been involved with the creation or maintenance of a large software project has probably experienced this problem. To help eliminate this type of frustrating error, most C compilers include a utility called MAKE that helps synchronize source and object files. (The exact name of the MAKE utility for your compiler may be something slightly different than MAKE, so be sure to check your compiler's user's manual.)

MAKE automates the recompilation process for large programs composed of several files. Often, many small changes will be made to many files in the course of program development. After the changes have been made, the program is recompiled and tested. Unfortunately, it is easy to forget which of the files need to be recompiled. In this situation, you may either recompile all the files—a waste of time—or accidentally not recompile a file that should be, potentially adding several hours of frustrating debugging. The MAKE program solves this problem by automatically recompiling only those files that have been altered.

The examples presented in this section are compatible with the MAKE programs supplied with Borland C/C++ and Microsoft C/C++. Borland calls its MAKE program MAKE. However, contemporary versions of Microsoft C/C++ call it NMAKE. The examples will also work with most other mainstream MAKE utilities, and the general concepts described are applicable to all MAKE programs.

> **NOTE:** *In recent years, MAKE programs have become very sophisticated. The examples presented here illustrate the essence of MAKE. You will want to explore the MAKE utility supported by your compiler. It may contain features that are especially useful to your development environment.*

MAKE is driven by a *make file*, which contains a list of target files, dependent files, and commands. A *target file* requires its *dependent files* to produce it. For example, T.C would be a dependent file of T.OBJ because T.C is required to make T.OBJ. MAKE work by comparing the dates between a dependent file and its target file. (As used here, the term *date* includes both the calendar date and the time.) If the target file has a date that is older than its dependent file (or if target does not exist), the specified command sequence is executed. If that command sequence contains target files defined by other dependencies, then those dependencies are also updated, as needed. When the MAKE process is over, all target files have been updated. Therefore, in a correctly constructed make file, all source files that require compilation are automatically compiled and linked, forming the new executable file. In this way, source files are kept in synchronization with object files.

The general form of the make file is

```
target_file1 : dependent_file list
    command_sequence

target_file2 : dependent_file list
    command_sequence

target_file3 : dependent_file list
    command_sequence
       .
       .
       .
target_fileN : dependent_file list
    command_sequence
```

The target file name must start in the leftmost column and be followed by a colon and its list of dependent files. The command sequence associated with each target must be preceded by at least one space or a tab. Comments are preceded by a # and may follow the dependent file list and/or the command sequence. If they appear on a line of their own, they must start in the leftmost column. Each target-file specification must be separated from the next by at least one blank line.

The most important thing that you need to understand about a make file is this: Execution of a make file stops as soon as the first dependency succeeds. This means that you must design your make files in such a way that the dependencies are heirarchical. Remember that no dependency can succeed until all subordinate dependencies relating it are also resolved.

To see how MAKE works, consider a very simple program. The program is divided into four files called TEST.H, TEST.C, TEST2.C, and TEST3.C. This situation is illustrated in Figure 26-2. (To follow along, enter each part of the program into the indicated files.)

If you are using Borland C/C++, the following make file will recompile the program when you make changes. (If you are using a Microsoft C/C++ compiler, change **bcc** to **cl**.)

```
test.exe:  test.h test.obj test2.obj test3.obj
        bcc test.obj test2.obj test3.obj

test.obj: test.c test.h
        bcc -c test.c

test2.obj: test2.c test.h
        bcc -c test2.c

test3.obj: test3.c test.h
        bcc -c test3.c
```

By default, a MAKE program will use the directives contained in a file called MAKEFILE. However, you will usually want to use another name for your make file. When using another name for the make file, you must use the –f option on the command line. For example, if the name of the preceding make file is TEST, you would type something like

    make –f test

at the command prompt to compile the necessary modules and create an executable program. (This applies to the Borland version of MAKE and to Microsoft's NMAKE. A different option may be needed if you use a different MAKE utility.)

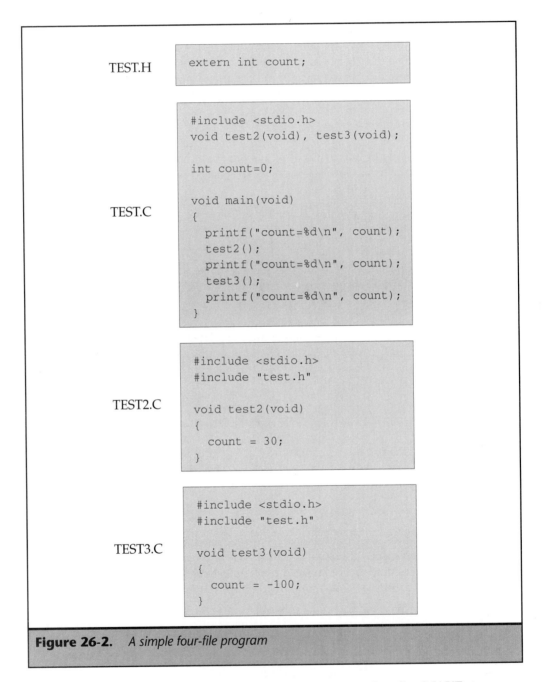

Figure 26-2. *A simple four-file program*

Order is very important in the make file because, as stated earlier, MAKE stops processing the directives contained in the file as soon as the first dependency is satisfied. For example, if the preceding make file were changed to look like this:

```
# This is an incorrect make file.
test.obj: test.c test.h
        bcc -c test.c

test2.obj: test2.c test.h
        bcc -c test2.c

test3.obj: test3.c test.h
        bcc -c test3.c

test.exe: test.h test.obj test2.obj test3.obj
        bcc test.obj test2.obj test3.obj
```

it would no longer work correctly when the file TEST.H (or any other source file were changed). This is because the final directive (which creates a new TEST.EXE) will no longer be executed.

Using Macros in MAKE

MAKE allows macros to be defined in the make file. These macro names are simply placeholders for the information that will actually be determined either by a command-line specification or by the macro's definition in the make file. Macros are defined according to this general form:

macro_name = definition

If there is to be any white space in the macro definition, you must enclose the definition within double quotes.

Once a macro has been defined, it is used in the make file like this:

$(*macro_name*)

Each time this statement is encountered, the definition linked to the macro is substituted. For example, this make file uses the macro **LIBFIL** to determine which library is used by the linker:

```
LIBFIL = graphics.lib

prog.exe: prog.obj prog2.obj prog3.obj
        bcc prog.obj prog2.obj prog3.obj $(LIBFIL)
```

Many MAKE programs have additional features, so it is very important to consult your user's manual.

Using an Integrated Development Environment

Most modern compilers are supplied in two different forms. The first form is the stand-alone, command-line compiler. Using this form, you use a separate editor to create your program, then you compile your program, and, finally, you execute your program. These events all occur as separate commands given by you on the command line. Any debugging or source file control (such as MAKE) also occurs separately. The command-line compiler is the traditional way compilers were implemented.

The second form of a compiler is found in an integrated development environment (IDE). In this form, the compiler is integrated with an editor, a debugger, a project manager (that takes the place of a separate MAKE utility), and a run-time support system. Using an IDE, you edit, compile, and run your program without ever leaving the IDE. When IDEs were first invented, they were somewhat cumbersome to use and tedious to work with. However, today the IDEs provided by the major compiler manufacturers have much to offer the programmer. If you take the time to set the IDE's options so that it is optimized for your needs, you will find that using the IDE streamlines the development process.

Of course, whether you use an IDE or the traditional command-line approach is also a matter of taste. If you like using the command line, then by all means, use it. Also, one point that is still in favor of the traditional approach is that you can personally select every tool you use, rather than taking what the IDE has to offer.

Chapter Twenty-Seven

Efficiency, Porting, and Debugging

The ability to write programs that make efficient use of system resources, are bug-free, and can be transported to new environments is the mark of a professional programmer. It is also in these areas that computer science becomes the "art of computer science," because there are so few formal techniques that ensure success. This chapter presents some of the methods that help achieve efficiency, enhance program debugging, and increase portability.

Efficiency

In programming, the term *efficiency* can refer to the speed of execution, the use of system resources, or both. System resources include such things as RAM, disk space, printer paper, and the like—basically anything that you can allocate and use up. Whether a program is efficient or not is sometimes a subjective judgment that can change from situation to situation. For example, consider a sorting program that uses 128K of RAM, requires 2MB of disk space, and has an average run time of seven hours. If this program is sorting only 100 addresses in a mailing-list database, it is not very efficient. However, if the program is sorting the New York telephone directory, it is probably quite efficient.

In addition, optimizing one aspect of a program often degrades another. For example, making a program execute faster also often means making it bigger when you use in-line code to eliminate the overhead of a function call. By the same token, making a program smaller by replacing in-line code with function calls makes the program run slower. In the same vein, making more efficient use of disk space means compacting the data, which can often make disk accesses slower. These and other types of efficiency trade-offs can be very frustrating—especially to nonprogrammers and end users who cannot see why one thing should affect the other.

Fortunately, there are some programming practices that are always efficient—or, at least, more efficient than others. Also, there are a few techniques that make programs both faster and smaller. This chapter examines these techniques.

The Increment and Decrement Operators

Discussions of the efficient use of C almost always start with the increment and decrement operators. In case you have forgotten, the increment operator, **++**, increases its operand by one, and the decrement operator, **--**, decreases it by one. For example, both of these statements are the same in final effect:

```
x = x + 1;
x++;
```

Both increase the value of **x** by one. However, the increment statement often executes faster (requiring fewer instructions) than its assignment statement counterpart. This is because of the way object code is generated by the compiler. Specifically, most CPUs can increment or decrement a word of memory without using explicit load and store instructions. For example, by using an imaginary assembly language that loosely approximates that found on many microprocessors, the statement

```
x = x + 1;
```

generates object code that looks something like this:

```
move A, x   ; load value of x from memory into
            ; accumulator
add A, 1    ; add 1 to the accumulator
store x     ; store new value back in x
```

If, however, you used the increment operator, the following code would be produced:

```
incr x   ; increase x by 1
```

As you can see, both the load and store instructions are eliminated, which means that the code executes faster and is smaller. Although many of the better compilers automatically optimize a statement like **x=x+1** into **x++**, you should not take this for granted.

Using Register Variables

One of the most effective ways to speed up your code is through the use of **register** variables. Although **register** variables may prove effective elsewhere, they are particularly well suited for loop control. Recall that any variable specified as **register** is stored in a manner that produces the shortest access time. For integer types, this usually means a register of the CPU. This is important because the speed with which the critical loops of a program execute sets the pace for the overall program speed.

To show how the code differs between a **register** variable and a regular memory variable, the following program will be compiled to an assembly-language program. As you may know, most C compilers provide an option that causes the compiler to create an assembly code file rather than an object code file. Using this option allows us to examine the code produced by the compiler, observing how each type of variable is handled. (Declaring **j** as a global variable ensures that no compiler optimization will automatically convert it into a **register** variable.)

```c
int j;

void main(void)
{
  register int i;

  for(i=0; i<100 ;i++) ;

  for(j=0; j<100; j++) ;
}
```

The assembly-code file produced by the preceding program is shown next. This file was produced by Borland C/C++. (The comments beginning with asterisks were added by the author.) Notice the differences in the instructions used by the register-controlled loop and the non-register loop. Although this code was produced by Borland C/C++, similar code will be produced by any C compiler.

```
.286p
        ifndef  ??version
?debug  macro
        endm
publicdll macro name
        public  name
        endm
$comm   macro   name,dist,size,count
        comm    dist name:BYTE:count*size
        endm
        else
$comm   macro   name,dist,size,count
        comm    dist name[size]:BYTE:count
        endm
        endif
        ?debug  V 301h
        ?debug  S "test.c"
        ?debug  C E93197931D056578352E63
```

```
_TEXT    segment byte public 'CODE'
_TEXT    ends
DGROUP   group   _DATA,_BSS
         assume  cs:_TEXT,ds:DGROUP
_DATA    segment word public 'DATA'
d@       label   byte
d@w      label   word
_DATA    ends
_BSS     segment word public 'BSS'
b@       label   byte
b@w      label   word
_BSS     ends
_TEXT    segment byte public 'CODE'
    ;
    ;        void main(void)
    ;
         assume  cs:_TEXT,ds:DGROUP
_main    proc    near
         push    bp
         mov     bp,sp
    ;
    ;        {
    ;           register int i;
    ;
    ;           for(i=0; i<100 ;i++) ;
    ;
; ****************************************************
;  The following code initializes the register
;  controlled loop. Notice how the loop control
;  variable is initialized using an XOR instruction.
;  ****************************************************
         xor     ax,ax
         jmp     short @1@86
@1@58:
; ****** This is a register increment.
         inc     ax
@1@86:
; ******  This is a register compare.
         cmp     ax,100
         jl      short @1@58
```

```
        ;
        ;
        ;          for(j=0; j<100; j++) ;
        ;
        ; *****************************************************
        ;   The following code initializes the memory
        ;   controlled loop.  Notice that a memory access is
        ;   required to initialize the loop control variable.
        ; *****************************************************
                mov     word ptr DGROUP:_j,0
                jmp     short @1@170
        @1@142:
        ; ****** Here, a memory access is required to increment j.
                inc     word ptr DGROUP:_j
        @1@170:
        ; ****** Here, a memory access  is required to compare j.
                cmp     word ptr DGROUP:_j,100
                jl      short @1@142
        ;
        ;          }
        ;
                pop     bp
                ret
        _main   endp
        _TEXT   ends
        _BSS    segment word public 'BSS'
        _j      label   word
                db      2 dup (?)
                ?debug  C E9
                ?debug  C FA00000000
        _BSS    ends
        _DATA   segment word public 'DATA'
        s@      label   byte
        _DATA   ends
        _TEXT   segment byte public 'CODE'
        _TEXT   ends
        _s@     equ     s@
                public  _j
                public  _main
                end
```

As you can see by looking at the assembly language file, the register-controlled loop requires no memory accesses. However, the memory-controlled loop requires numerous memory accesses. Since memory accesses are much more costly in terms of time than are register accesses, it is obvious which loop will execute faster.

Although you can declare as many variables as you like using **register**, in reality most compilers can only optimize the access time of a few. For example, generally only two integer variables can be held in registers of the CPU at any one time. Other types of fast storage, such as cache memory, are also easily exhausted. For this reason, the C compiler is allowed to disregard the **register** specifier and simply handle the variable normally. This provision also enables code created for one environment to be compiled in another environment in which there are fewer fast-access storage locations. Since fast-access storage is always limited, it is best to choose carefully those variables that you want to be optimized for fast access.

Pointers Versus Array Indexing

In many cases you can substitute pointer arithmetic for array indexing. Doing so often produces both smaller and faster code. (Pointers generally make your code run faster and take up less space than does array indexing.) For example, the following two code fragments do the same thing:

Array indexing

```
for(;;) {
  a = array[t++];
    .
    .
    .
}
```

Pointer arithmetic

```
p = array;
for(;;) {
    a = *(p++);
      .
      .
      .
}
```

The advantage of the pointer method is that once **p** has been loaded with the address of **array** (perhaps using an index register such as **SI** on the 8086-family of processors), only an increment must be performed each time the loop repeats. However, the array index version must always compute the array index based on the value of **t**—a more complex task. The disparity in the execution speeds of array indexing and pointer arithmetic gets wider as you use multiple indexes. Each index requires its own sequence of instructions, whereas the pointer arithmetic equivalent can use simple addition.

Be careful. You should use array indexes when the index is derived through a very complex formula and pointer arithmetic would obscure the meaning of the program.

It is usually better to degrade performance slightly than to sacrifice clarity. Also, the disparity between array indexing and pointer arithmetic may not be significant for highly optimizing compilers or on all processor types or in all environments. However, the general rule is still valid.

Use of Functions

Remember at all times that the use of stand-alone functions with local variables helps form the basis of structured programming. Functions are the building blocks of C programs and are one of C's strongest assets. Do not let anything that is discussed in this section be construed otherwise. Having been warned, you should know a few things about C functions and their ramifications on the size and speed of your code.

When a C compiler compiles a function, it uses the stack to hold the parameters (if any) to the function and any local variables used by the function. When a function is called, the return address of the calling routine is placed on the stack as well. (This enables the subroutine to return to the location from which it was called.) When a function returns, this address and all local variables and parameters have to be removed from the stack. The process of pushing this information is generally referred to as the *calling sequence*, and the popping process is called the *returning sequence*. These sequences take time—sometimes quite a bit of time.

To understand how a function call can slow down your program, look at these two code fragments:

version 1
```
for(x=1; x<100; ++x) {
   t = compute(x);
}


float compute(int q)
{
   return abs(sin(q)/100/3.1416);
}
```

version 2
```
for(x=1; x<100; ++x) {
   t = abs(sin(x)/100/3.1416);
}
```

Although each loop performs the same function, version 2 is much faster because the overhead of the calling and returning sequence has been eliminated through the use of in-line code.

Look at another example, this time one that involves assembly code output by the Borland C/C++ compiler. This program

```
max(int a, int b);

void main(void)
{
    int x;

    x = max(10, 20);
}

max(int a, int b)
{
    return a>b ? a : b;
}
```

produces the following assembly code. The calling and returning sequences are indicated by comments beginning with asterisks added by the author. As you can see, they amount to a sizable part of the program code.

```
        .286p
                ifndef  ??version
?debug  macro
        endm
publicdll macro name
        public  name
        endm
$comm   macro   name,dist,size,count
        comm    dist name:BYTE:count*size
        endm
        else
$comm   macro   name,dist,size,count
        comm    dist name[size]:BYTE:count
        endm
        endif
        ?debug  V 301h
        ?debug  S "test.c"
        ?debug  C E96B98931D056578392E63
_TEXT   segment byte public 'CODE'
_TEXT   ends
DGROUP  group   _DATA,_BSS
```

```
        assume  cs:_TEXT,ds:DGROUP
_DATA   segment word public 'DATA'
d@      label   byte
d@w     label   word
_DATA   ends
_BSS    segment word public 'BSS'
b@      label   byte
b@w     label   word
_BSS    ends
_TEXT   segment byte public 'CODE'
    ;
    ;       void main(void)
    ;
        assume  cs:_TEXT,ds:DGROUP
_main   proc    near
        enter   2,0
    ;
    ;       {
    ;           int x;
    ;
    ;           x = max(10, 20);
    ;
;   *********************************************
;   This is the start of the calling sequence.
;   *********************************************
        push    20
        push    10
        call    near ptr _max
;   *********************************************
;
;
;   *********************************************
;   The next line is part of the returning sequence.
;   *********************************************
        add     sp,4
        mov     word ptr [bp-2],ax
    ;
    ;       }
    ;
        leave
        ret
_main   endp
```

```
        ;
        ;       max(int a, int b)
        ;
                assume  cs:_TEXT,ds:DGROUP
_max    proc    near
;       **************************************************
;   More of the calling sequence.
;       **************************************************
                push    bp
                mov     bp,sp
                mov     dx,word ptr [bp+4]
                mov     bx,word ptr [bp+6]
;       **************************************************
   ;
   ;       {
   ;          return a>b ? a : b;
   ;
                cmp     dx,bx
                jle     short @2@86
                mov     ax,dx
                jmp     short @2@114
@2@86:
;       **************************************************
;   Here is the first part of the returning sequence.
;       **************************************************
                mov     ax,bx
@2@114:
                pop     bp
                ret
   ;
   ;       }
   ;
                pop     bp
                ret
_max    endp
                ?debug  C E9
                ?debug  C FA00000000
_TEXT   ends
_DATA   segment word public 'DATA'
s@      label   byte
_DATA   ends
_TEXT   segment byte public 'CODE'
```

```
_TEXT    ends
_s@      equ     s@
         public  _max
         public  _main
         end
```

The actual code produced depends on how the compiler is implemented and what processor is being used, but it will generally be similar to this.

Now you may think that you should write programs that have just a few very large functions so that they run quickly. This is probably not a good idea. First, in the vast majority of cases the slight time differential gained by avoiding function calls is not meaningful and the loss of structure is acute. But there is another problem. Replacing functions that are used by several routines with in-line code causes your program to become very large because the same code is duplicated several times. Keep in mind that subroutines were invented largely as a way to make efficient use of memory. In fact, this is why, as a rule of thumb, making a program faster means making it bigger, while making it smaller means making it slower.

In the final analysis, it really makes sense to use in-line code instead of a function call only when speed is the overriding priority. Otherwise, the liberal use of functions is definitely recommended.

Porting Programs

It is common for a program written on one machine to be transported to another computer with a different processor, operating system, or both. This process is called *porting*, and can be very easy or extremely hard, depending upon how the program was originally written. A program that can be easily ported is called *portable*. When a program is not easily portable, this is usually because it contains numerous *machine dependencies*—that is, it has code fragments that work only with one specific operating system or processor. C allows you to create portable code, but achieving this goal still requires care and attention to detail. This section examines a few specific problem areas and offers some solutions.

Using #define

Perhaps the single most effective way to make programs portable is to make every system- or processor-dependent "magic number" a **#define** macro. These magic numbers include things like buffer sizes for disk accesses, special screen and keyboard commands, memory allocation information, and the like—that is, anything that has the slightest possibility of changing when the program is ported. These **#define**s not only make all magic numbers obvious to the person doing the porting, but also simplify the job because their values have to be changed only once instead of throughout the program.

For example, here is an **fread( )** statement that is inherently non-portable:

```
fread(buf, 128, 1, fp);
```

The problem is that the buffer size, 128, is hardcoded into **fread( )**. This might work for one operating system but be less than optimal for another. Here is a better way to code this function:

```
#define BUF_SIZE 128

fread(buf, BUF_SIZE, 1, fp);
```

In this case, when moving to a different system, only the **#define** has to change and all references to **BUF_SIZE** are automatically corrected. This not only makes it easier to change, but also avoids many editing errors. Remember that there will probably be many references to **BUF_SIZE** in a real program, so the gain in portability is often great.

Operating-System Dependencies

Virtually all commercial programs contain code specific to the operating system that they are designed to run under. For example, a DOS-based spreadsheet program might directly access BIOS routines to achieve faster switching between screens, or a Windows-based accounting package may use special text fonts only found in that environment. The point is that some operating-system dependencies are necessary for truly good, fast, and commercially viable programs. However, operating system dependencies also make your programs harder to port.

While there is no hard and fast rule that you can follow to minimize your operating system dependencies, there is one piece of advice that can be offered: Separate the parts of your program that relate directly to your application from those parts that interface with the operating system. In this way, if you port your program to a new environment, only the interfacing modules will need to be changed.

Differences in Data Sizes

If you want to write portable code, you must never make assumptions about the size of a data type. As you probably know, the size of a word in a 16-bit processor is 16 bits; for a 32-bit processor it is 32 bits. Because the size of a word tends to be the size of an integer, code that assumes that integers are 16 bits, for example, will not work when ported to a 32-bit environment. To avoid size dependencies, use **sizeof** whenever your program needs to know how many bytes long something is. For example, this statement writes an integer to a disk file and works in any environment:

```
fwrite(&i, sizeof(int), 1, stream);
```

Sometimes, however, you cannot create portable code even with **sizeof**. For example, this function (which swaps the bytes in an integer) works with 16-bit integers but fails when integers are 32-bits.

```
void swap_bytes(int *x)
{
  union sb {
    int t;
    unsigned char c[2];
  } swap;

  unsigned char temp;

  swap.t = *x;
  temp = swap.c[1];
  swap.c[1] = swap.c[0];
  swap.c[0] = temp;
  *x = swap.t;
}
```

If you know in advance that you will need a 32-bit version of this function, you will need to create a second version and then use a conditional compilation directive (such as **#ifdef**) to compile the right version for each environment.

Debugging

To paraphrase Thomas Edison, programming is 10% inspiration and 90% debugging. All really good programmers are good debuggers. The types of bugs that can occur easily while you are using C are the topic of this section.

Order-of-Evaluation Errors

The increment and decrement operators are used in most C programs, and the order in which the operations take place is affected by whether these operators precede or follow the variable. Consider the following:

```
y = 10;                    y = 10;

x = y++;                   x = ++y;
```

These two sequences are not the same. The first one assigns the value of **10** to **x** and then increments **y**. The second increments **y** to **11** and then assigns the value **11** to **x**. Therefore, in the first case **x** contains **10**; in the second, **x** contains **11**. In the general case, a prefix increment (or decrement) operation occurs before the value of the operand is obtained for use in the larger expression. A postfix increment (or decrement) occurs after the value of the operand is obtained for use in the larger expression. If you forget these rules, problems will result.

The way an order-of-evaluation error usually occurs is through changes to an existing statement. For example, you may enter the statement

```
x = *p++;
```

which assigns the value pointed to by **p** to **x** and then increments the pointer **p**. Say, however, that later you decide that **x** really needs the value pointed to by **p** squared. To do this, you try

```
x = *p++ * (*p);
```

However, this can't work because **p** has already been incremented. The proper solution is to write

```
x = *p * (*p++);
```

Errors like this can be very hard to find. There may be clues such as loops that don't run right or routines that are off by one. If you have any doubt about a statement, recode it in a way that you are sure about.

Pointer Problems

A very common error in C programs is the misuse of pointers. Pointer problems fall into two general categories: misunderstanding indirection and the pointer operators, and accidentally using invalid pointers. The solution to the first problem is to understand the C language; the solution to the second is always to verify the validity of a pointer before it is used.

What follows is a typical C programming error:

```
/* This program has an error. */
#include <stdlib.h>
#include <stdio.h>

void main(void)
{
  char *p;

  *p = malloc(100); /* this line is wrong */
  gets(p);
  printf(p);
}
```

This program will most likely crash—probably taking the operating system with it. The reason is that the address returned by **malloc( )** was not assigned to **p** but rather to the memory location pointed to by **p**, which in this case is completely unknown. To correct this program, you must substitute

```
p = malloc(100); /* this is correct */
```

for the wrong line.

The program also contains a second and more insidious error. There is no run-time check on the address returned by **malloc( )**. Remember, if memory is exhausted, **malloc( )** returns **NULL**, which is never a valid pointer in C. The malfunction caused by this type of bug is difficult to find because it occurs rarely, when an allocation request fails. The best way to handle this problem is to prevent it. What follows is a corrected version of the program, which includes a check for pointer validity:

```
/* This program is now correct. */

#include <stdio.h>
#include <stdlib.h>

void main(void)
{
  char *p;

  p = malloc(100); /* this is correct */

  if(!p) {
    printf("Out of memory.\n");
```

```
    exit(1);
  }

  gets(p);
  printf(p);
}
```

The terrible thing about wild pointers is that they are so hard to track down. If you are making assignments through a pointer that does not contain a valid address, your program may appear to function correctly some of the time and crash at other times. The smaller your program, the more likely that it will run correctly, even with a stray pointer. This is because very little memory is in use and the odds are that the offending pointer is pointing to memory that is not being used. As your program grows, failures will become more common, but you will be thinking about current additions or changes to your program, not about pointer errors. Hence, you will tend to look in the wrong spot for the bug.

The way to recognize a pointer problem is that errors are often erratic. Your program will work right one time, wrong another. Sometimes other variables will contain garbage for no apparent reason. If these problems begin to occur, check your pointers. As a matter of procedure, you should always check all pointers when bugs begin to occur.

As a consolation, remember that although pointers can be troublesome, they are also one of the most powerful aspects of the C language and are worth whatever trouble they may cause you. Make the effort early on to learn to use them correctly.

One final point to remember about pointers is that you must initialize them before they are used. Consider the following code fragment:

```
int *x;

*x = 100;
```

This will probably be a disaster because you don't know where **x** is pointing. Assigning a value to that unknown location may destroy something of value, such as other code or data.

Bizarre Syntax Errors

Once in a while you will see a syntax error that does not make sense. Either the error message is cryptic or the error being reported doesn't seem like an error at all. However, in most cases the compiler is right about detecting an error; it is just that its reporting of it is less than perfect! Finding the cause of unusual syntax errors usually requires some backtracking on your part. If you encounter an error message that doesn't seem to make sense, try looking for a syntax error one or two lines earlier in your program.

One particularly unsettling error occurs when you try to compile the following code.

```
char *myfunc(void);

void main(void)
{
      .
      .
      .

}

myfunc(void)  /* error reported here */
{
      .
      .
      .

}
```

Your compiler will issue an error message similar to **Type mismatch in redeclaration of f( )** in reference to the line indicated in the listing. How can this be? There are not two **myfunc( )**s. The answer is that the prototype at the top of the program shows **myfunc( )** having a character pointer return type. This caused a symbol table entry to be made with that information. When the compiler encountered **myfunc( )** later in the program, there was no indication that it was to be returning anything other than an integer, the default type. Hence you were "redeclaring" or "redefining" the function.

Another syntax error that is difficult to understand is generated with the following code:

```
/* This program has a syntax error in it. */
#include <stdio.h>

void func1(void);

void main(void)
{
   func1();
}

void func1(void);
```

```
{
  printf("this is func1 \n");
}
```

The error here is the semicolon after the definition of **func1( )**. The compiler will see this as a statement outside of any function, which is an error. However, the way that various compilers report this error differs. Many compilers issue an error message like **bad declaration syntax** while pointing at the first open brace after **func1( )**. Because you are used to seeing semicolons after statements, it can be very hard to see the source of this error.

One-Off Errors

As you know, in C all array indexes start at 0. However, even experienced pros have been known to forget this well known fact while in the heat of programming! Consider the following program, which is supposed to initialize an array of 100 integers:

```
/* This program will not work. */

void main(void)
{
  int x, num[100];

  for(x=1; x<=100; ++x) num[x]=x;
}
```

The **for** loop in this program is wrong in two ways. First, it does not initialize **num[0]**, the first element of array **num**. Second, it goes one past the end of the array because **num[99]** is the last element and the loop runs to 100. The correct way to write this program is

```
/* This is right. */

void main(void)
{
  int x, num[100];

  for(x=0; x<100; ++x) num[x]=x;
}
```

Remember, an array of 100 has elements 0 through 99.

Boundary Errors

Both the C run-time environment and many standard library functions have very little or no run-time bounds checking. For example, you can easily overwrite arrays. Consider the following program, which is supposed to read a string from the keyboard and display it on the screen:

```c
#include <stdio.h>

void main(void)
{
  int var1;
  char s[10];
  int var2;

  var1 = 10;  var2 = 10;
  gets(s);
  printf("%s %d %s", s, var1, var2);
}
```

Here, there are no direct coding errors. Indirectly, however, calling **gets( )** with **s** may cause a bug. In the program, **s** is declared to be ten characters long, but what if the user enters more than ten characters? This causes **s** to be overwritten. The real problem is that **s** may contain all the characters, but either **var1** or **var2** will not contain the correct value. This is because all C compilers use the stack to store local variables. The variables **var1**, **var2**, and **s** will be located in memory as shown in Figure 27-1.

Your C compiler may exchange the order of **var1** and **var2**, but they still bracket **s**. When **s** is overwritten, the additional information is placed into the area that is supposed to be **var2**, destroying any previous contents. Therefore, instead of printing the number **10** for both integer variables, the variable destroyed by the overrun of **s** displays something else. This makes you look for the problem in the wrong place. Also, in this specific instance the return address of the function call may also be overwritten, causing a crash.

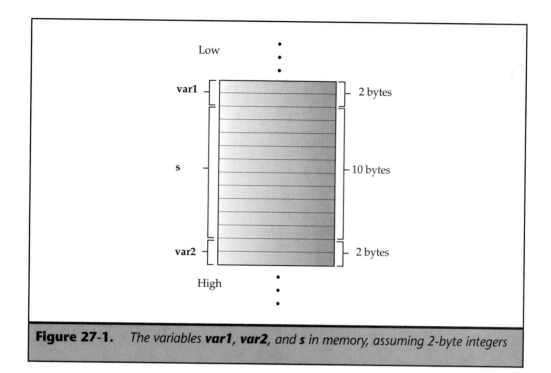

Figure 27-1.   *The variables **var1**, **var2**, and **s** in memory, assuming 2-byte integers*

Function Prototype Omissions

In today's programming environment, failure to use full function prototyping is an inexcusable lapse of judgment. To understand why, consider the following program, which multiplies two floating-point numbers:

```
/* This program is wrong. */
#include <stdio.h>

void main(void)
{
  float x, y;
```

```
   scanf("%f%f", &x, &y);
   printf("%f", mul(x, y));
}

float mul(float a, float b)
{
   return a*b;
}
```

Here, since no prototype for **mul( )** is used, **main( )** expects an integer value to be returned from **mul( )**. But in reality, **mul( )** returns a floating-point number. Assuming 2-byte integers and 4-byte **floats**, this means that only 2 bytes out of the 4 needed for a **float** are actually used by the **printf( )** statement within **main( )**. This causes the wrong answer to be displayed. Although a C compiler will catch this error if both **main( )** and **mul( )** are in the same file, it cannot if they are in separately compiled modules and no prototype for **mul( )** is included.

The way to correct this program is to prototype **mul( )**. The corrected version follows.

```
/* This program is correct. */
#include <stdio.h>

float mul(float a, float b);

void main(void)
{
   float x, y;

   scanf("%f%f", &x, &y);
   printf("%f", mul(x, y));
}

float mul(float a, float b)
{
   return a*b;
}
```

Here, the prototype tells **main( )** to expect **mul( )** to return a floating-point value.

Argument Errors

You must be sure to match whatever type of argument a function expects with the type you give it. An important example is **scanf( )**. Remember that **scanf( )** expects to receive the *addresses* of its arguments, not their values. For example,

```
int x;
char string[10];

scanf("%d%s", x, string);
```

is wrong, while

```
scanf("%d%s", &x, string);
```

is correct. Recall that strings already pass their addresses to functions, so you should not use the **&** operator on them.

Stack-Heap Collisions

Although some C compilers do not allow the stack to collide with the heap, many do. When this happens, the program either dies completely or continues executing in a bizarre fashion. This second symptom is due to the stack being corrupted. The worst thing about stack-heap collisions is that they generally occur without any warning and kill the program so completely that debugging is difficult. The only advice that can be offered is that some stack-heap collisions are caused by runaway recursive functions. If your program uses recursion and you experience unexplainable failures, check the terminating conditions in your recursive functions.

Debugging Theory in General

Everyone has a different approach to programming and debugging. However, certain techniques have, over time, proven to be better than others. In the case of debugging, incremental testing is considered to be the most cost- and time-effective method, even though it can appear to slow the development process at first. *Incremental testing* is the process of always having a working program. That is, very early in the development process, an operational unit is established. An *operational unit* is simply a piece of working code. As new code is added to this unit, it is tested and debugged. In this way, the programmer can easily find errors because the errors probably occur in the newly added code or in the way that it interacts with the operational unit.

Debugging time is proportional the total number of lines of code in which a bug could reside. With incremental testing, you can often restrict the number of lines of code that may contain a bug to only those that are newly added—that is, those not part of the operational unit. This situation is shown in Figure 27-2. As a programmer, you want to deal with the smallest possible area while debugging. Through incremental testing, you can subtract the area already tested from the total area, thereby reducing the region in which a bug may be found.

In large projects, there are often several modules that have little interaction. In these cases, you can establish several operational units to allow concurrent development.

Incremental testing is simply the process of always having working code. As soon as it is possible to run a piece of your program, you should do so, testing that section completely. As you add to the program, continue to test the new sections as well as the way they connect to the known operational code. In this way, you concentrate most possible bugs in a small area of code. Of course, you must always be alert to the possibility that a bug may have been overlooked in the operational unit. But, you have reduced the likelihood of this being the case.

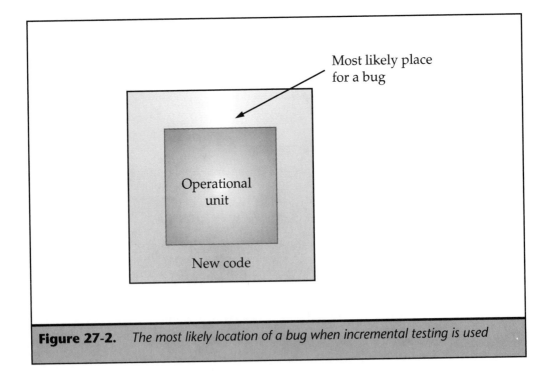

Figure 27-2.   *The most likely location of a bug when incremental testing is used*

The Art of Program Maintenance

Once a program has been written, tested, debugged, and—finally—judged ready for use, the program's development phase is over and its maintenance phase begins. Most programmers like the glamour and excitement of developing a new program but try to avoid being the one to maintain it. This is, in part, because the maintenance phase never ends. When a program is being developed, even a very large one, there is always light at the end of the tunnel. Someday the program will be done. However, the maintenance phase is a daily grind of quirks, anomalies, errors, and bugs. The maintenance programmer may never feel the thrill of accomplishment, and the only good part of the day may be quitting time. As bleak as it may seem, program maintenance can be a challenging and rewarding task if you approach it correctly.

The maintenance programmer has two responsibilities:

- Correcting bugs
- Providing source-code protection

Fixing Bugs

All nontrivial programs have bugs. This is one of the unprovable but irrefutable truths of computer science. The hard part about maintaining a program is that all of the easy bugs are found during the development stage. The bugs that the maintenance programmer must find and fix are often very obscure and only turn up under devilishly complex and difficult to re-create circumstances. If you like real challenges, perhaps program maintenance is for you.

There are basically three types of bugs: those that you must fix (category 1), those that you would like to fix (category 2), and those that you just plain aren't going to worry about (category 3). Category 1 bugs crash the system, scribble on the disk, or destroy data. For example, a bug that causes a database program to occasionally destroy the disk file that holds a database simply must be fixed because it renders the program unusable. Category 2 bugs get fixed only when there are no category 1 bugs to fix. An example of a category 2 bug is one that causes a word processor to, on rare occasions, incorrectly reformat a paragraph. Nothing is lost, the program doesn't die, and the user compensates by making a manual adjustment. Category 2 bugs are, for the most part, annoyances to the user but they can be worked around. These bugs should be fixed, but they are not a number one priority. Finally, category 3 bugs are a nuisance, such as a word processor that always ejects an extra sheet of paper at the end of a print session. While it is true that paper costs money, it does not cost very much, so this bug causes no real harm. Another type of category 3 bug is really not a bug at all, but a difference between the way the documentation says the program will work and the way it actually works. Category 3 bugs are rarely fixed; not because they shouldn't be, but because there are always too many category 1 and 2 bugs.

If you can organize the bugs you find into these three categories, you can budget your time accordingly.

Source-Code Protection

The maintenance programmer is often in charge of the source code to the program. Although most companies place a copy of the source code of the program in a bank box, it is usually out of date if it is ever needed. Generally, the code in the bank is viewed as the code of last resort. In reality, it is the maintenance programmer who is in charge of protecting the company's source code. What this really means is not losing it!

The most common way that source code is lost is during the bug-fixing process. It works like this: Programmer A "fixes" a bug. In the process and unknown to A, an editing error deletes five lines of code elsewhere in the file. Programmer A compiles the program and checks to see if the bug is fixed. The bug appears to be fixed, so—and here is the important part—programmer A copies the "fixed" source code from the work directory back into the storage directory. Now, five lines of code are missing and the program definitely has a new bug. But before this is discovered, programmer B, whose job it is to back up the hard disk, copies the new, mutilated copy of the program onto the off-site storage disk. Now the old source code is really gone.

There is only one way to prevent the preceding scenario: Never destroy old versions of the program. The real error that occurred, aside from sloppy editing, was not that programmer A copied the altered source code back into the storage directory. The error was that programmer B overwrote the off-site storage media.

Here is how you must handle the source code to an evolving program to prevent its loss. First, create three directories. The first holds the currently released version of the program. This directory is only updated when a new release is made. The second directory contains the latest stable but unreleased version of the program. The third directory contains the evolving code. Next, perform off-site storage backups on a regular basis—for example, weekly—always using a new disk (or tape). Keep on file all previous backups. In this way, the off-site storage is never more than five days out of date if it is needed for a recovery.

PART FIVE

A C Interpreter

Part Five concludes this book by developing an interpreter for C. As you will see, this accomplishes two important things. First, it illustrates several aspects of C programming that are common to most larger projects. Second, it gives insight into the nature and design of the C language. However, as you will see, the creation of a C interpreter is also just plain fun!

Chapter Twenty-Eight

A C Interpreter

L anguage interpreters are fun! And what could be more fun for a C programmer than a C interpreter?

To end this book I wanted a topic that would be of interest to virtually all C programmers and, at the same time, illustrate several features of the C language. I also wanted the topic to be fresh, exciting, and useful. After rejecting many ideas, I finally decided upon the creation of the Little C interpreter. Here's why.

As valuable and important as compilers are, the creation of a compiler can be a difficult and lengthy process. In fact, just the creation of a compiler's run-time library is a large task in itself. By contrast, the creation of a language interpreter is an easier and more manageable task. Also, if it is correctly designed, the operation of an interpreter can be easier to understand than that of a comparable compiler. Beyond ease of development, language interpreters offer an interesting feature not found in compilers—an engine that actually executes the program. Remember, a *compiler* only *translates* your program's source code into a form that the computer can execute. However, an *interpreter* actually *executes* the program. It is this distinction that makes interpreters interesting.

If you are like most C programmers, you use C not only for its power and flexibility but also because the language itself represents an almost intangible, formal beauty that can be appreciated for its own sake. In fact, C is often referred to as "elegant" because of its consistency and purity. Much has been written about the C language from the "outside looking in," but seldom has it been explored from the "inside." Therefore, what better way to end this book than to create a C program that interprets a subset of the C language?

In the course of this chapter an interpreter is developed that can execute a subset of the C language. Not only is the interpreter functional, but it is also well-designed—you can easily enhance it, extend it, and even add features not found in C. If you haven't thought about how C really works, you will be pleasantly surprised to see how straightforward it is. The C language is one of the most theoretically consistent computer languages ever developed. By the time you finish this chapter, you will not only have a C interpreter that you can use and enlarge, but you will also have gained considerable insight into the structure of the C language itself. Of course, if you're like me, you'll find the C interpreter presented here just plain fun to play with!

NOTE: *The source code to the C interpreter presented in this chapter is fairly long, but don't be intimidated by it. If you read through the discussion, you will have no trouble understanding it and following its execution.*

The Practical Importance of Interpreters

Although the Little C interpreter is interesting in and of itself, language interpreters do have some practical importance in computing.

As you probably know, C is generally a *compiled language*. The main reason for this is that C is a language used to produce commercially salable programs. Compiled code is desirable for commercial software products because it protects the privacy of the source code, prevents the user from changing the source code, and allows the programs to make the most efficient use of the host computer, to name a few reasons. Frankly, compilers will always dominate commercial software development, as they should; however, any computer language can be compiled or interpreted. In fact, in recent years a few C interpreters have appeared on the market.

There are two traditional reasons that interpreters have been used: they can be easily made interactive and they can allow substantial debugging aids. However, in recent years, compiler developers have created Integrated Development Environments (IDEs) that provide as much interactivity and debugging capability as any interpreter. Therefore, these two traditional reasons for using an interpreter no longer apply in any real sense. However, interpreters have their uses. For example, most database query languages are interpreted. Also, many industrial robotic control languages are interpreted.

The main reason that language interpreters are interesting is because they are easy to modify, alter, or enhance. This means that if you want to create, experiment with, and control your own language, it is easier to do so with an interpreter rather than a compiler. Interpreters make great language prototyping environments because you can change the way the language works and see the effects very quickly.

Interpreters are (relatively) easy to create, easy to modify, easy to understand, and, perhaps most important, fun to play with. For example, you can rework the interpreter presented in this chapter to execute your program backward—that is, executing from the closing brace of **main( )** and terminating when the opening brace is encountered. (I don't know why anyone would want to do this, but try getting a compiler to execute your code backward!) Or, you can add a special feature to C that you (and perhaps only you) have always wanted. The point is that while compilers absolutely make more sense when doing commercial software development, interpreters let you really have fun with the C language. It is in this spirit that this chapter was developed. I hope you will enjoy reading it as much as I enjoyed writing it!

The Little C Specifications

Despite the fact that ANSI standard C has only 32 keywords, C is a very rich and powerful language. It would take far more than a single chapter to fully describe and implement an interpreter for the entire C language. Instead, the Little C interpreter understands a fairly narrow subset of the language. However, this particular subset includes many of C's most important aspects. What to include in the subset was decided mostly by whether it fit one (or both) of these two criteria:

1. Is the feature fundamentally inseparable from the C language?

2. Is the feature necessary to demonstrate an important aspect of the language?

For example, features such as recursive functions and global and local variables meet both criteria. The Little C interpreter supports all three loop constructs (not because of the first criterion, but because of the second criterion). However, the **switch** statement is not implemented because it is neither necessary (nice, but not necessary) nor does it demonstrate anything that the **if** statement (which is implemented) does not. (Implementation of **switch** is left to you for entertainment!)

For these reasons, I implemented the following features in the Little C interpreter:

- Parameterized functions with local variables
- Recursion
- The **if** statement
- The **do-while**, **while**, and **for** loops
- Integer and character variables
- Global variables
- Integer and character constants
- String constants (limited implementation)
- The **return** statement, both with and without a value
- A limited number of standard library functions
- These operators: +, –, *, /, %, <, >, <=, >=, ==, !=, unary –, and unary +
- Functions returning integers
- Comments

Even though this list may seem short, it takes a relatively large amount of code to implement it. One reason for this is that a substantial "price of admission" must be paid when interpreting a structured language such as C.

One Important Little C Restriction

The source code for the Little C interpreter is quite long—longer, in fact, than I generally like to put in a book. In order to simplify and shorten the source code for Little C, I have imposed one small restriction on the C grammar: the targets of **if**, **while**, **do**, and **for** must be blocks of code surrounded by beginning and ending curly braces. You may not use a single statement. For example, Little C will not correctly interpret code such as this:

```
for(a=0; a<10; a=a+1)
  for(b=0; b<10; b=b+1)
```

```
      for(c=0; c<10; c=c+1)
        puts("hi");

  if(...)
     if(...) statement;
```

Instead, you must write the code like this:

```
for(a=0; a<10; a=a+1) {
  for(b=0; b<10; b=b+1) {
    for(c=0; c<10; c=c+1) {
      puts("hi");
    }
  }
}

if(...) {
  if(...) {
    statement;
  }
}
```

This restriction makes it easier for the interpreter to find the end of the code that forms the target to one of these program control statements. However, since the objects of the program control statements are often blocks of code anyway, this restriction does not seem too harsh. (With a little effort, you can remove this restriction, if you like.)

Interpreting a Structured Language

As you know, C is structured: it allows stand-alone subroutines with local variables. It also supports recursion. What you might find interesting is that, in some areas, it is easier to write a compiler for a structured language than it is to write an interpreter for it. For example, when a compiler generates code to call a function, it simply pushes the calling arguments onto the system stack and executes a machine language CALL to the function. To return, the function puts the return value in the accumulator of the CPU, clears the stack, and executes a machine language RET. However, when an interpreter must "call" a function, it manually has to stop what it is doing, save its current state, find the location of the function, execute the function, save the return value, and return to the original point, restoring the old environment. (You will see an example of this in the interpreter that follows.) In essence, the interpreter must emulate the equivalent of a machine language CALL and RETURN. Also, while support for recursion is easy in a compiled language, it requires some effort in an interpreted one.

In my book *The Art of C* (Berkeley, CA: Osborne/McGraw-Hill, 1991), I introduced the subject of language interpreters by developing a small BASIC interpreter. In that book, I stated that it is easier to interpret a language such as standard BASIC than C because BASIC was designed to be interpreted. What makes BASIC easy to interpret is that it is not structured. All variables are global and there are no stand-alone subroutines. I still stand by this statement; however, once you have created the support for functions, local variables, and recursion, the C language is actually easier to interpret than BASIC. This is because a language such as BASIC is full of exceptions at the theoretical level. For example, in BASIC the equal sign is an assignment operator in an assignment statement, but an equality operator in a relational statement. C has few of these inconsistencies.

An Informal Theory of C

Before we can begin to develop the C interpreter, it is necessary to understand how the C language is structured. If you have ever seen a formal specification for the C language (such as that found in the ANSI C standard specification), you know that it is quite long and filled with rather cryptic statements. Don't worry—we won't need to deal this formally with the C language to design our interpreter because most of the C language is so straightforward. While the formal specification of a language is necessary for the creation of a commercial compiler, it is not needed for the creation of the Little C interpreter. (Frankly, there isn't space in this chapter to explain how to understand the C formal syntax definition: it could fill a book!)

This chapter is designed to be understood by the widest variety of readers. It is not intended to be a formal introduction to the theory of structured languages in general or C in particular. As such, it intentionally simplifies a few concepts. However, as you will see, the creation of an interpreter for a subset of C does not require formal training in language theory.

Although you do not need to be a language expert to implement and understand the Little C interpreter developed in this chapter, you will still need a basic understanding of how the C language is defined. For our purposes, the discussion that follows is sufficient. Those of you who wish a more formal discussion may refer to the ANSI standard for C. Also, for an excellent theoretical introduction to languages, see *The Theory of Parsing, Translation, and Compiling* by Aho and Ullman (Englewood Cliffs, NJ: Prentice-Hall).

To begin, all C programs consist of a collection of one or more functions, plus global variables (if any exist). A *function* is composed of a function name, its parameter list, and the block of code associated with the function. A *block* begins with a { , is followed by one or more statements, and ends with a }. In C, a statement either begins with a C keyword, such as **if**, or it is an expression. (We will see what constitutes an expression in the next section.) Summarizing, we can write the following *transformations* (sometimes called *production rules*):

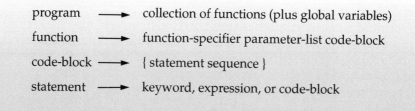

program ⟶ collection of functions (plus global variables)

function ⟶ function-specifier parameter-list code-block

code-block ⟶ { statement sequence }

statement ⟶ keyword, expression, or code-block

All C programs begin with a call to **main( )** and end when either the last } or a **return** has been encountered in **main( )**—assuming that **exit( )** or **abort( )** has not been called elsewhere. Any other functions contained in the program must either be directly or indirectly called by **main( )**; hence, to execute a C program, simply begin at the start of the **main( )** function and stop when **main( )** ends. This is precisely what Little C does.

C Expressions

C expands the role of expressions relative to many other computer languages. In C, a statement is either a C keyword statement, such as **while** or **switch**, or it is an expression. For the sake of discussion, let's categorize all statements that begin with C keywords as *keyword statements.* Any statement in C that is not a keyword statement is, by definition, an *expression.* Therefore, in C the following statements are all expressions:

```
count = 100;                    /* line 1 */
sample = i / 22 * (c-10);       /* line 2 */
printf("This is an expression."); /* line 3 */
```

Let's look more closely at each of these expression statements. In C, the equal sign is an *assignment operator.* C does not treat the assignment operation the way a language such as BASIC would, for example. In BASIC, the value produced by the right side of the equal sign is assigned to the variable on the left. But, and this is important, in BASIC, the entire statement does not have a value. In C, the equal sign is an assignment operator and the value produced by the assignment operation is equal to that produced by the right side of the expression. Therefore, an assignment statement is actually an *assignment expression* in C; because it is an expression, it has a value. This is why it is legal to write expressions such as the following:

```
a = b = c = 100;
printf("%d", a=4+5);
```

The reason these work in C is that an assignment is an operation that produces a value.
Line 2 shows a more complex assignment.

In line 3, **printf( )** is called to output a string. In C, all non-**void** functions return
values, whether explicitly specified or not. Hence, a non-**void** function call is an
expression that returns a value—whether the value is actually assigned to something
or not. Calling a **void** function also constitutes an expression. It is just that the
outcome of the expression is **void**.

Evaluating Expressions

Before we can develop code that will correctly evaluate C expressions, you need to
understand in more formal terms how expressions are defined. In virtually all
computer languages, expressions are defined recursively using a set of production
rules. The Little C interpreter supports the following operations: +, –, *, /, %, =, the
relational operators (<, ==, >, and so forth), and parentheses. Therefore, we can use
these production rules to define Little C expressions:

expression ⟶ [assignment] [rvalue]

assignment ⟶ lvalue = rvalue

lvalue ⟶ variable

rvalue ⟶ part [rel-op part]

part ⟶ term [+term] [–term]

term ⟶ factor [*factor] [/factor] [%factor]

factor ⟶ [+ or –] atom

atom ⟶ variable, constant, function, or (expression)

Here, *rel-op* refers to any of C's relational operators. The terms *lvalue* and *rvalue* refer to
objects that can occur on the left side and right side of an assignment statement,
respectively. One thing that you should be aware of is that the precedence of the
operators is built into the production rules. The higher the precedence, the further
down the list the operator will be.

To see how these rules work let us evaluate this C expression:

```
count = 10 - 5 * 3;
```

First, we apply rule 1, which dissects the expression into these three parts:

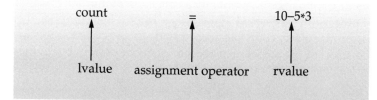

Since there are no relational operators in the "rvalue" part of the subexpression, the term production rule is invoked.

Of course, the second term is composed of the following two factors: 5 and 3. These two factors are constants and represent the lowest level of the production rules. Next, we must begin moving back up the rules to compute the value of the expression. First, we multiply 5*3, which yields 15. Next, we subtract that value from 10, yielding –5. Finally, this value is assigned to **count** and is also the value of the entire expression.

The first thing we need to do to create the Little C interpreter is to construct the computerized equivalent of the expression evaluation we just performed in our minds.

The Expression Parser

The piece of code that reads and analyzes expressions is called an *expression parser.* Without a doubt, the expression parser is the single most important subsystem needed by the Little C interpreter. Because C defines expressions more broadly than do many other languages, a substantial amount of the code that constitutes a C program is actually executed by the expression parser.

There are several different ways to design an expression parser for C. Many commercial compilers use a *table-driven parser,* which is usually created by a parser-generator program. While table-driven parsers are generally faster than other methods, they are very hard to create by hand. For the Little C interpreter developed here, we will use a *recursive-descent parser,* which implements in logic the production rules discussed in the previous section.

A recursive-descent parser is essentially a collection of mutually recursive functions that process an expression. If the parser is used in a compiler, then it is used to generate the proper object code that corresponds to the source code. However, in an interpreter, the object of the parser is to evaluate a given expression. In this section, the Little C parser is developed.

> *NOTE: Expression parsing is introduced in Chapter 22. The parser used in this chapter expands upon that simple foundation.*

Reducing the Source Code to Its Components

Fundamental to all interpreters (and compilers, for that matter) is a special function that reads the source code and returns the next logical symbol from it. For historical reasons, these logical symbols are generally referred to as *tokens.* Computer languages in general, and C in particular, define programs in terms of tokens. You can think of a token as an indivisible program unit. For example, the equality operator == is a token. The two equal signs cannot be separated without changing the meaning. In the same vein, **if** is a token. Neither *i* nor *f* by itself has any meaning to C.

In the ANSI C standard, tokens are defined as belonging to one of these groups:

keywords	identifiers	constants
strings	operators	punctuation

The *keywords* are those tokens that make up the C language, such as **while**. *Identifiers* are the names of variables, functions, and user-types (not implemented by Little C). Constants and strings are self-explanatory, as are operators. Punctuation includes several items, such as semicolons, commas, braces, and parentheses. (Some of these are also operators, depending upon their use.) Given the statement

```
for(x=0; x<10; x=x+1) printf("hello %d", x);
```

the following tokens are produced, reading left to right:

Token	Category
for	keyword
(	punctuation
x	identifier
=	operator
0	constant
;	punctuation
x	identifier
<	operator
10	constant
;	punctuation
x	identifier
=	operator
x	identifier
+	operator
1	constant
)	punctuation
printf	identifier
(	punctuation
"hello %d"	string
,	punctuation
x	identifier
)	punctuation
;	punctuation

However, in order to make the interpretation of C easier, Little C categorizes tokens as shown here:

Token Type	Includes
delimiter	punctuation and operators
keyword	keywords
string	quoted strings
identifier	variable and function names
number	numeric constant
block	{ or }

The function that returns tokens from the source code for the Little C interpreter is called **get_token( )**, and it is shown here:

```
/* Get a token. */
get_token(void)
{
  register char *temp;

  token_type = 0; tok = 0;

  temp = token;
  *temp = '\0';

  /* skip over white space */
  while(iswhite(*prog) && *prog) ++prog;

  if(*prog=='\r') {
    ++prog;
    ++prog;
    /* skip over white space */
    while(iswhite(*prog) && *prog) ++prog;
  }

  if(*prog=='\0') { /* end of file */
    *token = '\0';
    tok = FINISHED;
    return(token_type=DELIMITER);
  }

  if(strchr("{}", *prog)) { /* block delimiters */
    *temp = *prog;
    temp++;
    *temp = '\0';
    prog++;
    return (token_type = BLOCK);
  }

  /* look for comments */
  if(*prog=='/')
    if(*(prog+1)=='*') { /* is a comment */
      prog += 2;
      do { /* find end of comment */
        while(*prog!='*') prog++;
        prog++;
      } while (*prog!='/');
```

```
      prog++;
    }

if(strchr("!<>=", *prog)) { /* is or might be
                               a relation operator */
  switch(*prog) {
    case '=': if(*(prog+1)=='=') {
        prog++; prog++;
        *temp = EQ;
        temp++; *temp = EQ; temp++;
        *temp = '\0';
      }
      break;
    case '!': if(*(prog+1)=='=') {
        prog++; prog++;
        *temp = NE;
        temp++; *temp = NE; temp++;
        *temp = '\0';
      }
      break;
    case '<': if(*(prog+1)=='=') {
        prog++; prog++;
        *temp = LE; temp++; *temp = LE;
      }
      else {
        prog++;
        *temp = LT;
      }
      temp++;
      *temp = '\0';
      break;
    case '>': if(*(prog+1)=='=') {
        prog++; prog++;
        *temp = GE; temp++; *temp = GE;
      }
      else {
        prog++;
        *temp = GT;
      }
      temp++;
      *temp = '\0';
      break;
```

```c
  }
  if(*token) return(token_type = DELIMITER);
}

if(strchr("+-*^/%=;(),'", *prog)){ /* delimiter */
  *temp = *prog;
  prog++; /* advance to next position */
  temp++;
  *temp = '\0';
  return (token_type=DELIMITER);
}

if(*prog=='"') { /* quoted string */
  prog++;
  while(*prog!='"'&& *prog!='\r') *temp++ = *prog++;
  if(*prog=='\r') sntx_err(SYNTAX);
  prog++; *temp = '\0';
  return(token_type=STRING);
}

if(isdigit(*prog)) { /* number */
  while(!isdelim(*prog)) *temp++ = *prog++;
  *temp = '\0';
  return(token_type = NUMBER);
}

if(isalpha(*prog)) { /* var or command */
  while(!isdelim(*prog)) *temp++ = *prog++;
  token_type=TEMP;
}

*temp = '\0';

/* see if a string is a command or a variable */
if(token_type==TEMP) {
  tok = look_up(token); /* convert to internal rep */
  if(tok) token_type = KEYWORD; /* is a keyword */
  else token_type = IDENTIFIER;
}
return token_type;
}
```

The **get_token( )** function uses the following global data and enumeration types:

```
char *prog;  /* points to current location in source code */
extern char *p_buf;  /* points to start of program buffer */

char token[80]; /* holds string representation of token */
char token_type; /* contains the type of token */
char tok; /* holds the internal representation of token if
              it is a keyword */

enum tok_types {DELIMITER, IDENTIFIER, NUMBER, KEYWORD, TEMP,
                STRING, BLOCK};

enum double_ops {LT=1, LE, GT, GE, EQ, NE};

/* These are the constants used to call sntx_err() when
   a syntax error occurs. Add more if you like.
   NOTE: SYNTAX is a generic error message used when
   nothing else seems appropriate.
 */
enum error_msg
     {SYNTAX, UNBAL_PARENS, NO_EXP, EQUALS_EXPECTED,
      NOT_VAR, PARAM_ERR, SEMI_EXPECTED,
      UNBAL_BRACES, FUNC_UNDEF, TYPE_EXPECTED,
      NEST_FUNC, RET_NOCALL, PAREN_EXPECTED,
      WHILE_EXPECTED, QUOTE_EXPECTED, NOT_TEMP,
      TOO_MANY_LVARS};
```

The current location in the source code is pointed to by **prog**. The **p_buf** pointer is unchanged by the interpreter and always points to the start of the program being interpreted. The **get_token( )** function begins by skipping over all white space, including carriage returns and line feeds. Since no C token (except for a quoted string or character constant) contains a space, spaces must be bypassed. The **get_token( )** function also skips over comments. Next, the string representation of each token is placed into **token**, its type (as defined by the **tok_types** enumeration) is put into **token_type**, and, if the token is a keyword, its internal representation is assigned to **tok** via the **look_up( )** function (shown in the full parser listing that follows). The reason for the internal representation of keywords will be discussed later. As you can see by looking at **get_token( )**, it converts C's two-character relational operators into their corresponding enumeration value. Although not technically necessary, this step makes the parser easier to implement. Finally, if the parser encounters a syntax error, it calls the function **sntx_err( )** with an enumerated value that corresponds to the type of error found. The **sntx_err( )** function is also called by other routines in the interpreter whenever an error occurs. The **sntx_err( )** function is shown here:

```c
/* Display an error message. */
void sntx_err(int error)
{
  char *p, *temp;
  register int i;
  int linecount = 0;

  static char *e[]= {
    "syntax error",
    "unbalanced parentheses",
    "no expression present",
    "equals sign expected",
    "not a variable",
    "parameter error",
    "semicolon expected",
    "unbalanced braces",
    "function undefined",
    "type specifier expected",
    "too many nested function calls",
    "return without call",
    "parentheses expected",
    "while expected",
    "closing quote expected",
    "not a string",
    "too many local variables"
  };
  printf("%s", e[error]);
  p = p_buf;
  while(p != prog) {  /* find line number of error */
    p++;
    if(*p == '\r') {
      linecount++;
    }
  }
  printf(" in line %d\n", linecount);

  temp = p;  /* display line with error */
  for(i=0; i<20 && p>p_buf && *p!='\n'; i++, p--);
  for(i=0; i<30 && p<=temp; i++, p++) printf("%c", *p);

  longjmp(e_buf, 1); /* return to safe point */
}
```

Notice that **sntx_err( )** also displays the line number in which the error was detected (which may be one line after the error actually occurred) and displays the line in which it occurred. Further, notice that **sntx_err( )** ends with a call to **longjmp( )**. Because syntax errors are frequently encountered in deeply nested or recursive routines, the easiest way to handle an error is to simply jump to a safe place. Although it is possible to set a global error flag and interrogate the flag at various points in each routine, this adds unnecessary overhead.

The Little C Recursive-Descent Parser

The entire code for the Little C recursive-descent parser is shown here, along with some necessary support functions, global data, and data types. This code, as shown, is designed to go into its own file. For the sake of discussion, call this file PARSER.C. (Because of its size, the Little C interpreter is spread among three separate files.) Enter this file now.

```
/* Recursive descent parser for integer expressions
   which may include variables and function calls. */
#include <setjmp.h>
#include <math.h>
#include <ctype.h>
#include <stdlib.h>
#include <string.h>
#include <stdio.h>

#define NUM_FUNC        100
#define NUM_GLOBAL_VARS 100
#define NUM_LOCAL_VARS  200
#define ID_LEN          31
#define FUNC_CALLS      31
#define PROG_SIZE       10000
#define FOR_NEST        31

enum tok_types {DELIMITER, IDENTIFIER, NUMBER, KEYWORD, TEMP,
                STRING, BLOCK};

enum tokens {ARG, CHAR, INT, IF, ELSE, FOR, DO, WHILE, SWITCH,
             RETURN, EOL, FINISHED, END};

enum double_ops {LT=1, LE, GT, GE, EQ, NE};

/* These are the constants used to call sntx_err() when
```

```
   a syntax error occurs. Add more if you like.
   NOTE: SYNTAX is a generic error message used when
   nothing else seems appropriate.
*/
enum error_msg
     {SYNTAX, UNBAL_PARENS, NO_EXP, EQUALS_EXPECTED,
      NOT_VAR, PARAM_ERR, SEMI_EXPECTED,
      UNBAL_BRACES, FUNC_UNDEF, TYPE_EXPECTED,
      NEST_FUNC, RET_NOCALL, PAREN_EXPECTED,
      WHILE_EXPECTED, QUOTE_EXPECTED, NOT_TEMP,
      TOO_MANY_LVARS};

extern char *prog;  /* current location in source code */
extern char *p_buf;  /* points to start of program buffer */
extern jmp_buf e_buf; /* hold environment for longjmp() */

/* An array of these structures will hold the info
   associated with global variables.
*/
extern struct var_type {
  char var_name[32];
  enum variable_type var_type;
  int value;
}  global_vars[NUM_GLOBAL_VARS];

/*  This is the function call stack. */
extern struct func_type {
  char func_name[32];
  char *loc;  /* location of function entry point in file */
} func_stack[NUM_FUNC];

/* Keyword table */
extern struct commands {
  char command[20];
  char tok;
} table[];

/* "Standard library" functions are declared here so
   they can be put into the internal function table that
   follows.
 */
```

```c
int call_getche(void), call_putch(void);
int call_puts(void), print(void), getnum(void);

struct intern_func_type {
  char *f_name; /* function name */
  int (* p)();  /* pointer to the function */
} intern_func[] = {
  "getche", call_getche,
  "putch", call_putch,
  "puts", call_puts,
  "print", print,
  "getnum", getnum,
  "", 0  /* null terminate the list */
};

extern char token[80]; /* string representation of token */
extern char token_type; /* contains type of token */
extern char tok; /* internal representation of token */

extern int ret_value; /* function return value */

void eval_exp(int *value), eval_exp1(int *value);
void eval_exp2(int *value);
void eval_exp3(int *value), eval_exp4(int *value);
void eval_exp5(int *value), atom(int *value);
void eval_exp0(int *value);
void sntx_err(int error), putback(void);
void assign_var(char *var_name, int value);
int isdelim(char c), look_up(char *s), iswhite(char c);
int find_var(char *s), get_token(void);
int internal_func(char *s);
int is_var(char *s);
char *find_func(char *name);
void call(void);

/* Entry point into parser. */
void eval_exp(int *value)
{
  get_token();
  if(!*token) {
    sntx_err(NO_EXP);
```

```
      return;
  }
  if(*token==';') {
    *value = 0; /* empty expression */
    return;
  }
  eval_exp0(value);
  putback(); /* return last token read to input stream */
}

/* Process an assignment expression */
void eval_exp0(int *value)
{
  char temp[ID_LEN];   /* holds name of var receiving
                          the assignment */
  register int temp_tok;

  if(token_type==IDENTIFIER) {
    if(is_var(token)) {  /* if a var, see if assignment */
      strcpy(temp, token);
      temp_tok = token_type;
      get_token();
      if(*token=='=') {   /* is an assignment */
        get_token();
        eval_exp0(value);  /* get value to assign */
        assign_var(temp, *value);  /* assign the value */
        return;
      }
      else {  /* not an assignment */
        putback();  /* restore original token */
        strcpy(token, temp);
        token_type = temp_tok;
      }
    }
  }
  eval_exp1(value);
}

/* This array is used by eval_exp1(). Because
   some compilers cannot initialize an array within a
   function it is defined as a global variable.
```

```
*/
char relops[7] = {
  LT, LE, GT, GE, EQ, NE, 0
};

/* Process relational operators. */
void eval_exp1(int *value)
{
  int partial_value;
  register char op;

  eval_exp2(value);
  op = *token;
  if(strchr(relops, op)) {
    get_token();
    eval_exp2(&partial_value);
    switch(op) {  /* perform the relational operation */
      case LT:
        *value = *value < partial_value;
        break;
      case LE:
        *value = *value <= partial_value;
        break;
      case GT:
        *value = *value > partial_value;
        break;
      case GE:
        *value = *value >= partial_value;
        break;
      case EQ:
        *value = *value == partial_value;
        break;
      case NE:
        *value = *value != partial_value;
        break;
    }
  }
}

/*  Add or subtract two terms. */
void eval_exp2(int *value)
{
```

```
  register char  op;
  int partial_value;

  eval_exp3(value);
  while((op = *token) == '+' || op == '-') {
    get_token();
    eval_exp3(&partial_value);
    switch(op) {   /* add or subtract */
      case '-':
        *value = *value - partial_value;
        break;
      case '+':
        *value = *value + partial_value;
        break;
    }
  }
}

/* Multiply or divide two factors. */
void eval_exp3(int *value)
{
  register char  op;
  int partial_value, t;

  eval_exp4(value);
  while((op = *token) == '*' || op == '/' || op == '%') {
    get_token();
    eval_exp4(&partial_value);
    switch(op) { /* mul, div, or modulus */
      case '*':
        *value = *value * partial_value;
        break;
      case '/':
        *value = (*value) / partial_value;
        break;
      case '%':
        t = (*value) / partial_value;
        *value = *value-(t * partial_value);
        break;
    }
  }
}
```

```
}

/* Is a unary + or -. */
void eval_exp4(int *value)
{
  register char  op;

  op = '\0';
  if(*token=='+' || *token=='-') {
    op = *token;
    get_token();
  }
  eval_exp5(value);
  if(op)
    if(op=='-') *value = -(*value);
}

/* Process parenthesized expression. */
void eval_exp5(int *value)
{
  if((*token == '(')) {
    get_token();
    eval_exp0(value);    /* get subexpression */
    if(*token != ')') sntx_err(PAREN_EXPECTED);
    get_token();
  }
  else
    atom(value);
}

/* Find value of number, variable, or function. */
void atom(int *value)
{
  int i;

  switch(token_type) {
  case IDENTIFIER:
    i = internal_func(token);
    if(i!= -1) {  /* call "standard library" function */
      *value = (*intern_func[i].p)();
    }
```

```
    else
    if(find_func(token)){  /* call user-defined function */
      call();
      *value = ret_value;
    }
    else  *value = find_var(token);  /* get var's value */
    get_token();
    return;
  case NUMBER: /* is numeric constant */
    *value = atoi(token);
    get_token();
    return;
  case DELIMITER: /* see if character constant */
    if(*token=='\'') {
      *value = *prog;
      prog++;
      if(*prog!='\'') sntx_err(QUOTE_EXPECTED);
      prog++;
      get_token();
    }
    return;
  default:
    if(*token==')') return; /* process empty expression */
    else sntx_err(SYNTAX); /* syntax error */
  }
}

/* Display an error message. */
void sntx_err(int error)
{
  char *p, *temp;
  int linecount = 0;
  register int i;

  static char *e[]= {
    "syntax error",
    "unbalanced parentheses",
    "no expression present",
    "equals sign expected",
    "not a variable",
    "parameter error",
```

```
      "semicolon expected",
      "unbalanced braces",
      "function undefined",
      "type specifier expected",
      "too many nested function calls",
      "return without call",
      "parentheses expected",
      "while expected",
      "closing quote expected",
      "not a string",
      "too many local variables"
  };
  printf("%s", e[error]);
  p = p_buf;
  while(p != prog) {  /* find line number of error */
    p++;
    if(*p == '\r') {
      linecount++;
    }
  }
  printf(" in line %d\n", linecount);

  temp = p;
  for(i=0; i<20 && p>p_buf && *p!='\n'; i++, p--);
  for(i=0; i<30 && p<=temp; i++, p++) printf("%c", *p);

  longjmp(e_buf, 1); /* return to safe point */
}

/* Get a token. */
get_token(void)
{

  register char *temp;

  token_type = 0; tok = 0;

  temp = token;
  *temp = '\0';

 /* skip over white space */
```

```
    while(iswhite(*prog) && *prog) ++prog;

if(*prog=='\r') {
  ++prog;
  ++prog;
  /* skip over white space */
  while(iswhite(*prog) && *prog) ++prog;
}

if(*prog=='\0') { /* end of file */
  *token = '\0';
  tok = FINISHED;
  return(token_type=DELIMITER);
}

if(strchr("{}", *prog)) { /* block delimiters */
  *temp = *prog;
  temp++;
  *temp = '\0';
  prog++;
  return (token_type = BLOCK);
}

/* look for comments */
if(*prog=='/')
  if(*(prog+1)=='*') { /* is a comment */
    prog += 2;
    do { /* find end of comment */
      while(*prog!='*') prog++;
      prog++;
    } while (*prog!='/');
    prog++;
  }

if(strchr("!<>=", *prog)) { /* is or might be
                              a relation operator */
  switch(*prog) {
    case '=': if(*(prog+1)=='=') {
        prog++; prog++;
        *temp = EQ;
        temp++; *temp = EQ; temp++;
```

```
            *temp = '\0';
        }
       break;
     case '!': if(*(prog+1)=='=') {
          prog++; prog++;
          *temp = NE;
          temp++; *temp = NE; temp++;
          *temp = '\0';
        }
       break;
     case '<': if(*(prog+1)=='=') {
          prog++; prog++;
          *temp = LE; temp++; *temp = LE;
        }
       else {
          prog++;
          *temp = LT;
        }
       temp++;
       *temp = '\0';
       break;
     case '>': if(*(prog+1)=='=') {
          prog++; prog++;
          *temp = GE; temp++; *temp = GE;
        }
       else {
          prog++;
          *temp = GT;
        }
       temp++;
       *temp = '\0';
       break;
   }
   if(*token) return(token_type = DELIMITER);
}

if(strchr("+-*^/%=;(),'", *prog)){ /* delimiter */
  *temp = *prog;
  prog++; /* advance to next position */
  temp++;
  *temp = '\0';
```

```c
    return (token_type=DELIMITER);
  }

  if(*prog=='"') { /* quoted string */
    prog++;
    while(*prog!='"'&& *prog!='\r') *temp++ = *prog++;
    if(*prog=='\r') sntx_err(SYNTAX);
    prog++; *temp = '\0';
    return(token_type=STRING);
  }

  if(isdigit(*prog)) { /* number */
    while(!isdelim(*prog)) *temp++ = *prog++;
    *temp = '\0';
    return(token_type = NUMBER);
  }

  if(isalpha(*prog)) { /* var or command */
    while(!isdelim(*prog)) *temp++ = *prog++;
    token_type=TEMP;
  }

  *temp = '\0';

  /* see if a string is a command or a variable */
  if(token_type==TEMP) {
    tok = look_up(token); /* convert to internal rep */
    if(tok) token_type = KEYWORD; /* is a keyword */
    else token_type = IDENTIFIER;
  }
  return token_type;
}

/* Return a token to input stream. */
void putback(void)
{
  char *t;

  t = token;
  for(; *t; t++) prog--;
}
```

```c
/* Look up a token's internal representation in the
   token table.
*/
look_up(char *s)
{
  register int i;
  char *p;

  /* convert to lowercase */
  p = s;
  while(*p){ *p = tolower(*p); p++; }

  /* see if token is in table */
  for(i=0; *table[i].command; i++)
      if(!strcmp(table[i].command, s)) return table[i].tok;
  return 0; /* unknown command */
}

/* Return index of internal library function or -1 if
   not found.
*/
internal_func(char *s)
{
  int i;

  for(i=0; intern_func[i].f_name[0]; i++) {
    if(!strcmp(intern_func[i].f_name, s))  return i;
  }
  return -1;
}

/* Return true if c is a delimiter. */
isdelim(char c)
{
  if(strchr(" !;,+-<>'/*%^=()", c) || c==9 ||
     c=='\r' || c==0) return 1;
  return 0;
}

/* Return 1 if c is space or tab. */
iswhite(char c)
```

```
{
  if(c==' ' || c=='\t') return 1;
  else return 0;
}
```

The functions that begin with **eval_exp** and the **atom( )** function implement the production rules for Little C expressions. To verify this, you might want to execute the parser mentally, using a simple expression.

The **atom( )** function finds the value of an integer constant or variable, a function, or a character constant. There are two kinds of functions that may be present in the source code: user-defined or library. If a user-defined function is encountered, its code is executed by the interpreter in order to determine its return value. (The calling of a function will be discussed in the next section.) However, if the function is a library function, first its address is looked up by the **internal_func( )** function, and then it is accessed via its interface function. The library functions and the addresses of their interface functions are held in the **intern_func** array shown here:

```
/* "Standard library" functions are declared here so
   they can be put into the internal function table that
   follows.
*/
int call_getche(void), call_putch(void);
int call_puts(void), print(void), getnum(void);

struct intern_func_type {
  char *f_name; /* function name */
  int (* p)();  /* pointer to the function */
} intern_func[] = {
  "getche", call_getche,
  "putch", call_putch,
  "puts", call_puts,
  "print", print,
  "getnum", getnum,
  "", 0  /* null terminate the list */
};
```

As you can see, Little C knows only a few library functions, but you will soon see how easy it is to add any others that you might need. (The actual interface functions are contained in a separate file, which is discussed in the section "The Little C Library Functions.")

One final point about the routines in the expression parser file: To correctly parse the C language occasionally requires what is called *one-token lookahead*. For example, in order for Little C to know that **count** is a function and not a variable, it must read both **count** and the parenthesis that follows it, as shown here.

```
alpha = count();
```

However, if the statement had read

```
alpha = count * 10;
```

then the second token (the *) would need to be returned to the input stream. For this reason, the expression parser file includes the **putback( )** function, which returns the last token to the input stream.

There may be functions in the expression parser file that you don't fully understand at this time, but their operation will become clear as you learn more about Little C.

The Little C Interpreter

In this section, the heart of the Little C interpreter is developed. Before jumping right into the actual code of the interpreter, it will help if you understand how an interpreter operates. In many ways, the code of the interpreter is easier to understand than the expression parser because, conceptually, the act of interpreting a C program can be summed up by the following algorithm:

```
while(tokens_present) {
   get_next_token;
   take_appropriate_action;
}
```

This algorithm may seem unbelievably simple when compared to the expression parser, but this really is exactly what all interpreters do! One thing to keep in mind is that the "take appropriate action" step may also involve reading additional tokens from the input stream. To understand how the algorithm actually works, let's manually interpret the following C code fragment:

```
int a;

a = 10;

if(a<100)  printf("%d", a);
```

Following the algorithm, read the first token, which is **int**. The appropriate action given this token is to read the next token in order to find out what the variable being declared is called (in this case **a**) and then to store it. The next token is the semicolon that ends the line. The appropriate action here is to ignore it. Next, go back and get another token. This token is **a**. Since this line does not begin with a keyword, it must begin a C expression. Hence, the appropriate action is to evaluate the expression using the parser. This process eats up all the tokens in that line. Finally, we read the **if** token. This signals the beginning of an **if** statement. The appropriate action is to process the **if**. The sort of process described here takes place for any C program until the last token has been read. With this basic algorithm in mind, let's begin building the interpreter.

The Interpreter Prescan

Before the interpreter can actually start executing a program, a few clerical tasks must be performed. One characteristic of languages that were designed with interpretation rather than compilation in mind is that they begin execution at the top of the source code and end when the end of the source code is reached. This is the way traditional BASIC works. However, C (or any other structured language) does not lend itself to this approach for three main reasons. First, all C programs begin execution at the **main( )** function. There is no requirement that **main( )** be the first function in the program; therefore, it is necessary that the location of the **main( )** function within the program's source code be known so that execution can begin at that point. (Remember also that global variables may precede **main( )**, so even if it is the first function, it is not necessarily the first line of code.) Some method must be devised to allow execution to begin at the right spot.

Another problem that must be overcome is that all global variables must be known and accounted for before **main( )** begins executing. Global variable declaration statements are never executed by the interpreter, because they exist outside of all functions. (Remember: In C all executable code exists *inside* functions, so there is no reason for the Little C interpreter to go outside a function once execution has begun.)

Finally, in the interest of speed of execution, it is important (although not technically necessary) that the location of each function defined in the program be known so that a call to a function can be as fast as possible. If this step is not performed, a lengthy sequential search of the source code will be needed to find the entry point to a function each time it is called.

The solution to these problems is the *interpreter prescan*. Prescanners (or preprocessors, as they are sometimes called, although they have little resemblance to a C compiler's preprocessor) are used by all commercial interpreters regardless of what language they are interpreting. A prescanner reads the source code to the program before it is executed and performs whatever tasks can be done prior to execution. In our Little C interpreter, it performs two important jobs: first, it finds and records the location of all user-defined functions, including **main( )**; second, it finds and allocates space for all global variables. In the Little C interpreter, the function that performs the prescan is, strangely enough, called **prescan( )**. It is shown here:

```
/* Find the location of all functions in the program and
   store all global variables. */
void prescan(void)
{
  char *p;
  char temp[32];
  int brace = 0;   /* When 0, this var tells us that
                      current source position is outside
                      of any function. */


  p = prog;
  func_index = 0;
  do {
    while(brace) {  /* bypass code inside functions */
      get_token();
      if(*token=='{') brace++;
      if(*token=='}') brace--;
    }

    get_token();

    if(tok==CHAR || tok==INT) { /* is global var */
      putback();
      decl_global();
    }
    else if(token_type==IDENTIFIER) {
      strcpy(temp, token);
      get_token();
      if(*token=='(') {   /* must be a function */
        func_table[func_index].loc = prog;
        strcpy(func_table[func_index].func_name, temp);
        func_index++;
        while(*prog!=')') prog++;
        prog++;
        /* now prog points to opening curly
           brace of function */
      }
      else putback();
    }
    else if(*token=='{') brace++;
  } while(tok!=FINISHED);
  prog = p;
}
```

The **prescan( )** function works like this. Each time an opening curly brace is encountered, **brace** is incremented. Whenever a closing curly brace is read, **brace** is decremented. Therefore, whenever **brace** is greater than zero, the current token is being read from within a function. However, if **brace** equals zero when a variable is found, then the prescanner knows that it must be a global variable. By the same method, if a function name is encountered when **brace** equals zero, then it must be that function's definition.

Global variables are stored in a global variable table called **global_vars** by **decl_global( )**, shown here:

```c
/* An array of these structures will hold the info
   associated with global variables.
*/
struct var_type {
  char var_name[ID_LEN];
  int var_type;
  int value;
} global_vars[NUM_GLOBAL_VARS];

int gvar_index; /* index into global variable table */

/* Declare a global variable. */
void decl_global(void)
{
  get_token();  /* get type */
  global_vars[gvar_index].var_type = tok;
  global_vars[gvar_index].value = 0;  /* init to 0 */

  do { /* process comma-separated list */
    get_token();  /* get name */
    strcpy(global_vars[gvar_index].var_name, token);
    get_token();
    gvar_index++;
  } while(*token==',');
  if(*token!=';') sntx_err(SEMI_EXPECTED);
}
```

The integer **gvar_index** will hold the location of the next free element in the array.

The location of each user-defined function is put into the **func_table** array, shown here:

```
struct func_type {
  char func_name[ID_LEN];
  char *loc;  /* location of entry point in file */
} func_table[NUM_FUNC];

int func_index; /* index into function table */
```

The **func_index** variable will hold the index of the next free location in the table.

The main( ) Function

The **main( )** function to the Little C interpreter, shown here, loads the source code, initializes the global variables, calls **prescan( )**, "primes" the interpreter for the call to **main( )**, and then executes **call( )**, which begins execution of the program. The operation of the **call( )** function will be discussed shortly.

```
main(int argc, char *argv[])
{
  if(argc!=2) {
    printf("Usage: littlec <filename>\n");
    exit(1);
  }

  /* allocate memory for the program */
  if((p_buf=(char *) malloc(PROG_SIZE))==NULL) {
    printf("Allocation Failure");
    exit(1);
  }

  /* load the program to execute */
  if(!load_program(p_buf, argv[1])) exit(1);

  if(setjmp(e_buf)) exit(1); /* initialize long jump buffer */

  /* set program pointer to start of program buffer */
  prog = p_buf;
  prescan(); /* find the location of all functions
                and global variables in the program */

  gvar_index = 0;  /* initialize global variable index */
  lvartos = 0;     /* initialize local variable stack index */
  functos = 0;     /* initialize the CALL stack index */
```

```
/* setup call to main() */
prog = find_func("main");   /* find program starting point */
prog--; /* back up to opening ( */
strcpy(token, "main");
call();   /* start interpreting */
return 0;
}
```

The interp_block( ) Function

The **interp_block( )** function is the heart of the interpreter. It is the function that decides what action to take based upon the next token in the input stream. The function is designed to interpret one block of code and then return. If the "block" consists of a single statement, then that statement is interpreted and the function returns. By default, **interp_block( )** interprets one statement and returns. However, if an opening curly brace is read, then the flag **block** is set to 1 and the function continues to interpret statements until a closing curly brace is read. The **interp_block( )** function is shown here:

```
/* Interpret a single statement or block of code. When
   interp_block() returns from its initial call, the final
   brace (or a return) in main() has been encountered.
*/
void interp_block(void)
{
  int value;
  char block = 0;

  do {
    token_type = get_token();

    /* If interpreting single statement, return on
       first semicolon.
    */

    /* see what kind of token is up */
    if(token_type==IDENTIFIER) {
      /* Not a keyword, so process expression. */
        putback();   /* restore token to input stream for
                        further processing by eval_exp() */
        eval_exp(&value);   /* process the expression */
```

```
        if(*token!=';') sntx_err(SEMI_EXPECTED);
    }
    else if(token_type==BLOCK) { /* if block delimiter */
      if(*token=='{') /* is a block */
        block = 1; /* interpreting block, not statement */
      else return; /* is a }, so return */
    }
    else /* is keyword */
      switch(tok) {
        case CHAR:
        case INT:     /* declare local variables */
          putback();
          decl_local();
          break;
        case RETURN:  /* return from function call */
          func_ret();
          return;
        case IF:      /* process an if statement */
          exec_if();
          break;
        case ELSE:    /* process an else statement */
          find_eob(); /* find end of else block
                         and continue execution */
          break;
        case WHILE:   /* process a while loop */
          exec_while();
          break;
        case DO:      /* process a do-while loop */
          exec_do();
          break;
        case FOR:     /* process a for loop */
          exec_for();
          break;
        case END:
          exit(0);
      }
  } while (tok != FINISHED && block);
}
```

Calls to functions like **exit( )** excepted, a C program ends when the last curly brace (or a **return**) in **main( )** is encountered—not necessarily at the last line of source code. This is one reason that **interp_block( )** executes only a statement or a block of code, and not the entire program. Also, conceptually, C consists of blocks of code. Therefore, **interp_block( )** is called each time a new block of code is encountered. This includes both function calls as well as blocks begun by various C statements, such as **if**. This means that in the process of executing a program, the Little C interpreter may call **interp_block( )** recursively.

The **interp_block( )** function works like this. First, it reads the next token from the program. If the token is a semicolon and only a single statement is being interpreted, then the function returns. Otherwise, it checks to see if the token is an identifier; if so, the statement must be an expression, so the expression parser is called. Since the expression parser expects to read the first token in the expression itself, the token is returned to the input stream via a call to **putback( )**. When **eval_exp( )** returns, **token** will hold the last token read by the expression parser, which must be a semicolon if the statement is syntactically correct. If **token** does not contain a semicolon, an error is reported.

If the next token from the program is a curly brace, then either **block** is set to 1 in the case of an opening brace, or, if it is a closing brace, the function returns.

Finally, if the token is a keyword, the **switch** statement is executed, calling the appropriate routine to handle the statement. The reason that keywords are given integer equivalents by **get_token( )** is to support the **switch** instead of using a sequence of **if** statements and string comparisons (which are quite slow).

The interpreter file is shown here. Before we look at the functions that actually execute C keyword statements, enter this code into a file called LITTLEC.C.

```
/* A Little C interpreter. */

#include <stdio.h>
#include <setjmp.h>
#include <math.h>
#include <ctype.h>
#include <stdlib.h>
#include <string.h>

#define NUM_FUNC          100
#define NUM_GLOBAL_VARS   100
#define NUM_LOCAL_VARS    200
#define NUM_BLOCK         100
#define ID_LEN            31
#define FUNC_CALLS        31
#define NUM_PARAMS        31
#define PROG_SIZE         10000
#define LOOP_NEST         31
```

```
enum tok_types {DELIMITER, IDENTIFIER, NUMBER, KEYWORD,
                TEMP, STRING, BLOCK};

/* add additional C keyword tokens here */
enum tokens {ARG, CHAR, INT, IF, ELSE, FOR, DO, WHILE,
             SWITCH, RETURN, EOL, FINISHED, END};

/* add additional double operators here (such as ->) */
enum double_ops {LT=1, LE, GT, GE, EQ, NE};

/* These are the constants used to call sntx_err() when
   a syntax error occurs. Add more if you like.
   NOTE: SYNTAX is a generic error message used when
   nothing else seems appropriate.
*/
enum error_msg
     {SYNTAX, UNBAL_PARENS, NO_EXP, EQUALS_EXPECTED,
      NOT_VAR, PARAM_ERR, SEMI_EXPECTED,
      UNBAL_BRACES, FUNC_UNDEF, TYPE_EXPECTED,
      NEST_FUNC, RET_NOCALL, PAREN_EXPECTED,
      WHILE_EXPECTED, QUOTE_EXPECTED, NOT_TEMP,
      TOO_MANY_LVARS};

char *prog;  /* current location in source code */
char *p_buf; /* points to start of program buffer */
jmp_buf e_buf; /* hold environment for longjmp() */

/* An array of these structures will hold the info
   associated with global variables.
*/
struct var_type {
  char var_name[ID_LEN];
  int var_type;
  int value;
}  global_vars[NUM_GLOBAL_VARS];

struct var_type local_var_stack[NUM_LOCAL_VARS];

struct func_type {
  char func_name[ID_LEN];
  char *loc;  /* location of entry point in file */
```

```
} func_table[NUM_FUNC];

int call_stack[NUM_FUNC];

struct commands { /* keyword lookup table */
  char command[20];
  char tok;
} table[] = { /* Commands must be entered lowercase */
  "if", IF, /* in this table. */
  "else", ELSE,
  "for", FOR,
  "do", DO,
  "while", WHILE,
  "char", CHAR,
  "int", INT,
  "return", RETURN,
  "end", END,
  "", END  /* mark end of table */
};

char token[80];
char token_type, tok;

int functos;  /* index to top of function call stack */
int func_index; /* index into function table */
int gvar_index; /* index into global variable table */
int lvartos; /* index into local variable stack */

int ret_value; /* function return value */

void print(void), prescan(void);
void decl_global(void), call(void), putback(void);
void decl_local(void), local_push(struct var_type i);
void eval_exp(int *value), sntx_err(int error);
void exec_if(void), find_eob(void), exec_for(void);
void get_params(void), get_args(void);
void exec_while(void), func_push(int i), exec_do(void);
void assign_var(char *var_name, int value);
int load_program(char *p, char *fname), find_var(char *s);
void interp_block(void), func_ret(void);
int func_pop(void), is_var(char *s), get_token(void);
```

```
char *find_func(char *name);

main(int argc, char *argv[])
{
  if(argc!=2) {
    printf("Usage: littlec <filename>\n");
    exit(1);
  }

  /* allocate memory for the program */
  if((p_buf=(char *) malloc(PROG_SIZE))==NULL) {
    printf("Allocation Failure");
    exit(1);
  }

  /* load the program to execute */
  if(!load_program(p_buf, argv[1])) exit(1);
  if(setjmp(e_buf)) exit(1); /* initialize long jump buffer */

  /* set program pointer to start of program buffer */
  prog = p_buf;
  prescan(); /* find the location of all functions
                and global variables in the program */

  gvar_index = 0;  /* initialize global variable index */
  lvartos = 0;     /* initialize local variable stack index */
  functos = 0;     /* initialize the CALL stack index */

  /* setup call to main() */
  prog = find_func("main");  /* find program starting point */
  prog--; /* back up to opening ( */
  strcpy(token, "main");
  call();  /* call main() to start interpreting */
  return 0;
}

/* Interpret a single statement or block of code. When
   interp_block() returns from its initial call, the final
   brace (or a return) in main() has been encountered.
*/
void interp_block(void)
{
```

```
int value;
char block = 0;

do {
  token_type = get_token();

  /* If interpreting single statement, return on
     first semicolon.
   */

  /* see what kind of token is up */
  if(token_type==IDENTIFIER) {
    /* Not a keyword, so process expression. */
      putback();  /* restore token to input stream for
                      further processing by eval_exp() */
      eval_exp(&value);  /* process the expression */
      if(*token!=';') sntx_err(SEMI_EXPECTED);
  }
  else if(token_type==BLOCK) { /* if block delimiter */
    if(*token=='{') /* is a block */
      block = 1; /* interpreting block, not statement */
    else return; /* is a }, so return */
  }
  else /* is keyword */
    switch(tok) {
      case CHAR:
      case INT:      /* declare local variables */
        putback();
        decl_local();
        break;
      case RETURN:  /* return from function call */
        func_ret();
        return;
      case IF:       /* process an if statement */
        exec_if();
        break;
      case ELSE:    /* process an else statement */
        find_eob(); /* find end of else block
                       and continue execution */
        break;
      case WHILE:    /* process a while loop */
```

```
          exec_while();
          break;
        case DO:        /* process a do-while loop */
          exec_do();
          break;
        case FOR:       /* process a for loop */
          exec_for();
          break;
        case END:
          exit(0);
      }
  } while (tok != FINISHED && block);
}

/* Load a program. */
load_program(char *p, char *fname)
{
  FILE *fp;
  int i=0;

  if((fp=fopen(fname, "rb"))==NULL) return 0;

  i = 0;
  do {
    *p = getc(fp);
    p++; i++;
  } while(!feof(fp) && i<PROG_SIZE);
  if(*(p-2)==0x1a) *(p-2) = '\0'; /* null terminate the program */
  else *(p-1) = '\0';
  fclose(fp);
  return 1;
}

/* Find the location of all functions in the program
   and store global variables. */
void prescan(void)
{
  char *p;
  char temp[32];
  int brace = 0;   /* When 0, this var tells us that
                      current source position is outside
                      of any function. */
```

```
p = prog;
func_index = 0;
do {
  while(brace) {  /* bypass code inside functions */
    get_token();
    if(*token=='{') brace++;
    if(*token=='}') brace--;
  }

  get_token();

  if(tok==CHAR || tok==INT) { /* is global var */
    putback();
    decl_global();
  }
  else if(token_type==IDENTIFIER) {
    strcpy(temp, token);
    get_token();
    if(*token=='(') {  /* must be a function */
      func_table[func_index].loc = prog;
      strcpy(func_table[func_index].func_name, temp);
      func_index++;
      while(*prog!=')') prog++;
      prog++;
      /* prog points to opening curly brace of function */
    }
    else putback();
  }
  else if(*token=='{') brace++;
} while(tok!=FINISHED);
  prog = p;
}

/* Return the entry point of the specified function.
   Return NULL if not found.
*/
char *find_func(char *name)
{
  register int i;

  for(i=0; i<func_index; i++)
```

```
      if(!strcmp(name, func_table[i].func_name))
        return func_table[i].loc;

  return NULL;
 }

/* Declare a global variable. */
void decl_global(void)
{
  get_token();  /* get type */

  global_vars[gvar_index].var_type = tok;
  global_vars[gvar_index].value = 0;  /* init to 0 */

  do { /* process comma-separated list */
    get_token();  /* get name */
    strcpy(global_vars[gvar_index].var_name, token);
    get_token();
    gvar_index++;
  } while(*token==',');
  if(*token!=';') sntx_err(SEMI_EXPECTED);
}

/* Declare a local variable. */
void decl_local(void)
{
  struct var_type i;

  get_token();  /* get type */

  i.var_type = tok;
  i.value = 0;  /* init to 0 */

  do { /* process comma-separated list */
    get_token(); /* get var name */
    strcpy(i.var_name, token);
    local_push(i);
    get_token();
  } while(*token==',');
  if(*token!=';') sntx_err(SEMI_EXPECTED);
```

```
}

/* Call a function. */
void call(void)
{
  char *loc, *temp;
  int lvartemp;

  loc = find_func(token); /* find entry point of function */
  if(loc==NULL)
    sntx_err(FUNC_UNDEF); /* function not defined */
  else {
    lvartemp = lvartos;  /* save local var stack index */
    get_args();  /* get function arguments */
    temp = prog; /* save return location */
    func_push(lvartemp);  /* save local var stack index */
    prog = loc;  /* reset prog to start of function */
    get_params(); /* load the function's parameters with
                     the values of the arguments */
    interp_block(); /* interpret the function */
    prog = temp; /* reset the program pointer */
    lvartos = func_pop(); /* reset the local var stack */
  }
}

/* Push the arguments to a function onto the local
   variable stack. */
void get_args(void)
{
  int value, count, temp[NUM_PARAMS];
  struct var_type i;

  count = 0;
  get_token();
  if(*token!='(') sntx_err(PAREN_EXPECTED);

  /* process a comma-separated list of values */
  do {
    eval_exp(&value);
    temp[count] = value;  /* save temporarily */
    get_token();
```

```
      count++;
    }while(*token==',');
    count--;
    /* now, push on local_var_stack in reverse order */
    for(; count>=0; count--) {
      i.value = temp[count];
      i.var_type = ARG;
      local_push(i);
    }
}

/* Get function parameters. */
void get_params(void)
{
  struct var_type *p;
  int i;

  i = lvartos-1;
  do { /* process comma-separated list of parameters */
    get_token();
    p = &local_var_stack[i];
    if(*token!=')') {
      if(tok!=INT && tok!=CHAR) sntx_err(TYPE_EXPECTED);
      p->var_type = token_type;
      get_token();

      /* link parameter name with argument already on
         local var stack */
      strcpy(p->var_name, token);
      get_token();
      i--;
    }
    else break;
  } while(*token==',');
  if(*token!=')') sntx_err(PAREN_EXPECTED);
}

/* Return from a function. */
void func_ret(void)
{
  int value;
```

```
  value = 0;
  /* get return value, if any */
  eval_exp(&value);

  ret_value = value;
}

/* Push a local variable. */
void local_push(struct var_type i)
{
  if(lvartos>NUM_LOCAL_VARS)
    sntx_err(TOO_MANY_LVARS);

  local_var_stack[lvartos] = i;
  lvartos++;
}

/* Pop index into local variable stack. */
func_pop(void)
{
  functos--;
  if(functos<0) sntx_err(RET_NOCALL);
  return(call_stack[functos]);
}

/* Push index of local variable stack. */
void func_push(int i)
{
  if(functos>NUM_FUNC)
    sntx_err(NEST_FUNC);
  call_stack[functos] = i;
  functos++;
}

/* Assign a value to a variable. */
void assign_var(char *var_name, int value)
{
  register int i;

  /* first, see if it's a local variable */
  for(i=lvartos-1; i>=call_stack[functos-1]; i--)  {
```

```
      if(!strcmp(local_var_stack[i].var_name, var_name)) {
        local_var_stack[i].value = value;
        return;
      }
    }
  }
  if(i < call_stack[functos-1])
  /* if not local, try global var table */
    for(i=0; i<NUM_GLOBAL_VARS; i++)
      if(!strcmp(global_vars[i].var_name, var_name)) {
        global_vars[i].value = value;
        return;
      }
  sntx_err(NOT_VAR); /* variable not found */
}

/* Find the value of a variable. */
int find_var(char *s)
{
  register int i;

  /* first, see if it's a local variable */
  for(i=lvartos-1; i>=call_stack[functos-1]; i--)
    if(!strcmp(local_var_stack[i].var_name, token))
      return local_var_stack[i].value;

  /* otherwise, try global vars */
  for(i=0; i<NUM_GLOBAL_VARS; i++)
    if(!strcmp(global_vars[i].var_name, s))
      return global_vars[i].value;

  sntx_err(NOT_VAR); /* variable not found */
}

/* Determine if an identifier is a variable. Return
   1 if variable is found; 0 otherwise.
*/
int is_var(char *s)
{
  register int i;

  /* first, see if it's a local variable */
  for(i=lvartos-1; i>=call_stack[functos-1]; i--)
```

```
      if(!strcmp(local_var_stack[i].var_name, token))
        return 1;

  /* otherwise, try global vars */
  for(i=0; i<NUM_GLOBAL_VARS; i++)
    if(!strcmp(global_vars[i].var_name, s))
      return 1;

  return 0;
}

/* Execute an if statement. */
void exec_if(void)
{
  int cond;

  eval_exp(&cond); /* get left expression */

  if(cond) { /* is true so process target of IF */
    interp_block();
  }
  else { /* otherwise skip around IF block and
            process the ELSE, if present */
    find_eob(); /* find start of next line */
    get_token();

    if(tok!=ELSE) {
      putback();  /* restore token if
                      no ELSE is present */
      return;
    }
    interp_block();
  }
}

/* Execute a while loop. */
void exec_while(void)
{
  int cond;
  char *temp;
```

```
    putback();
    temp = prog;  /* save location of top of while loop */
    get_token();
    eval_exp(&cond);  /* check the conditional expression */
    if(cond) interp_block();  /* if true, interpret */
    else {  /* otherwise, skip around loop */
      find_eob();
      return;
    }
    prog = temp;  /* loop back to top */
}

/*Execute a do loop. */
void exec_do(void)
{
  int cond;
  char *temp;

  putback();
  temp = prog;  /* save location of top of do loop */

  get_token(); /* get start of loop */
  interp_block(); /* interpret loop */
  get_token();
  if(tok!=WHILE) sntx_err(WHILE_EXPECTED);
  eval_exp(&cond); /* check the loop condition */
  if(cond) prog = temp; /* if true loop; otherwise,
                            continue on */
}

/* Find the end of a block. */
void find_eob(void)
{
  int brace;

  get_token();
  brace = 1;
  do {
    get_token();
    if(*token=='{') brace++;
    else if(*token=='}') brace--;
```

```
  } while(brace);
}

/* Execute a for loop. */
void exec_for(void)
{
  int cond;
  char *temp, *temp2;
  int brace ;

  get_token();
  eval_exp(&cond);   /* initialization expression */
  if(*token!=';') sntx_err(SEMI_EXPECTED);
  prog++; /* get past the ; */
  temp = prog;
  for(;;) {
    eval_exp(&cond);   /* check the condition */
    if(*token!=';') sntx_err(SEMI_EXPECTED);
    prog++; /* get past the ; */
    temp2 = prog;

    /* find the start of the for block */
    brace = 1;
    while(brace) {
      get_token();
      if(*token=='(') brace++;
      if(*token==')') brace--;
    }

    if(cond) interp_block();   /* if true, interpret */
    else {   /* otherwise, skip around loop */
      find_eob();
      return;
    }
    prog = temp2;
    eval_exp(&cond); /* do the increment */
    prog = temp;   /* loop back to top */
  }
}
```

Handling Local Variables

When the interpreter encounters an **int** or **char** keyword, it calls **decl_local( )** to create storage for a local variable. As stated earlier, no global variable declaration statement will be encountered by the interpreter once the program is executing, because only code within a function is executed. Therefore, if a variable declaration statement is found, it must be for a local variable (or a parameter, which will be discussed in the next section). In structured languages, local variables are stored on a stack. If the language is compiled, the system stack is generally used; however, in an interpreted mode, the stack for local variables must be maintained by the interpreter. The stack for local variables is held by the array **local_var_stack**. Each time a local variable is encountered, its name, type, and value (initially zero) are pushed onto the stack using **local_push( )**. The global variable **lvartos** indexes the stack. (For reasons that will become clear, there is no corresponding "pop" function. Instead, the local variable stack is reset each time a function returns.) The **decl_local** and **local_push( )** functions are shown here:

```
/* Declare a local variable. */
void decl_local(void)
{
  struct var_type i;

  get_token();  /* get type */

  i.var_type = tok;
  i.value = 0;  /* init to 0 */

  do { /* process comma-separated list */
    get_token(); /* get var name */
    strcpy(i.var_name, token);
    local_push(i);
    get_token();
  } while(*token==',');
  if(*token!=';') sntx_err(SEMI_EXPECTED);
}

/* Push local variable */
void local_push(struct var_type i)
{
  if(lvartos>NUM_LOCAL_VARS)
  sntx_err(TOO_MANY_LVARS);

  local_var_stack[lvartos] = i;
  lvartos++;
}
```

The **decl_local( )** function first reads the type of the variable or variables being declared and assigns it an initial value of zero. Next, it enters a loop, which reads a comma-separated list of identifiers. Each time through the loop, the information about each variable is pushed onto the local variable stack. At the end, the final token is checked to make sure that it contains a semicolon.

Calling User-Defined Functions

Probably the most difficult part of implementing an interpreter for C is the execution of user-defined functions. Not only does the interpreter need to begin reading the source code at a different position and return to the calling routine after the function terminates, but it must also deal with these three tasks: the passing of arguments, the allocation of parameters, and the return value of the function.

All function calls (except the initial call to **main( )**) take place through the expression parser from the **atom( )** function by a call to **call( )**. It is the **call( )** function that actually handles the details of calling a function. The **call( )** function is shown here, along with two support functions. Let's examine these functions closely.

```
/* Call a function. */
void call(void)
{
  char *loc, *temp;
  int lvartemp;

  loc = find_func(token); /* find entry point of function */
  if(loc==NULL)
    sntx_err(FUNC_UNDEF); /* function not defined */
  else {
    lvartemp = lvartos;  /* save local var stack index */
    get_args();  /* get function arguments */
    temp = prog; /* save return location */
    func_push(lvartemp);  /* save local var stack index */
    prog = loc;  /* reset prog to start of function */
    get_params(); /* load the function's parameters with
                      the values of the arguments */
    interp_block(); /* interpret the function */
    prog = temp; /* reset the program pointer */
    lvartos = func_pop(); /* reset the local var stack */
  }
}

/* Push the arguments to a function onto the local
```

```
    variable stack. */
void get_args(void)
{
  int value, count, temp[NUM_PARAMS];
  struct var_type i;

  count = 0;
  get_token();
  if(*token!='(') sntx_err(PAREN_EXPECTED);

  /* process a comma-separated list of values */
  do {
    eval_exp(&value);
    temp[count] = value;  /* save temporarily */
    get_token();
    count++;
  }while(*token==',');
  count--;
  /* now, push on local_var_stack in reverse order */
  for(; count>=0; count--) {
    i.value = temp[count];
    i.var_type = ARG;
    local_push(i);
  }
}

/* Get function parameters. */
void get_params(void)
{
  struct var_type *p;
  int i;

  i = lvartos-1;
  do { /* process comma-separated list of parameters */
    get_token();
    p = &local_var_stack[i];
    if(*token!=')') {
      if(tok!=INT && tok!=CHAR) sntx_err(TYPE_EXPECTED);
      p->var_type = token_type;
      get_token();
```

```
      /* link parameter name with argument already on
         local var stack */
      strcpy(p->var_name, token);
      get_token();
      i--;
    }
    else break;
  } while(*token==',');
  if(*token!=')') sntx_err(PAREN_EXPECTED);
}
```

The first thing that **call( )** does is find the location of the entry point in the source code to the specified function by calling **find_func( )**. Next, it saves the current value of the local variable stack index, **lvartos**, into **lvartemp**; then it calls **get_args( )** to process any function arguments. The **get_args( )** function reads a comma-separated list of expressions and pushes them onto the local variable stack in reverse order. (The expressions are pushed in reverse order so that they can be more easily matched with their corresponding parameters.) When the values are pushed, they are not given names. The names of the parameters are given to them by the **get_params( )** function, which will be discussed in a moment.

Once the function arguments have been processed, the current value of **prog** is saved in **temp**. This location is the return point of the function. Next, the value of **lvartemp** is pushed onto the function call stack. The routines **func_push( )** and **func_pop( )** maintain this stack. Its purpose is to store the value of **lvartos** each time a function is called. This value represents the starting point on the local variable stack for variables (and parameters) relative to the function being called. The value on the top of the function call stack is used to prevent a function from accessing any local variables other than those it declares.

The next two lines of code set the program pointer to the start of the function and link the name of its formal parameters with the values of the arguments already on the local variable stack with a call to **get_params( )**. The actual execution of the function is performed through a call to **interp_block( )**. When **interp_block( )** returns, the program pointer (**prog**) is reset to its return point and the local variable stack index is reset to its value before the function call. This final step effectively removes all of the function's local variables from the stack.

If the function being called contains a **return** statement, then **interp_block( )** calls **func_ret( )** prior to returning to **call( )**. This function processes any return value. It is shown here:

```
/* Return from a function. */
void func_ret(void)
{
  int value;

  value = 0;
  /* get return value, if any */
  eval_exp(&value);

  ret_value = value;

}
```

The variable **ret_value** is a global integer that holds the return value of a function. At first glance you might wonder why the local variable **value** is first assigned the return value of the function and then is assigned to **ret_value**. The reason is that functions can be recursive and **eval_exp( )** may need to call the same function in order to obtain its value.

Assigning Values to Variables

Let's return briefly to the expression parser. When an assignment statement is encountered, the value of the right side of the expression is computed and this value is assigned to the variable on the left using a call to **assign_var( )**. However, as you know, the C language is structured and supports global and local variables. Hence, given a program such as this:

```
int count;

main()
{
  int count;

  count = 100;

  f();
}

f()
{
  int count;
```

```
    count = 99;

}
```

how does the **assign_var( )** function know which variable is being assigned a value in each assignment? The answer is simple: first, in C, local variables take priority over global variables of the same name; second, local variables are not known outside their own function. To see how we can use these rules to resolve the above assignments, examine the **assign_var( )** function, shown here:

```
/* Assign a value to a variable. */
void assign_var(char *var_name, int value)
{
  register int i;

  /* first, see if it's a local variable */
  for(i=lvartos-1; i>=call_stack[functos-1]; i--)  {
    if(!strcmp(local_var_stack[i].var_name, var_name)) {
      local_var_stack[i].value = value;
      return;
    }
  }
  if(i < call_stack[functos-1])
    /* if not local, try global var table */
    for(i=0; i<NUM_GLOBAL_VARS; i++)
      if(!strcmp(global_vars[i].var_name, var_name)) {
        global_vars[i].value = value;
        return;
      }
  sntx_err(NOT_VAR); /* variable not found */
}
```

As explained in the previous section, each time a function is called, the current value of the local variable stack index (**lvartos**) is pushed onto the function call stack. This means that any local variables (or parameters) defined by the function will be pushed onto the stack above that point. Therefore, the **assign_var( )** function first searches **local_var_stack**, beginning with the current top-of-stack value and stopping when the index reaches that value saved by the latest function call. This mechanism ensures that only those variables local to the function are examined. (It also helps support recursive functions because the current value of **lvartos** is saved each time a function is invoked.) Therefore, the line "count = 100;" in **main( )** causes **assign_var( )**

to find the local variable **count** inside **main( )**. In **f( )**, **assign_var( )** finds its own **count** and does not find the one in **main( )**.

If no local variable matches the name of a variable, then the global variable list is searched.

Executing an if Statement

Now that the basic structure of the Little C interpreter is in place, it is time to add some control statements. Each time a keyword statement is encountered inside of **interp_block( )**, an appropriate function is called, which processes that statement. One of the easiest is the **if**. The **if** statement is processed by **exec_if( )**, shown here:

```
/* Execute an IF statement. */
void exec_if(void)
{
  int cond;
  eval_exp(&cond); /* get left expression */

  if(cond) { /* is true so process target of IF */
    interp_block();
  }
  else { /* otherwise skip around IF block and
            process the ELSE, if present */
    find_eob(); /* find start of next line */
    get_token();

    if(tok!=ELSE) {
      putback();  /* restore token if
                     no ELSE is present */
      return;
    }
    interp_block();
  }
}
```

Let's look closely at this function.

The first thing the function does is to compute the value of the conditional expression by calling **eval_exp( )**. If the condition (**cond**) is true (non-zero), then the function calls **interp_block( )** recursively, allowing the **if** block to execute. If **cond** is false, then the function **find_eob( )** is called, which advances the program pointer to the location immediately after the end of the **if** block. If an **else** is present, the **else** is processed by **exec_if( )** and the **else** block is executed. Otherwise, execution simply begins with the next line of code.

If the **if** block executes and there is an **else** block present, there must be some way for the **else** block to be bypassed. This is accomplished in **interp_block( )** by simply calling **find_eob( )** to bypass the block when an **else** is encountered. Remember, the only time an **else** will be processed by **interp_block( )** (in a syntactically correct program) is after an **if** block was executed. When an **else** block executes, the **else** is processed by **exec_if( )**.

Processing a while Loop

A **while** loop, like the **if**, is quite easy to interpret. The function that actually performs this task, **exec_while( )**, is shown here.

```
/* Execute a while loop. */
void exec_while(void)
{
  int cond;
  char *temp;

  putback();
  temp = prog;   /* save location of top of while loop */
  get_token();
  eval_exp(&cond);   /* check the conditional expression */
  if(cond) interp_block();   /* if true, interpret */
  else {   /* otherwise, skip around loop */
    find_eob();
    return;
  }
  prog = temp;   /* loop back to top */
}
```

The **exec_while( )** works like this. First, the **while** token is put back into the input stream and the location of the **while** is saved into **temp**. This address will be used to allow the interpreter to loop back to the top of the **while**. Next, the **while** is reread to remove it from the input stream, and **eval_exp( )** is called to compute the value of the **while**'s conditional expression. If the conditional expression is true, then **interp_block( )** is called recursively to interpret the **while** block. When **interp_block( )** returns, **prog** (the program pointer) is loaded with the location of the start of the **while** loop and control returns to **interp_block( )**, where the entire process repeats. If the conditional expression is false, then the end of the **while** block is found and the function returns.

Processing a do-while Loop

A **do-while** loop is processed much like the **while**. When **interp_block( )** encounters a **do** statement, it calls **exec_do( )**, shown here:

```
/*Execute a do loop. */
void exec_do(void)
{
  int cond;
  char *temp;

  putback();
  temp = prog;   /* save location of top of do loop */

  get_token(); /* get start of loop */
  interp_block(); /* interpret loop */
  get_token();
  if(tok!=WHILE) sntx_err(WHILE_EXPECTED);
  eval_exp(&cond); /* check the loop condition */
  if(cond) prog = temp; /* if true loop; otherwise, continue on */
}
```

The main difference between the **do-while** and the **while** loops is that the **do-while** always executes its block of code at least once because the conditional expression is at the bottom of the loop. Therefore, **exec_do( )** first saves the location of the top of the loop into **temp** and then calls **interp_block( )** recursively to interpret the block of code associated with the loop. When **interp_block( )** returns, the corresponding **while** is retrieved and the conditional expression is evaluated. If the condition is true, **prog** is reset to the top of the loop; otherwise, execution will continue on.

The for Loop

The interpretation of the **for** loop poses a more difficult challenge than the other constructs. Part of the reason for this is that the structure of the C **for** is definitely designed with compilation in mind. The main trouble is that the conditional expression of the **for** must be checked at the top of the loop, but the increment portion occurs at the bottom of the loop. Therefore, even though these two pieces of the **for** loop occur next to each other in the source code, their interpretation is separated by the block of code being iterated. However, with a little work, the **for** can be correctly interpreted.

When **interp_block( )** encounters a **for** statement, **exec_for( )** is called. This function is shown here:

```
/* Execute a for loop. */
void exec_for(void)
{

  int cond;
  char *temp, *temp2;
  int brace ;

  get_token();
  eval_exp(&cond);  /*initialization expression */
  if(*token!=';') sntx_err(SEMI_EXPECTED);
  prog++; /* get past the ; */
  temp = prog;
  for(;;) {
    eval_exp(&cond);  /* check the condition */
    if(*token!=';') sntx_err(SEMI_EXPECTED);
    prog++; /* get past the ; */
    temp2 = prog;

    /* find the start of the for block */
    brace = 1;
    while(brace) {
      get_token();
      if(*token=='(') brace++;
      if(*token==')') brace--;
    }

    if(cond) interp_block();  /* if true, interpret */
    else {  /* otherwise, skip around loop */
      find_eob();
      return;
    }
    prog = temp2;
    eval_exp(&cond); /* do the increment */
    prog = temp;  /* loop back to top */
  }
}
```

This function begins by processing the initialization expression in the **for**. The initialization portion of the **for** is executed only once and does not form part of the loop. Next, the program pointer is advanced to a point immediately after the semicolon that ends the initialization statement, and its value is assigned to **temp**. A loop is then established, which checks the conditional portion of the loop and assigns

temp2 a pointer to the start of the increment portion. The beginning of the loop code is found, and, finally, if the conditional expression is true, the loop block is interpreted. (Otherwise, the end of the block is found and execution continues on after the **for** loop.) When the recursive call to **interp_block( )** returns, the increment portion of the loop is executed, and the process repeats.

The Little C Library Functions

Because the C programs executed by Little C are never compiled and linked, any library routines they use must be handled directly by Little C. The best way to do this is to create an interface function that Little C calls when a library function is encountered. This interface function sets up the call to the library function and handles any return values.

Because of space limitations, Little C contains only five "library" functions: **getche( )**, **putch( )**, **puts( )**, **print( )**, and **getnum( )**. Of these, only **puts( )**, which outputs a string to the screen, is described by the ANSI C standard. The **getche( )** function is a common extension to C for interactive environments. It waits for and returns a key struck at the keyboard. This function is found in many compilers. **putch( )** is also defined by many compilers that are designed for use in an interactive environment. It outputs a single character argument to the console. It does not buffer output. The functions **getnum( )** and **print( )** are my own creations. The **getnum( )** function returns the integer equivalent of a number entered at the keyboard. The **print( )** function is a very handy function that can output either a string or an integer argument to the screen. The five library functions are shown here in their prototype forms.

```
int getche(void);     /* read a character from keyboard and
                         return its value */
int putch(char ch);   /* write a character to the screen */
int puts(char *s);    /* write a string to the screen */
int getnum(void);     /* read an integer from the keyboard and
                         return its value */
int print(char *s);   /* write a string to the screen */
or
int print(int i);     /* write an integer to the screen */
```

The Little C library routines are shown here. You should enter this file into your computer, calling it LCLIB.C.

```
/****** Internal Library Functions *******/

/* Add more of your own, here. */
```

```
#include <conio.h>  /* if your compiler does not
                       support this header file,
                       remove it */

#include <stdio.h>
#include <stdlib.h>

extern char *prog; /* points to current location in program */
extern char token[80]; /* holds string representation of token */
extern char token_type; /* contains type of token */
extern char tok; /* holds the internal representation of token */

enum tok_types {DELIMITER, IDENTIFIER, NUMBER, KEYWORD,
                TEMP, STRING, BLOCK};

/* These are the constants used to call sntx_err() when
   a syntax error occurs. Add more if you like.
   NOTE: SYNTAX is a generic error message used when
   nothing else seems appropriate.
*/
enum error_msg
     {SYNTAX, UNBAL_PARENS, NO_EXP, EQUALS_EXPECTED,
      NOT_VAR, PARAM_ERR, SEMI_EXPECTED,
      UNBAL_BRACES, FUNC_UNDEF, TYPE_EXPECTED,
      NEST_FUNC, RET_NOCALL, PAREN_EXPECTED,
      WHILE_EXPECTED, QUOTE_EXPECTED, NOT_STRING,
      TOO_MANY_LVARS};

int get_token(void);
void sntx_err(int error), eval_exp(int *result);
void putback(void);

/* Get a character from console. (Use getchar() if
   your compiler does not support getche().) */
call_getche()
{
  char ch;
  ch = getche();
  while(*prog!=')') prog++;
  prog++;    /* advance to end of line */
  return ch;
}
```

```c
/* Put a character to the display. */
call_putch()
{
  int value;

  eval_exp(&value);
  printf("%c", value);
  return value;
}

/* Call puts(). */
call_puts(void)
{
  get_token();
  if(*token!='(') sntx_err(PAREN_EXPECTED);
  get_token();
  if(token_type!=STRING) sntx_err(QUOTE_EXPECTED);
  puts(token);
  get_token();
  if(*token!=')') sntx_err(PAREN_EXPECTED);

  get_token();
  if(*token!=';') sntx_err(SEMI_EXPECTED);
  putback();
  return 0;
}

/* A built-in console output function. */
int print(void)
{
  int i;

  get_token();
  if(*token!='(')  sntx_err(PAREN_EXPECTED);

  get_token();
  if(token_type==STRING) { /* output a string */
    printf("%s ", token);
  }
  else {  /* output a number */
   putback();
   eval_exp(&i);
```

```
    printf("%d ", i);
  }

  get_token();

  if(*token!=')') sntx_err(PAREN_EXPECTED);

  get_token();
  if(*token!=';') sntx_err(SEMI_EXPECTED);
  putback();
  return 0;
}

/* Read an integer from the keyboard. */
getnum(void)
{
  char s[80];

  gets(s);
  while(*prog!=')') prog++;
  prog++;  /* advance to end of line */
  return atoi(s);
}
```

To add library functions, first enter their names and the addresses of their interface functions into the **intern_func** array. Next, following the lead of the functions shown previously, create appropriate interface functions.

Compiling and Linking the Little C Interpreter

Once you have entered all three files that make up Little C, compile and link them together. If you use Borland C/C++, you can use a sequence such as the following.

```
bcc -c parser.c
bcc -c lclib.c
bcc littlec.c parser.obj lclib.obj
```

If you use Microsoft C/C++, use this sequence:

```
cl -c parser.c
cl -c lclib.c
cl littlec.c parser.obj lclib.obj /F 6000
```

By default, when compiling using Microsoft C/C++, Little C may not be given sufficient stack space. The /F option increases the stack to 6000 bytes, which is sufficient for most purposes. However, you might need to increase the size of the stack even more when interpreting highly recursive programs.

If you use a different C compiler, simply follow the instructions that come with it.

Demonstrating Little C

The following C programs demonstrate the features of Little C:

```
/* Little C Demonstration Program #1.

   This program demonstrates all features
   of C that are recognized by Little C.
*/

int i, j;   /* global vars */
char ch;

main()
{
  int i, j;  /* local vars */

  puts("Little C Demo Program.");

  print_alpha();

  do {
    puts("enter a number (0 to quit): ");
    i = getnum();
    if(i < 0 ) {
      puts("numbers must be positive, try again");
    }
    else {
      for(j = 0; j < i; j=j+1) {
        print(j);
        print("summed is");
```

```
        print(sum(j));
        puts("");
      }
    }
  } while(i!=0);
}


/* Sum the values between 0 and num. */
sum(int num)
{
  int running_sum;

  running_sum = 0;

  while(num) {
    running_sum = running_sum + num;
    num = num - 1;
  }
  return running_sum;
}

/* Print the alphabet. */
print_alpha()
{
  for(ch = 'A'; ch<='Z'; ch = ch + 1) {
    putch(ch);
  }
  puts("");
}


/* Nested loop example. */
main()
{
  int i, j, k;

  for(i = 0; i < 5; i = i + 1) {
    for(j = 0; j < 3; j = j + 1) {
      for(k = 3; k ; k = k - 1) {
        print(i);
        print(j);
```

```
        print(k);
        puts("");
      }
    }
  }
  puts("done");
}


/* Assigments as operations. */
main()
{
  int a, b;

  a = b = 10;

  print(a); print(b);
  while(a=a-1) {
    print(a);
    do {
        print(b);
    }while((b=b-1) > -10);
  }
}


/* This program demonstrates recursive functions. */
main()
{
 print(factr(7) * 2);
}

/* return the factorial of i */
factr(int i)
{
  if(i<2) {
    return 1;
  }
  else {
    return i * factr(i-1);
  }
}
```

```
/* A more rigorous example of function arguments. */
main()
{
  f2(10, f1(10, 20), 99);
}

f1(int a, int b)
{
  int count;

  print("in f1");

  count = a;
  do {
    print(count);
  } while(count=count-1);

  print(a); print(b);
  print(a*b);
  return a*b;
}

f2(int a, int x, int y)
{
  print(a); print(x);
  print(x / a);
  print(y*x);
}


/* The loop statements. */
main()
{
  int a;
  char ch;

  /* the while */
  puts("Enter a number: ");
  a = getnum();
  while(a) {
```

```
    print(a);
    print(a*a);
    puts("");
    a = a - 1;
  }

  /* the do-while */
  puts("enter characters, 'q' to quit");
  do {
    ch = getche();
  } while(ch!='q');

  /* the for */
  for(a=0; a<10; a = a + 1) {
    print(a);
  }
}
```

Improving Little C

The Little C interpreter presented in this chapter was designed with transparency of operation in mind. The goal was to develop an interpreter that could be easily understood with the least amount of effort. It was also designed in such a way that it could be easily expanded. As such, Little C is not particularly fast or efficient; however, the basic structure of the interpreter is correct, and you can increase its speed of execution by following these steps.

Virtually all commercial interpreters expand the role of the prescanner. The entire source program being interpreted is converted from its ASCII human-readable form into an internal form. In this internal form, all but quoted strings and constants are transformed into single-integer tokens, much the way that Little C converts the C keywords into single-integer tokens. It may have occurred to you that Little C performs a number of string comparisons. For example, each time a variable or function is searched for, several string comparisons take place. String comparisons are very costly in terms of time; however, if each token in the source program is converted into an integer, then much faster integer comparisons can be used. The conversion of the source program into an internal form is the *single most important change* you can make to Little C in order to improve its efficiency. Frankly, the increase in speed will be dramatic.

Another area of improvement, meaningful mostly for large programs, is the lookup routines for variables and functions. Even if you convert these items into integer tokens, the current approach to searching for them relies upon a sequential search. You could, however, substitute some other, faster method, such as a binary tree or some sort of hashing method.

As stated earlier, one restriction that Little C has relative to the full C grammar is that the objects of statements such as **if**—even if single statements—must be blocks of code enclosed between curly braces. The reason for this is that it greatly simplifies the **find_eob( )** function, which is used to find the end of a block of code after one of the control statements executes. The **find_eob( )** function simply looks for a matching closing curly brace to the one that starts the block. You might find it an interesting exercise to remove this restriction. One approach to this is to redesign **find_eob( )** so that it finds the end of a statement, expression, or block. Keep in mind, however, that you will need to use a different approach to finding the end of the **if**, **while**, **do-while**, and **for** statements when they are used as single statements.

Expanding Little C

There are two general areas in which you can expand and enhance the Little C interpreter: C features and ancillary features. Some of these are discussed briefly in the following section.

Adding New C Features

There are two basic categories of C statements you can add to Little C. The first is additional action statements, such as the **switch**, the **goto**, and the **break** and **continue** statements. You should have little trouble adding any of these if you study closely the way the statements that Little C does interpret are constructed.

The second category of C statement you can add is new data types. Little C already contains the basic "hooks" for additional data types. For example, the **var_type** structure already contains a field for the type of variable. To add other elementary types (for example, **float**, **double**, and **long**), simply increase the size of the value field to the size of the largest element you wish to hold.

Supporting pointers is no more difficult than supporting any other data type. However, you will need to add support for the pointer operators to the expression parser.

Once you have implemented pointers, arrays will be easy. Space for an array should be allocated dynamically using **malloc( )**, and a pointer to the array should be stored in the **value** field of **var_type**.

The addition of structures and unions poses a slightly more difficult problem. The easiest way to handle them is to use **malloc( )** to allocate space for them and simply use a pointer to the object in the value field of the **var_type** structure. (You will also need special code to handle the passing of structures and unions as parameters.)

To handle different return types for functions, add a **type** field to the **func_type** structure that defines what type of data a function returns.

One final thought—if you like to experiment with language constructs, don't be afraid to add a non-C extension. By far the most fun I've had with language interpreters is making them do things not specified by the language. If you want to add a Pascal-like **REPEAT-UNTIL** construct, for example, go ahead and do it! If something doesn't work the first time, try finding the problem by printing out what each token is as it is processed.

Adding Ancillary Features

Interpreters give you the opportunity to add several interesting and useful features. For example, you can add a trace facility that displays each token as it is executed. You can also add the ability to display the contents of each variable as the program executes. Another feature you might want to add is an integrated editor so that you can "edit and go" instead of having to use a separate editor to create your C programs.

Index

E

G

M

XOR

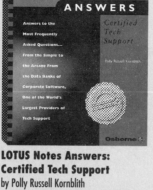
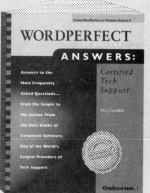

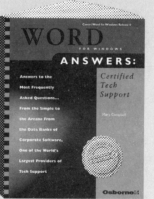

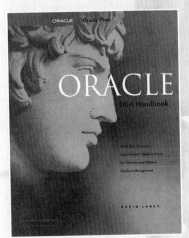

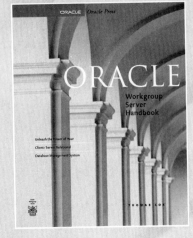
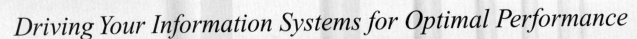

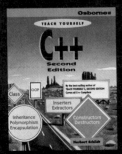

Secret Recipes
FOR THE SERIOUS CODE CHEF

BYTE's Mac Programmer's Cookbook
by Rob Terrell
Includes One 3.5-Inch Disk
$29.95 U.S.A., ISBN: 0-07-882062-6

No longer underground...the best-kept secrets and profound programming tips have been liberated! You'll find them all in the new BYTE Programmer's Cookbook series — the hottest hacks, facts, and tricks for veterans and rookies alike. These books are accompanied by a CD-ROM or disk packed with code from the books plus utilities and plenty of other software tools you'll relish.

BYTE's Windows Programmer's Cookbook
by L. John Ribar
Includes
One CD-ROM
$34.95 U.S.A.
ISBN: 0-07-882037-5

BYTE's DOS Programmer's Cookbook
by Craig Menefee, Lenny Bailes, and Nick Anis
Includes
One CD-ROM
$34.95 U.S.A.
ISBN: 0-07-882048-0

BYTE's OS/2 Programmer's Cookbook
by Kathy Ivens and Bruce Hallberg
Includes
One CD-ROM
$34.95 U.S.A.
ISBN: 0-07-882039-1

BYTE Guide to CD-ROM
by Michael Nadeau
Includes
One CD-ROM
$39.95 U.S.A.
ISBN: 0-07-881982-2